# THE GUINNESS BOOK OF
# ANIMAL RECORDS

*Written and photographed by*

*MARK CARWARDINE*

GUINNESS PUBLISHING

## ACKNOWLEDGEMENTS

A great many people around the world have helped with the research for this book. Some shared their knowledge; others read and commented on early versions of the text; and they all provided moral support and encouragement. I am indebted to everyone who has been involved. In particular, I would like to thank (in no particular order): Dr Robert Prys-Jones, Michael Walters, Peter Colston and the rest of the Bird Group at the Natural History Museum, Tring; Alwyne Wheeler; Jo Taylor and Carolyn Slicer at the Information Service of the World Conservation Monitoring Centre; Chris Wemmer, Chairman, IUCN Deer Specialist Group; Tom Langton and all the staff at Herpetofauna Conservation International Ltd; Colin Harrison; John Burton, the World Wide Land Conservation Trust; Ian Redmond; Alison Smith; Chris Stroud and Erich Hoyt at the Whale and Dolphin Conservation Society; John Gooders; Tony Hutson, the Bat Conservation Trust; Nick Garbutt; Robert Burton; Peter Jackson, Chairman, IUCN Cat Specialist Group; Cyril Walker, Department of Palaeontology, The Natural History Museum, London; Randall Reeves, Deputy Chairman, IUCN Cetacean Specialist Group; Mark Simmonds, University of Greenwich; Paul Thompson, University of Aberdeen; David Lavigne; and Chris Mattison.

I would also like to say a special thank you to everyone at Guinness Publishing – in particular Beátrice Frei, Stephen Adamson, David Roberts and Barbara Edwards – all of whom have been incredibly supportive and enthusiastic throughout. It has been a great pleasure working with them. At the same time, I would like to acknowledge the pioneering work of Gerald L. Wood, who first wrote *The Guinness Book of Animal Facts and Feats* back in the early 1970s.

Space does not permit me to list all the sources of reference used for this book. However, having consulted many thousands of journals, magazines and books over a period of several years, I would like to acknowledge the fact that I have drawn freely on the painstaking and pioneering research work of others. Finally, as new information comes to light, and as animals run faster, grow fatter, fly higher, and generally improve on their own personal bests, many records are likely to be beaten in the coming years. I would be most grateful to hear of such changes.

Mark Carwardine

*Illustrations supplied by the author except for the following:*
**David Carwardine** (p.7). **Bruce Coleman:** (p.76), Jen & Des Bartlett (p.103 *top*), Jane Burton (p.193), John Cancalosi (p.225), Adrian Davies (p.189), CB & DW Frith (p.215), Charles & Sandra Hood (p.168/9), David Hughes (p.219), Andy Purcell (p.228), Hans Reinhard (p.198), Jeffrey L. Rotmam (p.205), Jens Rydell (p.11), Rod Williams (p.82), Gunter Ziesler (p.13).
**Jacana:** König Rudolf (p.188). **Jacana Scientific Control** (p.27).
**Planet Earth:** Pete Atkinson (p.247), Ken Lucas (p.192, 199), Doug Perrine (p.245), James D. Watt (p.194).
**Science Photo Library:** A. B. Dowsell (p.249).
*Artwork* **Matthew Hillier**, *except those on p.217 and p.233, which are by* **Martin Camm**.

Editor: Beátrice Frei
Design: Stonecastle Graphics Ltd.
Layout: John Rivers
Picture editing and research: Image Select and Mark Carwardine

The Work Copyright © Mark Carwardine, 1995

Typeset in Palatino and Frutiger by Ace Filmsetting Ltd., Frome, Somerset
Printed and bound in Italy by New Interlitho SpA., Milan

A catalogue record for this book is available from the British Library

ISBN 0-85112-658-8

# CONTENTS

# AARDVARK

## *Orycteropodidae*

**Burrowing** The aardvark or ant bear (*Orycteropus afer*), which lives in the grasslands, scrub and open woodland of sub-Saharan Africa, is one of the fastest burrowing animals in the world. With its long, spoon-shaped claws and enormously powerful legs, it can dig a burrow in soft earth faster than several people with shovels. In fact, if it is unable to run away from its enemies, it will often dig an instant hole and hide instead; in exceptional cases, a complete burrow several metres long can be completed in under 5 minutes. Even hard, sun-baked earth is not an obstacle, although it does make the burrowing take a little longer. Baby aardvarks are able to dig their own burrows when they are about 6 months old.

**Most burrows** The aardvark (*Orycteropus afer*) is an elusive, nocturnal animal and often the only sign of its presence is its burrowing. Some individuals dig a large number of burrows: the record is 60 entrances in one small area approximately 300 m *984 ft* × 100 m *328 ft*. Since the majority of these entrances remain unused for long periods of time, many other animals take advantage of the aardvark's digging prowess and take up residence instead.

> When they are burrowing, aardvarks fold their ears back and close their nostrils to keep out the dirt and to ensure that ants and termites do not get inside.

> Since aardvarks frequently bump into bushes, tree trunks and other obstacles when they are running, it is believed that their eyesight is not particularly good

# ANTELOPES & WILD CATTLE

## *Bovidae*
130 species including: antelopes, kudu, buffalo, duiker, oryx, wildebeest, gazelles, chamois and sheep.

## *Antilocapridae*
Pronghorn only.

**Largest** A number of bovids are known to attain a height at the shoulder of nearly 2 m *6 ft 7 in* and a weight approaching 1000 kg *2205 lb*. These include the wild yak (*Bos mutus*), gaur (*Bos gaurus*), American bison (*Bison bison*), wild water buffalo (*Bubalus arnee*) and domestic cattle (*Bos taurus*). The tallest of all the wild species is probably the Asian gaur, by a narrow margin because of the male's large shoulder hump; it has a head-body length of 2.5–3.3 m *8 ft 2 in–10 ft 10 in*; a tail length of 70–100 cm *27½–39½ in*; a shoulder height of 1.6–2.2 m *5 ft 3 in–7 ft 3 in*; and a weight of 650–1000 kg *1433–2205 lb*. However, the heaviest bovid is probably the wild water buffalo (*Bubalus arnee*), which lives in India, Nepal, Bhutan and Thailand, and is the ancestor of the domestic water buffalo (*Bubalus bubalis*); it has a head-body length of 2.4–3 m *7 ft 10 in–9 ft 10 in*; a tail length of 60–100 cm *23½–39 in*; a shoulder height of 1.5–1.9 m *4 ft 11 in–6 ft 3 in*; and a weight of 700–1200 kg *1543–2646 lb*.

The largest of all the antelopes is the giant eland (*Tragelaphus derbianus*) of western and central Africa. It has a head-body length of 1.8–3.5 m *6–11½ ft*; a tail length of 50–90 cm *19.7–35.4 in*; a shoulder height of 1.3–1.83 m *51–72 in*; and a weight of 350–940 kg *772–2072 lb*. Males are normally larger than females. The common eland (*Tragelaphus oryx*) of eastern and southern Africa is a similar size but does not have such impressive horns; there is one record of a 1.65 m *5 ft 5 in* common eland bull shot in Malawi *c.* 1937 which weighed 943 kg *2078 lb*.

Giant eland, largest of all the antelopes, with a royal antelope, the world's smallest bovid.

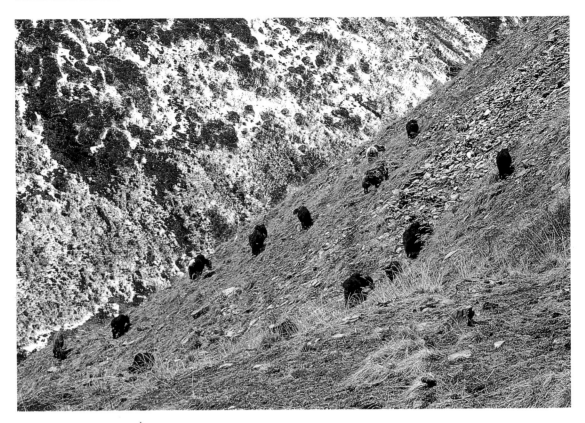

**Largest domestic** The heaviest domestic cattle (*Bos taurus*) on record was a Holstein-Durham cross named Mount Katahdin, which from 1906 to 1910 frequently weighed 2267 kg *5000 lb*. He stood 1.88 m *6 ft 2 in* at the shoulder and had a girth measuring 3.96 m *13 ft*. The animal was exhibited by A. S. Rand of Maine, USA, and died in a barn fire c. 1923.

The largest domestic goat ever recorded was a British Saanen named *Mostyn Moorcock*, owned by Pat Robinson of Ewyas Harold, Hereford & Worcester, UK, which reached a weight of 181.4 kg *400 lb* (shoulder height 1.12 m *44 in* and overall length 1.68 m *66 in*). He died in 1977 at the age of four.

The largest domestic sheep ever recorded was a Suffolk Whisper 23H, owned by Joseph and Susan Schallberger of Boring, Oregon, USA, which weighed 247.2 kg *545 lb* and stood 1.09 m *43 in* tall in March 1991.

**Smallest** The royal antelope (*Neotragus pygmaeus*) of western Africa is the smallest bovid and one of the smallest of all hoofed mammals (after certain chevrotains or mouse deer in the family Tragulidae). About the size of a large brown hare (*Lepus europaeus*), it has a head-body length of 45–55 cm *17¾–21¾ in*; a tail length of about 4–5 cm *1.6–2 in*; a shoulder height of 25–30.5 cm *9.8–12 in*; and a weight of 1.5–3 kg *3 lb 5 oz–6 lb 10 oz*.

**Smallest domestic** The smallest breed of domestic cattle (*Bos taurus*) is the Ovambo of Namibia, with bulls and cows averaging 225 kg *496 lb* and 160 kg *353 lb* respectively.

The smallest breed of sheep is the Ouessant, from the Ile d'Ouessant, Brittany, France, at 13–16 kg *29–35 lb* in weight and standing 45–50 cm *18–20 in* at the shoulder.

**Fastest** The pronghorn or American antelope (*Antilocapra americana*) of the western United States, south-western Canada and parts of northern Mexico is the fastest land animal over a sustained distance (the cheetah [*Acinonyx jubatus*] is the fastest over a short distance). It has been observed to run at 56 km/h *35 mph* for 6 km *4 miles*, at 67 km/h *42 mph* for 1.6 km *1 mile* and 88.5 km/h *55 mph* for 0.8 km *½ mile*. There are claims of speeds of up to 113 km/h *70 mph*, but these are considered unlikely (at least one such claim was the result of a faulty speedometer). Both speed and endurance may be essential for pronghorns to escape from wolves and other predators on the wide open prairies, where there is nowhere to hide.

Recent research has revealed some of the pronghorn's physiological secrets. Most important of all, it is able to consume oxygen with more than three times the expected efficiency of an animal of the same size. It has spectacularly large lungs and a big heart to

**Yaks are the highest-living large mammals in the world and are believed to reach an altitude of 6100 m *20 000 ft*; the herd in this photograph lives near the Tibetan plateau, south-western China.**

pump more blood; the blood itself is unusually rich in haemoglobin (which means that more oxygen can be delivered to the muscles in less time); and the muscle cells are densely-packed with mitochondria, the little powerhouses that use oxygen to supply energy.

The fastest of the other bovids are the gazelles. Species such as the springbok (*Antidorcas marsupialis*) have a top speed of 82–89 km/h *51–55 mph*. They can dodge and turn sharply when running flat out and can make long (but not high) jumps to escape still faster cheetahs (*Acinonyx jubatus*). However, they are relatively poor runners over long distances and overheat easily.

**Highest** The highest-living large mammal in the world is the yak (*Bos mutus*), which lives in China, India and Nepal (it is believed to be extinct in Bhutan and Afghanistan). It roams at high altitudes in the mountains of the Himalayas and the Tibetan plateau and is believed to reach a height of 6100 m *20 000 ft* when foraging (only the Asian large-eared pika [*Ochtona macrotis*] goes

**Common wildebeest, Serengeti National Park, Tanzania, forming part of the largest gathering of hoofed mammals in the world today.**

---

higher). A bull shot in 1899, in the Himalayas, was found at an altitude of 5639 m *18 500 ft*.

**Largest herds** The largest gathering of hoofed mammals today takes places in the Serengeti-Mara ecosystem, in Tanzania and neighbouring Kenya. During the rainy season, from November to May, this area may harbour as many as 1.3 million common wildebeest or white-bearded gnus (*Connochaetes taurinus*), some 200 000 Burchell's zebras (*Equus burchelli*), more than 250 000 Thomson's gazelles (*Gazella thomsonii*) and Grant's gazelles (*Gazella granti*), as well as common eland (*Tragelaphus oryx*), topi (*Damaliscus lunatus*), hartebeest (*Alcelaphus buselaphus*) and a variety of other species (plus all their

*There are no indigenous cattle, antelopes, sheep or goats in South America or Australia.*

attendant predators). There is a general movement off the plains as soon as the grasses lose their green flush, at the beginning of the long, dry season in May or June. During this migration, herds of wildebeest up to 40 km *25 miles* long have been observed from the air.

Spectacular herds of hoofed mammals once gathered in many parts of the world (particularly in Africa and North America) even during the last century. The largest on record were those of the springbok (*Antidorcas marsupialis*) on migration across the plains of the western parts of southern Africa in the 19th century. In 1849 John (later Sir John) Fraser observed a *trekbokken* that took three days to pass through the settlement of Beaufort West, Cape Province, South Africa. Another herd seen moving near Nels Poortje, Cape Province, in 1888, was estimated to contain 100 million head, although 10 million is probably a more realistic figure. A herd estimated to be 24 km *15 miles* wide and more than 160 km *100 miles* long was reported from Karree Kloof, Orange River, South Africa, in July 1896. These unbroken herds were so enormous that other animals met on the way were either trampled or had to move along with them.

**Country with largest stock of cattle** India has a larger stock of cattle

than any other country in the world. In 1993 (the year for which the latest figures are available), it had an estimated 271.3 million head from a world total of 1.05 billion head. The leading producer of milk in 1993 was the US, with 68.7 million tonnes.

**Country with most domestic sheep** The world's leading producer of sheep is Australia, with an estimated total of 147.1 million head in 1993 (the year for which the latest figures are available).

**Shortest horns** All adult male (and some female) bovids carry horns. The shortest horns of any member of the family belong to the royal antelope (*Neotragus pygmaeus*). Present only in the male, they are normally 1.2–2.5 cm *½–1 in* long.

**Longest horns** The longest horns grown by any living animal are those of the wild water buffalo (*Bubalus arnee*) which lives in India, Nepal, Bhutan and Thailand, and is the ancestor of the domestic water buffalo (*Bubalus bubalis*). The average spread is about 1 m *3 ft 3 in*, but one bull shot in 1955 had horns measuring 4.24 m *13 ft 11 in* from tip to tip along the outside curve across the forehead.

Among domestic cattle (*Bos taurus*), a record spread of 3.2 m *10 ft 6 in* was recorded for a Texas longhorn steer on exhibition at the Heritage Museum, Big Springs, Texas, USA.

**Most horns** The male four-horned antelope (*Tetracerus quadricornis*), which lives in India and Nepal, is the only mammal with four horns. The front pair are often poorly developed but average 2–5 cm *0.8–2 in* in length, the rear pair are a slightly longer 8–12 cm *3–4¾ in*.

**Horn shedding** The pronghorn or American antelope (*Antilocapra americana*) of the western United States, south-western Canada and parts of northern Mexico combines several characteristics of both antelopes (family Bovidae) and deer (family Cervidae), but none more striking than its horns. Male, and most female, pronghorns possess short horns. These consist of a bony core covered by an outer keratin sheath, like bovid horns, but they are shed annually after the breeding season, like deer antlers. Consequently, it is the only mammal with true horns to shed them every year.

**Most recently discovered** No fewer than four new bovid species have been discovered since the famous kouprey (*Bos sauveli*) – which lives in small numbers in Cambodia, Laos, Vietnam and, until recently, Thailand – was officially named in 1937. These are the Bilkis gazelle (*Gazella bilkis*), which may still survive in the Yemen, where it was discovered in 1951 (it was named in 1985); the dwarf blue sheep (*Pseudois schaeferi*), which lives in China and was discovered in 1963; the Vu Quang ox or sao la (*Pseudoryx nghetinhensis*), which was discovered in 1992 and lives in parts of northern Vietnam and probably in neighbouring Laos; and the mountain goat or linh duong (*Pseudonovibos spiralis*), which was discovered in Vietnam in 1994 and may also occur in north-western Cambodia.

The discovery of the Vu Quang ox was particularly exciting, because it was the first time in 50 years that an entirely new genus of large mammal had been found. It was discovered by Dr John MacKinnon, Vu Van Dung and their colleagues, in May 1992, during a survey of Vu Quang Nature Reserve, Ha tinh Province, Vietnam. Initially, they found three sets of long, straight horns in the houses of local hunters, but more than 20 specimens (including three complete skins) have been found since. The species has a head-body length of about 1.5–2 m *59–79 in* (plus a short tail of 13 cm *5 in* of bone with a fluffy black tassle); a shoulder height of

*When alarmed, an impala can make a spectacular jump 3 m 10 ft high and 11 m 36 ft long; when a predator comes within pouncing range, an entire herd of impala explodes in all directions.*

80–90 cm *31½–35½ in*; and a weight of about 100 kg *221 lb*. The first live specimen, a female calf estimated to be 4–5 months old, was caught by local hunters in a forest just outside Vu Quang Nature Reserve early in 1994 and was kept in a large enclosure at Vietnam's Forest Research and Planning Institute, Hanoi; she died of respiratory and digestive problems 3 months later. A second live animal, a young male, was brought to Hanoi in September 1994, but died soon afterwards. Information provided by local villagers suggests that a few hundred of these shy, goat-like animals may survive in the wild and scientists are currently

**Water buffalo, Kaziranga National Park, India, which grow the longest horns of any living animal.**

**M
A
M
M
A
L
S**

drawing up a conservation plan to protect them from hunting and habitat destruction.

The most recent find, the mountain goat or linh duong, also represented a new genus. A pair of black, twisted horns, found on a market stall in Ho Chi Minh, Vietnam, by biologist Wolfgang Peter, first brought it to the attention of the scientific world. It has yet to be seen alive by biologists, but is believed to live in the Vietnamese districts of Ban Me Thuot, Dac Lac and Kon Tum, and may survive in Cambodia's north-western districts.

**Most threatened** The World Conservation Union (IUCN) lists a total of 52 different bovids as threatened with extinction. The species considered to be most at risk include the addax (*Addax nasomaculatus*), of Mali, Mauritania, Chad and Niger, and may already be extinct in Algeria, Egypt, Libya and Sudan; the lowland anoa (*Bubalus depressicornis*), of Sulawesi, Indonesia; the wild yak (*Bos mutus*), of China, India and Nepal, and may already be extinct in Afghanistan and Bhutan; the markhor (*Capra falconeri*), of India, Pakistan, Afghanistan, Tajikistan, Turkmenistan and Uzbekistan; the kouprey (*Bos sauveli*), which lives in the war-damaged border areas of Laos, Cambodia and Vietnam, and may already be extinct in Thailand; the recently discovered Vu Quang ox (*Pseudoryx nghetinhensis*), of Vietnam and neighbouring Laos; and the Arabian oryx (*Oryx leucoryx*), which became extinct in the wild in 1972 but is now being reintroduced from captive-bred herds.

A further 63 bovid sub-species are threatened with extinction, as well as two sub-species of pronghorn: the Baja California pronghorn (*Antilocapra americana peninsularis*), from Mexico, and the Sonoran pronghorn (*Antilocapra a. sonoriensis*), from Mexico and the USA.

**Extinctions** Two bovids are known to have become extinct in recent times: the red gazelle (*Gazella rufina*), which disappeared from its home in Algeria in the 19th century, and the bluebuck

(*Hippotragus leucophaeus*), which disappeared from South Africa in 1800.

A further four sub-species of bovid are known or suspected to have become extinct in recent times: the bubal hartebeest (*Alcelaphus buselaphus buselaphus*), from Algeria, Egypt, Morocco and Tunisia; the Egyptian barbary sheep (*Ammotragus lervia ornatus*), from Egypt; the Saudi gazelle (*Gazella dorcas saudiya*), from Iraq, Kuwait, Saudi Arabia, Yemen and United Arab Emirates; and Robert's lechwe (*Kobus leche robertsi*) from Zambia.

**Most rapid decline** An estimated 50–60 million American bison or buffalo (*Bison bison*) roamed the great plains of North America in the early 1800s. Their vast migrating herds were the economic mainstay of the local Indians: they ate the meat and used the hides to make clothes, tepees and canoes; but they killed relatively small numbers and had no long-term effect on the bison population. However, when the European settlers arrived on the continent and, particularly, when they began to sweep westwards in the 1860s, a mass slaughter began. The white men killed bison (on foot, on horseback and, later, even from the comfort of passenger trains) specifically to deprive the Indians of their wild herds, but also to free the land for farming, to obtain the animals' tongues and hides, and for sport. At the peak of the slaughter, some 2.5 million bison were killed annually from 1870 to 1875 and the legendary 'Buffalo Bill' Cody claimed to have killed 4862 of the animals in one year alone. By the late 1890s there were no more than 800 left on the entire North American continent and the species was virtually extinct in the wild. Fortunately, a few hundred had been taken into captivity and, with strenuous conservation efforts, the bison survived. The total population today is about 130 000.

**First successful reintroduction** The first successful reintroduction of a mammal, after the extermination of its entire wild population, took place in 1982 when the Arabian oryx (*Oryx leucoryx*) was returned to its desert home in

Oman. The Arabian oryx was once abundant throughout suitable habitat on the Arabian peninsula but, from 1945, was hunted relentlessly by Arabs armed with automatic weapons and travelling in huge motorized convoys. The last herd of Arabian oryx, comprising just six animals, was destroyed on 18 Oct 1972 and this was the last confirmed sighting of the species in the wild. Fortunately, thanks to the far-sighted efforts of the Fauna & Flora Preservation Society, which set up Operation Oryx in 1962, a small number of animals had been captured and taken to zoos in the USA and Arabia for safekeeping. The first reintroduction to the wild took place in Oman on 31 Jan 1982, under the watchful eyes of local nomadic people, who have been employed to guard the animals as they wander over the desert. Further reintroductions are planned in Jordan and Saudi Arabia (the total wild population is now *c.* 230).

**Most inquisitive** The pronghorn or American antelope (*Antilocapra americana*) of the western United States, south-western Canada and parts of northern Mexico is renowned for its insatiable curiosity and must be one of the most inquisitive animals in the world. It will approach from a considerable distance to inspect moving objects (including people, vehicles and even predators) with no apparent concern for the potential risks involved. Early settlers took advantage of this unlikely behaviour by 'flagging' – tying handkerchiefs to poles and waving them in the air – to attract the inquisitive animals within gunshot range.

Flagging is now illegal but overhunting by early settlers, coupled with habitat loss, was the primary cause of a massive population decline in the pronghorn. Its numbers dropped from 35–50 million in 1850 to just 13 000 by 1920. Strenuous conservation efforts have helped the species to recover and the population now stands at a much more healthy 750 000, although there is concern that oil exploration and strip mining for coal pose serious threats to the relatively little remaining habitat.

# BATS

## *Chiroptera*
*c.* 1000 species:
165 Megachiroptera and 820 Microchiroptera

**Earliest** The earliest known fossil bat is a species called *Icaronycteris index*, which was found as an almost complete skeleton in rocks in Wyoming, USA. It lived during the Eocene some 50 million years ago and, according to its teeth, was probably insectivorous (significantly, insect-eating bats, and possibly all bats, are thought to have evolved from shrew-like insectivores). *Icaronycteris* was an active flier, suggesting that bats of one kind or another must have been around much earlier (perhaps 70–100 million years ago). A further 13 Eocene bat species – all belonging to the sub-order Microchiroptera (predominantly insect-eating species) – have been discovered in North America, Europe and Pakistan. In contrast, the sub-order Megachiroptera (fruit bats or flying foxes) is first represented in the fossil record from the Oligocene some 35 million years ago. Since all known fossil bats resemble modern species, and there is no record of an intermediate evolutionary stage (part bat and part something else), it is unknown when they first took to the air.

There are some significant anatomical and neurological differences between the two main bat groups, the Megachiroptera and the Microchiroptera, and recent studies support a theory that they may have evolved separately. Biologists at the University of Heidelberg, Germany, have used immunological studies (looking at the proteins in blood serum) to demonstrate a close taxonomical relationship between the megachiropterans and primates. If their controversial theory is correct, this means that the similarities between the two bat groups reflect adaptations to a similar way of life rather than a common ancestry (the ability to fly must have evolved twice) and that fruit bats are really 'flying primates'. The truth may come only with the discovery of additional fossil evidence.

**Largest** The largest bats in the world are the flying foxes (family Pteropodidae), particularly those living in south-east Asia. Several species in the genus *Pteropus* may have a head-body length of 45 cm *17¾ in*; a wingspan of at least 1.7 m *5 ft 7 in*; a forearm length of 23 cm *9 in*; and a weight of 1.6 kg *3½ lb*. Unfortunately, there is insufficient agreement among experts to identify the overall largest with certainty, although it is probably either the appropriately named gigantic or Indian flying fox (*Pteropus giganteus*), which lives on the Indian sub-continent and the Maldives or a population of large flying foxes (*Pteropus vampyrus*) also living on the Maldives. The other main contenders are the Bismarck flying fox (*Pteropus neohibernicus*) and the Samoan flying fox (*Pteropus samoensis*).

**Smallest** The smallest mammal in the world is the bumblebee or Kitti's hognosed bat (*Craseonycteris thonglongyai*), which is confined to the deepest and darkest chambers of about 21 limestone caves (population of only about 2000) on the Kwae Noi River, Kanchanaburi Province, south-west Thailand. With a body no bigger than a large bumblebee, it has a head-body length of 2.9–3.3 cm *1.14–1.30 in*; a forearm length of 2.2–2.6 cm *0.87–1.02 in*; a wingspan of approximately 15–16 cm *5.9–6.3 in*; and a weight of 1.7–2 g *0.06–0.07 oz*. It was discovered in October 1973 by the Thai mammal researcher Dr Kitti Thonglongya, who sadly died less than 5 months later. His sensational discovery was confirmed in 1974, when the bat was described for science – bearing his name.

*Nearly a quarter of the world's mammals are bats.*

**Longest ears** The spotted bat (*Euderma maculatum*), which occurs from northern Mexico through the western USA to south-western Canada, is an extraordinary-looking animal. Its ears are longer in proportion to its body than any other species of bat. An enormous 4.5–5 cm *1.8–2 in* long (compared with a head-body length of 6–7.7 cm *2.4–3 in*), they make the species unmistakable. Only some related species of long-eared bats in the genus *Plecotus* have ears that are proportionally almost as large (ears up to 4 cm *1.6 in* in length compared with a head-body length of 4.5–7 cm *1.8–2.8 in*).

**Longest lived** Bats are relatively long-lived for their size and, once an individual has survived the most dangerous period from birth to weaning, 5–8 years is fairly typical for most species. There are a number of records of Daubenton's bats (*Myotis daubentonii*), greater horseshoe bats (*Rhinolophus ferrumequinum*), little brown bats (*Myotis lucifugus*) and gigantic or Indian flying foxes (*Pteropus giganteus*) living for about 30 years. The greatest age reliably reported for a bat is 32 years for a banded female little brown bat in captivity in the USA; a gigantic flying fox died at London Zoo on 11 Jan 1979 at the age of 31 years 5 months.

The greatest reliable age in the wild is about 30 years for a greater horseshoe bat in the UK. There is also a record of at least 24 years for a female little brown bat, which was found on 30 Apr 1960 in a cave on Mt Aeolus, Vermont, USA. It had previously been banded as an adult at a colony in Mashpee, Massachusetts, USA, on 22 Jun 1937.

**Fastest** Because of their erratic flying patterns, and therefore the great practical difficulties in obtaining accurate measurements, few data on bat speeds have been published. In one US experiment in the 1960s, using an artificial mine tunnel and 17 different species of bat, only four of them managed to exceed 20.8 km/h *13 mph* in level flight. The fastest was a big brown bat (*Eptesicus fuscus*), which reached a maximum speed of 25 km/h *15½ mph* over a distance of 28 m *92 ft*. The greatest velocity reliably attributed to a bat is 51 km/h *32 mph* in the case of a Mexican free-tailed bat (*Tadarida brasiliensis*), but this may have been wind-assisted. Higher, unauthenticated speeds have been claimed. Fast-flying bats tend to have long, narrow wings, while agile, slow-flying species have broad wings.

**Longest gestation period** The longest known gestation period for any bat is 7 to 8 months in the common vampire (*Desmodus rotundus*); the baby then suckles for a further 9 months or more (changing its diet from milk to blood in stages). Several other species have exceptionally long delays between mating and birth of the young: either the egg is fertilized at mating and the development of the embryo is delayed, or fertilization itself is delayed. These long delays often coincide with hibernation. They give an 'apparent' gestation period of 9 months or more in the North American little brown bat (*Myotis lucifugus*) and, indeed, most other temperate bats; however, the true period of embryonic development in each of these species is only 6–8 weeks.

**Shortest gestation period** The shortest known gestation period in bats, by a very small margin, is probably 40–45 days in the common pipistrelle (*Pipistrellus pipistrellus*), which lives in Europe and south-western Asia. However, many other temperate species have similarly short gestation periods.

**Largest litter** Most bats give birth to only one young at a time, although twins occur regularly in some species. The only bats which *commonly* have more than two young are members of the genus *Lasiurus*: the hoary bat (*L. cinereus*), northern yellow bat (*L. intermedius*), seminole bat (*L. seminolus*) and, in particular, the red bat (*L. borealis*) all produce litters of up to four. There is one report of two female red bats with 5 young each, although it is possible that they were fostering orphans from other parents. The number of young varies between individuals as well as species, depending on latitude, food availability, the age and experience of the females, and a variety of other factors.

A small number of bats have more than one litter every year. The little free-tailed bat (*Tadarida pumila*), for example, has three litters of one young per year. But the record-holder is probably Wroughton's pipistrelle (*Pipistrellus mimus*), which lives in Asia; the female bears twins and may have as many as three litters annually. This species reaches sexual maturity at a young 5 months, which is probably earlier than in any other bat.

Despite their small litters, bats produce roughly the same *weight* of youngsters as non-flying mammals of a similar size. Baby bats are enormous at birth, weighing 12–43 per cent of the weight of the mother (the largest being the Japanese horseshoe bat, *Rhinolophus cornutus*); this compares with an aver-

age weight of 8 per cent for non-flying mammals of a similar size. However, if the whole litter weight is taken into account (most small mammals have relatively large litters) the average figures are 26 per cent for bats and 25 per cent for non-fliers.

**Male lactation** The relatively uncommon Dayak fruit bat (*Dyacopterus spadiceus*) is the only wild mammal in which the male is known to produce milk. This remarkable discovery, which overturns a fundamental assumption about mammals, was made by a team of scientists from the New York Zoological Society, Rhode Island College and Boston University during a study of bats in the Krau Game Reserve, Pahang, Malaysia, in 1992. They happened to catch 13 male Dayak fruit bats, 10 of which were sexually mature and had working mammary glands that were producing milk (albeit in small quantities). It is unknown if the bats were actually suckling young animals. Milk production by male mammals is not without precedent, but is isolated and rare and normally due to abnormalities such as extreme inbreeding in domestic animals and hormone treatment in humans.

**Midwife bats** The only bats known to give birth with the assistance of another are the rare Rodrigues fruit bat (*Pteropus rodricensis*) and the black flying fox (*Pteropus alecto*). Professor Thomas Kunz and colleagues from Boston University observed this for the first time on 5 Aug 1991, during a study of a small captive colony of Rodrigues fruit bats at the Lubee Foundation in Gainsville, Florida, USA. When an inexperienced mother-to-be was having problems giving birth, a female roostmate came to her aid: she fanned her, sometimes embraced her body with spread wings and even appeared to give her instructions; finally, after a rather difficult delivery lasting 1 hr 43 min, the 'midwife' helped to manoeuvre the pup into a suckling position. Similar observations were reported soon afterwards in a captive colony of black flying foxes (*Pteropus alecto*) at a research station in Queensland, Australia. It is possible that such cooperative behaviour is common in colonial bats and the fact that it had not been observed before may simply be because few people have ever seen a bat giving birth.

Midwife behaviour is uncommon in the animal world, and has been reported only for the common marmoset (*Callithrix jacchus*), Indian elephant (*Elephas maximum*), spiny mouse (*Acomys cahirinus*), bottlenose dolphin

(*Tursiops truncatus*), some domestic dogs and, of course, humans.

**Greatest sexual dimorphism** The greatest sexual dimorphism in bats is found in the African hammer-headed fruit bat (*Hypsignathus monstrosus*). The male is nearly twice the weight of the female (an average of 420 g *15 oz* compared with 234 g *8¼ oz*) and, while the female has a familiar fox-shaped head, the male has a square, hammer-shaped head and enormous, pendulous lips.

**Largest colonies** The largest concentration of bats anywhere in the world is a summer nursery of Mexican free-tailed bats (*Tadarida brasiliensis*) found in about a dozen caves in Texas, USA. These bats have the distinction of attaining a higher population density than any other mammal (including humans). At one time, there were estimated to be about 100 million of them but, after the indiscriminate and widespread use of DDT in North America in the 1960s, the population crashed to less than 3 million; their numbers have partly recovered in recent years. One particular cave (Bracken Cave near San Antonio) is probably the most populous bat cave in the world; 10 million females (which have migrated some 800–1800 km *500–1200 miles* from their wintering grounds in Mexico) give birth over a 7–10 day period, resulting in 10 million baby bats in one place. However, several of the other caves are almost as crowded, being home to no fewer than 5 million females and their young.

Since there can be as many as 3000 baby free-tailed bats per m² *280 per ft²* of ceiling, and because they are always jostling one another and moving around, it can be difficult for a female to locate her own baby. After a feeding flight, she enters the dark cave and uses memory to alight to within a few feet of where she had seen it last. She calls, waits for the baby to answer and then scrambles past the other youngsters (all trying to steal a drink of milk) until she is close enough to recognize it by smell. Research has shown that the females are successful in finding their own babies 85 per cent of the time.

Colonies of more than 1000 bats are now rare in Europe. Earlier reports suggest *c.* 100 000 pipistrelles (*Pipistrellus*

> *The Chinese word for bat is 'yeh yen', which means 'swallow of the night'.*

> *Injuries to bat wing membranes heal amazingly fast; for example, a hole with a 2 cm 0.8 in diameter in the wing of a flying fox will heal within about a month.*

Mexican free-tailed bats in Texas, USA, where many millions gather to form the largest concentration of bats in the world today.

---

*pipistrellus*) in a cave in Romania, but one of the largest today is a group of 60 000 Schreiber's bats (*Miniopterus schreibersii*) which was discovered in the 1980s in a cave at the north-east end of the Pyrenees, in Aude, France. But perhaps the most important – certainly in northern Europe – is a colony living in an old military underground tunnel system (built by the Germans before and during World War II) in western Poland. More than 20 000 bats of 12 different species hibernate in the tunnels of the former Miedzyrzecki Fortified Region in the Lubuskie Lake District, about 100 km *62 miles* west of Poznan. The tunnels comprise about 30 km *18½ miles* of reinforced concrete passages some 30 m *98 ft* below ground. The most numerous species (accounting for a little more than half the total population) is Daubenton's bat (*Myotis daubentonii*).

**Roost building** Sixteen different bat species have been recorded creating secure, dry day-time roosts, typically by turning single leaves into simple tents. But the champion is Peters' tent-making bat (*Uroderma bilobatum*), which has been studied on Barro Colorado Island, Panama, by Dr Jae Choe of Harvard University. This appropriately named species builds a sophisticated tepee-shaped tent, from as many as 14 leaves each about 44 cm *17¼ in* long and 21 cm *8¼ in* wide, and the bats simply fly in and out of the bottom. It gives excellent protection from downpours and is spacious enough to accommodate up to three bats. No females have yet been recorded using a tepee and, since the building process has also never been observed, it is uncertain whether a single bat makes it or if several bats cooperate.

**Burrowing** The New Zealand lesser short-tailed bat (*Mystacina tuberculata*) is the only bat able to excavate burrows. It uses its incisor teeth, and probably its talon-like claws, to produce burrows which can be as much as 50 cm *20 in* in depth and up to 10 cm *4 in* in diameter.

**Longest hibernation** In temperate zones, in order to survive the long, foodless winters, bats have a choice between migrating to warmer regions with a sufficient food supply or hibernating and surviving without food. Most species choose to hibernate and, indeed, some spend longer periods of time in uninterrupted hibernation than any other mammal. Under natural conditions, little brown bats (*Myotis lucifugus*) have been known to remain without movement for up to 86 days and big brown bats (*Eptesicus fuscus*) have been observed in the same state for 64–66 days. Under laboratory conditions, however, several species have been kept in uninterrupted hibernation for much longer (in one exceptional case a big brown bat was kept in a controlled refrigerator for 344 days before it died of starvation).

Hibernating bats spend the autumn

> *The US Air Force at Randolph Air Force Base, Texas, USA, schedules the flights of its aircraft around the activities of Mexican free-tailed bats, which live in enormous colonies nearby; one 12 g 0.42 oz bat can destroy an engine and could even cause a fatal crash.*

fattening up (increasing their total body weight by as much as 25–35 per cent) and survive the winter on their fat reserves. They spend up to 6 months in a state of extended lethargy, lowering their metabolism dramatically to reduce energy consumption. Their body temperature falls about to the level of their surroundings; their heart rate may decrease to around 25 beats/min (compared with more than 1000/min while flying); and their breathing may drop to a rate of as little as one breath every 45 minutes (some individuals have been known to go for 2 hours between breaths). Even hanging upside down costs no energy (indeed, it often continues after death) since there is a tendon that prevents the hook-like toes from straightening. Unlike many other hibernators, bats may not feed again until the following spring, but they do wake at intervals (on average every 20 days) to move to a different part of the hibernaculum or even to another site (and may eat if the opportunity arises). Waking is also essential for them to drink: they lose water by breathing and

Some moths have evolved ear-like organs, enabling them to hear an echolocating bat and to take evasive action; others produce a string of ultrasonic clicks that interfere with the bat's echolocation system and force it to give up the chase, or produce ultrasonic clicks that warn the bat that they do not taste very nice.

**Bats are by far the most efficient echolocators of all terrestrial animals, using the echoes of their ultrasonic calls and clicks to detect objects as small as midges from at least 20 m *65½ ft* away.**

dehydrate easily. Even though bats may be awake for only 2–4 per cent of the winter, these brief *natural* interludes consume more than 75 per cent of their total energy reserves; a single *forced* arousal caused by disturbance uses up so much extra energy (equivalent to up to 50 days in hibernation) that it can mean the difference between starvation and survival.

**Lowest body temperature** Many hibernating bats can allow their bodies to cool almost to freezing point. But the North American red bat (*Lasiurus borealis*) can withstand its body tissues actually freezing into ice at temperatures well below freezing, without suffering any serious ill effects. It has the thickest fur, the lowest heart rate at low temperatures and the highest red blood cell count of any bat.

The guano produced by a huge colony of Mexican free-tailed bats, in New Mexico, USA, was used as a major source of nitrates for manufacturing gunpowder during the American Civil War.

**Longest migration** A number of temperate bat species undertake seasonal migrations to avoid the extremes of winter; these include members of the genera *Nyctalus, Vespertilio, Lasiurus, Lasionycteris, Pipistrellus* and *Tadarida*. The longest true flight ever recorded was 2347 km *1458 miles* as the crow flies by a European noctule (*Nyctalus noctula*), which was ringed in August 1957 by Russian zoologist P.P. Strelkov, at Voronezh, Russia, and was found again in southern Bulgaria in January 1961. The North American red bat (*Lasiurus borealis*) is believed to migrate as far as 2000 km *1242 miles* on occasion, and a number of other long-distance migrants travel distances of 1000–1500 km *621–932 miles*.

There are also a number of cases where migrating bats have been *blown* thousands of kilometres off course. The record-holder for wind-assisted flights must be the hoary bat (*Lasiurus cinereus*), which managed to reach the Hawaiian Islands, USA, located some 3700 km *2300 miles* from the American mainland at the nearest point. It has now established itself as a separate island sub-species (*Lasiurus c. semotus*).

**Most northerly** The population of northern bats (*Eptesicus nilssonii*) living high above the Arctic Circle, in the north of Norway, is by far the most northerly population of bats anywhere in the world. One individual has even been seen at Austertana in Finnmark (70° 25′ N), which is the northernmost record for any bat. The first observation of breeding (69° 05′ N) was made in July 1991 by a team of scientists from Sweden, Norway and the UK; this is some 4° further north than the most northerly breeding bats elsewhere in

the world (a colony of the same species at 65°N near Luleä, Sweden). The presence of northern bats in the north of Norway has been known since last century and is probably influenced by the Gulf Stream which makes the climate there much warmer than in other areas at the same latitude.

**Echolocation** Echolocation is an extremely sophisticated form of sonar, in which an animal builds up a 'sound picture' of its surroundings by listening for the returning *echoes* of sounds it produces to *locate* objects in its path. In bats, which are by far the most efficient echolocators of all terrestrial mammals, it enables them to gather information on the distance, direction and relative velocity of an object, as well as its shape, size and texture; some species are able to detect objects as small as midges from at least 20 m *65½ ft* away.

The calls and clicks produced by echolocating bats are mostly ultrasonic (beyond the range of human hearing) and are very complex, made up of different sounds of varying frequencies. Most species use frequencies in the 20–80 kHz range, although some go as high as 120–250 kHz (the normal range of human hearing is 20 Hz to almost 20 kHz). Their ultrasonic pulses vary in duration from about 0.2 milliseconds to 100 milliseconds and are repeated at regular intervals, according to the bat's activity. A hunting bat will search using an emission rate of about 3–10 pulses/s; this increases to 15–50 per second once a flying insect has been detected; and, in the final approach stage, it increases still further to as much as 200 pulses/s, providing the bat with continuous information about its target. The sounds are produced in the larynx and, in most species, emitted through the open mouth; however, bats with nose leaves tend to 'call' through their nostrils (and, consequently, fly with their mouths closed).

It is presumed that all bats in the sub-order Microchiroptera are able to echolocate, although only a small number have been studied in detail. The only fruit bats or flying foxes (sub-order Megachiroptera) known to do it are a few members of the genus *Rousettus*, such as the Egyptian fruit bat (*R. aegyptiacus*). *Rousettus* species roost in caves and need to be able to find their way in and out in total darkness; they use a very simple form of echolocation and produce orientation sounds by clicking their tongue against the side of the mouth. A number of other animals are able to echolocate: dolphins and many toothed whales, certain birds such as cave swiftlets and oilbirds, a few gliding marsupials, and certain rodents and insectivores; like the fruit bats, all except the cetaceans use a rather crude form of echolocation to detect relatively large objects in total darkness.

Contrary to popular opinion, not all bat echolocation is beyond the range of human hearing. Among the sub-order Microchiroptera, the North American spotted bat (*Euderma maculatum*) and the European free-tailed bat (*Tadarida teniotis*) are unique in making echolocation calls which sweep between 9 kHz and 15 kHz; these sound as if they were being made by an insect rather than a bat. The 'song flight' of the male particoloured bat (*Vespertilio murinus*) goes down to 10 kHz, and echolocating fruit bats in the sub-order Mega-chiroptera also produce sounds that are partially audible to the human ear (in the range 5–100 kHz).

> *Contrary to popular belief, bats are not blind; they all have functional eyes and many have keen vision that compares well with our own.*

**Strongest flier** The female red bat (*Lasiurus borealis*) is stronger in flight than any other species of bat and is capable of carrying two or even three infants (easily exceeding her own body weight) as they cling to her fur. Vampire bats (family Desmodontidae) are able to fly on exceedingly full stomachs (*see Blood drinking*).

**Deepest** A colony of 1000 little brown bats (*Myotis lucifugus*) spends the winter at a record depth of 1160 m *3805 ft* in a zinc mine in New York, USA. This species normally roosts at a depth of about 200 m *656 ft*.

**Blood drinking** Vampire bats (family Desmodontidae) are the only mammals that feed exclusively on blood. They have the most extreme dietary specialization of any bat and are also the only true bat parasites. There are three species, found only in Central and South America: the hairy-legged vampire (*Diphylla ecaudata*) and the white-winged vampire (*Diaemus youngi*), both of which feed almost exclusively on bird blood; and the appropriately named common vampire (*Desmodus rotundus*), which feeds almost exclusively on mammalian blood. They are fairly small bats, with a head-body length of only 6.5–9 cm *2½–3½ in*; a wingspan of 32–35 cm *12½–13¾ in*; and a weight of about 40 g *1.4 oz*.

The common vampire is normally active on dark, moonless nights. Once it has found a victim, it lands on the ground a few feet away and walks, runs or hops its way across (vampires are more agile on the ground than any other species of bat); if it has chosen a horse or mule it may land on the tail or mane instead. With the help of a heat sensor on its nose, it identifies an area where the blood flows close to the skin (it does not bite into an artery or vein) and begins to lick over an area of about 0.5 cm *0.2 in* in diameter. If there is fur in the way it uses its large, razor-sharp upper incisor teeth to clip it away, and then carefully removes a flap of skin. The bite is normally painless (the vic-tim rarely wakes up) and the vampire's saliva contains an anticoagulant that prevents the blood from clotting. Contrary to popular belief, it does not suck the blood through its 'fangs', but has a special way of licking it up as it oozes freely from the wound. A vampire needs at least 20 g *0.7 oz* of blood every day to survive (equivalent to two table-spoons or half its own body weight), and normally takes about 20 minutes to drink its fill. Within 2 minutes of begin-ning to feed, it starts to urinate to get rid of the blood plasma, which is heavy and contains no nutritive value (it is easier to fly afterwards on a less full stomach). Each bat feeds only once in a night (after feeding it returns to its roost to digest the meal) but may return night after night to the same victim (reopen-ing the old wound on subsequent visits).

Blood loss is generally not a prob-lem with bites caused by vampire bats, as relatively small amounts are in-volved. The greatest risk is from infected bats transmitting diseases such as ra-bies and from subsequent invasion by screw worms and other parasites.

---

**Vampires are the only mammals that feed exclusively on blood and are the only true bat parasites; this is a common vampire.**

# MAMMALS

*Vampire bats have profited enormously from cattle ranching in Central and South America, because the unfortunate domestic animals provide an inexhaustible blood bank.*

**Most threatened** The World Conservation Union (IUCN) lists a total of 72 species of bat (7.3 per cent of the world total) as known or suspected to be threatened with extinction. The species considered most at risk include: the golden-capped fruit bat (*Acerodon jubatus*) of the Philippines; Bulmer's fruit bat (*Aproteles bulmerae*) of Papua New Guinea; the Philippines tube-nosed fruit bat (*Nyctimene rabori*), which lives on the island of Negros, in the Philippines; the Ryukyu flying fox (*Pteropus dasymallus*) of Taiwan and the Ryukyu Islands, Japan; Rodrigues flying fox (*Pteropus rodricensis*), which lives on the island of Rodrigues, 500 km *310 miles* east of Mauritius; the Seychelles sheath-tailed bat (*Coleura seychellensis*) of the Seychelles; and the grey bat (*Myotis grisescens*), which lives in the USA. The many and varied threats they face include the widespread use of persistent pesticides in agriculture and highly toxic insecticides for treating building timbers, habitat destruction, overhunting, disturbance at their roosts and natural factors such as tropical cyclones. Negative human attitudes towards them are also a major problem.

In addition, further sub-species of bat are known or suspected to be threatened with extinction. These include the Aldabra flying fox (*Pteropus seychellensis aldabrensis*), which lives on Aldabra Atoll, in the Seychelles, and is regarded by some as a separate species; and the Hawaiian hoary bat (*Lasiurus cinereus semotus*) of the Hawaiian Islands, USA.

The most threatened bats are the fruit bats or flying foxes (sub-order Megachiroptera): out of a total of about 165 species, no fewer than 48 (29 per cent) are listed by the World Conserva-

*It is a myth that bats fly into people's hair; they may swoop low over people to investigate but would hate to get tangled up.*

tion Union (IUCN) as known or suspected to be threatened with extinction, and a further eight are thought to have become extinct in recent years. A central problem is that 86 per cent of fruit bats live on islands – and island species are especially vulnerable to change as they have nowhere to escape.

**Rarest** It is almost impossible to identify the world's rarest bat. A considerable number of species – including the small-toothed fruit bat (*Neopteryx frosti*) from Tamalanti, Sulawesi (discovered in 1938–39) and *Paracoelops megalotis* from Vinh, Vietnam (discovered in 1945) – are known only from the type specimen. Yet they may survive, so far undiscovered, in reasonable numbers. Salim Ali's fruit

bat (*Latidens salimalii*) is a good example. It was first discovered on 2 May 1948 and, although it was originally identified wrongly as a common dog-nosed bat (*Cynopterus sphinx*), was re-examined in 1972 and recognized as both a new species and a new genus. For many years, it was feared extinct until, in April 1993, a small population was rediscovered on a remote coffee estate in the High Wavy Mountains of southern India.

**Extinctions** No fewer than 12 bat species are known or suspected to have become extinct in recent times. These include the Panay giant fruit bat (*Acerodon lucifer*), which disappeared from the island of Panay, in the Philippines, in 1888; the Guam flying fox (*Pteropus tokudae*), from the island of

The world's most threatened bats are the fruit bats or flying foxes; these Rodrigues fruit bats are being bred in captivity to save them from extinction on their island home in the Indian Ocean.

Guam, in 1968; the Philippine bare-backed fruit bat (*Dobsonia chapmani*), which is believed to have disappeared from the islands of Cebu and Negros, in the Philippines, in 1964; and the New Zealand greater short-tailed bat (*Mystacina robusta*), which probably disappeared from Big South Cape Island, off the coast of Stewart Island, in New Zealand and Solomon Island, in the 1960s.

**Longest absence** Bulmer's fruit bat (*Aproteles bulmerae*) was thought to have become extinct 9000–10 000 years ago, and was known only from 200 incomplete fossils excavated in the 1970s at a site called the Kiowa rock shelter in Chimbu Province, New Guinea. However, soon afterwards palaeontologist James I. Menzies discovered two skulls and two lower mandibles in a dirty old box full of fruit bat skulls in a back room at the Australian Museum, Sydney. They had been collected in 1975 by anthropologist D. Hyndman from a cave 0.8 km ½ *mile* underground in the Hindenburg ranges, western Papua New Guinea, and left unstudied. A startled Menzies recognized the remains as belonging to Bulmer's fruit bat – which had clearly survived right up to the present day. Investigations in

1977 revealed that the original colony had been wiped out by local people but, in May 1992, another colony containing 137 of the bats was found in a single cave within the Hindenberg ranges.

> There are two very distinct groups of bats: the herbivorous Megachiroptera or fruit bats (with about 165 species) and the predominantly insect-eating Microchiroptera (with about 820 species)

# BEARS

### *Ursidae*
8 species, including giant panda (still considered by some to be a member of the raccoon family)

**Largest** The largest bear (and, indeed, the largest of the carnivores) is the polar bear (*Ursus maritimus*). Adult males typically weigh 400–600 kg *880–1323 lb*, although the weight of individuals can fluctuate enormously during the course of a year; they have a nose-to-tail length of 2.4–2.6 m *95–102 in* (the tail itself

The male Kodiak bear is the most heavily built bear in the world: the largest confirmed record in the wild was of a specimen weighing 751 kg *1656 lb*.

measures 8–13 cm *3–5 in*). Adult females reach a maximum length of around 2 m *80 in* and are roughly half the weight of the males. The largest polar bear on record was a male that allegedly weighed 1002 kg *2210 lb* when it was shot at the polar entrance to Kotzebue Sound, Alaska, USA, in 1960; it is now on display at Anchorage Airport, where it stands 3.4 m *11 ft 2 in* tall.

A few brown bears (*Ursus arctos*) in Alaska, USA, have been known to reach a similar size. In 1981 an unconfirmed weight of over 907 kg *2000 lb* was reported for a brown bear from Alaska, USA, on exhibition at the Space Farms Zoological Park at Beemerville, New Jersey, USA.

The male Kodiak bear (*U. a. middendorffi*), a sub-species of brown bear found on Kodiak Island and the adjacent Afognak and Shuyak islands, in the Gulf of Alaska, USA, is generally smaller in length than the polar bear but is usually more robustly built. Again, the male is usually larger than the female. Male Kodiak bears weigh 475–530 kg *1050–1170 lb* and have a nose-to-tail length of 1.7–2.8 m *5 ft 7 in– 9 ft 2 in*, with the tail measuring 6–21 cm *2.4–8.3 in*; they stand up to 1.5 m *4 ft 11 in* at the shoulder. The largest Kodiak bear on record was a 'cage-fat' male in the Cheyenne Mountain Zoological Park, Colorado Springs, USA, which weighed 757 kg *1670 lb* at the time of its death on 22 Sep 1955. The largest confirmed record in the wild was a male shot at English Bay, Kodiak Island, in the Gulf of Alaska, USA, in 1894; it weighed 751 kg *1656 lb* and its stretched skin measured 4.11 m *13 ft 6 in* from nose to tail.

There is an unconfirmed report of a male brown bear, shot near Cold Bay, Alaska, USA, on 28 May 1948, with a nose-to-tail length of 3.05 m *10 ft* and an estimated weight of 726–771 kg *1600– 1700 lb*. The bear had just come out of hibernation and, with its fat reserves, may have weighed as much as 840 kg *1852 lb* at the end of the previous summer.

There are reports of giant bears weighing as much as 1134 kg *2500 lb* living on the Kamchatka Peninsula, Russia, but scientific evidence is virtually non-existent.

**Largest extinct** One of the largest known terrestrial carnivores was the extinct giant short-faced bear (*Arctodus simus*); an average male weighed 600– 1000 kg *1323–2204 lb*.

**Smallest** The sun bear (*Helarctos malayanus*) of tropical forests in southeast Asia, is the smallest of the bears, measuring 1.2–1.5 m *4–5 ft* in length and weighing 27–65 kg *60–145 lb*. Males are 10–20 per cent larger than females.

**Smallest cub** Newborn bears are extremely small compared to the newborn of other carnivores and are typically less than 1 per cent of their mother's weight. The smallest, in actual size as well as in relation to the size of its mother, is the giant panda (*Ailuropoda melanoleuca*) which weighs only 85–140 g *3–5 oz* at birth; this is roughly the same size as an adult mole. Since the weight of a female giant panda is 70–100 kg *155–220 lb* the cub is, on average, 0.13 per cent of the weight of its mother. The difference in size between mother and cub is also extreme in the polar bear (*Ursus maritimus*), brown bear (*Ursus arctos*) and Asiatic black bear (*Ursus thibetanus*): the cubs, respectively, weigh 0.28 per cent, 0.34 per cent and 0.34 per cent of their mothers. In comparison, a healthy newborn human child weighs 5–8 per cent of its mother.

**Weight gain** Several species of bear live a continuous cycle of feast and famine: they spend most of the winter asleep and most of their waking time searching for food and eating. They do not hide the food, but store it as a thick layer of fat on their bodies; as a result, their fat deposits may constitute more than 50 per cent of their total body weight by the end of the summer. The greatest increase in weight recorded was for an adult female polar bear (*Ursus maritimus*) weighed in western Hudson Bay, Canada; she increased her weight by a factor of five from 97 kg *214 lb* in late November to 505 kg *1112 lb* the following August.

In the spring and early summer, polar bears (*Ursus maritimus*) feed on recently weaned ringed seal pups, which can be up to 50 per cent fat. The seals are so plentiful from April to July that the bears sometimes eat only the layer of fat beneath the skin and leave the rest of the carcass untouched. For these few months of the year, the bears may have the highest kilojoule intake of fat of any mammal.

The brown bear (*Ursus arctos*) eats as much as 41 kg *90 lb* of food a day in the summer, resulting in a daily weight gain of up to 2.7 kg *6 lb*.

An American black bear (*Ursus americanus*) weighed 195 kg *430 lb* when it was captured as part of a research programme in Manitoba, Canada, on 25 Jun 1987, and weighed 364 kg *803 lb* when it was recaptured on 9 Sep 1987. The bear gained 169 kg *373 lb* in 75 days – an average of 2.3 kg *5 lb* per day – and almost doubled in weight.

**Weight loss** Brown bears (*Ursus arctos*), black bears (*Ursus americanus*) and female polar bears (*Ursus maritimus*) go into a deep sleep for the winter and survive not by eating but by burning up their fat reserves. Their body weight falls dramatically during this period. Losses of more than 1 kg *2.2 lb* per day have been recorded for brown bears, whose weight during the winter may halve.

**Hibernation** Bears do not hibernate in the true sense of the word: their body temperature rarely drops more than 5°C *9°F* below the normal 31–37.4°C *87.8–99°F* and they can wake in an instant. But four species do have a long winter sleep: American black bear (*Ursus americanus*), Asiatic black bear (*Ursus thibetanus*), brown bear (*Ursus arctos*) and polar bear (*Ursus maritimus*). During this period they have a lower metabolic rate, and reduced heart and breathing rates, and they do not eat, drink, urinate or defecate; if left undisturbed, they may sleep for as long as a month without changing position. American black bears living in northern Canada probably sleep for longer than any of the others, dozing off by October and waking in late April – a total of up to 7 months.

**Longest fast** Pregnant female polar bears (*Ursus maritimus*) in the Hudson Bay region of Canada survive entirely on their stored fat for a continuous period of about 8 months. They are forced ashore in June or July, when the sea ice melts, and are unable to feed again until they return to the ice the following March or April. During this period, they walk hundreds of miles to their breeding grounds, construct a den in the snow, survive the sub-zero temperatures of the Arctic winter, give birth to one or two cubs, nurse the cubs from less than 1 kg *2.2 lb* to about 10–12 kg *22–27 lb* and then, stimulated by an increase in the light shining through the den ceiling, break out and walk hundreds of miles back to their hunting grounds in the middle of the Bay.

**Best insulation** The combined insulation of fat and fur on a polar bear

**The female polar bear produces richer milk than any other bear, containing nearly 50 per cent fat; this is essential to help her cubs survive in cold, arctic conditions.**

(*Ursus maritimus*) is so effective that its body temperature and metabolic rate remain normal even when the outside temperature drops to as low as –37°C (–35°F).

**Richest milk** Milk produced by the female polar bear (*Ursus maritimus*) contains up to 48.4 per cent fat, making it as rich as cream; this is important in building up the fat reserves of the cubs to help them survive in extremely cold conditions. In comparison, the milk produced by a female sun bear (*Ursus malayanus*) contains only 5 per cent fat.

**Earliest** The first real bear-like carnivore evolved from a dog-like animal called *Cephalogale* and appeared around 5–6 million years ago. It ultimately gave rise to all other bears.

> *The giant panda appears to have an extra, sixth 'finger' on each forepaw; this is actually an enlarged wrist bone (the radial sesamoid) that is capable of independent movement.*

**Most primitive** The most primitive bear alive today is the giant panda (*Ailuropoda melanoleuca*). Current evidence suggests that it diverged from the other bears between 18 and 25 million years ago.

The spectacled bear (*Tremarctos ornatus*) diverged from the other bears between 12 and 15 million years ago and is also very primitive. It is the only living relative of the giant short-faced bear (*Arctodus simus*), a species that became extinct about 10 000 years ago. The two animals share several characteristics: a short muzzle and similar skull proportions, primitive auditory bullae (small projections of the skull enclosing the middle ear) and primitive teeth.

**Most herbivorous** Most bears are predominantly herbivorous, with plant material accounting for at least 75 per cent of their diet. The giant panda (*Ailuropoda melanoleuca*) is probably the most herbivorous member of the family and, indeed, is probably the most herbivorous of the carnivores. As much as 99 per cent of its diet consists of bamboo stems, branches and leaves.

**Most carnivorous** The polar bear (*Ursus maritimus*) lives almost exclu-

**The giant panda has a larger appetite, in relation to body weight, than any other bear; it spends over 60 per cent of its life feeding.**

sively on seals: primarily ringed seals but also, to a lesser degree, bearded seals. It may also eat walruses, beluga whales, narwhals and carrion. During the summer, however, it may feed on grass, berries and seaweed.

**Most specialized diet** Several bear species have very specialized diets. The sloth bear (*Ursus ursinus*) is almost entirely insectivorous and feeds mainly on termites, for example, while the polar bear (*Ursus maritimus*) eats primarily ringed seals. The giant panda (*Ailuropoda melanoleuca*) feeds almost exclusively on bamboo stems, branches and leaves, accounting for as much as 99 per cent of its diet. Although as many as 30 species of bamboo are eaten throughout the panda's range, each panda usually survives on only a handful of different species. Very occasionally, it will eat other plants, such as tufted grass, crocuses and vines, the carrion of dead deer or takin, and even fish, pikas and rodents.

> The name 'grizzly' bear came about because the tip of each hair in the fur is often light in colour, whereas the main body of the hair is dark; this gives the animal a grizzled appearance.

**Most varied diet** The spectacled bear (*Tremarctos ornatus*) probably has the most varied diet of all the bears, eating from a range of over 80 different food items, including rabbits, deer, vicuna, birds, berries, 32 species of fruit, 22 species of bromeliad, 11 species of cactus, mosses and orchid bulbs.

**Largest appetite** The giant panda (*Ailuropoda melanoleuca*) has to spend up to 15 hours a day feeding in order to survive. It eats more food in relation to its body weight than any other bear and, unlike other members of the family with large appetites, feeds all year round. It is able to digest no more than 21 per cent of the bamboo it eats and, consequently, every day it has to consume up to 15 per cent of its body weight in bamboo leaves and stems (which it eats mainly during winter) or as much as 38 per cent of its body weight in bamboo shoots (which it eats mainly in the spring); this is equivalent to 10–45 kg *22–99 lb* of food a day. One wild panda, in Wolong Natural Reserve, Sichuan Province, China, was observed to eat 3481 bamboo stems in one sitting.

**Largest prey** An adult male polar bear (*Ursus maritimus*) has a stomach capacity of around 68 kg *150 lb* and is known to kill animals as large as walruses (500 kg *1100 lb*) and beluga whales (600 kg *1320 lb*). Brown bears (*Ursus arctos*) are able to kill animals as large as moose (450 kg *990 lb*) and bison (500 kg *1100 lb*) and, in some cases, have even been observed carrying their carcasses. Even spectacled bears (*Tremarctos ornatus*), which themselves weigh only 64–155 kg *141–342 lb* have been known to kill domestic cattle.

**Most dangerous** All members of the bear family have been known to attack people at one time or another, though attacks are extremely rare in comparison with the large number of bear–human encounters. The only species which actively preys on people is the polar bear (*Ursus maritimus*). Most attacks occur during the night and are made by hungry sub-adult males that are probably inexperienced hunters and are more likely to be driven from their normal kills by larger bears. The most recent fatal attack took place in March 1995, when a German tourist was killed by a polar bear on the outskirts of Longyearbyen, Svalbard. Many more bears are killed in polar bear–human confrontations simply because more people carry firearms in the Arctic than in other bear habitats.

In North America, hundreds of thousands of people walk in bear country every year and close encounters are inevitable; however, there are relatively few injuries and few deaths. Since 1900 American black bears (*Ursus americanus*) have killed a total of 35–40 people; most attacks take place in remote areas where the bears have little experience of humans and, on the whole, this species is not considered to be a serious threat. North American brown bears (*Ursus arctos*) have killed an average of one person/year from 1984–94; in national parks, it has been estimated that one in 1–2 million visitors is injured by a brown bear and, in more remote areas, injury rates vary from one in every 5000 hiking days to one in every million hiking days.

In Japan, an average of two to three people are killed and another 10–20 injured by Asiatic black bears (*Ursus thibetanus*) and brown bears (*Ursus arctos*) every year.

**Least shaggy coat** The sun bear (*Ursus malayanus*) has a short coat compared to other members of the bear family, as an adaptation to the warm climate of its tropical rainforest home in south-east Asia. The fur of its sleek black coat is less than 1 cm *0.4 in* long.

**Highest living** During the *Daily Mail* 'Abominable Snowman Exhibition', in May 1954, expedition members reported seeing what appeared to be a brown bear (*Ursus arctos*) at a height of 5486 m *18 000 ft* on the Reipimu Glacier, in the Himalayas; they also found a fresh set of footprints which were believed to belong to this species. Sightings and tracks of the so-called 'Abominable Snowman' may well be attributable to brown bears, in which case there may well be a resident population of them living at high altitudes in the Himalayas.

Several bear species are able to live at high altitudes. The giant panda (*Ailuropoda melanoleuca*) consistently lives at 1200–3500 m *4000–11 500 ft* in the mountain forests of south-western China; the population in Wolong, western Sichuan, spends more than 85 per cent of its time in the forests above 2600 m *8530 ft*. Panda footprints and droppings have been found as high as 4040 m *13 250 ft*. The spectacled bear (*Tremarctos ornatus*), which lives in a much wider range of habitats, has been reported at altitudes of up to 4200 m *13 800 ft* in the Andes; its preferred habitat is cloud forest from 1800–2700 m *5900–8860 ft*. The Asiatic black bear (*Ursus thibetanus*) has also been reported at an altitude of around 4000 m *13 120 ft* in the Himalayas.

**Furthest north** The polar bear (*Ursus maritimus*) is found throughout the Arctic. Footprints of wandering individuals have been recorded as far north as 88°N, within 2° of the North Pole, although there would be few prey animals so far north and this is clearly beyond their normal range. The furthest south they live all year round is James Bay, Canada, at about 50°N.

Sign near the town of Churchill, Canada, which speaks for itself: the polar bear is the only member of the family which actively preys on people.

*Above:* polar bears live further north than any other bear: footprints of wandering individuals have been found within 2° of the North Pole.

*Below:* the brown bear is the most widespread of the bears; this individual was photographed fishing for salmon in Katmai National Park, Alaska.

**Most widespread** The brown bear (*Ursus arctos*) is the most widespread of the bears and is found over much of the northern hemisphere, albeit in localized pockets, and is the most

widespread member of the bear family. It occurs in parts of Europe, Asia and North America, from the edges of the Arctic seas southwards.

**Most restricted distribution** The giant panda (*Ailuropoda melanoleuca*) is found only along the eastern rim of the Tibetan Plateau, in south-western China. It is limited to six small mountainous areas in Sichuan, Shaanzi and Gansu provinces, with a total range of only 5900 km² *2277 miles²*.

**Largest concentration** Bears are usually solitary creatures, although there are occasions when large numbers come together. Every autumn countless polar bears (*Ursus maritimus*) gather along the western shores of Hudson Bay, Canada, waiting for the sea ice to melt and forming the largest concentration of polar bears anywhere in the world. For a few weeks from mid-October to early November some 600–1000 bears gather along a 160 km *100 mile* stretch of coast, between the Nelson and Churchill Rivers, waiting for the ice to refreeze; as soon as it does, the bears disperse across the frozen bay to hunt for seals.

Groups of brown bears can be seen feeding at garbage dumps and at salmon spawning streams in several parts of their range; at the peak of the

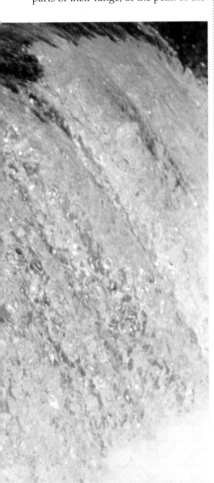

salmon season, as many as 67 bears have been recorded at one time along a 0.8 km *0.5 mile* stretch of the McNeil River, in Alaska. In such situations, they have been known to congregate in groups of 50 or more.

**Largest home range** Polar bears (*Ursus maritimus*) tend to have much larger home ranges than any other species of bear. The largest on record are for females in the Chukchi and Bering Seas, where they can be in excess of 300 000 km² *116 000 miles²*. Many polar bears travel great distances: one marked individual was killed a year later some 3220 km *2000 miles* from its original release point.

A male brown bear (*Ursus arctos*) living in the Alaskan interior was recorded roaming an area of 5700 km² *2200 miles²*. In Sweden, adult male brown bears have an average home range of 2163 km² *835 miles²*; newly-independent subadults may roam over even wider areas before they settle into a more permanent home range.

> Bear gall bladders are prized ingredients in traditional Chinese medicine and are prescribed as a cure for liver and heart disease, digestive disorders or as a general health tonic; thousands of bears are killed every year to supply the trade.

**Smallest home range** Female giant pandas (*Ailuropoda melanoleuca*) studied in the Qinling Mountains, Shaanzi Province, China, had overlapping home ranges with an average size of only 4.2 km² *1.6 miles²*. Few giant panda home ranges are larger than 6.5 km² *2½ miles²* – and these are normally shared with other pandas.

Female black bears have an average home range of 6–26 km² *3.7–16 miles²*; the males have home ranges of up to 132 km² *52 miles²*. Female sloth bears (*Ursus ursinus*) which were radio-collared in Royal Chitwan National Park, Nepal, in 1990, had a home range of as little as 9 km² *3½miles²*. On Kodiak Island, Alaska, adult female brown bears have a home range of only 28–92 km² *11–36 miles²*.

**Fastest** Bears are not really built for speed: they have few predators and rarely hunt by chasing their prey. However, they are capable of running surprisingly fast when it is necessary. The top speed reliably recorded is for a

> *Polar bears have been seen covering their dark noses with a paw or a piece of snow when stalking seals on the open ice.*

polar bear (*Ursus maritimus*) running along a road at Churchill, Canada, at a speed of 56 km/h *35 mph*. It is likely that the *actual* top speed is higher. The brown bear (*Ursus arctos*) is capable of short bursts of speed in excess of 64 km/h *40 mph*.

**Oldest** Bears are long-lived animals. The oldest ever recorded was a European brown bear (*Ursus arctos*) which died in Skansen Zoo, Stockholm, Sweden, aged 47 years. The oldest polar bear (*Ursus maritimus*) ever recorded was a 41-year-old male in London Zoo, UK. A female polar bear, born in the wild in 1947, died aged 42 at Detroit Zoo, USA, on 9 Sep 1989. In the wild, the oldest reliably aged bear is a 32-year-old female polar bear which died on Devon Island, North-West Territories, Canada.

A brown bear (*Ursus arctos*) nicknamed 'Red Collar', at the McNeill Sanctuary, Alaska, USA, was 24 when her last cub was born.

**Best sense of smell** It is very difficult to compare the sense of smell in different species of bear. However, it may be the most highly developed in polar bears (*Ursus maritimus*): researchers in Alaska have followed them walking in a straight line, over the tops of pressure ridges of uplifted ice and through open leads, to reach seals that they had apparently detected from up to 64 km *40 miles* away. There is also good evidence that they are able to detect a seal or whale carcass from as far away as 32 km *20 miles*.

**Commonest** The American black bear (*Ursus americanus*) is the commonest of all the bears. It is found throughout North America, from northern Alaska to the northern mountains of Mexico, inhabiting most of the continent's forested areas, and has an estimated

> *A polar bear's liver is extremely rich in Vitamin A and is toxic to people; several arctic explorers have died after eating it.*

*An American black bear in Yosemite National Park, California, USA, specialized in stealing food from Volkswagens. It discovered that this particular make of car is air-tight when the doors and windows are closed; so the bear used to climb on to the roof and jump up and down until it caved in: the resulting air pressure inside forced the doors to pop open.*

population of 400,000–750000. Although it has disappeared from many areas, especially in the east and Midwest, elsewhere it is regarded as a game animal and hunters kill more than 40000 every year.

**Most threatened** Five of the world's eight species of bears are endangered, and all but the American black bear (*Ursus americanus*) and the polar bear (*Ursus maritimus*) are in decline due to a variety of human activities from habitat destruction to hunting. The giant panda (*Ailuropoda melanoleuca*) is the rarest of the world's bears, with a population of fewer than 1000 surviving in just six remote areas in the mountains of south-western China: in Shaanzi, Gansu and Sichuan Provinces. Its range consists of a mere 25 isolated pockets of bamboo forest, more than two-thirds of which support fewer than 50 pandas; many of these sub-populations are considered too small to remain viable. A further 100–120 giant pandas survive in zoos, mostly in China.

The sun bear (*Ursus malayanus*), sloth bear (*Ursus ursinus*) and spectacled bear (*Tremarctos ornatus*) are also endangered. There may be as few as 2000 spectacled bears surviving in northern South America; there are estimated to be 7000–10000 sloth bears in the forests of Sri Lanka and parts of the Indian sub-continent; and, although there is no population figure, the sun bear's population is undoubtedly low in the forests of the Malay Peninsula, Java, Borneo, Sumatra, Burma, Thailand and north-eastern India. Major threats are habitat destruction, capture for the pet trade and hunting for the sale of the gall bladders, which are 'milked' of their bile to supply the lucrative traditional-medicine trade.

**Swimming** Polar bears (*Ursus mari-timus*) are powerful swimmers, using their front legs to do doggy-paddle and their hind legs as a rudder.

**Radio-tracking giant pandas in south-western China, where fewer than 1000 survive in the wild, making this the rarest of the world's bears.**

They are capable of swimming distances of at least 100 km *62 miles* without resting, at an average speed of 10 km/h *6.2 mph*.

Polar bears will sometimes swim underwater to catch seabirds resting on the surface or to stalk seals that are lying on ice next to the water's edge. The longest time recorded underwater was 2 minutes by a polar bear stalking a seal.

**Most varied colour** Most black bears (*Ursus americanus*) are, indeed, black. However, many colour variations are officially recognized in different parts of their range: black, brown, cinnamon, honey, blue, white and a host of variations in between, with black being the commonest and white the rarest. These are all classified as colour phases or geographical races, rather than subspecies, and all share one distinctive colour feature: a brown muzzle. The rare Kermode white 'black' bear, which has beautiful cream-coloured fur and brown eyes (proving that it is not albino) is found only in three small, isolated coastal areas of British Columbia; when first described to science in 1905 it was considered to be a distinct species, but is now believed to be simply a colour variation like all the others.

**Homing instinct** Several species of bear display an accurate homing instinct if they are removed from their home range. An adult male American black bear (*Ursus americanus*) in Michigan, USA, found its way home after being flown 250 km *156 miles* away. There are many examples of brown bears (*Ursus arctos*) finding their way home after being transplanted at least 200 km *125 miles* away.

Perhaps one of the most astonishing cases occurred in September 1973, when a young brown bear was captured near Cordova, Alaska, USA, and was moved by boat to Montague Island, Prince William Sound, some 93 km *58 miles* from its original territory. Twenty-eight days later, it was found dead just 100 m *328 ft* from where it had been captured. In order to return home, the bear had to swim 11 km *6.8 miles* to one island, another 1 km *0.6 mile* to a second island, then 3 km *1.9 miles* to the mainland – all the time swimming against the strong tides and in the frigid waters of Prince William Sound – before walking to its original point of capture.

*A bear's age can be determined by counting the rings in a cross-section of its tooth, in a way not dissimilar to counting the annual rings in the growth of a tree.*

# CAMELS & LLAMAS

---

### Camelidae

6 species: llama, alpaca, guanaco, vicuña, dromedary and bactrian camel; three of these (dromedary, llama and alpaca) are domesticated and do not normally live independently of people.

---

**Largest** The largest member of the Camelidae is the dromedary or one-humped camel (*Camelus dromedarius*), which is a native of the Middle East but survives today only as a feral animal in Australia and as a domestic animal elsewhere. It is also the largest artiodactyl or even-toed hoofed mammal, with a head-body length of 2.3–3.5 m *7½–11½ft*; a tail length of 55 cm *21.7 in*; a shoulder height of 1.8–2.1 m *6–7 ft* (maximum 2.4 m *7 ft 11 in*) and a weight of 450–690 kg *992–1521 lb*.

The Bactrian or two-humped camel (*Camelus bactrianus*), which survives in the wild only in the remote deserts of Mongolia and western China, and as a domestic animal elsewhere, is marginally smaller.

**Smallest** The smallest member of the Camelidae is the vicuña (*Vicugna vicugna*), which lives in the high Andes of South America. It has a head-body length of 1.3–1.9 m *4¼–6¼ft*; a tail length of 15–25 cm *6–9.8 in*; a shoulder height of 70–110 cm *27½–43 in*; and a weight of 35–65 kg *77–143 lb*.

**Highest living** The vicuña (*Vicugna vicugna*) and the domesticated alpaca (*Lama pacos*) both live on alpine grasslands at heights of 3700–4800 m *12 150–15 750 ft* and 4400–4800 m *14 450–15 750 ft* respectively, where the air is too thin for most mammals to lead a normal, active life. The highest authenticated record is for a vicuña, which was found above the snowline at 5486 m *18 000 ft* in the Peruvian Andes.

> *The vicuña's incisors are unique among hoofed mammals because they grow continuously.*

**Earliest domestication** The earliest domestication of llamas (*Lama glama*) and alpacas (*Lama pacos*), for their highly valued wool, meat and milk, and as beasts of burden, took place in Peru approximately 4000–5000 years ago – either in the Lake Titicaca region, or on the Junin Plateau, about 100 km *62 miles* to the north-west.

The two camels were domesticated independently. The dromedary (*Camelus dromedarius*) was first domesticated in central or southern Arabia some 4000–6000 years ago; it is believed to have become extinct in the wild about 2000 years ago. The Bactrian camel (*Camelus bactrianus*) was first domesticated on the plateaux of northern Iran and south-western Turkestan about 4500 years ago.

**Most threatened** Two members of the family Camelidae are known to be threatened with extinction: the wild bactrian camel (*Camelus bactrianus*), which survives in remote parts of the Gobi desert on the borders of China and Mongolia, and the vicuña (*Vicugna vicugna*), which is found in Argentina, Bolivia, Chile and Peru. The dromedary (*Camelus dromedarius*), the llama (*Lama glama*) and the alpaca (*Lama pacos*) are common as domestic animals but no longer survive in the wild (apart from a feral population of dromedaries in Australia); however, both the llama and alpaca are believed to be domesticated descendants of the guanaco (*Lama guanicoe*) and may never have lived independently of people.

---

The smallest member of the camel family, the vicuña is also the highest living and has been recorded at an altitude of 5486 m *18 000 ft* in the Peruvian Andes.

Camels are better adapted to life in the desert than almost any other mammal; this individual was photographed in Kirthar National Park, Pakistan.

---

**Most dramatic recovery** The vicuña (*Vicugna vicugna*) once occurred widely in the Andes from southern Ecuador south through Peru and Bolivia to Argentina and northern Chile. The Incas found them impossible to domesticate, but rounded up wild herds every 3 to 5 years to shear them: their golden-brown wool has long been highly prized as the finest in the world. After the Spanish conquest, the colonialists simply killed the animals for their skins and meat and, over a period of several hundred years, the population declined from more than 2 million to an all-time low of 6000 in 1965. Fortunately, strict protection pulled them back from the brink of extinction and the species is now relatively safe (although recent poaching pressure and the spread of livestock into their grazing lands are cause for concern). The estimated population figures for 1993/94 were: 48 000 in Peru; 25 000–28 000 in Argentina; 26 000 in Chile; 500 in Ecuador; and unknown numbers in small, scattered groups in Bolivia.

**Desert adaptations** Both species of camel – the dromedary (*Camelus dromedarius*) and the Bactrian (*Camelus bactrianus*) – are better adapted to life in the desert than almost any other mammal.

Contrary to popular belief, camels do not store water in their humps, but energy-rich fat. This can be broken down in the body to produce energy, carbon dioxide and water, and helps them to survive long periods of up to several months without food. A well-fed camel has a large hump (an individual weighing 500 kg *1100 lb* can store more than 50 kg *110 lb* of fat in its hump) but a camel that has had little or nothing to eat may have no hump at all.

Camels have a number of record-breaking adaptations to help conserve water. They do not begin to sweat until their body temperature reaches 40.5°C *105°F* (a high fever in a human); they have the ability to accumulate heat slowly within the body during the day, as the outside temperature rises, and then to dissipate it in the cool of the night; their thick coat restricts water loss through evaporation; their highly efficient kidneys ensure that the water content of their urine is kept to a minimum; they produce dry dung; and they can survive a water loss of up to 40 per cent of their body weight without harm (compared with less than 14 per cent in a human). They are also able to go for long periods without drinking (at least a week when working in very high temperatures and several months at other times) and then, when the opportunity arises, can drink huge quantities (up to 60 litres *13 gallons*) in a matter of minutes.

Camels are unique among mammals in having elliptical (rather than round) red blood cells; this prevents their blood from thickening with a rise in temperature. They also have webbed feet to stop them sinking into soft sand; long, thick lashes to keep wind-blown sand out of their eyes; and nostrils that can be kept tight shut to keep out the sand.

*Camel dung is so dry that it can be used as fuel as soon as it leaves the animal.*

# CATS

### *Felidae*
36 species

**Earliest** The first cat-like carnivores were the sabre-toothed cats (family Felidae), the earliest of which was a species called *Hoplophoneus* whose 35-million-year-old fossils have been found in North America. Their powerful jaw muscles and huge upper canines (typically 20 cm *8 in* long) were specially adapted to penetrate the thick skins of bison, mammoths and other large prey.

The best-known sabre-tooth (and one of the most recent) was a species called *Smilodon fatalis*, which was similar in size to the African lion (*Panthera leo*). It lived within the past 2 million years, becoming extinct some 10 000 years ago. Nearly 100 000 fossilized bones of this species (representing nearly 2000 animals) were discovered in 1913 in a former tar pit at Rancho La Brea, California, USA (now part of downtown Los Angeles). This extraordinary find also included the remains of extinct horses and pronghorns, mammoths, giant bison and ground sloths.

**Largest** The Siberian tiger (*Panthera tigris altaica*) is the largest and most massively built sub-species of tiger and, indeed, the world's largest cat. It has a total length of 2.7–3.3 m *8 ft 10 in–10 ft 10 in* (male) and 2.4–2.75 m *7 ft 11 in–9 ft* (female), as measured between pegs from the tip of the nose to the end of the extended tail; it stands 99–107 cm *39–42 in* at the shoulder; and it weighs 180–306 kg *397–675 lb* (male) and 100–167 kg *220–368 lb* (female). There are many old hunting records of animals reaching a length of 4 m *13 ft* or even more, but none of these has been authenticated (one problem is that skins can be stretched by as much as 30 per cent). The all-time record-holder is probably a male weighing 384 kg *846½ lb*, which was shot in 1950 in the Sikhote Alin Gory Mountains, Maritime Territory, Russian Federation. When the Siberian tiger was more numerous, it is possible that some individuals reached an even greater size.

An outsized male Bengal tiger (*P. t. tigris*) shot in northern Uttar Pradesh, India, in November 1967, measured 3.22 m *10 ft 7 in* between pegs (3.37 m *11 ft 1 in* over the curves) and weighed 389 kg *857 lb* (cf. a normal size range of 2.7–3.1 m *8 ft 10 in–10 ft 2 in* and 180–258 kg *397–569 lb* for an adult male). However, this record is a little artificial as the tiger had just killed a buffalo the previous evening and probably had an extremely full stomach (possibly adding as much as 63 kg *139 lb* to its overall weight). It is now on display at the US Museum of Natural History at the Smithsonian Institution, Washington, DC, USA.

The largest tiger ever held in captivity, and the heaviest cat on record, was a 9-year-old Siberian male named *Jaipur*, owned by animal trainer Joan Byron-Marasek of Clarksburg, New Jersey, USA. *Jaipur* measured 3.32 m *10 ft 11 in* in total length and weighed 423 kg *932 lb* in October 1986.

The African lion (*Panthera leo leo*) is the second largest of the cats; the Asiatic lion (*P. l. persica*) is slightly smaller. The average male African measures 2.4–2.8 m *7 ft 11 in–9 ft 2 in* overall including the tail, stands 91–97 cm *36–38 in* at the shoulder and weighs 150–189 kg *331–417 lb* (the female is considerably smaller). The heaviest wild specimen on record was a known man-eater which weighed 313 kg *690 lb* and was shot near Hectorspruit, Transvaal, South Africa, in 1936; this weight was so exceptional that it had to be checked several times on local railway scales before being accepted. In July 1970 a weight of 375 kg *826 lb* was reported for a black-maned lion named *Simba* (b. Dublin Zoo, 1959) at Colchester Zoo, Essex, UK; he died on 16 Jan 1973 at the now defunct Knaresborough Zoo, N Yorkshire, UK.

**Largest domestic** The heaviest reliably recorded domestic cat was a neutered male tabby named *Himmy*, which weighed 21.3 kg *46 lb 15¼ oz* (neck 38.1 cm *15 in*, waist 83.8 cm *33 in* and length 96.5 cm *38 in*) at the time of his death from respiratory failure on 12 Mar 1986 at the age of 10 years 4 months. *Himmy* was owned by Thomas Vyse of Redlynch, Cairns, Queensland, Australia.

**Smallest** The smallest wild member of the cat family is the rusty-spotted cat (*Prionailurus rubiginosus*) of southern India and Sri Lanka, albeit by a very small margin. It has a head-body length

A tiger, the largest member of the cat family, compared with a rusty-spotted cat, which is the smallest.

**MAMMALS**

of 35–48 cm *13.8–18.9 in*; a tail length of 15–25 cm *5.9–9.8 in*; and an average weight of 1.1 kg *2 lb 7 oz* (female) and 1.5–1.6 kg *3 lb 5 oz–3 lb 8 oz* (male).

The black-footed cat (*Felis nigripes*) of southern Africa is almost as small. It has a head-body length of 33.7–50 cm *13.3–19.7 in*; a tail length of 15–20 cm *5.9–7.9 in*; a shoulder height of about 25 cm *9.8 in*; and a weight of 0.8–1.6 kg *1 lb 12 oz–3 lb 8 oz* (female) and 1.6–2.1 kg *3 lb 8 oz–4 lb 10 oz* (male). Despite its size, it has gained a reputation for ferocity among several African tribes; however, in this instance, local folklore is not taken too seriously by most experts as it claims that the black-footed cat attacks and kills animals as large as giraffes.

**Smallest domestic** The smallest domestic cat on record is a male blue point Himalayan-Persian called *Tinker Toy*, which is just 7 cm *2¾ in* tall and 19 cm *7½ in* long. He is owned by Katrina and Scott Forbes of Taylorville, Illinois, USA.

**Earliest domestication** The first record of domestic cats comes from the ancient village of Dier el Medina, near Luxor, Egypt. In the village tombs, some 3500 years ago, people painted domestic scenes which included women sitting in their chairs with domestic cats

curled up next to them; these paintings suggest that cats were common household pets at the time. Indeed, it is likely that the transition from a wild to a domestic animal took place much earlier, because dogs, cows and sheep had already been domesticated for hundreds or even thousands of years. There is also circumstantial evidence of earlier domestication; for example, archaeologists excavating one of the earliest human settlements on Cyprus (*c.* 6000 BC) have unearthed the unmistakable remains of a cat's jawbone, although it is unknown whether the animal had actually been domesticated or, alternatively, whether it had been eaten.

Unfortunately, thousands of mummified Egyptian cats – deemed uninteresting by archaeologists at the end of the 19th century – were sold by the tonne as fertilizer or ship's ballast and, consequently, a great deal of information was lost forever. But the general consensus among experts is that the domestic cat is a sub-species of the wildcat (*Felis silvestris*) and, in particular is descended from the African wildcat (*F. s. libyca*). It is normally given the Latin name *Felis silvestris catus*. However, since the ancient Egyptians also mummified other species, such as the jungle cat (*Felis chaus*), and since there is evidence from a temple built by Queen Hatshepsut around 1470 BC that

the priests kept jungle cats as pets, it seems likely that at least one other species contributed to the domestic cat's ancestry. In fact, it is possible that several species of cat effectively domesticated themselves by entering human settlements to prey on the plentiful rats, mice and other vermin – and were then encouraged by the human inhabitants.

**Most social** The majority of cats are solitary (apart from females and their dependent offspring) but lions (*Panthera leo*) are a dramatic exception to the rule. Their main social unit is the pride, which usually consists of 5–15 related adult females, and their offspring, and 1–6 adult males originally from other prides. The pride members do not spend all their time together (they are often scattered individually or in small subgroups throughout the range) but the core membership is stable and they work as a team more fully than any other member of the family. Uniquely among cats, they hunt cooperatively, share their prey and even help to rear each other's cubs.

---

**Lions are exceptional members of the cat family in being highly social; this pride was photographed after a night-time hunt in Londolozi Game Reserve, South Africa.**

**The cheetah is the fastest land animal over short distances, capable of reaching its maximum speed of at least 96 km/h *60 mph* in just three seconds from a standing start.**

**Most names** The cougar (*Felis concolor*) has more names than any other mammal in the world and more than 40 are recognized in the English language alone. Cougar, puma, panther and mountain lion are the most commonly used, but painter, catamount (short for 'cat-of-the-mountain') and deer tiger are frequently used east of the Mississippi, USA. Some of the stranger names include mountain screamer, Indian devil and even purple feather. At the same time, as many as 29 sub-species or geographic races of the puma are recognized (12 of which live north of the Mexican/US border) and each of these has its own name as well; for example, there is the Florida panther, Yuma cougar, eastern cougar, Wisconsin puma and Colorado cougar. Then, to add to the complications, it also has at least 18 native South American names and a further 25 native North American names.

**Oddest-looking** The oddest-looking cat in the world is probably the flat-headed cat (*Prionailurus planiceps*) of Malaysia (Peninsular Malaysia, Sabah and Sarawak), Thailand, Indonesia (Kalimantan and Sumatra) and Brunei. About the size of a domestic cat, its head is strangely broad and flat, with a long, sloping forehead; it has unusually small ears, set low down on each side of the head; and it has comparatively large, close-set eyes. A secretive and poorly known animal, it appears to be largely nocturnal and feeds mainly

on fish, frogs and other aquatic creatures.

However, the flat-headed cat is clearly a cat and experts frequently consider the jaguarundi (*Felis yagouaroundi*) to be even stranger. Found from Arizona, USA, south to Argentina, this species closely resembles a mongoose (family Herpestidae).

**Longest jump** Two cat species are renowned for their extraordinary jumping abilities: the puma (*Felis concolor*) and the snow leopard (*Uncia uncia*). The record long-jump for a puma along level ground is an outstanding 11.7 m *38 ft 4½ in*. But even this is overshadowed by a snow leopard which was observed by Russian biologists leaping over a 15 m *49 ft 2 in* wide ditch. For comparison, the world record human long-jump is 8.95 m *29 ft 4½ in*, achieved by Michael Anthony 'Mike' Powell (USA) in Tokyo, Japan, on 30 Aug 1991.

Both species are also able to jump from a height of 15–18 m *49 ft 2 in–59 ft* to the ground, and land on their feet unharmed, while the puma is able to leap up to a tree or ledge to a record height of 5.4 m *17 ft 8½ in*. But perhaps most impressive of all is a record of another puma jumping 3.6 m *11 ft 10 in* into the fork of a tree – with the carcass of a deer in its mouth.

**Fastest** The cheetah (*Acinonyx jubatus*) is the fastest land animal over short distances (the pronghorn antelope

[*Antilocapra americana*] is the fastest over long distances). Measuring the running speed of wild animals is difficult to do accurately (there is a tendency to over estimate) and considerable disagreement shrouds the cheetah's maximum speed. However, over distances of up to 500 m *1640 ft* it is widely considered to be 96–101 km/h *60–63 mph* on level ground. Tests in London, UK, in 1937 showed that, on an oval greyhound track over 316 m *1037 ft*, a female cheetah's average speed during three runs was 69.8 km/h *43.4 mph*; but this animal was not running flat out and had great difficulty in negotiating the bends. In a study of 78 sprints in the wild, the maximum speed was 87 km/h *54 mph*. Speeds of 114 km/h *71 mph*, 135 km/h *84 mph* and even 145 km/h *90 mph* have been claimed, but these figures seem unlikely.

The fastest acceleration ever recorded was determined by careful analysis of a film sequence of a running cheetah taken in Kenya, in 1959. This revealed that the animal reached its maximum speed of 90 km/h *56 mph* from a standing start in just 3 seconds.

The cheetah is the only true pursuit predator in the cat family and has a longer strike distance than any other cat (90–200 m *295–656 ft*). But it has little endurance at maximum speed and appears to have evolved with a total focus on acceleration and short distance sprinting. At high speed it builds up massive amounts of heat (raising its body temperature to an almost lethal 40.6°C *105°F*) which means that it would probably die if it continued a strenuous chase over a distance much longer than 500 m *1640 ft*. Most cheetahs give up after 400–500 m *1312–1640 ft* or about 60 seconds and, indeed, the average chase is no further than 200–300 m *656–984 ft* and lasts for less than 20 seconds. Afterwards, it may take a full 20 minutes of rest for the animal to cool down and to pay back its huge oxygen debt (by breathing 150–160 times/min compared with a normal 15–20/min).

The cheetah's many anatomical specializations include exposed claws (which act like running shoes) and long legs combined with a flexible spine. Its

*The four largest cats (lion, tiger, jaguar, leopard) are distinguished from all the others by their ability to roar; most of the smaller species are able to purr and make shrill, high-pitched sounds instead.*

**M A M M A L S**

In optimal conditions, a lion's roar (which can reach a level of 114 decibels) can be heard up to 5 km 3 miles away.

strides are so fast and so long that all four feet are off the ground for more than 50 per cent of the distance covered when it is running at maximum speed: it is almost literally flying.

**Oldest** The greatest age recorded for any member of the cat family (excluding domestic cats) is at least 34 years for a bobcat (*Lynx rufus*), which was captured by Fred Space of the Space Wild Animal Farm, Mear Sussex, New Jersey, USA. It was captured as an adult in 1942 and eventually put to sleep on 10 May 1974. A small number of lions (*Panthera leo*) have lived for as long as 30 years in captivity.

**Oldest domestic** Domestic cats are generally longer-lived than dogs. The average life expectancy of undoctored, well-fed animals raised under household conditions and receiving good medical attention is 13–15 years for males and 15–17 years for females. Neutered males and females live on average one or two years longer. The oldest reliably recorded domestic cat was a female tabby named *Ma*, owned by Alice St George Moore of Drewsteignton, Devon, UK, which was put to sleep on 5 Nov 1957 at the age of 34.

A less well documented record beats *Ma* by about 2 years. The tabby *Puss*, owned by Mrs T. Holway of Clayhidon, Devon, UK, celebrated his 36th birthday on 28 Nov 1939 and died the next day.

**Greatest sexual dimorphism** Male and female lions (*Panthera leo*) are more easily distinguishable than the two sexes of any other species in the cat family. The males have distinctive manes (which serve to protect their necks during fights and make them look bigger and more menacing) but these are entirely absent in females. Since the manes are cumbersome and make the males conspicuous, the females do most of the hunting for the pride. There is also a considerable size difference between the sexes (females are up to 30 per cent lighter than males) but there are more extreme examples in other species; in particular, the female fishing cat (*Prionailurus viverrinus*) is almost half the size of the male.

**Longest gestation period** The longest gestation period for any member of the cat family is an average of 110 days (range 100–114 days) for the lion (*Panthera leo*). Four other species are close runners-up: snow leopard (*Uncia uncia*) with 93–110 days; jaguar (*P. onca*) with 91–111 days; leopard (*P. pardus*) with 90–105 days; and tiger (*P. tigris*) with 93–112 days.

**Shortest gestation period** A number of small cat species have gestation periods of around 60 days or slightly less. The shortest known are 56–63 days for the African wildcat (*Felis silvestris libyca*), 56–70 for the leopard cat (*Prionailurus bengalensis*), 59–67 for the sand cat (*Felis margarita*), and 58–62 for the Asian desert cat (*Felis silvestris ornata*). There is little information on the flat-headed cat (*Prionailurus planiceps*), but one individual studied had a gestation period of 56 days. The shortest ever recorded is 50 days for a bobcat (*Lynx rufus*), but this species has an average of 62 days and a range of up to 70 days.

**Largest litter** The European wildcat (*Felis silvestris silvestris*) has a litter size of up to eight, with an average of four (the same as in the domestic cat). Also cheetah (*Acinonyx jubatus*), Canadian lynx (*Lynx canadensis*), bobcat (*Lynx rufus*) and several other species also have as many as eight, although only on rare occasions.

---

A hybrid between a male tiger and female lion is called a tigon, but the reverse cross produces a liger; either way, the offspring are normally sterile.

---

**Smallest litter** Many members of the cat family have only one young in a litter at times, although the average is normally higher. The only species known to have just one consistently is African golden cat (*Profelis aurata*), the little spotted cat (*Leopardus tigrinus*) and the margay (*Leopardus wiedii*).

**Most prolific domestic** A tabby named *Dusty* (b. 1935) of Bonham, Texas, USA, produced 420 kittens during her breeding life. She gave birth to her last litter (a single kitten) on 12 Jun 1952.

**Infanticide** There are scattered records of adult male pumas (*Puma concolor*), Canadian lynxes (*Lynx canadensis*),

ocelots (*Leopardus pardalis*) and, in particular, tigers (*Panthera tigris*) killing kittens and cubs. But the only species in which this is known to be common and widespread is the lion (*Panthera leo*). Lions practice infanticide for two main reasons: to remove cubs sired by males they have driven away and to force the females to come into oestrus sooner. Infanticide is most common when males take over a new pride (females with dependent offspring normally lose their cubs within a month of takeover).

**Most dangerous** A number of wild cat species are known to attack people. The puma (*Felis concolor*), jaguar (*Panthera onca*) and leopard (*P. pardus*) have all killed on occasion, although they are not normally aggressive and rarely regard people as potential prey. The only regular man-eaters are the lion (*P. leo*) and tiger (*P. tigris*), both of which have killed thousands of people over the years. But even these two species normally try to avoid people and most attacks are the result of accidental close encounters or confrontations.

The individual man-eating record is held by a notorious tigress dubbed the 'Champawat man-eater', which operated first in Nepal and then in the Kumaon district of northern India. She killed 436 people in a period of just 8 years. Such was the fear of local villagers that, towards the end of her reign of terror, they lived behind locked doors and refused to go outside. When the tigress was eventually shot, in 1911, by the legendary Jim Corbett, author of *Man-Eaters of Kumaon*, she was found to have damaged teeth as the result of an earlier gunshot wound.

When records were kept by the British in India, during the early 1900s, tigers were claiming an average of 800–900 human victims per year (although many more tigers were killed by people in retribution). Even so, it was estimated at the time that no more than 1 in 300 tigers was ever guilty of attacking humans: a minority simply gained a bad reputation for the majority.

Nowadays, man-eating tigers are rare outside two key problem areas. The worst is a vast area of mangrove forests, tidal creeks and rivers known as the Sundarbans, which is shared by Bangladesh (5980 km² *2310 miles²*) and neighbouring India (3900 km² *1505 miles²*) and is home to the largest single population of tigers in the world (as many as 500). The area has had a reputation for man-eating tigers since at least the 17th century. During a recent 25-year period (1956–83) no fewer than 554 people were reportedly killed in

**The most widespread big cat is the leopard, which lives in a wide variety of habitats in much of Africa, the Middle East and Asia.**

---

the Bangladeshi section and just over 1000 people in the Indian section (and it is likely that many other deaths went unrecorded). Most victims are honey-collectors and wood-cutters, though it is not unusual for man-eating tigers to swim out to boats to kill fishermen as well. The number of deaths dropped dramatically (to fewer than 50 per year) after the introduction of boldly painted face masks, in November 1986. These are worn on the back of the head to confuse the tigers (which nearly always attack from behind) and there have even been occasions when tigers have followed people wearing the masks for up to 8 hours without attacking. The second problem area is Dudhwa National Park, Kheri District, Uttar Pradesh, India, which is near the border with Nepal. Since 1978 more than 200 people have been killed in and around the park. Local villagers grow sugar cane right up to the boundary and, since tigers regard these plantations as an extension of their usual tall grass habitat, there are many more close encounters than there were a few years ago.

There are numerous examples of prides of man-eating African lions (*P. l. leo*) killing large numbers of people and terrorizing entire villages. The worst case was a pride of 17 lions which persistently killed and ate people around Njombe, at the northern end of Lake Malawi, southern Tanzania, over a 15-year period (1932–47). They killed an average of nearly two people every week (a total of 1000–1500) before being shot in 1947. The most famous case involved the so-called 'man-eaters of Tsavo' which, in 1898, preyed on rail-workers who were building the Mombasa to Kampala railroad, in East Africa. While the men were putting the rails and bridge over the Tsavo River, Kenya, the lions killed 28 immigrant Indians and 'dozens' of natives over a 9 month period. The situation became so bad that, in the end, work had to be halted for 3 weeks while the lions were found and shot. Interestingly, in both these cases, the lions were found to be in good condition and, presumably, fully capable of hunting the abundant game in each area.

The Asiatic lion (*P. l. persica*), which survives only in the Gir National Park and Wildlife Sanctuary, Gujarat, western India, was long renowned for its lack of aggression towards people. During the 1970s and the early 1980s, the small relict population of fewer than 280 animals was responsible for

an average of only six attacks and less than one death per year. However, after a severe drought in the area, in 1987–8, the attack-rate suddenly increased dramatically. There were no fewer than 81 attacks in the 2-year period January 1988–April 1990, resulting in 16 deaths. As the lion population density increases in the sanctuary, more animals are straying into nearby agricultural land and human settlements and, perhaps inevitably, most recent attacks have been during these sorties. But the main cause of the increase is believed to have been the drought: many domestic livestock died and, in the past, they had accounted for at least half the lions' prey.

When leopards become man-eaters, they can be more difficult to deal with because of their stealth. The worst case was an Indian leopard known as the 'man-eater of Panar' which killed about 400 people before it was shot by Jim Corbett in 1910. But another leopard, dubbed the 'man-eater of Rudraprayag', received far more publicity. After killing its first person on

> *Lions sleep or doze for up to 20 hours every day.*

**MAMMALS**

Confined to the small island of Iriomote, Japan, the Iriomote cat has the most restricted distribution of any member of the cat family.

9 Jun 1918, it terrorized villagers for an 8-year period (1918–26) and killed more than 125 people in total. Somehow, it survived every conceivable effort to kill it: breaking out of a box trap, surviving a poisoning campaign and trip-guns set over kills, escaping from an ambush by British army officers, and even managing to extricate itself from a leg-hold trap. Its progress was followed by the press in at least 10 countries around the world and questions were even asked about it in the House of Commons, London. Eventually, soon after its last killing on 14 Apr 1926, and following a hunt which had lasted for several months, it was shot by Jim Corbett.

**Highest living** A number of cat species are known to ascend to a height of at least 4000 m *13 120 ft*, but only five are known to venture beyond 5000 m *16 400 ft*. The highest record is of a puma (*Felis concolor*) which was recently observed at 5800 m *19 024 ft* in the Andes; however, it is quite unusual for pumas to go above 4500 m *14 760 ft*. A very close runner-up is a leopard (*Panthera pardus*) whose carcass was discovered at the edge of the rim of Mt Kilimanjaro's Kibo Crater, in 1926, at a height of 5700 m *18 696 ft*; there is also a population of leopards on the highest slopes of the Ruwenzori and Virunga volcanoes, central Africa, at a height of 4000–5000 m *13 120–16 400 ft*. In the summer, snow leopards (*Uncia uncia*) are normally found in alpine meadows and rocky areas at a height of 2700–4500 m *8856–14 760 ft* (often below 1800 m *5904 ft* in the winter) and occasionally venture up to 5500 m *18 040 ft*. The Andean mountain cat (*Oreailurus jacobita*) is rarely found below 3000 m *9840 ft* and, in Peru at least, is known to range up to at least 5100 m *16 728 ft*. Similarly, the pampas cat (*Oncifelis colocolo*) has been recorded beyond 5000 m *16 400 ft* in parts of its range in the western half of South America.

On 6 Sep 1950 a 4-month-old kitten belonging to Josephine Aufdenblatten of Geneva, Switzerland, followed a group of climbers all the way to the top of the 4478 m *14 691 ft* Matterhorn, in the Alps.

**Most widespread** The wildcat (*Felis silvestris*) has three recognized sub-species which, between them, are more widely distributed than any other member of the cat family. The European wildcat (*F. s. silvestris*) is found throughout most of Europe (including the UK but excluding Scandinavia), through parts of the Middle East and into central Asia; the African wildcat (*F. s. lybica*) is found throughout Africa (except parts of west Africa) and much of the Middle East; and the Asian desert wildcat (*F. s. ornata*) lives in south-west Asia as far east as northern India. The IUCN/SSC Cat Specialist Group has calculated their combined geographical range to be approximately 34.17 million km² *13.2 million miles²* (an area slightly larger than the whole of Africa).

The most widespread big cat is the leopard (*Panthera pardus*), which lives in a wide variety of habitats throughout most of sub-Saharan Africa, north-west Africa, parts of the Middle East, in several areas in west Asia and through most of tropical Asia, with isolated populations in eastern Russia, northern China, North and South Korea, Sri Lanka and the Indonesian island of Java. It is also the least threatened of the big cats (although several sub-species are in serious trouble) with an estimated population of several hundred thousand. The IUCN/SSC Cat Specialist Group has calculated its geographical range to be approximately 23.14 million km² *8.93 million miles²* (an area slightly larger than twice the size of China).

With a range that extends 14 400 km *8940 miles* from south-eastern Alaska, USA, and southern Yukon, Canada, to Tierra del Fuego, at the southern tip of South America, the puma (*Felis concolor*) has the greatest north-south range of any cat. Although its range is patchy in many areas, the IUCN/SSC Cat Specialist Group has calculated it to be approximately 17.12 million km² *6.61 million miles²* (an area roughly the size of the whole of South America).

**Most restricted distribution** According to recent calculations by the IUCN/SSC Cat Specialist Group, several members of the cat family have extremely restricted distributions with a total estimated geographical range of under 1 million km² *0.39 million miles²* (roughly the size of Tanzania). These are the Spanish lynx (*Lynx pardinus*), kodkod (*Oncifelis guigna*), Bornean bay cat (*Catopuma badia*), Chinese mountain cat (*Felis bieti*), black-footed cat (*Felis nigripes*), Andean mountain cat (*Oreailurus jacobita*) and rusty-spotted cat (*Prionailurus rubiginosus*).

But the record-holder by far is the rare Iriomote cat (*Felis iriomotensis*), which is confined to the 293 km² *113 miles²* Japanese island of Iriomote. This remote and mountainous island lies at the southern end of the Ryukyu Islands, southern Japan, some 2100 km *1304 miles* south of Tokyo and 200 km

*The caracal can leap into the air and catch a bird in mid-flight, knocking it down with one of its front paws.*

*124 miles* off the east coast of Taiwan. First described in 1967, the Iriomote cat has an estimated population of less than 100; it is probably the rarest cat in the world.

**Most abundant** The most abundant member of the cat family is probably the widely distributed wildcat (*Felis silvestris*), although hybridization with domestic cats is threatening the genetic purity of populations in some areas (*see Most widespread*).

**Least known** The rare Bornean bay cat (*Catopuma badia*) is probably the least known member of the cat family. Until recently, its description rested on just a few skins and skulls (from five specimens collected between 1855 and 1900) which are now scattered in several museums around the world. The only confirmed sighting was in 1928, until a female was captured by trappers on the Sarawak–Indonesian border and taken to the Sarawak Museum on 4 Nov 1992; the only live member of the species to be studied, this unfortunate animal died soon afterwards.

The Andean mountain cat (*Oreailurus jacobita*) is also known mainly from museum skins and skulls. However, although almost nothing is known about its biology and behaviour, there have been two reasonable observations in the wild; during the only sighting by biologists, a single animal was followed for more than 2 hours on foot (at a distance of 15–50 m *49–164 ft*) at a height of 4250 m *13 940 ft* in the north-east of Tucuman province, Argentina.

**Most threatened** The World Conservation Union (IUCN) lists no fewer than 20 cat species (54 per cent of the total) as known or suspected to be threatened with extinction. The species considered to be most at risk are: the Spanish lynx (*Lynx pardinus*) of Portugal and Spain, which is down to a fragmented population of fewer than 1200 (including sub-adults and only 350 breeding females); the snow leopard (*Uncia uncia*) of Afghanistan, Pakistan, India, Nepal, Bhutan, China, Mongolia, the Russian Federation, Kazakhstan, Kyrgyzstan, Tajikistan and Uzbekistan, which has an estimated population of only 4500–7500; and the tiger (*Panthera tigris*) of Asia (*see below*).

A further 13 sub-species are also listed as threatened, including the Asiatic lion (*Panthera leo persica*) of the 1412 km² *545 miles²* Gir National Park and Wildlife Sanctuary, Gujarat, western India (with a small relict population of about 280 animals); and the Florida

puma or panther (*Puma concolor coryi*) of Florida, USA (with a surviving population of about 30–50 adult animals).

The tiger is widely distributed on the Indian sub-continent (India, Bangladesh, Bhutan, Myanmar, Nepal), in parts of south-east Asia (Peninsular Malaysia, Cambodia, Vietnam, Laos, Java and Sumatra, Thailand) and in China, the Russian Federation, Tajikistan, Kazakhstan, Kyrgyzstan, Turkmenistan and Uzbekistan. However, there are estimated to be only 5100–7400 left (2750–3750 of which are in India) and the species has already become extinct in recent times in Afghanistan and probably North Korea, and on various islands. Furthermore, some 95 per cent of the remaining populations consist of fewer than 120

---

**The snow leopard, which is one of the most threatened cats in the world, also lives at a higher altitude than most other species.**

tigers and inbreeding is a potential problem (it is estimated that a population consisting of fewer than 50 breeding adults may become genetically impoverished in 100 years). The main threat facing the tiger is hunting for its bones and, to a lesser extent in recent years, for its skin. But it also suffers from competition for space with ever-increasing numbers of people (India's population alone has increased by more than 50 per cent in the past 20 years) and from deforestation, overgrazing, mining and other forms of habitat destruction and fragmentation.

There are eight recognized sub-species of tiger. Three of these are already believed to be extinct: the Bali (*P. t. balica*) disappeared in the 1940s, the Caspian (*P. t. virgata*) in the early 1970s and, most recently, the Javan (*P. t. sondaica*) in the early 1990s. The last reliable sighting of a Javan tiger was in 1982, and tracks and dung were found in 1990, but a year-long survey in 1993–4 failed to find any survivors. The remaining five sub-species are at risk of

**M A M M A L S**

meeting the same fate in the near future. Counting tigers is difficult, but population figures were reviewed in detail for the Global Tiger Forum, held in New Delhi, India, in 1994, and these provide a reasonable picture of their status. The Siberian tiger (*P. t. altaica*), which lives mainly in the eastern territories of Khabarovsk and Primoriye, in the Russian Federation, was particularly hard-hit by poachers in the winter of 1993–4 (when 30–50 per cent of the population was killed); the current population is estimated to be 150–200. The South China tiger (*P. t. amoyensis*) population has plummeted from 4000 in 1949 to just 30–80 today. The Sumatran tiger (*P. t. sumatrae*) has an estimated 600–650 survivors. The Indo-Chinese tiger (*P. t. corbetti*) may have a total population of approximately 1050–1750; these are distributed as follows: 600–650 in Malaysia, 150–600 in Thailand, 200–300 in Vietnam, 100–200 in Cambodia, and extremely small numbers in Laos and Myanmar (formerly

---

**During the 20th century, the tiger population has declined by about 95 per cent, which is at a faster rate than that of any other cat.**

Burma). The Bengal tiger (*P. t. tigris*) is the commonest sub-species (although it is still rare) with 2750–3750 in India, 300–460 in Bangladesh, 150–250 in Nepal, and 50–250 in Bhutan (total approximately 3250–4700).

**Tiger smuggling** Tigers (*Panthera tigris*) are poached mainly for their bones, which are ground up to make tonics and traditional medicines; in 1994 the bones of a single animal could generate US$10 000 worth of business. Their skins are also sold, mainly to collectors, although these are no longer the primary product. China is the main market, although it is closely followed by South Korea and Taiwan. All three countries have officially banned the sale of tiger products, but the illegal trade continues. Other markets exist in Hong Kong, Malaysia, Singapore, Thailand and, to a lesser extent, anywhere else in the world where there are substantial Chinese communities (including Europe and North America). The single biggest haul of tiger bones was imported into South Korea in 1993 – weighing 1783 kg *3930 lb* and representing an estimated 160–300 tigers.

**Fastest decline** Since the turn of the

century, when there were estimated to be about 100 000 tigers (*Panthera tigris*) throughout Asia, the tiger population has probably declined faster than that of any other cat. Loss of habitat and, increasingly, relentless hunting took their toll. By the early 1970s, there were no more than 5000 left. In India alone, the population of Bengal tigers (*P. t. tigris*) dropped from some 40 000 to a dangerously low 2000.

In 1972 the World Wide Fund for Nature launched Operation Tiger (India's own Project Tiger was officially launched in partnership with the Indian government on 1 Apr 1973) and, over the next 15 years, the world's tiger population increased by some 50 per cent to an estimated 7500 (most of the increase in India). But then the conservation community let its guard down, and the poachers quickly resurfaced – steadily shooting, poisoning and snaring tigers throughout their range. The result has been another dramatic decline in numbers. The best known example is Ranthambhore Tiger Reserve, 200 km *124 miles* south of Delhi, India, where the tiger population is believed to have declined from 44–46 in 1991, to about 20 only a year or so later.

# DEER

## Cervidae

*Cervidae*: c. 40 species and several times that number of sub-species
*Moschidae*: 4 species (musk deer)
*Tragulidae*: 4 species (chevrotains)

**Earliest** Deer are believed to have evolved from forest-dwelling animals (not unlike modern chevrotains or mouse deer in the family Tragulidae) during the Oligocene, some 30 million years ago. The earliest true, antler-shedding deer was a species called *Dicroceros*, which first appeared in Europe about 20 million years ago; it was a small animal, with simple forked antlers, and is thought to have survived until about 3 million years ago.

**Largest** The largest deer is the moose or elk (*Alces alces*), which lives in the northern forests of North America, northern Europe and Siberia (it is known as the moose in North America and the elk in Europe). It has an average head-body length of 2.6–3 m *8½–10 ft*; a tail length of 5–12 cm *2–4¾ in*; a height at the shoulder of 1.6–2 m *5¼–6½ ft*; and a weight of 300–550 kg *661–1213 lb*. Males are typically 25 per cent larger than females.

The largest specimens recorded are bulls belonging to the sub-species known as the Alaskan moose (*Alces a. gigas*). A bull standing 2.34 m *7 ft 8 in* between pegs and weighing an estimated 816 kg *1800 lb* was shot on the Yukon River in the Yukon Territory, Canada, in September 1897. Unconfirmed measurements of up to 2.59 m *8 ft 6 in* at the shoulder and estimated weights as high as 1180 kg *2600 lb* have been claimed for this sub-species.

**Largest prehistoric** The extinct Irish elk (*Megaloceros* [formerly *Megoceros*] *giganteus*) was a giant among deer. It was at least as tall and heavy as the modern moose (*Alces alces*) and had even larger antlers. Despite its name, it was not an elk and did not live exclusively in Ireland (although more fossil

remains have been found in Ireland than anywhere else). Fossil evidence and some remarkably good cave paintings suggest that it reached a height of at least 2 m *6 ft 7 in* at the shoulders and looked rather like a giant fallow deer (*Cervus dama*). The Irish elk lived in the grassland areas of Europe, ranging as far east as Siberia and as far south as northern Africa. It became extinct in Ireland around 11 000 years ago, but probably survived in continental Europe until about 10 000 years ago.

**Smallest** The smallest true deer (family Cervidae) is the southern pudu (*Pudu puda*), which is 33–38 cm *13–15 in* tall at the shoulder and weighs 6.3–8.2 kg *14–18 lb*. Found in Chile and Argentina, it has short antlers with a length of only 7–10 cm *2¾–4 in*. The similar but slightly larger northern pudu (*P. mephistophiles*) is found in Ecuador, Colombia and the extreme north of Peru.

The lesser Malay chevrotain (*Tragulus javanicus*) is even smaller, but is not a true deer (*see Smallest artiodactyl*).

**Antlers** Deer are the only animals in the world to possess antlers. Despite their superficial similarity to the horns of antelopes, goats and other mammals, they differ in several ways: they do not grow directly from the skull (horns grow out from the frontal bone, or forehead); they are made entirely of bone (horns are covered by an outer sheath of keratin); they fall off after a year and regrow the following year (horns are permanent and grow throughout life); they are found almost exclusively on male deer (in most horned species, females as well as males have horns); and, in most species, they are branched (horns may be straight, curved, coiled or spiral – but never branched). They also serve different functions: horns are primarily used as weapons of combat or defence, while antlers are at least as important in social display.

While antlers are found almost exclusively on male deer, there are two exceptions: they are also found on female reindeer or caribou (*Rangifer*

*tarandus*) and the Chinese water deer (*Hydropotes inermis*) has no antlers at all. Musk deer (family Moschidae) and chevrotains or mouse deer (family Tragulidae) do not have antlers, but are not regarded as true deer.

*Reindeer are the only deer to be used regularly as draught animals; they pull sledges across ice and snow in many settlements north of the Arctic Circle; a single reindeer is capable of drawing a load of 200 kg 441 lb over snow, travelling up to 40 km 25 miles a day.*

**Largest antlers** The size of antlers varies according to the species, the quality of food available, characters inherited from both parents, the age of the animal and other factors. On average, the longest antlers are normally those of the American wapiti (*Cervus canadensis*) and the caribou (*Rangifer tarandus*), some of which exceed 1.5 m *59 in* in length. The moose (*Alces alces*) is a much larger animal, and its antlers are normally heavier, but they also tend to be shorter. However, the record antler spread or 'rack' for any modern species is 1.99 m *6 ft 6½ in* (skull and antlers 41 kg *91 lb*) from a moose killed near the head-waters of the Stewart River in the Yukon, Canada, in October 1897; the antlers are now on display in the Field Museum, Chicago, Illinois, USA.

**Largest prehistoric antlers** The extinct Irish elk (*Megaloceros* [formerly *Megoceros*] *giganteus*), found in continental Europe as recently as 10 000 years ago, had the largest antlers of any known animal. Indeed, they were 2.5 times larger than would be predicted from the animal's body size. One specimen recovered from an Irish bog had greatly palmated antlers measuring an amazing 4.3 m *14 ft* across and weighing 45 kg *99 lb*, which corresponds to a shoulder height of 1.83 m *6 ft* and a body weight of 500 kg *1100 lb*.

**Smallest antlers** The smallest antlers are found on the tufted deer (*Elaphodus cephalophus*) of Asia: they are unbranched and often completely hidden in a tuft of hairs which grow from the forehead. The Chinese water deer (*Hydropotes inermis*) and, indeed, the females of all other species except the reindeer or caribou (*Rangifer tarandus*) have no antlers at all.

*The sinews and tendons in a moose's long legs make a loud clicking noise when they walk.*

MAMMALS

**Oldest** Deer have a reputation for living a long time but, in reality, once they have survived the early, most vulnerable period of life, 10–20 years is a good age for most species. The oldest ever recorded is a hand-reared Scottish red deer (*Cervus elaphus scoticus*) named *Bambi* (b. 8 Jun 1963), owned by the Fraser family of Kiltarlity, Beauly, UK, which died on 20 Jan 1995 (aged 31 years 7 months 12 days).

There are several records of deer exceeding 26 years in captivity. A red deer, which lived at Milwaukee Zoo, Wisconsin, USA, was 26 years 8 months when it died on 28 Jun 1954. Another red deer, at the National Zoo, Washington, DC, USA, lived for 26 years 2 months 2 days. And a female sambar (*Cervus unicolor*) died on 11 Dec 1955 in New York Zoological Park, USA, aged 26 years 5 months 6 days.

**Most threatened** The World Conservation Union (IUCN) lists a total of 20 deer species as known or suspected to be threatened with extinction (approximately half the world total). The species considered most at risk are the following: the Calamian hog deer (*Axis calamianensis*), Calamian Islands, Philippines; Kuhl's hog deer (*Axis kuhlii*), Bawean Island, Indonesia; the Visayan spotted deer (*Cervus alfredi*), Visayan Islands, Philippines; the swamp deer (*Cervus duvauceli*), India and Nepal; the Persian fallow deer (*Dama mesopotamica*), Iran – it may already be extinct in Iraq; Père David's deer (*Elaphurus davidianus*), being reintroduced to its native home in China; the South Andean huemul (*Hippocamelus bisulcus*), Argentina and Chile; and Fea's muntjac (*Muntiacus feae*), China, Myanmar and Thailand. The recently discovered giant muntjac (*Megamuntiacus vuquangensis*) should probably be added to this list (*see Most recent discoveries*).

A further 12 sub-species of deer are listed as threatened, including the North China sika (*Cervus nippon mandarinus*), which lives in China, and the Key deer (*Odocoileus virginianus clavium*), which lives in the Florida Keys, USA. The many threats deer face include hunting, habitat destruction, and diseases and parasites passed on from domestic cattle.

**Extinctions** Only one species of deer is known or suspected to have become extinct in recent years: Schomburgk's deer (*Cervus schomburgki*), which disappeared from its home in Thailand in 1932. In addition, one sub-species – the Shansi sika (*Cervus nippon grassianus*) – is thought to have become extinct in its native China.

The prehistoric Irish elk had the largest known antlers of any animal, stretching up to 4.3 m *14 ft* across; alongside for scale is a red deer.

**Longest absence** For nearly a century, only two specimens of Fea's muntjac (*Muntiacus feae*) were known to science. Both originated from the borders of southern Myanmar (formerly Burma) and western Thailand, where they were found in the 1880s. Then, in December 1977, a female arrived at Dusit Zoo, Bangkok, Thailand, followed by two females in 1981 and three males and three females from Xizang, Tibet, between February 1982 and April 1983. Several other individuals have been taken into captivity since and the species is now known to occur in Myanmar (formerly Burma), Thailand, China, Vietnam and Laos, although there is still no estimate of the present population.

**Longest recovery** Père David's deer (*Elaphurus davidianus*) was once widely distributed in eastern China. But it became extinct in the wild about 1500–2000 years ago and survived only in captivity in the Chinese Emperor's Imperial Hunting Park, outside Beijing. It was unknown to western scientists until Père Armand David, the French missionary and naturalist, found it in 1865. He sent two skins back to Europe for identification (the new species was later named after him) and then shipped a number of live animals to zoos outside China. Soon afterwards, in 1900, the entire Chinese herd was eaten by hungry soldiers during the Boxer Rebellion – so, perhaps unwittingly, Père

Armand David had saved the species from extinction. Then the Duke of Bedford, in what was probably the first conscious effort to save a mammal from extinction, gathered together all 18 available specimens of Père David's deer from zoos in Europe to create one breeding herd at Woburn Park, Bedfordshire, UK. From this small nucleus herd, established at the beginning of the century, there are now about 1500 Père David's deer distributed in parks and zoos around the world (fortunately, inbreeding does not appear to have been a problem) and a reintroduction programme is underway in China.

**Most recently discovered** During the period 1937 to the present, at least 17 new large mammal species have been discovered. Four of these were deer (*see also Musk deer, p.36*) of which three are muntjacs: the dwarf brocket (*Mazama chunyi*), discovered in 1959, lives in southern Peru and northern Bolivia; the Bornean yellow muntjac (*Muntiacus atherodes*), discovered in 1982, lives in Borneo; the Gongshan muntjac (*Muntiacus gongshanensis*), discovered in 1990, lives in China and, possibly, Myanmar (formerly Burma); and the giant muntjac (*Megamuntiacus vuquangensis*), discovered in 1994, lives in northern Vietnam and neighbouring Laos.

The giant muntjac was officially dis-covered in April 1994, when Dr John MacKinnon and colleagues found various skulls and horns in the homes of local hunters in a village near Vu Quang Nature Reserve, northern Vietnam (on the border with Laos). The first live specimen had actually been seen a month earlier, by professional ornithologists Tom Evans and Rob Timmins; unlikely as it may seem, they found a male, by chance, sharing a cage with an Indian muntjac (*Muntiacus muntjac*) at the headquarters of a logging company in Laos. The giant muntjac stands about 80 cm *31½ in* high at the shoulders and weighs 40–50 kg *88–110 lb* (more than twice the weight of the Indian muntjac). It has a brown

**M A M M A L S**

and grizzled coat, a black patch on the top of its tail and antlers about 20 cm *7.9 in* long. Local people hunt this species for its meat and skin and it is believed to be the third most commonly killed mammal in the area (after wild pig and Indian muntjac). There are estimated to be a few thousand survivors, and the population is declining.

The Vu Quang Nature Reserve, Vietnam, has been in the news a great deal in recent years with a series of new zoological discoveries: the Vu Quang ox (*Pseudoryx nghetinhensis*), a monkey, a pheasant and a fish among them. It has been described as the single most important wildlife site in Indo-China.

## CHEVROTAINS

Chevrotains or mouse deer (family Tragulidae) are small, secretive animals, found in the tropical rainforests and swamps of western and central Africa, India and parts of south-east Asia. Intermediate in form between pigs and deer, they do not have antlers but the upper canines are well developed (especially in the males) and protrude below the lips like tusks. There are four known species.

**Most primitive ruminant** The chevrotains or mouse deer (family Tragulidae) are considered to be the most primitive ruminants (mammals with a four-chambered stomach containing micro-organisms that help to digest their cellulose-rich food). Providing a living link between non-ruminants and ruminants, they are thought to have remained virtually unchanged for approximately 30 million years. They share many features with ruminants, including a four-chambered stomach (although the third chamber is poorly developed); a lack of upper incisor teeth; and various behavioural patterns. They also share features with non-ruminants, including a lack of horns or antlers; four fully developed toes; and, again, various behavioural patterns. The water

chevrotain (*Hyemoschus aquaticus*) is generally considered to be the most primitive of the four species.

**Smallest artiodactyl** The world's smallest artiodactyl (even-toed hoofed mammal) is the lesser Malay chevrotain or lesser mouse deer (*Tragulus javanicus*), which lives in the tropical rainforests and mangroves of southeast Asia. Adults are no bigger than a rabbit, with a head-body length of 44–48 cm *15¾–19 in*; a tail length of 6.5–8 cm *2.6–3.2 in*; a shoulder height of 20–25 cm *7.9–9.8 in*; and a weight of 1.7–3 kg *3¾–6½ lb*. Males are generally smaller than females.

**Most threatened** The World Conservation Union (IUCN) lists only one sub-species of chevrotain or mouse deer as threatened: the Balabac chevrotain (*Tragulus napu nigricans*), which lives on Balabac Island, in the Philippines.

## MUSK DEER

Despite their name and deer-like appearance, musk deer (*Moschus* sp) are not normally included in the deer family (Cervidae): they show a number of important differences and are placed in a family of their own (Moschidae). They are small animals, with an average height at the shoulder of 50–60 cm *20–24 in* and a weight of 10–15 kg *22–33 lb* (unusually among deer, females are heavier than males). Both sexes lack antlers but, like a number of primitive members of the deer family, males have large canine tusks in the upper jaw. Found sporadically in high altitude forests in the mountainous areas of central and eastern Asia, they take their name from the male's musk gland. Classification is controversial but four species are currently recognized.

**Most valuable product** The waxy substance known as musk, which is secreted by male musk deer (family Moschidae), is one of the most expensive animal products in the world. Used in the manufacture of perfumes and soaps in the West and for traditional medicines in the Far East (to treat anything from asthma and epilepsy to pneumonia and typhoid), it fetched up to US$45/g *US$1280/oz* on the international market in the mid-1980s, although the price has since dropped to about US$30–40/g *US$850–1140/oz* today (still several times the price of gold). The annual international trade was about 1400 kg *3086 lb* at the turn of

the century, representing the slaughter of nearly 50 000 deer. The trade dropped to 300 kg *661 lb* by the mid-1980s (85 per cent of which goes to Japan). This decline has not been due to falling demand, but reflects the rapidly declining populations of musk deer in the wild. For comparison, the current market value of Asian rhino horn in Taiwan is US$60/g *US$1700/oz*.

The musk is stored in a fist-sized pouch on the belly of the deer, near the tail. A single mature male carries about 30 g *1.06 oz* (maximum 45 g *1.59 oz*) and, nowadays, this can be extracted without having to kill the animal. Therefore, because of the high value of musk and the need for stricter protection measures, musk deer ranches and farms have recently been established in China.

**Most powerful natural perfume** The musk produced by male musk deer (family Moschidae) is thought to be the most powerful natural perfume in the world. A tiny amount will scent more than 50 000 m³ *1.8 million ft³* of air quite distinctly.

**Most threatened** The World Conservation Union (IUCN) lists only one species of musk deer as threatened: the Siberian musk deer (*Moschus moschiferus*), which is found in parts of Russia, Mongolia, China, North Korea and South Korea. Reports indicate that the Russian population alone has declined by 70 per cent in the period 1993–95, primarily due to demand for musk on the world market.

**Most recently discovered** A new species of musk deer, named *Moschus fuscus*, was discovered a few years ago. The first live specimen was captured in March 1988, in the mountains of Gongshan County, Yunnan Province, China. At first, it was believed to be Fea's muntjac (*Muntiacus feae*), but chromosome analysis later revealed that it was a species new to science. Skins collected in Bome County, Tibet, in 1981, which were also believed to belong to Fea's muntjac, have now been re-examined and are known to belong to the new species.

# DOGS, FOXES & WOLVES

## Canidae

*c.* 35 species, including domestic dogs, foxes, jackals, coyotes, wolves, zorros and dholes

**Earliest** Canids originated in North America during the late Eocene, some 40 million years ago, when they were short-legged in appearance and more closely resembled mongooses and civets than modern species. The earliest known was the North American civet-like *Hesperocyon*, or dawn dogs which had an elongated muzzle, a long tail, and a fairly slender body shape; it grew to a length of about 80 cm *31½ in*. The oldest surviving dog is the grey fox (Urocyon cinereoargenteus) of North and Central America, which first appeared 6–9 million years ago; it lives much like the dawn dogs did in the late Eocene.

**Largest** The largest member of the dog family is the widely distributed grey or timber wolf (*Canis lupus*), which has a head-body length of 1–1.6 m *39½–63 in*; a tail length of 31–51 cm *12¼–20 in*; a shoulder height of 66–81 cm *26–32 in*; and a weight of 16–80 kg *35¼–176½ lb*. Males are usually about 15–20 per cent larger than females. Size varies noticeably throughout the range, with the largest animals living in mid-latitude Canada, Alaska and Siberia, and the smallest in the Middle East. There is also a general large-to-small trend from north to south. The largest widely accepted (albeit poorly documented) grey wolf on record is an individual from the Yukon, Canada, that reportedly weighed 103 kg *227 lb*.

The maned wolf (*Chrysocyon brachyurus*) of central and eastern South America has extremely long legs and, consequently, has an impressive shoulder height of 74–87 cm *29–34¼ in*, making it the tallest member of the family. However, it weighs only 20–23 kg *44–50¾ lb* and is therefore much smaller than the wolf in overall size. For comparison, its other measurements are: head-body length 1.24–1.32 m *48¾–52 in* and tail length 28–45 cm *11–17¾ in*.

**Largest domestic** The heaviest breeds of domestic dog are the St Bernard and the Old English mastiff. Males of both species regularly weigh 77–91 kg *170–201 lb*. The heaviest domestic dog ever recorded is *Aicama Zorba of La-Susa* (whelped 26 Sep 1981), an Old English mastiff owned by Chris Eraclides of London, UK. *Zorba* stands 94 cm *37 in* at the shoulder and weighed a peak 155.58 kg *343 lb* in November 1989.

The tallest breed is the Great Dane. The tallest domestic dog ever recorded was *Shamgret Danzas* (whelped 1975), a Great Dane owned by Wendy and Keith Comley of Milton Keynes, Buckinghamshire, UK. This dog stood 1.05 cm *41½ in* at the shoulder (1.07 cm *42 in* with hackles raised) and weighed up to a maximum of 108 kg *238 lb*. He died on 16 Oct 1984.

> In 1925 a Dobermann pinscher named Sauer, which had been trained by Det-Sgt Herbert Kruger, tracked a stock-thief by scent alone across 160 km 100 miles of the Great Karroo, in South Africa.

**Smallest** The smallest member of the dog family is the fennec fox (*Fennecus zerda*), which lives in the deserts of northern Africa and parts of Arabia. It has a head-body length of 24–41 cm *9½–16 in*; a tail length of 18–31 cm *7–12¼ in*; a shoulder height of 19–21 cm *7½–8¼ in*; and a weight of 1–1.5 kg *2 lb 3 oz–3 lb 5 oz*.

Little is known about Blandford's fox (*Vulpes cana*), which lives in parts of south-western Asia and, possibly, Arabia. It appears to be longer and taller than the fennec fox (head-body length about 42 cm *16½ in*; tail length 30 cm *12 in*; and shoulder height 28–30 cm *11–12 in*) but specimens studied in Israel had a weight range of only 0.9–1.3 kg *2 lb–2 lb 13 oz*.

The raccoon dog (*Nyctereutes procyonoides*) of Asia (and parts of Europe where it has been introduced) has such short legs that it stands only 20 cm *7.9 in* at the shoulder. However, it is a stocky animal with a head-body length of 50–60 cm *19¾–23½ in*; a tail length of 18 cm

*7 in*; and a weight of 7.5 kg *16½ lb* (making it six times heavier than the fennec fox).

**Smallest domestic** The smallest domestic dog on record was a matchbox-sized Yorkshire terrier owned by Arthur Marples of Blackburn, Lancashire, UK, a former editor of *Our Dogs*. This tiny creature, which died in 1945 aged nearly two, stood 6.3 cm *2½ in* at the shoulder, measured 9.5 cm *3¾ in* from the tip of its nose to the root of its tail, and weighed just 113 g *4 oz*.

**Longest legs** The maned wolf (*Chrysocyon brachyurus*) has the longest legs (in relation to body size) of any carnivore, giving it an impressive shoulder height of 74–87 cm *29–34¼ in* (*see Largest*). With a pointed muzzle, bright chestnut coat and bushy tail, in combination with such long, slender legs, it looks rather like a red fox (*Vulpes vulpes*) on stilts. It was once believed that the maned wolf had long legs as an adaptation for running but, in fact, it has a loping gait and is not particularly fast; they are more likely to enable it to peer over the tall grass of its pampas home.

**Largest ears** In relation to body size, the fennec fox (*Fennecus zerda*) has the largest ears of any carnivore. They measure an astonishing 15 cm *5.9 in* in length, almost doubling the animal's total height at the shoulder (*see Smallest*). Large ears give the fennec fox a rather comical appearance, but are essential to its survival: they act like radiators, dissipating heat to keep it cool in its desert home, and they help to locate termites and other prey by detecting the infinitesimally small sounds they make while scurrying underground.

Several other desert-living foxes have exceptionally large ears. The appropriately named bat-eared fox (*Otocyon megalotis*) of southern and eastern Africa has ears up to 12–13 cm *4¾–5 in* long (compared with a shoulder height of 30–40 cm *11¾–15¾ in*). It stands with its nose pointing downward and ears tilted forward, listening for insects, then turns its head from side to side to determine their precise location.

**Least toes** The African wild dog (*Lycaon pictus*) is unique among canids in having only four toes on its front feet; as in other species it has five on its hind feet, making a total of 18 altogether. All other members of the dog family have 20 toes.

**Earliest domestic** Dogs were probably domesticated for the first time about

12 000 years ago, although the earliest undisputed evidence dates from 11 000 years ago in Iran and from 9500 years ago in Yorkshire, UK. Numerous wild dog species have been domesticated at one time or another, but the grey wolf (*Canis lupus*) is generally accepted as the ancestor of all 350–400 modern domestic dog breeds. Selective breeding was first attempted by the Egyptians in around 2000 BC, in order to produce three distinct types of dog: a guard dog, a hunting dog and a decorative, friendly one. But the many different kinds around today are the result of highly selective breeding programmes during the past few hundred years.

**Oldest** Surprisingly little is known about the maximum lifespans of many wild members of the dog family. Most species live for less than 10 years in the wild and a little longer in captivity (at least partly because the threats of shoot-ing, trapping and poisoning are removed). The longest-lived species are the coyote (*Canis latrans*), which lives for up to 14½ years in the wild (maximum 21 years 10 months in captivity); the grey wolf (*Canis lupus*) and golden jackal (*Canis aureus*): up to 16 years in the wild (20 in captivity); the grey fox (*Urocyon cinereoargenteus*) and maned wolf (*Chrysocyon brachyurus*): up to 13 years in the wild (15 in captivity); and the Asiatic wild dog or dhole (*Cuon alpinus*): up to 10 years in the wild (16 in captivity).

Most domestic dogs live for 8–15 years. Authentic records of dogs living over 20 years are rare and generally involve the smaller breeds. The greatest reliable age recorded for a dog is 29 years 5 months for an Australian cattle-dog named *Bluey*, owned by Les Hall of Rochester, Victoria, Australia. *Bluey* was obtained as a puppy in 1910 and worked among cattle and sheep for nearly 20 years before being put to sleep on 14 Nov 1939.

**Noisiest** Grey wolves (*Canis lupus*) make a variety of sounds, including barks, growls, whimpers and squeaks, but their howling is the best-known and noisiest. Howling serves several different functions: it advertises the presence of a pack to avoid unneces-sary encounters with neighbouring wolves, it helps to maintain contact when the pack is split up or enables its members to reassemble after being separated on a long hunt, and it helps to strengthen social bonds within the pack. When a wolf howls, it is often accompanied by other members of the pack and, under ideal conditions, their combined effort can be heard from as far as 10 km *6.2 miles* away.

**Most dangerous** Several members of the dog family have been reported to attack people, particularly young children. But well-documented cases are extremely rare and a great deal of nonsense has been written about dangerous canids over the years. The truth is that most of them are nervous of people and, if possible, prefer to avoid close encounters.

The grey wolf (*Canis lupus*) is the only canid that represents a potential threat to people, and there is little doubt that if this species wanted to kill someone it could do so quite easily. But its evil reputation as a vicious and uncompromising killer is entirely undeserved. It is certainly not dangerous in North

**The tallest domestic dog ever recorded was a Great Dane which stood 1.05 m *41½ in* at the shoulder (seen here with the world's smallest breed of horse; see p.56).**

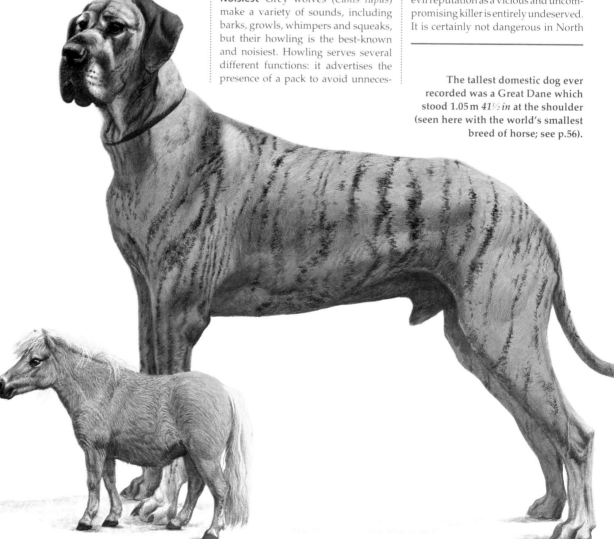

America where, despite a great many claims to the contrary, there has never been a serious attack by an unprovoked, healthy wild wolf. Indeed, when North American biologists walk up to packs of hungry wolves on their kills, the animals walk or run away until their food has been examined, and then return to resume feeding about 10 minutes after the biologists have left. There have been a number of well-documented minor incidents, but these have been under unusual circumstances; for example, in 1927, in Northwest Territories, Canada, a man was attempting to break up a fight between a wild wolf and his huskies and, as he tried to grab the wolf by the scruff of the neck, it bit him on the arm and ran away.

However, experts are divided over the situation in Europe and Asia. There is little doubt that apparently healthy, wild wolves have made unprovoked attacks on people in these regions, although there are few well-documented examples. Two exceptional cases have received considerable attention. The first concerned a rogue wolf dubbed the 'Beast of Gevauden' which, over a period of 2 years, attacked dozens of children and adults in the mountainous region of Lozère, France. More than 100 wolves were killed before the culprit itself was shot, on 19 Jun 1766; when it was cut open, the shoulder bone of a young child killed the previous day was found inside its stomach. The second case concerned a pack of wolves which suddenly appeared, in the summer of 1948, in the Darovskoye district, about 1000 km *620 miles* east of Moscow, Russia; the animals killed about 40 children and then disappeared almost as suddenly as they had arrived.

The main problem with wolves in Europe may be hybridization with large domestic dogs. The resulting dog-wolf hybrids are believed to be considerably more dangerous than pure-bred wolves, since they are often larger and more aggressive, and frequently show little fear of people. Commonly encountered in packs of 12 or more, they have become a major concern in some parts of Russia, in particular.

The greatest threat from members of the dog family is rabies. Most mammals are susceptible to this viral disease, but some canids are highly susceptible and can become major vectors. In Europe and much of North America, the main carrier is the red fox (*Vulpes vulpes*), but it is the arctic fox (*Alopex lagopus*) in the far north, the black-backed jackal (*Canis mesomelas*) in southern Africa, and a variety of other species elsewhere. The early stages of the

**The streetwise red fox has adapted to life in towns and cities more successfully than any other member of the dog family.**

disease (during which there are no obvious symptoms and the victim is not infective) may last for as little as three weeks or, in exceptional circumstances, as long as a year. A day or two before the symptoms begin to appear, the victim becomes infective and virus particles in the saliva can be passed on to others through bite wounds. After this stage has been reached, death is inevitable, usually within a few days. An oral vaccine, which was first tested in Switzerland in 1978, has proved to be a major breakthrough in the battle against rabies: it is both cheaper and more effective than efforts to eradicate the main carriers. Some scientists are now cautiously optimistic that rabies may now be virtually eliminated from most parts of Europe by the end of the millennium, and there are hopes that the vaccine can be used successfully in other parts of the world.

**M**
**A**
**M**
**M**
**A**
**L**
**S**

The African wild dog
is the most carnivorous
member of the canid family,
eating nothing but meat.

**Most urbanized** Several different canids have successfully adapted to city life, but none are quite as streetwise as the red fox (*Vulpes vulpes*) which, in some parts of the world, is more numerous in towns and cities than it is in the surrounding countryside. Red foxes have even been reported raising cubs in the 54 000-seater Yankee Stadium, New York, USA, and in the attic of a four-storey office block in Bristol, UK. One enterprising vixen, also in Bristol, would enter an occupied house via the cat-flap, run down the hall and squeeze through a broken board in the kitchen to reach her cubs under the floor; a dog and a cat also lived in the house, but she persevered and managed to raise the cubs successfully.

**Best climber** The red fox (*Vulpes vulpes*), corsac fox (*Vulpes corsac*) and several other canids are able to climb trees, but none do so as frequently or easily as the grey or tree-climbing fox (*Urocyon cinereoargenteus*) of North, Central and the northern tip of South America. It is an extremely agile climber, using its long claws to anchor itself to the tree trunk, and can even leap from branch to branch. The grey fox often seeks refuge in trees if it feels threatened (reversing down the trunk backwards once the danger has passed) but often climbs without provocation as well. Young cubs are able to climb trees when they are as little as 1 month old.

**Longest gestation period** The African wild dog (*Lycaon pictus*) has a gestation period of 69–73 days, which is the longest of all the canids. The bat-eared fox (*Otocyon megalotis*) has a lower average but can range from 60–75 days.

**Shortest gestation period** The fennec fox (*Fennecus zerda*) of northern Africa has the shortest gestation period of all the canids, typically 50–52 days. However, the cape fox (*Vulpes chama*) of southern Africa and the widely distributed red fox (*Vulpes vulpes*) both come a very close second, with 51–52 days being typical; in addition, the gestation period in the red fox can be as low as 49 days, which is the lowest recorded in the family (it ranges up to 55 days). The average for several other species is under 55 days.

**Largest litter** The African wild dog (*Lycaon pictus*) has the largest litter size in the family, with an average of 7–10 pups but as many as 19 recorded on occasion; the female has 12–14 teats (more than any other canid). The arctic fox (*Alopex lagopus*) typically has 6–16 pups in a litter, although in good lemming years on Wrangel Island, off the coast of north-eastern Siberia, as many

as 19 have been recorded; there is also an unconfirmed report of 25 pups in a single litter. As many as 18 pups have been recorded for the coyote (*Canis latrans*), but they probably represent the litters of two different females; the typical litter size for this species is six.

**Smallest litter** A number of canid species give birth to a single pup on occasion, but in most cases the average is higher. In this respect, the maned wolf (*Chrysocyon brachyurus*) and Blanford's fox (*Vulpes cana*) probably have the smallest litter sizes, typically ranging from a single pup to a maximum of three.

**Most carnivorous** The African wild dog (*Lycaon pictus*) is the only *exclusively* carnivorous member of the canid family (other species feed predominantly on other mammals, but invariably take invertebrates, fruit and vegetables as well).

*In parts of South America, it is believed that the cry of the maned wolf is a warning of a change in the weather, and that its hypnotic gaze is able to fell a chicken.*

**Most insectivorous** The bat-eared fox (*Otocyon megalotis*) is the most insectivorous canid. Unique among carnivores in having four to eight extra molars (which provide more chewing surfaces for feeding on insects) it is the only member of the dog family to have largely abandoned mammalian prey. Its range in southern and eastern Africa actually matches that of the harvester termite (*Hodotermes mossambicus*), which accounts for more than half its total food intake. It will also eat adult and larval beetles and grasshoppers, as well as the occasional spider and scorpion, but vertebrate prey such as lizards, birds and mammals seldom constitutes more than 10 per cent of its diet. Ironically, it still remains dependent on other mammals for its food, because its favourite insects are numerous only where large hoofed mammals abound.

**Most varied diet** Most canids eat whatever food is available in return for the least possible effort, and they vary their diets from day to day as well as from season to season. If necessary, even the grey wolf (*Canis lupus*) can live off mice and insects, or go vegetarian, until its favoured prey is more readily available. But, by a small margin, the red fox (*Vulpes vulpes*) probably has the most varied diet in the family. It will eat a wide range of vertebrates, from small hoofed mammals and rodents to birds and fish; a broad selection of invertebrates, including beetles, earthworms and grasshoppers; a variety of fruit, such as blackberries and apples, and vegetables; and a mixture of carrion, human debris and other scavenged items. Red foxes in Australia have taken to eating sheep placentae at lambing time, while those living in towns and cities in many parts of the world have been known to try anything from greasy chip papers to rubber bands. Absolutely nothing is wasted – to the point where even dead or dying foxes are occasionally cannibalized.

**Largest prey** Grey wolves (*Canis lupus*) have a varied mammalian diet, but will tackle prey as large as moose (200–825 kg *441–1820 lb*) and bison (350–1000 kg *772–2205 lb*), which are

many times their own weight (see *Largest*). Typically hunting in packs, they tend to concentrate on young animals, or elderly, sick or injured adults, but will occasionally tackle perfectly healthy, fully grown adults as well. Despite their indisputable hunting skills and strength, studies in North America reveal a hunting success rate of only 7–10 per cent and, consequently, they frequently go for several weeks without food.

African wild dogs (*Lycaon pictus*) normally prey on the most abundant mammals available in the 14–45 kg *31–99 lb* weight range but, hunting in packs, will tackle prey as large as greater kudu (200–300 kg *441–661 lb*) and Burchell's zebra (350 kg *772 lb*).

**Largest pack** A number of canids live in well-structured packs. The size of these packs is extremely variable (depending on the species, the time of year and local conditions) but the largest are normally formed by grey wolves (*Canis lupus*) and African wild dogs (*Lycaon pictus*).

The largest on record are for African wild dogs during the 19th century, when packs containing more than 100 animals were not unusual and some containing as many as 500 were reported on rare occasions. Nowadays, following drastic population declines throughout Africa (see *Most threatened*), the average pack size is about 10 adults and their pups; packs of over 30 animals are exceedingly rare. Each pack is typically composed of a dominant breeding pair, a number of non-breeding adults, and their dependent offspring (the dominant male and female inhibit breeding in the others by physiological and behavioural means); unusually among social mammals, it is the females rather than the males that leave their natal packs, on reaching maturity, to join unrelated packs.

Grey wolf packs are generally smaller. The largest occur when mature offspring fail to disperse (in times of food abundance) and where the prey is largest. Packs of 8–12 are most common, but as many as 36 animals have been reported living together. Their complex social organization is centred around a dominant breeding pair; there is a strict hierarchy among the other, non-breeding members of the pack, which help to raise the dominant pair's offspring until they are old enough to challenge the leader or his mate, or leave to begin their search for a new pack.

**Largest home range** The home range of the grey wolf (*Canis lupis*) varies greatly from one pack to another, de-

pending on prey density and availability, but can be considerably larger than in any other canid. The normal range is 80–2000 km² *31–772 miles²*, but the largest ever recorded was an amazing 13 000 km² *5000 miles²* for a pack in Alaska, USA.

The African wild dog (*Lycaon pictus*) also has an exceptionally large home range. A typical pack ranges over an area of 500–1500 km² *193–579 miles²* (overlapping with other packs by 50–80 per cent) but can have a range as large as 3900 km² *1505 miles²* (as recorded for a pack in South Africa).

**Oddest** The raccoon dog (*Nyctereutes procyonoides*) is the least dog-like member of the canid family. As its name suggests, it looks more like a raccoon: it is roughly the same size, and has long, thick body fur and even a black face mask. Believed to be the most primitive member of the family, it lives in woodland and forested river valleys in Asia and has been introduced into western Russia and Europe.

The similar-sized bush dog (*Speothos venaticus*) of Central and South America looks more like a stocky weasel or civet than a dog. It is a heavily built, broad-faced animal with small, rounded ears, squat legs, webbed feet and a short tail.

**Hibernation** The raccoon dog (*Nyctereutes procyonoides*) of Asia and parts of Europe is the only member of the dog family that hibernates. It puts on weight during the autumn (growing from 4–6 kg *8 lb 13 oz–13 lb 4 oz* to 6–10 kg *13 lb 4 oz–22 lb*) and then retreats to an underground burrow, where it lives off its fat store for the duration of the winter. In the extreme north of the range, where the weather is particularly harsh, it remains in a state of lethargy from as early as November until as late as April. But if the weather is mild it may emerge for a few days at a time and, in the south, may not hibernate at all.

**Hottest** The fennec fox (*Fennecus zerda*) probably has to survive higher temperatures in its home, deep in the Sahara

*A brown hare can run much faster than a red fox but, when it notices a fox approaching, it does not run away; instead, it stands up. Once the fox realizes that it has been seen, it does not bother to give chase and thereby saves both animals the effort of running.*

Desert, than any other canid. It is so well adapted to coping with the heat that, if the temperature drops to below 20°C *68°F*, it starts to shiver. Mainly active at night, it escapes the worst of the daytime heat by denning up in its underground burrow. It has exceptionally large ears that help to dissipate excess heat, like miniature radiators, the soles of its feet are furred to provide insulation against the hot sand, and it can survive for long periods without water. Perhaps most impressive of all, it is capable of panting at an astounding 690 breaths/min when the temperature reaches *c.* 38°C *100°F*.

**Coldest** The arctic fox (*Alopex lagopus*) regularly survives colder temperatures than any other canid. Found throughout the Arctic and sub-Arctic, it is well-suited to its extreme environment, where temperatures may drop to as low as –70°C *–94°F* (captives have even survived experimental temperatures down to –80°C *–112°F*). Its many adaptations include: a compact size, and short muzzle, ears and legs, to reduce heat loss; a thick winter coat (consisting of 70 per cent fine underfur) which provides unbeatable insulation; an ability to reduce blood flow to the skin; fur on the soles of the feet to protect them

> *The last authenticated British wild wolf was shot in Scotland in 1743, although hunters claimed to have killed one as recently as 1848.*

from frostbite; and extensive fat reserves in other parts of the body. These adaptations are so effective that the arctic fox's metabolic rate does not even start to increase until the outside temperature reaches –50°C *–58°C*.

**Highest living** Several members of the dog family have been observed at altitudes higher than 5000 m *16 400 ft*. The record-holders are: a small pack of five African wild dogs (*Lycaon pictus*) observed by a climber in the snows atop Mt Kilimanjaro, Tanzania, at 5345 m *17 532 ft*; a Tibetan fox (*Vulpes ferrilata*) at 5640 m *18 500 ft*; and a grey wolf (*Canis lupus*) at 5791 m *19 000 ft*.

**Most variable colour** Despite considerable colour variations between populations and individuals in many

canids, three species are exceptional: the grey wolf (*Canis lupus*), arctic fox (*Alopex lagopus*) and the African wild dog (*Lycaon pictus*).

The grey wolf varies from almost jet black on Princess Royal Island, BC, Canada, to almost pure white in some arctic areas such as Ellesmere Island.

The arctic fox occurs in two distinct colour phases. One is known as the white or polar form, and is uniformly white in winter and brown in summer (brown on the back and thighs, but yellow on the belly and sides). The other is known as the blue form, and is pale bluish-grey in winter and dark bluish-grey or chocolate-brown in summer. Both forms are genetically determined by a single gene, the white one being recessive, and vary in abundance from region to region (possibly according to the extent of winter snow cover). On mainland Alaska, USA, for example, 99 per cent of arctic foxes are the polar form; but offshore, on the Pribilof Islands, more than 90 per cent are the blue form.

The African wild dog (*Lycaon pictus*) is unusual because each individual has

---

**The arctic fox can survive colder temperatures than any other canid.**

**MAMMALS**

**Despite heavy persecution, the coyote is the most numerous and successful large predator in North America; these tracks were photographed in Baja California, Mexico.**

---

unique markings that are as distinctive as human fingerprints. The mottled black, yellow and white patterning on their fur occurs in almost every conceivable arrangement and proportion of colour; in combination with scars and other markings, these enable experts to tell one animal from another at a glance.

**Most successful** Perhaps surprisingly, a number of canid species are thriving,

*One arctic fox den on Wrangel Island, off the north-east coast of Siberia, is believed to have been occupied continuously by successive generations of foxes for more than 300 years.*

despite heavy persecution. Two of the best examples are the North American coyote (*Canis latrans*) and the Australian dingo (*Canis familiaris dingo*).

The coyote is the most numerous and successful large predator in North America. While the range of most predators is shrinking, its range is expanding. In the past century, it has spread northwards and eastwards (possibly taking advantage of the decimation of wolves in many areas) and is now found throughout the continent, from Alaska to Costa Rica and from California and British Columbia to Nova Scotia and New England. There are even large populations in the centre of Los Angeles, California, and in other major cities. In many areas, the persecution continues unabated – but the coyote population apparently thrives against all the odds.

Dingoes first came to Australia some 4000–6000 years ago. They were probably brought by south-east Asian seafarers, as a live food source to vary the diet on long ocean voyages, when they visited the north of the continent to trade. The dingoes were partly domesticated, but took to the wild with relish and quickly spread throughout mainland Australia. Nowadays, they thrive in a variety of habitats, from

*Native Americans have great respect for the coyote, which has been known by various tribes as little brother, song dog, first-born, God's dog and wise one.*

deserts to deep forest, and are found everywhere except where they are specifically excluded from sheep grazing areas by special fences. Similar forms are also found on many islands in southeast Asia. There is still discussion about the taxonomy of the dingo, but it probably descended from the Indian plains wolf (*Canis lupus pallipes*) and is currently considered to be a sub-species of the domestic dog (*Canis familiaris*).

**Most widespread** Only a few centuries ago, the grey wolf (*Canis lupus*) had the greatest natural range of any land mammal, apart from humans. It occupied much of the northern hemisphere, from the icy wastes of Greenland to the deserts of the Arabian peninsula, extending across North America, Europe, Asia and the Middle East. But heavy persecution has wiped out many

> *In the 1920s it was estimated that grey wolves killed about one million cattle in Russia; the result was a control programme involving the removal of 40 000–50 000 wolves a year for the next half a century.*

populations and today it is mainly an inhabitant of remote wilderness areas, where it does not conflict with human interests.

The red fox (*Vulpes vulpes*) is now the most widespread wild dog, occurring throughout much of the northern hemisphere and in parts of the southern hemisphere. It is found from the Arctic tundra to the deserts of northern Africa and from British Columbia across Europe and the Asian steppes to Japan. It lives on Ellesmere Island, Northwest Territories, Canada, at a latitude of 77°N or even higher, and is found in Australia (where it was introduced last century for hunting and in an attempt to control the rabbit population) at a latitude of about 38°S. Found in woodlands, deserts, moorland, farmland, cities and almost any other habitat, it is one of the most successful and widespread mammals in the world.

**Smallest range** Excluding the red wolf (*Canis rufus*), which became extinct in the wild and is now being reintroduced (*see Most threatened*), the island grey fox (*Urocyon littoralis*) has the smallest range of any member of the dog family. Until recently, it was believed to occur only on the six main Channel Islands, off the coast of southern California, USA; even the largest of these islands, Santa Cruz, is just 38 km *24 miles* long and 3–13 km *2–8 miles* wide. But recent evidence suggests that some nearby populations on the mainland, which were previously believed to be grey foxes (*U. cinereoargenteus*), may in fact be this species.

**Most threatened** The World Conservation Union (IUCN) lists a total of 18 canid species as known or suspected to be threatened with extinction. This accounts for more than half the total family. The species considered most seriously at risk are: the red wolf (*Canis rufus*) of the USA; the Ethiopian wolf or Simien jackal (*C. simensis*) of Ethiopia; and the African wild dog (*Lycaon pictus*). There is also special concern for the grey wolf (*C. lupus*), maned wolf (*Chrysocyon brachyurus*), Asiatic wild dog or dhole (*Cuon alpinus*), grey zorro or South American grey fox (*Dusicyon*

*griseus*) and bush dog (*Speothos venaticus*).

The Ethiopian wolf is endemic to the highlands of Ethiopia, where it is found on open moorlands from a height of 3000 m *9840 ft* to 4377 m *14 357 ft* on the summit of Tullu Deemtu. There may be fewer than 500 survivors, in only six locations. More than half of them (probably forming the only genetically viable population) are found in the Bale Mountains National Park, on the south-eastern rim of the Rift Valley, in the eastern Ethiopian Highlands. The most immediate threats they face are habitat degradation caused by high-altitude subsistence agriculture and over-grazing by livestock; competition and hybridization with domestic dogs; disease; and human persecution.

In the past 30 years, the African wild dog has all but disappeared from 19 of the 34 countries in which it once lived, including Algeria, Mauritania, Mali, Burundi, Rwanda, Uganda, Benin, Togo, Congo, Gabon, Ghana and Zaire. Only six countries support viable populations and in at least two of these numbers have halved in the past decade. The best remaining stronghold for the species is Selous Game Reserve, Tanzania, which has a population of about 800 adults (possibly as many as 40 per cent of the entire adult population). Mikumi National Park, which borders Selous to the north-west, probably holds another 90 adults. Elsewhere, there are widely scattered packs in unprotected, prey-depleted areas, and many of these are almost certainly doomed. The total population (including juveniles) is now about 5000 and the extinction of the species has been predicted within the next 20 years unless the current population decline can be reversed. The main threats are loss and fragmentation of suitable habitat, persecution and disease.

The red wolf was once abundant throughout south-eastern USA, from Pennsylvania to Texas. But habitat degradation, human persecution and hybridization with eastward-moving coyotes all took their toll and, at one point, it was cited as the world's rarest mammal. The species officially became extinct in the wild in 1980, when the last survivor died in south-eastern Texas. Fortunately, a small number had been taken into captivity and a reintroduction programme began on 14 Sep 1987, when the first captive-bred pair was released into the Alligator River National Wildlife Refuge, North Carolina. Further reintroductions have followed. The first reintroduction to a mainland site (the others were on more easily con-

trolled islands and a peninsula) was in 1991 in the Great Smoky Mountains National Park, straddling North Carolina and Tennessee. The plan is to establish at least 220 animals in the wild and a further 330 in captivity, although there is considerable opposition from local people. The current wild population is about 30 and second generation pups were first born in the wild in 1991. A further setback came in June 1991, when the results of mitochondrial DNA analysis were published, concluding that the red wolf may not be a separate species but rather a hybrid of the grey wolf (*Canis lupus*) and coyote (*C. latrans*).

**Extinctions** One species of canid is known to have become extinct in recent times: the Falkland Island wolf (*Dusicyon australis*). Resembling a grey wolf (*Canis lupus*) in appearance, albeit with shorter legs, it stood about 60 cm *24 in* high at the shoulder and was the only mammalian predator on its island home in the South Atlantic. When it was first discovered, in 1690, the Falkland Island wolf was still common. But it was renowned for being exceptionally tame (it would even wade into the sea to greet arriving boats) and made an easy target for early settlers. The Spanish killed large numbers simply by tempting the wolves within range with a piece of meat held in one hand – and then stabbing them with a knife held in the other. Many more wolves were killed by fur traders from the USA and, when Scottish settlers began to raise sheep on the islands in the 1860s, still more succumbed to poisoned baits. The last known survivor was killed in 1876 and all that remains of the species today is 11 specimens scattered in museums around the world.

A number of sub-species have also become extinct, including seven unique varieties of grey wolf. One of these was a Japanese form (*C. l. hodophilax*), which was hunted to extinction by 1905; standing just 36 cm *14 in* high at the shoulder, it was the smallest sub-species of grey wolf.

# EDENTATES

## Xenarthra

29 species, including 20 armadillos, 5 sloths and 4 anteaters; found only in North, Central and South America.

> *The giant anteater sleeps on its side, using its huge, fluffy tail as a blanket.*

**Largest** The giant anteater (*Myrmecophaga tridactyla*), which lives in the savannas and open woodlands of Central and South America, is the largest of the edentates. It has a head-body length of 1–1.2 m *39–47 in*; a tail length of 70–90 cm *27½–35½ in*; and a weight of 20–60 kg *44–132¼ lb*. Males are typically 10–20 per cent heavier than females.

In exceptional circumstances, giant armadillos (*Priodontes maximus*) have been known to attain a weight of 60 kg *132¼ lb*, but these have been over-fed zoo specimens; the average head-body length for this species is 75–100 cm *29½–39 in* (tail length about 50 cm *19½ in*).

**The giant anteater is the largest of the anteaters, measuring up to 2 m 6½ ft in length (including the long, bushy tail).**

**Largest prehistoric** Modern edentates are small compared with many of their prehistoric relatives. In particular, giant ground sloths in the family Megalonychidae, such as a species called *Megatherium*, were at least the size of today's elephants; they appeared during the early Oligocene some 34 million years ago, and were prevalent in North and South America and the Caribbean until between 8500 and 11000 years ago. For many years, there have been rumours of a giant, human-sized ground sloth – the South American equivalent of the abominable snowman – still living in the depths of the Amazon rainforest; according to Indians, rubber-tappers and illegal gold-miners, who claim to have seen the creature and call it the *mapinguari*, it gives off a cloud of noxious gas when approached. Some western scientists take the claims seriously and believe that such an animal may really exist.

The largest armadillo-like edentate was a rhinoceros-sized species called *Glyptodon*, which reached 5 m *16 ft 5 in* in length and carried a rigid 3 m *9 ft 10 in* long bony shell on its back. The huge shell was used as a roof or tomb by early South American Indians.

**Smallest** The lesser or pink fairy armadillo (*Chlamyphorus truncatus*), which lives in central Argentina, is the smallest of the edentates. It has a head-body length of 12.5–15 cm *5–6 in*; a tail length of 2.5–3 cm *1–1.2 in*; and a weight of 80–100 g *2.8–3½ oz*. Roughly the size of a small rat, its armour is pale pink in colour.

**Sleepiest** Some armadillos (family Dasypodidae), sloths (families Bradypodidae and Megalonychidae) and opossums (family Didelphidae) spend up to 80 per cent of their lives sleeping or dozing.

Sloths have a metabolic rate that is only 40–45 per cent of that expected for animals of their size. Subsisting entirely on leaves, which are a poor source of food, they are particularly economic with their use of energy and seem to live in perpetual slow motion. Even when they are alert, their movements are methodical and slow. Digestion, in particular, is so slow that it may take up to a month for foodstuffs to pass from the stomach to the small intestine.

The least active of all mammals are probably the three species of three-toed sloths in the genus *Bradypus*, which may occupy the same tree for two or more nights in a row (two-toed sloths in the genus *Choloepus* move from tree to tree as often as four times in a night).

**Slowest** The three-toed sloth (*Bradypus tridactylus*) of tropical South America is probably the slowest mammal in the world, with an average ground speed of

> *A giant anteater eats around 30000 ants and termites in a single day.*

**Three-toed sloth in the Amazon, Brazil: the slowest, and one of the sleepiest, mammals in the world.**

---

1.8–2.4 m/min *6–8 ft/min* (0.1–0.16 km/h *0.07–0.1 mph*). It descends to the ground about once a week to defecate and, like all sloths, is so highly modified for its arboreal life that it has lost the ability to walk or run. Its long, curved claws and weak hind legs (sloths have about half the muscle weight of other animals of a similar size) make normal locomotion impossible, so it lies on its belly, reaches forward to get a claw-hold in the soil and literally drags itself along the ground. In the trees it can accelerate to a slightly more impressive 4.6 m/min *15 ft/min* (0.27 km/h *0.17 mph*); peak acceleration is probably reached during the courtship 'pursuit', when amorous males go in search of females.

Strangely, sloths are adept at swimming and have considerable stamina in the water; they normally swim breaststroke, but sometimes do a very elegant front crawl.

**Most upside down** Sloths (families Bradypodidae and Megalonychidae) probably spend more of their lives hanging upside down than any other mammals (including non-hibernating bats). They eat, sleep, travel hand-over-hand, mate and give birth in an upside-down position. Indeed, even their fur grows upside down – or, at least, 'backwards' – from the wrist towards the shoulder and from the stomach towards the back. Even after they have died, they sometimes continue to hang in exactly the same way, firmly hooked on to a branch by their coathanger-like 8–10 cm *3–4 in* long claws. The only times they right themselves are when climbing up or down (which they do in an upright position) or when visiting the ground briefly to defecate (about once a week).

**Quadruplets** The nine-banded or common long-nosed armadillo (*Dasypus novemcinctus*), which lives in southern North America and Central and South America, is unique among mammals in producing litters of four chromosomally identical young. The four infants, which are all of the same sex (either male or female), are produced from a single fertilized egg that subdivides once development starts.

**Most threatened** The World Conservation Union (IUCN) lists six edentate species as known or believed to be threatened with extinction. The maned sloth (*Bradypus torquatus*) and the Brazilian three-banded armadillo (*Tolypeutes tricinctus*), both of which live in Brazil, are considered to be most seriously at risk. The other species are the greater pichi ciego or Chacoan fairy armadillo (*Chlamyphorus retusus*), of Argentina, Bolivia and Paraguay; the lesser pichi ciego or lesser fairy armadillo (*Chlamyphorus truncatus*), of Argentina; the giant armadillo (*Priodontes maximus*), from many parts of South America; and the giant anteater (*Myrmecophaga tridactyla*) of Central and South America. The many threats they face include hunting, collection for the live-animal trade and habitat destruction. No species is known to have become extinct in recent times.

**Longest tongue** The tongue of the giant anteater (*Myrmecophaga tridactyla*) can be pushed out a remarkable 61 cm *24 in* beyond the tip of the snout – up to 150 times/min. The sheath containing the tongue and tongue-retracting muscles is anchored to the breastbone.

**Lowest body temperature** Edentates have some of the lowest body temperatures of all mammals (excluding species in hibernation). The two-toed sloths in the genus *Choloepus* have the lowest and most variable on record, ranging from a low of 24°C *75°F* to a high of 33°C *91°F*; they move in and out of the sun in the same way that reptiles and other cold-blooded animals do to regulate their body temperatures. The pichi (*Zaedyus pichiy*) body temperature drops to a low of 24°C *75°F*, but is slightly more variable and also reaches a high of 35.2°C *95.3°F*.

---

*The word 'edentate' literally means 'without teeth', although only the anteaters are genuinely toothless (armadillos and sloths possess simple, peg-like molars and pre-molars).*

# ELEPHANTS

## *Proboscidea*
There are only two species of elephant: African and Asian.

> *The Asian elephant is easily distinguished from the African by its much smaller ears and its more rounded back.*

**Earliest** According to the fossil record, more than 300 species of trunked animals (proboscideans) have lived on Earth (on every continent except Australia and Antarctica); only two of them survive today. Remains of the earliest known proboscidean were first found at Lake Moeris, near El Fayyum, Egypt (about 60 km *37 miles* south-west of Cairo); subsequently, more remains have been found at various localities along the fringes of the Sahara. Named *Moeritherium*, it first appeared during the Eocene, about 50–55 million years ago, and was roughly the size of a large pig. It is thought to have been semi-aquatic, spending most of its life in and around water and feeding mainly on aquatic vegetation. There is no evidence to suggest that it possessed a trunk, although it may have had a thickened upper lip.

The first known elephant-like proboscidean was probably a species called *Palaeomastodon*, which appeared during the Oligocene about 35 million years ago. It grew to roughly the size of a cow and had a medium-length trunk and downward-curving tusks.

The family Elephantidae, which includes modern elephants and mammoths, first appeared about 5 million years ago; it is the only surviving family of all the proboscideans.

**Largest** The African bush or savannah elephant (*Loxodonta africana africana*) is the largest living land animal. The average adult stands 3–3.7 m *9 ft 10 in–12 ft 2 in* at the shoulder and weighs 4–7 tonnes; cows are considerably smaller than bulls of a similar age. The largest elephant ever recorded was a bull of this sub-species shot near Mucusso, southern Angola, on 7 Nov 1974. Lying on its side, it measured 4.16 m *13 ft 8 in* in a projected line from the highest point of the shoulder to the base of the forefoot, indicating a standing height of about 3.96 m *13 ft*. Other measurements for this record-breaking individual included an overall length of 10.67 m *35 ft* (measured from the tip of the trunk to the end of the tail) and a forefoot circumference of 1.8 m *5 ft 11 in*. The tusks (one broken) measured 2.26 m *7 ft 5 in* and 1.63 m *5 ft 4 in* respectively. Its weight was computed to be 12.24 tonnes.

The other sub-species of African elephant, the forest elephant (*Loxodonta a. cyclotis*), which lives in the equatorial forests of the central African basin and West Africa, is considerably smaller than the savanna elephant. It has an average height at the shoulder of 2–3 m

The African bush elephant, which is the largest terrestrial animal alive today, also has larger ears than any other animal on Earth.

*6 ft 7 in–9 ft 10 in* and an average weight of 2–4.5 tonnes.

The endangered desert elephant (a race of the African bush elephant) of Damaraland, Namibia, is the tallest elephant in the world because it has proportionately longer legs than other elephants. The tallest recorded individual was a bull shot near Sesfontein, Damaraland, on 4 Apr 1978 after it had allegedly killed 11 people and caused widespread crop damage. Lying on its side, this individual measured 4.42 m *14½ ft* in a projected line from the shoulder to the base of the forefoot, indicating a standing height of about 4.21 m *13 ft 10 in*. Other measurements included an overall length of 10.38 m *34 ft 1 in* and a forefoot circumference of 1.57 m *5 ft 2 in*. It weighed an estimated 8 tonnes.

Asian elephants (*Elephas maximus*) are lighter and shorter than African. The largest on record are generally bulls in the region of 3–3.4 m *9 ft 10 in–11 ft 1 in* high at the shoulder; in fact, their maximum height is slightly taller than this because, unlike the African elephant, which is tallest at the top of the shoulder, the highest point on an Asian elephant is at the top of its head.

An expedition to Nepal, mounted in 1992 by John Blashford-Snell, found two giant males near Bardia Reserve, in the west of the country. The largest was named *Raja Gag* ('king elephant') by local villagers. He was estimated to be 3.43 m *11 ft 3 in* tall at the shoulder and had a footprint 57.2 cm *22½ in* in diameter. Recent reports from Nepalese naturalists suggest that he has since grown and now stands a record-breaking 3.66 m *12 ft* at the shoulder (also an estimation).

The majority of *authenticated* record-breakers belong to the Sri Lankan sub-species, *Elephas m. maximus*, which is found in Sri Lanka and southern India. The largest individual measured properly was a bull shot in northern Sri Lanka, in 1882, which had a height at the shoulder of 3.4 m *11 ft 1 in* (standing height 3.23 m *10 ft 7 in*); other measurements included 3.58 m *11 ft 9 in* at the peak of the back; an overall length of 7.92 m *26 ft*; a girth of 6.81 m *22 ft 4 in* at the thickest part of the body; and an estimated weight of about 8 tonnes.

> **Elephant skin is extremely sensitive, enabling the animal not only to feel an irritating insect but also to pin-point its exact position, ready to be brushed off with the trunk or tail.**

**Largest prehistoric** The largest prehistoric elephant was the Steppe mammoth (*Mammuthus trogontherii*) which roamed the area that is now central Europe. A fragmentary skeleton found in Mosbach, Germany, indicates a shoulder height of 4.5 m *14¾ ft*.

> **Some tree seeds will not germinate unless they have passed through an elephant's gut.**

**Smallest prehistoric** The smallest known elephant was a dwarf species called *Elephas falconeri*, which had a maximum shoulder height of about 90 cm *35 in*. Fossil evidence has been found on the islands of Malta and Sicily, in the Mediterranean.

The smallest mammoth (and, indeed, the most recent known mammoth) was a dwarf version of the woolly mammoth (*Mammuthus primigenius vrangeliensis*), which lived up to between 3500 and 4000 years ago (the time the pyramids were being built in Egypt). According to fossil teeth and bones discovered on Wrangel Island, in the Arctic Ocean about 200 km *124 miles* off the north-east coast of Siberia, it was only about 1.8 m *5 ft 11 in* high and weighed around 2 tonnes. The fossil remains were found by Russian researchers Andrei Sher, Sergei Vartanyan and their colleagues at the Severtsov Institute of Evolutionary Animal Morphology and Ecology, in Moscow, Russia, and have been described as one of the most remarkable finds of the century. They are particularly exciting because scientists had previously thought that mammoths had become extinct at the end of the last Ice Age, some 10 000 years ago, but they seem to have survived longer on Wrangel Island than anywhere else in the world. Humans did not reach Wrangel until about 3000 years ago, by which time the mammoths were probably already extinct.

**Longest tusks** Tusks are found on both male and female African elephants (*Loxodonta africana*) but only on male Asian elephants (*Elephas maximus*), and continue to grow throughout life; in some Asian countries only a small proportion of males have tusks (5–7 per cent in Sri Lanka, for example) and, throughout their range, females either have no tusks at all or they are vestigial and do not protrude beyond the lip. The longest tusks from any living species are a pair from an African elephant

shot in the eastern Congo (now Zaïre) at the turn of the century and preserved in the National Collection of Heads and Horns kept by the New York Zoological Society in Bronx Park, New York City, USA. The right tusk measures 3.49 m *11 ft 5½ in* along the outside curve and the left 3.35 m *11 ft*; their combined weight is 133 kg *293 lb*. A single tusk of 3.5 m *11 ft 6 in* has also been reported.

**Heaviest tusks** The heaviest tusks from any animal (excluding prehistoric examples) are a pair from a bull African elephant (*Loxodonta africana*) shot at the foot of Mt Kilimanjaro, Kenya, in 1897, and now held in the The Natural History Museum, UK. They originally weighed 109 kg *240 lb* (length 3.11 m *10 ft 2½ in*) and 102 kg *225 lb* (length 3.18 m *10 ft 5½ in*) respectively, giving a total weight of 211 kg *465 lb*, but their combined weight today is 200 kg *440½ lb*. A single African elephant tusk collected in Benin and exhibited at the Paris Exposition in 1900 weighed 117 kg *258 lb*.

**Prehistoric tusks** The longest tusks of any known animal were those of the straight-tusked elephant (*Palaeoloxodom antiquus germanicus*), which lived in what is now northern Germany about 300 000 years ago. The average length for tusks of adult bulls was 5 m *16 ft 5 in*.

The tusks of woolly mammoths (*Mammuthus primigenius*) were slightly smaller, although one notable exception is preserved in the Franzens Museum at Brno, Czech Republic, which measures 5.02 m *16 ft 5½ in* along the outside curve.

The heaviest recorded fossil tusks (and, indeed, the heaviest tusks known) are a pair belonging to a 4.06 m *13 ft 4 in* tall Columbian mammoth (*Mammuthus columbi*) in the State Museum, Lincoln, Nebraska, USA. The specimens, which have a combined weight of 226 kg *498 lb* and measure 4.21 m *13 ft 9 in* and 4.14 m *13 ft 7 in* respectively, were found near Campbell, Nebraska, USA, in April 1915. A single fossil tusk (unknown species) weighing 150 kg *330 lb* is now preserved in the Museo Civico di Storia Naturale, Milan, Italy; the specimen, which is in two pieces, measures 3.58 m *11 ft 9 in* in total length and has a maximum circumference of 89 cm *35 in*.

**Largest ears** The African bush elephant (*Loxodonta a. africana*) has larger outer ears than any other animal on Earth. Their size, however, has less to do with hearing than with temperature control. They each have a large network of blood vessels which act rather like radiator pipes: as the blood passes across the ears it loses heat; the system is so effective that there can be a difference of as much

> **Elephant tusks are simply enlarged incisor teeth in the upper jaw; baby elephants even have milk tusks, which fall out when they are about a year old.**

as 19°C *66°F* between the arterial blood coming from the heart and the returning venous blood. To increase temperature loss, the elephant flaps its ears or holds them out to catch the breeze; and, to decrease temperature loss, it holds them tight against the body. The African forest elephant (*Loxodonta a. cyclotis*) and the Asian elephant (*Elephas maximus*) have proportionately smaller ears because they live in more shady forests and do not have such a problem with over-heating.

**Oldest** No other terrestrial mammal can match the age attained by humans (*Homo sapiens*), but the Asiatic elephant (*Elephas maximus*) probably comes closest. The greatest verified age is 78 years for a cow named *Modoc*, which was imported into the USA from Germany, in 1898, at the age of two. She had an extraordinarily varied career, including 35 years in a circus (during which she gained notoriety by rescuing caged lions from a fire), 20 years in a roadside zoo and 9 years as a TV star in programmes such as *Daktari* (for which she had to wear false ears to make her look African). She eventually died at Santa Clara, California, USA, on 17 Jul 1975, as a result of complications after surgery for an in-growing toe nail.

Since many Asian elephants live to be 55–70 year olds, it seems quite possible that some unauthenticated reports of individuals living for longer than 80 years may be accurate. *Raja*, Sri Lanka's bull elephant which led the annual Perahera procession through Kandi, carrying the Sacred Tooth of the Buddha from 1931, died on 16 Jul 1988 allegedly aged 81 years. Captive females have been known to give birth at 60 years of age.

The African elephant (*Loxodonta africana*) has a potential lifespan in the wild of about 60 years. However, in recent years, the majority have been killed by poachers before they reach old age and so the average lifespan has decreased considerably.

**Longest gestation period** The Asiatic elephant (*Elephas maximus*) has the longest gestation period of any mammal, averaging 20–22 months. The maximum ever recorded is 760 days (about 25 months), which is more than two

**The Asiatic elephant has the longest lifespan of any terrestrial mammal, after humans; the record-holder reached a grand old age of 78 years.**

and a half times the maximum gestation period of humans. The African elephant (*Loxodonta africana*) has a gestation period of about 18–22 months.

**Largest appetite** Elephants have huge appetites and African elephants (*Loxodonta africana*), in particular, spend about 18 hours a day feeding (usually in three main bouts – in the morning, afternoon and in the middle of the night – with time in between for other activities). A typical adult will consume 75–150 kg *165–330 lb* of vegetable matter every day (and will drink 80–160 litres *20–40 gallons* of water) but very large bulls may eat twice this amount.

**Swimming** There are many accounts of elephants swimming across rivers, lakes and oceans. The largest herd swimming together was a group of 79 animals, but individuals and smaller

groups have been reported swimming for as long as six hours at a time and as far as 48 km *30 miles* – without a break and without touching the bottom.

**Earliest domestication** There are records of tamed Asian elephants (*Elephas maximus*) being used as beasts of burden in the Indus Valley civilization, which thrived on the Indian subcontinent at least 4000 years ago. Since then, they have been widely used in agriculture and forestry, during wars, on ceremonial occasions and, more recently, for carrying tourists. Unfortu-

*Just as some people are left-handed or right-handed, elephants prefer to use one tusk rather than the other (usually the right).*

nately, since they are difficult animals to breed in captivity, most trained elephants are still obtained as youngsters from the wild.

It is a myth that African elephants (*Loxodonta africana*) cannot be tamed and used as working animals, although they have been used less widely than their Asian relatives. The best-known example was when the Carthaginian leader, Hannibal, used them in his wars against the Romans over 2000 years ago. Today, there are a small number of tamed African elephants at the long-established Elephant Domestication Centre, Gangala na Bodio, in Garamba National Park, Zaïre, which are used for short tourist safaris.

**Most threatened** Both species of elephant – Indian (*Elephas maximus*) and African (*Loxodonta africana*) – are threatened with extinction. The African elephant is threatened mainly by poaching: as many as 100 000 were being

**Domesticated elephant in Garamba National Park, Zaïre, dispelling the myth that African elephants cannot be tamed.**

slaughtered for their tusks every year at the peak of poaching operations in the early 1980s. But this is of secondary importance to the Indian elephant, which is threatened more by habitat destruction and competition for space with the growing human population in many parts of its range.

Asian elephants are found in Bangladesh, Bhutan, Brunei, Cambodia, China, India, Indonesia (Kalimantan and Sumatra), Laos, Malaysia (Peninsula Malaysia and Sabah), Myanmar, Nepal, Sri Lanka, Thailand and Vietnam. There are an estimated 34 500–53 700 survivors remaining (of which approximately one third are domesticated). Country populations vary from some 50–90 in

Nepal and 60–150 in Bhutan (mainly strays from across the border) to as many as 20 000 in India.

African elephants are found in 37 different countries (approximately 3 per cent in West Africa, 18 per cent in East Africa, 33 per cent in southern Africa and 46 per cent in Central Africa). The total population has declined dramatically from an estimated minimum 1.3 million in 1979 to about 600 000 since 1989 (it appears to have stabilized in the past 5 or 6 years). Although the frightening trend is not in dispute, the figures themselves are only a guideline since the population sizes for many African countries are poorly known.

The ivory trade has shown some revealing trends in recent years: 204 tonnes: 1950; 1000 tonnes: 1983; 600 tonnes: 1986; 300 tonnes: 1988. The decline in weight during the 1980s did not represent fewer dead elephants simply because, in 1979, one tonne of ivory represented 54 dead elephants but, by 1987, one tonne represented 113 dead elephants (not counting the many calves that would have been orphaned and left to die of starvation). The poachers

*An elephant herd normally consists of a wise old female, known as the matriarch, and her daughters and grand-daughters; some of her sisters, and their offspring, may also be part of the herd but adult bulls join only at brief intervals to mate with the females.*

killed all the mature bulls first, because they had the largest tusks, and then turned their attentions to cows and calves with smaller tusks.

**Biggest ivory cache** The world's biggest ivory cache was discovered in Namibia, in September 1989, when police managed to break a massive international smuggling syndicate and captured 25 people with 972 tusks weighing 6827 kg *15 050 lb*.

**Tool using** Both species of elephant are able to use tools, but the African elephant (*Loxodonta africana*) is obviously the largest animal to do so (excluding humpback whales which use bubbles as fishing nets). A recent study by Dr Suzanne Chevalier-Skolnikoff, of the University of California, and Dr Jo Liska, of the University of Colorado, in the USA, revealed that on average wild elephants use tools more than once an hour (captive ones use them ten times as often, perhaps because more objects are ready to hand). Most of the tool-use observed was to do with personal hygiene: for example, using vegetation to swat flies or scratch themselves, wiping cuts on their bodies with clumps of grass held in the trunk, and throwing dirt or blowing water over themselves to cool down or to relieve irritation from parasites. They also throw objects at unwanted intruders (other animals or vehicles). Some of the more unusual cases of tool-using records compiled by the researchers include a large bull picking up a young calf and throwing it against a fence to break it and captive elephants twisting hay into ropes and rings to adorn their bodies like jewellery.

# FLYING LEMURS

## *Dermoptera*
2 species
(otherwise known as colugos)

**Largest** Flying lemurs are cat-sized and the largest of all the gliding mammals. The largest of the two species, albeit by a small margin, is the Malayan flying lemur (*Cynocephalus variegatus*), which is widely distributed in the tropical rainforests and rubber plantations of south-east Asia. It has a head-body length of 34–42 cm *13.4–16½ in*; a tail length of 17.5–27 cm *6.9–10.6 in*; a 'wingspan' of 70 cm *27.6 in*; and a weight of 1–1.75 kg *2 lb 3 oz–3 lb 14 oz*.

**Smallest** The Philippine flying lemur (*Cynocephalus volans*) which, as its name suggests, lives in the Philippines, is slightly smaller than its relative. It has a head-body length of 33–38 cm *13–15 in*; a tail length of 17.5–27 cm *7–10.6 in*; and a weight of 1–1.5 kg *2 lb 3 oz–3 lb 5 oz*.

**Largest gliding membrane** Gliding has evolved independently in several mammalian groups: three marsupial families, two rodent families and the flying lemur family. The two species of flying lemur have a better-developed gliding membrane (known as the patagium) than any of the others. It extends all the way from the neck to the tips of the fingers and toes and right to the end of the tail (in other gliding mammals it does not incorporate the hands and feet or the tail). When a flying lemur stretches out its limbs, the membrane forms a taut gliding platform, but all the extraneous skin has to be tucked away under its arms to avoid being caught on twigs and branches while it is climbing.

**Longest glide** The two flying lemurs are efficient gliding mammals. Few glides have been measured accurately, but controlled glides greater than 70 m *230 ft* are believed to be fairly common. The longest on record is a glide of 136 m *446 ft* between two trees, during which the animal lost only 10.5–12 m *34½–39½ ft* in height.

Flying lemurs are primarily nocturnal and are therefore capable of launching themselves into the air, from the tops of the trees, in darkness. They have good night-time and stereoscopic vision, giving them the depth perception necessary for judging accurate landings. Indeed, they are able to determine their long, shallow glides with astonishing accuracy and normally land on a secure tree trunk selected beforehand; this may be only 3–4 m *10–13 ft* above the ground (landing on *terra firma* would be dangerous since they are so well adapted to life in the treetops that they are almost helpless on the ground). After landing, they climb up the tree trunk (in a rather clumsy and lurching fashion) ready for another glide.

*Flying lemurs always have a gap between their two front teeth.*

# GIRAFFE & OKAPI

## *Giraffidae*
2 species: giraffe and okapi

> *Male giraffes fight by head-butting their opponents and slamming their necks together.*

**Tallest** The tallest living animal is the giraffe (*Giraffa camelopardalis*), found in the dry savannah and open woodland areas of Africa south of the Sahara. Its great height enables it to feed on the leaves of trees that are out of reach of other herbivores living on the African savanna. The average measurements for adult giraffes are: 4.7–5.3 m *15ft 5in–17ft 5in* overall height (including horns of about 15–22 cm *6–9in*), 2.7–3.3 m *8ft 10in–10ft 10in* in height at the shoulder, and 900–1600 kg *1984–3527lb* in weight, for the male; and 3.7–4.7 m *12ft 2in–15ft 5in* overall height, 2.5–3 m *8ft 2in–9ft 10in* in height at the shoulder, and 600–1000 kg *1323–2205lb* in weight, for the female. Despite their long necks, giraffes have no more than the usual seven neck vertebrae found in most other mammals.

The tallest sub-species is the Masai giraffe (*Giraffa. c. tippelskirchi*) and the tallest specimen ever recorded was a Masai bull named *George*, who was received at Chester Zoo, UK, on 8 Jan 1959; he had arrived from Kenya, at the age of about 18 months. His horns *almost* grazed the roof of the 6.1 m *20ft* high Giraffe House when he was 9 years old. George died on 22 Jul 1969. Another Masai bull, shot in Kenya earlier this century, measured 5.87 m *19ft 3in* between pegs (standing height about 5.8 m *19ft*). Less credible and unauthenticated heights of up to 7 m *23ft* between pegs have been claimed for several other bulls shot in the field.

**Shortest** The okapi (*Okapia johnstoni*), which is restricted to the dense tropical rainforests of Zaïre, in central Africa, reaches an average size of 1.7–1.8 m *67–72in* overall height (maximum 2.1 m

The strange-looking okapi has an exceptionally long tongue, reaching a maximum length of about 50 cm *20in*.

83 *in*), 1.5–1.7 m *59–67in* in height at the shoulder (maximum 1.8 m *71in*), and 200–250 kg *441–551lb* in weight. It has a much shorter neck and shorter legs than its close relative the giraffe (*Giraffa camelopardalis*).

Nine different sub-species of giraffe are recognized and the smallest is Thornicroft's giraffe (*Giraffa camelopardalis thornicrofti*), which lives only in Luangwa Valley, Zambia. It is only slightly smaller than the others, males reaching a maximum height of about 5 m *16ft 5in* and females about 4.5 m *14ft 9in*.

**Most recent discovery** The elusive okapi (*Okapia johnstoni*) is one of the few large terrestrial mammals to have become known to science for the first time this century. It was first mentioned by the explorer Sir Henry Morton Stanley in his book *In Darkest Africa*, which was published in 1890. Stanley described a strange creature that was known to the Wambutti pygmies of the dense Ituri Forest, Zaïre (formerly contained within Uganda's borders); they called it the *o'api* (the apostrophe is pronounced like a 'k') and described it as shy and donkey-like, with a long neck, vivid zebra-like stripes on its legs and an extraordinary, long blue tongue. The first incontrovertible proof of the okapi's existence came in 1901, when Swede Karl Eriksson managed to obtain a complete skin and two skulls; it was formally described and named on 18 Jun 1901 (after Sir Harry Johnston, Governor of Uganda at the time, who had been enthusiastically following up Stanley's information). News of this striking animal made newspaper headlines around the world and, in 1982, the okapi was adopted as the official emblem of the International Society of Cryptozoology (for the study of 'hidden' animals).

> *Special valves in the blood vessels of a giraffe's neck help to regulate the blood supply to its head when the animal is reaching up to browse on high branches or bending down to drink at ground level.*

*No two giraffes have exactly the same body pattern, although all the animals living in one area tend to have the same basic pattern.*

**Most threatened** No member of the family Giraffidae is considered to be immediately threatened with extinction. However, the okapi (*Okapia johnstoni*) is at risk from habitat destruction and hunting, and only a few thousand survive in a small area of rainforest in eastern Zaïre. It has been officially protected by a government decree since 1933, but enforcement is difficult.

The range of the giraffe (*Giraffa camelopardalis*) has been drastically reduced and fragmented within historical times and, while it is still fairly common in many parts of Africa, its future survival outside protected areas is doubtful.

**Fastest** Despite its great size and rather gangly shape, the giraffe (*Giraffa camelopardalis*) is far from ungainly and can attain such high speeds over short distances that in a race a horse would have difficulty keeping up. The highest speed ever recorded is 56 km/h *35 mph* for an individual running across open ground. For long distance running (during which the giraffe does not tire easily) the animal usually lopes along at about 16 km/h *10 mph*. When running, the giraffe's long neck tends to sway sinuously from side to side, almost in a figure of eight.

**Longest tongue** Both members of the family Giraffidae have two of the longest and most mobile tongues in the animal kingdom. The giraffe (*Giraffa camelopardalis*) tongue has an average length of 45.6 cm *18.2 in* (maximum 53 cm *21 in*) and is used for gathering food. The okapi (*Okapia johnstoni*) has such a long tongue (up to 50 cm *20 in*) that it can reach up to lick and clean its own eyes.

**Eyesight** The giraffe (*Giraffa camelopardalis*) probably has the greatest range of vision of any mammal, thanks to its phenomenally good eyesight, its preferred open habitat and, of course, its height above the ground.

The world's tallest living animal is the giraffe, which can reach an astonishing height of nearly 6.1 m *20 ft.*

# HIPPOPOTAMUSES

### *Hippopotamidae*
There are only two species of hippo: the common and the pygmy.

*After sunset, and throughout the night, hippos leave their daytime haunts in lakes and rivers to graze on the surrounding grassland.*

**Largest** The common hippopotamus (*Hippopotamus amphibius*) is one of the world's heaviest terrestrial animals, second only in weight to elephants and some rhinos. It has an average head-body length of 2.8–4 m *9 ft 2 in–13 ft 1 in* (plus a tail of about 35–50 cm *14–20 in*), a height at the shoulder of about 1.4 m *55 in* and a weight of 1.3–2.5 tonnes (males are considerably larger than females of a similar age). The largest recorded individuals measure about 4.6 m *15 ft 1 in* head-body length (plus a tail of about 60 cm *24 in*) and a height at the shoulder of 1.65 m *65 in*; on rare occasions, they may weigh in excess of 4 tonnes.

**Smallest** The pygmy hippopotamus (*Choeropsis liberiensis*) has an average head-body length of 1.5–1.85 m *59–73 in* (plus a tail of about 15–21 cm *6–8¼ in*), a height at the shoulder of 70–100 cm *27½–39¼ in* and a weight of 160–275 kg *353–606 lb*. There is relatively little difference between the two sexes.

**Most threatened** The pygmy hippopotamus (*Choeropsis liberiensis*) is the only one of the two hippo species to be listed by the World Conservation Union (IUCN) as threatened with extinction. It is found primarily in Liberia, but the neighbouring countries of Côte d'Ivoire, Guinea and Sierra Leone also harbour small groups; there may be a very small number in Guinea-Bissau, but this is uncertain. There have been unauthenticated reports of the sub-species *Hexaprotodon l. heslopi* in the delta of the Niger, in Nigeria, but if the pygmy hippopotamus has not already disappeared from Nigeria it is certainly on the verge of extinction. The total population is estimated to be 'several thousand'. The main threats are deforestation and

*Hippos crop the grass so short when eating, that grass fires are unable to spread across areas where they have been feeding.*

**The pygmy hippo weighs just a fraction of its much larger relative.**

*When a male hippo yawns next to a female, it does not mean that he is bored: the yawn is part of courtship, rather like a gesture of 'affection'.*

**Heavyweight: exceptionally large hippopotamuses have been known to weigh in excess of four tonnes.**

land clearance, hunting for its meat, trophies and teeth, persecution by local human populations and pollution by the petrochemical industry.

The common hippopotamus (*Hippopotamus amphibius*) is not considered to be imminently threatened with extinction, but it suffers from habitat degradation caused by a variety of human activities and is hunted for its meat, skin and teeth; the teeth are an increasingly popular substitute for elephant ivory, which they resemble closely. The species is found, in varying numbers, in a total of 39 different countries – most of which have de-

clining or, at best, stable populations. The total numbers are estimated to be at least 160 000, with the majority of these living in eastern and southern Africa.

**Largest population** There are considerably more common hippopotamuses (*Hippopotamus amphibius*) in Zambia than in any other country in Africa (the Zambian population is estimated to be approximately 40 000). Zaïre is second with about 30 000 hippos. At the other extreme some countries, such as The Gambia and Ghana, have no more than 100 left.

*Hippos do not have sweat glands but, instead, have glands below their skin which secrete an oily pink fluid that protects the skin from sunburn (and may also have a protective function against infections); this strange-looking secretion prompted the early, erroneous idea that hippos sweat blood.*

# HORSES, ASSES & ZEBRAS

*Horses, zebras and asses have outstanding eyesight: their only blind spot lies directly behind the head, they have binocular vision in front, they can probably see colour and their acute night vision ranks with that of owls.*

### *Equidae*
6 living species: mountain zebra, Grevy's zebra, common or plains zebra, African wild ass, Asian wild ass and the wild horse; the domestic donkey and the domestic horse are normally considered to be sub-species of the African wild ass and the wild horse respectively.

The smallest breed of horse is the Falabella, which may stand as little as 38 cm *15 in* tall and weigh less than 12 kg *26½ lb.*

**Earliest** The evolutionary history of horses, asses and zebras is relatively well known. The earliest of the horse-like ancestors was a species called eohippus or the dawn horse (*Hyracotherium*), which appeared during the Eocene some 55 million years ago; it was a forest-dweller and probably weighed *c.* 5.4 kg *12 lb* and stood *c.* 36 cm *14 in* high at the shoulder. The genus *Equus*, to which all living species belong, first appeared during the early Pleistocene about 1.5–2 million years ago.

**Earliest domestication** The first domestication of the horse probably occurred in what is now the Ukraine approximately 6500 years ago, when paleolithic hunters tamed small numbers of wild horses (*Equus ferus*) for their flesh and milk (compared with 12 000 years ago for dogs and 9000 years ago for sheep). Evidence also from the Ukraine indicates that horses may have been ridden at about the same time.

**Largest** Wild equids are generally smaller in size than domestic breeds. The largest is Grevy's zebra (*Equus grevyi*), which has an average head-body length of 2.5–2.7 m *8 ft 2 in–8 ft 10 in*, a tail length of 50–70 cm *20–27½ in*, a height at the shoulder of 1.5 m *59 in* and a weight of 350–430 kg *772–948 lb* (maximum 450 kg *992 lb*). As with all members of the family, males are normally 10 per cent larger than females.

The tallest and heaviest domestic horse was the shire gelding *Sampson* (later renamed *Mammoth*), bred by Thomas Cleaver of Toddington Mills, Bedfordshire, UK. This horse (foaled 1846) measured 21.2½ hands (2.19 m *7 ft 2½ in*) in 1850 and was later said to have weighed 1524 kg *3360 lb*.

**Smallest** The African wild ass (*Equus africanas*) is the smallest of the wild equids. It has an average head-body length of 2 m *79 in*, a tail length of 42 cm *16½ in* and a weight of about 275 kg

606 lb. As with all members of the family, males are normally 10 per cent larger than females.

The smallest domesticated horse was the stallion *Little Pumpkin* (foaled 15 Apr 1973), which stood 35.5 cm *14 in* and weighed 9.07 kg *20 lb* on 30 Nov 1975. It was owned by J. C. Williams Jr of Della Terra Mini Horse Farm, Inman, South Carolina, USA.

The smallest breed of horse is the Falabella of Argentina (*see p.38*), developed by Julio Falabella of Recco de Roca. Most adult specimens stand less than 76 cm *30 in* and average 36–45 kg *80–100 lb* in weight. The smallest example was an adult mare which was 38 cm *15 in* tall and weighed 11.9 kg *26¼ lb.*

**Oldest** The greatest age reliably recorded for a domestic horse is 62 years for *Old Billy* (foaled 1760), believed to be a cross between a Cleveland and eastern blood, which was bred by Edward Robinson of Woolston, Lancashire, UK. In 1762/63 the horse was sold to the Mersey and Irwell Navigation Company and remained with them

in a working capacity (mainly marshalling and towing barges) until 1819, when he was retired to a farm at Latchford, near Warrington, UK. He died on 27 Nov 1822.

The average longevity of wild equids is believed to be about 10–25 years in the wild and can be up to 35 years in captivity.

**Most threatened** Despite the abundance of domestic horses, their wild relatives are generally in a precarious situation. According to the World Conservation Union (IUCN), four of the six living members of the family Equidae are threatened with extinction: the African wild ass (*Equus africanas*), which lives in Ethiopia and Somalia (free-living animals of uncertain pedigree also occur in other northern African countries); the Asian wild ass (*Equus hemionus*), which lives in China, India, Iran, Kazakhstan, Turkmenistan and Mongolia (and has been reintroduced to Israel and Uzbekistan); Grevy's zebra (*Equus grevyi*), which lives in Ethiopia and Kenya; and the mountain zebra (*Equus zebra*), which lives in Angola, Namibia and South Africa. The many threats they face include competition with livestock for food and water; hunting for skin, meat and trophies, and as pests; water extraction schemes; fencing (which blocks their migration routes); and interbreeding with domestic and feral horses and donkeys.

Wild population sizes for both threatened species and sub-species are estimated to be: 7000 Hartmann's mountain zebras (*Equus z. hartmannae*); 700 Cape mountain zebras (*Equus z. zebra*); 5000–6000 Grevy's zebras; a few hundred African wild asses; and unknown numbers of Asian wild asses (likely to be tens of thousands).

**Extinctions** The South African quagga (*Equus quagga*) is the only member of the family Equidae to have become extinct in modern times. In fact, it is one of only two large mammal species to have become extinct in sub-Saharan Africa in the past 200 years (the other being the bluebuck, *Hippotragus leucophaeus*, which disappeared from its former home in South Africa around 1800). A yellowish-brown zebra, which used to live in South Africa, it had stripes only on its head, neck and forequarters. The last wild specimen was shot in South Africa in 1878 and the last known survivor died in Amsterdam Zoo in 1883.

Several sub-species of equid are also known or suspected to have become extinct in the wild, including the North Mongolian kulan (*Equus hemionus hemionus*) and the Syrian wild ass (*Equus hemionus hemippus*). The Mongolian wild horse or Przewalski's horse (*Equus ferus przewalskii*), a sub-species of the wild horse which survived in the wild until recently in northern Sinkiang, China, and in the Altai Mountains, western Mongolia, became extinct in the wild in the 1960s. The last possible sighting was in 1966 on the Takhin-

> *Feral horses and donkeys live – often in large numbers – on every continent except Antarctica.*

---

Przewalski's horse is the most recent member of the horse family to become extinct in the wild, disappearing in the 1960s; fortunately, it is a common animal in zoos and there are plans to reintroduce the species back into its native Mongolia.

Shara-Nuru plateau, when the Hungarian zoologist, Z. Kaszab, counted a group of eight individuals which he believed to be one stallion and seven mares. Fortunately, about 1200 animals survive in zoos around the world (all descended from just 13 parents – including one domestic horse) and the ultimate conservation objective is to reintroduce the species back into the wild in its native Mongolia. (Note: there is not universal agreement about the

**Plains zebra is the only common and widespread member of the horse family in the wild.**

---

status of Przewalski's horse, but recent evidence indicates that it is a sub-species of the wild horse *Equus ferus* rather than a species in its own right.)

**Most abundant** Apart from the domestic horse (*Equus ferus caballus*), the common or plains zebra (*Equus burchellii*) is the only widespread and abundant member of the family. The total population is probably over ¾ million, making it one of the commonest ungulates (hoofed mammals) in Africa. Its range includes about a quarter of the continent. There are seven

> *No two zebras have stripes that are exactly alike; even the patterns on opposite sides of a zebra's body do not match exactly.*

recognized sub-species, varying significantly in stripe patterning, and by far the commonest of these is Grant's zebra (*Equus b. boehmi*): an estimated 390 000 live in Tanzania and 141 000 in Kenya, accounting for more than 70 per cent of the entire common zebra population.

**Most valuable** The world's most valuable animals (in terms of money) are racehorses. The most paid for a yearling is $13.1 million paid for *Seattle Dancer* on 23 Jul 1985 at Keeneland, Kentucky, USA, by Robert Sangster.

**Fastest** In horse racing, the highest speed record is 69.62 km/h *43.26 mph* by *Big Racket* (20.8 seconds for 402 m *¼ mile*) at Mexico City, Mexico, on 5 Feb 1945; the 4-year-old carried 51.7 kg *114 lb*. The record for 2414 m *1½ miles* is 60.86 km/h *37.82 mph* by 3-year-old *Hawkster* (carrying 54.9 kg *121 lb*) at Santa Anita Park, Arcadia, California, USA, on 14 Oct 1989 with a time of 2 min 22.8 s.

Wild horses (*Equus ferus*) living in an inhospitable region of Serrado, on Brazil's border with Venezuela, are reputed to accelerate faster than domestic

horses and, according to Embrapa, Brazil's national agricultural research institute, can maintain a top speed of 60 km/h *37¼ mph* for much longer than a racehorse. Known as the 'wild horses of Roraima', their numbers have dwindled in recent years to no more than a few hundred.

**Strongest** On 23 Apr 1924 a shire gelding named *Vulcan*, owned by the Liverpool Corporation, registered a pull equal to a starting load of 29–47 tonnes on a dynamometer at the British Empire Exhibition at Wembley, London. At the same event, a pair of shires *easily* pulled a starting load of 51 tonnes, the maximum registered on the dynamometer.

There is a widely reported record of a pair of draught-horses (combined weight 1587 kg *3500 lb*) which hauled a load, allegedly weighing 130.9 tonnes, on a sledge litter for a distance of 402 m *1319 ft* along a frozen road at the Nester Estate near Ewen, Michigan, USA, on 26 Feb 1893. However, this tonnage was exaggerated: the load, which comprised 50 logs of white pine measuring 36 055 board feet, actually weighed about 42.3 tonnes.

# HYENAS

## *Hyaenidae*
4 species: spotted hyena, brown hyena, striped hyena and aardwolf.

**Earliest** The hyenas form the youngest (and, indeed, the smallest) of all the carnivore families. They are thought to have evolved from early civets and mongooses (family Viverridae) *c.* 20–22 million years ago, when a civet-like creature called *Plioviverrops* lived in Asia. However, species closely resembling modern hyenas did not emerge as dominant scavengers until about 5 million years ago.

**Largest** The largest member of the family Hyaenidae is the spotted hyena (*Crocuta crocuta*), otherwise known as the laughing hyena. It is one of the world's largest carnivores, with a head-body length of 1.2–1.7 m *47–67 in;* a tail of 25–35 cm *9.8–13.8 in;* a shoulder height of 70–90 cm *31–35.4 in;* and a weight of 50–80 kg *110–176 lb.* Females are normally larger than males of the same age. It is a fairly common animal in the open country and grasslands of sub-Saharan Africa (except the southern reaches of South Africa and the forests of Zaïre).

**Largest prehistoric** The largest known hyena was an extinct animal called the cave hyena (*Crocuta crocuta spelaea*), which was almost twice the size of the modern spotted hyena (*Crocuta crocuta*).

**Smallest** The smallest hyena is the aardwolf (*Proteles cristatus*), which lives in open country and grassland in southern Africa and East Africa. It has a head-body length of 55–80 cm *21.7–31.5 in;* a tail length of 20–25 cm *7.9–9.8 in;* a shoulder height of 40–50 cm *15.8–19.7 in;* and a weight of 8–12 kg *17 lb 10 oz–26 lb 8 oz.*

**Most threatened** The World Conservation Union (IUCN) lists only the brown hyena (*Hyaena brunnea*) as being threatened with extinction. It survives in Botswana, Namibia, South Africa, Lesotho, the extreme west and south-west of Zimbabwe, south-western Mozambique and into south-western Angola. Botswana is believed to harbour the only large population of this species.

The sub-species of the striped hyena, known as the barbary hyena (*Hyaena hyaena barbara*), is also listed as endangered. It survives in Algeria, Morocco and Tunisia.

**Most specialized diet** The aardwolf (*Proteles cristatus*) has a highly specialized diet: it feeds mainly on a few species of snouted harvester termites in the genus *Trinervitermes*, with termites in the genus *Hodotermes* supplementing the diet occasionally. Although it lacks a long snout, digging forelimbs and strong claws (and therefore is unlike any of the other ant- and termite-eating mammals such as aardvarks, pangolins and anteaters) it is a highly efficient hunter. During the summer a single aardwolf will eat up to 300 000 termites (weighing about 1 kg *2.2 lb*) each night. It locates the termites by sound and smell and then licks them up – together with copious quantities of soil – by rapid movements of its long, sticky tongue.

**Most efficient scavenger** The spotted hyena (*Crocuta crocuta*) is not only a skilful and regular hunter but is also the world's most efficient mammalian scavenger. It utilizes the carcasses of large vertebrates such as zebras and wildebeest more efficiently than any other carnivore. Its jaw muscles and teeth are strong enough to crush large bones (the teeth exert a pressure of 800 kg/cm² *11 400 lb/in²*) and its powerful digestive system can break down the organic matter of bones, hooves, horns and hides; no other animal has this ability. In one extreme example, a group of 38 spotted hyenas was once seen to dismember an adult zebra in less than 15 minutes, leaving little more than a few scraps behind when they had finished. The few indigestible remains, such as fur and the unwanted parts of horns and hooves, are regurgitated as pellets within 24 hours. While most other carnivores waste up to 40 per cent of their kills, this remarkably efficient system enables the spotted hyena to extract the utmost nourishment from a carcass.

**Sibling attack** According to recent research by biologists at the University of California, the spotted hyena (*Crocuta crocuta*) is the only wild mammal whose infants appear to be genetically programmed to attack and, in many cases, kill their siblings. The animals are born with fully developed canine teeth and an apparent determination to use them. Most spotted hyenas produce twins, but this sibling aggression means that around half of all mothers are destined to bring up a single cub. In captivity, newborn cubs will attack any inanimate object that is about the same size and texture as a brother or sister, although studies in the wild suggest that the killing is confined to twins of the same sex. They have even been known to attack brothers or sisters that have not yet emerged from the amniotic sac. While this behaviour is believed to be unique among mammals, sibling attack is quite common among some large birds such as eagles, herons and egrets. In birds, the dominant fledglings kill their subordinates when food is scarce, but there are believed to be more complex factors involved in hyena sibling rivalry and the precise reasons for it happening are still unclear.

**The spotted hyena is the world's most efficient mammalian scavenger, eating everything from bones and hooves to horns and hides.**

# HYRAXES

## Procaviidae
(otherwise known as dassies or conies)
3–11 species (little agreement on classification).

The Verreaux's eagle feeds almost exclusively on hyraxes.

**Earliest** Hyraxes are believed to have descended from early ungulates (hoofed mammals) that were also ancestral to the elephants and sirenians; these animals, known as the paenungulata, lived about 55 million years ago; modern hyraxes still retain many of their original features, such as hoofed toes and a ridged structure on their teeth. Around 40 million years ago, hyraxes were the most important medium-sized grazing and browsing ungulates of the time. But they began to decline in numbers some 15 million years later, when competition from cattle and antelopes forced them to live in uncontested niches: in particular, around rocky outcrops, cliffs and trees.

**Largest** The largest hyrax is Johnston's rock hyrax (*Procavia johnstoni*), which grows to a maximum weight of 5.4 kg *12 lb* and has a head-body length of up to 58 cm *23 in*; as with all hyraxes, it does not have an external tail. The southern tree hyrax (*Dendrohyrax arboreus*) is marginally lighter in weight (maximum approximately 5 kg *11 lb*) but can grow to a slightly longer head-body length of 60 cm *24 in*.

**Largest prehistoric** Some early members of the extinct family Geniohyidae

Hyraxes are unable to regulate their body temperature as efficiently as other mammals; they often have to bask in the sun or huddle together in groups to keep warm.

Hyraxes such as this rock dassie, photographed in Cape Province, South Africa, are believed to be more closely related to elephants than to any other animal.

attained the size of a tapir or a small horse. One of the better known of these giant hyraxes was a species called, appropriately, *Titanohyrax*; fossil evidence has been found in northern Africa.

**Smallest** The smallest hyrax is Bruce's yellow-spotted hyrax (*Heterohyrax brucei*), which weighs as little as 1.3 kg *2 lb 14 oz* (maximum 2.4 kg *5 lb 5 oz*) and has a minimum head-body length of 32.5 cm *12¾ in* (maximum 47 cm *18½ in*) when adult; as with all hyraxes, it does not have an external tail.

**Highest living** Several different hyraxes in the genera *Procavia* and *Dendrohyrax* live in the alpine zone of mountains and mountain ranges at heights in excess of 3500 m *11 480 ft* above sea level. The highest living species are those found on Mt Kenya, in Kenya (5199 m *17 058 ft*); Mt Kilimanjaro, in Tanzania (5894 m *19 340 ft*) and in the Ruwenzori Mountains, on the border between Uganda and Zaïre

(5119m *16795ft* at Mt Stanley). It is highly unlikely that a hyrax would ever approach the summit of any of these mountains but the southern tree hyrax (*Dendrohyrax arboreus*), for example, is known to live among rock boulders in the Ruwenzoris at a height of at least 4500m *14760ft*.

**Lowest living** There is a population of Abyssinian hyraxes (*Procavia syriaca*) living at 400m *1312ft* below sea level along the shores of the Dead Sea.

**Most threatened** The World Conservation Union (IUCN) considers only one species of hyrax to be threatened with extinction: the eastern tree hyrax (*Dendrohyrax validus*), which lives in Kenya and Tanzania. It has been heavily hunted for its fur, particularly in the forest belt around Mt Kilimanjaro.

**Climbing** Hyraxes are the only true hoofed mammals that regularly climb trees. Although hoofed toes are not a particularly good adaptation for climbing, the soles of their feet are moist and

rubbery and therefore provide excellent traction. In addition, the centre part of each sole can be pulled inwards, by special muscles inside the foot, and the vacuum created by this strong 'suction cup' helps them to stick to whatever surface they happen to be climbing. Legend has it that the overall grip is so powerful that a hyrax will remain fixed to a nearly vertical surface even after it has died.

**Different species living together** Two species of hyrax – Bruce's yellow-spotted hyrax (*Heterohyrax brucei*) and Johnston's hyrax (*Procavia johnstoni*) – live together in harmony in the dense vegetation of the Serengeti kopjes, in Tanzania. Such a close association between different species is otherwise unknown in mammals except primates. The two different hyraxes spend the night sleeping in the same holes; they huddle together for warmth early in the morning; their newborn are greeted and sniffed enthusiastically by both species; the young animals form joint nurseries and play together; and they

*The similarity between rodents and hyraxes is only superficial; in fact, hyraxes are more closely related to elephants than any other mammal (they share a common ancestor and their feet, in particular, are remarkably similar).*

even use similar vocalizations to communicate with one another. There are two main reasons why they are able to coexist in this way: they do not interbreed (their mating behaviour is different and their sexual organs are incompatible) and they do not compete for food (Bruce's yellow-spotted hyrax browses on leaves while Johnston's hyrax feeds mainly on grass). But there is no doubt about the dominant species: whenever there is a limited resource, such as a dust bath or a pool of water, the much larger Johnston's hyrax always takes precedence.

# INSECTIVORES

## Insectivora
350–400 species (little agreement on classification): shrews, moles, tenrecs, hedgehogs, solenodons etc.

*An average adult European hedgehog has as many as 5000 needle-sharp spines, which are actually modified hairs, covering its back and sides; exceptionally large animals may have as many as 7500 spines.*

**Most primitive** Insectivores are considered to be the most primitive of the living placental mammals and moonrats (sub-family Galericinae) are probably the most primitive of them all. The world's first true mammals were shrew-like creatures, known from the late Triassic some 200–220 million years ago, and modern insectivores are considered to be similar to these ancestral species. They share a number of primitive features, such as relatively small brains, primitive teeth, a flat-footed gait, and a cloaca (a common chamber into which the genital, urinary and faecal passages all empty).

However, they are also well-equipped for life in the modern world, because superimposed upon these primitive features are many specializations that enable them to fill a wide variety of ecological niches.

**Largest** The moon rat (*Echinosorex gymnurus*), which is found in Myanmar (formerly Burma), Thailand, Malaysia, Sumatra and Borneo, is generally considered to be the world's largest insectivore (not including other insect-eating mammals in the orders Monotremata and Edentata). About the size of a rabbit, it has a head and body length of 26–46cm *10¼–18in*; a tail length of 17–25cm *6.7–9.8in*; and a weight of 1–2kg *2lb 3oz–4lb 6oz*. Females are slightly larger than males.

The European hedgehog (*Erinaceus europaeus*) is much shorter in overall length (20–30cm *7.9–11.8in*; tail length 2–4cm *0.8–1.6in*) and normally weighs

0.5–1.4kg *1lb 2oz–3lb 1oz*. However, well-fed specimens (especially captive ones with indulgent owners) have been known to weigh as much as 2.2kg *4lb 14oz*.

The giant otter-shrew (*Potamogale velox*), which lives in streams and pools in western and central Africa, is sometimes described as the world's largest insectivore. But its size can be deceptive because, in general appearance, it very closely resembles a small otter. It has a head-body length of 29–35cm *11.4–13.8in* and a tail length of 25–29cm *9.8–11.4in*.

The common or tail-less tenrec (*Tenrec ecaudatus*), which lives in Madagascar and the Comoro Islands, is also a possible contender, with a head-body length of 25-39cm *9.8–15.4in*; a tail length of 1–1.6cm *0.4–0.6in*; and a weight of 0.5–1.5kg *1lb 2oz–3lb 5oz* (maximum 2.4kg *5lb 5oz* in captivity).

*A golden mole can lift 150 times its own weight.*

The world's smallest non-flying mammals are shrews, which also have the shortest lifespans and, for their size, the largest appetites.

**Longest lifespan** Insectivores tend to have very short lifespans (an absolute maximum of 5–8 years for most species). However, the greatest reliable age recorded is over 16 years for a lesser hedgehog-tenrec (*Echinops telfairi*), which was born in Amsterdam Zoo, Netherlands, in 1966, and was later sent to Jersey Zoo, Channel Islands, UK, where it died on 27 Nov 1982.

**Shortest lifespan** Shrews (family Soricidae) are the shortest-lived mammals in the world. They are so active they burn themselves out very quickly and, consequently, have an even shorter lifespan than other mammals of a similar size. In the wild, most species live for an average of 9–12 months; however, they can live longer in captivity, the record being four years for a greater white-toothed shrew (*Crocidura russula*).

**Largest litter** The greatest number of young born to a 'wild' mammal at a single birth is 31 (30 of which survived) in the case of the common or tail-less tenrec (*Tenrec ecaudatus*), at Wassenaar Zoo, Netherlands, in 1972. This species is normally found in Madagascar and the nearby Comoro Islands, where individuals inhabiting relatively seasonal woodland/savanna regions have an incredible average of 20 young per litter (fewer in habitats with more stable climatic conditions). The females have up to 29 nipples – more than on any other mammal. There are records of rodents such as house mice (*Mus domesticus*) with slightly larger litters, but it is suspected that these may have been treated with fertility drugs.

**Smallest** The world's smallest land mammal (*see Smallest bat*) is the pygmy or Savi's white-toothed shrew (*Suncus etruscus*), otherwise known as the Etruscan shrew. It has a head-body length of 3.6–5.2 cm *1.32–2.05 in*; a tail length of 2.4–2.9 cm *0.94–1.14 in*; and a weight of just 1.5–2.5 g *0.05–0.09 oz*. So small, it can even creep into the holes made by large earthworms, it is found along the Mediterranean coast, eastwards as far as Sri Lanka and southwards to Cape Province, South Africa.

Several other shrews are almost as small. Two of the closest contenders are probably the least shrew (*Sorex minutissimus*), which occurs from Scandinavia eastwards to Japan, and the Eurasian pygmy shrew (*Sorex minutus*), which occurs from Europe across Siberia into parts of central Asia. They have a head-body length of 3.5–4.5 cm *1.38–1.77 in* (least) and 3.9–6.4 cm *1.54–2.52 in* (Eurasian pygmy); a tail length of 2.1–3.2 cm *0.83–1.26 in* (least) and 3.2–4.4 cm *1.26–1.73 in* (Eurasian pygmy); and a weight of 1.5–4 g *0.05–0.14 oz* (least) and 2–6.3 g *0.07–0.22 oz* (Eurasian pygmy).

The smallest freshwater mammal in the world is the southern or Miller's water shrew (*Neomys anomalus*), which lives in streams and marshes in southern and eastern Europe. It has an overall length of 6.7–8.7 cm *2.64–3.43 in*; a tail length of 4–5.2 cm *1.58–2.05 in*; and a weight of 8–17 g *0.28–0.6 oz*.

> *Some shrew families have a habit of 'caravanning' when they are on the move: the young form a line, each holding on to the rump of the animal in front, with the mother leading the way; their grip is so strong that an entire family can be lifted off the ground by holding up the mother.*

*The North American star-nosed mole has an extraordinary snout bearing 22 fleshy tentacles, which are found on no other mammal; these make its nose a more effective touch-sensitive organ for locating prey.*

**Youngest breeder** The streaked tenrec (*Hemicentetes semispinosus*) of Madagascar is weaned after only 5 days, and females can breed when they are only 3–5 weeks old.

**Most venomous** Only two groups of mammals are venomous: the monotremes and certain insectivores in the families Soricidae and Solenodontidae. The Cuban solenodon (*Solenodon cubanus*), the Haitian solenodon (*Solenodon paradoxus*), the American short-tailed shrew (*Blarina brevicauda*) and the Eurasian water shrew (*Neomys fodiens*) all have venomous bites. They have venom-producing salivary glands, which open near the bases of the lower incisors, and when they bite a special toxic saliva seeps into the puncture wounds. Once a prey animal has been located, it is normally attacked from behind and quickly bitten on the neck or at the base of the skull, where the neurotoxic venom is most readily introduced into the central nervous system. Even a small amount causes paralysis (the American short-tailed shrew carries enough venom to kill by intravenous injection about 200 mice) and enables the animals to tackle prey considerably larger than themselves. The venom is used mainly to subdue large creatures such as frogs, fish, lizards and small birds. In humans, a bite can cause considerable pain, hypersensitivity and reddening of the skin which may last for several days.

**Largest appetite** Shrews (family Soricidae) have a hectic pace of life and need to consume disproportionately large amounts of food for their body size. To satisfy their energy requirements they have to feed every 2 or 3 hours – day and night – and can die of starvation in as little as 4 hours. Indeed, it is not unusual for them to consume as much as 1.3 times their own body weight in a single day.

The streaked tenrec of Madagascar breeds at a younger age than any other insectivore.

**Most threatened** The World Conservation Union (IUCN) lists a total of 73 insectivore species as known or suspected to be threatened with extinction: 2 solenodons; 10 tenrecs and otter-shrews; 13 golden moles; 1 hedgehog; 1 moonrat; 2 desmans; 1 mole; and 43 shrews. The species considered to be most at risk are the Cuban solenodon (*Solenodon cubanus*) from Cuba; the Haitian solenodon (*Solenodon paradoxus*) from Haiti and the Dominican Republic; and the Mount Nimba otter-shrew (*Micropotamogale lamottei*) from Guinea, Liberia and Côte d'Ivoire. The many threats they face include habitat destruction, pollution, and competition and predation by introduced species such as rats, mongooses, dogs and cats.

**Extinctions** Five insectivore species are known to have disappeared in recent times. They were all solenodons in the extinct genus *Nesophontes* and lived in the Dominican Republic, Haiti, Cuba and the Cayman Islands. They were unable to cope with rats, mongooses, dogs and cats (which were introduced mainly with the arrival of the Spaniards) or with the extensive clearing of land for agriculture. The two remaining solenodons are struggling to survive against similar odds and many experts fear are destined to suffer the same fate (indeed, they have already been declared extinct, albeit mistakenly, on several occasions in the past).

## ELEPHANT-SHREWS

Elephant-shrews superficially resemble the true shrews and, indeed, used to be classified with them in the order Insectivora. They have also, at one time or another, been associated with the primates, tree shrews and even hoofed mammals. However, they possess a unique combination of features – including large eyes (true shrews have little beady eyes), a long flexible trunk-

*Despite their name, insectivores do not eat only insects: some species are partial to a variety of other invertebrates, small vertebrates and even plants.*

like snout, and long legs (true shrews have short legs that barely lift their bellies off the ground) – and have now been assigned their own order (Macroscelidea). There are 15 species in a single family (Macroscelididae), all with their hind legs longer than their fore legs; indeed, they are the only insect-eating mammals adapted for bounding. They are widespread in Africa, but are found nowhere else in the world.

**Largest** The largest elephant-shrews are the three members of the genus *Rhynchocyon*, known as the chequered elephant shrews. The largest of these is the golden-rumped elephant-shrew (*R. chrysopygus*), which lives in south-eastern Kenya; it has a head-body length of 27–31.5 cm *10.6–12.4 in*; a tail length of 23–26.5 cm *9–10.4 in*; and an average adult weight of approximately 500 g *1 lb 2 oz*.

**Smallest** The smallest elephant-shrew is the short-eared elephant-shrew (*Macroscelides proboscideus*), which lives in southern Africa; it has a head-body length of 10.4–11.5 cm *4.1–4½ in*; a tail length of 11.5–13 cm *4½–5.1 in*; and an average adult weight of about 45 g *1.6 oz*.

**Fastest** The golden-rumped elephant-shrew (*Rhynchocyon chrysopygus*) is able to run across the open forest floor at speeds of at least 25 km/h *15½ mph*, which is about as fast as a person would be able to run across similar terrain.

**Most threatened** The World Conservation Union (IUCN) lists two species of elephant-shrews which are known or suspected to be threatened with extinction: the golden-rumped elephant-shrew (*Rhynchocyon chrysopygus*) of Kenya and the black-and-rufous elephant-shrew (*R. petersi*) of Kenya and Tanzania.

A further three sub-species are thought to be threatened as well: the four-toed elephant-shrew (*Petrodromus tetradactylus sangi*) of Kenya, the chequered elephant-shrew (*Rhynchocyon cirnei cirnei*) of Mozambique, and Henderson's chequered elephant-shrew (*Rhynchocyon c. hendersoni*) of Malawi.

> *When they are handled, elephant-shrews often emit a sharp, high-pitched scream – but they are surprisingly gentle and rarely attempt to bite.*

# MANATEES & DUGONGS

## *Sirenia*
4 living species: 3 manatees and 1 dugong.

**Earliest** Relatively little is known about sirenian evolution and it appears that even at their zenith there were no more than about a dozen (mostly monotypic) genera worldwide. Ancestral forms date from the early Eocene, about 55 million years ago, and the oldest known fossils belong to a species called *Protosiren*, which has been found in Jamaica. The earliest known true manatee, a species called *Potamosiren*, lived in the middle Miocene some 13–16 million years ago; the main difference between this and modern species is in the teeth: *Potamosiren* lacked the extra teeth and the tooth replacement facility which is characteristic of today's manatees (as an adaptation for eating abrasive plant materials).

**Largest** The West Indian manatee (*Trichechus manatus*), which lives in the Caribbean, the Gulf of Mexico and the western Atlantic, is by a narrow margin the largest living sirenian. It is often split into two sub-species, both of which have an average length of 3 m *9 ft 10 in* and an average weight of 500 kg *1100 lb* (males and females are similar in size); however, the sub-species known as the Florida manatee (*Trichechus m. latirostris*) reaches a larger maximum size of 3.9 m *12 ft 10 in* and 1660 kg *3650 lb* than the slighly smaller Antillean manatee (*Trichechus m. manatus*). There is an unauthenticated report of a 4.7 m *15 ft 5 in* Florida manatee, caught off the coast of Texas, USA, in 1910, but information is lacking and this figure is treated as suspect by most experts.

There is an unauthenticated record of a dugong (*Dugong dugon*) caught off India on 23 Jul 1959 which allegedly measured 4.06 m *13 ft 4 in* in length and weighed 1016 kg *2240 lb*. However, the average size for this species is only 2.7 m *8 ft 10 in* and 250–350 kg *550–770 lb* and recent assessments suggest that a measurement error was made when this particular animal was examined. In one study of 310 adult-sized animals fewer than 2 per cent were more than 3 m *9 ft 10 in* in length. The maximum reliable measurement is 3.31 m *10 ft 10 in* for a female.

The extinct Steller's sea cow

(*Hydrodamalis gigas*), which lived in the cold waters of the Bering Sea (the only modern sirenian adapted to living in cold water), was the giant of the five recent species. Adults probably reached a length of at least 8 m *26¼ ft* (average about 7 m *23 ft*) and weighed an estimated 4–10 tonnes (depending on which model is used for estimation); the maximum body circumference on record was 6.2 m *20¼ ft*.

Some prehistoric species (such as *Hydrodamalis cuestae*, represented by 3–8-million-year-old fossils from California, USA) were even larger than Steller's sea cow and may have attained a length of well over 9 m *29½ ft*.

> *The dugong is the only truly sea-going mammal that is herbivorous.*

**Smallest** The Amazonian manatee (*Trichechus inunguis*) is the smallest sirenian and is both shorter and more slender than its relatives. The average size is about 2.5 m *8 ft 2 in* and 350 kg *661 lb*; the longest recorded specimens measure 3 m *9 ft 10 in* and the heaviest was an animal caught in Ecuador which weighed 480 kg *1058 lb*. Despite its *relatively* small size, it is still the largest herbivore living in South America's Amazon basin.

**Oldest** The normal lifespan of sirenians is not well known. But West Indian manatees (*Trichechus manatus*) have been known to live in captivity for more than 40 years and estimates of the ages of wild sirenians (by counting growth layers in the ear bones of manatees and in the tusks of dugongs) suggest a normal lifespan of 50–60 years. The record to date is 73 years in the case of a dugong (*Dugong dugon*).

**Freshwater living** The Amazonian manatee (*Trichechus inunguis*) is the only sirenian which lives exclusively in freshwater. The dugong (*Dugong dugon*) is a marine animal, although it enters brackish or freshwater occasionally; and the West Indian manatee (*Trichechus manatus*) and West African manatee (*Trichechus senegalensis*) both live in a mixture of freshwater and saltwater habitats.

**Longest dive** The average interval between breaths for the three manatee species is estimated to be approximately 2–4 minutes and for the dugong (*Dugong dugon*) approximately 1¼ minutes (although dive times vary with activity – active animals need to breathe more frequently). The longest authenticated dive recorded for any of the four species is 24 minutes for a West Indian manatee (*Trichechus manatus*) in Florida; however, since adults frequently dive for 15–20 minutes when resting, it is likely that some manatees are capable of holding their breath for even longer.

**Longest migration** Individual marking studies in Florida have shown that at least some Florida manatees (*Trichechus manatus latirostris*) migrate north in summer and south in winter; long-distance movements of more than

850 km *528 miles* have been recorded. There is little information on the migrations of the other two manatees, although short-range seasonal movements in response to shifts in food availability and changing weather patterns probably occur. Circumstantial evidence suggests that the dugong (*Dugong dugon*) may travel long distances. During one study, an individual equipped with a satellite transmitter travelled between two bays 200 km *124 miles* apart three times in 9 weeks; there are also occasional sightings of dugongs as far south as Sydney, Australia, which is 700 km *435 miles* south of the nearest known habitat area.

**Metabolic rate** The metabolic rate of manatees is about one-third that of a typical mammal of the same weight. They are capable of rapid movement when being pursued (swimming

---

The Amazonian manatee is the only sirenian which lives exclusively in freshwater; this injured animal is being cared for at a research centre near Manaus, Brazil.

> **Manatees are sometimes used for weed control; they are introduced to man-made waterways, such as irrigation canals or reservoirs, and keep them open by munching their way through as much as 75 kg 165 lb of vegetation every day.**

speeds of up to 25 km/h *15½ mph* have been recorded) but they are normally slow and languid in their movements.

**Longest gestation period** All sirenians have a gestation period of approximately one year, although the dugong (*Dugong dugon*) consistently has the longest (13–14 months) by a very narrow margin (the gestation period in wild West Indian manatees [*Trichechus manatus*] is 12–13 months and in captive individuals as long as 14 months).

**Most threatened** All four sirenians – dugong (*Dugong dugon*), Amazonian manatee (*Trichechus inunguis*), West

> *Manatees and dugongs can be distinguished by their tails: manatees have large, rounded tails while dugongs have fluke-shaped tails (like those of dolphins).*

Indian manatee (*Trichechus manatus*) and West African manatee (*Trichechus senegalensis*) – are threatened with extinction. Their slow movement, placid disposition, inland or inshore distribution and relatively poor hearing have made them exceedingly vulnerable; the many threats they face include hunting, habitat destruction, entanglement in fishing nets, pollution and heavy boat traffic. The only one for which the population size is known is the Florida manatee (*Trichechus m. latirostris*), a subspecies of the West Indian manatee found in the south-eastern USA, with an estimated 1850 survivors.

> *The nearest living relatives to the sirenians are the elephants and, according to some experts, the hyraxes.*

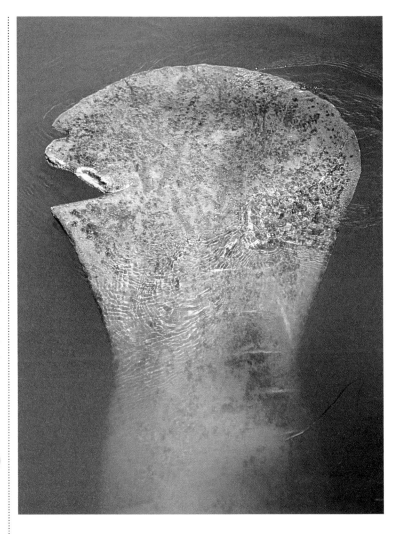

The injuries on the tail of this West Indian manatee, photographed in Florida, USA, were caused by boat propellers; all four sirenians are endangered by heavy boat traffic and a variety of other threats.

**Extinctions** One species of sirenian is known to have become extinct since 1600: Steller's sea cow (*Hydrodamalis gigas*). It has the unhappy distinction of being one of only two marine mammals to have disappeared in modern times (the other being the recently extinct Caribbean monk seal *Monachus tropicalis*). Fossil evidence suggests that *c.* 20000 years ago its range extended along northern Pacific coasts from Japan to California, but at the time of its discovery it occurred mainly on Bering Island and nearby Copper Island, between Kamchatka and the western tip of the Aleutian Islands in the western Bering Sea.

Steller's sea cow was discovered in November 1741 by the crew of the Russian brig *St Peter*, which was wrecked on an uninhabited island (later named Bering Island after Vitus Bering – the captain of the brig) near the remote Aleutian Islands, Alaska, USA. The survivors of the shipwreck lived on the huge, unknown marine mammals for 10 months, while they built a new boat to take them home. Fortunately, one of the shipwrecked survivors was the

naturalist George Wilhelm Steller, who spent much of his enforced time on the island recording information on the animals and plants he found; he made the only detailed written record of the habits and appearance of the sea cow that was later to bear his name. However, as the news spread, Bering Island, and nearby Copper Island, soon became the focus of countless Russian hunting expeditions. The crews lived almost exclusively on sea cow meat, while they hunted local fur-bearing animals such as seals and sea otters. At the time of their discovery, the total number of sea cows was probably in the region of 1500–2000, but so many of the slow, inoffensive animals were killed that the species disappeared altogether in the space of just 27 years. There is indirect evidence that a few

may have survived until the mid-1800s – and there are still occasional reports of unusual-looking creatures fitting the description of Steller's sea cows off the coast of Siberia – but the last definite sighting was in 1768 and this is when most experts consider it to have become extinct.

**Most abundant** The dugong (*Dugong dugon*), which is widely, though unevenly, distributed along the coasts of no fewer than 43 countries throughout the Indian Ocean and the western Pacific, is probably the most abundant sirenian. The largest population is found in Australian waters where there are an estimated 85000 animals.

> *Manatees never run out of teeth: they possess only molars and pre-molars and these are continuously being replaced by new teeth which appear behind the 'active' row and then-move forward.*

# MARSUPIALS

### Marsupialia

*c.* 275 species, including kangaroos, wallabies, wombats, bandicoots, phalangers, possums, marsupial mice, koala, opossums, numbat and thylacine.

**Earliest** There is evidence to suggest that marsupials diverged from placental mammals at least 100 million years ago. The earliest undisputed fossil is a tiny jaw from a mouse-sized marsupial (*Kokopellia juddi*) found in 100-million-year-old siltstone in central Utah, USA. Two fossil skulls belonging to *Pucadelphys andinus* and *Mayulestes ferox*, which were found in Bolivia, are believed to be about 75 million years old. An animal called *Holoclemensia texana*, which lived in Texas, USA, about 120 million years ago, may also be a marsupial – but many experts are not convinced.

The earliest undisputed marsupials yet found in Australia date from the Miocene, some 23 million years ago, by which time most of the modern families had become established. However, a tiny fragment of fossil tooth, found in northern Australia in 1985, is estimated to be 100 million years old and *could* belong to a marsupial; unfortunately, there is insufficient material for a definitive identification. It is generally considered that marsupials originated in the Americas some 75–100 million years ago, and from there spread to Australia via South America and Antarctica (all three continents were united as a single landmass until about 45 million years ago).

**Largest** The red kangaroo (*Macropus rufus*) of central, southern and eastern Australia is the world's largest marsupial. It has a head-body length of 1.3–1.65 m *4 ft 3 in–5 ft 5 in* (male) and 85–105 cm *33½–41¼ in* (female); a tail length of 1–1.2 m *39–47¼ in* (male) and 65–85 cm *25½–33½ in* (female); and a weight of 20–90 kg *44–198 lb* (rarely more than 55 kg *121¼ lb* in males and 30 kg *66 lb* in females). Old males may be 1.8 m *5 ft 11 in* tall when standing in the normal position, and considerably taller (up to 2.1 m *6 ft 11 in*) when standing on their toes, for example during aggressive encounters. Head-body lengths of up to 3.4 m *11 ft 2 in* and weights of up to 136 kg *300 lb* have been claimed by hunters in the past, but these are considered extremely unlikely. Old hunting reports suggest that some males of the Tasmanian race of the eastern grey kangaroo (*Macropus*

*giganteus tasmaniensis*) may rival the largest reds for size.

**Smallest** There are a number of very small, mouse-sized marsupials and opinions vary over which is the smallest. The two main contenders are the rare long-tailed planigale (*Planigale ingrami*), a flat-skulled shrew-like creature of northern Australia, and the rather similar pilbara ningaui (*Ningaui timealeyi*) of north-western Australia. The planigale has a head and body length of 5.5–6.3 cm *2.17–2.48 in*; a tail length of 5.7–6 cm *2.24–2.36 in*; and a weight of 3.9–4.5 g *0.14–0.16 oz*. The ningaui has a head-body length of 4.6–5.7 cm *1.81–2.24 in*; a tail length of 5.9–7.9 cm *2.32–3.11 in*; and a weight of 2–9.4 g *0.07–0.33 oz*.

**Largest prehistoric** There were many large marsupials in prehistoric times. The largest known was an Australian species called *Diprotodon*, which was rhinoceros-like (in size and appearance) and belonged to the now-extinct family Diprotodontidae; it may have survived until about 20 000 years ago. The largest known kangaroo was the 3 m *9 ft 10 in* tall species called *Procoptodon goliah*.

**Largest carnivorous marsupial** The dog-like thylacine or Tasmanian tiger (*Thylacinus cynocephalus*), which may be extinct (*see Extinctions*), is the largest carnivorous marsupial to have survived into historical times. It has a head-body length of 1–1.3 m *39½–51 in*; a tail length of 50–65 cm *20–25½ in*; a shoulder height of about 60 cm *23½ in*; and a weight of 15–35 kg *33–77 lb*. Its most distinctive features are the long, stiff tail and a series of 8–20 black or chocolate-brown stripes across its back. The scientific name is particularly descriptive and means 'pouched dog with a wolf head'.

**Largest burrowing** The largest burrowing marsupial is the common wombat

---

When feeling threatened, the eastern grey kangaroo is capable of hopping along at record-breaking speeds of up to 64 km/h *40 mph.*

(*Vombatus ursinus*) of south-eastern Australia, which is roughly the same weight as an Old English sheepdog. It has a head-body length of 70–120 cm *27½– 47¼ in* (the tail is almost non-existent); and a weight of 15–35 kg *33–77 lb*. It is a strong and powerful digger, using its claws and trowel-like teeth to burrow through soil at an incredible rate of up to 3 m *9 ft 10 in* per hour.

**Oldest** Most marsupials probably do not live to maturity but, having survived the dangerous period of youth, many of the larger species have fairly long potential lifespans. The greatest reliable age recorded is 26 years 22 days for a common wombat (*Vombatus*

---

*Tree kangaroos have been known to leap 10 m 33 ft or more between trees and can jump to the ground from heights of up to 30 m 98½ ft without apparently harming themselves.*

---

*ursinus*) which died in London Zoo on 20 Apr 1906. Another wombat lived to a similar age in Antwerp Zoo, Belgium, from 1928 until its death on 30 Nov 1954. Large kangaroos, especially the eastern grey (*Macropus giganteus*) and red (*M. rufus*), have been known to reach 20–24 years in captivity and may be able to live for as long as 28 years.

**Fastest** Kangaroos and wallabies are capable of attaining extremely high speeds, particularly over short distances. They hop with their two hind feet, holding their front paws up against their chests and using their big tails as counterbalances. The highest speed recorded for any marsupial is 64 km/h *40 mph* by a mature female eastern grey kangaroo (*Macropus giganteus*). The highest sustained speed is 56 km/h *35 mph* recorded for a large male red kangaroo (*Macropus rufus*), which unfortunately died from its exertions after being paced for 1.6 km *1 mile* (maximum speed is normally reached only under pressure, such as when being chased by a car).

**Most dangerous love-life** Broad-

---

footed marsupial mice in the genus *Antechinus* have an extremely peculiar trait: after mating frenetically for a 2-week period, all the exhausted males die. This remarkable phenomenon is best understood and most sudden in the brown antechinus (*A. stuartii*) of eastern Australia. The male begins to change dramatically in the period leading up to the breeding season: his testes grow and grow until they make up about a quarter of his total body weight; huge amounts of the male sex hormone, testosterone, enter his bloodstream; and he develops an insatiable sexual appetite. For a 2-week period every year, the entire adult male population goes on the rampage in a desperate bid to mate with as many females as they can. They are so busy chasing females and fighting rival males that they have no time (or simply forget) to eat. In a matter of days, they are all dead. Some die of starvation, others from stomach ulcers caused by all the stress, but most succumb to disease or infection (excessive amounts of testosterone suppress the immune system). Only the pregnant females, and their unborn offspring, are left. The females live for up to 3 years, while most males have a life expectancy of no more than 11–12 months.

**Highest jump** Large kangaroos normally do not jump higher than about 1.5 m *59 in*, and fences of this height will deter most animals. However, there are many records (mostly unauthenticated) of them jumping much higher, especially when under pressure to escape from predators or human hunters. The record-holder is probably a red kangaroo (*Macropus rufus*), which cleared a stack of timber 3.1 m *10 ft* high in a desperate bid to escape from a pack of hunting dogs in the 1960s. There is also a record of a captive male eastern grey kangaroo (*M. giganteus*) which reportedly cleared a 2.44 m *8 ft* fence when it was frightened by a car suddenly back-firing.

**Longest jump** When travelling at speed, it is not unusual for large kangaroos to leap enormous distances of 8 m *26¼ ft* or more in a single bound. Hopping is both rapid and, in terms of energy consumption, an efficient mode of travel. The record-holder may be an eastern grey kangaroo (*Macropus giganteus*) which jumped nearly 13.5 m

M
A
M
M
A
L
S

*44 ft 8½ in* on the flat, although this has not been verified. A very close runner-up is a female red kangaroo (*M. rufus*) which made a series of exceptional bounds, including one of 12.8 m *42 ft*, during a chase in New South Wales, Australia, in January 1951.

**Gliding** Three marsupial families include a total of six species which are capable of gliding flight: the Pseudocheiridae (one species: the greater glider *Petauroides volans*), Petauridae (four species in the genus *Petaurus*) and Burramyidae (one species: the feathertail glider *Acrobates pygmaeus*, which is the smallest gliding marsupial). All six have a membrane of skin stretched between their arms and legs which, when extended, forms a rectangular, kite-like aerofoil. The glider climbs to the top of a high tree, leaps into the air and glides a considerable distance before landing with all four feet on the trunk of another tree; steering is achieved by altering the tension of the membrane on either side of the body, and balance by using the outstretched tail as a rudder. When not in use, the gliding membrane is folded away and may be visible as a wavy line along each side of the body.

The feathertail glider has the least-developed membrane, extending from the elbows to the knees (compared with the elbows to the ankles in the greater glider, and the wrists to the ankles in all the others). The much heavier greater glider probably has the most limited gliding abilities, descending steeply and with relatively little control, but some species are capable of gliding further than 100 m *328 ft* and are highly manoeuvrable in the air.

**Best grip** The fingertips of the feathertail glider (*Acrobates pygmaeus*) have expanded pads to give the animal extra grip while it is climbing. Each pad is microscopically grooved (as in geckos), enabling it to cling to almost any smooth surface. This is such an effective system that the feathertail is able to walk up a clean window and can even hold itself, albeit briefly, to the underside of a horizontal sheet of glass.

**Most diurnal** The numbat or marsupial anteater (*Myrmecobius fasciatus*) is the most diurnal Australian marsupial. All the other marsupials are nocturnal, crepuscular or active on and off around the clock. Despite its alternative name, it spends most of the day actively searching for its favourite food – which is termites, not ants.

**Sleepiest** Two marsupials, in particular, are well-known for their sleepy habits: the marsupial mole (*Notoryctes typhlops*) and the koala (*Phascolarctos cinereus*). Limited observations on the mole suggest that it alternates without warning between periods of frenetic activity and sudden sleep. It may unexpectedly fall asleep in the middle of rushing about, only to wake just as suddenly a few minutes later and carry on as if nothing had happened. The koala's sleepy habits are a little more logical: since it has a very low quality diet (*see Most fussy eater*), it spends up to 18 out of every 24 hours sleeping or dozing to conserve energy.

**Most fussy eater** The koala (*Phascolarctos cinereus*) of eastern Australia feeds almost exclusively on the leaves of eucalyptus trees. It browses regularly on only half a dozen of the 500 species, prefers individual trees above others, and is even choosy about specific leaves (sometimes sifting through as much as 9 kg *20 lb* of leaves every day for the 0.5 kg *1¼ lb* it eventually eats). No one knows what it is that makes one particular tree or leaf more desirable than another, especially since the choice varies between populations, between individuals, and with the seasons. However, it is likely to be connected with the fact that eucalyptus leaves are not a particularly good source of food: they contain little protein, lots of difficult-to-digest fibre and essential oils that are toxic in high concentrations.

**Longest gestation period** The gestation period is relatively short in all marsupials, since they give birth to very small, poorly developed young (the period of growth and development after birth is considerably longer than the period inside the womb). The records (with average non-delayed gestation periods) are: 37 days in the eastern grey kangaroo (*Macropus giganteus*); 36 days in the whiptail wallaby (*M. parryi*); and 35 days in the parma wallaby (*M. parma*), swamp wallaby (*Wallabia bicolor*) and koala (*Phascolarctos cinereus*). In some species, development of the fertilized egg is delayed until the previous young leave the pouch or until there are more favourable environmental conditions; in the red kangaroo (*M. rufus*), for example, this delay (between

mating and development) can be as long as 28 weeks.

Newborn marsupials have been described as 'breathing foetuses': their skin is bare, thin and richly supplied with blood (possibly acting as a respiratory surface); their eyes and ears are embryonic and non-functional; and their hindlimbs are little more than short, five-lobed buds. Birth is extremely rapid: the baby simply pops out and, within a few minutes, has dragged itself through the forest of hairs on its mother's belly, into the pouch and on to a teat (it has long, powerful forelimbs with needle-sharp claws). It is unassisted by its mother and no one knows exactly how it finds its way to the teat; major clues may be its good sense of smell and a possibility that it can detect gravitational pull. The youngster (known as a 'pouch embryo') closes its mouth around the teat, which enlarges so much that it cannot fall off until its jaws are sufficiently developed for it to be able to release itself, which may take weeks or even months.

**Shortest gestation period** The shortest mammalian gestation period is 12–13 days, which is common in a number of species. These include the Virginia opossum (*Didelphis virginiana*) of North America; the water opossum or yapok (*Chironectes minimus*) of central and northern South America; the eastern quoll or native cat (*Dasyurus viverrinus*) of Australia; and the long-nosed bandicoot (*Perameles nasuta*), also of Australia. On rare occasions, gestation periods of as low as 8 days have been recorded for some of these species.

**Largest litter** Most marsupials give birth to small litters of 1–10 babies, the general trend being the smaller the animal the larger the litter. The record-holder is the Virginia opossum (*Didelphis virginiana*) of North America, which frequently gives birth to more offspring than can be accommodated on its teats. The female normally has 13 teats, but typically produces 21 young per litter; not all the teats are functional and, since babies unable to obtain milk

**M**
**A**
**M**
**M**
**A**
**L**
**S**

A mother kangaroo is able to suckle two youngsters of different ages simultaneously by producing two kinds of milk: one slightly diluted for the youngest and the other more concentrated (with extra fat) for the oldest.

soon perish, it is rare for more than eight of them to survive. This seems very wasteful, but competition to reach a teat ensures that the mother invests her time and energy in raising only the strongest offspring. The overall record-holder is a female Virginia opossum which gave birth to an incredible 56 babies at one time, each about the size of a baked bean.

**Smallest newborn** All newborn marsupials are tiny, weighing less than 1 g *0.035 oz*. Unfortunately, it is very difficult to identify the smallest because, at the lower end of the range there is little difference between species and a cer-

Like most marsupials, the brushtail possum has a very short gestation period: in this case, about 16–18 days.

tain amount of variation between individuals. However, a strong contender is the honey possum (*Tarsipes rostratus*) of south-western Australia, which gives birth to two, three or occasionally four young – each weighing just 0.005 g *0.0002 oz*. They still weigh only 2.5 g *0.088 oz* by the time they leave the pouch (when they are 8 weeks old) but, to put this into context, four of them together weigh nearly as much as their mother.

**Largest newborn** The female red kangaroo (*Macropus rufus*) gives birth to the largest marsupial baby, but even this weighs only 0.75 g *0.027 oz* (0.003 per cent of the average maternal weight, compared with more than 5 per cent in humans). It would take 36 000 of these babies to equal the weight of the mother. Interestingly, by the time the young are weaned, the ratio between the mother's weight and the weight of the offspring (whether a litter or a single individual) is roughly the same in both marsupials and placentals.

**Largest pouch** In most marsupials, the young are protected by a pouch of hair-covered skin, known as the marsupium. This covers the teat area and can open forwards (as in kangaroos) or backwards (as in bandicoots). The numbat (*Myrmecobius fasciatus*) is the only marsupial without such a pouch (the young are carried attached to teats on the outside of the mother's belly), although some other species have little more than

a fold of skin, or develop a pouch only during the breeding season. The most capacious pouches belong to the largest kangaroos in the genus *Macropus*, which normally produce only one young at a time. The baby kangaroo, or 'joey', remains in the pouch long after it has become detached from the teat; even once it has begun to venture into the outside world, it frequently uses the pouch as a means of transport, a place to sleep and somewhere to dive for cover in case of danger. The young red kangaroo (*Macropus rufus*) eventually leaves the pouch for good when it is about 8 months old. Species that produce large litters lack a sufficiently large pouch to carry them for a long time; once the youngsters have detached themselves from the teat, they are usually left in a nest while their mother is out foraging.

**Most waterproof pouch** The female South American water opossum or yapok (*Chironectes minimus*) carries her babies around in a special waterproof pouch. When she is underwater, strong sphincter muscles close the rear-opening pouch tightly shut, while long hairs and fatty secretions create a watertight seal; air trapped inside allows the youngsters to breathe. An accomplished swimmer, the yapok is the only marsupial highly adapted for an aquatic way of life; its other adaptations include dense, oily, water-repellent fur and webbed hind feet.

**Playing possum** The cat-sized Virginia or American opossum (*Didelphis virginiana*), which is the only marsupial in North America, sometimes feigns death in the face of danger – giving its name to the phrase 'playing possum'. The aim is to make its predators less cautious in their approach and to make them lose interest because of a lack of visual stimuli. With staring, unblinking eyes, the opossum curls up on its side, droops its head, opens its mouth slightly, and lets its tongue hang out. The act is extremely convincing, especially since it remains largely insensitive to touch and rarely flinches even if it is being shaken about in a predator's mouth or badly bitten. In this trance-like state, it can remain absolutely immobile for less than a minute or for as long as 6 hours. There are certain physiological changes which make playing possum analogous to fainting in humans, but the possum's brain remains fully operational, ready for the animal to snap back into life and seize a chance of escape the moment the predator puts it down or briefly relaxes its grip. Death feigning has been reported in other opossums, but only rarely.

**Most recently discovered** A new species of kangaroo was discovered in June 1994, at an altitude of 4526 m *14 850 ft*, in the Maokop mountain range of Irian Jaya, the Indonesian part of New Guinea. Called the bondegezou ('man of the alpine forest') by local Moni peo-

ple, and weighing about 15 kg *33 lb*, the black and white animal is puzzling scientists because it has characteristics of both arboreal and ground-dwelling kangaroos. Its official discovery was prompted by a series of photographs published in *BBC Wildlife* magazine; they had been taken in November 1990, by natural history photographer Gerald Cubitt, and no one recognized the species. A joint Australian/Indonesian expedition was launched, by Dr Tim Flannery of the Australian Museum in Sydney, to make a detailed search. They did not see a living specimen, but were able to examine dead animals – including one killed by hounds as they approached with a hunting party from the Dani tribe. Early indications are that it is actually a tree kangaroo, al-

> *Marsupials frequently bear a striking resemblance to placental mammals and fill similar ecological niches; for example, bandicoots are analogous to rabbits and hares, gliders to flying squirrels, marsupial moles to moles, wombats to woodchucks, the Tasmanian devil to the wolverine, marsupial mice to shrews, and the numbat to anteaters.*

**The Tasmanian devil is the marsupial equivalent of the wolverine, and is probably the most efficient marsupial scavenger.**

though reports from local people suggest that it is a poor climber and spends most of its time on the ground. It could be the missing link between the two lines of kangaroos – or yet another complication to puzzle taxonomists for a long time to come. There are believed to be thousands of bondegezous living in the mountains, but their apparent lack of fear makes them easy prey for hunters and there is concern for their future. The species is yet to be described for science.

**Most unlikely discovery** A possum previously known only from fossilized remains, and presumed extinct for 10–15 000 years, was discovered alive and well behind a rubbish bin in a ski hut, in the Australian Alps of eastern Victoria. One day in August 1966 Dr Kenneth Shortman was looking for something to eat in the kitchen of the Melbourne University Ski Lodge, high on the slopes of Mt Hotham, when he found the small, dormouse-like mammal hiding in a corner. He knew it was a possum, but did not recognize the species and took it to the Victorian Fisheries and Wildlife Department for identification. To

*The thylacine or Tasmanian tiger has one of the widest gapes of all mammals: it is able to open its mouth so wide that its jaws are almost in a straight line.*

everyone's amazement, palaeontologist Norman Wakefield identified it as the mountain pygmy possum (*Burramys parvus*), known only from a few fossil fragments found in an owl pellet in 1896, in the Wombeyan Caves, near Burra, New South Wales, and from some more fossilized remains later found at the Buchan Caves, in Gippsland, Victoria. After searching for more animals, biologists have found a small number elsewhere in Victoria, as well as in New South Wales.

**Most threatened** The World Conservation Union (IUCN) lists 57 marsupial species (21 per cent of the total) as known or suspected to be threatened with extinction. Among the many species considered to be in particularly serious danger are the numbat (*Myrmecobius fasciatus*), golden bandicoot (*Isoodon auratus*), Leadbeater's possum (*Gymnobelideus leadbeateri*) and the northern hairy-nosed wombat (*Lasiorhinus krefftii*), all of which live in Australia; and Goodfellow's tree kangaroo (*Dendrolagus goodfellowi*) and the alpine wallaby (*Thylogale calabyi*) of Papua New Guinea. The many threats they face include hunting, deforestation, overgrazing by rabbits, predation by feral cats and foxes, competition with domestic livestock, large-scale bushfires and disease.

**Extinctions** No fewer than 10 marsupial species have been declared extinct since the first European settlers arrived in 1788 (representing approximately one in six of the world's mammal extinctions during the same period). All these extinctions have occurred in Australia: the broad-faced potoroo (*Potorous platyops*), 1875; eastern hare-wallaby (*Lagorchestes leporides*), 1890; pig-footed bandicoot (*Chaeropus ecaudatus*), 1907; toolache wallaby (*Macropus greyi*), 1927; lesser bilby (*Macrotis leucura*), 1931; central hare-wallaby (*Lagorchestes asomatus*), 1931; desert bandicoot (*Perameles eremiana*), 1935; desert rat-kangaroo (*Caloprymnus campestris*), 1935; thylacine (*Thylacinus cynocephalus*), 1936 (*see Most unlikely extinction*); and the crescent nailtail wallaby (*Onychogalea lunata*), 1964. It is believed that other species are likely to have become extinct in recent times, but have never been recorded by scientists.

**Most unlikely extinction** The most controversial 'extinction' is undoubtedly that of the thylacine, otherwise known as the Tasmanian tiger or wolf (*Thylacinus cynocephalus*). The last known survivor was a male called *Benjamin*, which had been caught by a wallaby-trapper in the heavily forested Florentine Valley, 96 km *60 miles* northwest of Hobart, Tasmania, in 1933; he was kept in captivity at Beaumaris Zoo, Hobart, where he died on 7 Sep 1936. Ironically, less than 2 months later, in July 1936, a new law was passed to protect the thylacine from hunting, which was probably the main cause of its demise. Since then there have been no *authenticated* sightings and no positive evidence to prove it still exists. But a great many reported sightings, and considerable circumstantial evidence, have kept up hopes that it might still be alive in remote parts of rugged Tasmania – and, indeed, it has been dubbed 'the world's most common extinct animal'.

The frequency of reported thylacine sightings is intriguing, especially since many of the eyewitness accounts have come from reliable observers such as park rangers; in 1982, for example, a ranger claimed he watched a thylacine for several minutes in the spotlight of his parked car. Thylacine-like animals are even reported from time to time on mainland Australia, where the species is believed to have been extinct for about 3000 years; in particular, a complete carcass was found in a large subterranean cave on Mundrabilla Station, eastern Western Australia: no one disputes that it was a thylacine, but estimates of its age vary from less than 20 years to 4500 years.

Recent computer analysis has left little doubt that the thylacine still exists in remote areas of Tasmania. Henry Nix of the Australian National University's Centre for Resource and Environmental Studies has developed a programme called Bioclim that can accurately predict where a particular species should be found. After feeding his computer with information on the thylacine's favourite environmental conditions, and all the more reliable sightings since it was declared extinct, he has demonstrated statistically that it is extremely likely that people really are seeing thylacines – and are not just imagining them.

Fossil evidence suggests that the thylacine was once widespread in Australia and New Guinea, but throughout historical times it has been known only in Tasmania. It probably lived on wallabies, possums and other large vertebrate prey, but with the arrival of the European settlers quickly gained a reputation as a sheep-killer. A bounty of £1 for each adult and 10 shillings for each pup was offered by the Tasmanian Government for a 21-year period (1888–1909) in a determined effort to wipe out the species. At least 2268 bounties were claimed, although the total number killed during this period was believed to be nearer 5000 (many hunters claimed bounties from private land-owners instead); thousands more had been killed before the bounty scheme came into operation. The hunting, a virulent distemper-like disease, competition with dingos, and habitat modification, are all to blame for the thylacine's extinction or near-extinction.

**The thylacine has been dubbed 'the world's most common extinct mammal': although it officially became extinct in the 1930s, there have been many reported sightings in recent years.**

# MONGOOSES, CIVETS & GENETS

### Viverridae & Herpestidae
*c.* 74 species

**Most primitive appearance** The viverrids and herpestids closely resemble a group of animals in the extinct family Miacidae, which are believed to be the direct ancestors of modern carnivores. The miacids, as they were known, were small mammals (similar in both size and appearance to modern genets) which evolved directly from insectivore stock soon after the dinosaurs disappeared, some 60 million years ago. Miacids lived in the forests of the northern hemisphere until, about 40 million years ago, a burst of evolution and diversification produced two major mammalian groups: the bear-like arctoids (giving rise to modern bears, seals, dogs, raccoons, pandas and mustelids) and the cat-like aeluroids (which gave rise to modern cats, hyenas, genets, civets and mongooses).

**Largest** The world's largest viverrid or herpestid is the African civet (*Civettictis civetta*), of sub-Saharan Africa. It has a head-body length of 68–89 cm *27–35 in*; a tail length of 44–46 cm *17–18 in*; and a weight of 7–20 kg *15½–44 lb*. This makes it about 40 times heavier than the smallest member of the family, the dwarf mongoose (*Helogale parvula*).

The Celebes palm civet (*Macrogalidia musschenbroekii*) of Sulawesi (formerly Celebes), Indonesia, is longer (head-body length up to 1 m *3¼ ft* and tail length up to 60 cm *23½ in*) but weighs considerably less (3.5–6.1 kg *7 lb 11 oz–13 lb 7 oz*). Similarly, the binturong (*Arctictis binturong*) of south-east Asia has a head-body length of 61–97 cm *24–38 in* and a tail length of 56–89 cm *22–35 in*, but rarely exceeds 14 kg *31 lb* (normal range 9–14 kg *20–31 lb*).

**The direct ancestors of modern carnivores, known as the miacids, were similar in both size and appearance to modern genets; this is a large-spotted genet, photographed in Kenya.**

*The common palm civet is often called the toddy cat, because it has developed a taste for an alcoholic drink known as toddy; to make toddy, people in south-east Asia collect the sap from palm trees and allow it to ferment naturally – but the civets often get there first.*

> *Contrary to popular belief, mongooses do not live entirely on snakes, nor are they immune to snake venom; instead, they rely on their skill, agility and thick fur to avoid being bitten while they tire the snake before grabbing it from behind.*

**Smallest** The world's smallest viverrid or herpestid is the dwarf mongoose (*Helogale parvula*), which lives in many parts of sub-Saharan Africa. It has a head-body length of 18–28 cm *7–11 in*; a tail length of 12–20 cm *4¾–8 in*; and a weight of 230–680 g *8–24 oz* (average 320 g *11¼ oz*). This species is also one of the smallest carnivores in Africa.

**Most precocious young** The falanouc (*Eupleres goudotii*) and the fanaloka (*Fossa fossa*), both of which live in the rainforests of Madagascar, are the only carnivores that produce young that are active immediately after birth. The single babies (or twins) are born with their

---

The dwarf mongoose is the world's smallest viverrid and the smallest carnivore in Africa.

eyes open, and in an advanced state of development, and are able to follow their mothers around on foraging expeditions within about 8 days. However, they grow and mature at a slightly slower pace than other similar-sized carnivores.

**Prehensile tail** The binturong or bear cat (*Arctictis binturong*) is the only viverrid or herpestid with a long (56–89 cm *22–35 in*), thick, prehensile tail, which it uses as an extra hand to cling to branches while it moves through the trees. The only other carnivore with a truly prehensile tail is the Central and South American kinkajou (*Potos flavus*), which belongs to the raccoon family but has rather similar arboreal habits.

**Least known** A number of mongooses, civets and genets are poorly known. But the most extreme example is Lowe's otter-civet (*Cynogale bennetti lowei*), which is known from only one skin (no skulls or skeletons) of a juvenile collected in northern Vietnam in 1926. Originally described a separate species (*C. lowei*), it is now considered to be a sub-species.

**Most threatened** The World Conservation Union (IUCN) lists 18 mongoose, civet and genet species as known or suspected to be threatened with extinction. The species considered to be most seriously at risk are the Liberian mon-

goose (*Liberiictis kuhni*) of Liberia, Côte d'Ivoire and Guinea; the otter-civet (*Cynogale bennettii*) of Brunei, Indonesia (Kalimantan and Sumatra), Malaysia (Peninsular Malaysia, Sabah and Sarawak), Thailand, Vietnam and, possibly, Singapore; and the crested genet (*Genetta cristata*) of Cameroon and Nigeria. The status of many other species is unknown.

A further eight sub-species are listed as known or suspected to be threatened with extinction, including the Sokoke bushy-tailed mongoose (*Bdeogale crassicauda omnivora*) of Kenya and Tanzania; the Javan small-toothed palm civet (*Arctogalidia trivirgata trilineata*) of Java, Indonesia; and the Mentawai palm civet (*Paradoxurus hermaphroditus lignicolor*) of Sumatra, Indonesia.

> *Civet musk, produced by civets for scent marking, has been cherished by the perfume industry for centuries; nowadays, there are synthetic chemical substitutes, but in many parts of the world civets are still hunted or bred in captivity for this valuable product.*

# MONOTREMES

## Monotremata
3 living species: duck-billed platypus, the short-beaked echidna
and the long-beaked echidna; all egg-laying mammals.

The monotremes, such as this spiny anteater or echidna, are the only living mammals that lay eggs.

**Earliest** The oldest known monotreme is represented by a 110-million-year-old fossil jaw fragment from New South Wales, Australia. It belonged to a species since named *Steropodon galmani*, which is thought to have been an ancestor of the modern platypus. Only a few other monotreme fossils have been found and, strangely, these all represent either echidnas or platypuses; palaeontologists are puzzled by the absence of any intermediate forms.

It was long thought that monotremes had always been confined to Australia and New Guinea. But a fossil tooth discovered in 1991 by a team of Argentinian palaeontologists in the Golfo de San Jorge, on the coast of central Patagonia, Argentina, is believed to have come from an early platypus. The single upper right molar, about 1 cm *0.39 in* long, was found in deposits laid down in a freshwater lagoon or mangrove swamp about 62 million years ago. It was the first evidence of a monotreme living outside Australia and New Guinea, and the second oldest known monotreme fossil. A lower tooth, and a second upper tooth, were found in 1992. According to current theories of continental drift, the great southern continent of Gondwanaland had broken up by that time, but Australia was still connected to South America through Antarctica (which was much warmer than it is now). Modern duck-billed platypuses (*Ornithorhynchus anatinus*) are born with teeth (indicating that their ancestors relied on them) but these are lost within a few weeks of birth.

**Most primitive** The monotremes are generally assumed to be the most primitive of living mammals: they lay eggs

(which is unique among mammals) and retain a number of reptilian skeletal features. Indeed, the modern duck-billed platypus (*Ornithorhynchus anatinus*) is very similar to fossils found in rocks of the mid-Miocene some 10 million years old. However, monotremes do not form a link between reptiles and the more advanced mammals, as was once suspected, but seem to represent an earlier evolutionary sidetrack.

**Largest** The largest monotreme is the long-beaked echidna or spiny anteater (*Zaglossus bruijni*), which lives in the mountains of Papua New Guinea and Irian Jaya, Indonesia (the western half of the island of New Guinea). The adult has a head-body length of 45–90 cm *17¾–35½ in* (there is only a short, blunt tail) and a weight of 5–10 kg *11–22 lb*; within a given population, males are normally 25 per cent larger than females of the same age.

**Smallest** The lightest monotreme is the duck-billed platypus (*Ornithorhynchus anatinus*), which lives along the eastern coast of Australia and on Tasmania. The adult has a head-body length of 45–60 cm *17¾–23½ in* (male) and 39–55 cm *15¼–21½ in* (female); a bill length of 4.9–7 cm *2–2¾ in* (male) and 4.5–5.9 cm *1¾–2¼ in* (female); a tail length of 10.5–15.2 cm *4–6 in* (male) and 8.5–13 cm *3½–5 in* (female); and a weight of 1–2.4 kg *2 lb 3 oz–5 lb 5 oz* (male) and 0.7–1.6 kg *1 lb 9 oz–3 lb 8 oz* (female). The smallest platypuses are found in northern Australia.

The short-beaked echidna (*Tachyglossus aculeatus*), which lives in Australia, Papua New Guinea and Irian Jaya, Indonesia (the western half of the island of New Guinea), is considerably heavier than the platypus, but is shorter. The adult has a head-body length of 30–45 cm *11¾–17¾ in* (there is only a short, blunt tail) and a weight of 2.5–7 kg *5½–15½ lb*; within a given population, males are normally 25 per cent larger than females of the same age.

**Most venomous** Only three groups of mammals are venomous: certain insectivores in the families Soricidae and Solenodontidae, at least two species of

loris in the genus *Nycticebus* and the monotremes. Of the monotremes, only the male duck-billed platypus (*Ornithorhynchus anatinus*) is capable of producing – and delivering – venom. The venom-producing gland, which is located in its thigh, is connected via a duct to a horny spur on the inner side of the ankle of each hind foot; curved and hollow, the spurs may be up to 1.5 cm *0.59 in* long and can be erected from within folds of skin. The venom itself is delivered when the platypus clasps its victim with its hind legs – so strongly that it can be almost impossible to prize off. It can kill a dingo within minutes and causes agonizing pain in people. No human deaths from platypus stings have been recorded, but the affected limb may swell to three or four times normal size and can remain painful and useless for many months afterwards. The female duck-billed platypus loses her spurs in infancy; the structures which produce and deliver venom are present in male echidnas, but not functional.

No one knows why the male duck-billed platypus has these venomous spurs. If they are for defence, it is strange that the smaller female does not retain them; it seems unlikely that they are for catching prey, since the platypus feeds on tiny creatures such as small crustaceans, worms, tadpoles, insect larvae and the occasional small fish or frog; and, if they are for the male to hold on to the female during courtship, the venom seems to be superfluous. Since the venom glands become enlarged during the breeding season, they may be used for duels between males over females; but, even then, young animals are sometimes killed when they challenge adults, so the weaponry seems unnecessarily severe.

*During courtship, a female echidna may be followed by as many as 10 hopeful males, lined up nose-to-tail, for as long as 36 days; she mates with only one of them before the two animals part company for good.*

**Egg-laying** The three monotreme species – duck-billed platypus (*Ornithorhynchus anatinus*), long-beaked echidna (*Zaglossus bruijni*) and short-beaked echidna (*Tachyglossus aculeatus*) – are the only living mammals that lay eggs. Almost everyone remained sceptical about this unlikely phenomenon for nearly a century after they were first studied, but the irrefutable fact was finally announced to a startled scientific community on 2 Sep 1884.

Despite their egg-laying, the reproductive system of monotremes is in most respects typically mammalian. The egg (one in echidnas and normally two in platypuses) is soft and leathery and about the size of a small grape. The female echidna incubates her egg in a small pouch for 10–10.5 days before it hatches; not surprisingly, because of its aquatic lifestyle, the female platypus does not have a pouch but incubates her eggs in a nesting chamber at the end of a 5–10 m *16½–33 ft* long burrow (maximum 30 m *98 ft 5 in*), curling her body around them in a half-sitting position. The incubation period is only 10–12 days and the tiny hatchlings (1.3–1.5 cm *0.5–0.6 in* long) are born naked and blind. The females do not have teats, but have special glands that ooze milk, which the young suck from the fur. Lactation lasts for about 200 days in the echidnas and 90–120 days in the platypus.

**Most threatened** According to the World Conservation Union (IUCN), the only monotreme currently considered to be threatened is the long-beaked echidna (*Zaglossus bruijni*), which is found in Papua New Guinea and Irian Jaya, Indonesia (the western half of the island of New Guinea). It is protected by law in both Papua New Guinea and Indonesia, but enforcement is difficult and, in Irian Jaya at least, there is an almost total disregard for the law on protected species. The many threats it faces include habitat loss (especially due to logging, agriculture and mining), hunting and capture for the pet trade.

The duck-billed platypus (*Ornithorhynchus anatinus*) has been fully protected in Australia since the turn of the century, but is considered to be potentially vulnerable. In the latter part of last century it was persecuted as a hindrance to fishing and hunted for its highly-prized fur; consequently, its numbers are reputed to have declined dramatically. Nowadays, there is more concern for its freshwater habitats, which are under increasing pressure from human use and, in some areas, are threatened by pollution; there is also a local problem of platypuses drowning in fishing nets.

**Most widespread** The short-beaked echidna (*Tachyglossus aculeatus*) is the most widely distributed native mammal in Australia, and is reportedly common in many parts of its range (including New Guinea and Tasmania). Ironically, it is rarely seen in the wild and, even though scientists have been studying it for more than 200 years, it is also one of the least known Australian mammals. There are six recognized sub-species, classified according to the length of their spines, their hairiness and the relative length of their third hind claw.

**Fastest digger** When it is frightened, an echidna digs with all four feet at once, instead of burrowing headfirst like most other mammals. It can disappear vertically into the ground in less than a minute – so rapidly that it has often been likened to a sinking ship. When it has finished, all that remains to be seen is a small, impregnable forest of

**The strange-looking duck-billed platypus is the only mammal known to be able to detect electric fields; its soft muzzle contains special electrical receptors, known previously only in some fish and tadpoles.**

razor-sharp spines protruding through the loosened soil.

**Oldest** The natural longevity of monotremes is still largely unknown. The oldest ever recorded was a captive short-beaked echidna (*Tachyglossus aculeatus*), which lived for 49 years in Philadelphia Zoo, USA. The longest authenticated age in the wild is 16 years, for the same species.

Duck-billed platypuses (*Ornithorhynchus anatinus*) have been known to live for a maximum of 20 years in captivity and 12 years in the wild.

**Detecting electricity** The duck-billed platypus (*Ornithorhynchus anatinus*) is the only mammal known to be able to detect electric fields. It is totally blind and deaf underwater (its eyes and ears are sealed in a furrow of skin when it dives) and, as recently as the mid-1980s, it was believed to feel for food by rummaging around under rocks and along the river bed with its muzzle. But Australian and German scientists, working together at the Australian National University in Canberra, have discovered that the soft muzzle contains special electrical receptors, known previously only in some fish and tadpoles. These electroreceptors detect the minuscule electrical discharges produced during the muscle movements of its invertebrate prey (even if the tiny animals are under mud or stones) from a distance of about 7–10 cm *2¾–4 in*.

# MUSTELIDS

## Mustelidae

c. 67 species, including weasels, mink, martens, badgers, skunks, otters.

> *The European badger has a sense of smell some 700–800 times more powerful than our own.*

**Largest** The sea otter (*Enhydra lutris*), which lives in the North Pacific, is the heaviest of the mustelids. It has a head-body length of 1–1.2 m *3¼–4 ft*; a tail length of 25–37 cm *9.8–14.6 in*; and a weight of 22–45 kg *48½–99 lb* (males) and 15–32 kg *33–70½ lb* (females).

The rare giant otter (*Pteronura brasiliensis*), which lives in South America, is the longest mustelid. It attains a greater length than the sea otter (head-body length of 86–140 cm *34–55 in* and tail length of 33–100 cm *13–39½ in*) but is significantly lighter (26–34 kg *57¼–75 lb* for males and 22–26 kg *48½–57¼ lb* for females).

The bear-like wolverine or glutton (*Gulo gulo*), which lives in the tundra and taiga zones of the arctic and subarctic, is frequently named as the world's largest mustelid. However, its robust, stocky appearance and long, dense fur can be deceptive and it has a head-body length of only 65–105 cm *25½–41¼ in*; a tail length of 17–26 cm *6¾–10¼ in*; and a weight of 7–30 kg *15½–66 lb*.

> *Nothing is too old or frozen for a wolverine to eat; its powerful jaws and strong teeth are uniquely adapted for eating frozen flesh in the depths of winter.*

**Smallest carnivore** The world's smallest living carnivore is the least or dwarf weasel (*Mustela nivalis*), which has a wide but fragmented range in Europe, North America, Asia and northern Africa (and has been introduced to New Zealand). It has a head-body length of 11–26 cm *4.33–10.24 in*; a tail length of 1.3–8.7 cm *0.51–3.43 in*; and a weight of 30–200 g *1.06–7.06 oz*. This species varies in size more than any other mammal – between the sexes, between populations and from one individual to another. Females are roughly half the size of males and the smallest individuals are those living in the north of the range (especially Siberia) and in the Alps. Resembling a long, slender

mouse, its small size is an advantage in hunting mice, voles and other tiny mammals in their runways and burrows.

**Smallest marine mammal** The marine otter (*Lutra felina*) of western South America is the world's smallest marine mammal. With a maximum length of just 1.15 m *45¼ in* (from the end of the snout to the tip of the relatively short tail), and a weight of only 4–4.5 kg *8 lb 13 oz–9 lb 15 oz*, it is substantially lighter and slightly shorter than the smallest seals, dolphins and porpoises. However, it is not exclusively marine: it has been reported far upstream in rivers and comes ashore to breed. The only other mustelid confined to marine habitats is the sea otter (*Enhydra lutris*), which is equivalent in size to the smallest dolphins and porpoises; some individuals off the coast of California, USA, never come to shore.

**Most fearless** The ratel or honey badger (*Mellivora capensis*) will attack or defend itself against animals of any size, especially if they dare to wander too close to its breeding burrow. It has fairly good reason to be brave. Its skin is so tough that it is impervious to the stings of bees, the quills of porcupines and even the bites of most snakes; it is also so loose that if the honey badger is held by the scruff of the neck, for example by a hyena or leopard, it can turn inside its own skin and bite the attacker until it is forced to let go.

**Strongest** The strength of the wolverine or glutton (*Gulo gulo*) is legendary and probably unexcelled among mammals of a similar size. Even though it is no larger than a medium-sized dog, it has been known to pry apart steel trap jaws, drag and carry prey carcasses several times its own weight for several kilometres, and even to tackle prey as large as reindeer and moose. Its strength seems to give it unlimited confidence and it has been known to drive bears and pumas from their kills, sometimes distracting grizzlies and black bears by biting them on the backside while they are busily eating. The only serious problem it has to face (apart from people) is a chance encounter with

a pack of wolves, against which even the wolverine is in trouble.

**Tool using** The sea otter (*Enhydra lutris*) is one of the few tool-using mammals and, indeed the only marine mammal known to use tools (although humpback whales use bubbles for fishing). It feeds primarily on abalones, mussels, clams, sea urchins and other hard-shelled prey, which are too tough to break open with its teeth alone; instead, it uses a remarkable level of dexterity to smash them with the help of a stone. The otter first collects a suitable stone from the seabed and then uses it, like a hammer, to knock the shellfish off their rocks. It returns to the surface, rolls upside down, places the stone on its chest and proceeds to smash the shell down on it, using the rock as an anvil. The first smash is usually a tentative one, perhaps to check for accuracy, but then it smashes away (testing the shell after every five or six blows) until the tasty meal inside is exposed. On average, 35 blows in six bouts are needed to break open Californian mussels, but one particularly hard shell required 88 blows in no fewer than 15 bouts. While it eats, the otter may roll over in the water at intervals to clean all the debris off its fur and then, when it has finished, it dives again to find more food. One otter was observed feeding on mussels for a period of 86 minutes, during which time it dived 54 times and delivered 2237 blows at the surface. Favoured stones are normally quite smooth, about 15 cm *6 in* in diameter and weighing roughly 0.5 kg *1 lb 2 oz*; they may be used several times and are held under the otter's armpit while it is diving.

**Largest sett** All badgers dig burrows of one kind or another, although most of them are fairly simple. The Euro-

> *Male sea otters obtain as much as one-third of their food by stealing from the females; sometimes, they will even hold a cub 'hostage' until the mother gives up her catch.*

**The European badger digs record-breaking underground setts, with as many as 50 underground chambers and 178 separate entrances.**

---

pean badger (*Meles meles*), however, spends more than half its life underground and builds record-breaking burrow systems (known as setts) that can be used for decades or even centuries, by one generation after another. More than 20 setts have been excavated, measured and mapped by researchers. The smallest of these was an 'outlier' sett (used only sporadically) which consisted of a single entrance and a simple, blind, L-shaped tunnel only 2 m *6½ ft* long. But the largest was

> *So many American mink have escaped from fur farms in Europe that they have supplanted the native, and rarer, European mink in many areas.*

a main sett estimated to contain a tunnel network 879 m *2883 ft* long, with 50 underground chambers and no fewer than 178 entrances. In another sett, the badgers had dug out 25 tonnes of soil.

The size of a European badger sett is not always related to the size of its social group. As might be expected, main setts are normally larger than outliers and they tend to be larger in regions where the soil is more easily dug. But most important of all, since the badgers are like human DIY enthusiasts and tend to go on extending their setts for as long as they are in residence, they grow larger with age.

**Smelliest** Mustelids have well-developed anal scent glands, which are used for social communication and in defence. These glands produce a thick, oily, yellow, pungent fluid called musk, which is stored in a sac that opens into the rectum. When they are threatened, some species are able to spray this unpleasant fluid out through the anus towards their attacker. The fluid varies greatly in potency from species to species, between individuals and even with the time of year – and there is little agreement about which is the most re-

pulsive. But the main contenders are probably the zorilla or striped polecat (*Ictonyx striatus*), which has a patchy distribution in sub-Saharan Africa; the two aptly named species of stink badger in the genus *Mydaus*, which live in south-east Asia; and the nine species of New World skunks in the genera *Mephitis*, *Spilogale* and *Conepatus*.

Skunks are certainly the best known of the smelly mustelids. Their vivid black and white markings warn potential predators of their unpleasant, and exceedingly effective, means of defence. They will normally spray only under extreme provocation, preferring to strut around as a warning, with stiff legs, their backs arched, tails pointing skyward and hairs erect; spotted skunks in the genus *Spilogale* even dramatize the effect by performing impressive handstands as well. If their attacker is persistent, and they do have to spray, they have an accurate range of about 2 m *6½ ft* and an overall range of some 6–7 m *19¾–23 ft*. They discharge either an atomized spray or a stream of droplets and aim for the attacker's eyes, causing a burning sensation, severe irritation and even temporary blindness. The smell itself is sulphurous and so foul that it frequently causes nausea and retching; it can be detected up to 2.5 km *1.6 miles* downwind. The fluid clings to the victim and releases more of its vile-smelling agents over a period of several days. It is virtually impossible to remove from clothes, which are best thrown away after a close encounter. Young skunks as little as 1 month old can spray – but the skunks themselves, and their dens, do not give off the same odour. As a result of this extraordinary defence system most animals avoid skunks, although the great horned owl (*Bubo virginianus*) is a notable exception and does not seem to be bothered by the effects of the spray.

**Strangest partnership** A mutually beneficial partnership has evolved between the honey badger (*Mellivora capensis*) and a small bird known as the greater honeyguide (*Indicator indicator*). When the bird locates a bees' nest, it

> *Sea otter mothers have been known to carry their dead cubs around for days before finally letting them go.*

gives a characteristic call (that sounds like a box of matches being shaken) which attracts the attention of the badger. Continuing to call, while the badger grunts and growls in response, the honeyguide leads the way to its find. Then it waits while the badger, which is completely impervious to the inevitable stings, breaks open the nest and devours the grubs and honey; the honeyguide itself feeds on the newly exposed beeswax. Honeyguides sometimes try to lead other mammals in the same way, but the honey badger is normally the only one that follows.

**Most marine** The sea otter (*Enhydra lutris*) of the North Pacific is the only mustelid which is exclusively marine, even though it rarely strays further than about 1 km *0.6 miles* from the shore. It can live out its entire life without ever coming to land – feeding, sleeping and breeding in the water – although some individuals and certain populations (particularly in Alaska, USA) are frequently seen hauled out on shore. Life at sea requires some ingenious adaptations. Before falling asleep, most sea otters wrap themselves in strands of kelp to avoid drifting out to sea during the night; they often sleep with their paws over their eyes. Keeping warm can also be a problem, because they do

> *Sea otters are very buoyant in the water and sometimes have to carry rocks when they dive, in the same way that human divers wear weight belts.*

not have a thick layer of blubber like dolphins and seals; instead, they have a dense fur coat, which provides sufficient insulation by trapping a layer of air between all the hairs (*see Densest fur*). In addition, they are able to maintain their body temperature by having a rapid metabolism (about 2.5 times that of a terrestrial animal of similar size); to sustain this they have a hearty appetite and have to eat more than 25–30 per cent of their body weight every day. The female sea otter is the only member of the family to give birth in water: she seizes her newborn cub and, lying upside down on the water

**With the densest fur of any mammal, the sea otter is well insulated against the cold water in which it spends most of its life.**

**M
A
M
M
A
L
S**

surface, transfers it to her chest where she begins grooming and suckling.

**Densest fur** The sea otter has the densest fur of any mammal, with an average of 110 000–125 000 hairs per cm² *710 000–806 000 per in²* (which adds up to as many as 800 million individual hairs on the pelt of an adult animal). There are 60–80 underfur hairs to every guard hair. Unlike other marine mammals, it has no blubber to provide insulation – but just 1 cm *0.39 in* of this thick fur is as effective an insulator as 4 cm *1.6 in* of fat. At the same time, the fur is waterproof, and it provides the animal with buoyancy in the water. Unfortunately, it is also highly valuable (last century the Russians referred to it as 'soft gold') and in the past has proved to be the sea otter's undoing (*see Most dramatic recovery*).

**Most widespread** The most widespread mustelids are the ermine or stoat (*Mustela erminea*) and the least weasel (*M. nivalis*), both of which inhabit a wide variety of habitats across much of Europe, northern Asia, North America and (stoat only) parts of Greenland.

**Most threatened** The World Conservation Union (IUCN) lists 16 mustelids as known or suspected to be threatened with extinction. The species considered most seriously at risk are the Colombian weasel (*Mustela felipei*) of Colombia and Ecuador; the European mink (*Mustela lutreola*) of France, Romania, Spain, Russia, Georgia, Belarus, Estonia, Latvia and Lithuania (it is believed to have become extinct recently in Finland and Poland); and the black-footed ferret (*Mustela nigripes*), which has recently been reintroduced in the USA. The status of a number of other species has not been evaluated: several are known from only a few skins and skeletons and, in some cases, a handful of sightings in the wild. Habitat destruction, pollution, and hunting and

trapping are the main threats.

A further nine sub-species of mustelids are known or suspected to be threatened with extinction including, in particular, the big thicket hog-nosed skunk (*Conepatus mesoleucus telmalestes*), which may already have disappeared from its home in Texas, USA; the grey-headed tayra (*Eira barbara senex*) of Belize, Guatemala and Mexico; and the Javan yellow-throated marten (*Martes flavigula robinsoni*) of Java, Indonesia.

**Extinctions** There was a species called the sea mink (*Mustela macrodon*), which lived along the shores of the Bay of Fundy and Gulf of Maine, in north-eastern USA and south-eastern Canada, but it was trapped to extinction by the late 19th century. It had a head-body length of about 60–70 cm *24–27½ in* and a tail length of 25 cm *10 in* but very little is known about its behaviour and ecology and, indeed, it was exterminated before scientists had a chance to describe the species. It is believed that the last sea mink was trapped on Campobello Island, New Brunswick, Canada, in 1894.

*Least weasels
have the unpleasant habit
of lining their dens with the
fur of mice to keep their
infants warm during the
winter.*

**Most dramatic recovery** Two mustelids have been very close to extinction – one actually disappeared altogether in the wild – but were saved at the last moment by vigorous conservation efforts. The sea otter (*Enhydra lutris*) was hunted relentlessly by fur traders in the 18th and 19th centuries, but has made a dramatic recovery in many parts of its range; and the black-footed ferret (*Mustela nigripes*) has survived thanks to a successful captive breeding programme, and is now being reintroduced to some of its former haunts.

It is estimated that up to 1 million sea otters were killed for their valuable pelts in the period 1740–1911, mainly by Russian, American and European fur-trappers. By the time an international treaty was signed for their protection, in 1911, there were no more than 13 remnant colonies left, scattered around the North Pacific. These contained a total of 1000–2000 survivors. Several of the colonies dwindled to extinction soon afterwards but, with a

relaxation of the hunting pressure and the introduction of legal protection, others soon began to recover. Now the species has reoccupied more than half its historical range in North America and Russia, although it is still absent from a number of former strongholds. Current numbers are estimated to be: 100 000–150 000 in Alaska, 10 500–12 500 in the western Pacific, 350 in British Columbia, over 200 in Washington and about 1400 in California. Sea otters still face a great many threats, including net entanglement, illegal hunting and oil pollution, but their future now looks more secure than it has done for many years.

The North American black-footed ferret feeds exclusively on prairie dogs, burrowing members of the squirrel family that are regarded as serious agricultural pests. Following an enormous poisoning campaign by farmers and ranchers, the ferret population dwindled to dangerously low numbers and only a handful of animals survived – all in the western state of Wyoming, USA. The species was considered rare by 1970 and feared extinct just 10 years later. Then, on 25 Sep 1981, a male black-footed ferret was killed by a dog near the town of Meeteetse, Wyoming, USA. Excited biologists descended on the town and discovered a population of nearly 60 ferrets living in the area. The numbers increased to at least 129 by 1984, but then disaster struck: in 1985 the animals suddenly began to die from canine distemper. In a last-ditch effort to save the ferret from extinction, 18 survivors were taken into captivity to form the basis of a captive-breeding programme. It was a good move because, within a year, the species had become extinct in the wild. Apart from a few inevitable setbacks, it has done well in captivity and, in 1991, the first of a new generation of black-footed ferrets was reintroduced to one of their former haunts in Wyoming. The species is not saved yet, but now there are an estimated 40 back in the wild and more than about 380 in captivity (April 1995). So far, the programme has cost more than US$3 million.

*Stoats have been seen
'dancing' (leaping up and
down and chasing their tails)
to elicit the curiosity of
rabbits and other prey animals;
as soon as their audience is
off guard, they move in for
the kill.*

# PANGOLINS

## Pholidota

7 species (otherwise known as scaly anteaters):
4 in sub-Saharan Africa and 3 in Asia.

*When alarmed, pangolins curl up into such a tight ball that they are practically impossible to unroll.*

**Largest** The giant ground pangolin (*Manis gigantea*), which lives in parts of sub-Saharan Africa, has a head-body length of 80–90 cm *31½–35½ in*; a tail length of 65–80 cm *25½–31½ in*; and a weight of 25–33 kg *55–72¾ lb*. The male is much larger than the female.

**Smallest** The long-tailed pangolin (*Manis tetradactyla*), which lives in parts of sub-Saharan Africa, has a head-body length of 30–35 cm *11.8–13.8 in*; a tail length of 50–60 cm *19.7–23.6 in*; and a weight of 1.2–3 kg *2 lb 10 oz–6 lb 10 oz*.

The female is much smaller than the male.

**Scales** Pangolins are the only mammals to have an armour of horny, overlapping scales (other armoured mammals are protected by thickened skin or plates of bone with a horny covering). At first glance, the scales – which grow from the thick underlying skin – make them appear more reptilian than mammalian. They protect every part of the body except the underside and the inner surfaces of the limbs, and are shed and replaced individually.

**Longest tongue** The long tongue of the giant ground pangolin (*Manis gigantea*) can be extended 36–40 cm *14–15¾ in* beyond the end of the snout, and is some 70 cm *27½ in* in total length. Coiled up inside the animal's mouth when at rest, it has muscular roots that pass down through the chest cavity and anchor to the pelvis. It is flicked in and out to catch the pangolin's favourite food – ants and termites.

**Longest tail** The long-tailed pangolin (*Manis tetradactyla*) has no fewer than 46–47 vertebrae in its tail, which is more than in any other mammal.

# PIGS & PECCARIES

*While adult pigs are uniform in colour, the young of many species are beautifully striped.*

## Suidae & Tayassuidae

10 species of pig (including the domestic pig and the extinct Vietnam warty pig) and 3 species of peccary.

Giant forest hog, Aberdare National Park, Kenya: the largest of the pigs and peccaries.

**Largest** The largest of the pigs and peccaries is the giant forest hog (*Hylochoerus meinertzhageni*), which lives in scattered populations across central and parts of west and east Africa. It has a head-body length of 1.3–2.1 m *51–83 in*; a tail length of 30–45 cm *12–17¾ in*; a shoulder height of 85–105 cm *33½–41¼ in*; and a weight of 130–275 kg *287–606 lb*. The wild boar (*Sus scrofa*) and the Javan warty pig (*Sus verrucosus*) can attain maximum weights of 200 kg *441 lb* and 185 kg *408 lb* respectively.

**Largest domestic** The heaviest domestic pig (*Sus domesticus*) ever recorded was a Poland-China hog named *Big Bill*, weighing 1157.5 kg *2552 lb* just before being put down after accidentally breaking a leg en route to the Chicago World Fair for exhibition in 1933. His other statistics included a height of 1.52 m *5 ft* at the shoulder and a length of 2.74 m *9 ft*.

**Smallest** The smallest of the pigs and peccaries is the pygmy hog (*Sus salvanius*), which used to be fairly wide-

**The babirusa has the strangest tusks of all pigs: two of the four actually pierce the flesh and grow up through the top of the animal's muzzle.**

spread in the foothills of the Himalayas but today survives only in Assam, India (it is thought to be extinct in Bhutan and Nepal). It has a head-body length of 50–65 cm *20–25½ in*; a tail length of 3 cm *1.2 in*; a shoulder height of 25–30 cm *9.8–11.8 in*; and a weight of 6–10 kg *13¼–22 lb*.

**Smallest domestic** The smallest breed of domestic pig (*Sus domesticus*) is the Mini Maialino, developed by Stefano Morini of St Golo d'Enza, Italy, after 10 years' experimentation with Vietnamese pot-bellied pigs. The piglets weigh 400 g *14 oz* at birth and 9 kg *20 lb* at maturity.

**Most threatened** The World Conservation Union (IUCN) lists five different pigs and peccaries as threatened with extinction: the babirusa (*Babyrousa babyrussa*), of the Indonesian islands of Buru, Sula, Sulawesi and Togian; the Visayan warty pig (*Sus cebifrons*), of the Philippine islands of Cebu and Negros; the pygmy hog (*Sus salvanius*), living in the foothills of the Himalayas in India (may already be extinct in Bhutan and Nepal); the Javan warty pig (*Sus verrucosus*), of Bawean Island and Java, Indonesia; and the Chacoan peccary (*Catagonus wagneri*), of Bolivia, Paraguay and Argentina. The many threats

being faced by wild pigs and peccaries include habitat loss, human disturbance, hunting and, in some cases, possibly livestock diseases.

A further seven sub-species are considered to be threatened, including the Somali warthog (*Phacochoerus aethiopicus delameri*), of Kenya and Somalia; the western forest hog (*Hylochoerus meinertzhageni ivoriensis*), of west Africa; and the Ryukyu Islands wild pig (*Sus scrofa riukiuanus*), of the Ryukyu Islands, Japan.

**Extinctions** It is believed that the Vietnam warty pig (*Sus bucculentus*), known only from Vietnam, is now extinct. A sub-species of the common warthog (*Phacochoerus aethiopicus*), the Cape warthog (*Phacochoerus a. aethiopicus*), is also extinct; it lived in Cape Province, South Africa.

**Longest absence** The Chacoan peccary (*Catagonus wagneri*) was thought to have become extinct during the last Ice Age, some 10000 years ago, and for many years was known only from the fossil record. Since its discovery in 1930, there had been no evidence for its existence later than the Pleistocene (2 million to 10000 years ago). But it was unexpectedly discovered, in 1975, living in the dry thorn forest of the Gran Chaco region of western Paraguay. Dr Ralph Wetzel and his colleagues at Connecticut University discovered that local inhabitants recognized the existence of three species of peccary (only two were known at the time) and, after detailed enquiries, succeeded in obtaining some skulls. Wetzel compared his skulls with

the prehistoric peccary, which had already been named *Platygonus wagneri*, and realized that they belonged to one and the same species. However, he concluded that it was really more akin to members of the genus *Catagonus* than *Platygonus*, and it was later renamed.

The Chacoan peccary has subsequently been found in the Gran Chaco region of northern Argentina and southeastern Bolivia as well. Sadly, since its discovery, its numbers have plummeted due to overhunting, habitat destruction and possibly disease. There may be no more than a few thousand left, mainly in small, widely dispersed populations.

The world's scientists were shocked to discover some years later that, unbeknown to them, the Chacoan peccary's hide had routinely been used by New York furriers to trim hats and coats.

**Country with most domestic pigs** China was the world's largest pig farming nation in 1993 (the latest year for which information is available), with an estimated 384.2 million from a worldwide total of 754.3 million head.

**Strangest tusks** Instead of growing out of the side of the mouth and over the lips, as they do in all other wild pigs, two of the four tusks of the babirusa (*Babyrousa babyrussa*) pierce the flesh and grow up through the top of the animal's muzzle, then curve backward towards the forehead. The babirusa's name comes from a native word meaning 'pig-deer', referring to the fact that the tusks look more like the antlers of a deer than the tusks of a pig.

# PRIMATES

### Primates

*c.* 200 species, including lemurs, lorises, tarsiers, marmosets, monkeys, gibbons, apes.

**Earliest** The first known primate belonged to the genus *Purgatorius*, and was similar in appearance to modern tree shrews of the order Scandentia (*see p.93*). First discovered alongside dinosaur remains as a single molar tooth from Purgatory Hill, eastern Montana, USA, *Purgatorius* is known from North America and Europe and dates from the end of the Cretaceous period, some 65 million years ago. It had an estimated length of only 10 cm *3.9 in* and probably fed on small invertebrates.

*Australopithecus*, the first genus in the hominid or early human family, emerged in Africa more than 4.5 million years ago, during the Pliocene. There were several different species, frequently referred to as the 'southern apes', and all of them resembled apes as much as they resembled humans. They were bipedal, and stood almost upright, but were only 1.2 m *47 in* in height and had relatively small brains.

The first species in the human genus was *Homo habilis* (meaning 'handy man'), which appeared in Africa a little under 3 million years ago; it had a noticeably larger brain than *Australopithecus*, and built rough shelters and shaped crude stone tools. Then came *Homo erectus* ('upright man'), which appeared about 1.5 million years ago and moved out of Africa into Europe and Asia; this species lived in camps, made use of fire and probably had some form of language. An early form of *Homo sapiens* ('wise man') first appeared about 300 000 years ago, but fully modern humans (*Homo sapiens sapiens*) date from only about 30–40 000 years ago. Throughout this entire period of hominid evolution, there were two major trends: an increase in height and an increase in brain size (from some 500 cm³ *30½ in³* in volume in *Australopithecus* to approximately 1500 cm³ *91½ in³* in modern humans).

The earliest direct evidence of hominids walking bipedally is a trail of fossil footprints at Laetoli, north-west Tanzania. First excavated in 1977, the footprints were preserved in volcanic ash more than 3.5 million years ago. They run for 27 m *88½ ft* and consist of two parallel trails: one evidently made by a single individual and the other probably by two individuals (thought to have been an adult and a child).

**Largest** The gorilla (*Gorilla gorilla*) is the largest of all the primates, although many exaggerated reports over the years have given a false impression of its large size. It has a bipedal standing height (measured from the crown of the head to the base of the heels) of 1.4–1.8 m *4 ft 7 in–5 ft 11 in* (male) and 1.25–1.5 m *4 ft 1 in–4 ft 11 in* (female); a chest circumference of 1.25–1.75 m *49¼–69 in* (male) and 95–128 cm *37½–50½ in* (female); and an average weight of 135–175 kg *298–386 lb* (male) and 68–114 kg *150–251 lb* (female). There are three subspecies: the western lowland gorilla (*G. g. gorilla*) of west central Africa, which is the smallest (albeit by a small margin); the very rare mountain gorilla (*G. g. beringei*) of Rwanda, Zaïre and Uganda; and the eastern lowland gorilla (*G. g. graueri*) of eastern Zaïre, which is the largest.

The record authenticated size in the wild is a standing height of 1.95 m *6 ft 5 in*; an armspan of 2.7 m *8 ft 10 in*; and a weight of 219 kg *483 lb* for a male eastern lowland gorilla (considered to be a mountain gorilla at the time) collected by Commandant E Hubert and Dr Serge Freckhof in the Tchibinda Forest, northern Kivu province, Zaïre (for-merly Belgian Congo), on 16 May 1938. There is also an unconfirmed (but generally accepted) report of a male eastern lowland gorilla (reported as a mountain gorilla) shot by Commander Attilio Gatti, in 1932, for the Royal Museum of Natural History, Florence, Italy. Also found in the Tchibinda Forest, it reputedly had a standing height of 2.06 m *6¾ ft* and weighed 218.6 kg *482 lb*.

In captivity, gorillas tend to put on weight through lack of exercise, and

*A fully mature male gorilla (13–15 years old) is known as a silverback, because of a silvery-white 'saddle' of fur which appears on his back, contrasting with the black hair on the rest of his body.*

they can be quite obese. The heaviest on record is a male of uncertain sub-species named *N'gagi*, held at San Diego Zoo, California, USA, from 5 Oct 1931. Weighing 310 kg *683½ lb* at his heaviest in 1943, he had a bipedal standing height of 1.72 m *5 ft 7¾ in* and a record-breaking chest measurement of 1.98 m *78 in*. *N'gagi* weighed 289 kg *636 lb* at the time of his death on 12 Jan 1944. There have been several much-publicized claims of heavier gorillas, particularly by circuses, but these appear to have been dreamt up as publicity stunts rather than being factual.

The largest species of monkey is the mandrill (*Mandrillus sphinx*) of equatorial west Africa. The greatest reliable weight recorded is 54 kg *119 lb* for a captive male, but an unconfirmed weight of 59 kg *130 lb* has been reported (compared with an average weight of 25 kg *55 lb*). There is a high degree of sexual dimorphism and adult females are about half the size of males.

**Largest tree-living mammal** The orang utan (*Pongo pygmaeus*), surviving only on the south-east Asian islands of Borneo and Sumatra, is the largest predominantly tree-living mammal on Earth. It has an average bipedal standing height (measured from the crown of the head to the base of the heels) of 1.15 m *45¼ in* (female) and 1.37 m *54 in* (male) and a weight of 60–90 kg *132–198 lb* (male) and 30–50 kg *66–110 lb* (female). There is a record of an unusually large male, in Borneo, with a height of 1.8 m *6 ft*; captive animals sometimes grow considerably heavier, with a record of 188 kg *415 lb*. The only truly arboreal ape, it climbs slowly and deliberately, often with all four limbs stretched out in different directions to spread the weight.

Gorillas (*Gorilla gorilla*) are largely terrestrial. The youngsters climb regularly, and even the big silverbacks clamber into the trees to collect fruit, but gorilla troops always travel long distances on the ground.

**Largest prehistoric** The largest primate ever known to have lived on Earth was the extinct hominid *Gigantopithecus* of the middle Pleistocene, in what is now northern Vietnam and southern China. From the only remains discovered to date (three partial lower jaws and more than 1000 teeth), it has been estimated that males stood about 2.74 m *9 ft* tall and weighed some 272 kg *600 lb*. However, this size will remain conjecture until further fossil evidence is uncovered, since there is a possibility that *Gigantopithecus* had a disproportionately large head, jaws and teeth in relation to its body size.

**M
A
M
M
A
L
S**

**Smallest** The world's smallest primate is a newly discovered species, the western rufous mouse lemur (*Microcebus myoxinus*), which lives in western Madagascar. First described around 200 years ago, it was thought to have become extinct until its rediscovery in 1993. Not much larger than an overweight mouse, it has a head-body length of 6.2 cm *2.4 in*; a tail length of 13.6 cm *5.4 in*; and a weight of 24.5–38 g *0.87–1.34 oz*. Until this discovery the eastern rufous mouse lemur (*Microcebus rufus*), which is found in the eastern rainforests of Madagascar, was always considered to be the smallest. It has a head-body length of 10.1–12.5 cm *4–4.9 in*; a tail length of 12.8–15 cm *5–5.9 in*; and a weight of 45–90 g *1.6–3.2 oz*.

The closest runners-up are: the grey mouse lemur (*Microcebus murinus*) of western and southern Madagascar; the dwarf bushbaby or Demidoff's galago (*Galago demidovii*) of west, central and east Africa; and the recently rediscovered hairy-eared dwarf lemur (*Allocebus trichotis*) of northern Madagascar.

**Longest armspan** The longest armspan known for any non-human primate is a record-breaking 2.79 m *9 ft 2 in* for a male mountain gorilla (*Gorilla gorilla beringei*) collected by the Percy Sladen Expedition to northern Cameroon in 1932–3.

All apes, except humans, have exceptionally long arms. The longest in relation to body length are found in the gibbons (genus *Hylobates*) and the orang utan (*Pongo pygmaeus*). The orang utan is the record holder, with an armspan of up to 2.5 m *8 ft 2 in* or possibly even 3 m *9 ft 10 in* (nearly three times the head-body length of up to 97 cm *3 ft 2 in*). The siamang (*H. syndactylus*) is a close runner-up, with an armspan of up to 1.5 m *59 in* (1.7 times the maximum head-body length of 90 cm *35½ in*).

It was once believed that long arms are an adaptation for brachiating (swinging by the arms under branches) but there is now a more down-to-earth hypothesis. It has been suggested that

**Largest of all the primates, the gorilla can attain a standing height of up to 1.95 m *6 ft 5 in* and an impressive chest measurement of as much as 1.98 m *78 in*.**

great apes are lazy animals. They like to sit amongst their favourite food plants and pull them in with as little effort as possible: it may be that long arms simply enable them to reach a wider area without wasting energy.

**Longest nose** The proboscis monkey (*Nasalis larvatus*), which lives in the riverine and mangrove forests of Borneo, is named for its huge, pendulous nose. Shaped rather like a tongue, it grows until maturity and eventually droops over the mouth and chin. In elderly animals, it can reach a maximum length of 17.5 cm *7 in* (compared with a head-body length of 66–76 cm *26–30 in*). The precise function of the nose is uncertain. It has often been suggested that it may serve as a resonating

organ in the production of the male's long, drawn-out honking call (it straightens out during calling), but it is more likely to be some kind of visual signal for sexual selection. Young proboscis monkeys have fairly long, rigid noses, which point forward; in females, their noses simply stop growing when the monkeys reach maturity.

**Most colourful** The male mandrill (*Mandrillus sphinx*), a kind of forest baboon from the rainforests of west Africa, is the most colourful mammal in the world. It has an olive-brown coat with pale yellowish underparts; yellowish-orange side whiskers; a whitish moustache and goatee beard; a red and blue naked rump; pink ears; a brilliant red, purple, white and blue face; a black nose; and even a red penis and blue scrotum. All the skin colours become more pronounced when the mandrill gets excited. Females and youngsters are similarly coloured, but much duller in comparison with the male.

**Oldest** Primates tend to have long lifespans compared with many other mammals. The greatest irrefutable age recorded for a non-human primate is 59 years 5 months for a chimpanzee (*Pan troglodytes*) named *Gamma*, who was born at the Yerkes Primate Research Center in Florida, USA, in September 1932, and died of natural causes at the Atlanta, Georgia, branch of the Yerkes Center on 19 Feb 1992.

Several other chimpanzees have been known to live to their mid-50s and beyond. A male named *Cheeta*, who starred with Johnny Weissmuller in a string of Tarzan movies, is almost 59 years old and still sharing the occasional drink and cigarette with his trainer. Another male, named *Jimmy*, lived to the age of 55 years 6 months; he died at his home in Seneca Zoo, Rochester, New York, USA, on 17 Sep 1985.

A male orang utan (*Pongo pygmaeus*) named *Guas*, who died in Philadelphia Zoological Garden, Pennsylvania, USA, on 9 Feb 1977, is reported to have reached an age of about 59 years; he was at least 13 years old on his arrival at the zoo on 1 May 1931. An old silverback mountain gorilla (*Gorilla gorilla beringei*), named *Beethoven*, once lived in the Virunga Volcanoes region straddling the international borders of Zaïre, Rwanda and Uganda, and died in 1985 at an estimated age of late 40s/early 50s.

The world's oldest monkey, a male white-throated capuchin (*Cebus capucinus*) called *Bobo*, died on 10 Jul 1988 aged 53 years, following complications related to a stroke. He was

originally imported from South America and donated to the Mesker Park Zoo in Evansville, Indiana, USA, on 1 Jan 1935. When the zoo disbanded its monkey colony, he was given to Dr Raymond T. Bartus, founder of the Geriatric Research Programme at Lederle Laboratories, American Cyanamid Co., Pearl River, New York, USA, and lived there from 31 Oct 1981 until his death.

**Best swimmer** The most competent swimmer among the primates is probably the proboscis monkey (*Nasalis larvatus*), which is usually found near freshwater in the lowland rainforests and mangrove swamps of Borneo. It takes to the water readily, especially when feeling threatened and trying to escape danger, and swims both on the surface and underwater. Entire groups have been seen diving out of the trees from heights of up to 16 m *52½ ft*.

Several other primates are renowned for their swimming. Few swim in the sea, but Japanese macaques (*Macaca fuscata*) living on Koshima Islet, in the extreme south of Japan, are a notable exception. They learnt to swim after years of cleaning sweet potatoes at the water's edge (*see Cultural transmission*) and now frequently enter the sea for other reasons. They find it refreshing in the hot summer months and the juveniles, in particular, simply enjoy leaping off rocks, diving underwater for seaweed, and splashing about.

**Closest relative** The relationship between humans and all other apes is a much-studied and highly controversial subject. There are many who would like to place us in entirely separate families, preferably ones which separated on the evolutionary tree many millions of years ago, but this has more to do with vanity than biology. The fact is that humans are apes: there is no natural category that includes chimpanzees (*Pan troglodytes*), bonobos or pygmy chimpanzees (*Pan paniscus*), gorillas (*Gorilla gorilla*) and orang utans (*Pongo pygmaeus*), but excludes humans. We *are* great apes.

Our closest relatives are the chimpanzee and bonobo. Indeed, the relationship is so close that, genetically, we are almost identical and share 98.4

> *Gorillas and chimpanzees have a cluster of sweat glands under their arms and, like humans after strenuous exercise, tend to have smelly armpits.*

**M
A
M
M
A
L
S**

*A captive gorilla in the United States, named Koko, had a pet kitten to which she was totally devoted; when the kitten was hit by a car and died, Koko grieved intensely.*

per cent of our genes. Furthermore, gorillas, chimpanzees and bonobos are more closely related to humans than they are to orang utans. This is not surprising, since orangs branched off the evolutionary tree about 12.5 million years ago – more than 6 million years before the human and African ape lines parted company. It is uncertain whether the gorilla, chimpanzee and human lines diverged at the same time or, as many experts now believe, the gorilla line split off first. Biochemical and morphological studies certainly seem to support the theory that the chimpanzee and bonobo are more closely related to humans than they are to gorillas.

Molecular evidence suggests that the ancestor we share in common with chimpanzees lived, in Africa, some 5–7 million years ago. This is equivalent to half a million generations ago, which is not long by evolutionary standards. Richard Dawkins, author of *The Selfish Gene* and *The Blind Watchmaker*, has calculated an interesting way of illustrating this with the help of an imaginary human chain. If a girl stands with her left hand holding the right hand of her mother, who in turn is holding the right hand of her mother, who in turn is holding the right hand of *her* mother, and so on in a long chain, how far would the chain have to go to reach this common ancestor? The answer, allowing for about 90 cm *3 ft* per person, is an astoundingly short 480 km *300 miles*.

**Learning behaviour** There are numerous examples of primates learning different forms of behaviour by observing and imitating one another, and then retaining the knowledge for future use. There is very little evidence to suggest active teaching: in most cases, young animals learn by passive observation of adults, followed by trial and error, rather than by direct instruction. The two best-known examples of learning are potato-washing in Japanese macaques (*Macaca fuscata*), which provided the first evidence for cultural transmission of behaviour in a nonhuman species; and nut-cracking in chimpanzees (*Pan troglodytes*), which provided the first evidence for behav-

ioural techniques being passed from one group or community to another.

Biologists studying a troop of Japanese macaques on Koshima Islet, in the extreme south of Japan, began to provide the animals with frequent supplies of sweet potatoes. The potatoes were distributed on a beach and, before eating them, the macaques always rubbed off the worst of the sand with their hands. The food must still have been rather gritty to eat until, in September 1953, a 2-year-old female named *Imo* dipped a potato into a stream that ran across the beach – and immediately had a clean potato. Other animals in the group readily adopted the new behaviour and, by 1962, all but the older adults were potato-washers. Then they discovered that sweet potatoes washed in salty seawater tasted better than those washed in freshwater and, within a few years, most members of the troop were picking up armfuls of potatoes and carrying them down to the sea.

During a recent study of chimpanzees in west Africa, a 31-year-old female named *Yo* changed home, from her birth group in the Ivory Coast to a new one 10 km *6¼ miles* away across the border in Guinea. Her new group was already using a special technique to crack open almond-shaped oil palm nuts, using stones as a hammer and anvil. But when biologists presented them with some spherical coula nuts, which they had not encountered before, they did not know how to adapt this technique to crack them open. *Yo*, who was already familiar with coula nuts from her time in the Ivory Coast, immediately placed one on her stone anvil and cracked it open ready to eat. Within a matter of days, two youngsters in the group (a 5-year-old female and a 6-year-old male) had learned the new technique and soon acquired a taste for the coula nuts.

**Most proficient tool-user** Orang utans (*Pongo pygmaeus*), black-capped capuchin monkeys (*Cebus apella*) and several other primates are known to use simple tools. However, most records are of them doing so in captivity and, in many cases, similar behaviour has not been observed in the wild. But a major exception is the chimpanzee (*Pan troglodytes*), which is by far the most proficient non-human tooluser, both in the wild and in captivity.

No fewer than 24 out of 32 known wild chimpanzee groups use tools, in at least 20 different ways (as a general rule, the more demanding the environment the more tools they use). They use stone hammers and anvils to crack open nuts; twigs as toothpicks; a handful of chewed-up leaves to form a rough

sponge for soaking up water in otherwise inaccessible tree hollows; and even stones as missiles against predators such as leopards. One individual learned that banging empty water cans together made his aggressive display more effective and, quite recently, others have been observed using a leaf 'pestle' and a fibre 'sponge' to get sap from oil palms. There is no evidence yet of them using tools to create new tools (such as chipping a stone hammer with another stone) but they do alter their tools to fit the task; for example, they bite thin, spindly twigs to a required length, peel off the bark, strip the leaves, fray one end, and then use them to fish for termites in termite mounds.

Gorillas have very manipulative hands, and are impressively skilful at opening and eating the palatable parts of many different plants, but do not appear to use tools in the wild.

*Chimpanzees are truly omnivorous and eat a wide variety of food from leaves to prey as large as colobus monkeys and wild pigs; some troops split up into well-organized groups for a hunt, and the meat is shared out among all the participants.*

**Most intelligent** Intelligence is a difficult concept to measure in animals, not least because many recognized psychological tests require the use of hands (which some highly intelligent animals, such as dolphins, do not possess); this means that different species are better at some tasks than others simply because of their adaptations to certain ways of life. But it is generally considered that the great apes are the most intelligent non-human animals. They are quick learners; they can use logic and insight to solve complicated tasks and puzzles; and they can be trained to use symbols or sign language to communicate, albeit in a rudimentary way.

It has not been possible to teach orang utans (*Pongo pygmaeus*), gorillas (*Gorilla gorilla*) or chimpanzees (*Pan troglodytes*) how to speak, because they do not have the necessary vocal apparatus. But attempts to teach them sign language have been more successful. Chimpanzees, in particular, can use abstract terms such as 'like' and 'different', but how far these indicate capacity for thought or language is still open to question.

the gorilla (*Gorilla gorilla*), 260–270 days in the orang utan (*Pongo pygmaeus*), and 250–285 days in humans.

**Shortest gestation period** The shortest gestation period known for any primate is 54–68 days, a record held jointly by the rufous mouse lemur (*Microcebus rufus*) and the grey mouse lemur (*M. murinus*). Even this is long compared with other similar-sized mammals (22–24 days in the slightly smaller common dormouse, for example).

**Strangest** There are a number of strange-looking primates: for example, the red uakari (*Cacajao rubicundus*), with its bare, bright red face; the long, droopy-nosed male proboscis monkey (*Nasalis larvatus*); the emperor tamarin (*Saguinus imperator*), with its enormous white moustache; and the male orang utan (*Pongo pygmaeus*), with its rather splendid 'face mask'. But the rare and elusive aye-aye (*Daubentonia madagascariensis*) of Madagascar is probably the strangest of them all. Once described as having been assembled from bits of other animals, it looks like a large cat with a bat's ears, a beaver's continuously growing incisor teeth, an owl's large eyes, a squirrel's bushy tail, and a middle finger resembling a long, dead twig. In fact, it is a nocturnal lemur (the only member of the family Daubentoniidae) and is the largest nocturnal primate in the world (head-body length 36–44 cm *14¼–17¼ in* and tail length 50–60 cm *19¾–23½ in*).

*In one sub-species of chimpanzee, living in central Africa, the adults go bald on the crown: males in a triangle, narrowing back from the forehead, and females totally.*

**Noisiest** Howler monkeys (*Alouatta* sp) of Central and South America are among the noisiest terrestrial animals in the world. They have greatly enlarged lower jaws, accommodating an egg-shaped hyoid bone at the top of the windpipe that helps to reverberate the sound of their roaring and growling calls. This chamber is larger in the male, whose call is consequently much louder and deeper. It is difficult to quantify the loudness of the call – and many different figures have been published – but, once in full voice, a male can be heard at least 3 km *1.9 miles* away through the jungle and 5 km *3.1 miles* away across water. Howling sessions take place at dawn and are a form of territorial

**Chimpanzees are our closest relatives – so close, in fact, that 98.4 per cent of our genes are the same.**

Evolutionary biologists have long pointed to the human brain's much larger frontal lobe as evidence of our superior skills of creative thinking and language. But recent research shows that it does not differ strikingly from other primates: the frontal lobe amounts to 31.7 per cent of a gorilla's brain, 36.1 per cent of a chimpanzee's brain, and 36.8 per cent of a human's. There are more subtle differences, though; for example, within the frontal lobe, humans have a significantly larger 'white body', a structure from which nerve fibres begin to fan out and make contact with other parts of the brain.

**Longest gestation period** Primates have remarkably long gestation periods. The longest are found in the apes: about 220–245 days in the gibbons (genus *Hylobates*), 230–240 days in both the chimpanzee (*Pan troglodytes*) and bonobo (*Pan paniscus*), 250–270 days in

**There are a number of strange-looking primates, but the aye-aye is probably the strangest of them all: it appears to have been assembled from bits of other animals.**

---

defence, to keep neighbouring troops well spaced. From a distance, different species of howler monkey can be recognized by their howls: for example, mantled howlers (*A. palliata*) sound like a cheering crowd in a football stadium, while red howlers (*A. seniculus*) resemble the crashing of surf on a distant shore.

**Self-healing** A number of primates are known to eat food that, as well as being nutritious, also has medicinal properties. But it is likely that few of them realize the significance of what they are doing. This does not seem to be true of chimpanzees (*Pan troglodytes*), which are the only animals other than humans known to be able to link consumption of a particular food source with relief from sickness or pain. There is strong evidence from many parts of tropical Africa that they treat themselves for a range of ailments, seeking out certain leaves and seeds specifically for their medicinal properties. Indeed, they frequently select the same

plants that local people use for similar complaints, and may even know as much about herbal medicine.

The best-known example comes from a study of chimpanzees in the Gombe Stream National Park, Tanzania, by famous chimp watcher Jane Goodall and Richard Wrangham, professor of anthropology at Harvard University. It was discovered that the animals use a variety of medicinal plants but, in particular, they seek out three species in the genus *Aspilia*. The young leaves of these tall but rather nondescript members of the sunflower family contain high concentrations of a bright red oil called thiarubrine-A, which is known to be a potent antibiotic and is also an effective antifungal and deworming agent; among its other properties, it is even more potent than the anti-cancer drug vinblastine in *in vitro* toxicity tests. There is no conclusive evidence that the chimpanzees use the plants for medicinal purposes, but there is a great deal of circumstantial evidence. Normally, when they are feeding, chimpanzees stuff leaves into their mouths as fast as they can; but they select the *Aspilia* leaves very carefully, and at different times of day when the chemistry of the plants varies. They also roll them around in their mouths and swallow them whole, instead of chewing and swallowing as usual. It is unlikely that the leaves are ingested

either for food or to increase fibre intake – since they are passed through the gut undigested – but they are believed to release significant amounts of chemicals before passing out the other end. Perhaps most significant of all, the local Tongwe people make a special tea out of *Aspilia* leaves to treat stomach disorders and a variety of external ailments such as wounds and burns. Scientists are now studying the same plants in the hope that they may prove useful to western medicine but, significantly, the chimpanzees found them first.

The first time a chimpanzee's recovery from an illness could be linked directly to its self-medication was in Mahale Mountains National Park, Tanzania, in the late 1980s. One day, a female being observed by primatologists was noticeably lethargic and clearly suffering from bad diarrhoea. She searched for a plant called *Vernonia amygdalina*, sucked out

---

*The bushbaby-like tarsier has larger eyes than any other mammal of a similar size; for comparison, on a human they would be the size of grapefruits.*

the bitter-tasting juice from the shoots, and then rested in a tree while her companions stayed nearby. Within 24 hours, she was back in the swing of things and seemed to be fully recovered.

**Echolocation** The aye-aye (*Daubentonia madagascariensis*) is the only primate suspected of using a simple form of echolocation to find its food. When it is searching for insect larvae, hidden in hollow cavities beneath the surface of tree trunks and branches, studies have shown that it does not use sight, hearing or smell. It taps the surface of the wood with its long, twig-like middle finger and then apparently listens with its extra-large ears for any change in the returning echoes. The system, which has been dubbed 'percussive foraging', is so efficient that the aye-aye can detect cavities as deep as 2 cm ¾ in below the surface and can even tell if they contain insect larvae. Whether it is listening only for reverberations inside the cavities, or whether it is aided by the sudden rustling of larvae disturbed by all the tapping, is unclear. But once it has located a grub, it quickly uses its incisor teeth to gnaw into the cavity, and then its elongated finger to probe and scoop.

Aye-ayes seem to fill a remarkably similar niche to woodpeckers, which also bore through wood (with their beaks) and probe cavities beneath the surface for insect larvae (with their long tongues). Interestingly, Madagascar is devoid of woodpeckers and it may be that aye-ayes have evolved to fill the ecological niche they occupy in other parts of the world.

**Most dangerous** Before gorillas (*Gorilla gorilla*) were studied in the wild, they had a reputation as highly dangerous and savage animals. But in recent years, almost by way of an apology, there has been a tendency to portray them as harmless, gentle giants. The truth is somewhere in between: for much of the time, they are peaceful family animals, and yet irate silverbacks are potentially the most dangerous of all the primates. When defending their families, they rush towards intruders and emit ear-shattering roars; it is these spectacular displays of strength that gave them their legendary reputation. But, thanks to the strong nerves of field biologists and park rangers, it is now known that the vast majority of charges are bluff. Unfortunately, it is not always easy to distinguish between bluff and outright attack until it is too late, but only a small number end with the gorilla delivering a massive thump and, perhaps, a bite.

**Northernmost population** Japanese macaques or snow monkeys (*Macaca fuscata*) living in a mountainous area of central Honshu, Japan, known as Jigokudani, form the northernmost population of any living species of non-human primate. During the winter, temperatures drop to at least −15°C 5°F, and the ground is covered in snow. But the macaques in this particular region have learned to sit in naturally heated springs to keep warm. The water temperature can be as high as 43°C 109°F and they test it first, with a few tentative splashes, before easing themselves into the warmth. Whole troops of snow monkeys can often be seen taking hot baths together, with only

**One of the noisiest animals in the world: a howler monkey having a good howl in the Amazon jungle, Brazil.**

**MAMMALS**

their heads poking out of the water (sometimes with several centimetres of snow and ice balanced on top). They always leave the springs in time to dry off properly before nightfall, otherwise they might freeze to death when they sleep.

**Most arid habitat** In 1986 a troop of 15 chacma baboons (*Papio cynocephalus ursinus*) was discovered living in the most arid environment known to be inhabited by any non-human primate. Conrad Brain of the Desert Ecological Research Unit of Namibia found the animals in the lower reaches of the Kuiseb River Canyon, in the heart of the Namib Desert, southern Africa, and has been studying them ever since. The animals survive in an area where day-time temperatures frequently reach 45°C *113°F* and where there is no surface water for about 8 months of the year. The Namib Desert annually receives about 27 mm *1 in* of rain, and the Kuiseb river usually runs for only a few weeks between December and March.

**Baboons are capable of living in more arid environments than any other non-human primate.**

The pools left by the passing flood dry quickly under the fierce sun and, for the remainder of the year, the only sources of drinking water are a tiny seep from a crack high up in the wall of the canyon and excavations in the sand made by gemsbok and mountain zebra. These sources are meagre, forcing the baboons to drink from them one at a time, and they frequently fail towards the end of the dry season. Chacma baboons studied in other parts of Africa need to drink daily, but this particular troop regularly goes without water for more than a week at a time. The record was in the last months of 1992, when they were unable to drink for 116 days; they obtained some moisture from wild figs, but even these had come to an end by the time the floods eventually arrived. The baboons were so relieved to see the newly formed river that they drank almost continuously, and even swam.

**Most species** Brazil is home to more different primates than any other country in the world. It has no fewer than 68 known species, accounting for about 34 per cent of the world total.

**Only European primate** The only non-human primate found in Europe is the so-called barbary 'ape' (*Macaca sylvanus*) which, despite its name, is a kind of tailless macaque. Native to northern Algeria and Morocco, it was imported to the Rock of Gibraltar, on the southern coast of Spain, in the early 1740s for game hunting by the British garrison. A small, free-living colony has lived there ever since. The animals have been cared for and protected by the British Army since 1915, thanks to a legend claiming that when the apes cease to live on the Rock, Gibraltar will no longer belong to Britain. Numbers have fluctuated over the years, falling from 130 in 1900 to a record low of just four in 1943 (when Winston Churchill ordered 24 new animals to be imported from North Africa). Nowadays, the population stands at about 100, living in two main areas: Middle Hill and Queen's Gate.

**Most recently discovered** It is fairly surprising, considering the high level of interest and research in primates, that new species are still being discovered. But no fewer than 11 have been found in the past 10 years (1985–95), including the black-headed marmoset (*Callithrix nigriceps*), found in the Brazilian Amazon in 1992; Sclater's guenon (*Cercopithecus sclateri*) and the red

colobus monkey (*Colobus badius*), both found along the banks of the River Niger in Africa and due to be described in 1995; the Diane tarsier (*Tarsius dianae*), which was discovered in central Sulawesi in 1988; and a possible new slow loris (*Nycticebus* sp) from Vietnam. In addition, a recent review of bushbabies and galagos (family Lorisidae) may result in as many as five new species being described in the near future.

The Rio Maués marmoset (*Callithrix mauesi*) was first seen in April 1985, but was not officially named as a new species until October 1992. Adorned with faint zebra-like stripes and furry ear tufts, it was discovered on the Maués River, in Brazil's central Amazon, by Swiss primatologist Marco Schwartz.

Vanzolini's squirrel monkey (*Saimiri vanzolinii*) was found by primatologist Dr Marcio Ayres, from São Paulo's National Institute for Amazonian Research, in a tiny patch of rainforest between Brazil's Japura and Amazon Rivers. It was officially named in 1985.

The black-faced lion tamarin (*Leontopithecus caissara*) was discovered in January 1990, by Brazilian biologists working on the island of Superagui, in Parana state, only 250 km *155 miles* south of Brazil's biggest city, São Paulo. Only a handful of the yellow, squirrel-sized animals were seen alive (it is believed

that fewer than 200 live on the island), but biologists Dr Vanessa Guerra Persson and Dr Maria Lucia Lorini also found a dead one by the side of the road, which became the type specimen. Named officially on 21 Jun 1990, the black-faced lion tamarin probably has the most restricted distribution of any primate.

The sun-tailed guenon (*Cercopithecus solatus*) was first discovered by primatologist Dr Mike Harrison in 1984, on the dinner table of a local hunter in the Forêt des Abeilles, central Gabon. The beautiful monkey, with a striking golden colour on the tip of its tail, was described for science in 1988.

The golden bamboo lemur (*Hapalemur aureus*) was discovered in 1985, by French researcher Corrine Dague, inhabiting a rainforest near Ranomafana, 46 km *28½ miles* east of Fianarantsoa, SE Madagascar (although it was not recognized as a new species at the time). It was officially named in 1987.

The golden-crowned sifaka (*Propithecus tattersalli*) was described for science in 1989 by American zoologist Dr Elwyn Simons of the Primate Center at Duke University, North Carolina, USA. In fact, it had previously been seen in 1974, in a dry forest near Daraina, in Antseranana province, Madagascar, by mammalogist Dr Ian Tattershall; but, at the time, Tattershall had not considered it to be a new spe-

**Gibraltar is home to the only non-human primate found in Europe: the so-called barbary 'ape'.**

cies and his observation went virtually unnoticed. It is particularly strange that this species had not been discovered before, since its golden crown makes it highly conspicuous from a considerable distance.

**Back from the brink** Several primates have unexpectedly reappeared long after they were feared extinct. One of the best-known examples is the greater bamboo lemur (*Hapalemur simus*), which had supposedly disappeared at the turn of the century; but, in 1972, about 100 of the ruddy-grey animals were discovered by French zoologist Dr André Peyriéras, living in a small patch of degraded rainforest near the village of Ranomafana, south-eastern Madagascar.

Another lemur which, at one time, appeared to be extinct is the hairy-eared dwarf lemur (*Allocebus trichotis*), which was previously known from only four dead specimens collected last century and a single live animal captured in 1964. Rediscovered during an expedition to the rainforests of northern Madagascar, 40 km *25 miles* south-west of Mananara, in April 1989, it almost went unnoticed. Zoologist Bernhard Meier had virtually given up hope when the first hairy-eared dwarf lemur seen for years suddenly jumped into the light of his headlamp, paused for a moment, and then disappeared into the darkness. He later found two adults and one immature animal inside a burrow, and others have been found since. But there is little doubt that the hairy-eared dwarf lemur is still in a precarious situation.

**Hidden primates** There are many reports of unidentified human-like primates living in some of the wilder and more remote regions of the world.

Some have proved to be nothing more than elaborate hoaxes, others are disregarded for good scientific reasons by all but the most open-minded experts, but a few are taken seriously. Indeed, there have been many costly expeditions and research projects to investigate possible sightings in more detail, but so far with little success. Four of the most publicized examples are the orang pendele, the yeti, the yeren and the yahoo.

A bipedal primate, known as orang pendek, continues to elude investigators in the forests of western Sumatra, Indonesia. However, there is growing evidence that such an ape/hominid

really does exist. Zoologist Debbie Martyr had three brief encounters in 1994, adding weight to the numerous glimpses reported by local people. The picture emerging is of an intelligent biped standing up to 1.2 m *4 ft* tall, with silky, reddish coloured body hair and a bare face. An expedition to search for the animal is being conducted in Kerinci Seblat National Park, Sumatra, in 1995.

The yeti, or abominable snowman, is a creature that is believed by some to live at high altitudes in central Asia. It has been reported by foreign travellers and local people for centuries, and there have been many possible sightings by reliable observers. But no one has yet been able to provide concrete evidence of its existence. The most exciting discovery was a series of huge footprints photographed in the snow by the Everest explorer Eric Shipton, when he was crossing the Menlung Glacier, in the Himalayas, in 1951. His photograph, showing a single footprint with an ice-axe placed alongside to provide scale, caused a sensation around the world. The print measured 46 cm *18 in* in length and 33 cm *13 in* in width, and appeared to have been made by a two-legged creature with three small toes and a huge, rounded fourth toe (although it could have been made by a smaller animal before melting changed its shape). Three years later, in 1954, some 'yeti scalps' were found in monasteries in the Himalayas but, after careful examination, they were found to belong to a kind of goat called a serow. Since then, more footprints have been photographed on a number of occasions, but most experts remain resolutely unconvinced.

In many parts of China, villagers have been talking about an animal they call the yeren (which translates into English as the 'wildman') for more than 2000 years. It is certainly feasible that large animals remain undiscovered in the country, where there are vast areas of wilderness that have never been explored. Indeed, the Chinese Academy of Sciences has even sponsored expeditions to search for the yeren, which some experts believe may be a descendant of the Pleistocene ape *Gigantopithecus*. There is still no concrete evidence of its existence, although a small number of possible yeren hairs

Capture for the pet trade is just one of many threats facing the world's primates; this saddening photograph was taken of a gibbon in an animal market in Ho Chi Minh City, Vietnam.

> A vine in Madagascar relies exclusively on lemurs for pollination; it is the only plant known to rely on primates in this way.

have been found independently in Sichuan, Guizhou and Hunan provinces. These have been analysed in China and the UK, using a variety of sophisticated techniques, and appear to differ markedly from all known animals, including humans. Certain characteristics of the hairs suggest to some experts that they came from an unknown higher primate but, without a body, mainstream scientists continue to doubt or deny the existence of the wildman.

There are many reports, mainly from the last century, of a man-sized primate living in Australia. Vaguely resembling a marsupial species known as *Hulitherium thomasetti*, which is supposed to have been extinct for some 38 000 years, it was named the yahoo by early settlers. Most experts, however, remain unconvinced that any such animal really exists.

**Most threatened** The World Conservation Union (IUCN) lists 113 species of primates as known or suspected to be threatened with extinction (accounting for more than half the total group); among them, all 33 species and subspecies of Madagascar's lemurs are on the danger list. Forty-three primates are considered to be in particularly serious trouble, including: the orang-utan (*Pongo pygmaeus*) which survives only on the islands of Borneo and Sumatra, with a total population of about 27 000 in the wild; the black gibbon (*Hylobates concolor*) of Cambodia, Laos, Vietnam and China; the grizzled leaf monkey (*Presbytis comata*) of Java, Indonesia; the lion-tailed macaque (*Macaca silenus*) of India; the sun-tailed guenon (*Cercopithecus solatus*) of Gabon; the golden lion tamarin (*Leontopithecus rosalia*) of Brazil; and the aye-aye (*Daubentonia madagascariensis*) of Madagascar. The many threats they face include deforestation and other forms of habitat destruction or fragmentation, hunting for food, and capture for the pet trade.

A further 61 sub-species of primates are also threatened with extinction, including the northern brown howler monkey (*Alouatta fusca fusca*) of Brazil, the Colombian woolly monkey (*Lagothrix lagotricha lugens*) of Colombia, and the critically endangered mountain gorilla (*Gorilla gorilla beringei*) of Rwanda, Uganda and Zaïre (which numbers fewer than 650).

## TREE SHREWS

These are believed to be among the most primitive forms of placental mammals. They bear a striking resemblance to early fossil primates and, for many years, were classified as primitive members of the primate order themselves. They also share affinities with insectivores such as the true shrews, but differ in many aspects of behaviour, anatomy and reproduction. Now placed in a group of their own (the order Scandentia), there are 19 recognized species living mainly in the tropical rainforests of eastern India and southeast Asia.

**Largest** The longest member of the order Scandentia is the common tree shrew (*Tupaia glis*), which has a maximum head-body length of 23 cm *9 in*; a tail length of up to 20 cm *7.9 in*; and a maximum weight of 185 g *6½ oz*. The Philippine tree shrew (*Urogale everetti*) is shorter, with a maximum head-body length of 22 cm *8.7 in* and a tail length of up to 17.5 cm *6.9 in*, but a fully grown male weighs a relatively hefty 350 g *12.4 oz*.

**Smallest** The world's smallest tree shrew is the rare pen-tailed or feather-tailed tree shrew (*Ptilocercus lowii*), which has a head-body length of 10–14 cm *3.9–5½ in*; a tail length of 13–19 cm *5.1–7½ in*; and a weight of 25–60 g *0.9–2.1 oz*. There are several close runners-up, in particular the pygmy tree shrew (*Tupaia· minor*) and the northern smooth-tailed tree shrew (*Dendrogale murina*).

Madagascar has more threatened primates than any other country in the world; this ring-tailed lemur was photographed in the south of the country.

# RABBITS, HARES & PIKAS

## Lagomorpha
*c.* 78 species (little agreement on classification): 24 rabbits, 29 hares and 25 pikas.

*The enormous ears of the black-tailed jackrabbit are not only for hearing; they also act as radiators, helping this desert animal to lose excess heat.*

**Largest** The world's largest lagomorph is the Alaskan or tundra hare (*Lepus othus*), which lives on open tundra in west and south-west Alaska. It weighs 3.2–6.5 kg *7–14¼ lb* (average 4.8 kg *10½ lb* in a sample of 83 animals) and has a head-body length of 51–61 cm *20–24 in*.

The European or brown hare (*Lepus europaeus*), which is found over most of Europe except Ireland, the Mediterranean region and Scandinavia, is often quoted as the largest lagomorph. One particular individual which was shot near Welford, Northamptonshire, UK, in November 1956, weighed 6.83 kg *15 lb 1 oz*; however, the normal weight for this species is 3–5 kg *6 lb 10 oz–11 lb* (average 3.8 kg *8 lb 6 oz*). It has a head-body length of 52–60 cm *20½–23½ in*.

The Arctic hare (*Lepus arcticus*), which lives in Greenland and northern Canada, is also large, weighing an average 4–5 kg *8 lb 2 oz–11 lb*.

**Largest domestic** The largest breed of domestic rabbit is the Flemish giant. Adults weigh 7–8.5 kg *15.4–18.7 lb* (average toe-to-toe length when fully stretched 91 cm *36 in*), but weights up to 11.3 kg *25 lb* have been reliably reported for this breed. The largest domestic rabbit on record is a 5-month-old French lop doe weighing 12 kg *26 lb 7 oz* which was exhibited at the Reus Fair in north-east Spain in April 1980.

**Smallest** The smallest lagomorphs are the pikas and the record-holder is the tiny Steppe or little pika (*Ochotona pusilla*), which lives in steppe regions from the upper Volga River and southern Ural Mountains south and east to the Chinese border. It has a head-body length of only 18 cm *7 in* and weighs just 75–210 g *2.7–7.4 oz*.

**Smallest domestic** Both the Polish and the Netherland dwarf have a weight range of 0.9–1.13 kg *2–2½ lb*. In 1975 Jacques Bouloc of Coulommière, France, announced a new hybrid of these two breeds which weighed an average of 396 g *14 oz*.

**Longest ears** The antelope jackrabbit (*Lepus alleni*), which lives in the desert regions of southern USA and northwestern Mexico, has longer ears than any other lagomorph. They measure 13.8–17.3 cm *5.4–6.8 in* from the top of the head to the tip (average 16.2 cm *6.4 in*).

The longest ears in domestic rabbits are found in the lop family and, in particular, the English lop. The ears of a typical example measure about 61 cm *24 in* from tip to tip (taken across the skull) and 14 cm *5.51 in* maximum width. *Sweet Majestic Star*, a champion black English lop owned and bred by Therese and Cheryl Seward of Exeter, Devon, UK, had ears measuring 72.4 cm *28½ in* long and 18.4 cm *7¼ in* wide; he died on 6 Oct 1992, but the ears of his grandson, *Sweet Regal Magic*, are of a similar length. There is at least one record of longer ears, but it is believed that weights had been used to stretch them (since the veins inside were badly varicosed) and so the record has not been counted.

**Fastest** Some of the larger hares, which tend to live in open habitats and are adapted for running rather than burrowing (in contrast to most rabbits), reportedly reach speeds of 80 km/h *50 mph* when in full flight. They are also good long-distance runners and can maintain speeds of up to 50 km/h *31 mph* for long periods.

**Highest living** The highest-living mammal in the world is the large-eared pika (*Ochtona macrotis*), which also has the largest ears of all the pikas. It lives in the Himalayas, the Pamir Mountains, the Karakorum Range and other high-altitude mountain ranges in Asia at a height of 2500–6130 m *8200–20 106 ft* (marginally higher than the maximum elevation reached by the yak, *Bos mutus*).

A significant number of other lagomorphs live at elevations higher than 4000 m *13 120 ft*. In particular, the Ladak pika (*Ochotona ladacensis*) lives at 4300–5450 m *14 104–17 876 ft* in the mountains of Kashmir, in India, and Qinghai, Xizang and Xinjiang, in China. The woolly hare (*Lepus oiostolus*) lives in the mountains of Tibet, China, Nepal and Kashmir at a height of 2500–5400 m *8200–17 712 ft* (there is also a single reliable record of an individual seen at 6035 m *19 800 ft*). The Omilteme cottontail (*Sylvilagus insonus*), which lives in the Sierra Madre del Sur, in the vicinity of Omilteme, Guerrero, Mexico, occurs at elevations of 2300–5280 m *7544–17 318 ft*. And there is a single record of a moupin pika (*Ochotona thibetana*), which lives in China, northern Burma, Bhutan and India, sunning itself on a rock at a height of 5486 m *18 000 ft*, when the temperature was −17°C *1°F* (the normal elevation for this species is 1800–4100 m *5904–13 448 ft*).

**Most threatened** The World Conservation Union (IUCN) lists a total of 23 species of rabbits, hares and pikas as threatened with extinction. The species considered most at risk are the riverine or bushman rabbit (*Bunolagus monticularis*), of South Africa; the hispid hare (*Caprolagus hispidus*), of Bangladesh, India and Nepal; the Tehuantepec jackrabbit (*Lepus flavigularis*), of Mexico; the volcano rabbit (*Romerolagus diazi*), which is restricted to two volcanic sierras close to Mexico City (within a 30-minute drive of 17 million people); the Amami rabbit (*Pentalagus furnessi*), which is found only on two islands in the Japanese Ryukyu archipelago; the

*The spectacular boxing matches observed between brown hares in the spring (giving rise to the phrase 'mad as a March hare') are believed to be the females rejecting over-amorous males.*

*Rabbits and hares have a highly specialised digestive system – to cope with large quantities of vegetation – which requires them to eat their own faeces.*

> A strange rule of thumb can be applied to the weight of hares in different parts of the world: with a few exceptions, it is generally true to say that those living in the far north weigh up to 5 kg 11 lb, those in temperate regions weigh about 3 kg 6½ lb and the ones living around the equator are about 2 kg 4½ lb.

# RACCOONS

### *Procyonidae*
Up to 20 species (little agreement on classification): 7 raccoons, 4 coatis, 1 panda, 1 kinkajou, 5 olingos, 1 ringtail and 1 cacomistle.

Sumatran short-eared rabbit (*Nesolagus netscheri*), of Sumatra, Indonesia; the Tres Marias cottontail (*Sylvilagus graysoni*), of the Tres Marias Islands, Mexico; and the Omilteme cottontail (*Sylvilagus insonus*), of the Sierra Madre del Sur, in the vicinity of Omilteme, Guerrero, Mexico.

A further 10 sub-species are known or believed to be threatened with extinction, including the Lower Keys marsh rabbit (*Sylvilagus palustris hefneri*), which lives in the Florida Keys, USA.

**Extinctions** One species of lagomorph is known to have become extinct in recent times: the Sardinian pika (*Prolagus sardus*), which disappeared from the islands of Sardinia and Corsica, in the Mediterranean, in the 18th century.

**Population fluctuations** Most animal populations fluctuate irregularly or unpredictably. But the best-known exception is the snowshoe hare (*Lepus americanus*), whose populations in the boreal forests of North America undergo remarkably regular fluctuations which peak every 8–11 years. The fluctuations are broadly synchronized over a vast area from Alaska to Newfoundland and are so dramatic that the difference between a population high and a low may be more than 100-fold (normally 10–30-fold). This extraordinary cycle has been documented in fur-trade records kept by the Hudson's Bay Company, Canada, for over two centuries and has been studied in considerable detail. For many years, it was supposed that the predatory activity of the lynx (*Lynx canadensis*) was responsible, because this species also shows population highs and lows at roughly 10-year intervals (lagging a year or two behind those of the hare). But it is now believed that the driving force is a complex interaction between the hare and its food, while the lynx – rather than influencing the cycle – is actually being influenced by it.

**Largest** The largest member of the raccoon family is the common raccoon (*Procyon lotor*), which is found throughout much of North, Central and northern South America, and has been introduced to parts of Europe and Asia. Several of the other large species – such as the kinkajou (*Potos flavus*) and the white-nosed coati (*Nasua narica*) – are approximately the same length (or even longer, including the tail) but do not match the raccoon in maximum weight. However, there is a great deal of individual variation in many of the procyonids and it is not unusual for certain specimens to exceed the average by a large margin. The head-body length of the common raccoon is 46–71 cm *18–28 in*; the tail length is 20–35 cm *8–13¾ in*; and the weight range is normally 2.5–12 kg *5½–26½ lb*. There is one record of a male raccoon in Wisconsin, USA, which weighed 28.3 kg *62½ lb*.

**Smallest** Several members of the raccoon family compete for this title and, unfortunately, there is too much individual variation (and, in some cases, there are too few measurements) to identify a single record-holder. The species most commonly described as the smallest is the ringtail (*Bassariscus astutus*), which lives in southern and western USA and throughout Mexico.

**Ring-tailed coati: one of the largest members of the raccoon family.**

*During the night, when a kinkajou is feeding, it emits a shrill, quavering scream that can be heard for nearly 1.6 km 1 mile.*

**The red panda is one of the most threatened members of the raccoon family.**

This graceful animal has a head-body length of 31–38 cm *12¼–15 in*; a tail length of 31–44 cm *12¼–17¼ in*; and a weight of only 800–1100 g *1¾–2½ lb*.

**Most threatened** The World Conservation Union (IUCN) lists no fewer than 12 members of the raccoon family (more than half) as known or suspected to be threatened with extinction. These include the red or lesser panda (*Ailurus fulgens*), of Bhutan, Nepal, China, India, Myanmar and Laos (it is the only member of the raccoon family with a natural distribution outside the New World); the Central American cacomistle (*Bassariscus sumichrasti*), which lives in Mexico and all seven Central American countries (with the possible exception of Honduras); and the Cozumel Island coati (*Nasua nelsoni*)

and Cozumel Island raccoon (*Procyon pygmaeus*) which, as their names suggest, live on Cozumel Island, Mexico. The many threats include habitat loss and fragmentation (mainly due to deforestation), human disturbance and hunting.

**Extinctions** The Barbados raccoon (*Procyon gloveralleni*) is the only member of the raccoon family which is known or suspected to have become extinct in recent times.

**Most mischievous** The common raccoon (*Procyon lotor*) is frequently described as the most mischievous animal in the world (although there are several other well-qualified contenders for this title). A highly intelligent and adaptable species, it is cheeky, has an insatiable curiousity and has learnt to coexist successfully with humans (despite being a major target for hunters). Always experimenting and poking its fingers into crevices, it can use its hands almost as skilfully as monkeys use theirs. It raids people's dustbins, overturning them and stealing the contents (even unscrewing jars and taking the stoppers out of bottles); begs by the roadside, where it knows passers-by will stop to provide scraps; and breaks into tents and cabins at campsites. It even looks the part with its unmistakable 'bandit' mask.

**The common raccoon is frequently described as the most mischievous animal in the world; this guilty-looking individual has just been raiding a camp-site dustbin in the Everglades, Florida.**

# RHINOCEROSES

## *Rhinocerotidae*
5 species: 2 in Africa and 3 in Asia.

There are roughly 9–11 500 rhinos left in the world: the sum total for all five species; 10 years ago, there were almost twice as many.

**Earliest** Many different species of rhino are known from the fossil record (estimates vary from 100 to 300 species in more than 65 distinct genera). Their ancestors first appeared in the Eocene, some 50 million years ago, when they looked rather like modern horses: long-legged creatures in the families Hyracidae and Hyracodontidae. One of the most primitive was a fast runner called *Hyrachyus*, which was the size of a collie dog; the later *Juxia* was a horse-sized runner. The first animals resembling modern rhinos were *Caenopenes* and *Aceratheres*, which appeared in what is now North America and Europe during the Oligocene some 30 million years ago; they were distinctly rhinoceros-shaped, although they carried tusks instead of horns. All five modern rhino species are descended from a common ancestor; however, the African evolutionary line split from the Asian line about 10 million years ago.

**Most primitive** The Sumatran rhinoceros (*Dicerorhinus sumatrensis*) is the most primitive rhino alive today. Covered with dense, dark reddish-brown fur, it is believed to have survived al-most unmodified for millions of years. It is the only surviving member of the sub-family Dicerorhinae, which also included the extinct and very similar woolly rhinoceros (*Coelodonta*), a well-known species which lived into the last Ice Age about 15–20 000 years ago.

**Largest** The largest of the rhinos is the white or square-lipped rhinoceros (*Ceratotherium simum*), which is restricted to southern and central Africa. It can attain a height of up to 1.85 m *6 ft* at the shoulder and a length of 4.2 m *13¾ ft*; the maximum weight is about 3.6 tonnes (males are heavier than females). The black rhinoceros (*Diceros bicornis*) has been known to reach a similar height at the shoulder (1.8 m *5 ft 11 in*) but is usually shorter and considerably lighter (maximum weight about 1.45 tonnes).

**Smallest** The smallest of the rhinos is the Sumatran rhinoceros (*Dicerorhinus sumatrensis*), which is sparsely scattered in south-east Asia.

It can attain a maximum shoulder height of 1.5 m *4 ft 11 in* but the average is little more than 1 m *3¼ ft*; its average weight is about 800 kg *1764 lb*.

**Largest prehistoric** The largest land mammal ever recorded was the giant giraffe rhinoceros (*Indricotherium = Baluchitherium*), a long-necked, hornless rhinocerotid which roamed across western Asia and Europe about 35 million years ago. It is known from fossil bones which were first discovered in the Bugti Hills of Baluchistan, Pakistan, in 1907–8. A restoration in the American Museum of Natural History, New York City, USA, measures 5.41 m *17 ft 9 in* to the top of the shoulder hump and 11.27 m *37 ft* in total length. It was so tall, it had the reach of a modern giraffe and could feed on leaves high in the treetops. The most likely maximum weight of this browser was revised in 1993 to 11–20 tonnes from earlier

The largest of the rhinos is the white rhinoceros, which can stand as high as 1.85 m *6 ft* at the shoulder and can weigh up to 3.6 tonnes; this is the extremely rare northern sub-species, photographed in Zaïre.

**MAMMALS**

> The skin on the back and flanks of a white rhino is about 2.5 cm *1 in* thick to provide protection against the horns of other rhinos; if the rhino was a 'normal' mammal of the same weight it would be expected to have a skin thickness of about 4 mm *0.12 in.*

estimates of 34 tonnes; although there are well-established techniques for estimating the size of extinct animals from fragments of fossil bones (using living animals as a guide), rhinoceroses are deceptive because they have skeletons which are far more robust than is necessary to support their bulk. *Indricotherium* disappeared about 10 million years ago.

**Longest horn** The longest recorded anterior horn for a rhinoceros is one of 1.58 m *62¼ in* found on a female southern white rhinoceros (*Ceratotherium simum simum*) shot in South Africa in *c.* 1848. The posterior horn measured 57 cm *22¼ in.* There is also an unconfirmed record of an anterior horn measuring 2.06 m *6¾ ft.*

**Most threatened** All five species of rhinoceros – white (*Ceratotherium simum*), black (*Diceros bicornis*), Indian (*Rhinoceros unicornis*), Sumatran

---

The Javan rhino is probably the rarest species of large mammal in the world.

(*Dicerorhinus sumatrensis*) and Javan (*Rhinoceros sondaicus*) – are threatened with extinction. No family of large mammals gives cause for greater concern. The main threat is poaching for their horn, which is used as an ingredient in traditional Chinese medicines (particularly in China, Taiwan and South Korea) and is carved to make dagger handles which are worn by many men in Yemen. Dealing in rhino horn has become as lucrative as pushing drugs and, even for local villagers at the beginning of the chain of people involved in the trade, the temptation to poach is irresistible. Current population sizes are estimated to be (in 1994): northern white – 32; southern white – 5000–6750; black – fewer than 2550; Indian – 1700; Sumatran – 500–900; and Javan – 60–65.

**Rarest** The Javan rhinoceros (*Rhinoceros sondaicus*), a single-horned rhino, is considered to be the rarest species of large mammal in the world. Once widely distributed from Bangladesh east through Burma, Thailand, the Malaysian Peninsula and Indo-China to Sumatra and Java, its population has declined dramatically as a result of hunting and, to a much lesser extent, loss of habitat. Now there are just two known surviving populations: one in Udjung Kulon National Park on the remote western tip of Java, Indonesia; and the other along the Dong Nai River valley between Song Be and Lam Dong provinces, Vietnam. It is just possible that a handful still survive undetected in Cambodia and Laos; the species recently became extinct in Myanmar (formerly Burma) and Thailand.

The largest population is in Udjung Kulon National Park, but nevertheless a camera-trapping survey in 1993 revealed that only about 50 rhinos survive there. Thirty-four cameras were set up in likely locations within the park and they photographed an average of one rhino every five days (individuals were identified by skin markings, sex, size and estimates of age); the only encouraging sign was that some of the pictures showed mothers with calves in tow.

It was feared that the Javan rhinoceros had disappeared from Vietnam until, in 1988, a hunter shot an adult female *c.* 130 km *81 miles* north-east of Ho Chi Minh City (Saigon). He was arrested while attempting to sell the horn and hide and given a 1-year jail sentence (commuted after 2 months). His discovery prompted a survey of the area during February and March 1989 and this estimated that at most there are 10–15 animals surviving within an area of no more than 750 km² *290 miles².*

> A group of rhinoceroses is called a 'crash'.

The white rhinoceros (*Ceratotherium simum*) is separated into two sub-species: the northern white (*Ceratotherium s. cottoni*) and the southern white (*Ceratotherium s. simum*). The northern sub-species, which is now found only in Garamba National Park, Zaïre (4920 km² *19000 miles²*), is rarer than any other member of the family. In 1980, there were 800–850 (400 known in Zaïre, 400 in Sudan, 1 in Uganda and probably 0 in Central African Republic) but in the space of a few years rebel

**The population of black rhinoceroses in Africa has declined by about 97.5 per cent in the past 30 years, making it the fastest-disappearing large mammal in the world.**

---

soldiers and other poachers had killed almost all of them. By 1984–85 the population had reached an all-time low of just 13 animals. After intensive protection, the population has more than doubled – although it is still in a precarious situation with a total of only 32 animals.

**Fastest decline** Since 1970 the world's rhino population has fallen by an unbelievable 85 per cent. The fastest-disappearing species has been the black rhinoceros (*Diceros bicornis*), which has declined from an estimated population of 100 000 in the early 1960s, to 65 000 in 1970, to 3500 in 1991, and to 2550 in 1994 (the majority of survivors live in South Africa, Zimbabwe, Namibia, Kenya and Tanzania); a guestimate in early 1995 suggests a figure of just over 2000. This population crash has been caused solely by poaching for horn. Numbers seem to have stabilized, according to an unpublished report of a meeting held in May 1994 by the IUCN/SSC African Rhino Specialist Group, but poaching is still

rife in Africa and many experts fear the worst. A major concern is that the rapid decline in numbers has been accompanied by an equally alarming fragmentation into very small populations of dubious viability.

**Commonest** The commonest rhino is the southern white rhinoceros (*Ceratotherium simum simum*), a sub-species of the white rhino which lives in South Africa and has been reintroduced to Botswana, Kenya, Namibia, Swaziland, Zimbabwe and Zambia (where it may now be extinct). Unfortunately, 'common' is a relative word when talking about rhinos and the current population size is considerably less than 6750 (see below).

The number of southern white rhinoceroses living in South Africa (home to almost 95 per cent of the surviving population) is a subject of major controversy. At the biannual meeting of the Convention on International Trade in Endangered Species, which was held in Fort Lauderdale, Florida, USA, in November 1994, the South African government claimed a wild population of some 6300 (including 2000 in the Hluhluwe-Umfolozi Game Reserve in Natal – the world's most important white rhinoceros reserve). However, after a preliminary air count conducted in September 1994, field staff working for the Natal Parks Board came up with

a population figure of only 1210 for Hluhluwe-Umfolozi. The general consensus now seems to be that the actual figure is likely to be several hundred short of 2000 but, more importantly, the discrepancy raises a question about the accuracy of the estimated population figure for the entire country.

The southern white rhinoceros was considered to be extinct as long ago as 1882 but, at the turn of the century, a small population of 11 animals was discovered in Umfolozi, Zululand, South Africa. This prompted an extraordinary effort to protect them from extinction and, by the mid-1960s, the numbers had increased to about 500. A programme was then devised to split the population up, and they were transferred to parks and reserves elsewhere in South Africa and in other countries. Despite occasional setbacks, numbers have continued to rise mainly as a result of vigorous protective measures in South Africa.

*Rhinos have many ways of communicating with one another, but perhaps the most surprising is a highly complicated method of regulating their breathing, like a sort of Morse code.*

# RODENTS

### Rodentia
*c.* 1750 species
(nearly 40 per cent of all mammal species) including beavers, squirrels, mice, rats, porcupines, voles and guinea pigs

**Earliest** Rodents first appear in the fossil record in the late Palaeocene, some 57 million years ago, from localities in Asia and North America. They were squirrel-like and belonged to the extinct family Paramyidae. Unfortunately, the evolutionary origin of rodents is obscured by the fact that, by this time, all the main characteristics of the order had developed.

**Most primitive** The mountain beaver (*Aplodontia rufa*), which lives in coniferous forests in western North America, is the most primitive of all the living rodents. Something of a zoological mystery, it is neither a beaver nor a particularly mountain-loving animal and is classed in a family of its own called the Aplodontidae. Unlike most other mammals, it has difficulty regulating its body temperature and, since it is unable to conserve either body moisture or fat, cannot hibernate.

**Largest** The world's largest living rodent is the capybara (*Hydrochoerus hydrochaeris*) of northern South America, which lives in densely vegetated areas around ponds, lakes, rivers, marshes and other aquatic habitats. It has a head-body length of 1–1.4 m *3¼–4½ ft* (the tail is vestigial); a shoulder height of 50–62 cm *20–24½ in*; and a weight of 35–66 kg *77–145½ lb*. In captivity, this species can attain an even greater weight and there is one record of a cage-fat specimen of 113 kg *250 lb*. Some extinct forms of capybara were twice as long and up to eight times as heavy as the modern species.

**Smallest** The world's smallest rodent is the tiny Baluchistan pygmy jerboa (*Salpingotus michaelis*), which lives in north-western Baluchistan, Pakistan. It has a head-body length of 3.6–4.7 cm *1.42–1.85 in* and a tail length of 7.2–

Life-size comparison of the foot of a capybara, which is the biggest of all the rodents, with a harvest mouse, which is one of the smallest.

9.4 cm *2.84–3.70 in*. For its size, it has enormous hind feet of some 1.8–1.9 cm *0.71–¾ in* in length (as an adaptation for jumping).

**Most teeth** All rodents have a single pair of razor-sharp incisors on each jaw and no canines, but the number of molars and premolars varies considerably from species to species. The silvery mole-rat (*Heliophobius argenteocinereus*), from central and east Africa, is the record-holder with 24 (making a total of 28 teeth).

**Least teeth** The one-toothed shrew mouse (*Mayermys ellermani*) has four incisors and no canines, like all rodents, but is distinguished from the others by having no premolars and just four molars (making a total of eight teeth altogether). Its name refers to the fact that it has just one molar tooth on each side of each jaw.

**Oldest** The longest-lived rodents are the porcupines and, in particular, the 11 species of Old World porcupines (family Hystricidae). The greatest reliable age reported is 27 years 3 months for a Sumatran crested porcupine (*Hystrix brachyura*), which died in the National Zoological Park, Washington, DC, USA, on 12 Jan 1965. Many rodents have longer lives in captivity, but in the wild most small species have short lifespans of only 1–3 years and the larger ones fair a little better with an average of about 10 years.

---

*The Food and Agriculture Organization of the United Nations has estimated that the damage brought about by rodents worldwide amounts to 42.5 million tonnes of food (roughly equivalent to the world's total annual production of cereals and potatoes); however, only a handful of species are responsible.*

**Longest glide** Two rodent families have evolved the ability to glide between trees: the flying squirrels (family Sciuridae), which live in south-east Asia, North America and northern Europe, and the scaly-tailed squirrels (family Anomaluridae), which live in western and central Africa. There are 38 species of flying squirrels and 7 species of scaly-tailed squirrels (although the flightless scaly-tailed squirrel, *Zenkerella insignis*, does not have a gliding membrane and, as its name suggests, is incapable of flight). The longest recorded glide of any gliding mammal was an outstanding 450 m *1476 ft* for a giant flying squirrel in the genus *Petaurista*. The longest glide of any of the scaly-tailed squirrels was *c.* 250 m *820 ft* by a Lord Derby's flying squirrel (*Anomalurus derbianus*). Some 50–100 m *164–328 ft* is more typical for most species.

Despite their names, these flying rodents are not capable of true flight. But they glide from tree to tree with the help of a furry membrane along each side of the body (stretched between the forelimbs and hindlimbs); this acts as a kind of parachute. It is an economical way to travel through their tall forest homes and an effective means of escaping from tree-borne predators. After climbing to an elevated point in a tree, they carefully judge the distance to the proposed landing site and then leap out into space, extending their arms and legs to open the membrane (known as the patagium). They bank and turn by raising and lowering their arms, and use their tail as a stabilizer. Just before landing, they brake by turning their tail and body upwards.

The smallest gliding mammal in the world is the pygmy scaly-tailed squirrel (*Idiurus zenkeri*), which has a head-body length of just 6.8–7.9 cm *2.68–3.11 in*; a tail length of 9.1–11.7 cm *3.58–4.61 in*; and a weight of 14–17.5 g *0.49–0.62 oz* (the three species of pygmy flying squirrels in the genus *Petaurillus* are only slightly larger). The largest of the gliding mammals are the giant flying squirrels in the genus *Petaurista*, which have a head-body length of 30.5–58.5 cm *12–23 in*; a tail length of 34.5–63.5 cm *13.6–25 in*; and a weight of 1–2.5 kg *2 lb 3 oz–5 lb 8 oz*. A single woolly flying squirrel (*Eupetaurus cinereus*) has been reported with a head-body length of 61 cm *24 in* and a tail length of 38 cm *15 in*.

**Longest hibernation** Several ground squirrels in the genus *Spermophilus*, especially those living in areas with a severe climate, spend considerably more than half the year in hibernation. Some not only hibernate during the

*As soon as it lands on a tree trunk, a flying squirrel runs around to the other side in case an owl or another predator has been following its flight.*

winter but also sleep during part of the summer, when there is drought and the vegetation is poor. North American populations of the arctic ground squirrel (*Spermophilus parryii*), living in Alaska and northern Canada, are probably the record-holders. They hibernate for 9 months of the year and, during the remaining 3 months, they feed, breed and collect food to store in their burrows.

**Master engineer** With the exception of humans, no mammal is capable of modifying its environment as dramatically as the North American beaver (*Castor canadensis*) and the European beaver (*Castor fiber*). They are accomplished engineers, able to construct dams and artificial lakes, and a family home – complete with moat – that is safe from predators and the rigours of winter.

Beaver dams average about 23 m *75½ ft* in length, but many are considerably longer. The largest ever built was probably one recorded on the Jefferson River, in Montana, USA, which measured 700 m *2296 ft* and was so strong it could bear the weight of a rider on horseback. Measurements of up to 1220 m *4000 ft* have also been claimed, although these have not been verified.

Beavers build dams, which obstruct the course of a stream or river, to create artificial lakes. These ensure that the

**Crested porcupines live longer than any other rodents, with a record of over 27 years.**

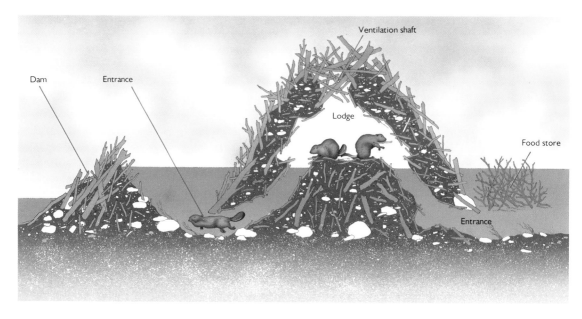

**Beaver lodge built by the most accomplished non-human engineer of all the mammals.**

water level around their home or 'lodge' is deep enough for the underwater entrances to be below ice-level during the winter freeze. Dams are made of logs (their massive incisor teeth are so strong that they can fell trees up to 1 m *3¼ft* in diameter), as well as branches and twigs, and are shored up by layers of mud, gravel and larger stones. The task of maintaining and extending the dams is continuous and may spread over several generations. In the middle of the new lake, they build a dome-shaped lodge of sticks and mud to avoid being caught by wolves and other predators. Ventilation is provided by looser construction on the top of the mound (which can extend more than 2 m *6ft 7in* above the surface of the water and may have a diameter at the base of over 12 m *39ft 4in*) and access is provided by underwater tunnels.

**Largest colonies** As recently as 100 years ago, western North America was teeming with prairie dogs (family Sciuridae) and the total population of all five species was probably more than 5 billion. The largest single colony or 'town' (indeed, the largest colony of mammals ever recorded) was one built by black-tailed prairie dogs (*Cynomys ludovicianus*) in western Texas. Discovered in 1901, it contained about 400 million individuals and was estimated to cover an area of 61 440 km² *24 000 miles²* (almost the size of The Republic of Ireland). For much of this century, prairie dog populations have declined dramatically as a direct result of shoot-

ing, poisoning and destruction of their grassland homes; however, the black-tails and others have been increasing once again in the past 20 years.

**Highest density** The highest density of rodents ever recorded was an astonishing 205 000 per ha *83 000 per acre* for a population of house mice (*Mus musculus*) in the dry bed of Buena Vista Lake, in Kern County, California, USA, in 1926–7. A similar 200 000 per ha *81 000 per acre* was later recorded for a population of house mice in Central Valley, California, in 1941–2.

**Most unique social organization** Naked mole rats (*Heterocephalus glaber*) are unique among mammals in the way they organize their colonies. There are clear divisions of labour, organized by a single breeding female, in a system which has parallels only in the social insects such as bees, wasps and ants. These almost hairless rodents live in underground colonies of 75–80 individuals (more than 250 have been recorded on occasion) in the dry savannas of Kenya, Somalia and Ethiopia. Breeding is entirely the preserve of a single female (the queen) and one or two male consorts. The other members of the colony are workers (which dig

> *Twenty-five per cent of a naked mole rat's muscle mass is concentrated in the jaw region (compared with one per cent in a human); this allows the rodent to cut through hard terrain (including concrete).*

tunnels, transport soil, forage, and carry food and bedding to the communal nest) and the larger non-workers (which spend most of their time in the nest, attending to the needs of the queen, caring for her offspring, defending the colony against snakes and other predators, and mending damaged tunnels). There is a distinct hierarchical system: the queen and the breeding males dominate the non-breeders, and larger animals dominate smaller ones, regardless of sex. The breeding female gives birth to between one and five litters a year, with an average of 14 pups in each, and suckles herself; the record-holder was a captive individual which had 27 pups in a single litter and 108 pups, in five different litters, in a single year. If the queen dies, another female in the colony, which was previously sexually inactive, quickly becomes active for the first time and takes over.

Naked mole rats build enormous tunnel systems, largely in their constant search for the succulent plant tubers. One record-breaking colony in Tsavo West National Park, Kenya, consisted of more than 3 km *1.9 miles* of tunnels and occupied an area greater than *100 000 m²* (about the size of 15 rugby pitches). The same colony – in an average month – excavated more than 200 m *656 ft* of new burrows (each about 4–7 cm *1.6–2.8 in* in diameter) and ejected more than 350 kg *772 lb* of soil through some 40 surface openings.

**Most inbred** Genetic fingerprinting and other studies by two independent research teams has shown that a naked mole rat (*Heterocephalus glaber*) colony is basically a clone. Hudson Kern Reeve and colleagues at Cornell University, New York State, USA, and Christopher Faulkes and colleagues at the Institute

Naked mole rats have such a unique social system that, genetically, members of a colony are almost identical – as if they had inbred for 60 generations.

of Zoology, London, have demonstrated that members of a colony are so similar genetically that it is as if they had inbred for 60 generations. Indeed, an estimated 85 per cent of matings are between parents and offspring or brother and sister. This has its advantages (*see Most unique social organization*) but is risky in case disease strikes, or environmental conditions alter, in which case all members of the colony are affected equally and it is more difficult for them to adapt.

**Most prolific** Many rodents are reproductively prolific: they breed frequently and have short gestation periods and large litters. The youngest breeding mammal is the female Norway lemming (*Lemmus lemmus*) of Scandinavia, which can become

The arctic ground squirrel frequently hibernates for a record-breaking 9 months of the year.

**M A M M A L S**

> The name 'rodent' is derived from the Latin verb meaning 'to gnaw'; rodent teeth are constantly worn down by the action of their opposite number on the other jaw and grow continuously throughout life, by as much as several millimetres per week.

pregnant when only 14 days old. Several rodent species have gestation periods of as little as 19–21 days but the shortest, by a small margin, is 15–16 days in the golden hamster (*Mesocricetus auratus*). In terms of frequency, the house mouse (*Mus musculus*) is capable of producing up to 14 litters in a year; and there is a record of a pair of Norway lemmings producing no fewer than eight litters in 167 days, after which the male died.

**Mass suicides** The compelling image of vast numbers of lemmings (subfamily Arvicolinae) hurling themselves over cliffs in mass suicide attempts is far from the truth. However, their extraordinary migrations – which inevitably result in many deaths – have never been properly explained. They remain one of the most intriguing puzzles of population ecology. A number of lemming species show dramatic population fluctuations, and migrations, but one of the best-known is the Norway lemming (*Lemmus lemmus*). It is a prodigious breeder and its population peaks roughly every 3–5 years. This leads to overcrowding which, according to one theory, forces many of the animals to leave in search of new places to live (normally in late summer or early autumn). At first, the migrations are fairly modest but, as numbers build up, they become more reckless and the animals seem to have a greater sense of urgency. There have even been reports of columns of lemmings marching across main roads and through busy town centres – with no intention of stopping. Eventually, there is mass panic and, driven on by those behind them, some of the lemmings fall over cliffs to their death or drown while attempting to swim across rivers that are too wide or too fast. It may *look* like mass suicide, but has a more logical explanation.

**Most dangerous** Some rodents are important transmitters of disease and have probably been responsible for more human deaths in the last millennium than all wars and revolutions put

together. They carry over 20 pathogens and spread bubonic plague, Lassa fever, murine typhus, *Salmonella* food poisoning, leptospirosis and rat-bite fever, among others. In this respect, the most dangerous are the species that habitually live near humans. The black or ship rat (*Rattus rattus*), in particular, was the main species responsible for transmitting the Black Death or bubonic plague (*see Most dangerous insects*) in Europe during the Middle Ages. This disease killed more than one-quarter of the population of Europe in a single 5-year period, from 1347 to 1352, and over the years has killed a great many more people in other parts of the world.

**Poorest thermoregulation** The naked mole rat (*Heterocephalus glaber*) has the poorest capacity for thermoregulation of any mammal and, indeed, is the only mammal in the world which is basically poikilothermic, or cold-blooded. This means that its body temperature fluctuates with the ambient temperature and has to be regulated behaviourally. Although it lives in well-insulated, underground burrows, and so seldom experiences any significant variation in temperature, it sometimes has to bask in warm soil near the surface or huddle together with its contemporaries during cold periods.

> A farmer in Australia once found 28 000 dead house mice on his veranda after one night's poisoning.

**Most widely distributed** The most widely distributed of all terrestrial mammals are probably the house mouse (*Mus musculus*) and the common or brown rat (*Rattus norvegicus*). They are found on every continent, including Antarctica, and even on many remote oceanic islands. The house mouse originally came from Asia and Mediterranean Europe, and the brown rat from northern China, but they have been able to extend their ranges by tolerating and, more importantly, by taking advantage of human habitation. Their ability to hitch rides on ships has also been essential.

**Most unlikely discovery** The Andes fishing mouse, a new species yet to be named but already placed in the genus *Chibchanomys*, is the only mammal to have been discovered on a TV screen. Scientists at a Mammal Society conference in 1994, in Ripon, North Yorkshire, UK, were watching a documentary about the wildlife of the Andes when a

fish-eating, stream-living mouse appeared on screen. Since no such animal was known to live in the Andes, it caused quite a stir and further investigations revealed that it was, indeed, a species new to science. Coincidentally, specimens of the mouse had previously been collected, at a height of 3600 m *11 800 ft* near Lake Luspa, in the Andes of southern Ecuador, in the early 1980s; although these had not been studied in detail at the time, they were recognized as being unusual and, fortunately, had been kept. They are now being used for the new scientific description of the now-famous TV mouse.

**Most threatened** The World Conservation Union (IUCN) lists a total of 118 rodent species as known or suspected to be threatened with extinction. The species considered to be most seriously at risk include: the Mexican prairie dog (*Cynomys mexicanus*) of Mexico; the Vancouver Island marmot (*Marmota vancouverensis*) of Vancouver Island, Canada; Poncelet's giant rat (*Solomys ponceleti*) of Bougainville, Papua New Guinea; the central rock-rat (*Zyzomys pedunculatus*) of Australia; and the little earth hutia (*Capromys sanfelipensis*) of Cuba.

A further 41 sub-species of rodents are known or suspected to be threatened with extinction. These include: the Carolina flying squirrel (*Glaucomys sabrinus coloratus*) of the USA; the broad-tailed beaver (*Castor canadensis frondator*) of Mexico; and the Key Largo cotton mouse (*Peromyscus gossypinus allapaticola*) of the USA.

**Extinctions** No fewer than 28 rodent species are known or suspected to have become extinct in recent times. These include: the rabbit-eared tree-rat (*Conilurus albipes*), which disappeared from Australia in 1875; Maclear's rat (*Rattus macleari*), which disappeared from Christmas Island in 1908; and the St Vincent rice rat (*Oligoryzomys victus*), which disappeared from the Caribbean island of St Vincent in 1897.

---

The Norway lemming is the only animal with a reputation for committing mass suicide, although the compelling image of thousands of lemmings hurling themselves over cliffs is far from the truth.

# SEALS, SEA LIONS & WALRUS

## Pinnipedia

34 species: 19 true seals, 5 sea lions, 9 fur seals and 1 walrus, including Caribbean monk seal.

**Largest** The largest of the pinnipeds is the southern elephant seal (*Mirounga leonina*), which lives mainly in the Southern Ocean around the Antarctic. Males typically grow up to 5.8 m *19 ft* in length from the tip of their inflatable snout to the end of their outstretched tail flippers, have a maximum girth of 3.7 m *12 ft 2 in* and weigh about 2000–3500 kg *4400–7720 lb*. Females are usually much smaller, growing up to 3 m *9 ft 10 in* in length and weighing up to 400–800 kg *882–1764 lb*. The largest accurately measured specimen is a male killed in the South Atlantic at Possession Bay, South Georgia, on 28 Feb 1913. He probably weighed at least 4000 kg *8820 lb* and measured 6.5 m *21 ft 4 in* after flensing (stripping of the skin and blubber); his original length was estimated to be 6.85 m *22 ft 6 in*.

The largest recorded live specimen is a male southern elephant seal, nicknamed *Stalin*, from South Georgia, in the South Atlantic. He was recorded by members of the British Antarctic Survey and the UK-based Sea Mammal Research Unit, on 14 Oct 1989, with a weight of 2662 kg *5870 lb* and a length of 5.10 m *16 ft 9 in*.

**Smallest** The Galapagos fur seal (*Arctocephalus galapagoensis*), which breeds on seven islands in the Galapagos archipelago, off the coast of Ecuador, is probably the world's smallest pinniped. Adult females average 1.2 m *47 in* in length and weigh 27 kg *60 lb*. Males are usually considerably larger, averaging 1.5 m *59 in* in length and weighing around 64 kg *141 lb*.

**Biggest teeth** The biggest pinniped teeth belong to the walrus (*Odobenus rosmarus*), which lives in the Arctic. Its two upper canines develop into long, curved tusks that protrude from its mouth and hang down well below the chin; they are used for fighting and display, as an anchor and as a lever to heave the animal along a rocky shore or out of the water on to floating ice. The tusks are heavier and larger in males. Many tusks are broken, and most are fairly worn, but they have been known to reach 1 m *39 in* in length and to weigh as much as 5.4 kg *12 lb*.

**Shortest lactation period** The hooded seal (*Cystophora cristata*) has the shortest lactation period known for any mammal. On average, the pups are weaned after only 4 days of nursing. They grow at an astonishing rate, their weight doubling from roughly 25 kg *55 lb* at birth to 50 kg *110 lb* at weaning.

**Longest lactation period** Compared with other pinnipeds, the female walrus (*Odobenus rosmarus*) consistently has the longest period of parental care, suckling her pups for as long as 2–2½ years. The Galapagos fur seal (*Arctocephalus galapagoensis*) has a 2-year lactation period and a small number of Australian fur seals (*Arctocephalus pusillus*), South American fur seals (*Arctocephalus australis*) and Steller's sea lions (*Eumetopias jubatus*) suckle their pups for 2 or, rarely, 3 years, though 1 year is more typical.

---

**The southern elephant seal is the largest of the pinnipeds; this heavyweight, which was photographed in the Falkland Islands, probably weighed at least 3 tonnes.**

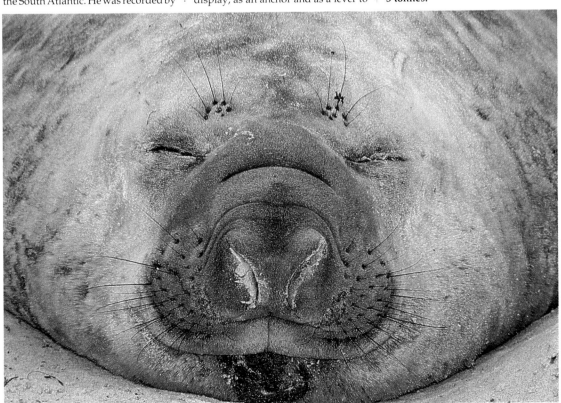

Appearances can be deceptive: California sea lions are capable of record-breaking swimming speeds of up to 40 km/h *25 mph*.

**Longest lived** Many pinnipeds, especially the females, have fairly long lifespans. The greatest authenticated age was recorded by scientists at the Limnological Institute, in Irkutsk, Russia, who have estimated that the maximum lifespan of the Baikal seal (*Phoca sibirica*) is 56 years for females and 52 years for males, based on cementum layers in the canine teeth. Female Caspian seals (*Phoca caspica*) are reputed to live to 50 years, and males to 47 years. A female grey seal (*Halichoerus grypus*) shot at Shunni Wick, Shetland, on 23 Apr 1969 was believed to be 'at least 46 years old' based on a count of dentine rings in its teeth. A 43-year-old ringed seal (*Phoca hispida*) was reported from the eastern Canadian Arctic. In all pinnipeds, except elephant seals, the females tend to have a slightly greater longevity than the males.

The captive record is 42–43 years for a male grey seal named *Jacob*. He was captured on 28 Oct 1901, at an estimated age of 2 years, and died at Skansen Zoo, Stockholm, Sweden, on 30 Jan 1942.

**Shortest lived** The shortest-lived pinniped in the wild is probably the Australian sea lion (*Neophoca cinerea*), which has a life expectancy of around 12 years.

**Most abundant** The crabeater seal (*Lobodon carcinophagus*) is the world's most abundant pinniped. The total population in its Antarctic home is estimated to be well over 10 million and, according to some estimates, may be as high as 35 million. The most widely accepted figures suggest a minimum of 9–11 million in the Weddell Sea, 1.3 million in the Amundsen and Bellinghausen Seas, 650 000 for the Oates and George V coasts, and 600 000 for the Adelie, Clairie and Banzare coasts.

**Greatest concentration** The greatest concentration of large mammals found anywhere in the world today is a herd of northern fur seals (*Callorhinus ursinus*) in the Pribilof Islands, Alaska. The herd reached a peak of about 2.5 million in the late 1950s, but numbers have declined since (partly due to many years of intensive hunting). Commercial harvesting of the animals is currently banned (though some 2500 are still allowed to be killed annually by subsistence hunters) and, every summer, the herd now contains an estimated 900 000 fur seals. These breed primarily on two main islands in the Pribilof group: St George and St Paul.

**Most recent extinction** Until quite recently, the Caribbean monk seal (*Monachus tropicalis*) lived on remote sandy beaches around the Bahamas, the Greater and Lesser Antilles and the Yucatan Peninsula, Mexico. The last reliable sighting was on Serranilla Bank, between Nicaragua and Jamaica, in 1952. The species is almost certainly extinct, in which case it is the only seal to have become extinct in recent times.

**Rarest** Assuming that the Caribbean monk seal (*Monachus tropicalis*) is extinct, the rarest species of pinniped alive today is the Mediterranean monk seal (*Monachus monachus*). There are estimated to be between 427 and 557 left, distributed as follows: Greece (200–250), Mauritania/Atlantic Morocco (130), Cyprus and Turkey (20–50), Algeria (10–30), Croatia (25), Albania (20), Mediterranean Morocco (10–20), Libya (0–20) and Deserta Grande island, Madeira (12). At least 2 were sighted in August 1994 on the coast of Sardinia, raising hopes that they may be re-establishing themselves there after an absence of more than a century. The main threats to the few survivors are hunting, habitat modification and disturbance.

The Hawaiian monk seal (*Monachus schauinslandi*) is also extremely rare, with an estimated population of 1000–1500, and is still threatened by disturbance, shark predation, entanglement in discarded fishing nets and packing bands, and disease.

A sub-species of the ringed seal (*Phoca hispida*) is on the verge of extinction. The mere 160–180 surviving Saimaa seals (*P.h.saimensis*), which live exclusively in Lake Saimaa, Finland, continue to be threatened by the building of summer cottages on the lake shore, incidental capture in fishing nets, pollution and artificial changes in water level.

**Fastest** The fastest swimming speed recorded for a pinniped is a short spurt of 40 km/h *25 mph* by a California sea lion (*Zalophus californianus*).

A leopard seal (*Hydrurga leptonyx*) of 275 kg can easily leap from water on to an ice floe 2 m *78 in* above the

Crabeater seal: the world's most abundant seal, with a total population of well over 10 million.

**The leopard seal is the only pinniped with a reputation for apparently unprovoked attacks on people, although experts generally believe that their fierce reputation is unjustified.**

surface, requiring an estimated exit speed of approximately 6 m/s or 22 km/h *14 mph*.

The fastest pinniped on land is the crabeater seal (*Lobodon carcinophagus*), which has been timed at 19 km/h *12 mph* across tightly packed snow on Signy Island, South Orkneys, near Antarctica, and in other instances has been estimated to be as high as 25 km/h *16 mph*.

**Most dangerous** When frightened, or molested, many pinnipeds will bite or chase intruders. But the carnivorous leopard seal (*Hydrurga leptonyx*) is the only species with a reputation for apparently unprovoked attacks on people. There are a number of documented cases of leopard seals suddenly lunging through cracks in the ice to snap at people's feet; divers have been attacked on at least one occasion; and several people have been chased across the ice over distances of up to 100 m *328 ft*. Leopard seals would certainly make powerful adversaries, growing to a maximum length of 3.6 m *11 ft 10 in*, weighing up to 450 kg *992 lb*, and armed with formidable teeth and powerful jaws – and they are undoubtedly short-tempered compared with other pinnipeds. However, experts generally believe that their fierce reputation is unjustified: most reported attacks seem to have been caused either by the seals making a genuine mistake (from underwater, the dark vertical shape of a man is not dissimilar to the shape of an emperor penguin) or by provocation.

**Deepest dive** Elephant seals are the only pinnipeds known to dive to depths in excess of 1000 m *3280 ft*. In May 1989, off the coast of San Miguel Island, California, an adult male northern elephant seal (*Mirounga angustirostris*) was documented on a small microprocessor-based time-depth recorder at 1529 m *5017 ft*. In the same experiment, which involved recording more than 36 000 dives by six different animals, a second seal dived to 1333 m *4374 ft*. In May 1988, when scientists from the University of California at Santa Cruz, USA, tested the diving abilities of northern elephant seals off Ano Nuevo Point, California, one female reached a record depth of 1257 m *4125 ft*. In similar experiments carried out on southern

**Elephant seals have been recorded diving deeper, and for longer, than any other member of the seal family; they are equally impressive animals on land.**

**M A M M A L S**

> *Leopard seals sometimes sing in their sleep, making a variety of chirps, whistles, gargles, grunts and sighing sounds.*

elephant seals (*M. leonina*), dives of 1256 m *4120 ft* and 1134 m *3720 ft* have been recorded.

**Longest dive** Experiments on the diving abilities of southern elephant seals (*Mirounga leonina*) in the Southern Ocean recorded a maximum dive time of 120 minutes, by a female. However, most southern elephant seal dives last for an average of 'only' 20–27 minutes. A 77-minute dive has been documented for the northern elephant seal (*Mirounga angustirostris*) and a 73-minute dive for the Weddell seal (*Leptonychotes weddelli*).

A study of northern elephant seals, in May 1989, off the coast of San Miguel Island, California, revealed that the animals rarely spent more than 5 minutes at the surface between dives, which typically lasted 21–24 minutes. During their many months at sea, it has been estimated that the seals are submerged about 86 per cent of the time.

**Most recently discovered** The Hawaiian monk seal (*Monachus schauinslandi*) was first described in 1905, from a skull found on Laysan Island, Hawaii, in 1899. No new species of pinniped has been named since.

**Longest gestation period** Research on wild Australian sea lions (*Neophoca cinerea*) suggests a total gestation period of 17.5 months; the gestation period in three captive individuals was estimated at 14–15 months. These figures include unknown periods of delayed implantation, during which attachment of the fertilized egg to the uterine wall is postponed. Walrus (*Odobenus rosmarus*) pups are born approximately 15 months after conception, including 4–5 months of delayed implantation. The gestation period in all other pinnipeds lasts 10–12 months, including varying periods of delayed implantation.

**Most southerly** The Weddell seal (*Leptonychotes weddelli*) consistently lives further south than any other pinniped. It occurs mainly along the land-fast ice close to the Antarctic continent, moving with the ice front (north in the winter and south in the summer) but usually remains within sight of land. The most northerly breeding colony is on South Georgia, in the South Atlantic, at a latitude of about 54°S. Several other pinnipeds, notably the leopard seal (*Hydrurga leptonyx*) and crabeater seal (*Lobodon carcinophagus*), live close to the Antarctic continent but occur mainly amongst the drifting pack ice a little further offshore.

**Most northerly** The ringed seal (*Phoca hispida*) has the most northerly distribution of any of the pinnipeds. The commonest seal in the Arctic, it is rarely found in the open sea or on floating pack ice, but occurs wherever there is sufficient open water in the more permanent ice. It has even been recorded as far north as the North Pole.

**Most limited range** Several pinnipeds have extremely limited ranges. Arguably, the most limited is that of the Guadalupe fur seal (*Arctocephalus townsendii*), which now breeds only along the eastern coast of Guadalupe Island, Mexico, approximately 200 km *124 miles* west of Baja California; however, since the early 1970s more than 50 sightings of this species have been made outside its normal breeding range, in particular around the Channel Islands, southern California. Other species with extremely limited ranges include: Juan Fernandez fur seal (*Arctocephalus philippii*), restricted to the Juan Fernandez and San Felix islands, both off the coast of Chile; Galapagos fur seal (*Arctocephalus galapagoensis*), which breeds on seven islands and hauls out on two others in the Galapagos archipelago, off the coast of Ecuador; Hawaiian monk seal (*Monachus schauinslandi*), found mainly on the small, mostly uninhabited, islands in the Leeward Chain, Hawaii; Caspian seal (*Phoca caspica*), found only in the Caspian Sea; and Baikal seal (*Phoca sibirica*), found only in Lake Baikal and, occasionally, some of the rivers flowing into the lake.

**Most widespread** The common seal (*Phoca vitulina*) is probably the most widespread pinniped, since its breeding range includes four major ocean areas: mainly the Temperate North Pacific and Temperate North Atlantic,

---

No other pinniped consistently lives further south than the Weddell seal.

but also the Pacific Arctic/sub-Arctic and Atlantic Arctic/sub-Arctic. The breeding range of the southern elephant seal (*Mirounga leonina*) includes the Temperate South Pacific, Temperate South Atlantic and Antarctic, but the majority of the population occurs in the sub-Antarctic. All other pinniped species occur in just one or two major ocean areas.

**Longest whiskers** All pinnipeds have whiskers on their faces, but fur seals tend to have the longest. The record is held by a male Antarctic fur seal (*Arctocephalus gazella*) whose longest whisker measured 48 cm *19 in*.

**Shortest whiskers** The shortest and thickest whiskers belong to the walrus (*Odobenus rosmarus*); they average only 8 cm *3 in* long and 2–3 mm *0.1 in* diameter.

**Most whiskers** The walrus (*Odobenus rosmarus*) has about 300 whiskers on each side of its 'moustache' – more than in any other pinniped.

**Most specialized diet** Despite its name, the crabeater seal (*Lobodon carcinophagus*) feeds almost exclusively on krill. These small, shrimp-like creatures account for 94 per cent of its diet, the remainder consisting of other invertebrates, fish and squid.

**Most varied diet** Many pinnipeds take a wide range of prey. The common seal (*Phoca vitulina*), for example, is known to feed on at least 50 different species of fish, as well as squid, whelks, crabs and molluscs. But the leopard seal (*Hydrurga leptonyx*) has by far the most varied diet and, indeed, has a reputation for eating almost anything that moves. It will take many species of penguins and other sea birds, fish, squid, octopus, krill, the pups of crabeater, Weddell, Ross, southern elephant and Antarctic fur seals, and even dead whales. The stomach of one male leopard seal contained an adult duck-billed platypus and another individual regurgitated a sea snake. Leopard seals also have voracious appetites: one was observed catching and eating six penguins in 70 minutes while another had 79 kg *174 lb* of penguin remains in its stomach.

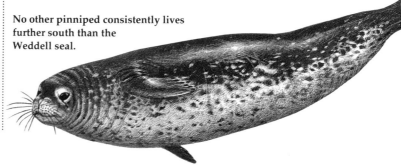

The Juan Fernandez fur seal, restricted to two small island groups off the coast of Chile, has one of the most limited ranges of all members of the seal family.

**Strangest** The strangest-looking pinniped is probably the hooded seal (*Cystophora cristata*) of the North Atlantic and Arctic. The adult male has an enlarged nasal cavity, which forms an inflatable hood on the top of its head: when not inflated, this is slack and wrinkled and its tip hangs down over the front of the mouth; but, when it is filled with air, it resembles a giant leathery football. The same animal is also able to blow up the internal membrane inside its nose to form a bright red or brown 'balloon' that usually extrudes from the left nostril. Both the hood and the balloon are inflated when the seal is disturbed and during courtship display, though it sometimes appears to 'play' with the hood by moving air gently from the front to the back.

**Furthest from the sea** The Baikal seal (*Phoca sibirica*) is effectively confined to Lake Baikal, a huge freshwater lake 630 km *395 miles* long in Russia, immediately north of Mongolia. The oldest and deepest lake in the world, Lake Baikal is approximately 1700 km *1056 miles* from the nearest coastline, which is on the Sea of Okhotsk. A single Baikal seal was recorded 400 km *248 miles* down the Angara River, which flows out of the lake's southern end, at which point it would have been approximately 1900 km *1180 miles* from the nearest coastline, on the Laptev Sea.

**Most precocious** Common seals (*Phoca vitulina*) are often born in the intertidal zone, so their pups must be ready to enter the sea soon after birth. They usually begin swimming within hours of birth but, if necessary, can cope in the water after just a few minutes. They can swim and dive efficiently almost straight away but, during the first week of their lives, will often ride on their mothers' backs if they get tired or if there is danger nearby.

Recent research suggests that the 'whitecoat' pups of grey seals (*Halichoerus grypus*) can also swim, although not as proficiently as the young common seals.

**Weight loss** The male northern elephant seal (*Mirounga angustirostris*) fasts for a total of 4 months in every year. During the breeding season, from early December to the end of February, it is unable to abandon the harem of females on shore in case another male attempts to mate with them and, consequently, is unable to enter the sea to feed. It loses up to half its body weight (in extreme cases, as much as 1000 kg *984 lb*) during this 3-month period. Then it fasts again during the month-long moult in late June and July. Newly weaned elephant seal pups fast for up to 3 months before they learn to fish for themselves, although they often try to sneak a meal from other lactating females in the harem after their natural mothers have left. In both adults and juveniles, the thick blubber layer serves as a food store during these fasting periods.

**Longest nose** The male northern elephant seal (*Mirounga angustirostris*) has an extremely long, inflatable proboscis; when relaxed, it hangs down over the animal's mouth by about 30 cm *12 in*. The proboscis begins to appear at puberty (3–4 years old) and is fully developed when the seal is about 8 years old. The male southern elephant seal (*M. leonina*) does not have such a pendulous nose: it overhangs its mouth by only about 10 cm *4 in*.

**Teeth** There is little variation in the number of teeth found in most pinniped species, with a total of 30–36 being typical. There are just two exceptions: the walrus (*Odobenus rosmarus*) which

*In hot weather, many pinnipeds flip sand and tiny pebbles on to their backs with their front flippers. This helps to keep them cool and probably alleviates skin irritation caused by drying out on land.*

The most widely publicized commercial seal hunt of recent years has been the hunt for harp seals off the coast of Newfoundland and in the Gulf of St Lawrence, in eastern Canada.

___

normally has only 18 teeth; and the California sea lion (*Zalophus californianus*) which has 34–38 teeth.

**Size difference** The greatest size difference between the sexes is found in the southern elephant seal (*Mirounga leonina*). At birth, pups of both sexes are roughly the same size (1.3 m *51 in* long and 40–50 kg *88–110 lb* in weight) but the males become substantially larger as they grow older. Adult males average 4–5 m *13–16 ft* in length and weigh about 3500 kg *7720 lb*; females average 2–3 m *78 in–9 ft 10 in* in length and weigh about 500–800 kg *1102–1764 lb*. This makes the males almost twice as long and more than five times as heavy as the females.

**Longest migration** Female northern fur seals (*Callorhinus ursinus*) leave their breeding grounds on the Pribilof Islands, Alaska, in late September and early October and swim some 5000 km *3100 miles* south to spend the winter off the coast of California; they begin their return journey as winter ends, arriving back in the Pribilofs some time in June. The males and youngsters make a shorter journey to spend the winter in the Gulf of Alaska.

A population of hooded seals (*Cystophora cristata*) routinely undertakes a 3250 km *2000 miles* annual migration from its breeding grounds in the Gulf of St Lawrence, Canada, to its moulting grounds between 66° and 68°N in the Denmark Strait, off the south-east coast of Greenland.

Hooded seals are great wanderers and often turn up in the most unexpected places, well outside their normal arctic and sub-arctic range in the North Atlantic. On 23 Jul 1990, a fairly healthy female, estimated to be about 3 years old, came ashore in San Diego, California; she must have travelled at least 13 000 km *8073 miles* through the Northwest Passage, into the Bering Sea and down through much of the North Pacific to get there.

**Most variable colour** A walrus (*Odobenus rosmarus*) changes colour depending on whether it is in or out of the water. Its basic body colour is cinnamon brown. However, in the water, blood is drawn away from the skin to maintain a high core body temperature, and the walrus turns a much paler colour; it may even appear ghostly white. On land, blood is directed towards the skin to release excess heat, and the walrus turns a grey to reddish-brown colour; it may appear bright pink, as if it were sunburnt.

**Most killed** No species of pinniped has escaped from human exploitation, although Ross seals (*Ommatophoca rossi*), leopard seals (*Hydrurga leptonyx*) and Weddell seals (*Leptonychotes weddellii*), in particular, have never been exploited to a significant degree. Most historical records are too sparse to be certain of the precise numbers of some other species killed over the years and, in some cases, the actual number is likely to be higher than official figures suggest. However, there is no doubt that tens of millions of seals have been killed commercially, particularly in the past two centuries, to obtain food, oil, fur and leather.

The highest kills on record took place on the Juan Fernandez Islands, off the coast of Chile, where commercial sealing began in 1687 and continued until the Juan Fernandez fur seal (*Arctocephalus philippii*) was believed to be extinct, which was towards the end of the 19th century. Two examples illustrate the scale of the killing: in 1801 a single ship carried a cargo of 1 million fur seal skins from the island of Más a Tierra to London; and, not long afterwards, as many as 3 million fur seals were killed during one 7-year period 1817–24.

The highly publicized commercial hunt for harp seals (*Phoca groenlandica*) off the coast of Newfoundland and in the Gulf of St Lawrence, in eastern Canada, first began in the mid-17th century. The annual catch exceeded 500 000 seals 11 times between 1825

___

*Many pinnipeds deliberately swallow stones and pebbles. No one knows what they are for, but there are several possible theories: they may help to allay hunger pangs during long periods of fasting, they could help to grind up food in the stomach, or they may play a role in buoyancy control. One southern fur seal had 11 kg 24 lb of stones and pebbles in its stomach, some as large as tennis balls.*

and 1860 and reached nearly 750000 in a few years during this period; in 1857 a maximum of 370 vessels and 13600 men participated in the hunt. The catch declined to approximately 250000 every year until 1911 and then averaged about 160000 (with a brief reduction during and immediately after World War II) until the early 1980s. Since then catches have been: 200162 (1981); 166739 (1982); 57889 (1983); 30900 (1984); 18225 (1985); 24532 (1986); 49000 (1987); 94024 (1988); 65072 (1989); 60040 (1990); 52565 (1991); 67428 (1992); 25175 (1993); and 56465 (1994).

The next highest 1-year kills on record include 460000 harp seals in the White Sea, Russia, in 1925; nearly 250000 antarctic fur seals (*Arctocephalus gazella*) on the South Shetland Islands, Antarctica, in 1821; some 250000 northern fur seals (*Callorhinus ursinus*) on the Pribilof Islands, Alaska, in 1868; and 227000 Caspian seals (*Phoca caspica*) in the Caspian Sea, in 1935.

**Longest hunt** Commercial hunting of the walrus (*Odobenus rosmarus*) began at least as long ago as the 9th century and still continues today. It has taken place sporadically in many parts of the arctic and sub-arctic (though nowadays it is restricted to the Bering and Chukchi Seas) for the animal's valuable ivory tusks, tough hide and oil.

The Uruguayan fur sealing industry is the longest sustained operation of its kind in the world. Extensive commercial exploitation of South American fur seals (*Arctocephalus australis*) began in Uruguay in 1724 and has been regulated by the local government since 1808. Some 4500–14000 animals were killed each year until 1982; the hunting continues today, though on a smaller scale due to a decline in the demand for furs.

**Most polygamous** A male northern fur seal (*Callorhinus ursinus*) living in the Pribilof Islands, Alaska, USA, was recorded mating with 161 females, making it the most polygamous pinniped and probably the most polygamous mammal. Most male northern fur seals mate with 15–30 females.

The northern elephant seal (*Mirounga angustirostris*) is also highly polygamous. A single dominant male typically mates with 40–50 females during a brief period of receptivity within a single breeding season. There are records of individuals mating with as many as 100 different females in the space of a few weeks, but competition is fierce and with this number it is difficult for them to keep out the lower ranking males. Only 1 in 100 males lives to be 9 or 10 years old, which is the optimum age for being dominant in the social hierarchy, and many of these die without mating at all. Even the successful males, having reached their reproductive peak, can remain sufficiently dominant for no more than 1 or 2 years before they die.

# TAPIRS

### *Tapiridae*
4 species: Malayan, south-east Asia; and the Brazilian, Central American and mountain tapirs, Central and South America.

> *Tapirs are good swimmers and, if they feel threatened, can hold their breath long enough to hide underwater for several minutes.*

**Earliest** Tapirs are among the most primitive large mammals in the world and, indeed, it is thought that they are still very similar to the common ancestors of all perissodactyls which lived more than 40 million years ago. The modern genus *Tapirus* first appeared in the Miocene nearly 20 million years ago.

**Largest** The largest tapir is the Malayan or Asian tapir (*Tapirus indicus*), which is well known for its striking black and white markings. It has a head-body length of 2.2–2.5 m *7¼–8¼ ft*; a tail length of 5–10 cm *2–4 in*; a height at the shoulder of 95–110 cm *37½–43¼ ft*; and weighs 250–360 kg *551–794 lb*. One individual is reputed to have weighed 540 kg *1191 lb*.

**Smallest** The mountain or woolly tapir (*Tapirus pinchaque*) is the smallest member of the tapir family. It has an average head-body length of 1.8 m *71 in*; a tail length of 5 cm *2 in*; a shoulder height of 75 cm *29½ in*; and an average weight of 225 kg *496 lb*.

**Most threatened** According to the World Conservation Union (IUCN), three of the four tapir species are considered to be threatened with extinction: the Central American or Baird's tapir (*Tapirus bairdii*), which lives in Colombia, Ecuador, possibly Mexico (where it may already be extinct), and six Central American countries (not El Salvador); the Malayan tapir (*Tapirus indicus*), which lives in Indonesia (Sumatra), Malaysia (Peninsula Malaysia), Thailand, Myanmar, Laos and Vietnam; and the mountain or woolly tapir (*Tapirus pinchaque*), which lives in Colombia, Ecuador, Peru and Venezuela. The many threats to tapirs include hunting for sport, food and for their highly-prized skins; capture of live animals for trade; and, most importantly, habitat destruction caused by logging, clearance for agriculture and major development projects.

**Highest living** The mountain tapir (*Tapirus pinchaque*) lives consistently at a height of 2000–4500 m *6560–14760 ft* in the upper reaches of the Andes. This is a region of low temperatures and almost perpetual mist and so, not surprisingly, it is the only member of the family with a long, thick coat of hair. Other tapirs live at high altitudes, but they also occur down to sea level.

**The striking black and white Malayan tapir is the largest member of the tapir family.**

# WHALES, DOLPHINS & PORPOISES

## Cetacea
79–80 species.

*The easiest way to tell a whale, dolphin or porpoise from a fish is by the tail: the cetacean's tail (called a fluke) is horizontal and swings up and down, while the fish's tail (called a caudal fin) is vertical and swings from side to side.*

**Earliest** The first whale-like animals, called Archaeocetes, or ancient whales, appeared about 50 million years ago. They were not the direct ancestors of modern whales but were probably very similar. However, they were more primitive in many ways – for example, in having nostrils which had not completely moved to the tops of their heads for easier breathing at the surface. There were many different kinds of Archaeocete, ranging in length from 2 m *6½ft* to 21 m *69ft*, but they all lived in coastal swamps and shallow seas. Their bodies were torpedo-shaped and their front limbs had turned into paddles. Known only from fossils, they eventually died out about 30 million years ago.

The 'missing link' between whales

**The largest toothed whale is the sperm whale, with an average male measuring about 15 m *49ft 2 in* in length and weighing some 45 tonnes.**

and their four-legged land-living ancestors is believed to have been a creature called *Ambulocetus natans* (Latin for 'walking and swimming whale') which lived some 50 million years ago, just when the first whales were colonizing the seas. The first fossil to be discovered was an incomplete skeleton in the Kala Chitta Hills, Pakistan, in 1993. In some ways, *Ambulocetus* resembled a sea lion, in particular by being able to hobble around on land on its legs and chest. But, unlike sea lions, which swim mainly with their forelimbs, it used its forelimbs for steering and probably swam by beating its enlarged, webbed hind feet and tail up and down. It is uncertain whether *Ambulocetus* was the actual whale ancestor or a hangover from earlier stages of whale evolution.

**Largest** The blue whale (*Balaenoptera musculus*) is the heaviest and longest animal on Earth. The average adult length is 25 m *82ft* in males and 26.2 m *86ft* in females, with body weights of

90–120 tonnes. Blue whales in the southern hemisphere tend to be the largest, and females are larger than males of the same age.

No blue whale has ever been weighed 'whole'. All known weights have been obtained either by cutting them into smaller pieces, or by adding up the total number of known-capacity cookers filled with the meat, bone and blubber of individual whales at shore stations or on floating factory ships. The heaviest recorded blue whale was a female, caught in the Southern Ocean on 20 Mar 1947, which weighed 190 tonnes. Another female blue whale, brought to the shore station at Prince Olaf Harbor, South Georgia, Southern Ocean, in 1931, was 29.5 m *97ft* long and was calculated to weigh, from the number of cookers filled, 166 tonnes; however, after transposing the figures, correcting an error in the published arithmetic, and adding 6.5 per cent for loss of blood and other body fluids, this makes a total estimated weight of 199 tonnes.

The longest blue whale ever recorded was another female, landed in 1909 at Grytviken, South Georgia, in the South Atlantic, which measured 33.58 m *110 ft 2 in* from the tip of her snout to the end of her tail.

The largest toothed whale is the sperm whale (*Physeter macrocephalus*). The average size for a male is about 15 m *49 ft 2 in* and 45 tonnes; females are considerably smaller, averaging 12 m *39 ft 4 in* and 20 tonnes. The largest officially measured was a record-sized male, some 20.7 m *67 ft 11 in* in length, which was captured in the summer of 1950 off the Kurile Islands, in the northwest Pacific. However, the 5 m- *16 ft 5 in*-long lower jaw of a sperm whale exhibited in The Natural History Museum, UK, is reputed to have belonged to a male measuring nearly 25.6 m *84 ft*. The heaviest animal reliably weighed was an 18.1 m *59 ft 5 in* male which stranded in the Netherlands on 24 Feb 1937; it weighed 57.1 tonnes. Even larger males were reported in the early days of whaling, though there are no authenticated records.

The largest member of the dolphin family is the killer whale or orca (*Orcinus orca*). Males typically grow to 8 m *26 ft 3 in* long, though females are considerably smaller and rarely exceed 7 m *23 ft*. The longest individual recorded was a 9.8 m *32 ft* male in the western North Pacific.

**Largest held in captivity** A female grey whale (*Eschrichtius robustus*) was captured in Scammon's Lagoon, Baja California, Mexico, on 13 Mar 1971 by a collecting expedition from Sea World. At the time, she was approximately 6–10 weeks old and 5.54 m *18 ft 2 in* long.

She arrived (by boat) in San Diego, USA, four days later, where she was named *Gigi*. By the time she was 1 year old, *Gigi* was 8.23 m *27 ft* long and weighed an estimated 6.35 tonnes. She was seriously outgrowing her surroundings and, on 13 Mar 1972, was returned to the sea about 6.4 km *4 miles* north of Port Loma, California, USA. Her release was timed to coincide with the annual migration of the grey whales travelling from their calving grounds in Mexico to their feeding grounds in the Arctic. *Gigi* joined up with the herd and was observed for 5 days as she moved northwards. In the autumn of 1979, she was sighted in San Ignacio Lagoon, Baja California, Mexico, with a new-born calf.

**Smallest** The black dolphin (*Cephalorhynchus eutropia*), Hector's dolphin (*Cephalorhynchus hectori*), finless porpoise (*Neophocaena phocaenoides*) and vaquita (*Phocoena sinus*) are probably equal contenders for the world's smallest cetacean. All four species can be as short as 1.2 m *3 ft 11 in* when fully grown although, taking *average* lengths, the shortest are Hector's dolphin and vaquita by a narrow margin. In terms of weight, the finless porpoise is probably the lightest, weighing 30–45 kg *66–99 lb*; nearly 3000 finless porpoises would weigh roughly the same as one

> When whales and dolphins open their eyes underwater, special greasy tears protect them from the stinging salt.

**This female humpback whale, known affectionately as 'Salt' by biologists off the east coast of the United States, is probably the most studied wild whale in the world.**

blue whale. The black dolphin, vaquita and franciscana (*Pontoporia blainvillei*) can all weigh as little as 30 kg *66 lb* when fully grown, though their average weights are higher. Commerson's dolphin (*Cephalorhynchus commersonii*) is also very small; weights of 19 animals off the coast of South America ranged from 26–44.5 kg *57–98 lb*.

The smallest baleen whale is the pygmy right whale (*Caperea marginata*). The maximum lengths recorded are 6.45 m *21 ft* for a female and 6.09 m *20 ft* for a male. Only two animals have been weighed: a female of 6.21 m *20 ft 4 in* was 3.2 tonnes and a male of 5.47 m *18 ft* was 2.85 tonnes; both were taken from the South Atlantic.

**Most studied whale** The most studied whale in the wild is probably a female humpback (*Megaptera novaeangliae*) called *Salt*. She was first sighted on 1 May 1976 by biologists studying the whales around Stellwagen Bank, off the coast of New England, USA. A huge animal, estimated to measure 14–15 m *46–49 ft* long and weighing about 30 tonnes, she was named after a distinctive white patch and a sprinkling of white spots on her dorsal fin. *Salt* has been observed and photographed by dozens of scientists, and thousands of whale watchers, around Stellwagen Bank and nearby Jeffrey's Ledge every summer since 1976. She has also been

*The black and white markings on the underside of humpback whale tails are so distinctive that they can be used like fingerprints, to tell one animal from another; they range from pure white to jet black and include an endless number of variations in between.*

studied in her Caribbean breeding grounds for many years, after she was first sighted off the coast of the Dominican Republic in 1978. For several years no one knew whether *Salt* was male or female, until she turned up with a calf by her side in 1980. She has had many calves since and became a grandmother for the first time in 1992.

Killer whale (*Orcinus orca*) pods living along the coasts of British Columbia, Canada, and Washington State, USA, have been studied since the early 1970s. There is now a registry containing photographs and names for each of more than 300 individual whales currently living in the area. Biologists have worked out most of their family trees, and have accumulated details on everything from the year they were born and their home ranges to injuries they have sustained and their more unusual habits.

**Largest baby** In the 2 months before it is born, the weight of a blue whale (*Balaenoptera musculus*) increases by as much as 2 tonnes – it grows about 1000 times faster than a human baby in the womb. The newborn calf is a record-breaking 6–8 m *20–26 ft* long and weighs 2–3 tonnes. Every day, the baby drinks about 200 litres *360 pints* of its mother's milk and gains as much as 90 kg *198 lb* in weight (roughly equivalent to the weight of a grown man). By the time it is weaned, at 7 months old, it has roughly doubled in length and weighs an amazing 20 tonnes.

The blue whale calf is not exceptionally large in proportion to the size of its mother: one-third of the adult length is typical for most newborn cetaceans. Several species give birth to calves which are closer to half their own length, including belugas (*Delphinapterus leucas*), northern bottlenose whales (*Hyperoodon ampullatus*), tucuxis (*Sotalia fluviatilis*), Atlantic white-sided dolphins (*Lagenorhynchus acutus*) and Dall's porpoises (*Phocoenoides dalli*).

**Gestation period** The longest known gestation period is 15–17 months (with a possible record of 18 months 28 days) for the sperm whale (*Physeter macrocephalus*) and up to 17 months for Baird's beaked whale (*Berardius bairdii*). The shortest gestation period is unknown, although 10–12 months is typical in many species and there have been reports of even shorter periods: 7 months for a Dall's porpoise (*Phocoenoides dalli*), 8 months for a harbour porpoise (*Phocoena phocoena*) and 9 months 15 days for a long-snouted spinner dolphin (*Stenella longirostris*); however, these are probably extreme cases. The gestation period is not dependent on body size: in the blue whale (*Balaenoptera musculus*), the largest animal on Earth, it is a little less than 12 months.

**Baleen** Most large whales have hundreds of furry, comb-like structures hanging down from their upper jaws, called baleen plates, or whalebones; these form a sieve to filter food from the sea-water. The size and number of baleen plates varies greatly from species to species and from one individual to another. The longest baleen is found in the bowhead whale (*Balaena mysticetus*): there are many records within the 3–4 m *10–13 ft* range, but lengths of up to 5.18 m *17 ft* have been reported for animals killed during the 19th century. A plate taken from a bowhead killed in 1849 was reputed to

be 5.8 m *19ft*, though this claim has been disputed since. The shortest baleen is found in the minke whale (*Balaenoptera acutorostrata*), with a maximum length of about 30 cm *12 in*. The total number of baleen plates inside the mouth ranges from a minimum of 280 in the grey whale (*Eschrichtius robustus*) to a maximum of 946 in the fin whale (*Balaenoptera physalus*).

**Weight loss** While nursing her calf, a 120-tonne female blue whale (*Balaenoptera musculus*) can lose up to 1 tonne per week – equivalent to more than 25 per cent of her body weight during the 7-month lactation period.

**Longest tooth** The male narwhal (*Monodon monoceros*) has two teeth. The one on the right normally remains invisible, but the one on the left grows to a remarkable length. It pierces the animal's upper lip, develops into a long tusk and eventually looks rather like a gnarled and twisted walking stick. When viewed from the root, it always spirals in a counter-clockwise direction. At least a third of all narwhal

**Sperm whales have been known to make record-breaking dives, lasting up to 1 h 52 min, to depths of more than 2000 m *6560 ft*.**

tusks are broken, but unbroken tusks reach an average length of about 2 m *6 ft 7 in* and weigh 8–9 kg *17½–19¼ lb*. In extreme cases, they exceed 3 m *9 ft 10 in* and 10 kg *22 lb* (with a maximum girth of about 23 cm *9 in*). Approximately one male in 500 has two tusks and one female in 30 grows a single tusk. There is only one record of a female with two tusks: the skull, with each tusk just over 2 m *6 ft 7 in* long, was given to a museum in Hamburg, Germany, in 1684, by a whaling captain who had killed the animal near Spitzbergen, in the Arctic. The tusk is probably used in establishing sexual dominance, in a way not dissimilar to the use of antlers in male deer.

The male strap-toothed whale (*Mesoplodon layardii*) has two teeth which grow from its lower jaw, curl upwards and backwards and then extend over the top of its upper jaw. In older animals, they can grow to a length of 30 cm *12 in* or more, and may actually meet in the middle. When this happens, the teeth form a muzzle, preventing the whales from opening their jaws properly (though they can still catch squid, their main prey, by using their mouths like vaccuum cleaners).

The largest 'normal' teeth of any animal species belong to the sperm whale (*Physeter macrocephalus*). In males, these can be nearly 25 cm *10 in* tall and weigh over 1 kg *2.2 lb* each; they are roughly half this size in females. The largest on record are two sperm whale teeth housed at the Old Dartmouth Historical Society Whaling Museum, Massachusetts, USA, which both measure 27.9 cm *11 in* in height and weigh 1.98 kg *4 lb 6 oz* and 1.90 kg *4 lb 3 oz* respectively. There are usually 36–50 teeth in the lower jaw of a sperm whale, but none in the upper jaw.

**Most teeth** The long-snouted spinner dolphin (*Stenella longirostris*) has more teeth than any other cetacean, the exact number varying from 172 to 252. The franciscana (*Pontoporia blainvillei*) is a close runner-up with a range of 208 to 228 (exceptionally 240).

**Worst eyesight** Ganges river dolphins (*Platanista gangetica*) and Indus river dolphins (*Platanista minor*) are the only cetaceans with eyes that lack a crystalline lens. The optic opening is no bigger than a pin prick and barely large enough to allow light to penetrate. For all intents and purposes they are blind, although recent evidence suggests that they can probably detect the direction, and perhaps intensity, of light. Also known as the blind river dolphins, they live in muddy rivers where eyes would be useless; they find their way around

by building up a 'sound picture' of their surroundings with a system known as echolocation, which is similar to the one used by bats to find their way around in the dark.

**Best-selling record** Male humpback whales (*Megaptera novaeangliae*) are the only animals that can boast a top-selling record in the pop charts. When their plaintive songs were first heard in the 1970s, many people were captivated by their eerie moans, groans, roars, snores, squeaks and whistles.

> *Humpback whales sometimes use bubbles to make their own fishing nets.*

**Longest song** Male humpback whales (*Megaptera novaeangliae*) sing the longest and most complex songs in the animal kingdom. Each song lasts for half an hour or more and consists of several main components; these are always sung in the same order, but are forever being refined and improved. All the humpbacks in one area sing broadly the same song, constantly incorporating each other's improvisations. Those in other parts of the world sing a completely different version. Most of the singing takes place at the breeding grounds, where the whales serenade one another throughout the day and night, with only brief one-minute pauses for breath. The aim of the singing is probably to woo females and to frighten off rival males.

Belugas (*Delphinapterus leucas*) make such a bewildering variety of whistles, squeals, clangs, moos, belches and yelps that early sailors nicknamed them 'sea canaries'. They also make resonant bell-like tones, a noise rather like an echo-sounder and even something resembling a giggling crowd of children. In calm conditions, these sounds are often audible above the surface of the water and through the hulls of boats.

**Deepest dive** The sperm whale (*Physeter macrocephalus*) is believed to dive deeper than any other cetacean. Most long, deep dives are made by older males and the depths they reach may be limited by time rather than water pressure. The deepest dives known were recorded in 1991 off Dominica, in the Caribbean, by scientists from the Woods Hole Oceanographic Institute. The scientists tagged a pair of male sperm whales and found that they regularly reached depths of 400–600 m *1312–1968 ft*, remaining underwater for

**M**
**A**
**M**
**M**
**A**
**L**
**S**

an average of 30–40 minutes. On one occasion, the bigger of the two – which was some 15 m *49 ft* in length – made a dive of 2000 m *6560 ft* to the seabed; it descended at a speed of up to 4 m/s *8 mph* and spent a total of 1 h 13 min underwater. The other animal managed a maximum dive of 'only' 1185 m *3887 ft*, but even this beat previous recorded dive depths.

*Indirect* evidence suggests that sperm whales may be able to dive to depths of at least 3000 m *9840 ft*. On 25 Aug 1969 a male sperm whale was killed 160 km *99 miles* south of Durban, South Africa, after it had surfaced from a dive lasting 1 h 52 min. Inside its stomach there were two small sharks which experts estimated had been swallowed about an hour earlier; these were later identified as *Scymnodon* sp, a type of dogfish found only on the seafloor. The water in the area exceeds a depth of 3193 m *10 473 ft* for a radius of some 48–64 km *30–40 miles*, suggesting that the sperm whale had been to a similar depth when seeking food.

Many beaked whales are believed to be deep divers and certain species may challenge the sperm whale for this record. However, there has been little research in this area and, currently, there is limited evidence to support such a claim.

**Longest dive** Early whalers reported dive times of more than 2 hours for northern bottlenose whales (*Hyperoodon ampullatus*), although their evidence is anecdotal. Sperm whales (*Physeter*

The unicorn – a mythical white horse with a horn growing out of its forehead – was really a whale, called a narwhal. Long before the narwhal itself was widely known, its tusks were on sale in Europe and many people were fooled into believing they came from unicorns.

*macrocephalus*) may also be capable of two-hour dives. On 25 Aug 1969, a male sperm whale was killed 160 km *99 miles* south of Durban, South Africa, after it had surfaced from a dive lasting 1 h 52 min.

**Fastest** On 12 Oct 1958 a bull killer whale (*Orcinus orca*) was timed swimming at 55.5 km/h *34 mph* in the eastern North Pacific. Similar speeds, albeit in short bursts, have also been reported for Dall's porpoises (*Phocoenoides dalli*).

**Most threatened** The World Conservation Union (IUCN) lists all the world's cetaceans as known or suspected to be threatened with extinction. Five species are considered to be in imminent danger: northern right whale (*Eubalaena glacialis*), blue whale (*Balaenoptera musculus*), vaquita (*Phocoena sinus*), baiji or Yangtze river dolphin (*Lipotes vexillifer*) and Indus river dolphin (*Platanista minor*).

**Rarest** The baiji, or Yangtze river dolphin (*Lipotes vexillifer*) is probably the rarest of all the cetaceans, with a population estimated at 150 and falling due to competition with fisheries, incidental capture in fishing nets, hunting,

pollution, disturbance and habitat destruction. The few survivors live mainly in the middle reaches of the Yangtze River, in China. Many experts believe that the baiji is at risk of becoming the first cetacean ever to become extinct as a direct result of human activity.

Longman's beaked whale (*Mesoplodon pacificus*) is known from only two skulls; one was discovered in 1922 on a beach near MacKay, Queensland, Australia, and the second in 1955 near Mogadishu, Somalia. However, the total lack of observations in the wild does not necessarily mean that this species is rare, especially since few beaked whales are seen regularly.

There are several other seriously endangered cetaceans with small and, in most cases, dwindling populations. In particular, there are only 'a few hundred' (minimum 100 maximum 500) vaquita (*Phocoena sinus*), all living in the northern end of the Sea of Cortez, Mexico. At a conference in 1990 one

**The world's rarest cetacean is believed to be the Yangtze river dolphin, or baiji, which has a total estimated population of 150 – and falling.**

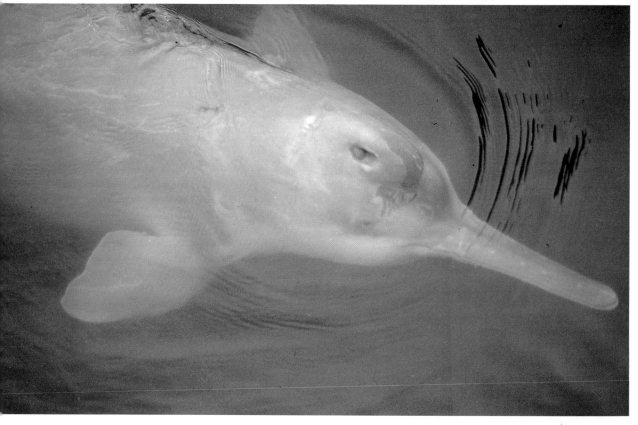

**The grey whale was long believed to undertake the longest migration of any mammal, although recent research has shown the humpback whale to be a close rival; the spyhopping grey whale in this picture was photographed in its breeding lagoon in Baja California, Mexico.**

vaquita researcher made a dismal prediction: 'Probably in less than 10 years the vaquita will be extinct'; others are not quite so pessimistic.

There are only about 500 Indus river dolphins (*Platanista minor*) in the Indus river, in Pakistan; and approximately 300–600 northern right whales (*Eubalaena glacialis*) in certain parts of the North Atlantic and North Pacific. The blue whale (*Balaenoptera musculus*) is also considered seriously endangered, as a direct result of whaling. Although the total population is unknown, it is likely to be in the low thousands; the population around Antarctica is believed to have declined from nearly a quarter of a million at the turn of the century to an estimated 460 today.

**Longest migration** The grey whale (*Eschrichtius robustus*) is believed to undertake the longest known migration of any mammal. Hugging the North American coastline, it swims from its winter breeding grounds in Baja California, Mexico, to its summer feeding grounds in the rich waters of the Bering Sea, and back again, every year. This amounts to a total annual distance of 12 000–20 000 km *7452–12 420 miles*. In a grey whale's lifetime of 40 years or more, this is equivalent to a return trip to the Moon.

Recent studies on migrating humpback whales (*Megaptera novaeangliae*) suggest that they may travel as far as the grey whales, and possibly even further. For example, one population migrates between Hawaii and Alaska every year, another between the Caribbean and Greenland and Iceland, and a third between parts of the Antarctic and Colombia.

**Tallest blow** A 'blow' or 'spout' is the cloud of water droplets produced above a whale's head when it blows out. The tallest blow belongs to the blue whale (*Balaenoptera musculus*); slender and

**The dorsal fin of a bull killer whale can be roughly as tall as a man, making it by far the tallest in the animal kingdom.**

vertical in shape, it reaches a height of 6–9 m *19 ft 8 in–29½ ft*, though blows of up to 12 m *39 ft 5 in* have been reported.

**Tallest dorsal fin** The huge, triangular dorsal fin of the bull killer whale (*Orcinus orca*) can reach a remarkable height of 1.8 m *6 ft*, which makes it roughly as tall as a man. In comparison, the blue whale's (*Balaenoptera musculus*) dorsal fin is relatively small, rarely reaching more than 40 cm *16 in* in height.

**Largest appetite** A blue whale (*Balaenoptera musculus*) eats up to 4 tonnes of krill (small, shrimp-like creatures) every day. Since each of these tiny animals weighs only about 1 g *0.04 oz*, a daily intake of no fewer than 4 million of them is required to keep the whale going. In terms of weight, this is equivalent to eating a fully grown African elephant every day. The whale does not feed all year round, but often gorges itself for about 4 months of the year – gaining as much as 770 kg *1698 lb* in weight per week – at its feeding grounds in polar waters, and then fasts for most of the time while on migration and at its breeding grounds in warmer waters.

There is a report from the mid-1860s, in which a male killer whale (*Orcinus orca*) was found to have no fewer than 13 porpoises and parts of 14 seals in its stomach (although it did not necessarily eat all of these on its own).

A sperm whale (*Physeter macrocephalus*) eats up to a tonne of squid every day, each animal ranging in size from a few centimetres to over 12 m *39 ft 4 in* long. One whale's stomach was reported to contain 28 000 of the smaller species.

**Largest prey** Killer whales (*Orcinus orca*) have been known to prey on more than 25 different whale and dolphin species, including sperm whale (*Physeter macrocephalus*), southern right whale (*Eubalaena australis*), grey whale (*Eschrichtius robustus*), humpback whale (*Megaptera novaeangliae*) and several others that are considerably larger than themselves. In one well-documented case, in May 1978, a young blue whale (*Balaenoptera musculus*) was surrounded and attacked by a pod of killers off the coast of Cabo San Lucas, Baja California, Mexico; after sizeable chunks of flesh had been torn away, the blue whale escaped as fast as it could, but probably died afterwards.

The largest 'giant squid' known to be taken by a sperm whale (*Physeter macrocephalus*) was 14.5 m *47 ft 7 in* long, including its tentacles; it was caught on Great Bahama Bank, in the Bahamas. Stories of fights between sperm whales and giant squid have probably been exaggerated, though there is little doubt that they make formidable adversaries and frequently turn on the whales, wrapping their tentacles around their heads to resist capture.

**Most contaminated** Belugas (*Delphinapterus leucas*) living in the Gulf of St Lawrence, Canada, are so badly contaminated with heavy metals, organochlorines and benzoapyrene (a byproduct of aluminium smelting and a potent carcinogen) that, when they

Two different forms of common dolphin have been identified in recent years; if they are declared as distinct species, they will be the latest of several new cetaceans to have been discovered in recent years.

die, their bodies could qualify as toxic waste.

**Most offspring** Unlike most other mammals, whales, dolphins and porpoises usually have just one baby at a time. There are records of up to six foetuses in individual fin whales (*Balaenoptera physalus*) but, in most cases, multiple foetuses die before birth; and, even if more than one calf is born, the mother cannot usually provide sufficient milk for more than one to survive. There are, however, a small number of records of twins being born and raised successfully by killer whales (*Orcinus orca*), belugas (*Delphinapterus leucas*) and bowhead whales (*Balaena mysticetus*).

**Most recently discovered** Several previously unknown cetaceans have been discovered in recent years. The most recent species to be named is the lesser beaked whale (*Mesoplodon peruvianus*). Scientists first became aware of it in 1976, when a skull was discovered at a fish market near San Andres, Peru; the first complete specimen was found in 1985, at another fish market just south of Lima, Peru, and the new species was

**M**
**A**
**M**
**M**
**A**
**L**
**S**

officially named in 1991

The so-called 'unidentified beaked whale' (*Mesoplodon* sp) is known from about 30 positive sightings at sea in the Eastern Tropical Pacific, but no specimens have been available for close examination and, consequently, it has yet to be named.

Several dolphins have been assigned species status for the first time in recent years. For example, the short-snouted spinner dolphin (*Stenella clymene*), which was previously considered to be one of many variations of the long-snouted spinner dolphin (*Stenella longirostris*), was officially classified as a separate species in 1981. Taxonomy of the common dolphin (*Delphinus delphis*) is very complicated, as there are so many individual variations, but recent research has revealed two distinct forms: the long-beaked and the short-beaked; these show many physical, behavioural and genetic differences and, in the near future, are likely to be declared as two separate species (*D. capensis* and *D. delphis* respectively).

**Noisiest** The low-frequency pulses made by blue whales (*Balaenoptera musculus*) and fin whales (*Balaenoptera physalus*) when communicating with each other across enormous stretches of ocean have been measured at up to 188 decibels, making them the loudest sounds emitted by any living source. The sounds themselves are infrasonic (below the range of human hearing) but, using specialist equipment, have been reliably detected from a distance of 850 km *528 miles* away. Biologists have established that blue whales calling off the coast of Newfoundland, Canada, can be heard throughout the western North Atlantic possibly as far south as the West Indies; and a fin whale calling off the coast of North Carolina, USA, can be heard off Nova Scotia, Canada; Bermuda; and Puerto Rico.

**Heaviest brain** The sperm whale (*Physeter macrocephalus*) has the world's heaviest brain, although it amounts to only 0.02 per cent of the animal's total body weight. During a Japanese whaling expedition to the North Pacific, in 1949–50, the brains of 16 mature males were weighed: the heaviest was 9.2 kg *20 lb 5 oz*, the lightest 6.4 kg *14 lb 2 oz* and the average 7.8 kg *17 lb 3 oz*. This compares with an average 1.4 kg *3 lb 1 oz* for the brain of an adult human.

**Size difference** The bottlenose dolphin (*Tursiops truncatus*) shows the most striking range in size between individuals of the same species. Physically mature adults vary in length from 1.9 m

> *Whales and dolphins are believed to have an extra sense, called 'biomagnetism', which enables them to detect variations in the Earth's magnetic field; some scientists think they may use this, like a map, to find their way around.*

*6 ft 3 in* to 3.9 m *12 ft 10 in* and in weight from 150 kg *331 lb* to 650 kg *1433 lb*.

The greatest size difference between the sexes is probably found in the short-finned pilot whale (*Globicephala acrorhynchus*). Males average 5.6 m *18 ft 4 in* and 2.2 tonnes, while females average 4.2 m *13¾ ft* and 0.88 tonnes. This makes the females 25 per cent shorter and 60 per cent lighter than the males.

**Thickest blubber** The blubber layer of the bowhead whale (*Balaena mysticetus*) is thicker than in any other animal, averaging 43–50 cm *17–20 in*, and providing the whale with protection against the freezing cold waters of its Arctic home.

**Most restricted distribution** The vaquita or Gulf of California porpoise (*Phocoena sinus*) probably has the most limited distribution of any marine cetacean. Nowadays it is found only within a 48 km *30 miles* radius in the

extreme northern end of the Gulf of California (Sea of Cortez), in western Mexico, although it may once have occurred further south along the Mexican mainland. It is most commonly seen around the Colorado River delta.

Several river dolphins also have extremely limited ranges. The Indus river dolphin (*Platanista minor*) lives exclusively in the Indus river, within the Pakistani provinces of Sind and Punjab. Its upstream limit appears to be the Jinnah barrage, in north-western Punjab, while the downstream limit is probably the Kotri barrage, in Sind. However, more than 80 per cent of the population lives exclusively along a 170 km *106 miles* stretch in the lower reaches of the river between the Sukkur and Guddu barrages.

**Most parasites** The grey whale (*Eschrichtius robustus*) is more heavily infested with a greater variety of external parasites than any other cetacean. This may be partly because it moves relatively slowly compared to most other species. It carries two major types: barnacles and whale lice. Each whale may have 100–200 kg *221–441 lb* of bar-

There is a more striking range in size between different bottlenose dolphins than in any other cetacean; some individuals weigh more than four times as much as others.

**M
A
M
M
A
L
S**

> *Whales and dolphins do not sleep like we do, but they rest on the surface of the sea or catnap for a few moments while they are swimming; each side of the brain takes it in turns to 'switch off' while the other half stays vigilant.*

nacles attached to its head and body for most of its life; every barnacle is firmly anchored, through the whale's skin and into its blubber, but is really just hitch-hiking and does its host no serious harm. One species of barnacle, *Cryptollepas rhachianecti*, attaches itself exclusively to the grey whale and is found nowhere else. The whale lice are not lice at all, but tiny crustaceans called amphipods; they actually feed on the skin of the whale and, if it is injured, will congregate in the wound and keep it clean by eating the decaying tissues. One hundred thousand whale lice have been found on a single whale. Perhaps surprisingly, the grey whale has relatively few internal parasites.

**Longest lived** Cetaceans are long-lived animals. However, it is difficult to assess their ages accurately and the maximum longevity is unknown for most species. The limited information available suggests that larger species tend to have longer life spans. The fin whale (*Balaenoptera physalus*) is prob-

ably the longest lived, with a maximum attainable lifespan estimated to be as high as 90–100 years. Baird's beaked whale (*Berardius bairdii*) comes a close second, with a maximum recorded age of 82 years, for a male killed off the coast of Japan in 1975.

A male killer whale (*Orcinus orca*), known affectionately as 'Old Tom', was reportedly seen every winter from 1843 to 1932 in Twofold Bay, New South Wales, Australia; this would have made him at least 89 years old. However, the record has never been authenticated and a recent study of the skeleton reputed to be of 'Old Tom' aged him at only 35 years at the time of his death.

**Shortest lived** The harbour porpoise (*Phocoena phocoena*) probably has the shortest life span of any cetacean, with most individuals dying before they are 8 years old. The oldest harbour porpoise recorded was 15 years.

**Oldest breeder** Male sperm whales (*Physeter macrocephalus*) reach sexual maturity at about 18–21 years, which is believed to be older than in any other cetacean. Even then, they have to wait until they are 20–25 years old before being strong and large enough to gain access to receptive females.

Female short-finned pilot whales (*Globicephala macrorhynchus*) reach sexual maturity when they are around 9 years old and, thereafter, have a calf every 4–6 years. They give birth for the last time when they are about 37 years

old, but sometimes continue to produce milk and to suckle other calves in the group until they are in their early forties.

**Youngest breeder** The female harbour porpoise (*Phocoena phocoena*) reaches sexual maturity at about 3 years old and begins to breed the year afterwards, which is probably at a younger age than in any other cetacean.

**Most acrobatic** Many cetaceans are known for their spectacular aerial displays. Among the larger species, southern right whales (*Eubalaena australis*), humpbacks (*Megaptera novaeangliae*) and killer whales (*Orcinus orca*) are particularly well known for their acrobatics. Humpbacks have been known to leap almost clear of the water 70–80 times repeatedly (Hawaii, USA); this is a phenomenal achievement, considering an average-sized humpback weighs the equivalent of 400 people.

There are many outstanding acrobats in the dolphin family. Some of the better known include the bottlenose dolphin (*Tursiops truncatus*), pantropical spotted dolphin (*Stenella attenuata*), striped dolphin (*Stenella*

---

**Female short-finned pilot whales give birth for the last time when they are approaching the grand old age of 40, which is much older than in most other cetaceans.**

*Above:* the dusky dolphin has a well-deserved reputation as one of the most acrobatic animals in the world.

*coeruleoalba*) and dusky dolphin (*Lagenorhynchus obscurus*); they have been known to hurl themselves as high as 7 m *23 ft* into the air and frequently turn somersaults before re-entering the water. Arguably, the most spectacular acrobat is the long-snouted spinner dolphin (*Stenella longirostris*), which hurls itself high into the air, then spins around on its longitudinal axis as many as seven times in a single leap.

**Longest flippers** The longest flippers belong to the humpback whale (*Megaptera novaeangliae*). They grow to 23–31 per cent of the length of the whale (making a potential maximum of over 5.5 m *18 ft*) but typically measure around 4.6 m *15 ft* in large animals. They are used to herd fish, to manoeuvre while swimming, to touch their young and to slap the surface of the water.

The record-breaking flippers of a humpback whale are frequently more than 4 m *13 ft 2 in* in length.

# BIRDS

## Aves

8500–9700 species (no universally accepted figure due to lack of agreement on bird classification)

## PREHISTORIC BIRDS

**Earliest** *Archaeopteryx lithographica* is the earliest unambiguous fossil bird. It displays a mixture of both reptilian and avian characteristics, providing palaentologists with their most conclusive evidence that birds evolved from reptiles, and is therefore one of the most important fossils of all time. It was discovered in 1861 (although the imprint of a single feather had been unearthed a year before) and is known from only six complete specimens, all found in the Solnhofen limestone beds of what is now Bavaria, southern Germany. Roughly the size of a magpie, *Archaeopteryx* had many reptilian features as well as two features distinctive of birds: feathers (which are unique) and a wishbone (which has recently been discovered in some advanced dinosaurs). Despite the presence of feathers, it is uncertain whether *Archaeopteryx* was capable of powered flight or if it was simply a glider. It lived during the late Jurassic period, about 150 million years ago.

However, the earliest fossil bird may

**Roughly the size of a magpie, *Archaeopteryx* is the earliest unambiguous fossil bird and probably lived about 150 million years ago.**

be a species called *Protoavis texensis*, which is known from only two partial skeletons discovered in Texas, USA, in 1984, in rocks dating from 220 million years ago. Named in 1991, this pheasant-sized creature has caused much controversy by possibly pushing the age of birds back many millions of years from the previous record, that of the more familiar *Archaeopteryx*. It is still unclear whether *Protoavis* will be widely accepted as a true bird, particularly since some prominent avian palaeontologists claim that the find is more likely to be a collection of bones from several unrelated species of small dinosaurs rather than the bones of a single individual bird.

**Number of species** More than 900 fossil bird species have been discovered to date.

**Heaviest** The heaviest prehistoric bird (and, indeed, the heaviest bird that has ever lived) was the flightless *Dromornis stirtoni*, a huge emu-like creature which lived in central Australia between 25 000 and 15 million years ago. Fossil leg bones found near Alice Springs, in 1974, indicate that the bird must have stood approximately 3 m *10 ft* tall and weighed about 500 kg *1100 lb*.

For a long time, the elephant bird (*Aepyornis maximus*), a flightless species which lived in Madagascar, was believed to be the heaviest bird. But recent estimates suggest that it weighed 'only' 450 kg *992 lb*, although it also reached a height of about 3 m *10 ft*. The elephant bird is often said to have been the inspiration for the legendary Rukh, or Roc, which carried off elephants to feed its young in *A Thousand and One Nights* (although the Roc could fly and a recently described extinct eagle, *Stephanoaetus mahery*, also from Madagascar, is a more likely candidate).

**Tallest** The tallest bird ever was probably the flightless giant moa (*Dinornis maximus*), from New Zealand. At 227 kg *500 lb*, it was about half the weight of *Dromornis stirtoni* and comparatively slender, but attained a maximum height of at least 3 m *10 ft*. The largest skeleton found measures 3.7 m *12 ft 1 in*. There were 12–20 different species of moa in

New Zealand before the Polynesians and Europeans arrived, but it is believed that they all became extinct before or during the 17th century.

**Most formidable** The most formidable birds were probably the so-called terror birds or phorusrhacoids. Believed to be the dominant terrestrial carnivorous animals of South America from 62 million years ago until about 2 million years ago, these flightless birds were powerful flesh-eaters and some may have reached a height of nearly 3 m *10 ft*. It has been suggested that they were capable of speeds of up to 70 km/h *44 mph*, although there is no way of estimating this with certainty. Their large heads and laterally flattened eagle-like bills suggest that they fed by tearing flesh and, indeed, they may have been predominantly carrion feeders. About 25 species of terror birds have been identified to date; their closest living relatives are believed to be the seriemas (family Cariamidae) of northern South America.

**Largest flying** The largest prehistoric flying bird (and, indeed, the largest flying bird of all time) was the giant teratorn (*Argentavis magnificens*) which lived on the South American pampas about 6–8 million years ago. Fossil remains discovered at a site 160 km *100 miles* west of Buenos Aires, Argentina, in 1979, indicate that this gigantic vulture-like bird had a wingspan of over 6 m *19 ft 8 in* (possibly up to 7.6 m *25 ft*), making it about the size of a small glider. The available evidence suggests that it was probably a soaring bird and flapped its wings only occasionally, but its discovery rocked the bird world and forced experts to re-examine their theories relating to size limitations in flight. *Argentavis* might have weighed as much as 80 kg *176 lb*, which is well above the theoretical limit for flapping flight, and had a standing height of 1.5 m *5 ft*. Its primary feathers are believed to have been as long as 1.5 m *5 ft* and as much as 18 cm *7 in* wide.

The largest ever flying creature was a reptile known as the pterosaur *Quetzalcoatlus northropi* ('feathered serpent'). About 70 million years ago it soared over what is now Texas, Wyoming and New Jersey, USA; Alberta, Canada; Senegal; and Jordan. Partial remains discovered in Big Bend National Park, Texas, USA, in 1971, indicate that this reptile must have had a wingspan of 11–12 m *36–39 ft* and may have weighed about 86–113 kg *190–250 lb*.

**Largest egg** The largest egg ever laid on Earth belonged to the extinct elephant bird *Aepyornis maximus* from

Madagascar. The largest known specimen was collected in 1841 and is currently housed in the Académie des Sciences, Paris, France, and measures 39 cm *15.4 in* in length and 32.6 cm *12.8 in* in width. This would give it a fluid capacity of more than 12 litres *2.6 gal*, equivalent to 16000 bee hummingbird eggs, 220 domestic chicken eggs, 9 ostrich eggs or 3–4 of the largest known dinosaur eggs. It would have weighed about 12.2 kg *27 lb* with its contents. It is not unusual for elephant bird eggs to wash out of the sand on certain beaches in southern Madagascar, where local people sometimes use them for carrying water; these have an average fluid capacity of 8–10 litres *1.8–2.2 gal*.

**Most primitive alive today** Only two modern bird groups are known to have existed for more than 65 million years: the sub-order Charadrii (shorebirds, gulls, terns, skuas and auks) and the superfamily Procellarioidea (albatrosses, petrels, penguins, loons and frigatebirds). They are both known from fossils dating as far back as the late Cretaceous. There is reason to believe that a number of other extant bird taxa pre-date these two groups, but fossil evidence has not yet been discovered.

Traditionally, the hoatzin (*Opisthocomus hoazin*) of tropical South America has often been regarded as the modern world's most primitive bird. It is certainly rather prehistoric-looking and has some unique characteristics, including an extraordinarily large crop and chicks with clawed wings. Its bizarre appearance has led to speculation that it is closely related to *Archaeopteryx*, one of the earliest birds of all time, and that it provides the 'missing link' between modern birds and their ancient ancestors. However, recent evidence from genetic analysis suggests that it may in fact be related to the cuckoos (order Cuculiformes) and that its unique features evolved relatively recently (some 25 million years ago).

## BIRD STATISTICS

**Largest** The largest living bird is the ostrich (*Struthio camelus*), which is found in Africa (although there is also an introduced population in Australia). Five sub-species are recognized. The tallest is the North African ostrich (*Struthio c. camelus*), which occurs south of the Atlas Mountains, from Upper Senegal and Niger across to the Sudan and central Ethiopia. Males are larger than females and have been recorded up to 2.74 m *9 ft* (including a head and neck of up to

1.4 m *55 in*); the average height is closer to 2 m *79 in*. The heaviest sub-species is the southern African ostrich (*Struthio c. australis*) which is reputed to weigh up to 160 kg *353 lb*.

**Smallest** The smallest bird in the world is widely claimed to be the bee hummingbird (*Mellisuga helenae*), a beautiful, red-faced little bird from Cuba and the Isle of Pines. Males measure 57 mm *2¼ in* in total length, half of which is taken up by the bill and tail, and weigh as little as 1.6 g *0.056 oz*. Females are slightly larger, but even they are so tiny that they are dwarfed by many butterflies and moths in their rainforest home. However, the little woodstar (*Acestrura bombus*) of Ecuador and northern Peru is considered by some experts to be slightly smaller.

**Smallest flightless bird** The smallest flightless bird may have been the tiny Stephens Island wren (*Xenicus lyalli*) from New Zealand, which was discovered and became extinct in the space of a few months in 1894. It measured only 10 cm *4 in* in length. However, although it was never seen to fly and reportedly ran like a mouse, its bone structure, short, rounded wings and soft plumage suggest that it may have been

The ostrich is the world's largest living bird, with an average height of around 2 m *79 in.*

capable of weak flight. If this is true, the smallest unambiguous flightless bird would then be the Inaccessible Island rail (*Atlantisia rogersi*) of the remote Tristan da Cunha island group, in the South Atlantic. About the size of a newly hatched domestic chick (12.5 cm *5 in* in length and 35 g *1¼ oz* in weight), the rail is still alive today and lives in burrows amongst tangled undergrowth.

**Largest marine bird** The heaviest marine bird is the emperor penguin (*Aptenodytes forsteri*), which averages 30 kg *66 lb* in weight and 1.15 m *45 in* in length (its standing height, with the head held horizontal, is about 1 m *40 in*). The heaviest ever recorded was an individual captured in the Ross Sea, during a British Antarctic Expedition in November 1915, which weighed 42.6 kg *94 lb*; it had a chest measurement of 1.32 m *52 in*.

The longest marine bird is the wandering albatross (*Diomedea exulans*), which has a body length of 1.1–1.4 m *43–55 in* and weighs 6–11 kg *13–24 lb*.

**Smallest marine bird** The least storm petrel (*Halocyptena microsoma*) is the smallest marine bird, with a length of 12.5–15 cm *5–6 in*, a weight of 28–34 g *1–1.1 oz* and a wingspan of only 32 cm *12½ in*. It is restricted to the eastern Pacific Ocean.

**Largest bird of prey** The heaviest individual bird of prey ever recorded was a female harpy eagle (*Harpia harpyja*) called *Jezebel*. Owned by the former manager of the Dadanawa cattle ranch, Guyana, she weighed 12.3 kg *27 lb*. However, this was really

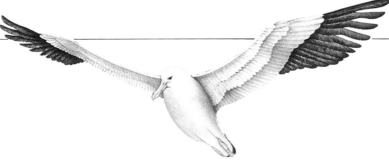

B
I
R
D
S

exceptional, since the average weight for this species from the rainforests of Central and northern South America is only 4.5 kg *10 lb*. Females are larger than males.

Strictly speaking, condors are not birds of prey; however, they are commonly included as members of the group. With this in mind, the largest, taking *average* weight as the measure, is the Andean condor (*Vultur gryphus*) which lives in South America, predominantly in the Andes Mountains. Large males weigh 9–12 kg *20–27 lb* and have an incredible wingspan of 3 m *10 ft* or more.

A weight of 14.1 kg *31 lb* has been claimed for a male California condor (*Gymnogyps californianus*), now preserved in the California Academy of Sciences at Los Angeles, USA. However, this figure seems very unlikely (this species is generally smaller than the Andean condor and rarely exceeds 10.4 kg *23 lb*) and is of dubious origin.

**Smallest bird of prey** The smallest bird of prey in the world is a title held jointly by the black-legged falconet (*Microhierax fringillarius*), distributed from southern Burma through Malaya, Sumatra, Borneo and Java, as far as Bali, and the white-fronted or Bornean falconet (*M. latifrons*), restricted to north-western Borneo. Both species have an average length of 14–15 cm *5½–6 in* (including a 5 cm *2 in* tail) and a weight of about 35 g *1¼ oz*. They feed mainly on insects, such as dragonflies, darting out from tree-perches to catch them in the same way that flycatchers hunt their prey.

**Largest owl** The European race of the eagle owl (*Bubo bubo*) is the world's largest owl, with an average length of 66–71 cm *26–28 in*, a weight of 1.6–4 kg *3½–8¼ lb* and a wingspan of more than 1.5 m *5 ft*.

**Smallest owl** Three species vie for this title, though the elf owl (*Micrathene whitneyi*), from south-western USA and Mexico, is usually quoted as the smallest. The other two contenders are the least pygmy owl (*Glaucidium minutissimum*), from Mexico, Central and South America, which is perhaps a little more sturdily built; and the long-whiskered owlet (*Xenoglaux loweryi*), from north-

ern Peru. All three species are about the size of a sparrow, averaging 12–14 cm *4¾–5½ in* in length and weighing less than 50 g *1¾ oz*.

**Largest wingspan** The wandering albatross (*Diomedea exulans*) of the southern oceans has the largest accurately measured wingspan of any living bird. Its wings average 2.54–3.51 m *8 ft 4 in–11½ ft* at full stretch, but the largest recorded specimen was a very old male with a wingspan of 3.63 m *11 ft 11 in*, caught by members of the Antarctic research ship *USNS Eltanin* in the Tasman Sea on 18 Sep 1965. Unconfirmed measurements of up to 4.22 m *13 ft 10 in* have also been claimed for this species and, since only a relatively small number have ever been measured, lengths of this order may prove to be feasible. The royal albatross (*Diomedea epomophora*), which also lives in the southern oceans, has a similar average wingspan of 3.05–3.51 m *10–11½ in*.

The largest wingspan among landbirds is found in the vulture-like marabou stork (*Leptoptilos crumeniferus*) of tropical Africa. The average length for the male's wingspan is 2.63 m *8½ ft* but up to 2.87 m *9 ft 5 in* is not uncommon. There is an unconfirmed report of

a specimen, shot in 1934, which had an estimated wingspan of 4.06 m *13 ft 4 in*.

The Andean condor (*Vultur gryphus*) of South America is a possible rival for this record, with a wingspan that may exceed 3 m *10 ft* in some individuals.

The extinct giant teratorn (*Argentavis magnificens*) had a surprisingly large wingspan of over 6 m *19 ft 8 in* (possibly up to 7.6 m *25 ft*), making it about the size of a small glider and by far the largest flying bird of all time.

**Longest bill** The spectacular bill of the Australian pelican (*Pelecanus conspicillatus*) is 34–47 cm *13–18½ in* long and is the longest bill of any bird.

The longest bill in relation to overall body length belongs to the sword-billed hummingbird (*Ensifera ensifera*), an inhabitant of South America that lives mainly in the high Andes from Venezuela south to Bolivia. Its bill measures an astonishing 10.2 cm *4 in*, making it longer than the bird's body length excluding the tail. Its length enables the sword-billed hummingbird

**The strange-looking marabou stork has the largest wingspan of any landbird, with a possible maximum of a little over 4 m *13 ft*.**

**The sword-billed hummingbird has a longer bill, in relation to overall body length, than any other bird in the world.**

to gather nectar from a number of different plants with very deep trumpet-shaped flowers. When perching, the bird (which measures up to 25 cm *10 in* from the tip of its bill to the end of its tail) tilts its head back and slants its bill steeply upwards to support the tremendous weight.

**Shortest bill** The shortest bills in relation to body length belong to the smaller swifts (family Apodidae) and, in particular, to the glossy swiftlet (*Collocalia esculenta*), whose bill is almost non-existent (measuring less than 4 mm *0.157 in* in length). Despite the shortness of their bills, the insect-eating swifts have huge gapes.

**Longest legs** The longest legs of any living bird belong to the ostrich (*Struthio camelus*), which is found in Africa (although there is also an introduced population in Australia). Males are normally larger than females and, in extreme cases, their powerful legs may stand up to 1.3 m *51 in* tall.

The longest legs in relation to body length belong to the black-winged stilt (*Himantopus himantopus*), a striking black and white wader widely distributed in many parts of Europe, Africa and Asia. Its long, pinkish-red legs measure 17–24 cm *7–9 in*, which is up to 60 per cent of the total body length of 35–40 cm *14–16 in*. When the stilt is flying, its legs trail up to 18 cm *7 in* beyond the end of the tail and act as a useful counterbalance to the long outstretched neck and bill.

**Shortest legs** The shortest legs belong to several species of swift. The family name (Apodidae), literally translated, means 'lacking legs'. Swifts spend so much of their time in the air that their legs have become almost non-existent and, in some species, only the feet are visible outside the plumage.

**Longest toes** The longest toes in relation to body length belong to the eight species of jacana or lily-trotter (family Jacanidae), which live in many parts of tropical and sub-tropical Africa, Asia, Australasia and Latin America. Their splayed, long-nailed toes can each be considerably longer than the tarsus (the length of leg between the 'ankle' and the 'knee') and are designed to dis-

perse the birds' weight, enabling them to walk on lily pads and other floating vegetation. Some of the larger species, which grow to a maximum overall length of 31 cm *1 ft*, have a 'toespan' of at least 15 cm *6 in*. In flight their long legs and toes trail behind.

**Longest feathers** The longest feathers grown by any bird are those of the Phoenix fowl or Yokohama chicken (a strain of red jungle fowl *Gallus gallus*), which has been bred in south-western Japan for ornamental purposes since the mid-17th century. Its upper tail coverts are moulted very infrequently and can grow continually for up to 6 years. In 1972 a tail covert measuring 10.6 m *34 ft 9½ in* was reported for a rooster owned by Masasha Kubota of Kochi, Shikoku Island, Japan.

Among flying birds, the tail feathers of the male crested pheasant or crested argus (*Rheinartia ocellata*) of south-east Asia regularly reach 1.73 m *5 ft 8 in* in length and 13 cm *5 in* in width. The central tail feathers of Reeves' pheasant (*Syrmaticus reevesii*) of central and northern China have reached 2.43 m *8 ft* in exceptional cases.

The longest feathers *relative to body length* among wild birds belong to the male ribbon-tailed bird of paradise (*Astrapia mayeri*) which lives in the mountain rainforests of New Guinea. Its ribbon-like central tail feathers, which play a key role in courtship display, measure up to 91.5 cm *3 ft* long and quadruple the overall length of their 28.5 cm *11 in* owner. The female has a much shorter tail.

Many species have tail feathers that more than double their overall lengths, including the resplendent quetzal (*Pharomachrus mocinno*) of southern Mexico and Central America; the marvellous spatule-tail (*Loddigesia mirabilis*), a hummingbird from northern Peru; the Asiatic paradise flycatcher (*Terpsiphone paradisi*); and the blue bird of paradise (*Paradisaea rudolphi*) from the rainforests of New Guinea.

Other species have extraordinarily long feathers on other parts of their bodies and the most striking of these is probably the male pennant-winged nightjar (*Macrodipteryx vexillarius*) of southern Africa. During the breeding season the 25–28 cm *10–11 in* nightjar grows a spectacular white streamer

from the middle of each wing that may grow up to 60 cm *2 ft* long; these streamers are moulted at the end of the breeding season. The two 'flag-bearing' head feathers of the King of Saxony bird of paradise (*Pteridophora alberti*), from New Guinea, are also very impressive.

**Shortest tail** Several non-flying bird families, including the kiwis (family Apterygidae), cassowaries (family Casuariidae), rheas (family Rheidae) and emus (family Dromaiidae) are virtually tailless. Unlike most other birds, which require tails for steering in flight, they do not have special tail feathers which are recognisably different from the other feathers on their bodies.

**Most feathers** The total number of feathers on a bird varies according to the species, the size of the individual, its sex, age and health, and the season and geographic distribution. In a series of feather counts on various bird species by a team of (very patient) ornithologists between 1937 and 1949, the maximum number were found on a tundra swan (*Cygnus columbianus*) which had a total of 25 216 feathers (80 per cent of which were on its head and neck).

**B**

**I**

**R**

**D**

**S**

**Least feathers** The lowest number of feathers so far recorded on an individual bird is 940 on a ruby-throated hummingbird (*Archilochus colubris*). Ironically, this tiny species (which is only 9 cm *3½ in* in length) has more feathers relative to its body size than most other birds. Smaller birds tend to have more feathers relative to body size than larger birds: while a tundra swan (*Cygnus columbianus*) is 2000 times the size of a hummingbird, it only has about 27 times more feathers.

## BIRDS IN FLIGHT

**Heaviest flying** The world's heaviest flying birds are the kori bustard or paauw (*Ardeotis kori*) of north-eastern and southern Africa and the great bustard (*Otis tarda*) of Europe and Asia. Weights of 19 kg *42 lb* have been reported for the kori bustard, and there is an unconfirmed record of 21 kg *46 lb 4 oz* for a male great bustard shot in Manchuria, although it was too heavy to fly. The heaviest reliably recorded great bustard weighed 18 kg *39 lb 11 oz*.

The mute swan (*Cygnus olor*) can reach 18 kg *40 lb* on very rare occasions, and there is an exceptional record from Poland of a cob (male) weighing 22.5 kg *49 lb 10 oz*, although it had temporarily lost the power of flight.

**Tallest flying** The tallest of the flying birds are the sarus crane (*Grus antigone*) of Asia and the whooping crane (*Grus americana*) of Texas, USA, which stand almost as tall as a man (up to 1.53 m *5 ft*).

Relative to body size, the rufous hummingbird is one of the world's most impressive long-distance migrants, capable of flying a round-trip of at least 10 000 km *6200 miles*.

**Smallest flying** The smallest flying bird is the bee hummingbird (*Mellisuga helenae*), from Cuba and the Isle of Pines. It is also the smallest bird on Earth. Males measure 57 mm *2¼ in* from the tip of the bill to the end of the tail, and

weigh as little as 1.6 g *0.056 oz*.

The little woodstar (*Acestrura bombus*) of Ecuador and northern Peru is considered by some experts to be slightly smaller.

**Fastest flying** The fastest flying bird (and, indeed, the fastest animal of any kind) is the peregrine falcon (*Falco peregrinus*). When 'stooping' or 'plunge-diving' from great heights to catch birds in mid-air, or during territorial displays, it is able to reach a maximum speed of at least 200 km/h *124 mph*. However, this is a much-debated figure. It has been calculated, using precise mathematical formulae, that a peregrine weighing just over 1 kg *2.2 lb* (with its wings folded and tail feathers closed to form a sleek projectile) would reach a maximum velocity of 385 km/h *239 mph* in a 1524 m *5000 ft* free-fall. Experiments in both Germany and Russia have recorded a velocity of 270 km/h *168 mph* at a 30° angle of stoop, rising to a maximum of 350 km/h *217 mph* (Germany) and 360 km/h *224 mph* (Russia) at steeper angles; however, there is still some controversy over the accuracy of these figures. Even at lower speeds, no one knows how this jet fighter among birds manages to pull out of such astonishing dives without blacking out or tearing itself apart.

It is often quoted that the brown-throated spine-tailed swift (*Hirundapus giganteus*) of Asia is capable of attaining a speed of 320 km/h *199 mph*. However, this speed was calculated by timing the birds with a stopwatch as they flew past a bungalow in Assam, India, and then disappeared over a ridge of hills 'exactly 2 miles away' and is generally considered to be inaccurate.

The fastest fliers in steady level flight are found among the ducks and geese (Anatidae). Some powerful species such as the red-breasted merganser (*Mergus serrator*), eider (*Somateria mollissima*), canvasback (*Aythya valisineria*) and spur-winged goose (*Plectropterus gambiensis*) can probably reach 90–100 km/h *56–62 mph* on rare occasions.

The fastest sustained flight ever recorded was accomplished by six wandering albatrosses (*Diomedea exulans*) moving across the south-western Indian Ocean in the late 1980s. They easily maintained a speed of 56 km/h *35 mph* over a distance of more than 800 km *497 miles*.

**Slowest flying** Probably at least 50 per cent of the world's flying birds cannot exceed 64 km/h *40 mph* in level flight. The slowest-flying birds are the American woodcock (*Scolopax minor*) and the Eurasian woodcock (*S. rusticola*), which

have been timed during their courtship displays at 8 km/h *5 mph* without stalling. Hovering birds, which often have a zero ground speed, are not considered to be in true level flight.

**Fastest wingbeat** Hummingbirds have the fastest wingbeats in the bird world. As a general rule, the smaller the bird the faster the wingbeat and, in many species, the wings move so fast that they are a blur and impossible to see with the human eye. They have to be measured with a stroboscope or similar sophisticated equipment. The maximum wingbeat recorded is for the horned sungem (*Heliactin cornuta*), a hummingbird living in tropical South America, at 90 beats/s. Similar rates have been claimed for the amethyst woodstar (*Calliphlox amethystina*), another hummingbird from South America, and several other members of the family have been recorded at 70–80 beats/s. At these speeds, the wings make the strange humming sound that gives the hummingbirds their family name.

Previous claims for wingbeats of up to 200 beats/s were for the narrow tips of the primary feathers only and not for the complete wing.

**Slowest wingbeat** Many larger birds, such as condors and albatrosses, are able to cruise on air currents for long periods without flapping their wings at all or by flapping them very rarely. However, the slowest wingbeats recorded during true level flight include 1/s for several species of New World vulture (family Cathartidae), 2/s for the grey heron (*Ardea cinerea*) and 2.3/s for the rook (*Corvus frugilegus*).

**Hovering** Few species are capable of true hovering flight, although many can hover for short periods or can use the wind in a technique called 'wind-hovering' (to remain stationary relative to the ground, they must fly into a moderate wind at the same speed as they are being blown back). The largest bird able to hover for sustained periods in windless conditions is the pied kingfisher (*Ceryle rudis*) of Africa and Asia, which is 25–29 cm *10–11½ in* in length and hovers with its body almost vertical and its bill pointed downwards while hunting for freshwater fish.

Hummingbirds (family Trochilidae) are the experts at hovering for prolonged periods in still air. Under experimental conditions, one bird hovered continuously for 50 minutes.

**Most acrobatic** Many birds are built for precision, speed and agility in the air. Even simple manoeuvres, such as landing on a perch or flying in dense flocks, require very fine coordination and split-second timing. The ultimate in flight control is found in predatory birds that have to capture moving targets at high speed, without harming themselves. In this respect, the hobby (*Falco subbuteo*) of Europe, North Africa and many parts of Asia is widely considered to be one of the best aerial acrobats. It catches nearly all its prey in mid-air and is fast enough to catch a swallow (*Hirundo rustica*) or a swift (*Apus apus*) on the wing and yet agile enough to catch bats and large insects such as dragonflies.

In terms of aerial manoeuvrability, hummingbirds (family Trochilidae) are probably the record-holders. By tilting their wings, in the same way that a pilot alters the angle of the rotors on a helicopter, they can fly forwards, backwards or sideways, spin on their axis and even turn over to fly upside down.

**Longest flight** Several bird species are thought to fly continuously between leaving their breeding colonies as

During its spectacular stooping dives, the peregrine falcon can reach speeds of at least 200 km/h *124 mph* – making it the fastest animal on Earth.

youngsters and returning several years later as adults. Most notable among these are the sooty tern (*Sterna fuscata*) and various swifts (family Apodidae) which, consequently, make the longest non-stop flights of any bird. It has been calculated that the common swift (*Apus apus*) completes a non-stop flight of 500 000 km *310 700 miles* between fledging late one summer and its first landing at a potential nesting site two years later.

Traditonally, the arctic tern (*Sterna paradisaea*) has been credited with the longest flight and, certainly, it makes the longest migratory journey of any bird. It breeds mainly around the shores of the Arctic Ocean and then flies to the other side of the world to spend the remainder of the year in the Antarctic – a total distance, if it were to travel in a straight line, of at least 16 000 km *9940 miles*. In a lifetime of 25 years, this is equivalent to flying to the Moon and back. Many individuals travel even further (strangely, birds that nest farthest north also go the farthest south) and limited evidence suggests that most of them take a more roundabout route, hugging the continental coastlines. Including their daily flights while foraging in the north and south, many arctic terns probably cover more than 50 000 km *31 000 miles* each year.

The greatest distance in a straight line covered by a ringed bird is 22 530 km *14 000 miles* by an Arctic tern,

banded as a nestling on 5 Jul 1955 in the Kandalaksha Sanctuary on the White Sea coast of Russia and captured alive by fishermen 13 km *8 miles* south of Freemantle, Western Australia, on 16 May 1956. The bird had probably flown south via the Atlantic Ocean and then circled Africa before crossing the Indian Ocean. It did not survive to make the return journey.

Other birds travel long distances while foraging but, since they rarely maintain a steady course, the distances covered are difficult to measure. When finding food for their chicks, swifts (*Apus apus*), for example, are believed to fly up to 1000 km *620 miles* a day. In 1990, six foraging wandering albatrosses (*Diomedea exulans*) were tracked across the Indian Ocean by satellite via miniature radio transmitters fitted by Pierre Jouventin and Henri Weimerskirch of the National Centre for Scientific Research at Beauvoir, France. Their results showed that the birds covered 3600–15 000 km *2240–9320 miles*, flying at speeds of up to 80 km/h *50 mph*, in single feeding trips, each lasting 10–33 days. According to the two researchers, the birds' long journeys were made possible by making the most of the prevailing weather: on the outward journey, they exploited the winds; and on the return journey they tacked their way home to avoid facing directly into the wind.

Relative to body size, the tiny 10 cm *3¾ in* long rufous hummingbird (*Selasphorus rufus*) is one of the greatest of all long-distance migrants. It occurs in western North America where, twice every year, it flies the length of the continent from as far north as Alaska, where it spends the summer, all the way to Mexico, where it spends the winter. For some individuals, this requires a round-trip of at least 10 000 km *6200 miles*.

**Most airborne** The most aerial of all birds is the sooty tern (*Sterna fuscata*), which is widespread throughout the tropical oceans. After leaving its nesting grounds as a youngster, it is reputed to remain aloft continuously for 3–10 years until it is old enough to breed for the first time. Although this is impossible to prove, research suggests that it

**Bar-headed geese have been seen flying over the Himalayas at altitudes approaching an impressive 9000 m *29520 ft*, although a single Ruppell's griffon vulture has been recorded even higher.**

does not need to return to land to rest but, as long as there is enough food available, can stay in the air indefinitely. It does not even need to settle on the sea to feed, preferring to catch fish or squid by picking them from the surface while hovering or by seizing them in mid-air when they jump to escape underwater predators.

The most aerial land bird is the common swift (*Apus apus*), which remains airborne for 2–4 years after fledging, during which time it sleeps, drinks, eats and even mates on the wing. Its flight is about 70 per cent more efficient than that of other birds of comparable

size, because it has long wings and a low body mass in relation to wing area (to reduce energy expenditure) and a shallow, forked tail that reduces drag and increases lift. Like the sooty tern, it has to come to land only when it is ready to breed.

**Shortest migration** The shortest true migrations are made by various species of grouse and quail (family Phasianidae) which move up or down mountain slopes to take advantage of seasonal food sources. The record-holder is probably the blue or dusky grouse (*Dendragapus obscurus*) from North America, which spends the winter in mountain pine forests and descends just 300 m *984 ft* to nest in deciduous woodland where there is an early crop of fresh leaves and seeds.

Mountain quails (*Oreortyx picta*) nest at altitudes of up to 2900 m *9500 ft* in central California but, with the onset of winter in September, groups of 10–30

walk in single file down to more sheltered valleys at an altitude of around 1500 m *4920 ft*. They do the return journey, again on foot, the following spring.

**Highest flying birds** Most bird species fly at altitudes below 1500 m *4920 ft*, even on migration. However, the highest confirmed altitude recorded is 11 277 m *37 000 ft* for a Ruppell's griffon vulture (*Gyps rueppellii*), which collided with a commercial aircraft over Abidjan, Ivory Coast, on 29 Nov 1973. The impact damaged one of the aircraft's engines, causing it to shut down, but the plane landed safely without further incident. Sufficient feather remains of the bird were recovered to allow the US Museum of Natural History (Washington) to make a positive identification of this high-flier, which is rarely seen above 6000 m *20 000 ft*. No mammal of a similar size could breathe enough air even to remain conscious at such an altitude.

Bar-headed geese (*Anser indicus*) have been seen flying over the Himalayas at altitudes approaching 9000 m *29 520 ft*. On 9 Dec 1967 about 30 whooper swans (*Cygnus cygnus*) were recorded at an altitude of just over 8230 m *27 000 ft*, flying in from Iceland to winter at Lough Foyle, which borders Northern Ireland and the Republic of Ireland; they were spotted by an airline pilot over the Outer Hebrides, and their height was confirmed on radar by air traffic control.

**Lowest living birds** The coal miners of 19th-century Britain used caged canaries (*Serinus canaria*), which originally came from the Canary Islands, Madeira and the Azores, to gauge the health of the air inside their mines; if the canaries keeled over, the miners were alerted to the fact that the air was probably contaminated with deadly methane gas. The lowest known resident population of wild birds is three house sparrows (*Passer domesticus*) which lived in Frickley Colliery, Yorkshire, UK, from the summer of 1975 to the spring of 1978 at a depth of 640 m *2100 ft*. Two of the birds even nested and raised three chicks, although they died soon afterwards.

## BIRD NUMBERS

**Total numbers** It has been estimated that some 150 000 bird species have inhabited the Earth since birds first evolved. Nearly 94 per cent of them have become extinct. Estimates of the total number of species alive today vary widely between 8500 and 9700 though, for the purposes of this book, *c.* 9200 species are recognized.

There have been several attempts to estimate the total number of individual birds on Earth, although it is almost impossible to take into account widely fluctuating seasonal variations in population sizes and, of course, all the species for which there have been no detailed censuses. Consequently, the results vary enormously between about 100 000 million and 300 000 million.

**Largest order** The passerines, or songbirds, form by far the largest order of birds. According to the system of classification used for this book, there are an incredible 5425 members of the order Passeriformes, which is equivalent to nearly 60 per cent of all the bird species in the world. This order includes all the most familiar garden birds, such as tits, robins and sparrows, as well as a host of other species from a wide range of land habitats. The passerines are perching birds and are usually small or medium-sized.

**Smallest order** The smallest order of birds is the Struthioniformes, which contains just one species: the ostrich (*Struthio camelus*).

**Largest family** According to the classification system used for this book, the Emberizidae forms the largest family of birds, with a total of 286 species. It includes buntings, sparrows, finches, cardinals and tanagers. Members of the same family are regarded as having descended from a common ancestor.

**Smallest family** There are several bird families that are monotypic (that is, they consist of only a single species): Struthionidae (ostrich), Dromaiidae (emu), Scopidae (hammerkop), Balaenicipitidae (shoebill), Pandionidae (osprey), Sagittariidae (secretary bird), Eurypygidae (sunbittern), Rhynochetidae (kagu), Aramidae (limpkin), Pedionomidae (plains wanderer), Ibidorhynchidae (ibis bill), Dromadidae (crab plover), Opisthocomidae (hoatzin), Steatornithidae (oilbird), Leptosomatidae (cuckoo roller), Upupidae (hoopoe), Oxyruncidae (sharpbill), Dulidae (palm-chat) and Coerebidae (bananaquit).

**The brown pelican is just one of 150 000 different bird species estimated to have inhabited the Earth since birds first evolved.**

**B**
**I**
**R**
**D**
**S**

**Most abundant** Excluding domestic fowl, the red-billed quelea (*Quelea quelea*), a seed-eating weaver of the drier parts of Africa south of the Sahara, is the most abundant bird alive today. It has an estimated adult breeding population of 1500 million. Densely packed flocks, containing hundreds of thousands or even millions of birds, are so highly synchronized as they wheel and turn in flight that they look like smoke clouds from a distance. Each bird weighs only about 20 g ¾oz but, when vast flocks descend on trees, they frequently break branches with their combined weight.

The North American passenger pigeon (*Ectopistes migratorius*) is widely believed to have been the commonest bird that has ever lived on Earth. It is impossible to give an accurate estimate of the population at its peak, but conservative estimates suggest that it may have been as high as 10 000 million in the first half of the 19th century. At the time, it is likely that 35–45 per cent of all the birds in North America were passenger pigeons. They lived in huge, densely packed flocks (some containing more than 2000 million birds) which darkened the sky and could take up to 3 days to pass overhead. But huge numbers were killed for their meat, and by sports hunters, and hunting competitions were organized in which more than 30 000 dead birds were needed to claim a prize; forest destruction and fragmentation also took its toll. The last passenger pi-

---

**The most abundant bird in the world is the red-billed quelea, which has an estimated adult breeding population of 1500 million.**

geon to be seen in the wild was shot by a young boy on 24 Mar 1900: the species had been hunted to extinction in less than 100 years. On 1 Sep 1914 the last of all the passenger pigeons, affectionately known as 'Martha', died in captivity in Cincinnati Zoo, USA.

**Largest gatherings** The largest bird gatherings tend to be at night-time roosts, either during cold winters when the birds huddle together to keep warm, or at focal points within areas where large numbers of them feed during the day. There are many cases where several million birds or more have been observed together. Among living species, the record is held by an extraordinary roost of bramblings (*Fringilla montifringilla*) in Switzerland. For several weeks, during the winter of 1951/52, an estimated 70 million of the birds assembled to roost together every night near the town of Hünibach.

One red-billed quelea (*Quelea quelea*) roost observed in the Sudan reportedly contained 32 million birds, though there are counter-claims that this estimate should have been substantially lower. Nightly gatherings of more than 1 million birds are not uncommon for red-winged blackbirds (*Agelaius phoeniceus*), starlings (*Sturnus vulgaris*), swallows (*Hirundo rustica*) and several other species.

Many sea birds breed in extremely large colonies. The breeding population of macaroni penguins (*Eudyptes chrysolophus*) on South Georgia, in the South Atlantic, for example, may exceed 5 million pairs, and many non-breeding birds are also present. On the Peruvian coast, guanay cormorants (*Phalacrocorax bougainvillei*) breed at densities of 5000

nests/ha *12 355/acre* and may attain a total colony size of 4–5 million birds.

**Most abundant sea bird** The most abundant sea bird in the world is probably Wilson's storm petrel (*Oceanites oceanicus*). There are thought to be more than 50 million pairs of this small, sparrow-sized bird nesting in the Antarctic and adjacent sub-Antarctic islands. Outside the breeding season, they range far north into the world's three main oceans.

---

## BIRD DISTRIBUTION

**Most species** Colombia, South America, has over 1700 indigenous breeding bird species, which is more than any other country in the world. In comparison, Canada and the USA combined have just over 600 breeding species.

By far the richest avifauna is found in the Neotropical region, consisting of tropical Mexico, Central and South America and the Caribbean. With some 3425 indigenous species of breeding birds, it is home to almost twice as many species as any other region and considerably more than a third of the world total. A further 175 species use the region as regular migrants. Diverse areas of a few square kilometres in the Amazon may hold well over 500 species, compared to 300–350 species in a comparable area of tropical Africa or Asia.

When the different continental regions of the world are compared according to their size, the Indomalayan region (India and south-east Asia

through western Indonesia) is the richest in breeding bird species with 196 per 1 million km² of land; the Neotropical region is next with 177; the Australasian region (New Guinea, Australia, New Zealand and related islands) has 154; the Afrotropical region (sub-Saharan Africa and south Arabia) has 66; the Nearctic region (North America and temperate Mexico) has 34; the Palearctic region (Europe, North Africa and Asia north of the Himalayas) has 31; and the Antarctic region (Antarctica and islands south of the Antarctic Convergence) has only three. The two remaining regions of the world are the Malagasy region (Madagascar and the western Indian Ocean islands) and the Pacific region (oceanic islands of the tropical Pacific) which have theoretical totals of 328 indigenous breeding bird species per 1 million km² of land and 4894 respectively; however, since these regions are non-continental, and include many small but widely dispersed islands, it would be misleading to compare their figures directly with the others.

**Least species** Within the limits of the Antarctic Convergence, only 51 indigenous bird species breed regularly: 31 albatrosses and petrels, 7 penguins, 2 cormorants, 2 skuas, 2 terns, 2 sheathbills, 3 ducks, 1 gull and 1 pipit. In addition, mallards (*Anas platyrhynchos*) have been introduced to the island of Kerguelen, and wekas (*Gallirallus australis*) to the island of Macquarie; and common starlings (*Sturnus vulgaris*) and redpolls (*Acanthis flammea*), introduced to New Zealand, have subsequently colonized Macquarie. Only 12 species breed on the Antarctic Continent itself and just three of these are endemic as nesting birds: the south polar skua (*Catharacta maccormicki*), the emperor penguin (*Aptenodytes forsteri*) and the Antarctic petrel (*Thalassoica antarctica*).

**Most introduced species** At one time or another, more than 150 species of birds have been introduced to the oceanic islands of the tropical Pacific, either intentionally or through accidental escapes of cagebirds. These birds have caused many problems for the native species, either as direct predators or as competitors for their food and nesting sites. Many of the introductions died out fairly quickly, but over 60 species are now completely naturalized. The Hawaiian islands have suffered more than most, with at least 50 introduced species firmly established. Among the most common are

> The first birds to be domesticated were Asian red junglefowl, more than 5000 years ago.

These blue-footed boobies share their home in Colombia with more than 1700 other breeding bird species; Colombia has more indigenous breeding birds than any other country in the world.

---

the grey francolin (*Francolinus pondicerianus*), barred ground dove (*Geopelia striata*), common mynah (*Acridotheres tristis*), house sparrow (*Passer domesticus*), Indian silverbill (*Lonchura malabarica*) and house finch (*Carpodacus mexicanus*). Since it was first introduced on the island of Oahu, Hawaii, in 1930, the Japanese white-eye (*Zosterops japonica*) has become the most numerous of all Hawaiian birds.

**Most successful introduced species** The natural breeding range of the house sparrow (*Passer domesticus*) is Eurasia; but it has been deliberately introduced to many other parts of the world, mainly by travellers keen to surround themselves with familiar creatures wherever they went. It has already colonized over two-thirds of the world's land surface (in particular, the vast former British Empire) and is continuing to spread. In many places it has become a serious pest. In the 1870s, for example, it was introduced to Argentina to control insects, but now causes problems itself by damaging grain and fruit, contaminating food, distributing parasites and

**B**
**I**
**R**
**D**
**S**

competing with indigenous species for suitable nest sites.·

**Most widespread species** Worldwide distribution is extremely rare at the species level, although the barn owl (*Tyto alba*), osprey (*Pandion haliaetus*), swallow (*Hirundo rustica*) and several others are virtually cosmopolitan. The peregrine falcon (*Falco peregrinus*) is generally considered to be the most widespread bird species of all, breeding on every continent except Antarctica and on many oceanic islands. Within its range, it shows great geographical variation, with the northern forms being the largest and generally the palest, and the southern forms being smaller and either darker or brighter in colour. Worldwide distribution does not, of course, imply great abundance and the

---

**The region south of the Antarctic Convergence has fewer breeding bird species than any other area of a similar size; the snowy sheathbill is one of only 51 species which breed there on a regular basis.**

peregrine still faces many threats and its status continues to be cause for concern in a number of countries throughout its range.

**Most successful natural spread in historic times** The collared dove (*Streptopelia decaocto*) has dramatically increased its range in recent years. It originated in northern India but, by the 16th century, had spread to parts of south-eastern Europe. Then there was a lull in the action, for unknown reasons, until about 1930, when it suddenly continued its spread across Europe. It reached Britain in 1952 (the first recorded British nesting was at Cromer, Norfolk, in 1955) and, by the 1970s, was breeding in the Faeroe Islands and Iceland. It has also been travelling in other directions and has already reached southern Asia and Japan.

The cattle egret (*Bubulcus ibis*) has also expanded its natural range dramatically in recent years, from its original home in Africa to many other parts of the world.

**Highest living** The alpine chough (*Pyrrhocorax graculus*) has been recorded

at a higher altitude on land than any other bird species. In the Himalayas, it is found year-round at altitudes of 3500–6250 m *11 480–20 500 ft*, but an Everest expedition observed a small party of the birds at a record height of 8235 m *27 010 ft*. Some Himalayan snowcocks (*Tetraogallus himalayensis*) may nest at heights of more than 5000 m *16 400 ft*. For comparison, laboratory mice in a pressure chamber are barely able to crawl at the altitude equivalent to 6100 m *20 008 ft*.

**Most southerly** Most Antarctic birds breed on islands in the Southern Ocean or along the coastal strip of the continent itself. Few species breed 'inland' on a regular basis. The most southerly breeder is the snow petrel (*Pagodroma nivea*), which nests among the rocky mountain peaks that poke through the ice, up to 240 km *150 miles* inland. Adelie penguins (*Pygoscelis adeliae*) breed almost as far south; the most southerly rookery is just in front of Sir Ernest Shackleton's hut at Cape Royds, Ross Island, where 1250 pairs of adelies nest at approximately 77° 34'S, 167° 07'E.

The most southerly nests ever recorded belong to Antarctic petrels (*Thalassoica antarctica*), which have bred in the Thiel Mountains, at 80° 30'S, 25° 00'W; snow petrels, on Mount Provender, in the Shackleton Mountains, at 80° 23'S, 29° 55'W; and south polar skuas (*Catharacta maccormicki*), in the Theron Mountains, at 79°S 30'W.

Antarctic skuas (*Catharacta antarctica*) and south polar skuas forage wherever humans leave something to scavenge upon and have even been recorded at the South Pole itself. Penguins may also wander far south: on 31 Dec 1957, the tracks of an emperor penguin (*Aptenodytes forsteri*) were found by a party of explorers traversing the Antarctic continent, over 400 km *248 miles* from the nearest sea.

**Most northerly** On average, the ivory gull (*Pagophila eburnea*) has the most northerly breeding range of all birds. It occurs almost exclusively north of 70°N, with major breeding grounds on Svalbard, Franz Josef Land, Novaya Zemlya, northern Canada and northern Greenland.

Several bird species have been recorded breeding at the extreme northern limits of land, in Greenland at 83°N, including knot (*Calidris canutus*), Ross's gull (*Rhodostethia rosea*), ivory gull and arctic tern (*Sterna paradisaea*). Some of their nests have been within 750 km *466 miles* of the North Pole. Turnstones (*Arenaria interpres*), snow geese (*Anser caerulescens*), snow buntings (*Plectrophenax nivalis*) and several

It is impossible to travel further south than the Antarctic skua, which occasionally turns up at the South Pole.

other species are regular breeders in the Lake Hazen area, Ellesmere Island, Canada, at 82°N. The gyrfalcon breeds as far north as 82°N in Greenland.

Although some 145 bird species breed regularly in the Arctic, relatively few of these are truly high-Arctic species, and even fewer are year-round residents. The only species which remain in the Arctic all year round are: ptarmigan (*Lagopus mutus*), raven (*Corvus corax*), snowy owl (*Nyctea scandiaca*), gyrfalcon (*Falco rusticolus*), redpoll (*Acanthis flammea*), Ross's gull, ivory gull, black guillemot (*Cepphus grylle*) and eider (*Somateria mollissima*). When food is available, the snowy owl may live further north than any other bird species during the winter; it has been recorded coping with the darkness and bitter cold of mid-winter on Ellesmere Island, Canada, at 82°N.

Only three birds have been recorded at the North Pole itself: a snow bunting (*Plectrophenax nivalis*) in May 1987; a

The well-camouflaged ptarmigan is one of only a handful of bird species known to remain in the Arctic all year round.

kittiwake (*Rissa tridactyla*) in July 1992; and a northern fulmar (*Fulmarus glacialis*) in August 1993.

**Smallest natural range** A number of bird species are confined to single mountain tops, tiny patches of forest or remote oceanic islands. In theory, those with just one or two survivors in the wild have the smallest natural ranges, although even they may wander over large distances. Taking this into account, the smallest natural range of any species belongs to the Aldabra brush warbler (*Nesillas aldabranas*) which has a total known range of only 10 ha *24.7 acres*. This consists of a 2 km *1¼ miles* long, 50 m *164 ft* wide, coastal strip on the western tip of Ile Malabar on the northern rim of Aldabra atoll, Sey-

**B**
**I**
**R**
**D**
**S**

chelles. Habitat analysis of this site has shown that the maximum likely distribution of the species is bounded by the same 50 m *164ft* strip but, in theory, it could extend a further 7 km *4.4 miles* up the coast; however, since 1976 feral goats and giant tortoises have penetrated and probably degraded the suitable vegetation in most of this area. The warbler has never been seen outside the basic 10 ha *24.7 acre* site. Sadly, the last confirmed record of the species was in September 1983 and it may now be extinct.

The Ascension frigatebird (*Fregata aquila*) breeds only on Boatswainbird islet, near the remote South Atlantic island of Ascension. The islet is just 3 ha *7.4 acres* in size. However, the species ranges across a wide area of sea when feeding and, of course, outside the breeding season. It once bred on Ascension itself, but egg collecting, human disturbance and introduced predators forced it to move to a safer home offshore. It is still a fairly numerous species with a population of about 10 000 birds.

Historically, the smallest known range belonged to the Chatham Island black robin (*Petroica traversi*), which lives on an isolated group of islands of the same name, 800 km *500 miles* east of New Zealand. When the entire population was reduced to just seven individuals, in 1976, it was restricted to a tiny islet of no more than 0.4 ha *1 acre* in size.

## BREEDING BIRDS

**Largest clutch** The number of eggs laid in a single clutch varies markedly from species to species, from individual to individual and according to latitude, habitat, time of year, age of the female, population density and local environmental conditions. The upper limit depends upon how many eggs the female can produce and incubate properly and how many young the parents can feed at any one time.

Some domestic chickens lay almost daily (i.e. up to 360 eggs per year). Among wild birds, the grey partridge (*Perdix perdix*) is generally considered consistently to lay the most eggs (typically 15–16 but up to 20) in a single

During a rather cruel experiment, in the 1920s, a female mallard reportedly laid a record-breaking 146 eggs in its effort to produce a full clutch.

*Not all ducks quack: some whistle, bark, squeak, coo and make a wide variety of other sounds.*

clutch. Other species may lay even more on rare occasions, for example bobwhites (*Colinus virginianus*) have been known to lay as many as 28, and blue tits (*Parus caeruleus*) and greater scaups (*Aythya marila*) as many as 22.

Even larger clutches may occur as a result of 'dump-nesting', where two or more females lay their eggs in the same nest. The ostrich is a well-known example, in which the male mates with as many as six females, all of whom lay their eggs in the same scrape in the ground; there may be more than 40 eggs in the scrape, before the dominant female selects which ones to keep (usually about 20) and simply rolls the others away. However, the record for dump-nesting is held by a North American redhead (*Aythya americana*), which had a nest containing no fewer than 87 eggs.

If eggs are removed from a nest, females often continue to lay more and may greatly exceed their normal clutch size. In one experiment of this kind, held in the 1920s, a female mallard (*Anas platyrhynchos*) reportedly laid an incredible 146 eggs in her effort to produce a full clutch; the normal clutch size is only 10–12. In a similar experiment, a common flicker (*Colaptes auratus*) was persuaded to lay 71 eggs in 73 days, despite normally laying only six to eight.

Certain parasitic birds, such as the females of several species of African cuckoo (family Cuculidae) have been known to lay as many as 24 eggs in rapid succession, but these are distributed between the nests of many host birds and therefore are not considered to be part of a single clutch.

**Smallest clutch** Many birds lay just one egg. This is a particularly common phenomenon in sea birds such as petrels and albatrosses (families Procellariidae and Diomedeidae), but is also found in several large eagles (family Accipitridae), king penguins (*Aptenodytes patagonicus*), emperor penguins (*A. forsteri*) and a variety of other species.

**Most clutches** In captivity, there are reports of zebra finches (*Poephila guttata*) raising as many as 21 consecutive broods and, indeed, there are other examples of birds laying one brood after another under artificial conditions.

In the wild, the stock dove (*Columba oenas*) in Britain probably has more broods in one year than any other species. It frequently attempts up to five broods, which it is able to do simply because its dependence on arable weed seeds allows it a very long breeding season (from mid-February to mid-November). A small number of other species may have five or even six broods in one year, but only on rare occasions.

The female spotted sandpiper (*Actitis macularia*) mates with as many as four different males, producing four clutches of eggs in rapid succession. Each male takes care of his own clutch, though the female usually gives the

Ostriches lay the largest eggs on Earth today; this medium-sized specimen is shown in comparison with a hen's egg.

*major*), for example, lays an average of 11 eggs, each weighing about 1.7 g *0.06 oz*.

**Smallest egg** The egg of the vervain hummingbird (*Mellisuga minima*), which lives in Jamaica and on two nearby islets, is barely the size of a pea and is the smallest egg laid by any bird on record. Two specimens measuring less than 10 mm *0.39 in* in length weighed 0.365 g *0.0128 oz* and 0.375 g *0.0132 oz*. However, the eggs are still unknown for many species and, with further research, this record may yet be broken.

The smallest egg in relation to the size of the female is laid by the emperor penguin (*Aptenodytes forsteri*). The female lays a single egg which weighs just 1.4 per cent of her own body weight of around 30 kg *66 lb*. Surprisingly, an average sized female ostrich (*Struthio camelus*) lays an egg which weighs about 2 per cent of her own body weight.

A few species lay eggs which are highly variable in size; for example, the macaroni penguin (*Eudyptes chrysolophus*) normally lays two to three eggs, the second of which is on average 71 per cent heavier than the first.

**Highest yolk content** The eggs of kiwis (family Apterygidae) have the highest yolk content of any bird, making them such a rich source of food for the developing chicks that they usually do not have to feed for several days after hatching.

**Rarest egg** There are several extinct bird species for which only one egg survives. Two good examples are held at The Natural History Museum, UK: *Cabalus modestus* and *Parendiastes pacificus*, both of which are rails.

**Largest nest** A nest measuring 2.9 m *9½ ft* wide and 6 m *20 ft* deep was built by a pair of bald eagles (*Haliaeetus leucocephalus*), and possibly their successors, near St Petersburg, Florida, USA; it was examined in 1963 and was estimated to weigh nearly 3 tonnes. The golden eagle (*Aquila chrysaetos*) also constructs huge nests, and one 4.57 m *15 ft* deep was reported from Scotland in 1954; it had been used for 45 years.

The incubation mounds built by several species of megapode or moundbuilder (family Megapodiidae) are even larger. The male begins by digging a

final one a helping hand with rearing the young. In several other species, including the red-legged partridge (*Alectoris rufa*) and Temminck's stint (*Calidris temminckii*), the female mates with just one male but produces two clutches of eggs in rapid succession: the male looks after the first and the female looks after the second.

**Least clutches** Most non-passerine birds, and many of the larger passerines, have such extended nesting cycles, or such long periods of parental care, that they are unable to produce more than one clutch in a year. The Philippine eagle (*Pithecophaga jefferyi*), formerly known as the monkey-eating eagle, has such a slow reproductive rate that it produces only a single egg every 2–3 years which is, on average, less than half a clutch a year.

Several species of albatross (family Diomedeidae) breed only in alternate years; since most of them do not even start breeding until they are 10–15 years old, they also have among the lowest total egg outputs of any bird.

**Largest egg** The egg of an ostrich (*Struthio camelus*) normally measures 15–20 cm *6–8 in* long, 10–15 cm *4–6 in* in diameter and weighs 1.0–1.78 kg *2.2–*

*3.9 lb* (on average, roughly equivalent in capacity to two dozen hens' eggs). The shell, although only 1.5 mm *0.06 in* thick, can easily support the weight of an adult man. The largest egg on record weighed 2.3 kg *5.1 lb* and was laid on 28 Jun 1988 by a 2-year-old northern/ southern hybrid (*Struthio c. camelus × S. c. australis*) at the Kibbutz Ha'on collective farm, Israel.

The largest eggs in relation to body size are laid by kiwis (family Apterygidae) and each weighs about 25 per cent of the adult female's weight. The brown kiwi (*Apteryx australis*), from New Zealand, is about the size of a chicken but lays an egg that is more than ten times the volume of a chicken's egg. Each kiwi egg (which is laid after 34 days of development inside the female – another record for birds) weighs about 450 g *1 lb*; the 1.7 kg *3¾ lb* female kiwi normally lays just one or two. Wilsons's storm petrels (*Oceanites oceanicus*), blue-grey noddies (*Procelsterna cerulea*) and Puerto Rican todies (*Todus mexicanus*) have also been known to lay eggs weighing as much as 25 per cent of the adults.

Over a period of several days, or several weeks, many species lay a clutch of eggs that in total weighs more than themselves. A 17 g *0.6 oz* great tit (*Parus*

hole in the ground about 1–1.5 m *39–59 in* deep. In the process, he may have to move some very large objects: a 1 kg *2.2 lb* bird was once seen to shift a rock weighing 6.9 kg *15.2 lb*. Then he fills the hole and makes a huge mound of leaf litter and soil or sand, in which the female lays the eggs. These are incubated by the sun and by fermentation of the decaying vegetation (it is rather like being inside a compost heap). However, the male is still kept busy maintaining the mound in such a way as to ensure a stable temperature inside for the eggs, which have to be kept at a constant 32–35°C *90–95°F*. The best-known megapode is the mallee fowl (*Leipoa ocellata*) of southern Australia, which builds a huge mound of leaf litter and soil measuring up to 4.57 m *15 ft* in height and 10.6 m *35 ft* in length. A mound of this size would involve the collection and movement of up to 250 m³ *8829 ft³* of vegetation and soil weighing more than 300 tonnes in a typical year. The mound is kept in use year after year.

**Smallest nest** The smallest nests are built by hummingbirds (family Trochilidae). They are typically incon-

The hoatzin, a large, strange-looking bird from South America, is such a poor flier that most of its landings are little more than controlled crashes.

spicuous cups of plant material, held together with silky threads from spiders' webs, and often adorned with tiny pieces of moss or lichen. The shallowest nest is made by the vervain hummingbird (*Mellisuga minima*), which lives in Jamaica and two nearby islets, and is about half the size of a walnut shell. The slightly deeper but narrower nest of the bee hummingbird (*M. helenae*), which lives in Cuba and the Isle of Pines, has a cup which is thimble-sized.

A number of birds make no nest at all or, for example, lay their eggs in a simple scrape in the ground. The guillemot (*Uria aalge*) lays its single egg on the bare ledge of a sea cliff; the fairy, or white, tern (*Gygis alba*) lays its egg directly on to a tree branch, where it is in constant danger of being knocked to the ground; many owls (family Tytonidae) and falcons (family Falconidae) use the abandoned nests of other birds and do not bother to make their own; and king penguins (*Aptenodytes patagonicus*) and emperor penguins (*A. forsteri*) simply keep their single eggs balanced on their feet.

**Most nests** Male wrens (family Troglodytidae) and weavers (family Ploceidae) construct large numbers of nests for evaluation by their prospective mates. Marsh wrens (*Cistothorus palustris*) are the record-holders: bigamous males build an average of 24.9 nests and monogamous males build 22.1 nests for the obviously fussy females to compare. The nests that are rejected for egg-laying serve as dummy nests that help to confuse potential predators.

**The incubation mounds built by megapode birds are even larger than the record-breaking nests built by other birds; this particularly impressive mound was photographed on the island of Komodo, in Indonesia.**

**Longest nest burrow** The rhinoceros auklet (*Cerorhinca monocerata*), a puffin-like sea bird which nests on small, grass-covered islands in the North Pacific, digs a nesting burrow that is usually 2–3 m *6½–10 ft* long. However, 6 m *19½ ft* burrows are not unusual and, in one exceptional case, a burrow of 8 m *26 ft* was recorded. Both sexes do the digging and, once the burrow is complete, a single white egg is laid at the end. Exactly why these 35 cm *14 in* birds should make such extensive excavations is still a mystery.

**Most populous nest** The aptly named sociable weaver (*Philetairus socius*), which lives in the dry grasslands of south-west Africa, builds an enormous communal nest that hangs from a tree or telegraph pole and looks surprisingly like a giant haystack. The 'haystack' contains up to 300 individually woven grass nests, each housing a single pair of weavers and their brood, all of which are clustered under one dome-shaped thatched roof. The communal nest is constantly being repaired and extended and may be as large as 2 m *6½ ft* high and 8 m *26 ft* long. The

The beautiful white or fairy tern does not bother to build a nest: it simply lays its single egg directly on to the branch of a tree (*below*).

main limit to its size is weight: it is not unusual for a sociable weaver nest to get so heavy that the tree collapses; when this happens, the birds simply start building a new home elsewhere.

**Strangest nesting material** There are many examples of birds using a variety of strange and unlikely materials to build their nests. In 1909 the 600 kg *1455 lb* nest of a white stork (*Ciconia ciconia*) was removed from the tower of a cathedral in Colmar, France, when it started to lean over; inside the walls of the nest the workmen found 17 ladies' black stockings, 5 fur caps, 3 old shoes, the sleeve of a white silk blouse, a large piece of leather and 4 buttons from a railway porter's uniform. A pair of house crows (*Corvus splendens*) in Bombay, India, made their nest entirely of gold spectacle frames, which they had stolen from an open shop window. In the Galapagos Islands, Ecuador, mockingbirds (*Nesomimus trifasciatus*) occasionally take hair from the heads of passing tourists for their nests; and, in Australia, magpies (*Gymnorhina tibicen*) have a particular fondness for wire offcasts from farm fencing (one nest contained no fewer than 243 pieces of wire with a total length of 100 m *330 ft*).

Many other birds use equally strange, but more natural, nesting materials. The violaceous trogon (*Trogon violaceous*) of Central and South America, for example, takes over a wasp's nest (having eaten all the adult wasps first) and then digs out the comb to make its own nesting cavity. Just as strange is the water thick-knee or dikkop (*Bruhinus vermiculatus*), from Africa, which frequently lays its eggs on the sun-dried droppings of large mammals such as hippos.

*All flying birds have hollow bones to make them lighter for flight.*

**Most valuable nest** The most valuable nests in the world belong to several species of cave swiftlet, in particular the white-nest or edible-nest swiftlet (*Aerodramus fuciphagus*), from southeast Asia. All swifts and swiftlets (family Apodidae) use a substance secreted from a pair of enlarged salivary glands situated beneath their tongues to glue their nests together, but in cave swiftlet nests saliva is the principal ingredient. Made into a gelatinous soup, which is essentially a protein-sugar solution, they have been eaten by the Chinese for some 1500 years. Nowadays they are considered a special delicacy (although, to the western palate, 'birds' nest soup' is almost tasteless) and have become extremely valuable. Collecting this so-called 'white gold' from the roofs and walls of deep caves can be very hazardous, but the demand is great. Hong Kong, which consumes more than 60 per cent of all the nests taken, imports some 8 million of them (worth nearly £20 million) every year. It takes two nests to make one bowl of soup.

**Longest incubation** A very small number of birds incubate their eggs for longer than 70 days. There is an isolated case of an egg laid by a mallee fowl (*Leipoa ocellata*) in Australia taking 90 days to hatch (compared with its average of 62 days) but the longest

King penguins look after their chicks, which spend the winter in crèches on starvation rations, for a record-breaking 360 days after hatching; very few other species are entirely dependent on their parents for as long as a year.

normal incubation period is shared by six species: two albatrosses and all four kiwis (in 1993, it was discovered by DNA analysis that the brown kiwi (*Apteryx australis*) is actually two distinct species). The wandering albatross (*Diomedea exulans*) has an average incubation period of 75–82 days; the royal albatross (*Diomedea epomophora*) also has a long incubation period, averaging 75–81 days; and the kiwis (family Apterygidae) incubate for an average of 78–82 days, although this frequently varies from 71 to 84 days. In exceptional circumstances, incubation periods of up to 85 days have been recorded for all these birds.

> *A marsh tit can memorize the locations of hundreds of hidden seeds.*

The male emperor penguin (*Aptenodytes forsteri*) has the longest *continuous* incubation period, incubating its single egg on the top of its feet without relief for 62–67 days. In contrast, the albatrosses and kiwis leave their nests at intervals to feed.

**Shortest incubation** No bird is known to have a normal incubation period of less than 10 days. However, a number of small passerines are known to incubate their eggs for as little as 10 days, including the shore lark (*Eremophila alpestris*) 10–14 days; hawfinch (*Coccothraustes coccothraustes*) 10–14 days; lesser whitethroat (*Sylvia curruca*) 10–11 days; and linnet (*Carduelis cannabina*) 10–14 days.

**Youngest incubator** The female white-rumped swiftlet (*Aerodramus spodiopygius*), of Australia and New Guinea and several Pacific islands, lays two eggs several weeks apart. By the time she has laid the second one, the first has hatched and the young chick is old enough to do the incubating.

**Longest interval between eggs** The longest laying interval between eggs is found in the maleo fowl (*Macrocephalon maleo*), a kind of megapode living in Sulawesi, Indonesia. The eggs are laid at 10–12 day intervals and, since there

are six to eight eggs in a clutch, laying can take more than 3 months to complete. In many cases the first chicks hatch before the last eggs have been laid.

**Shortest interval between eggs** As far as is known, no bird regularly lays more than one egg within a 24-hour period. However, there is a single record of a common flicker (*Colaptes auratus*), in the early 1900s, laying two eggs in 13 hours.

**Hatching time** The length of time between the first crack appearing in an eggshell and the emergence of the chick varies within a clutch in order to synchronize hatching and also varies from species to species. The total hatching time ranges from about 30 minutes in many small passerines (order Passeriformes) to as long as 6 days in some of the larger albatrosses (family Diomedeidae). For most small- to medium-sized birds it takes anything from a few hours to most of a day.

**Shortest chick-rearing period** There are basically two kinds of newly hatched chick: *altricial* and *precocial*. Altricial species are born blind and with little or no down, they cannot walk or fly and are even unable to regulate their own body temperatures; they are totally dependent on their parents for many days, weeks or even months after hatching. Precocial species, in contrast, hatch from the egg in an advanced state of development, usually leave the nest soon afterwards and are often capable of leading an independent existence within about 24 hours of hatching. The best-known examples of precocial birds are found among the 19 species of megapode (family Megapodiidae), many of which have chicks that are completely independent and receive absolutely no parental care after hatching; in many cases, they never even see their parents.

**Longest chick-rearing period** Frigate birds (family Fregatidae), king penguins (*Aptenodytes patagonicus*) and California condors (*Gymnogyps californianus*) have longer chick-rearing periods than any other birds. In frigatebirds, the young begin to fly when they are 5–6 months old, but keep returning to the nest to be fed until they are up to a year old. Endangered California condors feed and tend their young on their nesting cliffs for a year or more. King penguins lay their single eggs early in the sub-Antarctic summer, but their chicks fail to grow and moult in time to fledge before the onset of winter; they survive the bad weather by delaying the moment of independence from their parents, and spend the winter in crèches on starvation rations, before fledging the following spring – some 360 days after hatching. A number of other species continue to receive food from their parents for up to a year after hatching, although they are not entirely dependent.

**Quickest to fly** Young megapodes (family Megapodiidae) are born with extremely advanced contour-like feathers, instead of the down of most other young birds, enabling them to fly and escape from predators very soon after hatching. The best-known example is the mallee fowl (*Leipoa ocellata*) of southern Australia, which builds a huge nest consisting of a mound of leaf litter and soil. The newly hatched chick takes 2–15 hours to work its way up through the mound and on to the surface, where it opens its eyes for the first time, then tumbles down the side and staggers to the relative safety of the nearest bush to recover from its exertions. Within an hour, the baby mallee fowl can run confidently; after 2 hours it can flutter above the ground for 10–15 m *33–49 ft*; and, just 24 hours after its escape from the mound, it is capable of strong flight.

---

The slowest birds to reach maturity are the albatrosses, some of which do not breed until they are at least 10 years old; this is a young blackbrowed albatross, photographed in the Falkland Islands.

**Slowest to fly** The wandering albatross (*Diomedia exulans*) has the longest known interval between hatching and being able to fly. On average the chick flies from the nest for the first time some 278–280 days after hatching. It takes so long for the young bird to prepare itself that the adults can breed only once in 2 years.

**Fastest to maturity** Five species of quail in the genus *Coturnix* reach breeding maturity faster than any other bird: they are able to reproduce when only 5 weeks old. Even so, they are still in immature plumage at this stage and do not attain the full adult plumage for another 5–7 weeks.

**Slowest to maturity** The slowest birds to reach breeding maturity are the albatrosses (family Diomedeidae) and, in particular, the royal (*Diomedea epomophora*) and wandering (*D. exulans*) albatrosses. They become sexually mature at around 8 years old but often do not breed until they are 10 years old; there are even reports of first breeding attempts at 15 years old. When they do eventually form pairs, before settling down they spend a year of 'keeping company'; after that the partners stay together for life. Despite this protracted period of adolescence, in many cases their first breeding efforts are unsuccessful.

## BIRDS IN DANGER

**Rarest** It is virtually impossible to establish the identity of the world's rarest bird, because of the practical difficulties in assessing bird populations in the wild and, of course, because their numbers are constantly changing. However, in the wild, Spix's macaw (*Cyanopsitta spixii*) is as rare as it is possible to be without actually going extinct. Ornithologists searching for the bird in June–July 1990 managed to locate only one survivor, believed to be a male, living in the remote Tabebuia riverine forest of north-eastern Brazil. It has since been given round-the-clock protection. The main reason for the demise of the species has been trapping for the pet trade and, as recently as 1987, two of the birds were confiscated from men who were planning to sell them in Germany for about £25000. The macaw has also suffered from direct hunting for meat, competition with introduced African bees for nesting holes and habitat destruction. The only hope for its survival now lies in 31 individuals

Spix's macaw is probably the rarest bird in the wild, with only one known survivor, although there are at least 31 individuals in captivity.

population began to decline and, by the turn of the century, only about 25 pairs remained. By 1976 there were only seven birds left – two pairs and three extra males – and a daring and dramatic operation to save the species was launched. There was no room for mistakes, but translocation to safer areas within the Chathams, the use of foster parents for some of the eggs and clever manipulation of the breeding pairs increased the population to 37 by 1986. It was the first time cross-fostering had been used to manage an endangered passerine bird in the wild. There was a major setback in the same year, when a massive storm wiped out 14 of the robins, but the population has risen slowly since and there are now 160 on two islands. Much of the credit for the success of this remarkable rescue operation is often given to one particular bird, called *Old Blue* (named for the colour of her leg band). In 1976 *Old Blue* was one of the two surviving females. She began to breed in 1979, at the age of nine, by which time she was the only productive bird. Had she not lived to the grand old age of 13 (extraordinarily old for a black robin), and had she not bred every year until her death, the species would almost certainly have become extinct.

known to be kept in captivity. Indeed, in August 1994, a captive female was taken from a Brazilian collection to a holding facility near the wild male's favourite tree; the two birds began to interact soon afterwards and the female's release is imminent.

Sadly, there are many other strong contenders for the 'rarest bird in the world' record. Taking the *total* (including captive individuals), a number of species are even rarer than Spix's macaw. For example, there are only about 28 echo parakeets (*Psittacula echo*), on the island of Mauritius; 48 kakapos (*Strigops habroptitus*) in New Zealand; and only 26 Hawaiian crows (*Corvus hawaiiensis*): 12 in the wild and 14 in captivity.

Many birds are known from only one specimen and, assuming they have not simply escaped the notice of ornithologists, are probably extremely rare or may even be extinct. These include the orange-necked partridge (*Arborophila davidi*), discovered in 1927 near Ho Chi Minh City, Vietnam, and the Red Sea cliff swallow (*Hirundo perdita*), discovered at a lighthouse off Port Sudan, Sudan, in 1984. Many others have been seen only once or twice this century. The Cebu flowerpecker (*Dicaeum quadricolor*), for example, was rediscovered in 1992 on the island of Cebu, Philippines, after an 'absence' of 80 years; deforestation on Cebu, which is the bird's only home, is so severe that extinction had seemed inevitable.

**Back from the brink** Strenuous conservation efforts have successfully brought a number of species back from the brink of extinction. The best-known examples are probably the California condor (*Gymnogyps californianus*), the Mauritius kestrel (*Falco punctatus*) and the Chatham Island black robin (*Petroica traversi*).

The California condor was once widespread throughout many parts of

the south-western United States, but shooting, egg collecting, lead poisoning from bullets, predator baiting, high-voltage power lines and pesticides all contributed to its downfall. The population dropped to such low levels that, in the 1980s, it was decided to take all known survivors into captivity for safe-keeping. The last wild female was caught on 5 Jun 1986 and the last wild male on 19 Apr 1987. This brought the total to 27 birds in captivity – in San Diego Wild Animal Park and Los Angeles Zoo – and, for the first time in 2 million years, none left in the wild. The world's first captive-bred California condor chick hatched on 29 Apr 1988, in San Diego; since then a number of others have been hatched and reared successfully. Reintroduction into the wild began in January 1992, when two 8-month-old birds, called Chocuyens (a male) and Xewe (a female), were released into Los Padres National Forest, 120 km *75 miles* north of Los Angeles, California. By early 1994 the world population stood at 75, all but nine of them in captivity. Reintroductions are planned to continue until there are at least two separate self-sustaining populations of about 100 birds each.

In 1973, when the Mauritius Kestrel Conservation Programme started, there were only four individuals left in the wild. But captive breeding saved the species from extinction and there are now more than 300 free-living kestrels, including at least 60 wild breeding pairs. They live in three areas on Mauritius: the Bambou Mountains, Moka Mountains and Black River Gorges. The plan is to continue releasing captive-bred birds into the wild, and monitoring their progress, until there are at least 100 breeding pairs on the island.

The Chatham Island black robin lives on an isolated group of islands of the same name, 800 km *500 miles* east of New Zealand. When cats and rats were introduced to the Chathams, the robin

**Sightings of 'extinct' birds** It is not unusual for extremely rare birds to survive unnoticed for a great many years, and literally dozens of them have 'come back from the dead'. The most dramatic rediscovery of recent times must be of the Fiji petrel (*Pterodroma macgillivrayi*), which was formerly known from only one specimen collected on the island of Gau, Fiji, in 1855. It was not seen again until the night of 30 Apr 1984, also on Gau, when one reputedly collided with ornithologist Dick Watling's head. The bird was examined, photographed and released. The following year a fledgling was found on the same island, but there have been no further records.

Strangely, there are several other examples of petrels (family Procellariidae) being rediscovered after a long 'absence'. The longest interval between 'extinction' and rediscovery so far recorded is for the cahow or Bermuda petrel (*Pterodroma cahow*), which was first discovered nesting in vast numbers in Bermuda in the early 1500s, but was feared extinct in the mid-17th century; it went unnoticed for nearly 300 years until, after a few dead birds were identified in 1916, several nests were found on five offshore islets known as the Castle Rocks, in Bermuda, in 1951. The Chatham Island taiko or Magenta petrel (*Pterodroma magentae*) was first seen in 1867, in the Chatham Islands, New Zealand, and then not again until 1970; small numbers still survive on the islands, though they are hardly ever seen.

Other rediscoveries from around the world are equally extraordinary. Pelzeln's tody-tyrant (*Hemitriccus inornatus*) was rediscovered in 1992, in a patch of forest on the east bank of the Rio Negro, Brazil, no less than 161 years after the sole record of the species was made in 1831. Gurney's pitta (*Pitta gurneyi*), a brightly coloured, thrush-sized bird from south-east Asia, was declared extinct in 1985, after a long absence, but was promptly found a year later. The Madagascar red owl (*Tyto soumagnei*) had been recorded only once since 1934, until an individual was found being kept as a pet in Andapa, Madagascar, in 1994; the bird was reportedly captured almost 300 km

*186 miles* further north than any previous sightings. Only four specimens of the strange-looking takahe (*Notornis mantelli*) were identified in New Zealand during the entire 19th century, and none at all until the middle of the 20th century; then, in 1948, no fewer than 200 pairs were suddenly discovered in the Murchison Mountains and two neighbouring ranges rising from the western shores of Lake Te Anau; the species continues to live in the area, although its survival in the wild is still of major concern.

Perhaps the most unlikely rediscovery was of Vo Quy's pheasant (*Lophura haitiensis*), which was believed to be extinct until ornithologists found it turning up on the dinner plates of Vietnamese farmers. The farmers, who said they trapped and regularly ate the bird, agreed to keep alive two males, with their striking blue plumage and distinctive long white tails, and one female for captive breeding in Hanoi. These were the first live birds seen by ornithologists since the species was first discovered in 1964.

**Most recent extinction** Since the year 1600, 114 species and many more subspecies of bird are known to have become extinct. Many others, which have not been seen for years, may have disappeared unnoticed and still more inevitably disappear without us ever knowing of their existence; the precise dates of these extinctions will, of course, always remain uncertain.

The most recent acknowledged extinction is probably the ivory-billed woodpecker (*Campephilus principalis*), a large black, white and red bird which was widely distributed in south-eastern USA and Cuba only a century ago. It has not been seen in the USA since the early 1970s. In Cuba it was last sighted in March 1987, in a small forested area in Ojito de Agua, towards the east of the island; but a recent 3-month intensive search of Ojito de Agua, by ornithologists from the Netherlands and the Instituto de Investigaciones Forestales in Cuba, found no trace of the bird. The only suitable forest remaining for the species in Cuba is at Sierra Maestra, Granma Province, but there are no records of it ever having lived there, local people have never seen the bird and a 2-week search

**With the help of captive breeding, the Mauritius kestrel was brought back from the brink of extinction after its wild population dropped to an all-time low of only four individuals.**

B
I
R
D
S

*The gannet has a system of air sacs beneath its skin that act as shock absorbers, reducing the impact of plunging headfirst into the sea from a great height.*

proved fruitless. The experts finally gave up hope in 1993.

**Most precise extinction** The actual date and, in some cases, the precise time of extinction is known for a number of bird species and sub-species. The two best-known examples are the great auk (*Pinguinus impennis*) and the North American passenger pigeon (*Ectopistes migratorius*). The last two survivors of the flightless great auk (a breeding pair guarding their single egg) were found on the rocky skerry of Eldey, a few kilometres off the south-western tip of Iceland, on 3 Jun 1844. Jon Brandsson and Sigurdur Isleifsson killed the two adult birds with their clubs and Ketill Ketilsson accidentally smashed the egg with his boot; the skins were sold to a dealer and the egg was left to rot. The

**The greak auk is one of very few birds for which the precise date of extinction is known: in this case, 3 Jun 1844; this particular specimen was purchased for £9300 in 1971 by the people of Iceland which, at the time, was the highest price ever paid for a stuffed bird.**

Fuglinn sem hér er til sýnis var drepinn um 1820. Hann var keyptur fyrir samskotafé á uppboði í Lundúnum árið 1971, og er einn af fáum geirfuglum sem til eru. Enn færri egg hafa varðveist, en það sem hér er eignaðist safnið árið 1954.

three Icelandic fishermen were probably the last human beings ever to see a great auk alive (subsequent sightings have been claimed and may be genuine). The last North American passenger pigeon, a 29-year-old affectionately known as 'Martha', died in captivity in Cincinnati Zoo, USA, at 13.00 h Eastern Standard Time on 1 Sep 1914.

**Fastest extinction** The Stephens Island wren (*Traversia lyalli*), which lived on tiny Stephens Island, in Cook Strait, New Zealand, was discovered in 1894 and became extinct later in the same year. When a new lighthouse keeper arrived on the island, one of his cats caught a total of 16 of the wrens in rapid succession, including both the first and the last of the species. The lighthouse keeper was the only person to see one alive.

**Extinct raptor** The only bird of prey known for certain to have become extinct in the last 400 years is the Guadalupe caracara (*Polyborus lutosus*), which used to live on Guadalupe Island, 250 km *155 miles* off the coast of Baja California, Mexico. Last recorded in 1900, it was wiped out by settlers who believed that it preyed on the kids of their introduced goats.

**Threatened species** According to the World Conservation Union (IUCN), there are currently 971 bird species which are known or suspected to be globally threatened, representing more than 10 per cent of all known species.

**Most threatened group** There are more threatened songbirds (order Passeriformes) than any other major group of birds, with a total of 478 species (representing nearly 10 per cent of the order). However, *proportionately* more cranes and their allies (order Gruiformes) are threatened, with 52 out of a total 190 species (27 per cent) considered to be threatened. Gamebirds (order Galliformes), albatrosses and petrels (order Procellariiformes), parrots (order Psittaciformes) and grebes (order Podicipediformes) have approximately 23 per cent, 22 per cent, 19 per cent and 19 per cent of their species on the threatened list respectively.

**Country with the most threatened species** Indonesia has 123 internationally threatened bird species, which is more than any other country in the world. Brazil comes a close second, with 100 threatened species, and China is third with 88.

**Most extinct species** The island of Mauritius, in the Indian Ocean, was the

only or final home of 21 extinct bird species, which is more than for any other country in the world and accounts for 18.4 per cent of all bird species known to have become extinct since 1600.

**Least extinct species** No bird species is known to have become extinct on mainland Africa, in South America or on the continent of Antarctica in the past 400 years. Several species have been recorded only once, or just a handful of times, and may indeed be extinct – but the experts have yet to give up hope. It is also very likely that some species have become extinct before they were discovered and named.

**Period with most extinctions** The most disastrous period for bird extinctions was the 23 years between 1885 and 1907, when 24 species, 14 races and 38 forms were officially lost.

**Most threatened sea bird** The world's most threatened breeding sea bird is probably the Madeira petrel or freira (*Pterodroma madeira*), which breeds only in the high mountains of Madeira. After a dramatic decline through severe predation from rats, cats and people, the estimated breeding population now stands at only 20–30 pairs. It had its most successful breeding season for many years in 1993, with a record eight chicks fledging.

**Largest hunt** Every year over 6 billion birds of 140 different species follow one of Europe's most important migratory routes, from the Basque region of the Pyrenees to North Africa and beyond. As many as 900 million of them – 15 per cent of the total – are killed each year by hunters.

**Most hunters** The Mediterranean island republic of Malta has the highest concentration of bird hunters in the world. The Maltese countryside has more than 60 licensed hunters per km² – equivalent to roughly 1 in 20 of its 350 000 population. Between them, they shoot more than 3 million birds every year, including 50–100 000 birds of prey, 80 000 golden orioles, 200 000 skylarks and 400 000 swallows. No species is regarded as an unsuitable target, even if it is officially protected. The hunters use modern automatic weapons and a variety of other firearms and, in the process, an estimated 10 million cartridges are fired – so many, in fact, that there are fears that the tonnes of falling lead weight may be polluting public water supplies.

The Maltese hunters also trap a further 3 million birds every year; these

*Above:* the pink pigeon is just one of 971 bird species which are known or suspected to be threatened with extinction around the world.

*Below:* the echo parakeet is one of the rarest birds in the world, with only a handful of individuals surviving; it lives on the island of Mauritius, which has been the only or final home of more extinct bird species than any other country in the world.

are mainly finches, destined for brief lives as pets in cages.

**Most wasteful hunt** There are many distressing examples of wasteful bird hunts, from all over the world, but one is particularly bizarre. More than 80 000 Hawaii mamos (*Drepanis pacifica*), members of the Hawaiian honeycreeper tribe, were reputedly killed to make the famous cloak worn by Kamehameha I, the King of Hawaii (1810–19). The cloak was manufactured through the reigns of eight monarchs before it came to Kamehameha himself. The bird catchers were forbidden to kill the 'royal' birds and had to release them once the yellow feathers had been plucked. However, it seems that few birds were released and, of course, having had their feathers plucked, their chances of survival were slight. The Hawaii mamo became extinct in 1899 largely as a result of hunting for its highly prized, brilliant-yellow rump feathers and, to a certain extent, because of habitat destruction.

## FEEDING BIRDS

**Largest prey** The largest recorded wild animal killed and carried away by a bird was a 7 kg *15 lb* young male red howler monkey killed by a harpy eagle (*Harpia harpyja*) in Manu National Park, Peru, in 1990. This eagle, which lives in the tropical forests of Central and South America, is widely considered to be the world's most powerful bird of prey, although itself weighs only 9 kg *20 lb*. The harpy is also known to kill and eat 5 kg *11 lb* two-toed sloths on a regular basis. An American bald eagle (*Haliaeetus leucogaster*) has been reported flying with a 6.8 kg *15 lb* mule deer in its talons.

Stories of eagles carrying off human babies, children and even adults are generally unsubtantiated and treated with suspicion by most experts. However, there is one well documented case. In 1932, a 4-year-old Norwegian girl, Svanhild Hansen, who was apparently small for her age, was taken by a white-tailed sea eagle (*Haliaeetus albicilla*) from near her parents' farmhouse. It dropped her 1.6 km *1 mile* away, on a narrow ledge below its eyrie, and circled overhead while the girl was rescued, unharmed.

**Most food** Hummingbirds (family Trochilidae) require at least half their own body weights in food (primarily nectar and tiny insects) every day. With the possible exception of shrews, the birds have the highest metabolic rate of any known animal.

**Most specialized diet** Many birds have specialized diets. Some have such highly adapted bills and feet that they are unable to change diet if their normal food supplies are unavailable; these species are particularly vulnerable to fluctuations in their food supply and, not suprisingly, a number of them are threatened. One of the most extreme examples is the Everglade kite

B
I
R
D
S

> **On the most productive Rift Valley lakes, in East Africa, a million lesser flamingos may eat 60 tonnes of algae every day.**

(*Rostrhamus sociabilis*), which eats only snails of the genus *Pomacea*; the subspecies living in southern Florida (*R.s. plumbeus*) feeds exclusively on the large freshwater apple snail (*Pomacea paludosa*). Another good example is the lesser flamingo (*Phoeniconaias minor*), which lives in Africa, Madagascar and parts of India and is almost totally dependent on the filamentous blue-green algae *Spirulina*.

Pigeons (family Columbidae) and flamingos (family Phoenicopteridae) of both sexes, and male emperor penguins (*Aptenodytes forsteri*), feed their chicks exclusively on a high-protein secretion from the cells lining the crop (or oesophagus in flamingos); this is similar in composition to mammalian milk.

**Most varied diet** Specialized diets are the exception among birds and most species eat a wide variety of foods. The ruffed grouse (*Bonasa umbellus*) from North America is one of the better-known examples: it is known to have

**Flamingos are the only true filter-feeding birds, employing a system similar to the one used by baleen whales to strain krill or fish from seawater; this colourful flock was photographed in the Ngorongoro Crater, Tanzania.**

eaten part of at least 518 animal species and 414 plant species. Crows (family Corvidae) and gulls (family Laridae) are also cosmopolitan in their tastes and will eat a wide range of plant material, many species of live vertebrates and invertebrates, carrion and even the discarded waste products around human settlements.

**Filter feeding** The only birds that are true filter feeders are flamingos (family Phoenicopteridae). Holding their heads and bills upside-down in freshwater, they employ a system that is similar to the one used by baleen whales to strain krill and fish from seawater. They use their tongues as fast-action plungers, driving water and mud across the length of the bill and past special filters, or lamellae, that catch all the suspended food particles.

**Longest fast** The longest known period of fasting for any waking bird is endured by the male emperor penguin (*Aptenodytes forsteri*), which spends several months without feeding on the frozen wastes of the Antarctic sea ice. The female lays a single egg in late May or early June and then leaves the male to incubate it for 62–67 days until it has hatched. Having travelled overland from the sea to the breeding colony, courted the female, incubated the egg, waited for the female to return and then travelled back to the open sea, he may have had to go without food for as long as 115–120 days. The longest continuous fast recorded for a male emperor penguin was an incredible 134 days. Surviving on reserves of subcutaneous fat, which can be 3–4 cm *1.2–1.6 in* thick, his weight may drop from 40 kg *88 lb* at the beginning of winter to just

20 kg *44 lb* towards the end.

The North American nightjar or poorwill (*Phalaenoptilus nuttallii*) fasts for up to 5 months while it hibernates in a rock crevice or under a desert shrub, during the worst of the winter weather.

**Feather eating** The only birds known to pluck and eat their own feathers are grebes (family Podicipedidae). They often feed them to their young as well: more than 300 adult feathers were found in the stomach of one western grebe (*Aechmophorus occidentalis*) chick. One theory to explain this strange behaviour, which is most common in the fish-eating species, is that it helps in forming regurgitated pellets of bones and scales.

**Strangest diet** When it died, an ostrich (*Struthio camelus*) that had been living in London Zoo, UK, was found to have swallowed an alarm clock, a roll of film, a handkerchief, 91 cm *3 ft* of rope, a cycle valve, a pencil, three gloves, a comb, part of a gold necklace, a collar stud, a Belgian franc, four halfpennies and two farthings.

**Blood drinking** The sharp-beaked ground finch (*Geospiza difficilis*), which may be the only truly parasitic bird, drinks blood from holes it pecks between feathers in the wings of nesting masked boobies (*Sula dactylatra*) and red-footed boobies (*Sula sula*); surprisingly, the boobies do not seem to be particularly bothered by its activities.

**Strongest gizzard** The gizzard is the part of a bird's stomach that performs the function of mammalian teeth by grinding the food into small pieces; in most birds, it contains sand grains or

Grebes such as this western grebe photographed in California, USA, are the only birds known to pluck and eat their own feathers.

## BIRD SENSES

**Keenest vision** There are many unsubstantiated records of incredible visual acuity in birds; unfortunately, these are mainly based on anecdotal field observations. In reality, not much is known about how well they can see and, although some clearly have an outstanding ability to discriminate fine detail in distant objects, there is surprisingly little definitive data. Birds of prey are believed to have the keenest eyesight, with a slightly magnified area in the centre of their field of view. Large species, with eyes similar in size to our own, can probably resolve details at two and a half to three times the distance we can. To put this into perspective, under ideal conditions a golden eagle (*Aquila chrysaetos*) can detect the slight movements of a rabbit from more than 2 km *1¼ miles* away, while a peregrine falcon (*Falco peregrinus*) can spot a pigeon at a range of over 8 km *5 miles*.

small stones to aid the grinding process. The strongest gizzard belongs to a turkey (*Meleagris gallopavo*), which was capable of completely crushing 24 walnuts (in the shell) in under 4 hours and could turn surgical lancet blades into grit in less than 16 hours.

**Worst pest** The red-billed quelea (*Quelea quelea*) is probably the worst bird pest in the world. With each quelea consuming an average 3 g *⅛ oz* of seeds

every day, a flock of 1 million birds would need 3 tonnes of food every day and the population as a whole needs an estimated 4500 tonnes. A quarter of the population is believed to attack grain crops for about 30 days every year, costing Africa an estimated £15 million annually. At least 200 million of these 'feathered locusts' are slaughtered annually – breeding colonies and roosts containing literally millions of them are attacked with flame-throwers, dynamite bombs and poisonous aerial sprays – without having any obvious long-term impact on the population.

**Seeing in the dark** Nocturnal birds, such as owls (families Tytonidae and Strigidae) and nightjars (family Caprimulgidae), have eyes with the best light-gathering power, or visual sensitivity. It would be untrue to say that they can literally 'see in the dark', since in total darkness they can see no better than we can; but total darkness rarely occurs in nature and they can see extremely well on nights so dark that we would be utterly helpless. Controlled experiments have shown that several species of owl are able to see lifeless objects at light intensities of as little as 1 per cent of those we would require to see the same objects. Their eyes are not simply giant versions of our own, but actually have more light-sensitive cells on the retina and a variety of other special adaptations.

Birds of prey are believed to have the keenest eyesight of all birds; this is a black kite, photographed in Pakistan.

**Colour vision** As a group, birds probably have better colour vision than any other group of animals on Earth. They have a unique combination of light receptors in the retina, which are colour-sensitive, and oil droplets, which act as filters by narrowing the band of wavelengths absorbed and deciphered by each receptor; together, they create a powerful system for discerning subtle hues. The specific arrangement of these receptors and filters varies from

species to species, according to their particular needs, but it is likely that most, if not all, birds have colour vision of one kind or another.

**Ultraviolet vision** There is direct evidence that mallards (*Anas platyrhynchos*), black-chinned hummingbirds (*Archilochus alexandri*), belted kingfishers (*Megaceryle alcyon*) and several other species can see into the near-ultraviolet or even ultraviolet part of the light spectrum. Given the taxonomic diversity of the species tested to date, the majority of birds probably possess this ability, enabling them to appreciate colours that are not visible to mammals. Ultraviolet vision has several possible advantages. For example, it may help hummingbirds to detect flowers, which often strongly reflect ultraviolet light; and, since ultraviolet light penetrates thin cloud cover, migrating birds may use it to determine the position of the Sun on cloudy days.

**Field of vision** The field of vision in birds ranges from only a few degrees to a full 360° and is an excellent indication of whether they are predators or prey. Prey species tend to have eyes on the sides of their heads, giving them 360° vision; this enables them to scan as much of the world as possible to spot

> *The collective name for a group of crows is a 'murder'.*

approaching danger. The woodcock (*Scolopax rusticola*) is the best example because, in addition to having complete wrap-around vision horizontally, it can also see above itself – without having to move its head. The drawback of this arrangement is that the woodcock has only a very limited field of binocular vision (directly in front and behind) which limits its ability to judge size and distance, and to see finer details, and reduces the sensitivity of its eyes when the light is poor. However, these are all essential attributes for predatory species; they tend to have eyes nearer the front of the head, giving them a wide field of binocular vision but an extensive blind area behind. The tawny owl (*Strix aluco*) is an excellent example, with around 60° of binocular vision in front and an extensive blind area of around 130° behind. The field of vision of most other birds falls within these two extremes.

**Largest eyes** The ostrich has the largest eyes of any living bird (and, indeed, the largest eyes of any living land animal). They each measure up to 5 cm 2 *in* in diameter. All birds have relatively large eyes: compared to its body size, the eyes of a starling (*Sturnus vulgaris*), for example, are at least eight times larger than human eyes.

**Keenest hearing** It is very difficult to measure hearing acuity in birds although, in many species, it is certainly very impressive. It is likely that barn owls in the genus *Tyto* have the most exceptional hearing of all birds. They

are able to catch live prey, in total darkness, guided by sound cues alone. It has been shown under laboratory conditions that a barn owl (*Tyto alba*) is able to pinpoint the slightest sounds to within one degree in both the vertical and horizontal planes. It does this by measuring the differences in intensity and time of arrival of sounds at its two ears – and, indeed, can distinguish time delays of as little as 100 microseconds. Not only can the owl hear and locate noises accurately, it can also identify what is making them.

Oilbirds (*Steatornis caripensis*) and certain cave swiftlets (family Apodidae) also have a keen sense of hearing, which they use for echolocation. Each click an oilbird emits lasts for about 0.01 seconds and is not a single sound but a burst of pulses each only about 0.001 seconds long. We are able to hear only the click, but the oilbird's ears are so sensitive that it can hear each pulse as a distinct sound – and then interpret its echo.

**Hearing range** Collectively, birds have a narrower range of good hearing than mammals. However, their sensitivity to sounds of different frequencies is by no means uniform and varies considerably from species to species. Using sensitive equipment in a laboratory, scientists have found that pigeons (family Columbidae) can detect sounds as low as 0.1 hertz (that is, one vibration every 10 seconds). Since pigeons do not seem to have particularly exceptional ears, it seems likely that many other birds can pick up such low-frequency sounds as well (although there is a possibility that the birds cannot actually 'hear' the sounds but, instead, detect them via touch receptors on other parts of the body). There are many possible advantages in hearing low-frequency sound (infrasound); for example, it may enable the birds to hear the deep sounds generated by storms and thus give them advance warning of bad weather. At the other end of the scale, some owls (families Tytonidae and Strigidae) have a high-frequency hearing limit of around 15–20 kHz, which is essential for detecting prey in almost total darkness. For comparison, the human range of hearing extends from about 20 hertz to almost 20 kHz.

**Echolocation** The only birds known to echolocate are certain cave swiftlets

**Pigeons can detect sounds as low as 0.1 hertz, which is only one vibration every 10 seconds.**

(family Apodidae) living in south-east Asia, and oilbirds (*Steatornis caripensis*), which live in South America. Both birds nest and roost in the total darkness of caves and use a fairly simple system of echolocation to navigate; even in total darkness, and when flying at considerable speed, they can sense the walls of their caves and any other major obstacles in their path in time to take evasive action. As with bats and many cetaceans, they emit pulses of sound and build up a 'sound picture' of their surroundings by analysing the returning echoes. However, unlike echolocating mammals, they are restricted to the use of low frequency sounds (which are within the human range of hearing and can be heard as deep clicks) and, consequently, are not as efficient at finding their way around in the dark. Oilbirds, for example, cannot reliably detect objects less than about 20 cm *7¾ in* in diameter – a level of performance actually matched by some blind humans, who can also be guided by sound. Cave swiftlets are more sensitive and can avoid objects as small as 6 mm *¼ in*, though even this does not match the sensitivity of mammals using high-frequency ultrasound.

**Keenest sense of smell** Most birds have a poor sense of smell, although its importance varies markedly between species. Indeed, a small number rely on smell to find food and have large areas of their brain devoted to this sense. The New Zealand kiwis (family Apterygidae), uniquely, are noted for their ability to smell out worms, slugs and other prey animals amongst leaf litter and in the soil; no one knows how they prevent the soil from blocking their nostrils. But perhaps the most impressive example is the black-footed albatross (*Diomedea nigripes*), which lives in the North Pacific and can be attracted by the smell of bacon fat being poured on to the ocean surface from a distance of at least 30 km *19 miles*. Other birds with a relatively well-developed sense of smell include the New World vultures (family Cathartidae), honeyguides (family Indicatoridae), petrels and shearwaters (family Procellariidae), grebes (family Podicipedidae) and nightjars (family Caprimulgidae).

## BIRD ATHLETES

**Fastest swimmer** The gentoo penguin (*Pygoscelis papua*) is probably the fastest swimming bird in the world and has been recorded at a maximum speed of about 27 km/h *17 mph* during short bursts of 'flying' underwater. Earlier claims of speeds reaching 60 km/h *37 mph* are now considered to be inaccurate by most authorities.

**Deepest dive** The deepest dive accurately measured for any bird was recorded during a study of emperor penguins (*Aptenodytes forsteri*) in the Ross Sea, Antarctica, from October–December 1990. A team of French and American scientists from the Centre National de la Recherche Scientifique, in Strasbourg, and the Scripps Institution of Oceanography, in San Diego, obtained a complete record of diving depths reached by one particular penguin over a period of 14 days. They found that, although most dives were to mid-water depths, some were at or near the bottom. On day six the penguin made a series of four dives ranging from 444 to 483 m *1456–1584 ft* over a bottom depth of about 450–500 m *1476–1640 ft*.

**Longest dive** The longest dive accurately measured for any bird was recorded in 1969 for a small group of ten emperor penguins (*Aptenodytes forsteri*) at Cape Crozier, Antarctica, by a team of US scientists. They recorded a maximum dive time of 18 minutes.

**Walking on water** The storm petrels (family Hydrobatidae) are the only birds capable of 'walking on water'. They feed on small animals which they pluck from the sea while pattering on the surface. In fact, they are wind-hovering (flying slowly into the wind) while trailing their webbed feet in the water like sea anchors.

Jacanas (family Jacanidae) are able to walk on floating lily pads (*see Longest toes*).

**Worst walker** Several bird families are essentially incapable of walking, for example hummingbirds (family Trochilidae), swifts (family Apodidae) tropicbirds (family Phaethontidae) and loons or divers (family Gaviiformes); when ashore, a loon rests its weight entirely on its breast and 'leap-frogs' over short distances by kicking its legs out backwards.

**Longest stride** When running at sprint speed, the stride of an ostrich (*Struthio camelus*) may exceed 7 m *23 ft*.

**Fastest runner** In 1964 a male ostrich (*Struthio camelus*) was timed at 72 km/h *45 mph* over a distance of 732 m *2400 ft*; this would be fast enough to win most horse races. Another ostrich has been clocked over a short distance on the Mara plains, Kenya, at a speed of 60 km/h *37.3 mph*. In short bursts, ostriches can probably run even faster than these two records and there are even claims of them reaching speeds of up to 96.5 km/h *60 mph*, though these do seem excessively high and have yet to be proven. At slightly slower speeds

**The fastest-swimming bird in the world is probably the gentoo penguin, which literally 'flies' underwater at speeds of up to 27 km/h *17 mph*.**

of 45–48 km/h *28–30 mph* most ostriches can keep running for as long as 20 minutes without apparently tiring.

Flying birds are generally slow runners compared to similar-sized mammals, presumably because they have stronger wing muscles and weaker leg muscles; many flying birds also tend to have shorter legs, designed primarily for perching. The fastest running flying bird is the roadrunner (*Geococcyx californianus*), a member of the cuckoo family living in the dry, scrubby deserts of south-western USA. It has been clocked at speeds of at least 42 km/h *26 mph* and can even turn at right angles without slowing down. It straightens out its neck, opens its wings slightly to act as stabilizers and uses its long tail as a rudder, in order to dash around the desert catching insects, lizards and rattlesnakes.

**Energy expenditure** Hummingbirds use more fuel in relation to their size than a jet fighter aircraft. They consume half their body weight in high energy nectar every day and expend more energy in relation to their size than any other bird. If human beings were to expend energy at the same rate, it has been estimated that their body temperature would rise to nearly 400°C *750°F.*

# BIRD BEHAVIOUR

**Tool using** More than 30 species of birds are known to use tools. Some of the better-known examples include Egyptian vultures (*Neophron percnopterus*), which throw stones at the thick-shelled eggs of ostriches (*Struthio camelus*) in order to break them and eat the nutritious contents; woodpecker finches (*Camarhynchus pallidus*), which use cactus spines held in their bills to remove grubs from holes in trees; song thrushes (*Turdus philomelos*), which crack the shells of snails using rocks as anvils; and green-backed or striated herons (*Butorides striatus*), which have been seen angling for fish by throwing small pieces of twig, biscuit or anything else to hand into the water as bait (some individuals have even been seen to fashion twigs into the right shape and size).

**Most aggressive** Many wild birds are aggressive during the breeding season, when they are defending territories or competing for nest sites and mates. Perhaps surprisingly, one of the most aggressive birds in the world is the European robin (*Erithacus rubecula*). Fights between males can be extremely vicious and not infrequently result in death (up to 10 per cent of adult robins die as a result of territorial disputes).

Mass killings are very unusual, but biologists studying starlings (*Sturnus vulgaris*) in Wellington, New Zealand, have discovered that a severe housing shortage can have a devastating effect on the birds' behaviour. The starling population exploded from 300 to 3000 in just 10 years, after hundreds of nest boxes had been erected in the area, but there were soon too many birds for the available nest sites. Competition was severe and fights over suitable accommodation became the major cause of death. At the last count, more than 200 birds had been killed by their own kind.

**Most dangerous** Birds are not particularly dangerous to people and most 'attacks' are the result of molestation or provocation. Terns (family Laridae), skuas (family Stercorariidae), owls (families Tytonidae and Strigidae) and many others will vigorously defend their nests, while a great many birds will peck or kick if they are handled.

The only birds known to have attacked and *killed* people in the wild are ostriches (*Struthio camelus*), mute swans (*Cygnus olor*) and, perhaps the most dangerous of all, the three species of cassowary (family Casuariidae). Cassowaries, which live in New Guinea and north-eastern Queensland, Australia, are large birds (up to 2 m *79 in* tall) and have dagger-like claws up to 12 cm *4.7 in* long. A cornered, or wounded, bird can be extremely dangerous and will leap into the air and kick, damaging vital organs or causing massive bleeding.

Mid-air collisions with planes can be a major problem, causing human deaths and costing hundreds of millions of pounds in damage every year. Gulls (family Laridae), kites (family Accipitridae), pigeons (family Columbidae), swallows and martins (family Hirundinidae), swifts (family Apodidae) and lapwings (*Vanellus vanellus*) are among the most commonly involved. The first mid-air collision ever recorded was at Long Beach, California, USA, in 1910, when a plane struck a gull and crashed; the pilot did not survive. The worst air disaster proved to have been caused by birds was on 4 Oct 1960, in Boston, USA, when a Lockheed LI88 Electra aircraft struck a cloud of starlings (*Sturnus vulgaris*) on take off; the airliner nose-dived into a river and, of the 72 passengers and crew on board, 62 were killed and 9 seriously injured.

Crows (family Corvidae) are frequently associated with doom and disaster, presumably because of their 'black as death' plumage and their habit of eating carrion. But, although they strike fear into the hearts of superstitious people across the world, they are not dangerous.

**Most bossy** The kea (*Nestor notabilis*), a rowdy member of the parrot family living in New Zealand, is the only bird known to have a society in which higher-status individuals can force others to work for them. A study on a captive breeding colony of keas at the Konrad Lorenz Institute, Austria, provided the birds with a wooden see-saw with a perch at one end that lifted the lid of a feeding box at the other. It was designed so that the percher could not reach to feed itself and, as soon as it left the perch, the lid closed. It was found that the dominant birds always fed at the box while their subordinates did the perching. If the subordinates dared to neglect their duties, their superiors would chase them back. There was no evidence of the birds taking it in turns to feed and work the see-saw.

**Most avid collector** Male bowerbirds (family Ptilonorhynchidae) go to great

> *Japanese cranes are enthusiastic dancers, leaping into the air, flapping their wings, throwing their heads back and bobbing them up and down, bowing deeply, and running around; when one member of the flock takes to the floor the others cannot resist joining in.*

lengths to impress the females. In their forest homes in Australia and New Guinea, they spend many months building and maintaining ornate 'bowers' on the ground. These vary in design, depending on the species, from simple clearings and avenues of grass to substantial roofed huts; sometimes the bowers are painted with berry juice. They are all liberally decorated with bright objects such as berries, flowers, mushrooms, stones, shells, bones, kangaroo droppings and even tin foil, pieces of plastic or glass. There is great rivalry between the males and they often steal sought-after objects from each other's collections. Generally speaking, the duller the male, the more elaborate his bower – apparently to make up for his own shortcomings – and there appears to be a correlation between the colour of his plumage and

that of the treasures he collects. When a female begins to show interest, the male cackles and dances around, carefully displaying his decorations as if showing her valuable jewels. If all goes well, they mate inside or near the bower, and the female then goes away to build a nest.

## TALKING BIRDS

**Most talkative** A number of birds are renowned for their talking abilities (i.e. the reproduction of human words) but the African grey parrot (*Psittacus erithacus*) excels in this ability. A female named *Prudle*, formerly owned by Lyn Logue (died January 1988) and then in the care of Iris Frost of East Sussex, UK, won the 'Best-Talking Parrot-like Bird' title at the National Cage and Aviary Bird Show in London each December for 12 consecutive years (1965–76). *Prudle*, who had a vocabulary of nearly 800 words, was taken from a nest at Jinja, Uganda, in 1958. She retired undefeated and was still talking two days before her death, on 13 Jul 1994. For their talking abilities, many African grey parrots have been taken from the wild as pets; in the period 1983–9, an incredible 346 782 of them were recorded being exported from 20 African countries.

However, the record holder is a budgerigar (*Melopsittacus undulatus*) called *Puck* owned by Camille Jordan of Petaluma, California, USA, which had a vocabulary estimated at 1728 words on 31 Jan 1993.

A male budgerigar named *Candy*, and owned by Eileen Trapnell of Bristol, UK, has a vocabulary of over 500 words. He can recite his own name,

**Birds rarely attack people, but a few species can be quite aggressive when defending their eggs or chicks; this arctic skua, seen mobbing an intruder near its nest in Spitzbergen, eventually managed to draw blood after dive-bombing the man's head.**

**B**
**I**
**R**
**D**
**S**

*Parrots are normally either left-footed or right-footed.*

address and telephone number, knows eight nursery rhymes and one joke (Why did the chicken cross the road?) and often asks his owner to turn the television off. One of his favourite party tricks is to say '*Candy* can count up to 10 . . . 1, 2, 3, 4, 5, 6, 7, 8, 9, 10'. His first language is English, but he can also say phrases in French, Russian, Spanish, Welsh and Icelandic, and is currently learning some German. *Candy* was born on 14 Aug 1993.

Learning to imitate human words is basically a variation of the vocal mimicry that is found among many birds in the wild. Interestingly, some species, such as the marsh warbler (*Acrocephalus palustris*), are able to mimic a bewildering variety of other birds but have never been known to mimic people; yet, in contrast, species such as the Indian hill mynah (*Gracula religiosa*) are able to

---

**The kea is the only bird known to have a society in which higher-status individuals can force others to work for them.**

imitate the spoken words of their owners but, in the wild, never mimic the sounds of other birds.

**Best mimic** Many wild birds are able to mimic the sounds made by other animals, or even human machinery, but few are able to mimic a broad range of sounds. In this respect, the marsh warbler (*Acrocephalus palustris*) is generally considered to be the world record-holder. Each individual has a song which contains elements of up to 100 different species. A typical male imitates 70–80 species: about half from its European breeding range and the other half from its African wintering range. These appear to be copied indiscriminately from birds in the local community, since marsh warblers living near the coast, for example, have more marine species in their repertoires than those living further inland. Almost the entire marsh warbler repertoire is made up of mimicry, including elements 'borrowed' from a total of more than 200 different species.

**Loudest song** Low-frequency sounds, such as the calls of grouse (family Phasianidae), cuckoos (family Cuculidae) and large owls (family Strigidae) are the most effective for long-distance communication. On the ground, the most far-carrying song of any bird is the deep boom of the male kakapo (*Strigops habroptilus*), a rare nocturnal

parrot now restricted to two small islands off the coast of New Zealand. The bird inflates two enormous air sacs, which swell his breast and throat until he is the size and almost the shape of a football, to make a deep booming sound that reverberates through the night air. He may boom all night, every night, for as long as 3 months, in his untiring efforts to attract a female. The song can readily be heard by people within 5 km *3.1 miles* of a booming kakapo and has been heard from a record distance of 7 km *4.4 miles*.

The deep boom of the Eurasian bittern (*Botaurus stellaris*), which lives in parts of Europe, Asia and Africa, is also far-carrying and can be heard from as far as 5 km *3.1 miles* away. Its deep, very distinctive sound is more reminiscent of a distant foghorn, or even a cow, than a bird.

For its size, the 9–10 cm *3½–4 in* common wren (*Troglodytes troglodytes*) has one of the loudest songs of any bird. Certain elements of the song, which consists of a loud warble ending in a harsh, rattling *cherrr*, can be heard from a distance of over 500 m *1640 ft* away.

**Double song** Several birds are able to make two or more sounds simultaneously. The record-holder is the brown thrasher (*Toxostoma rufum*) of North America which, at one point during its song, utters four different sounds all at the same time. The

The most far-carrying song of any bird is the deep boom of the male kakapo; this rain-soaked individual is being examined by a professional kakapo tracker on Codfish Island, New Zealand, before release.

---

Gouldian finch (*Chloebia gouldiae*) of northern Australia is able to make a bagpipe-like drone while it sings two tunes at once. The reed warbler (*Acrocephalus scirpaceus*) is also able to sing two tunes at once, with different notes coming from each half of the syrinx (sound-producing organ).

**Most songs** The red-eyed vireo (*Vireo olivaceus*) of North and South America has been recorded singing 22 197 songs in one 10-hour period, which is more per unit of time than has been recorded for any other bird.

## BIRD ODDITIES

**Highest g-force** American experiments have shown that the beak of the red-headed woodpecker (*Melanerpes*

*erythrocephalus*) hits the bark of a tree with an impact velocity of 20.9 km/h *13 mph*, subjecting its brain to a deceleration of about 10 g when its head snaps back. Little research work has been done in this field and other woodpeckers may experience an even higher g-force.

**Sideways bill** The only sideways-curving bill belongs to the wry-billed plover or wrybill (*Anarhynchus frontalis*) from New Zealand. The tip of the bill (up to a third of its total length) turns sharply to the bird's right at an angle of 12–22°. This appears to be an adaptation for feeding: the wrybill feeds along the seashore, and around estuaries, by wading across the mud and sweeping its bill down and to the right, trapping all the tiny crustaceans in its path.

**Longest lower mandible** The only birds with a lower mandible much longer than the upper mandible are the three species of skimmer (family Rynchopidae), which live in the Americas, Africa and Asia. The birds fly low over the water, skimming the surface with their lower mandibles, and snap down on any fish or crustacean with which they come into contact.

**Head turning** Some owls (order Strigiformes) can rotate their heads by as much as 280° – and then rapidly swivel them round in the opposite direction in order to maintain visual contact. Accounts of them being able to swivel their heads a full 360° have been exaggerated.

**Hibernation** The only known hibernating bird is the desert-dwelling North American nightjar or poorwill (*Phalaenoptilus nuttallii*). Its hibernating habits were first discovered by scientists in the Chuckwalla Mountains of the Colorado Desert, California, USA, in December 1946, although the Hopi Indians have always known it as *Holchko* – 'the sleeping one'. With the onset of winter, it chooses a narrow cleft in a south-facing rock, or a comfortable spot under a desert shrub, and stays there for up to 5 months

during the worst of the weather. Its heart and respiration rates drop to almost unmeasurable levels, and its temperature falls from about 41°C *106°F* to as low as 6°C *43°F*. After waking, it requires about 7 hours to warm up fully.

Many other birds can enter into a dormant state overnight, or even for a few days at a time, if the weather is particularly severe or if food is in short supply. By allowing their body temperatures to fall, they slow their metabolic rates and, consequently, make considerable energy savings. A ptarmigan (*Lagopus mutus*), for example, can cope with a blizzard by settling into a comfortable spot in the snow and allowing its body temperature to drop to within a degree or two above the point of death. Many hummingbirds (family Trochilidae) cope in a similar way when food is in short supply; if they allow their body temperatures to drop by just 10°C *50°F* overnight, they can decrease their metabolic demands by as much as 25 per cent.

**Most daylight** The arctic tern (*Sterna paradisaea*) spends the northern summer in the Arctic and the southern summer in the Antarctic and, consequently, experiences more daylight per year than any other animal.

**Sexual dimorphism** The most remarkable example of sexual dimorphism in birds (in which the two sexes look quite different) was found in the huia (*Heteralocha acutirostris*), from New Zealand. For many years, male and female huias were thought to be separate species, because their bills were so different. They were both large and predominantly black, crow-sized birds, and each had a bright orange 'wattle' on either side of its face. But the male's beak was short, thick and starling-like for breaking up rotten bark in search of insects, while the female's was long, delicate and downcurved for picking up insects that were hiding in crevices out of reach of the male. Sadly, this extraordinary bird became extinct at the beginning of this century.

Skimmers are the only birds with a lower mandible significantly longer than the upper mandible.

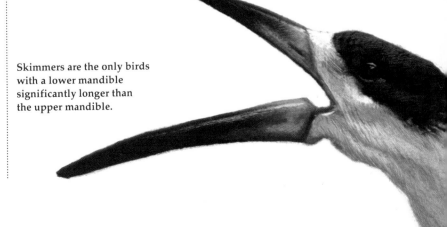

No other animal experiences as much daylight in a year as the globe-trotting arctic tern.

**Poisonous bird** The only poisonous birds known are three species of pitohui (pronounced 'pitohooey') from Papua New Guinea: the hooded pitohui (*Pitohui dichrous*), the rusty pitohui (*P. ferrugineus*) and the variable pitohui (*P. kirhocephalus*). The hooded pitohui is the deadliest of the three. In 1992 an ecology student from Chicago, USA, who was studying other birds in the pitohui's forest home, was scratched on his hand by a 'particularly feisty' individual as he released it from a mist net. After sucking the wounds, he experienced a 'numb and tingly' sensation in his mouth. It was a year before he caught another specimen and was able to investigate further, initially by licking one of its feathers and then by chemical analysis. He discovered that the skin and feathers of the songbird contain a homobatrachotoxin almost identical to the chemical toxin secreted by the celebrated poison-arrow frogs in the Amazon. An extract from just 10 mg of the bird's skin, injected into a mouse, killed the animal in 20 minutes; and tests imply that a single gram of the poison would be enough to dispatch roughly 20 million mice. The poison is believed to be a defence mechanism against hawks and snakes – and the birds' striking black and orange plumage is probably a warning.

**Avoiding land** The emperor penguin (*Aptenodytes forsteri*) is probably the only bird in the world that may never set foot on solid land. It spends its entire life at sea, feeding in the water during summer and breeding on the frozen pack ice in the depths of the Antarctic winter.

**Most similar** Closely related bird species are often very similar, but examples of convergent evolution in which unrelated species look similar is more unusual. One of the best-known examples is the Eastern meadowlark (*Sturnella magna*), a kind of blackbird found in North America, which is almost identical to the yellow-throated longclaw (*Macronyx croceus*), a kind of pipit from southern Africa. Both birds live in open grasslands, feed on the same types of food and occupy similar niches. The only variations between the two are small differences in the head patterning and in the claws; otherwise, their plumage, shape and size are almost identical.

**Fastest heartbeat** The resting heartbeats of birds are about half those of similar-sized mammals and range from around 93/min in a turkey (*Meleagris gallopavo*) to over 500/min in a hummingbird (family Trochilidae). In flight, the heartbeat increases dramatically to a maximum of 1300/min in certain hovering hummingbirds.

**Cold endurance** The male emperor penguin (*Aptenodytes forsteri*) is one of the hardiest creatures on Earth. It spends the height of the Antarctic winter – when temperatures of –60°C –76°F and icy winds gusting up to 200 km/h *124 mph* are not unusual – coping with some of the worst weather the planet can offer. While most other animals are moving northwards, as the surface of the Southern Ocean starts to freeze with the onset of winter, the emperors head south to breed. The males incubate their single eggs continuously for 62–67 days, much of the time in total darkness, holding them between their feet and a loose fold of skin on their bellies. When the weather gets really bad they huddle together in groups of up to 6000 for warmth, taking it in turns to go inside the huddle (where the temperature can be as much as 60°C *140°F* higher than on the periphery) and then on the leeward side and, finally, on the windward side. In this way, they can reduce their heat loss by as much as 50 per cent compared with standing alone.

The effectiveness of the insulation provided by an incubating emperor penguin was demonstrated in an Antarctic study in which egg temperatures were taken. It was found that if the eggs were exposed to outside temperatures for more than a few seconds, they chilled. But during incubation the heat transfer from the male's brood patch to the egg was so efficient that, when the external temperature was –26°C –15°F, the internal egg temperature was 31°C *88°F* – some 57°C *103°F* higher than the surrounding environment.

Under experimental conditions, Eurasian goldfinches (*Carduelis carduelis*), purple finches (*Carpodacus purpureus*), pine siskins (*Carduelis pinus*) and several other small passerines are able to sustain their normal body temperatures for several hours when subjected to an outside temperature of –70°C –94°F, as long as they have enough stored food energy.

**Heat endurance** Many desert-living birds regularly endure air temperatures of 40°C *104°F* or even higher. They do not have sweat glands, but have developed many physical and physiological tricks to keep their body temperatures below the fatal level (around 46–48°C *115–118°F* in most species). One extreme example is the African skimmer (*Rynchops flavirostris*) nesting on the shores of Lake Rudolph, Kenya, where the ground surface temperature may exceed 60°C *140°F* and the air temperature just above the ground may reach 40°C *104°F*.

The gray gull (*Larus modestus*) endures similarly high temperatures (air: up to 40°C *104°F*; ground: up to 50°C *122°F*) at its breeding grounds in the deserts of northern Chile.

**Longevity** The life expectancy of most small birds in the wild is only 2–5 years and few larger species live for longer than 20–30 years. However, it is very difficult to determine the maximum age of wild birds and, consequently, there are few extreme records. The highest ever reported is an unconfirmed age of about 82 years for a male Siberian white crane (*Grus leucogeranus*) named 'Wolf' at the International Crane Foundation, Baraboo, Wisconsin, USA. Said to have been hatched at a zoo in Switzerland in about 1905, 'Wolf' died in late 1988 after breaking his bill while repelling a visitor who approached too close to his pen.

Reports of captive members of the parrot family (Psittacidae) reaching a ripe old age of 100 years or more have never been authenticated and are extremely unlikely. The greatest irrefutable age reported is 'over 80 years' for a male sulphur-crested cockatoo (*Cacatua galerita*) named *Cocky*, who died in London Zoo on 28 Oct 1982. He was presented to the zoo in 1925, and had been with his previous owner since 1902 when he was already fully mature.

The oldest brooding bird and, indeed, the oldest ringed sea bird on record is a female royal albatross (*Diomedea epomophora*) named *Blue-White*. She was first banded as an adult when she arrived to breed on Taiaroa Head, New Zealand, in 1937. Since most royal albatrosses do not start breeding until they are at least 9 years old, she was probably born in 1928 or even earlier. Since then, she has come back

every other year to breed on the same headland and has raised 10 chicks of her own and fostered 3 others with her mate *Green White Green*. She even laid an egg at the age of 60, in November 1988, when her name was changed to *Grandma*. She failed to return to her colony at the end of 1990 and has not been seen since.

**Smelliest** The smelliest bird in the world is probably the South American hoatzin (*Opisthocomus hoazin*), which smells like cow manure. Indeed, some Columbians call it *pava hedionda* which, roughly translated, means 'stinking pheasant'. The cause of the smell is believed to be a combination of the hoatzin's diet, which consists almost exclusively of green leaves, and its highly specialized digestive system (which, unique among birds, involves a kind of foregut fermentation that is strikingly similar to the one found in cows, sheep, deer and a number of other ruminant mammals).

Several other birds are well known for being smelly. For example, the kiwis (family Apterygidae) exude an earthy, sweet and rather mammal-like odour that may linger for days.

The hoopoe (*Upupa epops*) is said to have the foulest-smelling nest. The penetrating stench, which is produced by the large preen gland, is believed to function as a predator deterrent.

---

## WATCHING AND STUDYING BIRDS

**Twitching** The world's leading bird-spotter or 'twitcher' is Phoebe Snetsinger of Webster Groves, Missouri, USA, who has logged 7772 species (based on a world list of 9672 known species) since 1965. This represents over 80 per cent of the available total.

The greatest number of species spotted in a 24-hour period is 342 by Kenyans Terry Stevenson, John Fanshawe and Andy Roberts on day two of the Birdwatch Kenya '86 event held on 29–30 November. The 48-hour record is held by Don Turner and David Pearson of Kenya, who spotted 494 species at the same event.

**Ringing** The first record of a ring being placed on a bird's leg dates back to the early 1700s, when a grey heron (*Ardea cinerea*) was ringed in Turkey. The first record of a ring recovery was in 1710, when the same bird was found in Germany.

The earliest known bird-marking for message transmission occurred between 218–201 B.C., when Quintus Fabius Pictor, a Roman officer, tied a thread to the leg of a swallow (family Hirundinidae) and released it to inform a besieged Roman garrison when relief could be expected.

**Largest egg collection** The Natural History Museum, UK, has the largest egg collection in the world. In 1994, it contained over 1 million individual eggs.

**Most recently discovered species** On average, three to four new bird species are added to the world list each year (in addition to new species which are sometimes unearthed when scientists re-classify particular groups). Most newly discovered birds tend to be small, drab, solitary insect-eaters that skulk around in thick undergrowth, and have simply escaped the attention of scientists, but there have been some dramatic exceptions over the years. For example, the Udzungwa forest partridge (*Xenoperdix udzungwensis*) was discovered in the Udzungwa Mountains, Tanzania, in 1991, and the chestnut-bellied cotinga (*Doliornis remseni*), discovered in montane forests in the Andes of southern Ecuador, was officially described in 1994.

**DNA analysis** The first new bird species to be discovered entirely by DNA analysis, without an individual having to be killed to provide a type specimen, is the bulo burti boubou (*Laniarius liberatus*). A single bird was first seen in the grounds of a hospital in Bulo Burti, central Somalia, on 27 Aug 1988, and was eventually captured a year later. Blood samples were taken and flown in a deep-frozen package to the UK for examination although, unfortunately, they were lost in transit. The DNA analysis was eventually carried out with blood samples taken from the ends of a few feathers the bird had lost while in captivity. On the basis of comparison with the DNA from museum skins and blood samples from all likely species, it became clear that it was indeed a species new to science. Having been closely studied in captivity, the only known bulo burti boubou was later released.

**Latest wild sighting** The blue-throated macaw (*Ara glaucogularis*) was located in the wild for the first time in August 1992. It was previously known only from museum skins and from birds in the pet trade, but had never before been located in its natural habitat by an ornithologist. The species appears to be uncommon and is apparently confined to the lowlands of Bolivia.

---

*When feeding on certain types of over-ripe, fermenting fruit, birds sometimes become intoxicated and have been known to fall to the ground in a stupor.*

# CROCODILES & ALLIGATORS

***Crocodylia***
22 species (or 23 if the Yacare caiman considered a unique species)

*Although people generally view crocodilians with fear, the harm they do us is minuscule compared to the devastation we have reaped on them.*

**Earliest** The first crocodilians appeared in the Late Triassic period, some 200 million years ago, and apart from birds, the 22 species alive today are more closely related to the dinosaurs than any other creature on Earth.

**Largest** The black caiman (*Melanosuchus niger*), American alligator (*Alligator mississippiensis*), American crocodile (*Crocodylus acutus*), Nile crocodile (*Crocodylus niloticus*), Orinoco crocodile (*Crocodylus intermedius*), saltwater crocodile (*Crocodylus porosus*) and gharial (*Gavialis gangeticus*) have all been known to attain lengths of 5.5 m *18 ft* or more. However, in most cases, such extreme sizes are exceptional.

The largest living crocodilian (and, indeed, the largest reptile in the world)

is the saltwater or estuarine crocodile which ranges throughout the tropical regions of Asia and the Pacific. Males are mature when they reach a length of about 3.2 m *10 ft 6 in* and females when they reach about 2.2 m *7 ft 3 in* and they continue to grow for many years afterwards. Extreme lengths of 9–10 m *29½–33 ft* are generally considered to be within the realms of possibility. However, the pressure of hunting has been so great that few have been able to grow to their maximum potential, at least during the 20th century.

The largest specimen in modern times may have been a saltwater crocodile which, in the early part of the 20th century, was considered sacred by the Seluke people of the Segama River, northern Borneo. On one occasion, local rubber plantation owner James Montgomery saw the huge animal on a sandbank in the river and, when it moved off, measured the impression left behind in the sand. This suggested that the crocodile measured 10.05 m *33 ft* in length.

A leading authority on saltwater crocodiles, Ron Pawlowski, reportedly measured 10 287 'salties' in his life and all but one measured less than 5.5 m *18 ft*. The single exception was an individual shot by his wife, Kris, in Norman River, northern Australia, in July 1957, that reportedly measured 8.64 m *28 ft 4 in*. Unfortunately, although a photographic record existed until 1968, it has since been lost; and no skeletal evidence is available to verify the claim, since even the head was apparently too heavy to move. This record is still controversial but is considered by many to have a high probability of accuracy.

The longest authenticated record of recent years is a male saltwater crocodile just over 7 m *23 ft* long, which lives in the Bhitarkanika Wildlife Sanctuary,

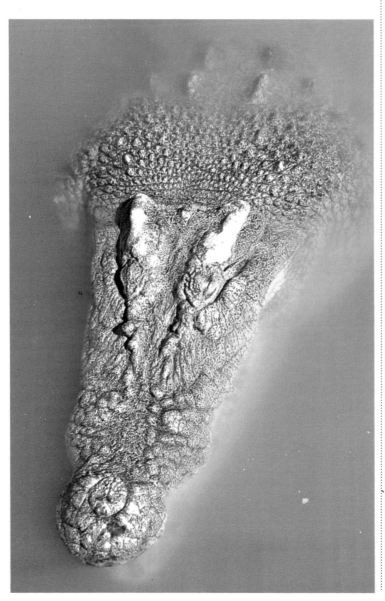

**The largest reptile in the world today is the saltwater or estuarine crocodile which, in extreme cases, may reach a length of 9–10 m 29½– 33 ft.**

Orissa State, India. There are currently three other individuals, in the same sanctuary, measuring more than 6 m *19 ft 8 in* in length.

The largest crocodile ever held in captivity is a saltwater/Siamese hybrid named 'Yai' (b. 10 Jun 1972) at the Samutprakarn Crocodile Farm and Zoo, Thailand. He is 6 m *19 ft 8 in* long and weighs 1115 kg *2465 lb*.

There are many eyewitness reports of 'giant crocodiles' reaching around 9.15 m *30 ft* in remote regions, but recent analysis of their skull measurements suggests that these were greatly exaggerated and were probably all under 6.1 m *20 ft* in length. The first ever recorded was a notorious man-eater killed at Jala Jala, Philippines, in 1823, by Paul de la Gironiere and George Russell after a 6-hour struggle. Forty natives were required to pull it out of the river. Russell's measurement was given as 8.85 m *29 ft*, including a skull length of a little under 91 cm *36 in*. However, the skull, which now resides in Harvard University's Museum of Comparative Zoology, USA, miraculously appears to have shrunk and now measures 64.8 cm *25½ in* (it is normal for the skull bones to shrink during the 'drying out' process – but rarely by more than 5 per cent). The head:body ratio for saltwater crocodiles up to 4.9 m *16 ft* in total length is a fairly constant 1:7.5, although the body length increases faster than head length in longer individuals, with 1:8.5 probably being more typical for much larger specimens; this would have made the Philippines croco-

> **Crocodilians can shut their jaws with devastating force, but the muscles for opening them are extremely weak; indeed, with a crocodilian up to 2 m *6 ft 7 in* in length, a rubber band is usually sufficient to keep its mouth closed.**

dile roughly 6.1 m *20 ft* in life. One possible explanation is that the original figure quoted may have been a 'curve measurement' taken along the belly rather than a 'straight-line measurement'.

Lengths in excess of 6.1 m *20 ft* have also been reliably reported for the gharial or gavial (*Gavialis gangeticus*), which lives in the river systems of India and Pakistan. The largest on record was one killed by Matthew George in the Kosi River, north Bihar, India, in January 1924, which measured 7.1 m *23 ft 4 in*. Unconfirmed measurements of up to 9.1 m *30 ft* have been claimed for this species.

**Largest prehistoric** The largest ever land predator may have been an alligator found on the banks of the Amazon in rocks dated as 8 million years old. Estimates from a skull 1.5 m *5 ft* long (complete with 10 cm *4 in* long teeth) indicate a length of 12 m *40 ft* and a weight of about 18 tonnes, making it larger than the fearsome dinosaur *Tyrannosaurus rex*. It was subsequently identified as a giant example of *Purussaurus brasiliensis*, a species named in 1892 on the basis of smaller specimens.

The longest predator on Earth was probably the eusuchian *Deinosuchus riograndensis* ('terrible crocodile') from the lakes and swamps of what is now Texas, USA, about 75 million years ago. Fragmentary remains discovered in Big Bend National Park, Texas, indicate a hypothetical length of 15–16 m *49–52 ft 6 in* and a weight of at least 6 tonnes. A virtually complete skull of this species measures over 2 m *6 ft 6 in*.

**Smallest** The dwarf caiman (*Paleosuchus palpebrosus*) of northern South America is the smallest species of crocodilian in the world today. Females rarely exceed a length of 1.2 m *4 ft* and males rarely grow to more than 1.5 m *4 ft 11 in*.

The dwarf crocodile (*Osteolaemus tetraspis*) of west and central Africa is also very small, although a number of individuals reach a length of 2 m *6 ft 6 in* and a few grow even longer.

**It has been estimated that the saltwater crocodile kills up to 2000 people every year, making it by far the most dangerous member of the crocodile family.**

**Highest living** The smooth-fronted caiman (*Paleosuchus trigonatus*) has been reported at elevations up to 1300 m *4264 ft* in Venezuela.

In 1971 a captive dwarf caiman (*Paleosuchus palpebrosus*) that had been kept without artificial heating at the Institute of National Sciences in Bogotá, Colombia, 2650 m *8692 ft* above sea level, managed to escape and was eventually found thriving on a diet of frogs in a small pool nearby.

**Most widely distributed** The saltwater crocodile (*Crocodylus porosus*) is the most widely distributed of all the crocodilians, occurring throughout the tropical regions of Asia and the Pacific, from the west coast of India, through Sri Lanka, Bangladesh, the Malay Peninsula, Indonesia and the Philippines, New Guinea and Australia, to the Solomon Islands and Fiji. It occurs in freshwater localities up to 1130 km *700 miles* inland and has even been found more than 1000 km *620 miles* out to sea.

**Most restricted distribution** The Cuban crocodile (*Crocodylus rhombifer*) has the smallest known natural distribution of any crocodilian. It is currently restricted to the Zapata Swamp in

*The myth of crocodile tears dates back to 1565, when explorer Sir James Hawkins mistook the warning roar of an alligator for crying, supposedly to deceive sympathetic humans to approach within range of its jaws; but, in truth, crocodiles cannot cry.*

south-western Cuba. Until recently, a small remnant population still survived in the Lanier Swamp on the nearby Isle of Pines, but this has apparently become extinct.

A sub-species of the spectacled caiman (*Caiman crocodilus*), the Apaporis River caiman (*C. c. apaporiensis*), is confined to a 200 km *124 mile* length of the Rio Apaporis, located in the south-east of Colombia.

**Most marine** Several crocodilians live in coastal habitats and a few have been found far out to sea. But the saltwater crocodile (*Crocodylus porosus*) is notable for being able to inhabit saltwater indefinitely and for travelling great distances across the sea. The record was a 3.8 m *12 ft 6 in* male which was found alive on Ponape, part of the eastern Caroline Islands, in the Pacific Ocean, at least 1360 km *845 miles* away from the nearest known population. Another individual managed to swim 1100 km *680 miles* from the Andaman Islands, in the Bay of Bengal, to the Krishna Sanctuary in Andhra Pradesh, India. And a third swam all the way to the Cocos (Keeling) Islands, in the Indian Ocean, more than 1000 km *620 miles* from the nearest land. As a protection against becoming overloaded with salt, the saltwater crocodile has special glands at the back of its tongue which secrete a concentrated sodium chloride solution.

**Most dangerous** At least 7 of the 22 species of crocodilian have been known to prey on people on occasion: black caiman (*Melanosuchus niger*), American alligator (*Alligator mississippiensis*), Nile crocodile (*Crocodylus niloticus*), saltwater crocodile (*Crocodylus porosus*), American crocodile (*Crocodylus acutus*), Orinoco crocodile (*Crocodylus inter-*

*The oldest confirmed age for a crocodilian is 66 years for an American alligator, although there have been many claims of older individuals over the years.*

*medius*) and the mugger (*Crocodylus palustris*). Human remains and jewellery have been found inside the stomachs of gharial (*Gavialis gangeticus*) on a number of occasions, but it is likely the animals feed on human corpses drifting down the Ganges from the burn-ing ghats and that they do not kill people at all. Several other species are large enough to inflict serious or even fatal injuries if they feel threatened; the relatively small Cuban crocodile (*Crocodylus rhombifer*), for example, has a reputation for being aggressive towards people and therefore children may be vulnerable. However, only the Nile and saltwater crocodiles are justly accused of being regular man-eaters and, on occasion, will even attack small boats; some individuals have been accused of killing up to 400 people, though such reports are probably exaggerated.

It has been estimated that the saltwater crocodile kills up to 2000 people every year, the vast majority of which go unrecorded. The largest death toll is reputed to have occurred during the night of 19–20 Feb 1945, when Allied troops invaded Ramree Island, off the west coast of Burma, in the Bay of Bengal, and trapped 800–1000 Japanese infantrymen in a coastal mangrove swamp. During the night, some of the infantrymen fell to gunfire, some drowned and some fell to other causes. But by far the majority are believed to have been taken by crocodiles, which moved in *en masse* as soon as darkness fell. In recent years, the authenticity of this often-quoted account has been questioned, but observers at the time reported that, by morning, only 20 of the men were left alive. There is little doubt that a large population of salt-water crocodiles *could* have killed all those men, given the opportunity. In a more widely accepted account, in December 1975, over 40 people were attacked and eaten by saltwater croco-diles when their holiday boat sank in the Malili River of central Sulawesi (Celebes), Indonesia.

The Nile crocodile (*Crocodylus niloticus*) also has a bad reputation and may kill as many as 1000 people every year. When this species was more nu-merous, some estimates put the total number of human deaths as high as 20 000 every year.

**Largest prey** There are many reliable reports of large crocodilians, in par-ticular saltwater crocodiles (*Crocodylus porosus*) and Nile crocodiles (*Crocodylus niloticus*), tackling enormous prey. Earlier in the century, a saltwater croco-dile seized a 1 tonne stallion which had recently been imported from the UK, and dragged it into the river. Other 'salties' have been known to take feral buffalo and domestic cattle. There are also records of Nile crocodiles success-fully tackling fully grown black rhino-ceroses, wildebeest, giraffes, lions and other big game. In the 1860s, in Natal, South Africa, a Nile crocodile was ob-served to seize the hind leg of a fully grown African elephant at a water hole; but the elephant dragged its attacker out of the water where another member of the herd killed it under its feet.

The stomach of a notorious Nile crocodile, which was killed in the Okavango Delta, Botswana, in Novem-ber 1968, was found to contain the remains of a local woman, two goats and about half a donkey.

**Oldest** Estimates for the maximum lifespan of crocodilians in the wild vary widely from around 50 years to as much as 200 years, although very little is known. In captivity, the greatest claimed age is for an American alliga-tor (*Alligator mississippiensis*) called 'Jean-qui-rit' ('Laughing John'), which reputedly lived in the Menagerie du Jardin des Plantes, Paris, France, for 85 years (1852–4 Apr 1937). However, the validity of this record is uncertain. The greatest authenticated age is 66 years for a female American alligator which

arrived at Adelaide Zoo, South Aus-tralia, on 5 Jun 1914, as a 2-year-old, and died there on 26 Sep 1978.

**Longest incubation period** The incu-bation period for eggs laid by the dwarf crocodile (*Osteolaemus tetraspis*) can be as long as 115 days, which is longer than for any other crocodilian.

**Most eggs** The record number of eggs laid in a single clutch by any crocodilian is 97 by a gharial (*Gavialis gangeticus*) in 1982; 69 of the eggs subsequently hatched in a hatchery incubator. How-ever, the *average* number of eggs in a gharial clutch is only 40, which is rela-tively low. The average clutch size of the black caiman (*Melanosuchus niger*) is larger than for any other crocodilian, being 50–60. Nest-sharing occurs in some species, in which two different females may lay their eggs in the same nest, accounting for unusually large numbers in certain cases.

The Nile crocodile (*Crocodylus niloticus*) and the saltwater crocodile (*Crocodylus porosus*) have both been known to lay as many as 90 eggs in a single clutch.

**Least eggs** Several crocodilian species lay exceptionally small clutches: Schneider's dwarf caiman (*Paleosuchus trigonatus*) rarely lays more than 15 eggs; Johnstone's crocodile (*Crocodylus johnsoni*) lays from just 4 to 18 eggs; the

dwarf crocodile (*Osteolaemus tetraspis*) lays from about 10 to 17 eggs; and the Philippine crocodile (*Crocodylus mindorensis*) lays from just 7 to 14 eggs.

**Largest eggs** The female false gharial (*Tomistoma schlegelii*) lays the largest eggs of any crocodilian, typically meas-uring 10 × 7 cm *4 × 2.8 in*.

**Maternal care** The female American alligator (*Alligator mississippiensis*) looks after her young for as long as 3 years or, exceptionally, 4 years, which is longer than for any other crocodilian. In con-trast, young Nile crocodiles (*Crocodylus niloticus*) are left to make their own way in the world after only a few weeks. No maternal care at all has been observed in the Chinese alligator (*Alligator sinensis*) and certain other species, al-though this is most likely to be because they have not been studied closely enough in the wild.

**Most variable** The Nile crocodile (*Crocodylus niloticus*) is the most geo-graphically variable species of crocodilian, with as many as seven sub-species officially recognized: Sudanese Nile crocodile (*C. n. niloticus*); East African Nile crocodile (*C. n. africanus*); West African Nile crocodile (*C. n. chamses*); South African Nile crocodile (*C. n. corviei*); Madagascan Nile croco-dile (*C. n. madagascariensis*); Kenyan Nile crocodile (*C. n. pauciscutatus*); and Cen-

The Nile crocodile is the most geographically variable species of crocodilian.

tral African Nile crocodile (*C. n. suchus*).

The spectacled caiman (*Caiman crocodilus*) is also highly variable, with four sub-species generally being recognized: Apaporis River caiman (*C. c. apaporiensis*); common caiman (*C. c. crocodilus*); brown or American caiman (*C. c. fuscus*); and the Yacare or red caiman (*C. c. yacare*). Several other sub-species have been described for the spectacled caiman but are not widely accepted.

**Rarest** It is very difficult to be precise about the rarest crocodilian, since the total population size in the wild is often unknown. However, there is little doubt that in several species it has dropped to below 1000 survivors. In recent years, the Siamese crocodile (*Crocodylus siamensis*) has been known from only two small populations in the wild. One is located in the Bung Boraphet Reservoir, in the province of Nakhon Sawan, Thailand, but there have been no recent sightings and the population may now be extinct. The other is in Kalimantan, Indonesia, where a small number may still survive. Further wild populations may remain undiscovered in Cambodia, Laos or Vietnam, but numbers are undoubtedly low. A large captive population exists, most notably in the Samut Prakan Crocodile Farm, near Bangkok, Thailand.

The total wild population of the protected Chinese alligator (*Alligator sinensis*) of the lower Yangtze River, in the Anhui, Zhejiang and Jiangsu provinces of China, is currently estimated at no more than a few hundred. This tiny population is spread over a total area of about 25 000 km² *9650 miles²*. Although

captive breeding programmes are proving successful, the alligator cannot easily be reintroduced into the wild because of the on-going destruction of its habitat and because it is still being killed or collected for sale to zoos or government-sponsored farms. Its extinction outside captivity is expected before the end of the century.

**Most threatened** The World Conservation Union (IUCN) currently recognizes 12 species of crocodilian as known or suspected to be threatened with extinction, representing more than 50 per cent of the world total. Seven of these are considered to be critically threatened (ranked according to severity of threat, with the most threatened first): Siamese crocodile (*Crocodylus siamensis*) of south-east Asia; Philippine crocodile (*Crocodylus mindorensis*) of the Philippines; Chinese alligator (*Alligator sinensis*) of China; Cuban crocodile (*Crocodylus rhombifer*) of Cuba; false gharial (*Tomistoma schlegelii*) of south-east Asia; Orinoco crocodile (*Crocodylus intermedius*) of South America; and gharial (*Gavialis gangeticus*) of the Indian sub-continent. Heavy exploitation for their valuable skins, indiscriminate killing, habitat loss and pollution are largely to blame.

**Country with the most threatened species** Several countries each have three internationally threatened crocodilian species: India, Indonesia, Malaysia, Colombia and Venezuela. Bangladesh and Thailand are both within the natural ranges of three threatened species, but one or more of these may already be extinct.

**First to be hunted** The American alligator (*Alligator mississippiensis*) was the first crocodilian to be widely commercially exploited, early in the 19th century. This was mainly for oil to grease the machinery of steam engines and cotton mills but, during the 1870s, demand for skins increased when alligator hide products became fashionable.

**Skin trade** The peak in the crocodilian skin trade came in the late 1950s and early 1960s, when 5–10 million hides entered the world market every year. Today, the figure has dropped to some 1.5 million skins; most of these are illegal and come from the spectacled caiman (*Caiman crocodilus*) and Yacare caiman (*Caiman yacare*).

**Most dramatic recovery** Conservation efforts literally managed to bring the gharial (*Gavialis gangeticus*) back from the brink of extinction. In the early 1970s there were only 60–70 left in the wild. Nowadays, since a reintroduction programme began in 1975, there are 1500 in the wild and a further 500 in captivity. The wild populations are currently restricted to the northern part of the Indian sub-continent, in four river systems: the Indua (Pakistan), the Ganges (India and Nepal), the Mahanadi (India) and the Brahmaputra (Bangladesh, India and Nepal).

**Fastest** The fastest crocodilian motion on land is the rarely seen gallop. The hindlimbs push the crocodile forward in a leap, the forelimbs reach out and hit the ground at the end of the leap, then the hindlimbs swing forward as the back bends and push once again. Only a few species are capable of galloping. The fastest ever recorded is Johnston's crocodile (*Crocodylus johnsoni*) which can reach speeds of up to 17 km/h *10.6 mph*.

Crocodile and alligator eggs frequently 'talk' to one another, as the young animals communicate by tapping from inside their shells; this may help to synchronize hatching of the clutch.

**Most aquatic** The gharial (*Gavialis gangeticus*) is arguably the most aquatic of all the crocodilians. Adults have weak legs, cannot walk in a semi-upright stance (as other crocodilians are able to do) and seldom move more than a few metres from the water.

**Longest submersion** Most crocodilians normally stay underwater for no more than a few minutes, although many species have the ability to stay under for an hour or more. In a series of gruesome experiments conducted in 1925, during which animals were held underwater until they drowned, an American alligator (*Alligator mississippiensis*) survived for 6 hours 5 minutes.

**Coldest** The Chinese alligator (*Alligator sinensis*) and the American alligator (*Alligator mississippiensis*), live in areas where the temperature can fall below freezing during the winter. Both species excavate burrows into which they can retreat for the worst of the weather which, in the northern parts of their range, is from about October until March. If they remain in water they keep the tip of the snout exposed, enabling them to breathe, but allow the rest of the head and body to be frozen into the ice. They can survive like this until the ice melts, even though their internal body temperature may plummet to just 5°C *41°F* (compared with a normal figure of around 33°C *91°F*).

**Noisiest** Crocodilians are the noisiest of all the reptiles, capable of making a wide variety of coughs, hisses, roars and bellows. It is even possible to distinguish individuals on the basis of their calls. The most vocal of them all is the American alligator (*Alligator mississippiensis*), possibly because of its habitat, where visual communication may be hard to maintain. Its bellowing, which vaguely resembles the roaring of a lion, can be heard easily at a distance of 150 m *492 ft*; from a distance of 5 m *16 ft*, it is almost as loud as standing next to the engine of a small propeller aircraft. Bellows are used during courtship and may serve to maintain the integrity of a group.

**R
E
P
T
I
L
E
S**

# DINOSAURS

### Dinosauria
1300 formally recognized species and new ones being found all the time

The most primitive dinosaur so far discovered is this small meat-eating theropod, known as *Eoraptor lunensis* or the 'dawn stealer'.

**First to be found** Dinosaur remains have been found on many occasions in the ancient past. The earliest recorded discovery dates back to a description in a book by Chinese scholar Chang Qu, writing around AD 300, of a fossil found at Wucheng, in what is now Sichuan Province, China; at the time, it was considered to be the bones of a dragon. In the years that followed, many dinosaur bones and teeth were dug up in China in areas that are now known, from modern research, to have dinosaur remains; they have long been prized for their magic and medicinal powers.

Dinosaur remains were not recognized as such until 1822, when fossil teeth found by Mary Mantell, in Sussex, UK, were identified as belonging to a huge, previously unknown reptile; they were later identified as being from a dinosaur that was officially named *Iguanodon*, in 1825.

**First to be described** The first dinosaur to be described scientifically was *Megalosaurus bucklandi* ('great fossil lizard') in 1824, by Dean William Buckland, Professor of Geology at the University of Oxford, UK. Remains of this bipedal flesh-eater (a theropod) were found by workmen in 1818 in a slate quarry near Woodstock, Oxfordshire, UK, and later placed in the

1·78 metres
(5 ft 10 ins)

University Museum, Oxford. The first fossil bone of *Megalosaurus* was actually a thigh bone found near Oxford, in 1677, but its true nature was not realized until much later.

It was not until 1841 that the name 'Dinosauria' (from the Greek words *deinos*, meaning 'terrible' and *sauros*, meaning 'reptile') was given to the

newly discovered giants. Coined by the anatomist Professor Richard Owen, the name was first used at a meeting of the British Association for the Advancement of Science at Plymouth, Devon, UK in 1841.

**Earliest** The most primitive dinosaur so far discovered is *Eoraptor lunensis* ('dawn stealer'). Named in 1993, from a skeleton found in the foothills of the Andes, in Argentina, it was removed from rocks dated as 228 million years old. One of the most primitive features of this 1 m *39 in* long dinosaur, which is believed to be a meat-eating theropod, is the fact that it lacks the dual-hinged jaw present in all other members of the group. The exact age of the volcanic ash found in the rocks containing the *Eoraptor* fossil was calculated using argon radioisotopic dating in a new and very precise technique by Carl Swisher III of the Institute of Human Origins in Berkeley, California, USA. Previous fossil dating techniques were relatively inaccurate.

Another dinosaur from the same area and rocks is *Herrerasaurus*, a carnivore known best from an almost complete skeleton discovered in 1989 at the foot of the Andes, in Argentina, by an expedition led by Paul Sereno of the University of Chicago, Illinois, USA. *Herrerasaurus* was about 2–2.5 m *6½– 8 ft* in length and weighed over 100 kg *220 lb*. Although of the same age as *Eoraptor*, it had the dual-hinged jaw.

Other dinosaurs of a similar age from the Late Triassic are known from incomplete remains found in Brazil, Morocco, India and the UK.

**Disappearance** The Age of Dinosaurs ended some 65 million years ago; many other animals, and plants, died out at the same time. However, the precise timescale is unknown. The extinction might have happened over a very short period, or it could have taken thousands or even millions of years. Evidence from Hell Creek Formation, Montana, USA, suggests that dinosaurs

> Despite the impression given by the fictional story of **The Flintstones**, cavemen did not live alongside any of the dinosaurs. If it were possible to compress into one day all the time elapsed since dinosaurs first lived on Earth, they would have appeared at midnight and died out at around 5 o'clock the following afternoon; by comparison, people would have been on Earth since less than one minute to midnight the same evening.

dwindled in importance over a period of 5–10 million years and were replaced progressively by small mammals, possibly because of long-term climatic changes taking place as a result of continental drift, mountain-building and sea level changes. But it is equally plausible that dinosaurs were wiped out by a catastrophic event that affected the Earth's climate and was so dramatic they had no chance to adapt before the new conditions killed them.

Perhaps the most popular current hypothesis for a sudden elimination of the dinosaurs is that a giant asteroid, up to 10 km *6.2 miles* in diameter, hit the Earth 65 million years ago and threw a vast mass of dust high into the stratosphere. Strong winds would have carried this cloud around the planet, causing global darkness lasting for many months. This theory is supported strongly by the discovery of significant levels of the element iridium, a metal common in meteorites but rare on Earth – and therefore a good indicator of extraterrestrial impact – in rocks dated as 65 million years old. There is also fossil proof of a sudden loss of flowering plants in North America at around the same time. Further evidence came to light in 1991, when the possible impact crater was found on the seabed off

the north-western tip of the Yucatán Peninsula, Mexico. Called the Chicxulub Crater, it measures some 180 km *112 miles* across, dates to 65 million years ago and is associated with iridium, melt gasses and evidence of tsunamis (giant sea-waves) around the proto-Caribbean. But what has yet to be explained is why the crocodiles – and many other animals – survived.

Another popular hypothesis is that there was a period of severe volcanic activity, which poured huge amounts of carbon dioxide and acids into the air. This could have caused an overheating of the Earth's surface, lethal acid rain, the destruction of atmospheric ozone that shuts out deadly solar radiation – and ultimately the extinction of the dinosaurs.

***Supersaurus* was one of the heaviest dinosaurs ever to have lived on Earth, estimated to have exceeded a weight of 50 tonnes.**

*Tyrannosaurus rex* is well-known as the largest flesh-eating dinosaur ever recorded, reaching a maximum height of 5.9 m *19½ ft* and an estimated weight of up to 7.4 tonnes.

**Most recent** The last known dinosaurs probably lived in western North America towards the end of the Mesozoic era as recently as 75 million years ago. Among them were two of the best-known of all the dinosaurs: *Tyrannosaurus* and *Triceratops*. Dinosaur fossils, believed to be from the Cainozoic era (from 65 million years ago to the present day) have been found in Europe, the Americas and Asia, but they are little more than scraps of bone and may simply have been dislodged from older rocks long before their discovery.

**Largest** The largest known land animals ever to have lived on Earth were the sauropod dinosaurs, a group of long-necked, long-tailed, four-legged plant-eaters that lived in many parts of the world during the Jurassic and Cretaceous periods 65–208 million years ago. Unfortunately, it is difficult to determine precisely which of these sauropods was the absolute largest (longest, tallest or heaviest). Estimating dinosaur lengths and heights is feasible, but only when a complete skeleton is available for study; in most cases, only incomplete remains have been found and therefore current evidence is severely limited. The world's largest sauropods have been identified variously as: *Brachiosaurus* and *Breviparopus*, both members of the family Brachiosauridae; *Antarctosaurus*, a member of the family Titanosauridae; and *Seismosaurus* and *Diplodocus*, both members of the family Diplodocidae.

**Tallest** The tallest dinosaur species known from a complete skeleton is *Brachiosaurus brancai* ('arm reptile' – a name referring to its front legs, which were much longer than its hind legs) from the Tendaguru site in Tanzania, dated as Late Jurassic (144–150 million years ago). The site was excavated by German expeditions during the period 1909–11 and the bones prepared and assembled at the Humboldt Museum für Naturkunde, Berlin, Germany. A complete skeleton was constructed from the remains of several individuals and put on display in 1937, forming the largest mounted dinosaur skeleton in the world. Resembling a massive giraffe, it measures 22.2 m *72 ft 9½ in* in overall length, with a height at the shoulder of 6 m *19 ft 8 in* and a raised head height of 14 m *46 ft*.

In recent years, two new giant sauropods have been reported: *Supersaurus*, a member of the family Diplodocidae, and *Ultrasauros* (recently respelled to avoid confusion with the previously named *Ultrasaurus*), a member of the family Brachiosauridae. The limited remains of both species, which were found in rocks dated as Late Jurassic, in Colorado, USA, suggest that they may have been considerably larger than *Brachiosaurus*. *Ultrasauros* has been estimated at lengths of up to 27 m *89 ft* and *Supersaurus* at more than 30 m *98 ft*. Unfortunately, there are too few fossil remains of either to be more certain.

**Heaviest** The main contenders for the heaviest dinosaur are probably the titanosaurid *Antarctosaurus giganteus* ('Antarctic lizard') from Argentina and India (40–80 tonnes); the brachiosaurid *Brachiosaurus altithorax* (45–55 tonnes); and the diplodocids *Seismosaurus halli* ('earthquake lizard') and *Supersaurus vivianae* (both over 50 tonnes).

Such weights do not necessarily represent the ultimate limit for a land vertebrate, and theoretical calculations suggest that some dinosaurs may have approached the maximum body weight possible for a terrestrial animal, around 120 tonnes. In theory, at weights greater than this, such massive legs would have been needed that the dinosaur could not have moved.

**Longest** Based on the evidence of footprints, the brachiosaurid *Breviparopus* may have attained a length of 48 m *157 ft*, which would make it the longest vertebrate on record. However, a diplodocid from New Mexico, USA, named *Seismosaurus halli*, was estimated in 1991 to be 39–52 m *128–170 ft* long based on comparisons of individual bones.

The longest dinosaur known from a complete skeleton is the diplodocid *Diplodocus carnegii* ('double beam'), assembled at the Carnegie Museum in Pittsburgh, Pennsylvania, USA, from remains found in Wyoming in 1899. Once described as a 'walking suspension bridge', *Diplodocus* was 26.6 m *87½ ft* long, with much of that length consisting of a long neck and an extremely long whip-like tail. It probably weighed 5.8–18.5 tonnes, with an estimate of around 12 tonnes being the most likely. The mounted skeleton was so spectacular that casts were requested by other museums, and copies can be seen in London, La Plata, Washington, Frankfurt and Paris.

> **The name Brontosaurus means 'thunder lizard' and was given to an enormous 25-tonne dinosaur to celebrate the supposed sound of its heavy tread; unfortunately, the name had to be changed when the so-called Brontosaurus fossils were found to belong to those of a dinosaur that had already been named Apatosaurus.**

**Longest neck** The sauropod dinosaur known as *Mamenchisaurus* ('Mamen Brook lizard'), which was discovered in China (Taihezhen, Sichuan Province) in 1957, in rocks dating back 160 million years, had the longest neck of any animal that has ever lived on Earth. Some individuals may have had necks in excess of 11 m *36 ft* long, which they probably used to browse on branches high above the ground. The total length of a *Mamen-chisaurus* may have been around 22–25 m *72–82 ft*. For comparison, a giraffe, which has the longest neck of any animal alive today, has a *total* body length of 4–6 m *13–20 ft*.

The sauropod dinosaur known as *Barosaurus* (meaning 'heavy lizard') also had an extremely elongated neck that projected 9 m *29 ft 6 in* beyond its shoulders. Rising on its hind legs, it could have reached food up to 15 m *49 ft* above the ground.

Experts are unable to agree on how animals with such long necks were able to pump blood so far up to their brains; one theory suggests that they required a massive 1–2 tonne heart, another that they managed with one moderately large heart aided by special arterial valves and strong muscles in the neck to stop the blood falling back down, and a third even suggests that they had a number of separate hearts.

**Largest predatory dinosaur** The largest flesh-eating dinosaur recorded so far is *Tyrannosaurus rex* ('king tyrant lizard'), which reigned over what is now Colorado, Montana, New Mexico and Wyoming, in the USA, and the

provinces of Alberta and Saskatchewan, Canada, about 75 million years ago. The largest and heaviest example, discovered in South Dakota, USA, in 1991, was 5.9 m *19½ ft* tall, had a total length of 11.1 m *36½ ft* and weighed an estimated 6–7.4 tonnes. It is believed that *Tyrannosaurus* grew up to 12 m *39 ft* in length: a man or woman would hardly have reached its knees. Despite its enormous size, its puny two-fingered 'hands' and 'arms' were no longer than our own.

The longest predatory dinosaur was probably an allosaur called *Epanterias amplexus*. Specimens from Masonville, Colorado, USA, suggest that it reached a length of 15.24 m *50 ft* and a weight of 4 tonnes, but the remains are incomplete. Similar lengths were also attained by *Spinosaurus aegyptiacus* ('thorn lizard') of Niger and Egypt.

The tallest predatory dinosaur was probably *Dynamosaurus imperiosus* ('dynamic lizard') of Shandong Province, China, which had a standing height of 6.1 m *20 ft* and an overall length of 14 m *46 ft*. However, this tyrannosaurid was not as heavily built as *Tyrannosaurus* was in North America.

**Smallest** The delicately built dinosaur *Compsognathus* ('pretty jaw') of southern Germany and south-eastern France, was as little as 70 cm *27½ in* in length and probably weighed around 3 kg *6 lb 8 oz*. It is the smallest adult dinosaur known. Standing no taller than a domestic chicken, *Compsognathus* probably used to feed on invertebrates and lizards.

An undescribed plant-eating fabrosaurid from Colorado, USA, measured 75 cm *29½ in* from the snout to the tip of the tail and weighed an estimated 6.8 kg *15 lb*.

**Largest egg** The largest known dinosaur eggs are those of *Hypselosaurus priscus* ('high ridge lizard'), a 12 m *40 ft* long titanosaurid which lived about 80 million years ago. Examples found in the Durance Valley near Aix-en-Provence, France, in October 1961 would have had, uncrushed, a length of some 30 cm *12 in* and a diameter of 25.5 cm *10 in* (capacity 3.3 litres *5.8 pt*).

**Longest teeth** The longest teeth of any known dinosaur belonged to the well-known predatory species *Tyrannosaurus rex*; its teeth, which were serrated like steak knife blades, were up to 18 cm *7 in* long.

**Longest claw** The therizinosaurids ('scythe lizards') from the Late Cretaceous period of the Nemegt Basin, Mongolia, had the largest claws of

any known animal. In the case of *Therizinosaurus cheloniformis* they measured up to 91 cm *36 in* along the outer curve (cf. 20.3 cm *8 in* for *Tyrannosaurus rex*). It has been suggested that these talons were designed for grasping and tearing apart large prey, but this creature had a feeble skull, and few or no teeth, and probably lived on termites.

The dinosaur *Baryonyx walkeri* ('heavy claw'), which lived in Europe and Africa about 120 million years ago, takes its name from the sharp, curved claws that were attached to its two thumbs. Together with the horny sheath, each claw measured about 30 cm *11.8 in* round the curve. There are two theories about how these claws were used: one is that *Baryonyx* (a spinosaur measuring more than 9 m *29½ ft* overall) hunted other large dinosaurs and used them for slashing; the other is that it used them to catch fish (the only known fossil of *Baryonyx* has fish scales in the stomach region, suggesting that fish was at least part of its last meal). The claw was discovered in January 1983 by William Walker, an amateur fossil collector, in a clay pit near Dorking, Surrey, UK.

**Noisiest** Dinosaurs probably made a wide variety of squeaks, grunts, chirps, snarls, roars and bellows. But the only real evidence so far discovered of them being able to make noises is found in the hadrosaurs, or 'duck-billed' dinosaurs, with their selection of nasal trumpets and air sacs. One of the better known of these is the 10 m *33 ft* long *Parasaurolophus*, which had a bony tube up to 1 m *39 in* long on the top of its head. The hollow interior of the tube housed a complex arrangement of pipes and chambers. At first, it was believed to act as a kind of snorkel, enabling the animal to feed on aquatic plants; however, it is now known that there was no hole at the top of the crest, so this would have been impossible. Alternatively, it may have been important visually, helping duck-billed dinosaurs to recognize other individuals of their own species. But the most popular explanation is that it acted as a resonator, rather like the pipes in a trombone, to produce a distinctive, deep bellowing or trumpeting sound. Since a note of low frequency travels over long distances and yet, at the same time, is very difficult to locate, it could have enabled the dinosaur to alert other members of the herd to approaching danger without becoming the centre of attention itself.

**Strangest defence** The dinosaur *Ankylosaurus*, which grew to a length of about 10 m *33 ft*, had a huge bony club at the end of its tail. If it was attacked by a larger dinosaur, it would turn its back and swing the club: the force of the blow was probably enough to break its attacker's legs or severely damage its body.

**Largest skull** The skulls of the long-frilled ceratopsids were the largest of all known land animals and culminated in the long-frilled *Torosaurus* ('piercing lizard'). This herbivore, which measured about 7.6 m *25 ft* in total length and weighed up to 8 tonnes, had a skull measuring up to 3 m *9 ft 10 in* in length (including the fringe) and weighing up to 2 tonnes. It ranged from Montana to Texas, USA.

**Most brainless** A large number of dinosaur skulls have been preserved well enough for scientists to estimate the volume of the brain case (the bony box within the skull containing the brain) for several dinosaur species. Allowing for the fact that the brain does not necessarily fill the entire case, it is possible to compute its approximate volume. Perhaps not surprisingly, these calculations have revealed widely ranging brain sizes.

However, weight for weight, most dinosaurs had smaller, lighter brains than birds or mammals and some had very tiny brains indeed. The 9 m *29'₂ft* long *Stegosaurus* ('plated lizard'), which roamed across Colorado, Oklahoma, Utah and Wyoming, USA, about 150 million years ago, had one of the smallest brains of any dinosaur. Indeed, its brain was barely walnut-sized

and weighed only 60–70 g *2–2½ oz*. This represented 0.002 per cent of its computed body weight of 3.3 tonnes (thirty times less than for an elephant of the same weight). The ratio of brain to body weight in the large sauropods is an even more dramatic 0.001 per cent (100 000:1).

Small brains do not necessarily imply stupidity: the size of the brain in relation to body size is more important, combined with the proportion used to handle relatively straightforward tasks such as sight, smell and limb coordination (as opposed to the 'thinking part').

**Brainiest** Although many dinosaurs had relatively small brains for their size, a few had brains more comparable in size to those of mammals and birds. The brainiest dinosaurs were probably the speedy, agile, keen-eyed coelurosaurs, such as *Troodon*, which hunted small mammals and lizards. Even so, *Troodon's* brain was still little more than 0.1 per cent of the weight of its body (compared with about 2.0–2.5 per cent for the human brain).

According to research by Professor James Hopson of the University of Chicago, USA, the dinosaur 'league table' of intelligence runs (with the least brainy first): sauropods, ankylosaurs, stegosaurs, ceratopians, ornithopods, carnosaurs and coelurosaurs.

**Largest meal** Presumably, the largest meals were eaten by the plant-eating sauropods, the largest dinosaurs. The nearest modern equivalent would be

the African elephant, which eats around 185 kg *408 lb* of plants every day to survive, equivalent to nearly 4 per cent of its own body weight. At this rate, a 30 tonne *Brachiosaurus* probably required more than 1 tonne of plants every day.

**Longest trackway** In 1983 a series of four *Apatosaurus* (= *Brontosaurus*) trackways running parallel for over 215 m *705 ft* were recorded from 145 million-year-old Morrison strata in south-eastern Colorado, USA.

**Largest footprint** The largest footprints on Earth were made by a large bipedal hadrosaurid, or 'duck-billed' dinosaur, and measured an incredible 1.36 m *53½ in* in length and 81 cm *32 in* wide. They were discovered in 1932, in Salt Lake City, Utah, USA.

Other reports from Colorado and Utah, USA, refer to footprints 95–100 cm *37–40 in* wide which are mainly attributed to the largest brachiosaurids. It is possible that even larger footprints may be discovered in the future.

**Fastest** It is possible, albeit extremely difficult, to estimate the running speeds of extinct dinosaurs by their trackways. One from Texas, USA, which was discovered in 1981, indicated that a carnivorous dinosaur had been moving at 40 km/h *25 mph*. Some ornithomimids were even faster, and the large-brained, 100 kg *220 lb* *Dromiceiomimus* ('emu mimic lizard') of the Late Cretaceous of Alberta, Canada, may even have been able to outsprint an ostrich, which has a top speed in excess of 60 km/h *37.3 mph*.

**The enormous *Stegosaurus* has the unenviable distinction of being one of the most brainless dinosaurs ever to have walked the Earth.**

# LIZARDS

## *Sauria*
*c.* 3800 species

**Earliest** The world's oldest fossil reptile, nicknamed 'Lizzie the Lizard', was found in March 1988 by palaeontologist Stan Wood, in a small quarry at Bathgate, near Edinburgh, UK. The 20 cm *8 in* long reptile (whose sex is, in fact, indeterminable) is estimated to be about 340 million years old. This is some 40 million years older than the previous oldest known reptile, which came from Canada. 'Lizzie' was officially named *Westlothiana lizziae*, in 1991, and was sold by her finder to the National Museums of Scotland for £195 000 (£170 000 plus VAT).

Recently, painstaking study of the animal's palate, and the discovery of a second specimen, have thrown doubt on its reptilian pedigree.

**Lizzie the Lizard: the world's oldest fossil reptile.**

**Largest** The largest lizard in the world is the Komodo dragon (*Varanus komodoensis*), otherwise known as the Komodo monitor or ora. Found on the Indonesian islands of Komodo, Rintja, Padar and Flores, males average 2.25 m *7 ft 5 in* in length and weigh about 59 kg *130 lb*; females are typically about two-thirds this size. Lengths of up to 9.15 m *30 ft* have been claimed for this species, though these are likely to be wild exaggerations. The largest accurately measured specimen

**The world's largest lizard is the threatened Komodo dragon, which lives only on a handful of islands in Indonesia.**

was a male presented to an American zoologist, in 1928, by the Sultan of Bima. In 1937 it was put on display in St Louis Zoological Gardens, Missouri, USA, for a short period, by which time it was 3.10 m *10 ft 2 in* long and weighed 166 kg *365 lb*. There are fewer than 5000 Komodo dragons surviving and Komodo itself has been made a national park – one of very few of the world's protected areas set aside

specifically for a lizard.

Most geckos (family Gekkonidae) are fairly small, with a maximum length of about 30 cm *12 in*, but there is one dramatic exception: the giant gecko (*Hoplodactylus delcourti*) which measures a staggering 60 cm *24 in* from the tip of its snout to the end of its tail. It was first discovered in the 1980s as a mounted specimen in the Marseilles Natural History Museum, France. No records exist to indicate where it came from, and no other specimens have been found, but it is believed to belong in the New Zealand genus *Hoplodactylus* and was probably collected by a 19th-century French expedition.

**Longest** The longest lizard in the world is the slender Salvadori or Papuan monitor (*Varanus salvadorii*) of Papua New Guinea. It is normally shorter than the Komodo dragon (*Varanus komodoensis*), and far less bulky, but has been reliably measured at lengths of up to 4.75 m *15 ft 7 in*. However, typically for this species, nearly 70 per cent of the total length is taken up by its tail. There are unsubstantiated claims of the Salvadori monitor reaching a length of just over 6.1 m *20 ft*, though this is considered highly unlikely by most experts.

**Smallest** *Sphaerodactylus parthenopion*, a tiny gecko indigenous to the island of Virgin Gorda, one of the British Virgin Islands, is believed to be the world's smallest lizard. It is known from only 15 specimens, including some pregnant females found between 10 and 16 Aug 1964. The three largest females measured 1.8 cm *0.70 in* from snout to vent, with a tail of approximately the same length.

It is possible that another type of gecko, *Sphaerodactylus elasmorhynchus*, may be even smaller. The only known specimen was an apparently mature female with a snout–vent measurement of 1.7 cm 0.67 in and a tail of approximately the same length. This specimen was found on 15 Mar 1966 among the roots of a tree in the western part of the Massif de la Hotte, Haiti.

The world's smallest chameleon is another close contender. The stump-tailed or pygmy chameleon (*Brookesia peyrieresi*), from Madagascar, has a maximum snout-vent measurement of only 1.9 cm ¾ in and a tail length of 1.6 cm 0.63 in. It has swivelling eyes and a projectile tongue, but lacks other chameleon features.

**Slimmest** The slimmest lizards in relation to body length are the snake lizards (family Pygopodidae) and the slow worm (*Anguis fragilis*) and glass lizards (family Anguidae), all of which are elongated, slender and limbless. The best example is probably the Australian legless snake lizard (*Lialis burtoni*) which attains a length of 50 cm *20 in* or more, but is no thicker than a pencil at mid-body.

**Broadest** The broadest lizards in relation to body length are probably the horned lizards in the genus *Phrynosoma*, which grow to about 15 cm *6 in* – and are saucer-shaped. The Latin *Phrynosoma* actually means 'toad-bodied' and

they are often called horned 'toads' because of their toad-like shape. There are 14 species altogether, living in the drier regions of the USA and Mexico.

**Most venomous** The only known venomous lizards are the gila monster (*Heloderma suspectum*), which lives in the south-western USA and Mexico, and the Mexican beaded lizard (*Heloderma horridum*), which lives in the western coastal region of Mexico south to Guatemala. They both have well-developed venom glands in their lower jaws (venomous snakes have them in their upper jaws) and carry enough venom to kill two adult humans. The venom is not injected but seeps into the wound caused by the bite; consequently, in a serious attack, the lizard may continue to hang on and actively chew for several minutes (the powerful jaws may have to be prized open to release the victim). The bite is both unpleasant and potentially dangerous, since the venom contains a pain-producing substance called serotonin, enzymes which break down tissue, anti-clotting agents and a powerful neurotoxin. In the wild, both species seem reluctant to bite unless they are handled or provoked; however, when they are sufficiently aggravated, they can attack with surprising agility – despite their heavy-bodied, plump and rather sluggish appearance. In one study of 34 people bitten by these animals (mostly

in captivity) there were eight fatalities, most of whom were either in bad health or drunk at the time. It is believed that the venom is used almost exclusively for defence and is not needed to subdue the relatively small and harmless invertebrate prey or birds' eggs that are the mainstay of their diet. The gila monster reaches a total length of about 50 cm *20 in*, making it the largest lizard in the USA; the Mexican beaded lizard is considerably larger, reaching a maximum length of 90 cm *35½ in*.

**Most bizarre defence** Three species of horned lizard (*Phrynosoma solare, P. cornutum* and *P. coronatum*) can squirt blood from their eyes over a distance of up to 1.2 m *47 in*, by increasing the blood pressure in the sinuses of their eye sockets until the walls burst. However, this is normally a last resort for these strange-looking lizards from the desert areas of western North America: they also have more traditional means of defence at their disposal when they feel threatened. They can change colour to match the desert sand or rock (when they flatten themselves against the ground and remain perfectly still, this

**The gila monster is one of only two lizard species known to be venomous, carrying enough venom to kill two adult humans; this individual was photographed in Death Valley, California, USA.**

makes them almost invisible) or they can inflate themselves to look more intimidating and then jump forward and hiss. But if their camouflage and intimidation strategies fail to work, blood-squirting usually has the desired effect.

**Tail shedding** Most lizard species are able to shed their tails (a process called autotomy) when danger threatens. Usually the tail breaks off only when it is grasped by a predator but, in some species, it can be ejected voluntarily. Although the fracture occurs on the spine, it is across a specific fracture-plane and the loss causes the creature little discomfort. Special muscles cause the tail to wriggle on its own, to hold the predator's interest while the lizard makes its escape. Eventually the lost tail regrows (though it is never quite the same as the original and is always supported by cartilage rather than bone); there is no limit to the number of times regrown tails can be lost. Tail-shedding is completely unknown in all species of chameleons (Chamaeleonidae), beaded lizards (Helodermatidae), monitors (Varanidae) and xenosaurs (Xenosauridae) and in the Bornean earless monitor (*Lanthonotus borneensis*).

The most extraordinary tail shedding probably occurs in the 1.5 m *5 ft* Pallas's glass snake (*Ophisaurus apodus*), which is really a lizard without legs. It is named for its extraordinary ability to shatter its own body. If under stress, it fractures its tail (which amounts to two-thirds the total length of the body) at all or most of the joints. Each piece of tail then wriggles convulsively on its own for several minutes, while the 'body' of the lizard makes its escape – sometimes reduced to as little as one-third of its original length.

**Longest tongue** All lizards possess well-developed, extendable tongues but the longest by far belong to the 140 known species of chameleons (family Chamaeleonidae). Their tongues can be catapulted forward and extended to a length at least as long as their own bodies (in some species up to 1.5 times their body length). After aiming the entire head at a suitable and unsuspecting insect, the chameleon is ready to fire – with great accuracy. A sticky mucus on the end of the tongue (which

can pull in about half the chameleon's own body weight) helps to capture the animal. Only very high speed photography can catch the tongue in action, since it can spring more than a body length away, hit a tiny and sometimes moving target and reel it back to the mouth in less than half a second – all in the blink of an eye. A special bone with its own muscle is used to propel the tongue forward and different muscles retract it.

**Largest meal** Unlike snakes, lizards cannot dislocate their jaws and therefore the upper limit of food items they can swallow is less than the width of their heads. However, they are able to tear food and many species can chew. As a result, the larger monitors (family Varanidae) will eat any animal they can catch and the record-holder in this respect is the Komodo dragon (*Varanus komodoensis*). This huge 2.25 m *7 ft 5 in* lizard feeds mainly on carrion, but has been known successfully to tackle animals as large as horses and, in one case, a 590 kg *1300 lb* adult water buffalo. Local villagers on the island of Komodo, Indonesia, also fall prey to the dragons from time to time; and, since the animals have become a tourist attraction, there have been several, well-documented occasions on which the tourists themselves have been added to their diet. In relation to body size, the largest single meal on record is a 41 kg *90 lb* wild pig which was eaten by a 46 kg *101 lb* Komodo dragon in one sitting.

**Most specialized diet** Many lizards have highly specialized diets. Most geckos (family Gekkonidae) and chameleons (family Chamaeleonidae), for example, are exclusively insectivorous, while horned lizards (genus *Phryno-soma*) feed mainly on ants and the snake lizard *Pygopus nigriceps* on scorpions. But many of these are adaptable and will vary their diets according to local conditions and seasonal changes in the availability of food. However, there are several species with very specific and unwavering diets, including caiman lizards in the genus *Dracaena*, which eat only molluscs; the marine iguana (*Amblyrhynchus cristatus*), which eats only seaweed; and, perhaps most extraordinary of all, the Australian thorny

The Komodo dragon will eat any animal it can catch and sometimes even tackles local villagers on its island home of Komodo, Indonesia; the owner of this scarred leg is one of the few survivors of a Komodo dragon attack.

devil (*Moloch horridus*), which eats only ants of the genus *Iridomyrmex*.

**Food storage** Several desert-dwelling lizards are able to store fat in their tails in preparation for periods of food shortage. The best example is probably the slow-moving gila monster (*Heloderma suspectum*), which lives in the south-western USA and Mexico and feeds on invertebrates, small reptiles, birds' eggs and small rodents. When food is plentiful, the gila monster is able to consume more than 35 per cent of its own body weight in a single sitting. But when food is scarce, it can manage on very few meals by breaking down the fat stored in its tail. After a long period without food, the girth of the tail can become reduced by as much as 80 per cent.

**Most recently discovered** New lizard species are discovered fairly frequently and, indeed, entirely new genera are still being found. For example, a recent major herpetological survey of Madagascan forests, carried out by Ron Nussbaum and Chris Raxworthy (1988–93), discovered many species new to

---

*Chameleons are among the few creatures that can move each eye independently, enabling them to look in two different directions at the same time; when hunting, they use one to look for tasty insects while the other keeps a wary lookout for predators and other enemies.*

*Right:* Guenther's gecko is one of the rarest lizards in the world, restricted to a small group of trees on Round Island, off the coast of Mauritius, in the Indian Ocean.

science. These include the day gecko (*Phelsuma antanosy*) (formally described in 1993) and no fewer than six new species of dwarf chameleon in the genus *Brookesia* (formally described in 1995).

A new species of iguana (*Brachophylus vitiensis*) was discovered on Yaduatabu, in the Fiji Islands, in January 1979. Several specimens were taken into captivity at the Fijian Cultural Centre, Orchid Island, and one of the females laid three eggs which were successfully hatched. It was the first time a new species of animal had been bred in captivity before it had been formally classified and given a scientific name.

**Most threatened** According to the World Conservation Union (IUCN) 149

*Below:* the iguana family lives further south than any other group of lizards; this is a green iguana, which is a common animal in Central and South America.

lizard species (4 per cent of the world total) are known or suspected to be threatened with extinction. More species are likely to be added to this list as research progresses. No fewer than 18 of these are considered to be in particularly serious danger, including five iguanas, five skinks, two geckos and one chameleon. Both species of tuatara (order Rhynchocephalia) are also listed as threatened. The many threats to lizards and their relatives include habitat destruction; exploitation for food, skins and the pet trade; and the careless introduction of predators and competitors from other parts of the world.

**Country with the most threatened species** South Africa harbours more internationally threatened lizards than any other country in the world, with a total of 25 (not including Peringueyi's leaf-toed gecko [*Phyllodactylus peringueyi*] whose status in the country is uncertain). Australia comes a close second with 22 threatened species and Chile third with 20. These figures may reflect high levels of research as well as a high incidence of threatened species.

Round Island, 24 km *15 miles* off the north coast of Mauritius, in the Indian Ocean, has more threatened lizard species per hectare than anywhere else in the world: one per 50 ha. The 151 ha *374 acre* island has no fewer than six lizard species, three of which are threatened and two endemic. The threatened species are: Durrell's night gecko (*Nactus serpensinsula durrelli*); the Round Island day gecko or Guenther's gecko (*Phelsuma guentheri*); and the Round Island or Telfair's skink (*Leiolopisma telfairii*).

**Extinctions** A total of 11 lizard species are known or suspected to have become extinct since 1600. All but two of them (*Hoplodactylus delcourti*, from New Zealand, and *Tetradactylus eastwoodae*, from South Africa) used to live on islands, including the Rodrigues day gecko (*Phelsuma gigas*), the Cape Verde giant skink (*Macroscincus coctei*) and the Martinique giant ameiva (*Ameiva major*). However, it is likely that at least some other species become extinct be-

*After an uncomfortably close encounter with a predator, some skinks have been known to return to the spot where they lost their tails and eat them – a unique example of self-cannibalism.*

**The marine iguana is the only truly marine lizard, and is capable of diving for as long as 20 minutes at a time.**

fore the status of their populations has been properly assessed or even before they are known to science – and therefore go unrecorded.

**Highest density** The highest densities so far recorded for any species of lizard are up to 20 000/ha *8100/acre* for several different anoles (family Iguanidae) on certain West Indian islands.

**Most northerly** The viviparous or common lizard (*Lacerta vivipara*) lives further north than any other species of lizard, occurring high above the Arctic Circle at the northern extremes of mainland Norway.

**Most southerly** Several species of iguana (family Iguanidae) live further south than any other species of lizard. One particular species, *Liolaemus magellanicus*, occurs on Tierra del Fuego, at the southern tip of Argentina.

**Most marine** The only truly marine lizard is the marine iguana (*Amblyrhynchus cristatus*), which lives in the Galapagos Islands, off the coast of Ecuador. This 1.75 m *5 ft 9 in* lizard feeds almost exclusively on seaweed and can dive to depths of up to 9.3 m *30½ ft* and stay underwater for as long as 20 minutes. While foraging, its heart rate and blood flow slow down to about half normal speed to cut down on heat loss (the waters of the Humboldt Current are extremely cold) and to reduce oxygen requirements to a minimum. It swims gracefully and with ease, using its long flattened tail and partially webbed feet for propulsion; it also has special glands in its nasal cavity which secrete excess salt. Despite all these adaptations, it only feeds every 3–5 days and spends most of its time basking on the black volcanic rocks in the hot tropical sun.

**Worst climber** Among the tree-living lizards, the western fence lizard (*Sceloporus occidentalis*) is probably the world's worst climber. Researchers working in the Hastings Natural History Reservation in Monterey County, California, USA, have calculated that the lizards fall out of their oak tree homes, landing with a thump on the forest floor, at a rate of around 12 000 falls/ha *4860/acre* every year. One particularly clumsy individual fell at least five times in 2 months, the final fall

proving fatal. This lack of sure-footedness is believed to be due to their over-enthusiastic pursuit of canopy insects, desperate efforts to escape from predators and, in the case of males, over-vigorous showing off before prospective mates.

Many lizards are arboreal, but the European glass lizard (*Ophisaurus apodus*) is the only legless species known to climb. However, it rarely ascends higher than low shrubs and tends to climb down to the ground if disturbed.

**Fastest** Lizards are renowned as much for their powers of acceleration as for their overall speed: some species can accelerate from a standing start to 95 per cent of their maximum speed within a quarter of a second. The highest speed accurately measured for any reptile on land is 34.9 km/h *21.7 mph* for a spiny-tailed iguana (*Ctenosaura* sp) from Costa Rica, in a series of experiments by Professor Raymond Huey from the University of Washington, USA, and colleagues at the University of California, Berkeley, USA. A special lizard racetrack was used, with a series of light beams and a computerized tim-

Basically, lizards differ from snakes in having four legs and movable eyelids; the few lizards that have lost their legs through evolution still retain both their shoulder and hip bones.

ing device: as the animals dashed down the track, they broke the beams and their times were automatically fed into the computer. The system is so accurate that it is claimed to rival the ones used in the Seoul Olympics.

A close runner-up is a six-lined race runner (*Cnemidophorus sexlineatus*) which was clocked at 29 km/h *18 mph* near McCormick, South Carolina, USA, in 1941. It was being chased by a car and maintained its speed on all four legs for over a minute before darting into the undergrowth by the side of the road.

Some lizards lay eggs, others give birth to live young.

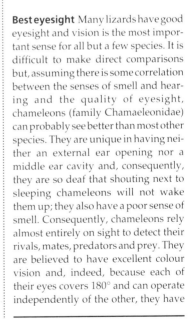

**Best eyesight** Many lizards have good eyesight and vision is the most important sense for all but a few species. It is difficult to make direct comparisons but, assuming there is some correlation between the senses of smell and hearing and the quality of eyesight, chameleons (family Chamaeleonidae) can probably see better than most other species. They are unique in having neither an external ear opening nor a middle ear cavity and, consequently, they are so deaf that shouting next to sleeping chameleons will not wake them up; they also have a poor sense of smell. Consequently, chameleons rely almost entirely on sight to detect their rivals, mates, predators and prey. They are believed to have excellent colour vision and, indeed, because each of their eyes covers 180° and can operate independently of the other, they have

Chameleons are so deaf that shouting next to them when they are asleep will not wake them up; however, they are believed to have better eyesight than most other lizards.

> *The green-blood skink is unique among vertebrates in having a green pigment in its blood; it is unclear what the pigment is for.*

both 3-D vision and the advantage of seeing to the side and behind.

**Worst eyesight** Burrowing lizards have the worst eyesight. In particular, blind lizards (family Dibamidae) have only rudimentary eyes which are covered by skin. They are probably unable to distinguish anything other than light from dark.

**Most vocal** Sound is an important means of intra-specific communication in the geckos (family Gekkonidae) and the snake lizards (family Pygopodidae), both of which are primarily nocturnal and use a variety of barks, grunts and squeaks to keep in touch with one another. Several species have reputations for being very loud or for their elaborate vocal repertoires. Barking geckos (*Ptenopus garrulus*), which live in the deserts of south-west Africa, are unique among lizards because the males all call together just as many frogs do in their choruses; at night, and on cloudy days, each male sits in the entrance to his burrow and calls loudly, using the burrow to amplify the sound. The tokay gecko (*Gecko gecko*), which lives in south-east Asia and grows to an impressive 50 cm *20 in* in length, has a staccato bark

**The enormous tokay gecko of south-east Asia has such a loud voice that its staccato barking is about as loud as the noise of a barking dog.**

that is so loud it would compete with a barking dog. The appropriately named talkative or barking gecko (*Ptenopus garrulus*) also has a reputation for its varied and loud vocal repertoire.

**Walking on water** The leafy plum-tree basilisk or Jesus Christ lizard (*Basiliscus basiliscus*) can run across the surface of water at speeds of up to 12 km/h *7½ mph*. It lives among the dense vegetation lining rivers and streams in Central America and, when threatened, runs away on its hind legs. If it is suddenly confronted with water, it simply keeps on running – and does not sink. It is able to do this by running incredibly fast (it has the most highly developed form of bipedal locomotion of all the lizards) and with the help of its powerful hind legs which end in long, fringed toes that act like flippers. One 80 cm *32 in* basilisk was seen to cross a 40 m *131 ft* wide lake without sinking, but normally a basilisk will begin to sink after a few paces. When it does finally sink, it is a good swimmer and can hold its breath long enough to avoid most predators.

**Best glider** No lizard has the power of flight, although some species are capable of gliding from tree to tree or from a branch or trunk down to the ground. The best-known glider is the flying dragon (*Draco volans*), an inhabitant of the rain forests of south-east Asia. Like other lizards of the genus *Draco*, which are the most highly adapted lizards for

gliding, it even has its own 'wings'. These comprise several pairs of elongated ribs, with a wide flap of skin stretched between them, and can be opened and closed voluntarily. As with all flying lizards, the flying dragon steers with its tail.

Two other genera have independently evolved their own special adaptations for gliding. Flying geckos in the genus *Ptychozoon*, which are also from south-east Asia, have webbed feet, a fringed tail and flaps of skin along their flanks; however, the flaps have no skeletal support and are opened purely by air resistance during gliding. Also, the African blue-tailed tree lizard (*Holaspis guentheri*) is known to leap from tree to tree and its tail and toes are fringed by large flattened scales, which may be an adaptation to reduce air resistance. Surprisingly, no gliding lizards have evolved in South America.

**Virgin birth** The ability of females to breed and produce viable offspring without the need for males to fertilize their eggs is fairly common among insects and other invertebrates, but rare among vertebrates. Parthenogenesis, as this process is called, is known or suspected in several different lizard species but is most extreme in the whiptail lizards (genus *Cnemidophorus*), which live in North and Central America. Some species are exclusively parthenogenetic – males are completely unknown in the Chihuahuan spotted whiptail (*Cnemidophorus exsanguis*) of southern Texas, USA, and northern Mexico, for example – and all-female populations are known for a number of others. The benefit of parthenogenesis is obvious in environments where periodic disasters such as floods or

devastating fires are likely, because only a single female needs to survive for the population to re-establish itself. The main disadvantage is that the offspring are identical to their mother (they are literally clones of one another) and so, if local conditions change, they have little chance of adapting.

**Most prolific** There are two major strategies for producing a large number of offspring: lay a single large clutch (or have a large number of young) once a year or lay a number of smaller clutches throughout the year. Iguanas (family Iguanidae) and geckos (family Gekkonidae), for example, choose the strategy of laying many small clutches (usually one or two eggs at a time). But the record-holder – the species which regularly lays the most eggs in any given year – is Meller's chameleon (*Chamaeleo melleri*) which lays an annual average of 70.

A number of females of the same species may lay all their eggs together in a large 'cache'. The largest recorded cache belonged to an unknown number of female teiid lizards *Kentropyx calcaratus* and contained a total of 800 eggs (whole and broken). It is believed that the cache had been used over a period of several years.

**Oldest** There is little information on lizard lifespans in the wild and, consequently, most authenticated information relates to species in captivity. However, it is known that few lizards live very long lives and, indeed, some smaller species such as the side-blotched lizard (*Uta stansburiana*) rarely live for more than a year. The average lifespan for the entire group (ignoring the high mortality of newly-hatched or newborn babies) is probably in the region of 5–10 years. Members of the families Anguidae (glass lizards, alligator lizards and the slow worm) and Lacertidae (wall and sand lizards) are exceptional in regularly exceeding 20 years. The greatest age recorded is over 54 years for a male slow worm (*Anguis fragilis*) kept in the Zoological Museum, Copenhagen, Denmark, from 1892 until 1946.

**Most tolerant to freezing** Only a handful of vertebrate species are known to be able to tolerate intercellular freezing: four amphibians, several turtles, one snake and two lizards. The lizards are the European wall lizard (*Podarcis muralis*), of central and southeastern Europe, and the spiny lizard *Sceloporus grammicus*, which lives at a high altitude on the slopes of Iztaccihuatl Volcano, Mexico. The tolerance of *S. grammicus* was discovered by accident by scientists from the University of Nebraska-Lincoln, USA. On 29 Jun 1991 they collected a total of 14 lizards from the slopes of Iztaccihuatl Volcano: seven *S. grammicus* and seven members of a closely related species of spiny lizard called *S. mucronatus*. They were all placed in a home freezer (inside temperature about 0°C 32°F) to kill them prior to preservation. The following day (after 28 hours) all the solidly frozen lizards were removed. However, after about half an hour of warming at room temperature, the scientists noticed movement among the *S. grammicus* species. When all the lizards had completely thawed, all seven *S. grammicus* were alive and well while all seven *S. mucronatus* were dead.

The alpine water skink (*Sphenomorphus quoyi*), which lives in the subalpine and montane regions of south-east Australia, can remain active even when its body temperature drops below freezing. Its optimum body temperature is 26–34°C 79–93°F but, thanks to small amounts of an anti-freeze agent (glycerol) in its blood, it can still move about when the temperature drops to –1.2°C 29.8°F.

**Most efficient thermo-regulator** Like all reptiles, lizards are unable to produce heat internally and rely primarily on the sun to raise their body temperature to the optimum level. The black-coloured lava lizard (*Liolaemus multiformis*), which lives in the Peruvian Andes, is believed to be more efficient at absorbing solar radiation than any other lizard. In near-freezing conditions, it can raise its body temperature to 33°C 91°F after only an hour in the sun, while the surrounding air temperature has barely risen to 1.5°C 35°F. Incredibly, its preferred body temperature is 35°C 95°F – which is never reached by the surrounding air.

## TUATARA

In 1867 Albert Günther of the British Museum announced to a startled scientific community that the lizard-like tuatara (*Sphenodon punctatus*) was not a lizard after all, but the sole surviving member of an ancient order of reptiles called the Rhynchocephalia. The order lived in many parts of the world during the reign of the dinosaurs and all but the tuatara died out more than 65 million years ago. Recent studies have substantiated Günther's statement: it is not a lizard because its jaw teeth are not separate but simple serrations of the jaw bone, the structure of its skull is different, it does not have an ear drum or a middle ear, and for many other reasons. The studies have also revealed that there are, in fact, two surviving species: the individuals living on North Brother Island, in Cook Strait, between New Zealand's North and South Islands, are genetically distinct and now belong to a new species called Brother's Island tuatara (*Sphenodon guntheri*); the original species is known as the Cook Strait tuatara.

The tuataras are rare animals, weighing up to 1.3 kg 2 lb 14 oz and attaining a maximum overall length of 61 cm 24 in (males are larger than females). Mainly nocturnal, they are found only on about 30 remote, windswept islands off the coast of New Zealand. Compared with the lizards, they break a number of significant records: longest period between mating and eggs hatching (37 months); longest incubation period (15 months – which is the longest known for any reptile species); oldest age to reach sexual maturity (20 years); longest period of growth (60 years); and longest lifespan (possibly more than 100 years).

## WORM LIZARDS

Despite their name, worm lizards are not true lizards but are placed in a separate sub-order (Amphisbaenia) within the reptilian order Squamata (which includes both snakes and lizards). There are about 130 species altogether, most of them similar in size, colour and general appearance to earthworms. All but three have no legs (in certain members of the genus *Bipes* the front limbs are retained) and they are all believed to feed mainly on burrowing invertebrates and small vertebrates. The majority are 15–35 cm 6–14 in long, but the largest is a species called *Amphisbaena alba*, from the rain forests of northern South America and the island of Trinidad, which grows to about 75 cm 29½ in. The shortest is only 10 cm 3.9 in long. As a group, worm lizards are found in North and South America, Africa, western Asia, the Middle East and extreme southern Europe.

*Many lizards, and both tuataras, have a 'third eye': a small opening on the top of the skull; this is believed to register daylight and may be used to control activities such as basking, hibernation and seasonal courtship.*

# SNAKES

## *Serpentes*
### c. 2700 species

> *No snake species is known to look after its offspring: once born, they are left to survive on their own.*

**Earliest** Snakes evolved from lizard-like ancestors and are believed to have appeared for the first time during the early Cretaceous period, perhaps 120 million years ago. The oldest snake fossils were found in Algeria, in deposits about 100 million years old, although they consist of little more than a few damaged vertebrae. The oldest complete snake fossil, found in the Middle East in deposits about 94–96 million years old, measured about 1 m *3 ft 4 in* long and belonged to a species called *Paryachis problematicus*; however, some experts still question whether this was a very elongated lizard (it had minimal hind legs) or a primitive snake.

**Longest** Giant snake stories abound – due to the wild imaginations of many early explorers, the difficulties in estimating or measuring the length of live animals which refuse to stay still and the fact that large snake skins can be deliberately stretched by more than 30 per cent without causing much noticeable distortion. In reality, even among the pythons (Pythoninae) and boas (Boinae), giant individuals are very rare. However, there are a few authenticated records of snakes exceeding a length of 9.14 m *30 ft*. The record-holder is the reticulated python (*Python reticulatus*) of south-east Asia, Indonesia and the Philippines, which regularly exceeds 6.25 m *20½ ft*. The greatest proven length for this species is 10 m *32 ft 9½ in* for a specimen shot on the north coast of Celebes, Indonesia, in 1912; it was accurately measured with a surveying tape by civil engineers working at a nearby mining camp. The closest runner-up is an African rock python (*Python sebae*) measuring 9.81 m *32 ft 2¼ in*, which was shot in 1932 by Mrs Charles Beart, in the grounds of a school in Bingerville, Ivory Coast, West Africa; however, this particular individual was truly exceptional, since the average length for this species is only 3–5 m *9 ft 10 in–16 ft 5 in*.

The largely aquatic anaconda (*Eunectes murinus*) of South America is a close contender for the longest snake record, although it has probably been the subject of more exaggerated claims regarding its size than any other living animal. Early Spanish settlers in South America spoke of individuals measuring 18–24 m *60–80 ft* and even larger specimens have been reported. But, in reality, it rarely exceeds 6.25 m *20½ ft* Perhaps the most famous of the claims that have been taken seriously was made in 1907 by Lt Col Percy Fawcett of the Royal Artillery. He shot an unusually large anaconda while navigating the Rio Abuná near its confluence with the Rio Negro, in the Amazon, Brazil, as it made its way out of the water and up a riverbank. He claimed that 'as far as it was possible to measure, a length of 45 feet [*13.7 m*] lay out of the water, and 17 feet [*5.2 m*] in it, making a total length of 62 feet [*18.9 m*]'. Fawcett was very meticulous in all the observations he entered in his journal, but his explorations often read like a comic-book adventure so the reliability of his giant anaconda has often been questioned. The truth will probably never be known for sure.

The longest (and heaviest) snake ever held in captivity was a female reticulated python named 'Colossus' which was 8.68 m *28 ft 6 in* long and weighed 145 kg *320 lb* at her heaviest. She died at Highland Park Zoo, Pennsylvania, USA, on 15 Apr 1963.

Most modern herpetologists have a healthy scepticism about any snake claimed to be longer than 9.14 m *30 ft*. However, it has been calculated, by taking into account the biomechanical and physiological stresses imposed on a large snake moving over land, that the upper length limit is probably about 15 m *49 ft*; a longer snake would have to spend most of its time in the water, to support its enormous weight. These calculations, combined with many unauthenticated reports of giant snakes, suggest that specimens in the 12–15 m *40–50 ft* range may well be found in the future.

**Longest sea snake** The longest of all the sea snakes is *Hydrophis spiralis*, from the northern Indian Ocean and many parts of south-east Asia, which can grow up to 2.75 m *9 ft* in length.

**Longest venomous** The longest venomous snake in the world is the king cobra (*Ophiophagus hannah*), also called the hamadryad, which has a wide range over India and south-east Asia, and averages 3.65–4.57 m *12–15 ft* in length. A 5.54 m *18 ft 2 in* specimen captured alive near Fort Dickson in the state of

The longest venomous snake in the world is the king cobra, which can attain a length of nearly 6 m *19½ ft*.

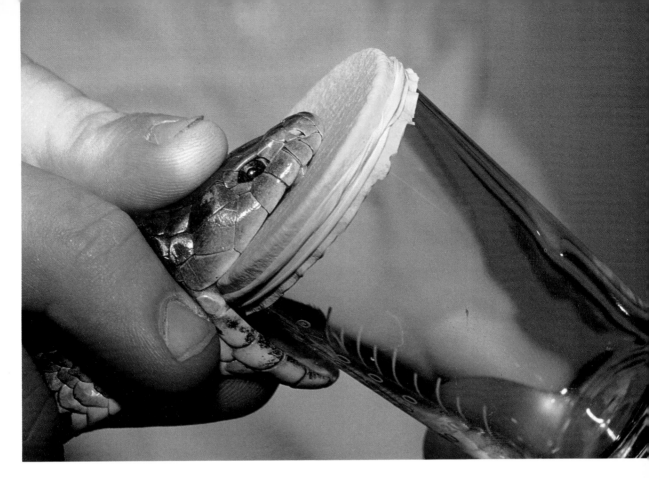

Negri Sembilan, Malaysia, in April 1937, later grew to 5.71 m *18 ft 9 in* in London Zoo, UK. It was destroyed at the outbreak of war, in 1939, to avoid the risk of escape. The king cobra is one of the few snakes known to feed almost exclusively on other snakes.

**Longest prehistoric** While giant dinosaurs roamed the earth, snakes were basically the same size as they are now. The longest prehistoric snake was the python-like *Gigantophis garstini*, which inhabited what is now Egypt about 38 million years ago. Parts of a spinal column and a small piece of jaw discovered at Fayum, in the Western Desert, indicate a probable length of some 11 m *36 ft*.

**Shortest** The world's shortest snakes are the thread snakes (family Leptotyphlopidae). There are about 60 species, widely distributed in tropical America, Africa and parts of western Asia, and they are all shorter than 40 cm *16 in*. The shortest of all is the very rare thread snake *Leptotyphlops bilineata*, which is known only from Martinique, Barbados and St Lucia, in the Caribbean. The longest known specimen measured 10.8 cm *4¼ in* and had such a small, matchstick-thin body it could have entered the hole left in a standard pencil after removing the lead.

Some worm-like blind snakes (family Typhlopidae), which are widely distributed in the warmer parts of the world, are also very small. *Typhlops*

*fornasinii* of East Africa, *T. caecatus* and *T. hallowelli* of West Africa, and *T. anchietae* of Angola all measure 12.7–15.2 cm *5–6 in*. Most blind snakes (there are 150 species in total) feed on small invertebrates, especially ants and termites.

The shortest of the 'giant' snakes (the boas and pythons – all of which kill their prey by constriction) is the dwarf boa *Tropidophis pardalis*, found in Cuba, which has a length of about 30 cm *12 in*. It feeds mainly on lizards, but probably takes small mammals and frogs when the opportunity arises.

**Shortest venomous** The namaqua or spotted dwarf adder (*Bitis schneideri*), which occurs mainly in coastal areas around the mouth of the Orange River, Namibia, has an average length of 18–24 cm *7–9½ in*. It occasionally bites people and, although its venom is mildly toxic and causes local swelling and pain, it is not serious and there have been no recorded fatalities. Mainly nocturnal, the namaqua dwarf adder eats small geckos and frogs.

**Heaviest** The heaviest snake in the world is the anaconda (*Eunectes murinus*) of tropical South America and Trinidad: it attains a considerably greater body weight than the much more slender reticulated python (*Python reticulatus*); for example, a 5.2 m *17 ft* anaconda would weigh roughly the same as a 7.3 m *24 ft* reticulated python. The record-holder is a female

**South African Bernard Keyter personally milked a record-breaking 780 000 venomous snakes over a 10-year period – and was never bitten.**

---

anaconda shot in Brazil in *c.* 1960. It was 8.45 m *27 ft 9 in* long, with a girth of 1.11 m *44 in*, and was estimated to have weighed nearly 227 kg *500 lb*.

**Heaviest venomous** The heaviest venomous snake is probably the eastern diamondback rattlesnake (*Crotalus adamanteus*) of sparse woodland and lowland coastal regions in the southeastern United States. It averages 5.5–6.8 kg *12–15 lb* (1.52–1.83 m *5–6 ft* in length), although the heaviest on record weighed 15 kg *34 lb* and was 2.36 m *7 ft 9 in* long.

The gaboon viper (*Bitis gabonica*) of tropical Africa is probably bulkier than the eastern diamondback, but its average length is only 1.22–1.52 m *4–5 ft*. An exceptionally long 1.83 m *6 ft* female

> *Snakes inject venom through the fangs which are especially adapted teeth. The forked tongue of a snake is used only for feeling and smelling and cannot sting or harm in any way.*

**The gaboon viper has the distinction of possessing the longest fangs of any snake; they can each be up to 5 cm *1.96 in* in length.**

weighed 11.34 kg *25 lb* and another female measuring 1.74 m *5 ft 8½ in* weighed 8.2 kg *18 lb* with an empty stomach.

**Largest meal** Snakes cannot chew or tear their food, so they have no choice but to swallow it whole. They are superbly adapted to swallowing prey considerably larger in girth than themselves because, as the wider parts of the body enter the mouth, the bones of the lower jaw can be temporarily dislocated and certain bones in the skull are capable of pulling apart. Once the prey has been swallowed, the snake yawns a few times to return the various parts of the skull to their original positions. The largest prey item on record was a 59 kg *130 lb* impala, which was removed from a 4.87 m *16 ft* African rock python (*Python sebae*). African rock pythons regularly take large prey but, when swollen with food, are vulnerable to attack by wild dogs and hyenas and so prefer to eat more moderate meals at shorter intervals.

There are many examples of snakes swallowing other snakes which are much longer than themselves. In 1955 a captive cottonmouth moccasin (*Ancistrodon piscivorous*), which was 35.5 cm *14 in* long, swallowed a very slender 73.6 cm *29 in* ribbon snake (*Thamnophis sauritus*) sharing the same cage. The stomach of a 1.51 m *59½ in* long file snake (*Mehelya capensis*) killed

in Kruger National Park, South Africa, contained a 1.09 m *47.2 in* olive grass snake (*Psammophis sibilans*), an 85 cm *33½ in* African rock python (*Python sebae*), a 54 cm *21.3 in* brown water snake (*Lycodonomorphis rufulus*) and a 49 cm *19.3 in* ring-necked spitting cobra (*Hemachatus haemachatus*). A king cobra (*Ophiophagus hannah*) was once placed by a misguided keeper in a cage with six Asiatic cobras (*Naja naja*); by the following morning, the king cobra had eaten all its room-mates.

**Man-eating** There are many stories of snakes swallowing people, but only a few have been authenticated – and, in most of these cases, the victims have been either young children or babies. One of the best-known examples occurred in November 1979, in northern Transvaal, South Africa, when a young Tswana herdsman was seized by an African rock python (*Python sebae*) measuring 4.5 m *14 ft 9 in* in length. His friend ran to get help but when he returned with two elders, about 20 minutes later, the victim had already been entirely swallowed by the snake. The men pelted the snake with stones and attempted to kill it with a pick-axe until, eventually, it regurgitated its prey; unfortunately, the young man was already dead.

**Longest fast** Most snakes do not feed every day but, on average, do so about once a week. If necessary, for example when they are hibernating or if they are unable to find suitable prey species due to adverse environmental conditions, they can survive without food for considerably longer. The longest known fasts are carried out by the highly ven-

omous Okinawa habu (*Trimeresurus flavoviridis*), the largest of the Asiatic pit vipers, found in the Ryukyu Islands between Japan and Taiwan in the western Pacific. On 10 Sep 1977, the Amami Kanko Pit Viper Centre in Naze City, Kagoshima Prefecture, Japan, started a fasting experiment with five of these snakes. Four of them died on the 207th, 696th, 1101st and 1184th days respectively, but the fifth was still alive and apparently healthy (if approached, it reared up in preparation for an attack) when the experiment was terminated on the 1189th day (12 Dec 1980). It had survived for 3 years 3 months without food, which is a record for any vertebrate animal. Although its weight decreased by 60.9 per cent during the fast, its length unaccountably *increased*. With special care, the snake was restored to full physical health.

**Most venomous sea snake** All 50 of the world's sea snakes are venomous, but the most venomous – and, indeed, the most venomous snake in the world – is probably the sea snake *Hydrophis belcheri* of the Australo-Pacific region (particularly common in the waters around Ashmore Reef in the Timor Sea, off north-west Australia). It has a myotoxic venom many times more effective than the venom of any land snake. However, fatalities are rare since the potency of the venom is matched only by the snake's friendly temperament (it has to be subjected to severe treatment before it can be induced to bite) and because people and sea snakes rarely encounter one other. Most bites are of fishermen handling nets – and even then only about 25 per cent of those bitten ever show signs of poisoning, since the snake rarely injects much of its venom.

**Most venomous land snake** Some 680–700 of the world's 2700 snake species are venomous (almost one third of which are harmless to people). By far the most venomous land snake in the world is the 1.7 m *5 ft 7 in* small-scaled

*All snakes are deaf, and unable to hear airborne sounds, which means that they cannot be charmed by music (snake charmers 'charm' their snakes with the movements of their instruments); instead, they can detect vibrations on the ground through their bodies.*

or fierce snake (*Oxyuranus micro-lepidotus*), found in isolated patches over a very large area of east-central Australia. It appears to be most common in the Diamantina River and Cooper Creek drainage basins, Queensland and western New South Wales, where it feeds mainly on the plague rat; a bitten rat would probably drop dead within a few seconds, since the snake's venom is strongly neurotoxic. The average venom yield after milking is 44 mg *0.00155 oz*, but one male specimen yielded a record 110 mg *0.00385 oz* – enough to kill 250 000 mice. Fortunately, because of the remoteness of its habitat, the fierce snake rarely comes into contact with people and, so far, no human fatalities have been reported.

**Largest yield of venom** The gaboon viper (*Bitis gabonica*) of tropical Africa probably has the highest *average* yield of venom (350–600 mg *0.012–0.021 oz*); only 60 mg *0.002 oz* of gaboon viper venom is enough to kill a fully grown man. However, the highest yield ever recorded was 1530 mg *0.054 oz* dry weight from a jararacussi (*Bothrops jararacussi*), which lives in southern Brazil, eastern Bolivia, Paraguay and northern Argentina; this was clearly exceptional, since the average yield for this species is 150–200 mg *0.005–0.007 oz*.

**Champion milker** Over a 10-year period ending in December 1970, Bernard Keyter (b. 1918), a supervisor at the South African Institute for Medical Research in Johannesburg, South Africa, personally milked 780 000 venomous snakes and obtained 3960 litres *870 gallons* of venom for research and serum production. He was never bitten.

**Longest fangs** The longest fangs of any snake are those of the highly venomous gaboon viper (*Bitis gabonica*) of tropical Africa. In a specimen of 1.83 m *6 ft* in length they measure up to 5 cm *1.96 in*.

**Country with most deaths from snakebite** Around the world, an estimated 1 million people are bitten by snakes every year. However, few of the snakes responsible are highly dangerous and, indeed, research has shown that in as many as 50 per cent of bites no venom is injected. Consequently, in most countries there is more chance of being killed by a bolt of lightning than there is of being killed by a snake. Nevertheless, the World Health Organisation estimates that 30–40 000 people are killed every year by snakes (although this figure is little more than a rough calculation) and, in some areas, the risk is relatively high.

More people die from snakebite in India than in any other country in the world, with the total death toll estimated to average 10–12 000 annually. This is partly due to a high incidence of venomous snakes, but also because in many areas medical care is not always readily available and, consequently, more bites prove fatal; death can often be prevented by prompt medical treatment and, indeed, most deaths from snakebite occur well away from hospitals and other treatment centres. In some areas, local habits and conditions also encourage a higher incidence of snakebite; in Bombay, for example, poor hygiene attracts large numbers of rats and other rodents which, in turn, attract large numbers of cobras (family Elapidae).

More people die of snakebite in Sri Lanka than in any other comparable area. An average of 800 people are killed by snakes every year on the 65 610 km² *25 332 miles²* island – equivalent to one person every 82 km² *32 miles²* annually. Over 95 per cent of the fatalities are caused by the common krait (*Bungarus caeruleus*), the Sri Lankan cobra (*Naja n. naja*) and Russell's viper (*Vipera russelli pulchella*).

The approximate number of deaths by snakebite, and the species most likely to have been responsible, according to major regions of the world are as follows: North America (10–12): western diamond-backed rattlesnake (*Crotalus atrox*) and eastern diamond-backed rattlesnake (*C. adamanteus*); Europe (10–15): sand viper (*Vipera ammodytes*); Australia (2–4): tiger snake (*Notechis scutatus*) and eastern brown snake (*Pseudonaja textilis*); Africa (1000): puff adder (*Bitis arientans*), saw-scaled viper (*Echis carinatus*) and Egyptian cobra (*Naja haje*); South America (2000): pit viper (*Bothrops atrox*), other *Bothrops* species, the rattlesnake *Crotalus durissus* and coral snakes in the genus *Micrurus*; India (10–12 000): Indian cobra (*Naja naja*), Russell's viper (*Vipera russelli*) and the saw-scaled viper (*Echis carinatus*).

**Country with highest incidence of snakebite** Certain islands of the Ryukyu group, between Japan and Taiwan in the western Pacific, have the highest incidence of snakebite in the world. On average, 0.2 per cent of the population – 1 in every 500 people – is bitten by a snake every year. Every person in the area has at least a one in seven chance of being bitten by a snake at one time or another during their lives. The snake most responsible is the

Madagascar is unique in having a rich and varied population of snakes, none of which are dangerous to people.

**R
E
P
T
I
L
E
S**

Okinawa habu (*Trimeresurus flavoviridis*); fortunately, most of its victims recover.

### Country with least venomous snakes

Several countries and islands have no snakes at all, including: Iceland, Greenland, Newfoundland, Ireland, New Zealand and the Falkland Islands. Most of the islands of the Pacific Ocean, and many Caribbean islands, have no poisonous land snakes, although those in equatorial waters are likely to have poisonous sea snakes just offshore. Madagascar is unusual in having a large and varied population of snakes – a total of nearly 90 species altogether – but no dangerous ones (a small number are venomous, but the arrangement of their fangs makes them completely harmless to people).

The adder or viper (*Vipera berus*) is the only venomous snake in Britain. Its bite has caused 10 human deaths since 1890, including six children. The most recent recorded death was on 1 Jul 1975, when a 5-year-old died 44 hours after being bitten at Callander, Perthshire, UK.

### Country with most venomous snakes

Australia has more venomous snakes than any other country in the world. It also has the unenviable distinction of being home to no fewer than 9 of the top 10 most venomous snakes in the world. Interestingly, it is the only continent with a higher proportion of venomous snakes to non-venomous ones: out of a total of nearly 170 species

(including more than 30 sea snakes) around 120 of them are venomous. Some 20–25 of these are considered to be highly dangerous to people, the commonest cause of serious snakebite being the tiger snake (*Notechis scutatus*).

Even though few parts of Australia are entirely free of dangerous snakes – and an estimated 3000 Australians are bitten by venomous snakes every year – deaths due to snakebite are relatively uncommon. Fatalities have dropped dramatically since the beginning of the century as anti-venoms have become more readily available: every year 200–500 of the snakebite victims require treatment with anti-venoms without which their chances of survival would have been limited. Between 1981 and 1991 only 18 deaths from snakebites were reported to the Commonwealth Serum Laboratory, Melbourne; four of these were people bitten after picking up the snakes or playing with them. Brown snakes (genus *Pseudonaja*) were responsible for 11 deaths; tiger snakes (*Notechus scutatus*) for four; taipans (*Oxyuranus scutellatus*) for two; and a death adder (*Acanthopis australis*) for one.

**Most dangerous** It is difficult to identify the most dangerous snake in the world, because the effect of a snakebite depends on the combination of many factors above and beyond the species itelf: the age, weight and health of the victim; the size of the snake, the number of bites and the volume of venom injected; and, of course, the speed and

efficiency of first aid treatment. However, taking into account the five most widely accepted features for comparison (venom toxicity, venom yield, fang length, temperament and frequency of bite) the saw-scaled or carpet viper (*Echis carinatus*) is generally considered to be the most dangerous snake in the world. Ranging from West Africa through the Middle East to India and Sri Lanka, it probably bites and kills more people in the world than any other species. In Asia alone, it is reported to kill 8000 people annually. Its venom is more toxic than in any other viper, it is small and easy to overlook and, above all, it becomes extremely aggressive when frightened or disturbed. Indeed, many snake experts put it on the top of their list of short-tempered species.

The beaked sea snake (*Enhydrina schistosa*) is generally considered to be the world's most dangerous sea snake. Blamed for many deaths in south-east Asia, in particular, it normally grows to about 1.2 m *4 ft* long and hunts catfish in shallow estuaries and tidal creeks.

**Resistance to venom** Some people have a higher than average resistance to snake venom. There are numerous

---

**The dangerous tiger snake is just one of nearly 170 snake species found in Australia, which has more venomous snakes than any other country in the world.**

examples of snake handlers and performers, particularly from the turn of the century, who appear to have suffered few ill effects after being bitten.

A series of bizarre experiments was carried out by Saul Wiener, in 1958, to test the theory that people can develop an immunity to snake venom. His willing human guinea pig was 46-year-old Charles Tanner, animal curator of the Alfred Hospital, in Melbourne, Australia. Tanner had already been bitten several times by venomous snakes and was allergic to anti-venom. The experiments involved injecting Tanner with venom milked from tiger snakes (*Notechis scutatus*), the dosage gradually being increased from 0.002 mg *0.00000007 oz* to 25 mg *0.0008825 oz* over a period of 13 months. The result of his final injection – which, under normal circumstances, would have been enough to kill 30 men – was nothing more than tenderness and muscle stiffness.

August Eichorn, a household name in Australia at the turn of the century, spent many years developing a remedy to snake bite. He was so confident in his new product (which almost certainly gave no immunity at all) that he became quite a performer – and coaxed snakes to bite him to demonstrate its efficacy. There are numerous photographs taken at the time, showing Eichorn 'accepting' the bites of some of Australia's most dangerous snakes – tigers (*Notechis scutatus*) and browns (*Pseudonaja textilis*) among them – on his arms, hands and face. There are photographs of tiger snakes clinging to his cheeks and hanging from his throat and he would even allow them to bite him under the tongue. On one occasion, he encouraged three tiger snakes to bite him simultaneously – and still showed no ill effects. He eventually died in 1943, at the grand old age of 85, from blood poisoning.

In general, venomous snakes are fairly resistant to their own venom and to the venom of other individuals of their own and closely related species. However, the level of immunity is unclear and may even vary from individual to individual. There are cases of venomous snakes being bitten by one of their contemporaries and surviving with little more than swelling, but there are also cases of venomous snakes accidentally biting themselves and dying within a couple of days. When one poisonous snake eats another, it apparently suffers no ill-effects from the venom because of a 'protective factor' in the blood; it is hoped that this factor could help to make a 'multi-purpose' anti-venom for people bitten by deadly snakes (existing anti-venoms

> *No one knows for certain why a rattlesnake has a rattle on the end of its tail; for many years it was believed to act as an audible warning, but its main function is probably to focus the attention of predators and prey onto the tail rather than the head.*

act only against specific snake species).

**Longest illness after snakebite** The most prolonged illness ever recorded after a snake bite occurred near Noosa, Queensland, Australia, in 1978. A 9-year-old boy, who had been bitten by a rough-scaled snake (*Tropidechus carinatus*) suffered cardiac arrest, kidney failure, muscle wastage and paralysis that kept him in hospital for a total of 18 weeks; for more than half this time, his life depended on mechanical ventilation and life-supporting drugs. When he eventually returned to school, a further 6 months later, he still found eating difficult because of a throat constriction.

**Longest snake sit-in** In the spring of 1986, Austin James Stevens spent a record-breaking 107 days and nights in a cage just 4 m *13 ft* long and 3 m *10 ft* wide – in the company of 36 highly venomous snakes. His feat took place at the Hartebeespoort Dam Snake and Animal Park, South Africa, and his companions in the cage were: 6 boomslangs (*Dispholidus typus*), 18 Egyptian cobras (*Naja haje*), 6 black mambas (*Dendroaspis polylepis*) and 6 puff adders (*Bitis arietans*). During the stunt, which was designed to raise funds for the Park, one of his most nerve-wracking experiences was to wake up one morning to find 7 cobras fast asleep in his pyjama legs; a Park colleague had to enter the cage to extract them, one by one, with a hook-stick. Stevens was bitten only once – on day 92 – by an Egyptian cobra which injected a large dose of venom into his wrist and left him seriously ill, though still in the cage, for 4 days.

**Most accurate spitter** Several cobras (family Elapidae) are able to spit or, more precisely, to eject their venom over considerable distances, thanks to a slight adaptation of the fangs. When the venom lands on human skin it has a minimal effect (unless it happens to enter an open wound) but when it hits the eyes it causes a painful burning sensation, leads to severe irritation and may even cause temporary blindness. For this reason, spitting cobras need to be able to aim accurately for maximum effect. A Mozambique spitting cobra (*Naja mossambica*) can aim its venom with remarkable accuracy at the eyes of

an approaching person when still 3 m *10 ft* or more away.

**Most variable** Several snake species show a startling degree of variation in their markings. One of the best examples is the common garter snake (*Thamnophis sirtalis*): individuals may have brilliant stripes, bright spots or heavy speckling, they may have rather subtle or even dull markings or, in some parts of their range, they may even be completely black.

**Largest hunt** Snakes are hunted all over the world: as food, as vermin, for their skin and because of their undeserved image as forces of evil. The largest organized hunts take place in the USA, where community-wide rattlesnake hunting dates back to 1680, ostensibly to rid the surrounding countryside of dangerous snakes. However, since the mid-1800s the hunts have become popular festival activities. More than 50 'Rattlesnake Round-Ups' are held in Texas, Oklahoma, Pennsylvania, Georgia, Alabama and Florida every year. The largest and most publicized of these is the Sweetwater Rattlesnake Round-Up, held in the town of Sweetwater, about 320 km *200 miles* from Dallas-Fort Worth, west Texas. Held annually on the second weekend of March, it attracts up to 35 000 spectators and results in the capture and killing of as many as 18 000 western diamondbacks (*Crotalus atrox*). The Round-Up began in 1958, and, in the period up to and including the 1991 event, a total of 174 996 snakes were killed. Captured snakes are brought to the Nolan County Coliseum, headquarters for the festival, where they are weighed and deposited in a snake pit for live demonstrations and, eventually, to be butchered and sold to dealers. Other snake species caught during the hunt include: prairie rattlesnakes (*Crotalus viridis*), coachwhips (*Masticophis flagellum*) and western bull snakes (*Pituophis melanoleucus*).

> *The venom produced by Russell's viper is used to stop bleeding in haemophiliacs.*

**Oldest** The greatest reliable age recorded for a snake is 40 years 3 months 14 days for a male common boa (*Boa constrictor constrictor*) named 'Popeye', which died at Philadelphia Zoo, Pennsylvania, USA, on 15 Apr 1977. In the wild, the oldest natural longevity known is about 30 years for the black ratsnake (*Elaphe obsoleta*).

**Fastest** The fastest land snake in the world is the much-feared black mamba (*Dendroaspis polylepis*) of the eastern part of tropical Africa. There are many stories of this species overtaking people on galloping horses but, although moving snakes do give an illusion of speed, such stories are greatly exaggerated. However, top speeds of 16–19 km/h *10–12 mph* have been recorded for black mambas in short bursts over level ground – certainly fast enough to catch up with a person on foot – and speeds of 10–11 km/h *6–7 mph* are probably not unusual.

**Most threatened** The World Conservation Union (IUCN) currently lists 71 snake species as known or suspected to be threatened with extinction, representing 2.6 per cent of the world total. Ten of these are believed to be in serious trouble: woma (*Aspidites ramsayi*) from Australia; Round Island keel-scaled boa (*Casarea dussumieri*) from Round Island, off the north coast of Mauritius; Antiguan racer (*Alsophis antiguae*) from Great Bird Island, in Antigua and Barbuda; black racer (*Alsophis ater*) from Jamaica; St Lucia racer or couresse (*Liophis ornatus*) from Maria Major Island, St Lucia; Martinique racer (*Liophis cursor*) from Rocher de Diamant, Martinique;

Round Island, off the coast of Mauritius, in the Indian Ocean: home of the Round Island boa which, if it is not already extinct, is the rarest snake in the world.

Kikuzato's brook snake (*Opisthotropis kikuzatoi*) from Nansei-shoto, Japan; black-striped snake (*Simoselaps calonotus*) from Australia; Latifi's viper (*Vipera latifii*) from the Lar Valley, Elburz Mountains, in Iran; and Cyclades blunt-nosed viper (*Vipera schweizeri*) from Greece. Some of these have not been seen for many years and may already be extinct.

Assuming the Round Island burrowing boa (*Bolyeria multicarinata*), one of two boas endemic to Round Island, off the north coast of Mauritius, is already extinct, the world's rarest snake is considered by many experts to be the St Lucia racer or couresse. Estimates by Dr David Corke of the Polytechnic of East London, UK, put its population at under 100 in 1989, with no specimens held in captivity.

**Extinct species** The only snake species *known* to have become extinct in recent times are *Typhlops cariei*, a kind of blind snake in the family Typhlopidae which disappeared from its home on Mauritius in the 17th century, and the Saint Croix racer (*Alsophis sancticrucis*), which disappeared from the US Virgin Islands some time during this century. The Round Island burrowing boa (*Bolyeria multicarinata*), one of two boas endemic to Round Island, off the north coast of Mauritius, has been sighted only four times since 1935 (the

last time in 1975) and, although its status is unknown for certain, it may already be extinct.

**Country with the most threatened species** Australia has more internationally threatened species of snake than any other country in the world, with a total of nine. Turkey comes a close second with eight threatened species and South Africa third with seven. These figures may reflect high levels of research in these countries as well as the actual number of threatened species in each case.

**Jumping** A number of snakes can jump or glide. The golden tree snake (*Chrysopelea ornata*), found in southeast Asia, is able to glide from tree to tree over distances of at least 10 m *33 ft*; during the 'flight' it holds its body rigid, like an arrow, and its ventral surface caves in to offer greater resistance to the air.

As its name suggests, the jumping viper *Bothrops nummifer*, from Central America, strikes so fiercely that its entire body moves forward. It is able to clear a height of up to 1 m *3 ft 4 in* high, by curling its body into an S-shape and using it as a spring or coil.

**Sperm storage** The females of many species are able to store sperm in their reproductive tracts before using it to fertilize their eggs. These are nature's sperm banks, enabling the females to be fertilized by the best males whenever they happen to be available, regardless of whether it is also the best time for young to be brought into the world. Implantation finally takes place in anticipation of a time when food is plentiful and the weather more suitable. Domestic sheep can store sperm for up to 2 days, humans for up to 5 days, domestic turkeys for up to 117 days and certain snakes and turtles for up to 5 years. The world record-holder is the Javan wart snake or elephant-trunk snake (*Acrochordus javanicus*), which can store sperm for up to 7 years.

**Egg incubation** Several species of snake guard their eggs, but female pythons (family Boidae) are the only ones known to incubate them. Since they are cold-blooded animals, keeping the eggs warm can be difficult. However, some species can raise their temperature by as much as 7°C *13°F* above that of the surroundings, by rapidly contracting their own body muscles or by gently shuffling the eggs in and out of the sun.

**Playing dead** A number of snakes, including the European grass snake (*Natrix natrix*) and the North American

Snakes will sometimes swallow one another accidentally; in particular, when they are both fighting over the same prey, one snake frequently gets swallowed by the other along with its catch.

hog-nosed snakes (*Heterodon* sp), pretend to be dead when they are threatened; lying belly-up, with a sagging jaw, lolling tongue and a deathly expression on their 'faces', they are really convincing. But probably the most impressive 'death display' is used by the West Indian wood snake (*Tropidophis* sp) of Cuba. When threatened, this small boa twists itself into a tight coil to mimic the stiffness of death and, with the help of fluids coating its scales, gives off a foul stench of decomposing flesh. To add to the illusion, it even has special blood vessels which burst to flush the eyes with blood and to form a trickle of blood from its gaping mouth. The overall effect successfully convinces most predators that the snake has been dead for some time. Another impressive death display is shown by the board snake (*Erpeton tentaculatum*) of Indochina, a strictly aquatic species up to 90 cm *35 in* long. Its name comes from its strange reaction when caught: it becomes totally rigid and holds itself straight, like a stick.

**Most recently discovered** A new species of hook-nosed snake (*Ficimia hardyi*) was discovered in northern Hidalgo, Mexico, in the upper headwaters of the Rio Pánuco, on 12 Jan 1985. It was officially named in 1993. A number of new species in the genus *Pseudo-xyrhopus* are currently being described for Madagascar.

**Rediscoveries** The colubrid snake *Chironius vincenti*, which is endemic to St Vincent, in the West Indies, had not been reported since 1894. Then one was collected by the Department of Forestry early in 1987 and interviews with local people since have revealed that they are familiar with the species, although it may not be common.

**Largest concentration** In 1932 millions of sea snakes of the species *Astrotia stokesii* congregated in the Strait of Malacca, off Malaysia, forming a solid line 3 m *9 ft 10 in* wide and 100 km *62 miles* long.

The greatest regular concentrations of snakes on land are formed by red-sided garter snakes (*Thamnophis sirtalis parietalis*) in Manitoba, Canada. In the autumn, hundreds or even thousands of the snakes gather at their wintering sites (normally pits in rocks) where they huddle together to survive temperatures as low as −40°C *−40°F*. They emerge again in April or May.

The floodplain of the Adelaide River, near Darwin, Australia, has the highest density of top predators in the world. Australian scientists have counted no fewer than 30 water pythons (*Liasis fuscus*) per km² (*78 per mile²*). This is equivalent to 400 kg *882 lb* of snake per km² (1036 kg *2284 lb per mile²*) which far exceeds the density of predators in the next most crowded location, the Ngorongoro Crater, Tanzania, where there are 30 kg *66 lb* of predator per km² (78 kg *172 lb per mile²*). The floodplain is perhaps the only place in the world where it is possible to find a wild python within 10 minutes of searching.

**Highest altitude** The Himalayan pit viper (*Agkistrodon himalayanus*) has been found at greater altitudes (4900 m *16 072 ft*) than any other snake. The ridge-nosed rattlesnake (*Crotalus*

*willardi*) of Mexico is not far behind, frequently being found at altitudes of over 4000 m *13 120 ft*.

**Lowest altitude** Healthy sea snakes are rarely recorded diving to depths of more than 100 m *328 ft*. Most species and, indeed, most individuals of deep-diving species are usually found in much shallower water.

**Most pelagic** Most of the world's 50 or so sea snakes are restricted to relatively shallow, coastal waters and are capable of existing for long periods out of water. The only truly pelagic species is the yellow-bellied sea snake (*Pelamis platurus*), which lives in the Indian and Pacific Oceans. A surface feeder that drifts with the warm currents, it may be found hundreds of kilometres from land.

**Longest dive** Research on yellow-bellied sea snakes (*Pelamis platurus*) equipped with pressure sensitive acoustic transmitters has shown that they spend an average of 87 per cent of their time below the surface. The longest dive observed lasted for 3 h 33 min and 20 per cent of all dives lasted for more than 1 hour. The time at the surface between dives was as little as one second.

**Mimicry** One of the best examples of mimicry in snakes is probably between a highly venomous coral snake known as the harlequin (*Micrurus fulvius*) and the false coral snake (*Lampropeltis triangulum*). Their physical resemblance – both have black, white, yellow and red bands – is astonishing. Since both species are secretive, nocturnal and live together in the rainforests of Central America, the harmless coral snake probably benefits because potential predators believe they are dealing with a dangerous animal and consequently do not attack.

The oldest snake on record is a captive boa constrictor, which reached the grand old age of 40 years 3 months 14 days.

# TURTLES & TORTOISES

### *Chelonia*
265 species

> *No tortoises or turtles have teeth; they rely on the sharp cutting edges of their jaws to tear food.*

**Earliest** The first chelonians appeared on Earth during the late Triassic or early Jurassic, at least 185 million years ago. Fossil species, such as *Proganochelys* and *Proterochersis*, found in Triassic deposits in Germany, resemble modern species in many ways. However, they also reveal some significant differences; for example, the fossil animals still had teeth on both jaws and were unable to withdraw their heads into their shells.

**Largest** The largest living chelonian is the widely distributed leatherback turtle (*Dermochelys coriacea*), which nests on tropical beaches in the Atlantic, Indian and Pacific Oceans and forages widely in temperate waters. The overall length from the tip of the beak to the end of the tail is normally 1.83–2.13 m *6–7 ft* (shell length averages 1.52–1.67 m *5–5½ ft*) and the front flipper-span is about 2.13 m *7 ft*. Mature specimens typically weigh at least 450 kg *1000 lb*. The largest leatherback turtle reliably recorded was a male found dead on the beach at Harlech, Gwynedd, UK, on 23 Sep 1988. It had an overall length of 2.91 m *9 ft 5½ in* (shell length 2.56 m *8 ft 5 in*) and measured 2.77 m *9 ft* across the front flippers. It weighed 961.1 kg *2120 lb*. Although most museums refuse to exhibit large turtles (because they can drip oil for up to 50 years) this specimen was put on display at the National Museum of Wales, Cardiff, on 16 Feb 1990. There are claims of leatherback turtles reaching 3.7 m *12 ft* in length (in particular, by the crew of a British trawler in 1962) but these have never been authenticated.

The largest freshwater turtle in the world is the alligator snapping turtle (*Macrochelys temminckii*) of the southeastern USA. The really large individuals tend to be most common in the northern extremes of the range, where the species is only rarely encountered. Males are much larger than females and may reach an overall length of 90 cm *35 in* and an upper weight of about 100 kg *220 lb*. There is an unconfirmed report of a giant individual living in Fulk's Lake, near the town of Churubusco, Indiana, which was first seen in the summer of 1948; despite repeated attempts, it was never captured and properly measured, but eye-witness accounts described it as being 'the size of a dining-room table' and

estimated its weight to be around 227 kg *500 lb*. There is another unconfirmed record of 183 kg *403 lb* for an enormous specimen caught in the Neosho River, Cherokee County, Kansas, USA, in 1937.

Several species of soft-shell turtle (family Trionychidae) can match the alligator snapping turtle (*Macrochelys temminckii*) in length, but not in weight. An overall length of 90 cm *35 in* has been recorded for the Nile soft-shell (*Trionyx triunuis*), the narrow-head soft-shell (*Chitra indica*) and the Asian giant soft-shelled turtle (*Pelochelys bibroni*); the record length for the latter species is said to be 127.5 cm *50 in*.

The largest living tortoises are the Aldabra giant tortoise (*Geochelone gigantea*), which is found on Aldabra Atoll, a group of four major islands in the Seychelles (there are also several introduced populations on other islands in the western Indian Ocean), and the Galapagos giant tortoise (*Geochelone elephantopus*), which is

found on a handful of islands in the Galapagos archipelago, in the Pacific. The normal maximum size attained by certain sub-species of the Galapagos giant tortoise is greater than that attained by the Aldabra giant tortoise (a shell length of 1.22 m *48 in* and a weight of 270 kg *595 lb* compared with 1.05 m *41 in* and 100–200 kg *220–440 lb*). The largest living specimen on record is a Galapagos giant tortoise named *Goliath*, who has resided at the Life Fellowship Bird Sanctuary in Sessner, Florida, USA, since 1960. He measures 1.36 m *53½ in* long, 1.02 m *40½ in* wide, 68.5 cm *27 in* high and 385.1 kg *849 lb* in weight. He is still growing. An Aldabra giant tortoise presented to London Zoo, UK, at the beginning of this century, had a shell length of 1.4 m *55 in*; although its weight was never recorded, it was estimated to be in excess of 318 kg *700 lb*. A male of the same species, called *Esmerelda*, a long-time resident of Bird Island, in the Seychelles, weighed 304 kg *670 lb* in early 1995.

**Largest prehistoric** The largest prehistoric chelonian was a turtle called *Stupendemys geographicus* (family Pelomedusidae) which lived about 5 million years ago. Fossil remains found by Harvard University palaeontologists in northern Venezuela, in 1972, indicate that this turtle had an overall length of about 3 m *9 ft 10 in* (shell length 2.18–2.30 m *7 ft 2 in–7 ft 6½ in*). It had a computed weight of 2040 kg *4500 lb*.

The largest prehistoric tortoise was probably *Geochelone atlas*, which lived in what is now northern India, Burma, Java, the Celebes, and Timor, about 2 million years ago. In 1923 the fossil remains of a specimen with a shell 1.80 m *5 ft 11 in* long (2.23 m *7 ft 4 in* over the curve) and 89 cm *35 in* high were discovered near Chandigarh in the Siwalik Hills, India. This animal had a total length of 2.44 m *8 ft* and is computed to have weighed 850 kg *2100 lb*.

**Smallest** The world's smallest chelonian is the stinkpot or common musk turtle (*Sternotherus odoratus*),

---

**The largest tortoises are the giant tortoises of the Seychelles and Galapagos Islands, which have attained a maximum length of 1.4 m *55 in* and a weight of 385 kg *849 lb*.**

which ranges from southern Canada to northern Mexico and has an average shell length of 7.62 cm *3 in* when fully grown and a weight of only 227 g *8 oz*; it is named for the offensive smell it emits when feeling threatened. A subspecies of the freshwater striped mud turtle (*Kinosternon baurii baurii*), which ranges from southern Georgia in a southerly direction through the Florida Keys, USA, is also very small with a maximum shell length of only 9.7 cm *3.82 in*.

The smallest tortoise in the world is the speckled Cape tortoise or padloper (*Homopus signatus*), which lives in western South Africa and south-western Namibia. It has a maximum shell length of about 9.6 cm *3.78 in* when fully grown (average length 6–8 cm *2.4–3.2 in*).

The smallest of the seven species of sea turtle (and, indeed, the most critically endangered) is the Atlantic or Kemp's ridley (*Lepidochelys kempii*), which nests mainly at Rancho Nuevo, on the Gulf coast of Mexico. It has an average shell length of 50–70 cm *19.7–27.6 in* and a maximum weight of around 80 kg *176 lb*.

**Longest neck** A number of species of snake-necked turtle (family Chelidae), as their name suggests, have exceptionally long necks in relation to the size of their bodies. The most notable are members of the Australian genus *Chelodina* (eight species) and the South American genus *Hydromedusa* (two species), in which the neck can be almost as long as the shell. The giant snake-necked turtle (*Chelodina expansa*), for example, has a shell size of up to 30 cm *11.8 in* but its overall length is nearly doubled when its head and neck are fully extended.

**Strongest jaw** The strength in the jaws of a large alligator snapping turtle (*Macrochelys temminckii*) is almost legendary. There are stories of individuals biting broomsticks in half and, although such claims may well be exaggerated, there is more than a little truth in them. The species is certainly quite capable of removing a human finger or toe if given the opportunity.

**Oldest** The greatest authenticated age for a chelonian – and, indeed, the oldest authenticated age for any land animal – is over 152 years for a male Marion's tortoise (*Geochelone gigantea sumeirei*), a sub-species of the Aldabra giant tortoise. Five individuals were brought from the Seychelles to Mauritius in 1766 by Marion de Fresne, the French explorer, and were presented to the army garrison at Port Louis, the island's capital. When the British captured Mauritius

in 1810, the tortoises were officially handed over, along with the island, by the surrendering French forces. The last survivor of the five became the British mascot. It went blind in 1908 and was accidentally killed, in 1918, when it fell through a gun emplacement. Since it was fully mature at the time of its capture, this ancient animal could have been nearly 200 years old at the time of its death – although any estimate beyond 152 years is purely speculation. It was the last surviving member of its sub-species, which officially became extinct in 1918.

There have been many unauthenticated claims of tortoises living for nearly 200 or even 300 years. Perhaps the most famous was a much-battered radiated tortoise (*Geochelone radiata*), known affectionately as 'Tu'imalilia' (King of the Malilia), which reputedly reached the grand old age of 193 years. It was said to have been a gift from Captain Cook to the King of Tonga in 1773 and, after an eventful life during which it was run over by a cart, kicked by a horse and escaped from two forest fires, it eventually died on 19 May 1966. Even if the story is true (unfortunately, there is no record of the original gift in Captain Cook's journals) the record may have been the composite of two or more tortoises living on the island in sequence.

Stories of pet tortoises staying 'in the family' for generations are difficult to authenticate. A large size and well-worn shell are not reliable indications of great age; neither are the growth rings in the shell, since the number laid down each year varies according to weather conditions and the availability of food. Many 'record-holders' are probably the result of dead animals secretly being replaced by thoughtful parents keen to avoid unnecessary upset and, since some tortoises undoubtedly outlive their original owners, the continuing existence of one individual is very difficult to prove one way or the other. Nevertheless, there are numerous reliable records of Mediterranean spur-thighed tortoises (*Testudo graeca*), European pond tortoises (*Emys orbicularis*) and several other species reaching in excess of 100 years.

Aquatic turtles seem to have relatively shorter lives than their more

---

*Some birds of prey feed on tortoises by dropping them from a great height, often several times in a row, in order to split open their shells.*

Tortoises are notoriously slow and laborious creatures, with an average walking speed of around 0.2–0.5 km/h *0.12–0.3 mph;* this is an Indian starred tortoise taking life slowly.

terrestrial counterparts, though there is even less reliable documentation. The oldest turtle on record was an alligator snapping turtle (*Macrochelys temminckii*) at Philadelphia Zoo, Pennsylvania, USA. When it was accidentally killed on 7 Feb 1949 it was 58 years 9 months and 1 day old.

**Slowest** The land-based tortoises (family Testudinidae) are notoriously slow and laborious creatures simply because their large, cumbersome shells severely restrict mobility. Unfortunately, it is very difficult to identify the slowest of them all because speed has to be measured over a sensible distance to be meaningful. However, tests carried out on the Californian desert tortoise (*Gopherus agassizii*) revealed an average walking speed of 0.22–0.48 km/h *0.14–0.3 mph.* Similar tests carried out on an Aldabra giant tortoise (*Geochelone gigantea*) in Mauritius revealed that, even when hungry and enticed by a cabbage, it could not exceed 0.27 km/h *0.17 mph.* Interestingly, Charles Darwin clocked a Galapagos giant tortoise (*Geochelone elephantopus*) at '6.4 km *4 miles* per day' which, when spread over a 24-hour period, is equivalent to an *average* speed of 0.27 km/h *0.17 mph.*

**Fastest** The fastest chelonians are the sea turtles (families Cheloniidae and Dermochelyidae). The highest speed claimed for any reptile in water is 35 km/h *22 mph* by a frightened Pacific leatherback turtle (*Dermochelys coriacea*).

The UK National Tortoise Championship record is 5.48 m *18 ft* up a 1:12 gradient in 43.7 seconds (0.45 km/h *0.28 mph*) by 'Charlie' at Tickhill, South Yorkshire, UK, on 2 Jul 1977. However, limited evidence suggests that wild tortoises regularly exceed this speed (*see Slowest*).

**Longest migration** Sea turtles (families Cheloniidae and Dermochelyidae) are renowned for making prodigious migrations between their feeding grounds at sea and their nesting beaches thousands of kilometres away. The record-holders are probably loggerhead turtles (*Caretta caretta*) born in Japan, which are known to travel 10 000 km *6200 miles* across the Pacific to feed off the coast of Baja California, Mexico. They begin their journey as hatchlings and, after being swept along

by strong ocean currents, arrive at their destination some two years later. They feed and grow for the next five years and then swim back to Japan as adults.

Leatherback turtles (*Dermochelys coriacea*) nest on tropical beaches in the Atlantic, Indian and Pacific Oceans and forage widely in temperate waters. For example, five leatherbacks tagged in the Guianas, northern South America, travelled over 5000 km *3105 miles* to recapture sites in Ghana, Mexico and the USA. However, the record-holder is a leatherback tagged at its nest site on a beach in Surinam, northern South America, which was recovered alive on the other side of the Atlantic, some 6800 km *4223 miles* away.

**Deepest dive** In May 1987 it was reported by Dr Scott Eckert that a leatherback turtle (*Dermochelys coriacea*) fitted with a pressure-sensitive recording device had reached a depth of 1200 m *3973 ft* off the Virgin Islands, in the West Indies. However, leatherbacks are believed to dive to depths of more than 1500 m *4920 ft* to reach dense aggregations of jellyfish.

**Rarest** The world's rarest chelonian (though not necessarily the most threatened) is the protected short-necked swamp tortoise or western swamp turtle (*Pseudemydura umbrina*), which is confined to Ellen Brook (65 ha *161 acres*) and Twin Swamps (155 ha *383 acres*) near Perth, Western Australia. The first specimen was discovered in 1839 and it was not seen again until 1953, when a schoolboy found one in the middle of

the road in a suburb north of Perth. He took it home and later exhibited his new pet at a local wildlife show in Warbrook, Western Australia. The director of the Western Australian Museum happened to be visiting and recognized it as the world's rarest chelonian which, at the time, was believed by many experts to be extinct. A meticulous search was made of the area where the schoolboy had made his unwitting discovery and more survivors were found. Captive breeding efforts in recent years have pushed the world population to over 180 (including 42 in the wild) and a reintroduction programme is under way.

There is just one known survivor of a sub-species of Galapagos giant tortoise known as the Abingdon giant tortoise (*Geochelone elephantopus abingdoni*). Affectionately called 'Lonesome George', he has been living at the Charles Darwin Research Station, on the island of Santa Cruz, since he was found in 1972. Tortoise droppings, not more than a few years old, were found on Pinta (formerly Abingdon) Island in 1981 and raised everyone's hopes that a second individual of this sub-species still existed, but none has been found.

**Most threatened** The World Conservation Union (IUCN) lists a total of 82 turtle and tortoise species as known or suspected to be threatened with extinction, representing 31 per cent of the world total. At least another 25 species are known to require priority conservation action in part or all of their range. The Madagascar tortoise or angonoka

(*Geochelone yniphora*) is generally regarded as the most seriously threatened; confined to an area of just 100 km² *39 miles²* around Baly Bay, in north-western Madagascar, it is suffering from habitat degradation, egg predation by feral pigs and collection by local people. There are believed to be only 400 remaining.

The next most seriously threatened are the batagur (*Batagur baska*) and the painted terrapin (*Callagur borneoensis*), from south-east Asia; the bolson tortoise (*Gopherus flavomarginatus*), from Mexico; the South American river turtle (*Podocnemis expansa*); the western swamp turtle (*Pseudemydura umbrina*), from Australia; and five species of sea turtle: green (*Chelonia mydas*), hawksbill (*Eretmochelys imbricata*), Kemp's ridley (*Lepidochelys kempii*), olive ridley (*L. olivacea*) and leatherback (*Dermochelys coriacea*).

**Country with the most threatened species** The USA currently has 16 internationally threatened species of turtles and tortoises within its borders, which is more than any other country in the world; this includes Kemp's

*Above:* one population of green turtles regularly migrates 2250 km *1397 miles* between feeding grounds off the coast of Brazil and nesting grounds on Ascension Island, in the middle of the South Atlantic.

*Below:* on beaches near Karachi, Pakistan, the eggs of threatened green and olive-ridley turtles are collected immediately after laying and transferred to well-protected enclosures.

**R
E
P
T
I
L
E
S**

> *The incubation temperature of turtle and tortoise eggs directly influences the sex of the hatchlings in many species.*

ridley turtle (*Lepidochelys kempii*), which nests sparsely within the USA while attempts are being made to establish a breeding colony at Padre Island. Mexico comes a very close second with 15 known threatened species. These figures may reflect high levels of research as well as a high incidence of threatened species.

**Extinctions** Seven species of giant tortoises are known or suspected to have become extinct in the last 300 years. These are all in the genus *Geochelone* and were found on the islands of Mauritius, Rodrigues, Réunion and the Seychelles, in the Indian Ocean.

---

The hawksbill turtle is one of the most threatened of the chelonians, yet many are still being killed for the tourist trade; this stuffed specimen is on sale as a tourist curio in Bali, Indonesia.

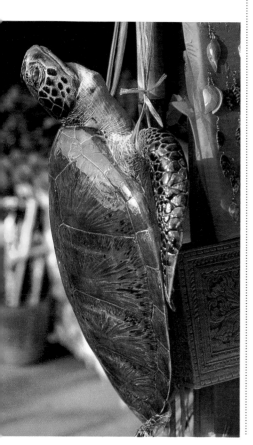

**Most restricted range** The black soft-shell turtle (*Trionyx nigricans*) exists only as a single semi-captive population in an artificial pond forming part of the sacred shrine of the Islamic saint Hazrad Sultan Byazid Bostami, at Nasirabad, near the town of Chittagong, Bangladesh. The pond is currently 100 m *328 ft* long and 50 m *164 ft* wide and contains fewer than 200 turtles. The animals depend almost entirely on food provided artificially by people. The origin of the population is unknown (although it was described as long ago as 1875) and no specimens of the dark soft-shell turtle have been found anywhere else in the world.

**Most belated discovery** A new genus and species of short-necked turtle (family Chelidae) was named and described for the first time in 1994 – even though scientists had known of its existence for approximately 25 years. The turtle had been turning up in Australian pet shops in Adelaide, Brisbane, Melbourne and Sydney since 1961, but no one would reveal where the animals were being caught. Then, in October 1990, biologist John Cann found four adults in the Mary River, in the extreme south-east of Queensland, Australia, and for the first time much of the crucial missing information could be pieced together. The species has been named the Mary River tortoise (*Elusor macrurus*): *Elusor* alludes to the fact that it remained frustratingly elusive for so long and *macrurus* refers to its long, fleshy tail.

**Most eggs** All turtles and tortoises lay eggs. The largest clutches are laid by sea turtles (families Cheloniidae and Dermochelyidae), which lay anything from a little under 70 to more than 180 eggs in multiple clutches at intervals of 9–30 days. The overall record-holder for a single clutch is a hawksbill turtle (*Eretmochelys imbricata*) which nested on Cousin Island, in the Seychelles, and laid a total of 242 eggs. However, the most prolific – and, indeed, the most prolific of all reptiles – are the green turtles (*Chelonia mydas*) which nest on Sarawak, Malaysian Borneo; in a single breeding season, each female lays up to a record of 11 clutches, each containing over 100 eggs – a total of more than 1100 eggs in less than 5 months.

**Least eggs** The pancake tortoise (*Malacochersus tornieri*) and the big-headed turtle (*Platysternon megacephalum*) are among many species that lay just one egg (sometimes two) in a clutch.

**Largest eggs** Most turtles and tortoises lay eggs which are either spherical or

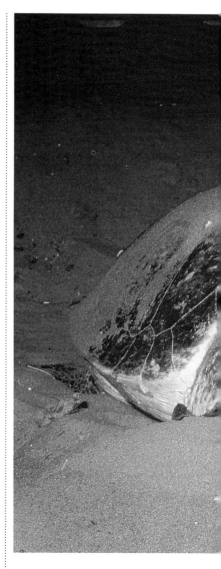

elongated. Since egg size tends to increase with body size, it is not surprising that the largest spherical eggs are laid by leatherback turtles (*Dermochelys coriacea*) and Galapagos giant tortoises (*Geochelone elephantopus*); these have an average diameter of 5–6 cm *2–2.4 in*. Among the species which lay elongated eggs, the largest are laid by the Malaysian giant turtle (*Orlitia borneensis*), which has a carapace length of about 80 cm *31.5 in*; on average, its eggs measure 7.6 cm *3 in* in length and 4.05 cm *1.6 in* in diameter, but can be as much as 0.5 cm *0.2 in* longer in both directions. However, there are exceptions in the relationship between body size and egg size and the largest eggs in relation to body size are laid by the black wood turtle (*Rhinoclemmys funerea*); this species has a maximum shell length of about 33 cm *13 in* and yet lays eggs which, on average, are 6.7 cm *2.6 in* in length and 3.7 cm *1.4 in* in diameter; one female, herself only 20 cm *7.9 in* long, laid eggs with a length of 7.5 cm *3 in*.

Sea turtles lay more eggs than any other turtle or tortoise; this female loggerhead turtle is about to lay her eggs at the back of a beach on the Greek island of Zakinthos.

**Longest hibernation** Many chelonians enter a state of dormancy when the temperature drops or during prolonged periods of drought. The length of time spent hibernating depends on local environmental factors and varies from a few days to many months. Certain populations of Horsfield's tortoise (*Testudo horsfieldii*) in Kazakhstan, on the border with Russia, are active for only about 3 months of the year, from the end of March to the middle of June. Apart from a very brief appearance at the end of the summer, they spend the remainder of the year buried underground.

**Freezing** The only reptiles known to freeze solid during the cold winter months, and survive, are young painted turtles (*Chrysemys picta*), adult box turtles (*Terrapene* sp) and garter snakes (*Thamnophis sirtalis*). Instead of leaving their nests after hatching in late summer, newly hatched painted turtles stay put, well hidden from predators until the following spring. Laboratory tests held at Carleton University in Ottawa, Ontario, Canada, show that the turtles freeze whenever the temperature falls below –3°C 26.6°F. When frozen, they show no movement, respiration, heart beat or blood circulation, and barely detectable neurological activity. Since winter temperatures continually fluctuate, the hatchlings must freeze and thaw repeatedly before finally emerging in the spring.

**Underwater nesting** Most reptiles lay their eggs on dry land for the simple reason that the developing embryos need oxygen to survive, and would drown under water. But the northern long-necked turtle (*Chelodina rugosa*) of Australia is unique in laying its eggs under water, usually in holes dug into the muddy bottom at depths of 15–20 cm 6–8 in. The eggs survive in a state of arrested development until the floodwaters subside and then start developing under the hardened mud. Tests have shown that, once they have started developing, the embryos cannot survive immersion under water.

*Local Indians claim that the Chiapas cross-breasted turtle, from Central America, is able to eat its way out of a crocodile.*

**Maternal care** The Burmese brown tortoise (*Geochelone emys*) is the only species of tortoise or turtle known to show any degree of maternal care. After laying, some species spend up to an hour concealing their eggs and the nest site, but then take no further interest. In contrast, the female Burmese brown tortoise is unique in remaining close to her nest site for a few days afterwards.

**Largest congregation** Once every year a 10 km 6.2 mile stretch of Gahirmatha beach in Orissa, eastern India, hosts the largest congregation of nesting sea turtles (and, indeed, the largest congregation of chelonians) anywhere in the world. In one week during February 1994, an estimated 520 000 olive ridley turtles (*Lepidochelys olivacea*) emerged from the surf after dark to lay their eggs on the beach; by dawn they had all left. A peak of 610 000 nesting turtles was counted in 1991. Each year, the nesting turtles lay more than 50 million eggs between them. Unfortunately, the government of Orissa is completing a fishing quay within 13 km 8 miles of the turtle rookery and work has already begun on three more quays lying south of the nesting area; each quay will add at least 500 fishing trawlers to the surrounding seas. Despite plans by the government to introduce regulations designed to reduce harm to the turtles, conservationists fear that the fishermen's gill and drag nets will devastate the population.

*Desert tortoises, always ready to make the most of water when it is available, have been known to drink over 40 per cent of their own body weight in little more than an hour.*

# CAECILIANS

Caecilians are easily mistaken for large earthworms, but are long-bodied, limbless amphibians.

## Gymnophiona
*c.* 170 species (exclusively in the tropics and sub-tropics)

**Earliest** Until recently, the fossil record of caecilians was almost non-existent and consisted of just two vertebrae (one from the Palaeocene of Brazil and the other from the late Cretaceous of Bolivia). However, the exciting discovery of an extensive series of early Jurassic caecilians in Coconino County, Arizona, USA, was announced by scientists from Harvard University and the University of London in 1993. The 200 million-year-old fossils are believed to belong to a prehistoric species known as *Eocaecilia micropodia* and reveal numerous features (such as limbs) which are unknown in modern caecilians.

This find is also exciting because it provides evidence of substantial evolutionary divergence between caecilians and other modern amphibian groups. The new species is older than the earliest known salamanders but younger than the earliest known frogs, confirming that the three groups were well differentiated by Jurassic times and thus all probably originated during the Triassic period or earlier.

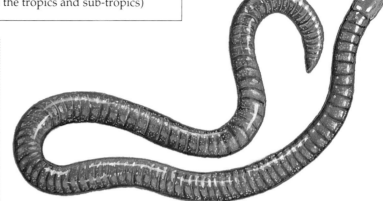

**Largest** The world's largest caecilian is a species called *Caecilia thompsoni*, which lives in Colombia and attains a maximum length of about 1.5 m *59 in* and a width of up to 3 cm *1.2 in*. This size is really exceptional and most caecilian species are within the 30–70 cm *12–27½ in* range.

A number of other species are shorter but much bulkier than *C. thompsoni*. For example, *C. nigricans* is 80 cm *31½ in* long and has a body diameter of 4 cm *1.6 in*. Body shapes vary between caecilians, with some stout-bodied species having a length:diameter ratio of 15:1 and more slender-bodied species having a length:diameter ratio of 100:1.

**Smallest** The world's smallest caecilian is a species in the genus *Idiocranium*, which lives in West Africa and attains a maximum length of about 8 cm *3.2 in* from the end of the snout to the tip of the tail. It matures at a length of 7 cm *2.8 in*.

# FROGS & TOADS

*The barking tree frog, which lives in North America, has a call which sounds very similar to a barking dog.*

## Anura
*c.* 3800 species (typically 15–25 new species formally described every year)

**Earliest** Our knowledge of early frogs and toads is almost non-existent. The earliest frog-like creature known is a species called *Triadobatrachus*, which has been found in France in deposits dating from the early Triassic period some 210–225 million years ago. *Triadobatrachus* was about 10 cm *3.9 in* long and had a wide, flat skull (like modern frogs) as well as a short tail. The first species believed to be almost identical to modern frogs appeared during the early Jurassic, about 150 million years ago.

**Most primitive** The world's most primitive frogs are members of the genera *Ascaphus* and *Leiopelma*. Three species live in New Zealand and one in north-western North America (which alone is circumstantial evidence that these frogs are survivors of an ancient time when the continents were joined together to form great land masses). A number of curious anatomical features (such as the presence of a tail or tail-wagging muscles and, in *Ascaphus*, the lack of a free-swimming tadpole stage) suggest that these frogs are survivors of a time when frog evolution was still in its infancy.

**Largest** The largest of all frogs and toads is the African giant or goliath frog (*Conraua goliath*) of West Africa, which frequently attains a snout-to-vent length of 30 cm *12 in*. A specimen captured in April 1989 on the Sanaga River, Cameroon, had a snout-to-vent length of 36.83 cm *14½ in* (87.63 cm *34½ in* overall with legs extended) and weighed 3.66 kg *8 lb 1 oz* on 30 Oct 1989.

There are a small number of records of longer frogs, though none exceed the Sanaga River specimen in weight. The longest authenticated record is of an American bullfrog (*Rana catesbeiana*) which was caught in Martha Lake, Alderwood Manor, Washington, USA, in 1949. It reportedly measured 91.4 cm *36 in* in overall length (with legs extended) and weighed 3.29 kg *7 lb 4 oz.*

The largest toad ever recorded was a male cane or marine toad (*Bufo marinus*) named Prinsen ('The Prince'), owned by Håkan Forsberg of Åkers Styckebruk, Sweden, which weighed 2.65 kg *5 lb 13½ oz* and measured 38 cm *15 in* snout-to-vent (53.9 cm *21.2 in* when extended) in March 1991. The largest female ever recorded was a cane toad nicknamed 'Totally Awesome' and owned by Blank Park Zoo, Des Moines, Iowa, USA; she attained a peak weight of 2.31 kg *5 lb 1½ oz* and a snout-to-vent length of 24.13 cm *9.5 in* on 19 Nov 1987 (she died on 8 Apr 1988, most probably from old age). However, the average size of the cane toad (which lives in tropical South America and Queensland, Australia, where it was introduced) is considerably smaller; an average specimen weighs 453 g *1 lb* and and measures about 15 cm *5.9 in* (snout-to-vent). Several toad species exceed this *average* size: in particular, Blomberg's toad (*Bufo blombergi*) of Colombia frequently attains a length of 24 cm *9.5 in*.

**Smallest** The world's smallest frog – and, indeed, the smallest known amphibian – is the tiny Cuban frog (*Sminthillus limbatus*), which is 0.85–1.2 cm *0.34–½ in* long (snout-to-vent) when fully grown. A number of other species vie for this title: several *Eleutherodactylus* sp (which range from northern Mexico south into Argentina and across to the West Indies), the smallest members of the widely distributed family Microhylidae, and *Psyllophryne didactyla*, from Brazil, all have an average adult length (snout-to-vent) of just under 10 mm *0.4 in*.

The world's smallest toad is the subspecies *Bufo taitanus beiranus*, which lives in Africa and attains a diminutive 2.4 cm *0.95 in* in length (snout-to-vent). The smallest full species is the oak toad (*Bufo quercicus*), which attains a maximum length of 3 cm *1.18 in*.

**Smallest adult in relation to tadpole**
The aptly-named paradoxical frog (*Pseudis paradoxus*), which lives in the Amazon and on the island of Trinidad, metamorphoses from a giant tadpole into a tiny frog. The tadpole usually grows to a length of 16.8 cm *6.6 in* (the record is 25 cm *9.8 in*) but then its whole body, including the heart and other vital organs, shrinks when it metamorphoses into a much smaller frog (the adult frog is a tiny 5.6–6.5 cm *2.2–2.6 in* or even less). The difference is so dramatic that for many years scientists could not believe that the two animals belong to the same species – and even now no one knows the reason for such a size change.

---

*A wild African bullfrog once entered a snake enclosure at Pretoria Zoo, in South Africa, and ate 16 live ringhal cobras; it was in the middle of eating the 17th when it was caught in the act.*

---

**Most poisonous** Frogs and toads are incapable of inflicting a poisonous bite or sting to deter their predators, but instead some secrete a toxic or distasteful substance from their skin. The most deadly toxins are produced by the 60 or so species of poison-arrow frogs in the genera *Dendrobates* and *Phyllobates*. These brightly coloured species (the garish colours warn potential predators that they are highly poisonous and should be disregarded as potential meals) are found in Central and South America. Several of them secrete some of the most deadly biological toxins known to science and, indeed, their secretions are so toxic that a tiny smear is enough to kill a horse.

The skin secretion of the golden poison-arrow frog (*Phyllobates terribilis*) of western Colombia is the most poisonous. This brilliant yellow or orange species, which was not discovered until 1973 and was first described in 1978, grows to a length of about 3.5 cm *1.4 in*. The combination of batrachotoxins and homobatrachotoxins found in its secretion is 20 times more toxic than that produced by any other poison-arrow frog. An average adult specimen carries

enough poison (0.0019 g *0.000067 oz*) to kill nearly 1000 people, making the species so dangerous that scientists have to wear thick gloves to pick it up to protect themselves. The golden poison-arrow frog has only two enemies: the frog-eating snake (*Leimadophis epinephelus*), which is believed to be immune to its toxin; and Choco Indians, who use the toxin to poison their blowpipe darts which can then kill large prey in a matter of seconds (in the old days, they also used poisoned darts to kill neighbouring hostile tribesmen).

For many years, it was assumed that poison-arrow frogs produce the toxins themselves. But recent research suggests that, although they do synthesize some of their own, they also obtain significant quantities from their food. Indeed, for this reason, they may actively choose toxic insects as prey.

**Worst smelling** The worst smelling of all the anurans is the aptly named Venezuela skunk frog (*Aromobates nocturnus*), which was described as new to science in 1991. Found in the cloud forests of the Venezuelan Andes, it attains a length of 6.2 cm *2.44 in* and is the largest of the poison-arrow frogs (family Dendrobatidae). Unlike other members of the family, which rely on toxic secretions from their skin for defence, the skunk frog releases a vile-smelling secretion instead. Appropriately enough, the chemical responsible for the smell is the same organosulphur compound as the one emitted by more familiar mammalian skunks.

The longest authenticated record of a frog is 91.4 cm *36 in* (with legs extended) for an American bullfrog, caught in 1949 in Washington, USA.

**Most eggs** The female cane or marine toad (*Bufo marinus*) lays as many as 30000–35000 eggs per spawning. However, she leaves them to the mercy of the weather and predators, so the mortality rate is extremely high.

**Least eggs** The tiny female Cuban frog (*Sminthillus limbatus*), a kind of poison-arrow frog, lays just a single egg – but does everything possible to make sure that it survives. A number of other anuran species (particularly small terrestrial ones) lay only 3–6 eggs.

**Viviparity** The only anurans which are truly viviparous (in which the young live inside their mother's uterus and are nourished by her 'uterine milk') are two species of toad from central Africa: *Nectophrynoides liberiensis* and *N. occidentalis*. In addition, three species are known to be ovo-viviparous (in which the eggs develop inside their mother's body but are nourished by their own yolk): two more toads from central Africa, *N. tornieri* and *N.*

*viviparus*, and a frog from Puerto Rico called *Eleutherodactylus jasperi*.

**Stomach brooding** The only animals in the world known to brood their young in the female's stomach are the northern or Eungella gastric brooding frog (*Rheobatrachus vitellinus*) and the gastric brooding platypus frog (*R. silus*), both of which live in Australia. They certainly show the most remarkable form of parental care among anurans: the female swallows her fertilized eggs, which develop into tadpoles and then froglets inside her stomach; after a 'gestation period' of 6 or 7 weeks, she eventually gives birth through her mouth. For the whole of this period the female is unable to feed (the tadpoles have sufficient yolk to be able to feed themselves) and the mechanism for digestion is 'switched off', with the help of a chemical produced by her youngsters, to ensure that her digestive juices do not break them down. The gastric brooding platypus frog was first discovered in 1972 but, within a few

**Golden poison-arrow frogs produce such a highly toxic skin secretion that scientists have to wear thick gloves when handling them; an average adult specimen carries enough poison to kill nearly 1000 people.**

---

years, seemed to have become extinct and has not been seen alive since 1983. Strangely, the northern gastric brooding frog was discovered just a couple of months later, although there is now concern that it has also become extinct (it was last seen in 1985).

**Longest leap** There is tremendous variation in jumping ability both between species and between individuals. It is not necessarily the largest ones that make the longest jumps: in one detailed study of the performance of 82 different species from around the world, the longest jumps were recorded by some of the smallest individuals. Indeed, the world record-holder is the South African sharp-nosed frog (*Ptychadena oxyrhynchus*), which is only 5.5 cm *2.2 in* (male) and 6.6 cm *2.6 in* (female) in length. In 1975, at the annual Calaveras County Jumping Frog Jubilee held at Angels Camp, California, USA, an individual named 'Ex Lax' jumped an amazing 5.35 m *17 ft 6 in* –

> *The difference between frogs and toads is fairly vague: terrestrial, walking species with warty skins are usually called toads and aquatic, jumping species with smooth skins tend to be called frogs; however, there are many exceptions to this rule.*

the longest single leap recorded for any amphibian.

Competition frog jumps are normally taken as the aggregate of three consecutive leaps. The greatest distance covered by a frog in a triple jump is 10.3 m *33 ft 5½ in* by a South African sharp-nosed frog (*Ptychadena oxyrhynchus*) named *Santjie* at a frog Derby held at Lurula Natal Spa, Paulpietersburg, Natal, South Africa, on 21 May 1977.

**Colour variations** Some frogs and toads have a number of contrasting colour phases. One of the best examples is the African reed frog *Hyperolius marmoratus*, which has three very distinctive phases: brilliantly striped, heavily speckled, and plain-coloured. All of these may occur within the same population – often side-by-side with other species sharing similar phases – and are so different that it is hard to believe they all belong to *H. marmoratus*. This can make identification extremely difficult, since two similarly striped frogs from the same pond may belong to different species, while a striped frog and a heavily speckled one may belong to the same species.

There is little sexual dimorphism (in terms of colour) among frogs and toads: in most species, the males and females are very similar. The main exceptions are several toad species in the genus *Bufo*, an African reed frog called *Hyperolius hieroglyphicus* and Couch's spadefoot toad (*Scaphiopus couchi*).

> *Fire-bellied toads are unusual in having eyes with heart-shaped pupils.*

**Breathing through skin** All frogs and toads have functional lungs in the adult stage but they are also able to absorb oxygen through their skin (either from water or air). The species most efficient at breathing through its skin is the Lake Titicaca frog (*Telmatobius culeus*). It has a very folded and wrinkled appearance because the surface area of its skin has been greatly increased to maximize the area over which oxygen can diffuse. This enables the frog, if it so wishes, to stay underwater for the whole of its life.

**Most transparent** Some glass frogs (family Centrolenidae) look as if they were made of frosted glass – and are partially transparent when seen from below. Found in the cloud and rain-forests of Central and South America, these rather delicate frogs are usually green in colour above but have such transparent skin on their bellies that all their bones, muscles and internal organs are readily visible.

**Most threatened** The World Conservation Union (IUCN) lists a total of 130 frogs and toads which are known or suspected to be threatened with extinction (more are likely to be added to this list as research progresses). The survival of no fewer than 27 of these, including the Table Mountain ghost frog (*Heleophryne rosei*) from South Africa and the spotted frog (*Litoria spenceri*) from Australia, is considered unlikely if current threats continue to operate.

**Country with the most threatened species** Australia currently has 37 internationally threatened species of frogs and toads. Chile comes a fairly distant second with 21 known threatened species. These figures may reflect high levels of research as well as a high incidence of threatened species.

---

**The common toad holds two world records: one for the highest altitude and the other for the lowest.**

> *A chemical extracted from the skin of an Ecuadorian frog has turned out to be a painkiller 200 times more potent than morphine.*

**Extinctions** Four species of frog are known to have become extinct in recent years: the Israel painted frog (*Discoglossus nigriventer*), which used to live in Lake Huleh, Israel; the Vegas Valley leopard frog (*Rana fisheri*), which disappeared from its home in the USA in 1960; a species called *Arthroleptides dutoiti*, which lived on Mt Elgon, Kenya; and *Rana tlaloci*, which lived in Mexico. A further three species are suspected to have become extinct: the golden toad (*Bufo periglenes*) from Costa Rica, which was seen in 1987 when more than 1000 gathered in one area to mate and then again during a survey in 1990 which found only 11 (a recent drought is probably to blame for their disappearance); and the northern gastric brooding frog (*Rheobatrachus vitellinus*) and gastric brooding platypus frog (*R. silus*), both from Australia. One sub-species of anuran may also be extinct: the Italian spadefoot toad (*Pelobates fuscus*

**A M P H I B I A N S**

*insubricus*), which lived in Italy and Switzerland. It is likely that at least some other species and sub-species become extinct before the status of their populations has been properly assessed or even before they are known to science – and therefore go unrecorded.

**Highest and lowest altitude** The common toad (*Bufo bufo*) is a remarkable species holding two interesting amphibian records – for both the highest and the lowest altitude. The highest altitude record is held by an individual found at a height of 8000 m *26 246 ft* in the Himalayas. The lowest is for another individual found at a depth of 340 m *1115 ft* in a coal mine. A third possible record is of a common toad found by scuba divers in a flooded quarry in Leicestershire, UK: it was sitting, alive and well, on a stone at a depth of 22.5 m *74 ft* (where the water temperature was 8°C *46°F*).

**Most restricted range** Hamilton's frog (*Leiopelma hamiltoni*) has been found only on two offshore islands in Cook Strait, New Zealand. One population (discovered in 1919) lives among a pile of rocks known as 'Frog Bank' on Stephens Island; the second (discovered in 1958) lives in a small patch of forest on Maud Island.

The Mallorcan midwife toad (*Alytes muletensis*) also has a severely restricted range, occurring only in a few small colonies in crevices in limestone cliffs on the island of Mallorca, in the Mediterranean.

**Fastest spread** The cane or marine toad (*Bufo marinus*), a native of Central and South America, has spread throughout eastern and northern Australia in the space of just 50 years. In 1935, 100 adult toads were imported to control the greyback cane beetle (*Dermolepida albohirtum*), which was devastating sugar cane in Queensland. The toads laid more than 1.5 million eggs of which 62 000 hatched and reached young adult stage. These were released into the wild and the species quickly established a niche in Australia – a country with no native toads – and began to spread at a rate of up to 35 km *21¾ miles* per year. In some areas it has reached plague proportions and hundreds of squashed bodies litter the roads. Many experts are concerned for the native wildlife, because the toad does not only eat pests but has an appetite for almost anything of a suitable size that moves. It is also poisonous to eat – and has been known to kill small crocodiles, koalas, goannas, lizards, snakes and many other animals (in some cases within minutes of being swallowed).

**Highest species diversity** The highest species diversity known for frogs and toads is found in a small outpost called Santa Cecilia, in Ecuador's Amazon basin. A recent survey revealed a total of 81 species inhabiting a little over 1 ha *2.47 acres* of rainforest; this is approxi-

mately the same number of species known to be living in the entire USA. A team of scientists working in the Santa Cecilia area once collected an incredible 56 different frog and toad species in a single evening.

Central and South America is by far the richest region of the world for frogs and toads, having over one third of all known species and genera.

**Antibiotics** The toxins secreted by two species of toad – the African clawed toad (*Xenopus laevis*) and the yellow-bellied toad (*Bombina variegata*) – have been found to have antibiotic properties. These appear to be effective against a broad spectrum of disease-carrying bacteria that cause problems to other animals, including the famous food-poisoner found in the human gut, *Escherichia coli*. The secretions may enable the toads to be protected by their own medicines – the yellow-bellied toad, for example, lives in stagnant water and may need to protect itself against skin infections.

---

**The fastest range increase recorded for any frog or toad occurred after 100 adult cane toads were introduced to Australia, in 1935; within 50 years, they had reached plague proportions in many parts of the country.**

# NEWTS & SALAMANDERS

## Caudata
*c.* 355 species (330 salamanders and 25 newts)

**Earliest** The earliest known amphibian – and, indeed, the earliest known land vertebrate – is a species called *Ichthyostega*. Looking rather like a modern salamander (with four well-formed limbs and a long tail) but with many fish-like features as well, *Ichthyostega* appeared towards the end of the Devonian period some 360 million years ago. Found in Devonian deposits in Greenland, it was about 1 m *39 in* in length and is believed to have died out about 100 million years ago.

Despite many similarities between *Ichthyostega* and newts and salamanders, it was not the direct ancestor of modern amphibians. The earliest known caudate appeared during the late Triassic period about 200 million years ago.

**Largest** The largest amphibians are the giant salamanders (family Cryptobranchidae) of which there are three species. The record-holder is the Chinese giant salamander (*Andrias davidianus*), which lives in mountain streams in north-eastern, central and southern China. The average adult measures 1.14 m *45 in* in length and weighs 25–30 kg *55–66 lb*. One specimen collected in Hunan Province measured 1.8 m *71 in* in length and weighed 65 kg *143 lb*. Unfortunately, this species is considered to be a great delicacy in China and, as a result of hunting, has become highly endangered.

The Japanese giant salamander (*Andrias japonicus*), which lives in south-west Honshu and central Kyushu, Japan, can grow to a similar length but has a proportionately longer tail and therefore weighs considerably less. The third species is the hellbender (*Cryptobranchus alleganiensis*), which is the largest of the North American salamanders; however, it is less than half the size of its two Asian relatives, reaching a maximum length of only 74 cm *29.2 in*.

The largest land salamander is the tiger salamander (*Ambystoma tigrinum*) which can attain an overall length of 33 cm *13 in*.

**Largest prehistoric** During the late Triassic period, around 200 million years ago, there were a number of giant amphibians far exceeding modern species in size. The largest was the crocodile-sized *Mastodonsaurus*, which attained a length of 4 m *13 ft* from the tip of the snout to the end of the tail. Its skull alone was 1.25 m *49 in* long.

**Smallest** The world's smallest caudate is the Mexican lungless salamander (*Bolitoglossa mexicana*), which attains a maximum length of about 2.54 cm *1 in* including the tail.

**Oldest** The greatest age reliably recorded for an amphibian is 55 years for a Japanese giant salamander (*Andrias japonicus*), which died in Amsterdam Zoo, Netherlands, in 1881. Another individual at the same zoo was born there on 10 Nov 1903 and died on 6 Jul 1955 aged 51 years 7 months and 2 days.

**Longest gestation** The beautiful black-coloured alpine salamander (*Salamandra atra*), which lives in the alpine regions of Europe, notably in Switzerland, Bosnia, Croatia and Albania, has a gestation period of up to 38 months – the longest of any vertebrate. Individuals at high altitudes (above 1400 m *4600 ft*) tend to have the longest gestation period; those living at lower altitudes (below 600 m *1968 ft*) have the shortest recorded for this species of 24–26 months. One or two young are born, on land, usually within a few hours of each other.

*When many species of salamander lose an eye, limb or tail, their missing pieces may regenerate within a few months (though often in a different colour and, sometimes, in a different shape).*

**Least development** In some newts and salamanders, the larval stage never develops into a 'normal' adult capable of living on land, although it does become sexually mature and can reproduce (a condition called neoteny). The best-known example is the axolotl (*Ambystoma mexicanum*), which was once common in highland lakes of Mexico (it is rarer nowadays due to hunting for food and predation by introduced trout). This species looks rather like a giant newt tadpole (up to 25 cm *9.8 in* in length) and has small limbs, a vertically flattened tail and bright red, feathery gills. It is capable of metamorphosing into an adult terrestrial form – for example, if its water source dries up – but normally breeds in its aquatic form. The name 'axolotl' stems from an Aztec word meaning 'water monster'.

Other species with similar development restrictions include the North American mudpuppy (*Necturus maculosus*) and the European olm (*Proteus anguinus*), which lives in cold, underground limestone caves and rivers along the Adriatic coast of Italy and Croatia.

A small group of eel-like amphibians, called sirens, are permanent larvae which retain external gills throughout their lives and have small front legs but no hind legs. They are so strange that some scientists classify them in a separate, fourth group of amphibians; normally, however, they are classified with the newts and salamanders (in the family Sirenidae). There are only three species, living in the south-eastern USA and Mexico, and they range in size from about 25 cm *9.8 in* in the tiny dwarf siren (*Pseudobranchus striatus*) to more than 90 cm *35½ in* in the greater siren (*Siren lacertina*).

**Strangest ribs** The sharp-ribbed salamander (*Pleurodeles waltl*), which lives

*In some mountain forests of eastern North America, there are so many salamanders that their total mass may exceed that of all the birds and mammals put together.*

in Morocco and parts of south and west Iberia, has a row of wart-like protruberances along its flanks. These mark the points where the ends of the ribs push against the animal's skin. In some individuals, the ribs actually poke through the skin (looking like rows of teeth) and the ends may be so sharp that they can easily draw blood if the salamanders are handled. It is uncertain why the ribs protrude, but it may be a form of defence to prevent the 30 cm *12 in* long animal from being swallowed by its many predators.

The spiny newt (*Echinotriton andersoni*), which lives in China, has a similar system. If it is grabbed by a predator, its long, sharp-pointed ribs push out through poison glands in the skin and give the attacker an intensely painful injection in the mouth.

**Cannibalism** The alpine salamander (*Salamandra atra*), which lives in the

---

**The Chinese giant salamander holds the record as the largest amphibian in the world; one outstanding specimen measured 1.8 m *71 in* in length.**

alpine regions of Europe, is the only amphibian whose young are cannibalistic before birth. The female carries as many as 60 fertilized eggs in her body, but most of them are devoured by the first few embryos as they develop. She finally gives birth to between one and four young.

The Arizona tiger salamander (*Ambystoma tigerinum nebulosum*) is often cannibalistic. The individuals which eat their own kind (some grow into relatively benign omnivores while others are predominantly carnivorous) are more heavily armed with elongated curved teeth and a wider head than their unfortunate contemporaries. Strangely, the cannibals are quite choosy about who they eat, preferring to dine on their more distant relatives than their next of kin.

**Most poisonous** Many newts and salamanders secrete poisons from numerous poison glands in their skin. In some species, this poison is quite mild and either acts as an irritant or simply makes the animal taste unpleasant. But in other species it can be extremely toxic. The skin, muscles and blood of the California newt (*Taricha torosa*) contain the highly

toxic substance tetrodotoxin, a powerful nerve poison also found in puffer fish and some other animals. Indeed, this toxin is so powerful that one tiny drop is sufficient to kill several thousand mice (although the newt itself is immune to extremely high concentrations).

**Poison spraying** The painted salamander (*Ensatina eschscholtzi*) of the western USA is the only caudate known to spray noxious chemicals to repel its predators. The 15–18 cm *6–7 in* long animal secretes a powerful, milky neurotoxin from glands at the base of the tail which it can squirt with considerable accuracy over a distance of at least 2.1 m *7 ft*. It shifts its body to direct the spray – frequently towards the attacker's face and, in particular, the eyes; in people, a direct hit causes excruciating pain and even temporary blindness. The only other amphibian known to be able to do this is the cane or marine toad (*Bufo marinus*), which can squirt toxic secretions from its paratoid glands (just behind the head) into the eyes or mouth of a predator from as far as 1 m *39 in* away. It is expected that other poison-spraying amphibians will be discovered as research progresses.

The strange-looking axolotl is unusual because it becomes sexually mature, and can reproduce, in the larval stage.

**Hardiest** Many salamanders are capable of withstanding extremely cold conditions, but the Siberian salamander (*Hynobius keyserlingii*) is often called the hardiest in the world. This 10 cm *4 in* long creature lives across the length of Russia, in marshes and ponds throughout the huge belt of conifer and birch forest, where the winter temperatures fall as low as –56°C *–68°F*. It is unable to burrow deep into the soil to escape the cold because of the permafrost and, consequently, is frequently trapped in the frozen soil and water near the surface. When warmer weather arrives, it literally 'thaws out' and for the duration of the summer its life resembles that of other salamanders.

**Most vegetarian** The Santa Cruz climbing salamander (*Aneides flavipunctus niger*), which lives in the Santa Cruz Mountains on the west coast of the

USA, is the only salamander known to eat vegetable matter intentionally (although it eats insects and other animals as well). It feeds on pieces of fungus, which it rips from the bark of trees. It is uncertain whether this unlikely food is a direct source of nutrients or if the salamander is benefiting more from the numerous bacteria which coat it.

**Most threatened** The World Conservation Union (IUCN) lists a total of 39 salamanders which are known or suspected to be threatened with extinction (more are likely to be added to this list as research progresses). The survival of five of these is considered unlikely if current threats continue operating: Abe's salamander (*Hynobius abei*) and the Hokuriku salamander (*H. takedai*), both of which live on the island of Honshu, Japan; and the desert slender salamander (*Batrachoseps aridus*), the shenandoah salamander (*Plethodon shenandoah*) and the Texas blind salamander (*Typhlomolge rathbuni*), all of which live in the USA. No salamanders or newts are known to have become extinct in recent years, although it is likely that at least some species and sub-species become extinct before the status of their populations has been properly assessed or even before they are known to science – and therefore go unrecorded.

The great crested newt (*Triturius cristatus*) is the only newt species con-sidered to be internationally threatened and is now protected by the European Community Habitats and Species Directive.

**Country with the most threatened species** The USA currently has 14 internationally threatened species of salamander which is more than any other country in the world. Italy comes a fairly distant second with eight known threatened species and Japan third with seven. These figures may reflect high levels of research as well as a high incidence of threatened species.

**Most restricted distribution** A number of newts and salamanders have very restricted ranges. The strangely named Peaks of Otter salamander (*Plethodon hubrichti*) probably has the most limited distribution of any known species. It lives along a 19 km *11.8 miles* stretch in the Blue Ridge Mountains in the state of Virginia, USA. A survey conducted in 1991 estimated a population density of up to 4.5 salamanders per m² in optimum areas.

**Most widely distributed** The Siberian salamander (*Hynobius keyserlingii*) has the largest continuous distribution of any newt or salamander. It is found in marshes and ponds across the entire length of Russia, from the western foothills of the Ural Mountains to the Bering Strait.

# FISHES

## Chondrichthes, Osteichthyes & Agnatha
*c.* 24 000 species (approx. 100 new species discovered every year)

> There are as
> many species of fish as
> all the amphibians, reptiles,
> birds and mammals
> put together.

**Earliest** The earliest fossil fish – and, indeed, the earliest known vertebrates (animals with backbones) – date from the late Cambrian/early Ordovician period, some 515 million years ago. Known as conodonts, they were up to 4.5 cm *1.8 in* long with teeth up to about 2 mm *0.08 in* long. The presence of teeth is highly significant, allowing them for the first time to bite and chew on food items that were too large to swallow in a single gulp, and making them the earliest of our own ancestors. The first complete fossil conodont was discovered in a coal seam near Edinburgh, UK, in 1983.

**The world's largest fish is the whale shark, which has been verified at lengths of more than 12 m *39 ft 4 in* and may even approach 18 m *59 ft* in exceptional cases.**

**Largest** The world's largest fish is the whale shark (*Rhincodon typus*), which is found in tropical and warm temperate waters of the Atlantic, Pacific and Indian Oceans. There have been many claims of specimens in the 17–18 m *56–59 ft* range and it is likely that this is the maximum attainable length of this species. However, most experts believe that the majority of whale sharks never exceed a length of 12 m *39 ft 5 in*. Few have actually been caught and weighed or measured and, consequently, the majority of records are based on unauthenticated visual assessments (which are notoriously unreliable). It is especially difficult to estimate the length of a large animal in the water and, unfortunately, the tendency is to overestimate. The largest scientifically measured specimen was captured off Baba Island, near Karachi, Pakistan, on 11 Nov 1949. It was 12.65 m *41½ ft* long and 7 m *23 ft* around the thickest part of

the body; its weight was estimated to be 15–21 tonnes. Despite its enormous size, the whale shark feeds on plankton and is harmless and unaggressive by nature.

The basking shark (*Cetorhinus maximus*), which is most common in the North Atlantic but can also be found in temperate waters in the South Atlantic and Pacific, is the world's second largest fish. Circumstantial evidence suggests a maximum length of approximately 14–15 m *46–49 ft* but, despite several claims for specimens of this length and even longer, there are no authenticated records. The largest accurately measured individual on record is a 12.3 m *40¼ ft* basking shark which became entangled in a herring-gill net in Musquash Harbour, Bay of Fundy, New Brunswick, Canada, on 6 Aug 1851. An 11.12 m *36½ ft* specimen was washed ashore at Brighton, East Sussex, UK, in 1806. Like its larger relative,

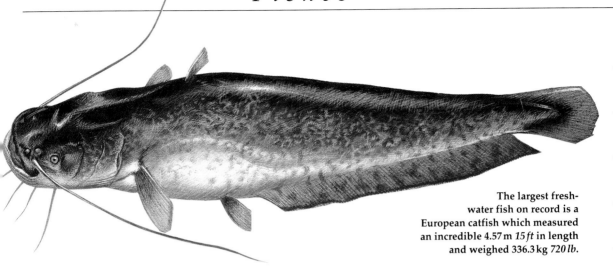

**F
I
S
H
E
S**

**The largest fresh-water fish on record is a European catfish which measured an incredible 4.57 m *15 ft* in length and weighed 336.3 kg *720 lb*.**

the basking shark is a harmless plankton feeder.

**Largest predatory** The largest predatory fish (excluding plankton-eaters) is the comparatively rare great white or white pointer shark (*Carcharodon carcharias*), which is most abundant in the cool, temperate waters of North America, southern Africa, and southern and western Australia, as well as New Zealand, Chile, Japan, and parts of the Mediterranean and Adriatic. Adult specimens (females are larger than males) average 4.3–4.6 m *14–15 ft* in length and generally weigh 522–771 kg *1150–1700 lb*. Stories about the size of great whites have often been greatly exaggerated and there are many claims of huge specimens in the 6–7.5 m *20–25 ft* range; some writers and fishermen even quote lengths in excess of 10 m *33 ft*. However, under close scrutiny, most of these claims prove to be either wild exaggerations or genuine mistakes; and, unfortunately, the few remaining records may never be properly authenticated. Therefore the difficulty is that, while there is plenty of circumstantial evidence to suggest that great whites grow to more than 6 m *20 ft* in length, reliable measurements are virtually non-existent. Consequently, there is no single universally accepted record. There are several verified lengths of 5.9 m *19 ft 4 in* but, in general terms, the largest great white accepted by a significant number of experts is probably a 7.01 m *23 ft* specimen caught by Alfred Cutajar off the island of Malta, in the Mediterranean, in 1987.

There are two widely published records which deserve a mention. A female great white shark caught off Castillo de Cojimar, Cuba, in May 1945, after taking a baited hook attached to a floating oil drum, reputedly measured 6.4 m *21 ft* in length and weighed an estimated 3314 kg *7300 lb*. However,

photographs of this individual were re-evaluated in 1987 and show conclusively that it was no more than 5 m *16½ ft* long. Some years later, in June 1978, another female was harpooned and landed by fishermen in the harbour of San Miguel, Azores, and was claimed to be 8.9 m *29 ft 3 in* long; unfortunately, detailed research by shark expert Richard Ellis in the 1980s proved this record to be a gross exaggeration.

The only other 'predatory' shark species known or suspected to approach a length of 6.1 m *20 ft* are the tiger shark (*Galeocerdo cuvier*), Greenland shark (*Somniosus microcephalus*), Pacific sleeper shark (*Somniosus pacificus*), thresher shark (*Alopias vulpinus*) and the great hammerhead (*Sphyrna mokarran*).

**Largest bony** The longest of the bony or 'true' fish (class Osteichthyes) is the oarfish (*Regalecus glesne*), which has a worldwide distribution in temperate and tropical seas. It is a striking fish, looking rather like a flattened silvery band with a red crest and a long red fin along its back. A specimen seen swimming off Asbury Park, New Jersey, USA, by a team of scientists from the Sandy Hook Marine Laboratory on 18 Jul 1963, was estimated to measure 15.2 m *50 ft* in length. Although this is purely an estimate, it is accepted by many experts because it was seen by experienced observers who, at the time, were aboard the 26 m *85 ft* research vessel *Challenger*, which gave them a

*Lemon sharks have been taught to ring bells and even swim through mazes to receive rewards of food.*

yardstick for measuring the fish's length. With regard to scientifically measured records, there are a number of oarfish exceeding 7 m *23 ft* in length; for example, in *c*. 1885, a specimen 7.6 m *25 ft* long, weighing 272 kg *600 lb*, was caught by fishermen off Pemaquid Point, Maine, USA.

The heaviest and broadest bony fish in the world is the ocean sunfish (*Mola mola*), which is found in all tropical, sub-tropical and temperate waters. The average size of an adult specimen is 1.8 m *6 ft* from the tip of the snout to the end of the tail fin (horizontal length) and 2.4 m *7 ft 10 in* between the tip of the dorsal fin and the tip of the anal fin (vertical length); the average weight is up to 1 tonne. On 18 Sep 1908 a specimen was accidentally struck by the SS *Fiona* off Bird Island about 65 km *40 miles* from Sydney, New South Wales, Australia, and towed to Port Jackson. It measured 3.1 m *10 ft* in horizontal length and 4.26 m *14 ft* in vertical length and weighed 2235 kg *4927 lb* – and was the largest specimen ever recorded.

The Russian sturgeon or 'beluga' (*Huso huso*) has also been known to grow to an enormous size, especially in former times when it was more abundant. The largest specimen on record was a gravid female caught in the estuary of the Volga in 1827, which measured 7.3 m *24 ft* in length and weighed 1474 kg *3249 lb*, though the average size for this species is considerably less. A monster sturgeon widely reported in 1992 to be 'as big as a minibus', which was reputedly caught in the Yangtze River, China, turned out to be a hoax by a junior reporter working for a Chinese news agency; it is unknown if he is still working for the agency.

**Largest freshwater** The largest fish spending its whole life in fresh or brackish water is the rare pla buk or pa beuk (*Pangasianodon gigas*), found only in the

**FISHES**

Mekong River and its major tributaries in China, Laos, Cambodia and Thailand. The largest specimen, captured in the River Ban Mee Noi, Thailand, was reportedly 3 m *9 ft 10¼ in* long and weighed 242 kg *533½ lb*.

However, the individual record for the largest freshwater fish is held by a European or wels catfish (*Silurus glanis*), which was caught in the Dnieper River, Russia, in the 19th century, and was 4.57 m *15 ft* in length and weighed 336.3 kg *720 lb*. The European catfish used to grow to an exceptional size before it was heavily fished – there were often sinister reports of the largest specimens eating small dogs and even children – but nowadays anything over 1.83 m *6 ft* and 90 kg *200 lb* is considered large.

Sturgeons (family Acipenseridae) are also strong contenders, although some live in the sea and only breed in freshwater. The largest species are the white sturgeon (*Acipenser transmontanus*) of North America, the Russian beluga (*Huso huso*) and the Kaluga sturgeon (*Huso dauricus*). The longest on record was a white sturgeon caught in the Columbia River, USA and Canada, in 1912, which was 3.8 m *12½ ft* long and weighed 580 kg *1280 lb*. A number of individuals, of several species, have been recorded with weights in excess of 1000 kg *2205 lb*.

The arapaima or pirarucu (*Arapaima gigas*), from the Amazon and other South American rivers, is often claimed to be the largest freshwater fish in the world. However, the largest authentically recorded specimen, which was caught in the Rio Negro, Brazil, in 1836, measured 'only' 2.48 m *8 ft 1½ in* in length and weighed 147 kg *325 lb*. The average size for this species is 2 m *6½ ft* in length and 68 kg *150 lb* in weight.

The longest eel ever recorded was a 3.7 m *12 ft 2 in* leopard moray eel (*Gymnothorax flavimarginatus*) found in the Coomera River, Queensland, Australia. Its body was said to be as thick as a man's thigh.

**Largest prehistoric** No known prehistoric fish grew significantly larger than either the whale shark (*Rhincodon typus*) or the basking shark (*Cetorhinus maximus*), the two largest species alive today. However, a prehistoric shark called megalodon (*Carcharodon megalodon*) – an extinct relative of the modern great white shark (*Carcharodon carcharias*) – was by far the largest known predatory (as opposed to plankton-feeding) shark known to have lived on Earth. Recent studies suggest that it attained a maximum length of 13.7 m *45 ft*, although the size of megalodon has been a subject for discussion since the first fossil teeth were found in the early 1800s. Some length estimates have ranged up to about 30 m *98½ ft*, but many of the early assumptions made are now known to have been in error. All estimates are based on ratios from fossil teeth (which are up to 17.8 cm *7 in* measured from the tip along one edge to the base) since these are the only evidence currently available for the existence of such an extraordinary species. Megalodon abounded in the world's oceans during the middle and late Tertiary, some 4.5–50 million years ago.

The sailfish is probably the fastest fish over short distances, with a maximum speed in excess of 100 km/h *62 mph*.

**Smallest** The shortest recorded fish (and, indeed, the shortest known vertebrate) is the marine dwarf goby *Trimmatom nanus* of the Chagos Archipelago in the central Indian Ocean. Average lengths recorded for a series of 92 specimens collected by the 1978–79 Joint Services Chagos Research Expedition of the British Armed Forces were 8.6 mm *0.34 in* for males and 8.9 mm *0.35 in* for females.

The shortest fish (and, again, the shortest known vertebrate) in Europe is another goby, *Economidichthys trichonis*, which was recently discovered in western Greece; the female is only 2.7 cm *1.06 in* long, the male just a little bigger.

**Smallest shark** The spined pygmy shark or dwarf shark (*Squaliolus laticaudus*), which is widely distributed in deep, tropical waters, is probably the world's smallest shark. The male matures at a length of only 15 cm *5.9 in* (females at 18 cm *7.1 in*) and older adults can reach a maximum length of only 25 cm *9.8 in*.

Approximately half of all living sharks are less than 1 m *39 in* in length

The South American arapaima is often claimed to be the largest freshwater fish in the world, although many 'records' appear to have been exaggerated.

and, not surprisingly, there are several other possible contenders for the title of smallest shark. In particular, the pygmy ribbontail catshark (*Eridacnis radcliffei*), a deep water inhabitant of the Indian Ocean and parts of the South Pacific, matures at 18 cm *7.1 in* (males) and 16 cm *6.3 in* (females); and the dwarf dogshark (*Etmopterus perryi*), a deep water inhabitant of the Caribbean Sea that was only described in 1985, matures at 16–17 cm *6.3–6.7 in* (males) and 19–20 cm *7.5–7.9 in* (females).

**Smallest freshwater fish** The shortest and lightest freshwater fish is the dwarf pygmy goby (*Pandaka pygmaea*), a colourless and nearly transparent species found in the streams and lakes of Luzon in the Philippines. Males are only 7.5–9.9 mm *0.28–0.38 in* long and weigh 0.004–0.005 g *0.00014–0.00018 oz*.

**Smallest commercial fish** The world's smallest commercial fish is the now endangered sinarapan (*Mistichthys luzonensis*), a goby found only in Lake Buhi, Luzon, Philippines. Males are 1–1.3 cm *0.39–0.51 in* long. It has been estimated that a dried 454 g *1 lb* fish cake would

contain about 70 000 of these tiny fish.

**Lightest vertebrate** The lightest of them all and the smallest catch possible for any fisherman is the dwarf goby *Schindleria praematurus*, from Samoa, which weighs only 0.002 g (equivalent to 14 184 to the ounce) and is 12–19 mm *½–¾ in* long.

**Longest fin** All three species of thresher shark (family Alopiidae) have a huge scythe-shaped caudal fin (tail fin) which is roughly as long as the body itself. The largest and commonest species, *Alopias vulpinus*, which is found worldwide in temperate and tropical seas, may grow to a length of 6 m *19 ft 8 in* of which almost 3 m *9 ft 10 in* consists of this greatly elongated upper tail fin; the body itself is rather sleek and relatively small. Also known as the thrasher or whiptailed shark, the thresher is believed to use its extraordinary tail to herd and then stun schools of milling fish ready for eating (although this behaviour is speculative and has never been observed in the wild).

**Strongest bite** Experiments carried out with a 'Snodgrass gnathodynamometer' (shark-bite meter) at the Lerner Marine Laboratory in Bimini, Bahamas, revealed that a 2 m *6 ft 6¾ in* long dusky shark (*Carcharhinus obscurus*) could

exert a force of 60 kg *132 lb* between its jaws. This is equivalent to a pressure of 3 tonnes/cm$^2$ or *19.6 tons/in$^2$* at the tips of its teeth. The bite of a larger shark such as the great white (*Carcharodon carcharias*) must be considerably more spectacular, but it has never been measured.

**Fastest** The cosmopolitan sailfish (*Istiophorus platypterus*) is considered to be the fastest species of fish over short distances, although practical difficulties make accurate measurements extremely difficult to secure. This large oceanic fish has a torpedo-shaped body and is streamlined for fast swimming. In a series of speed trials carried out at Long Key Fishing Camp, Florida, USA, one sailfish took out 91 m *300 ft* of line in three seconds, which is equivalent to a velocity of 109 km/h *68 mph* (cf 96 km/h *60 mph* for the cheetah on land).

Some American fishermen believe that the bluefin tuna (*Thunnus thynnus*) is the fastest fish in the sea, and bursts of speed up to 104 km/h *64.6 mph* have been claimed for this species; however, the highest authenticated speed recorded to date is 70 km/h *43.4 mph* in a 20 second dash. The marlin (*Makaira sp*), yellowfin tuna (*Thunnus albacares*) and the wahoo (*Acanthocybium solandri*) are also extremely fast, having been timed at 80 km/h *50 mph*, 74.6 km/h *46.4 mph* and 77.1 km/h *47.9 mph* respectively during 10–20 second sprints.

Most sharks are slow swimmers (even the larger species normally cruise at 1–4 km/h *0.6–2.5 mph*) but many of them are capable of rapid bursts of speed when chasing prey. The fastest shark is believed to be the 2.4–3.9 m *8–13 ft* shortfin mako (*Isurus oxyrinchus*) which may be able to attain speeds of up to 88.5 km/h *55 mph*.

**Slowest** The slowest-moving marine fish are the sea horses (family Syngnathidae) of which there are about 35 species. Their swimming ability is severely limited by a rigid body structure and, indeed, the only parts which can be moved rapidly are the pectoral fins on either side of the back of the head and the dorsal fin along the back. The major source of propulsion is the wave motion of the dorsal fin: this makes a ripple which drives the fish

**The oldest fish on record is an 88-year-old female European eel which died in 1948.**

forward in an erect posture. In still water, some of the smaller species such as the dwarf sea horse (*Hippocampus zosterae*), which reaches a maximum length of only 4.2 cm *1.7 in*, probably never attain speeds of more than 0.016 km/h *0.01 mph*. Sea horses are incapable of swimming against the current and, to avoid being swept away, hang on to coral and marine plants with their prehensile tails.

**Longest migration** Many fish species undertake long annual migrations, for example between their breeding grounds and favoured feeding grounds. However, it is very difficult to ascertain the maximum distances covered either by different species or by record-breaking individuals. The longest straight-line distance known to have been covered by a fish is 9335 km *5800 miles* for a bluefin tuna (*Thunnus thynnus*) which was dart-tagged off Baja California, Mexico, in 1958, and caught

*In April 1991 South Africa became the first country in the world to ban the killing of the great white shark – which is threatened throughout much of its range by commercial and recreational fishing.*

483 km *300 miles* south of Tokyo, Japan, in April 1963. During its journey, its weight increased from 16 kg *35 lb* to 121 kg *267 lb*.

**Longest flight** No species of fish is capable of true flight but several are able to glide over the surface of the water. Flying fish in the family Exocoetidae, which have specially adapted pectoral (and sometimes pelvic) fins, are the record-holders in terms of long-distance flying. Depending on the wind and sea conditions, some species are able to remain airborne for as long as 30–40 seconds, can reach a height of up to 10 m *33 ft* (when they catch good air currents) and are able to cover a distance of more than 400 m *1312 ft*. They normally fly when they are being pursued by predators, and can launch themselves into the air at speeds of up to 30 km/h *18.6 mph* with a rapid flick of the tail; if they are still being chased when they begin to fall back into the water they flick their tail again and are quickly launched into another flight. When flying fish are swimming, their enormous fan-like fins are folded away against the body.

Small river-dwelling South American hatchet fish in the genus *Carnegiella* possess powerful pectoral fin muscles and have been reported beating their fins up and down as if they were flapping true wings. Although there is speculation that this may represent the beginning of true flight, hatchet fish rarely travel for distances of more than about 10 m *33 ft* above the surface.

**Oldest** There is little reliable information on the maximum attainable age of

fish in the wild and, consequently, most records are for individuals which have been kept in captivity for extended periods. The oldest fish on record is an 88-year-old female European eel (*Anguilla anguilla*) named 'Putte', which used to live in the aquarium at Hälsingborg Museum, Sweden. She was allegedly born in 1860 in the Sargasso Sea, North Atlantic, and was caught in a river as a 3-year-old elver. She died in 1948.

It is possible to *estimate* the age of wild fish through long-term tagging studies or by counting the growth rings in their scales and bones. Growth ring research suggests that the lake sturgeon (*Acipenser fulvescens*) of North America is one of the longest-lived species in the wild. In one study of the growth rings in the largest ray of the pectoral fin of 966 specimens caught in the Lake Winnebago region, Wisconsin, USA, between 1951 and 1954, the oldest sturgeon was found to be a male (length 2.01 m *6 ft 7 in*), which gave a reading of 82 years. There are several unauthenticated claims for even older lake sturgeon, notably a specimen caught in 1953 which was estimated to be 154 years old.

In July 1974 a growth-ring count of 228 years was reported for a female ornamental koi (*Cyprinus carpio*), named *Hanako*, living in a pond in Higashi Shirakawa, Gifu Prefecture, Japan, but the greatest authoritatively accepted age for this species is little more than 50 years.

Most sharks are believed to have a lifespan of approximately 20–40 years, but the spiny dogfish (*Squalus acanthias*) has been reasonably estimated to live for more than 70 years and may even reach 100 years in certain North Pacific populations. A similar figure is sometimes suggested for the great white shark (*Carcharodon carcharias*).

**Oldest goldfish** Goldfish (*Carassius auratus*) have been reported to live for over 50 years in China, although there are few authenticated records. A goldfish named Fred, owned by A.R. Wilson of Worthing, West Sussex, UK, died on 1 Aug 1980 aged 41 years.

**Shortest lived** The shortest-lived fish are probably certain species of killifish (family Aplocheilidae), which are found in Africa. They normally live for about 8 months in the wild.

**Most abundant** The most abundant fish is probably the 7.6 cm *3 in* long deep-sea bristlemouth (*Cyclothone elongata*), which has a worldwide distribution (except for the Arctic). It would take about 500 of them to weigh 0.45 kg *1 lb*.

**Most abundant shark** The commonest member of the shark family is the spurdog or spiny dogfish (*Squalus acanthias*), which grows to a maximum length of about 1.6 m *63 in* and is found in temperate and cold waters worldwide. Over the years, this species has supported important fisheries in sev-

eral countries: the record catch was probably in 1904–05 when some 27 million spiny dogfish were taken off the coast of Massachusetts, USA, alone.

**Most restricted range** The devil's hole pupfish (*Cyprinodon diabolis*) is confined to a small part of a spring-fed pool (known as Devil's Hole) in Ash Meadows, Nevada, western USA (although a small number have been recently translocated to another spring nearby). It is believed to have the most restricted range of any vertebrate on Earth. Measuring about 20 m *65½ ft* long and 2.5–3.1 m *8¼–10 ft* wide, the pool is in the middle of an otherwise waterless desert. It is about 15 m *49 ft 2 in* below ground level and was once part of a water-filled cave – until the roof collapsed many years ago and exposed it to the desert sun. The pupfish depends for its food on a limited supply of invertebrates living in the algae on a rock shelf just 6 m *19 ft 8 in* long and 3 m *9 ft 10 in* wide, which lies just below the water surface. Fortunately, its precarious home is within a protected area in the Death Valley National Monument. However, its future survival depends on the maintenance of the water table (if the rock shelf is exposed its food supply will be destroyed) and, already, this has been affected by distant pumping of subterranean water. The total population varies

from 200–500, depending on local conditions.

**Rarest** It is almost impossible to identify the world's rarest fish: many species have yet to be discovered and the populations of others are completely unknown. However, a number of species are known from just one or, at most, a handful of specimens. For example, the largespine velvet dogfish (*Centroscymnus macracanthus*) is known from just one specimen found in the Straits of Magellan at the turn of the century; the comb-toothed lantern shark (*Etmopterus decacuspidatus*) is known from only one specimen described in 1966; and the enormous megamouth (*Megachasma pelagios*) is known from only six specimens (*see Longest unknown to science*).

The percid fish *Romanichthys valsanicola* survives only in a 1 km *0.6 mile* stretch of stream in Romania; a survey in 1993 found only eight survivors.

**Most threatened** According to the World Conservation Union (IUCN), no fewer than 979 fish species (4 per cent of the world total) are known or

---

The deep-sea bristlemouth is probably the most abundant species of fish in the world.

> *Sharks have a never-ending 'conveyor-belt' of new teeth which replace older ones throughout their lives: whenever an old tooth is lost, a new one moves forward from behind to replace it; a single shark may lose many thousands of teeth in its lifetime.*

suspected to be threatened with extinction (more species are likely to be added to this list as research progresses). No fewer than 158 of these are considered to be in particularly serious danger, including the Dalmatian barble-gudgeon (*Aulopyge hugeli*) from Yugoslavia and the Cape Fear shiner (*Notropis mekistocholas*), from the USA. These figures include 252 species of Lake Victoria cichlids in the family Cichlidae (*see Country with the most threatened species*). The many threats to fish worldwide include habitat destruction, commercial fishing, sports fishing, the aquarium trade, pollution and the careless introduction of predators and competitors from other parts of the world.

**Country with the most threatened species** The USA harbours more internationally threatened fish than any other country in the world, with a total of 174 (although this figure may reflect high levels of research as well as a high incidence of threatened species).

This does not take into account 252 species of Lake Victoria cichlids in the family Cichlidae, for which there is insufficient data on the range and status of individual species. The introduction of the Nile perch (*Lates niloticus*) into the lake (which is shared by Kenya, Tanzania and Uganda) in 1960 was an unmitigated disaster for the endemic fish already present. The perch is a voracious predator and, with a maximum length of 2 m *79 in*, is Africa's largest freshwater fish.

**Extinctions** A total of 33 fish species are known or suspected to have become extinct since 1600. These include (with year of extinction in brackets) the Miller Lake lamprey (*Lampetra minima*) (USA 1953); the Mexican dace (*Evarra tlahuacensis*) (1970); the New Zealand grayling (*Prototroctes oxyrhynchus*) (1920s); and the deepwater cisco (*Coregonus johannae*) (Great Lakes, Canada and USA 1955). It is likely that other species may have become extinct before the status of their populations had been properly assessed or even before they were known to science – and therefore went unrecorded.

**Survival out of water** The six species of lungfish (families Lepidosirenidae, Protopteridae and Ceratodidae), which can reach a length of up to 1.5 m *59 in*, live in freshwater swamps that frequently dry out for months or even years at a time. One species is found in the Amazon region of South America, one in the Mary and Burnett Rivers of northern Queensland, Australia, and

**Shark fins for sale on a market stall in Sri Lanka: the future of many shark populations is threatened by the wasteful trade in their fins.**

**The coelacanth 'went missing' for about 65 million years: formerly known only from fossilized remains, it was unexpectedly rediscovered in 1938 and nearly 200 specimens have been found since.**

four in west, central and southern Africa. In adverse conditions, they can all survive for long periods out of water, but two of the African lungfish are considered to be the real experts. As the water recedes, they burrow deep into the ground and secrete a mucus to form a moisture-saving cocoon around their bodies. Then they build a porous mud plug at the entrance to the burrow, curl up – and wait. Abandoning gill-breathing in favour of their air-breathing lungs, they can live for up to 4 years in this dormant condition until the rains finally return. As water fills the swamp again, they come to life within the space of a few hours, wriggle out of their burrow and swim away.

A number of other fish are able to survive varying lengths of time out of water, provided their skin can remain moist. The European eel (*Anguilla anguilla*), the walking catfish (*Clarias batrachus*) and the climbing perch or gourami (*Anabas testudineus*) are among them. Mudskippers (family Gobiidae) are probably the best known and, indeed, spend most of their time out of water. They live in the tropical mudflats and mangrove swamps of Africa, south-east Asia and Australasia, where they scurry and leap about on the mud and will even climb up the roots of mangrove trees. They breathe by way of an 'aqualung', in the form of water kept in their large gill chambers, and can also absorb some oxygen directly from the air through their moist skin; this means that they have to return to the water every few minutes to wet their skin and to take a fresh mouthful of water.

**Longest absence** The coelacanth (*Latimeria chalumnae*) is a large, deep-water fish that 'went missing' for about 65 million years. Formerly known only from fossilized remains some 65–400 million years old, it was assumed to have become extinct at around the same time as the dinosaurs. Then completely out of the blue, on 22 Dec 1938, a coelacanth was captured in a trawler's net off the mouth of the Chalumna River, near East London, South Africa, at a depth of 67 m *220 ft*. The scientific world was stunned: the discovery was almost equivalent to finding a living dinosaur and many experts considered it to be the zoological find of the century. Several years passed before another specimen was caught, this time by a fisherman 1600 km *994 miles* away off the coast of the Comoros, an isolated archipelago north-west of Madagascar in the Indian Ocean. Further research revealed that the local fishermen had been hauling in the odd coelacanth for many years and, indeed, almost all 200 coelacanths found since 1938 have come from the Comoros. The only exceptions have been, ironically, the 1938 discovery itself and one caught in August 1991 off the coast of Quelimane, Mozambique. None of the caught coelacanths have survived for more than a few minutes or, in exceptional cases, a few hours.

A living coelacanth was observed under water for the first time in 1987, by German biologist Hans Fricke. He had been searching for the fish off the Comoros Islands from a specially designed, two-man submarine at a depth of about 200 m *656 ft*. Professor Fricke and his colleagues have since observed live coelacanths on a number of occasions, including groups of up to 10 hiding away in caves at depths of 180–250 m *590–820 ft*.

The living coelacanth, which grows up to 1.9 m *6¼ ft* in length, does not differ significantly from its fossil coun-

terparts and has been dubbed a 'living fossil'. Some scientists believe that its muscular, paddle-like fins may hold clues to the crucial stage of evolution when aquatic creatures first developed limbs and took to the land.

**Longest unknown to science** The megamouth (*Megachasma pelagios*) holds the world record for being the biggest surviving animal to remain unknown to science for the longest. This strange plankton-feeding shark, with an exceptionally large mouth, rubbery lips and thousands of tiny teeth, was discovered for the first time on 15 Nov 1976. The naval research vessel *AFB-14*, operating in deep water (4600 m *15 088 ft*) some 42 km *26 miles* north-east of Oahu, Hawaii, deployed two parachutes as sea anchors at a depth of about 165 m *540 ft*. When the chutes were hauled to the surface, one of them had been swallowed by a bizarre-looking member of this species. It proved to be a male and was some 4.46 m *14 ft 8 in* in length and 750 kg *1653 lb* in weight. A second individual was caught by commercial fishermen off Catalina Island, southern California, USA, on 29 Nov 1984. The megamouth is so unlike any other known species of fish that it has been assigned a family of its own: Megachasmidae.

A healthy megamouth was seen for the first time on 21 Oct 1990, when a fisherman caught one alive off Dana Point, southern California, USA, and towed it into the harbour. On 23 October, after hordes of ichthyologists had studied it and film crews had filmed it, the shark was released back into the Pacific.

The first ever female megamouth – and the seventh specimen known – was washed up in Hakata Bay, Kyushu, Japan, in November 1944.

**Freshwater sharks** Sharks are geared to life in the sea, but several are able

to tolerate brackish water for short periods and two are known to spend a significant amount of time in freshwater: the bull shark (*Carcharhinus leucas*) and the Ganges shark (*Glyphis gangeticus*). The bull shark is found further from the sea – up to 3700 km *2300 miles* away in the upper Amazon – than any other member of the family. It is found in many other rivers, including the Hooghly, the Zambezi and the Mississippi, and was once believed to be land-locked in Lake Nicaragua, Central America, but is now known to negotiate rapids and return to the sea. The relatively rare Ganges shark is known only from the Ganges and Hooghly Rivers in India, and possibly in nearby inshore waters; it has a terrible reputation for man-eating, but most human deaths attributed to it are probably caused by the bull shark.

**Deepest** Brotulids of the genus *Bassogigas* are generally regarded as being the deepest-living vertebrates. The greatest depth from which one of these fish has been recovered is 8300 m *27 230 ft* in the Puerto Rico Trench (8366 m *27 488 ft*) in the Atlantic, by Dr Gilbert L. Voss of the US research vessel *John Elliott*, who captured a 16.5 cm *6½ in* long *Bassogigas profundissimus* in April 1970. It was only the fifth such brotulid ever caught.

Dr Jacques Piccard and Lt Don Walsh of the US Navy reported seeing a sole-like fish about 33 cm *1 ft* long (tentatively identified as *Chascanopsetta lugubris*) from the bathyscaphe *Trieste* at a depth of 10 918 m *35 820 ft* in the

**Deep-sea fish are some of the strangest-looking of all creatures; from top to bottom: Sloane's viperfish, gulper eel and *Linophryne arborifera* (which does not have an English name).**

---

Challenger Deep (Marianas Trench) in the western Pacific on 24 Jan 1960. This widely reported sighting, however, has been strongly challenged by many authorities, who still regard the brotulids of the genus *Bassogigas* as the deepest-living vertebrates.

More than 40 species of fish, belonging to over a dozen different families, spend their entire lives in lightless, underground caves or even in aquifers (water-bearing rock). Most of them live in tropical or warm temperate countries and tend to be colourless and have minute eyes or no eyes at all. Some of the better-known 'cave-dwellers' include a small catfish in the genus *Horaglanis*, which lives in wells in Kerala, southern India, and a subterranean loach (family Cobitidae) which lives in Iran.

**Highest** The world's highest living fish is the Tibetan loach (family Cobitidae), which is found at an altitude of 5200 m *17 056 ft* in the Himalayas.

**Most eggs** The ocean sunfish (*Mola mola*) produces millions of eggs, each measuring about 1.3 mm *0.05 in* in diameter. The record is a 1.37 m *4½ ft* long female which was carrying 300

million eggs, although larger individuals probably carry many times this number.

**Least eggs** The mouth-brooding cichlid *Tropheus moorii* of Lake Tanganyika, east Africa, produces seven eggs or fewer during normal reproduction. Not all fish lay eggs: some species, especially sharks, are viviparous and give birth to live young like mammals do.

**Largest egg** The largest egg produced by any living fish is that of the whale shark (*Rhincodon typus*). The largest on record measured 30.5 × 14 × 8.9 cm *12 × 5½ × 3½ in* and contained a live embryo 35 cm *13.8 in* long, although this particular specimen may have been aborted. It was found on 29 Jun 1953 by a shrimp trawler in the Gulf of Mexico fishing about 200 km *124 miles* south of Port Isabel, Texas, USA.

**Longest gestation period** Sharks have some of the longest gestation periods known in the animal kingdom, with a minimum of about 9 months. The

**The Russian sturgeon is the world's most valuable fish: specially prepared, its eggs become best-quality caviar.**

longest recorded is 22–24 months in the piked dogfish (*Squalus megalops*), which gives birth to an average of ten 25 cm *10 in* pups.

**Greatest size difference** The greatest size difference between a newborn vertebrate and an adult of the same species is found in the ocean sunfish (*Mola mola*). The adult measures up to 4 m *13 ft* across (though usually a little under 1 m *39 in*) and yet the newborn are each smaller than a pea (only 2.54 mm *0.1 in* in length). It is believed that the eggs are laid in the open ocean.

**Most valuable** The world's most valuable fish is the Russian sturgeon (*Huso huso*). Rubbed gently to remove the mucus, washed in wine or vinegar, and then dried or salted, the sturgeon's eggs become caviar – the most expensive fish dish in the world. One 1227 kg *2706 lb* female caught in the Tikhaya Sosna River in 1924 yielded 245 kg *540 lb* of best-quality caviar, which would be worth nearly £200 000 on today's market. The sturgeon is also one of the largest freshwater fish in the world, frequently growing to a length of 5 m *16 ft 5 in* and a weight of 1524 kg *3360 lb*: a large fish produces up to 8 million eggs in one spawning. Numbers of sturgeon fish have decreased greatly in recent years and there is now serious concern for the future of the species.

A 76 cm *30 in* long ginrin showa koi, which won the supreme championship in nationwide Japanese koi shows in 1976, 1977, 1979 and 1980, was sold 2 years later for 17 million yen (about £50 000). In March 1986 this ornamental carp (*Cyprinus carpio*) was acquired by Derry Evans, owner of the Kent Koi Centre near Sevenoaks, Kent, UK, for an undisclosed sum, but the 15-year-old fish died 5 months later.

**Most electric** More than 250 species of fish have evolved the capacity to generate electrical pulses from specialized 'electric organs'. These are used variously for communication (the pulses emitted are recognized by other mem-

bers of the same species); in a form of electrical echolocation (small electrical pulses are emitted and then bounce back from objects in the water to special electro-receptors in the skin); and to stun or kill both prey and predators (many species can deliver a painful or even fatal electric shock). The most powerful electric fish is the electric eel (*Electrophorus electricus*) from the slow, turbid rivers of northern South America. Despite its name, it is not a true eel but is related to characins in the order Cypriniformes. It has three electric organs (which are derived from muscle tissue and innervated by spinal nerves) occupying up to 80 per cent of its body. An average-sized specimen can discharge 1 amp at 400 volts, but measurements of up to 650 volts were recorded for a 41 kg *90 lb* individual in the New York Aquarium in the 1930s. This would be sufficient to kill a person on contact or to stun a horse at a distance of 6 m *20 ft*.

**Best sense of smell** Sharks have a better sense of smell, and more highly developed scent organs, than any other fish. Well known for detecting blood from great distances they can, indeed, detect one part of mammalian blood in 100 million parts of water. It is believed that they can even detect the scent of other fish's fear.

**Most ferocious** The razor-toothed piranhas of the genera *Serrasalmus* and *Pygocentrus* are generally considered to be the most ferocious freshwater fish in the world. They live in the sluggish waters of the large rivers of South America, and will attack any creature, regardless of size, if it is injured or making a commotion in the water. Carnivorous piranhas live mainly on fish, but their razor-sharp teeth and powerful jaws mean that, given a chance, they can also tear mammalian flesh to shreds. The danger piranhas represent to humans has been greatly exaggerated over

*The 18 cm 7 in Jack Dempsey is the only fish named after a heavy-weight boxer (the famous American heavy-weight champion from 1919 until 1926); it is named for its aggression towards other fish.*

the years and, indeed, not all of them are voracious predators: some of the 20 or so species are almost exclusively vegetarian, feeding on seeds, fruits, leaves and flowers. Nevertheless, some of the larger members of the genus *Serrasalmus*, in particular, can be a hazard and will attack *en masse*. On 19 Sep 1981 more than 300 people were reportedly killed and eaten when an overloaded passenger-cargo boat capsized and sank as it was docking at the Brazilian port of Obidos. According to one official, only 178 of the estimated number of people aboard the boat survived.

The bluefish (*Pomatomus saltatrix*) is often described as the most ferocious marine fish. Found in tropical and warm temperate seas in many parts of the world, it grows to a length of 1.2 m *47 in* and is best known for its strong conical teeth. A schooling fish, it sometimes hunts in packs of thousands that form feeding frenzies, attacking schools of mackerel, herring and other fish – by snapping at their prey indiscriminately and leaving a trail of dead and dying fish in their wake.

**Most venomous** Many fish are venomous, including the stingrays (family Dasyatidae), chimaeras (family Chimaeridae), catfish (families Ariidae, Clariidae and Plotosidae), weeverfish (family Trachinidae),

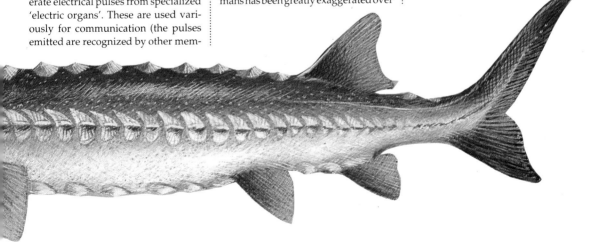

F
I
S
H
E
S

**Piranhas are generally considered to be the most ferocious freshwater fish in the world: their razor-sharp teeth and powerful jaws are certainly capable of tearing flesh to shreds in seconds.**

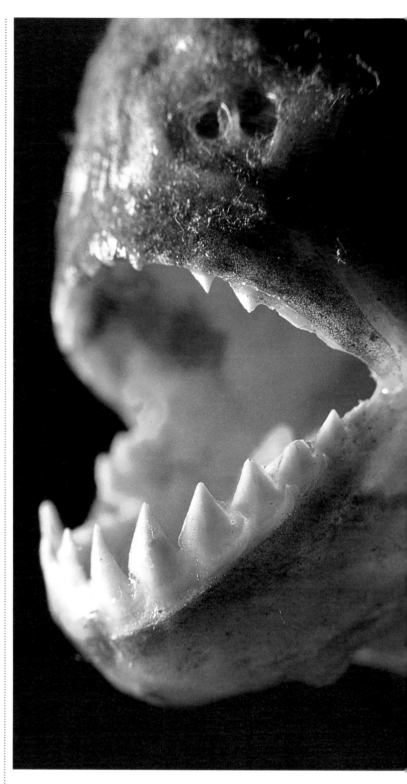

toadfish (family Batrachoididae), surgeonfish (family Acanthuridae), stargazers (family Uranoscopidae), scorpionfish (family Scorpaenidae) and the stonefish (family Synanceidae). The most venomous are the stonefish, whose spines inflict excruciatingly painful wounds which often prove fatal; the pain is so intense that victims frequently become delirious and frenzied, striking or biting anyone trying to help them. Most injuries are caused by people accidentally treading on the fish, which freeze and erect their spines when danger threatens – and are so well camouflaged that they are almost impossible to see.

The most venomous of all the 20 or so species of stonefish is the 60 cm *24 in* Indian stonefish (*Synanceia horrida*), which is found in shallow waters throughout the Indo-Pacific, Australia, China and India. It has the largest venom glands of any known fish, each of which is connected to one of 13 grooved dorsal spines. These spines are so sharp that they are capable of piercing the sole of a beach shoe – and inject the strong neurotoxic poison (each gland contains as much as 0.01 g *0.00035 oz*) into the wound as efficiently as a hypodermic syringe.

Two species of shark are known to be venomous (*see Most poisonous*): the 1.5 m *59 in* spurdog or spiny dogfish (*Squalus acanthias*) and the similar-sized Port Jackson shark (*Heterodontus portusjacksoni*), both of which have specially adapted venomous spines located at the front part of each of their two dorsal fins.

> **South American Indians sometimes use the jaws of piranha fish as razor blades.**

**Most poisonous** Many species of fish are poisonous to eat, but the most poisonous are the puffer fish (family Tetraodontidae), named for their ability to inflate themselves into a balloon shape by swallowing water or air whenever they feel threatened. The overall record-holder is the notorious death puffer or maki-maki (*Arothron hispidus*), which is found in a broad stretch of ocean from the Red Sea across the Indian Ocean and into much of the South Pacific. Its ovaries and eggs, blood, liver, intestines and, to a lesser extent, its skin contain a virulent poison (called tetrodotoxin) which can kill anyone who eats even a moderate amount. Less than 0.1 g *0.004 oz* is enough to kill an adult in as little as 20 minutes. Sufferers of tetrodotoxin poisoning experience extremely unpleasant symptoms: they may remain conscious but cannot swallow, see, speak or move.

In Japan, where the puffer fish is known as *fugu*, its flesh is considered to be a great delicacy and affluent Japanese pay high prices to eat it in specially licensed restaurants. After a 3-year apprenticeship, highly qualified chefs remove the poisonous parts without contaminating the rest of the fish: their objective is to retain just enough of the

**More attacks on humans are attributed to the great white shark than to any other species, although it is not always to blame.**

poison to produce a numbing sensation in the lips and tongue – and, of course, the thrill of flirting with death – but not enough to cause tetrodotoxin poisoning. Unfortunately, many non-experts also prepare the fish; consequently, there are about 50 deaths every year – making tetrodotoxin the number one cause of fatal food poisoning in Japan.

The liver (and sometimes other internal organs) of many sharks can be poisonous and may cause 'elasmobranch poisoning'. However, the flesh of only one species of shark is known to be poisonous to eat: the Greenland shark (*Somniosus microcephalus*), which is an inhabitant of the Arctic and cold temperate waters. It is most toxic when fresh but can be eaten if dried and prepared by an expert.

**Most dangerous shark** Sharks have a bad public image which is largely undeserved. There are more than 380 known species and most of them are harmless to people; indeed, more people die each year from bee stings than from shark attacks. However, nearly 40 species have been known to attack people (or are suspected of attacking people) and about half of these are considered to be highly dangerous. A number of others have the potential to be dangerous. The most dangerous species are those which habitually at-

tack people and these are the great white shark (*Carcharodon carcharias*), the tiger shark (*Galeocerdo cuvier*), the bull shark (*Carcharhinus leucas*) and, according to some experts, the oceanic whitetip (*Carcharhinus longimanus*).

More attacks on humans are attributed to the great white shark than to any other species. However, in reality, the identification of the shark in many of these attacks is suspect: telling one species from another can be very difficult at the best of times, but it is not surprising that the great white is often the first shark that comes to mind in an attack situation. The fact is that most attacks occur in the tropics, whereas the great white is normally found in cool, temperate waters. It is also relevant that the great white is not a particularly common animal; in recent years, it has suffered from a bad press (particularly after the release of the film *Jaws*) and the resulting human predation has caused population declines in some parts of its range. But none of this detracts from the undeniable fact that the great white accounts for a significant proportion of all fatal shark attacks (20–35 per cent depending on which estimates are to be believed) and that it is certainly one of the world's most dangerous sharks.

Many experts believe that the bull shark has probably attacked more people than any other species of shark. This certainly seems possible. It is a large shark with massive jaws; it has an indiscriminate appetite with a propensity for large prey; it occurs close to shore in tropical waters and therefore is more likely to come into contact with human swimmers and divers; and it is

far more common than the great white.

Like most animals, even small sharks will retaliate aggressively if they are provoked or feel threatened and many attacks on people are by sharks that are as little as 2 m *6 ft 7 in* long: these species have been dubbed 'man-attackers' rather than 'man-eaters'. The attacks normally consist of quick 'keep-your-distance' bites – normally aimed at divers who deliberately approach or try to touch the animals. In this category, the blacktip reef shark (*Carcharhinus melanopterus*) and the grey reef shark (*C. amblyrhnchos*), which reach lengths of 1.8 m *6 ft* and 2.5 m *8 ft 2 in* respectively, can be highly aggressive and are probably the most dangerous species of small shark.

It is estimated that only about 30–100 people are attacked by sharks every year, and on average 30 per cent of these attacks prove fatal (these figures do not include the victims of shipwrecks which succumb to unknown numbers of shark attacks). There is little documentation for many parts of the world and it is likely that more attacks and fatalities go unrecorded. Interestingly, only 25 per cent of all attack victims receive the kind of wounds that suggest the sharks were feeding – rather than giving a sharp warning – and even fewer are struck by the shark more than once. This evidence suggests that, despite popular opinion, sharks are not particularly interested in actually *eating* people.

**Country with most shark attacks** Australia has recorded more shark attacks than any other country on Earth (although many shark attacks go unrecorded, especially after shipwrecks at sea and around the coasts of developing countries, so the available evidence may be rather misleading). An analysis of 1165 cases in the International Shark Attack File (1958–67) reveals the following distribution of attacks: Australia 27 per cent; USA 19 per cent; Pacific Islands 12 per cent; and South Africa 8 per cent; the rest of the world combined accounted for the remaining 34 per cent. Since the first recorded death from a shark attack, in 1791, more than 150 people have been killed in Australian waters; however, since 1957, thanks to efficient beach protection, and better first aid knowledge and medical facilities, fatal attacks have averaged fewer than one a year.

The most dangerous places, with regard to frequency of shark attack, tend to be where large numbers of people congregate. However, this illustrates human preferences far more than the activities of dangerous sharks. More than half of all attacks occur in the tropics (where the water temperature range is 20–30°C *68–86°F*), within 60 m *197 ft* of the shore and in water less than 1.5 m *5 ft* deep. This is to be expected simply because people spend more time in warm, shallow water close to shore and so, inevitably, this is where there are likely to be more close encounters with sharks. The ratio of males to females attacked is 13.5:1 but, again, this is because more men spend more time in the water.

**Worst shark attack beach** Since the beginning of World War II, the highest incidence of shark attack within a small

area has been recorded at the beach resort of Amanzimtoti, 27 km *17 miles* south of Durban, South Africa. Since 1940 there have been 11 attacks, 2 of them fatal, all around a small area named Inyoni Rocks. Despite the high incidence of shark attack at Amanzimtoti, very few sharks get caught in the beach's protective nets; one theory is that temporary food chains build up in the area, bringing more sharks close to shore and causing increased abnormal predatory activity for a limited period.

Since 1950 more than 100 shark attacks can be reliably attributed to the great white (*Carcharodon carcharias*) worldwide. More than 40 per cent of these have taken place along a 200 km *124 mile* stretch of coastline between Monterey Bay and Tomales Point, California, USA.

**Worst shark attack** It is believed that sharks killed hundreds of men during one attack on 28 Nov 1942. When a German U-boat fired a salvo of torpedoes into the hull of the Liverpool steamer *Nova Scotia* some 48 km *30 miles* off the coast of Zululand, South Africa, the ship went down in 7 minutes and 900 men (including 765 Italian prisoners of war) were thrown into the sea. According to the 192 survivors, who were rescued by a Portuguese sloop, at least half of the men that died were taken by sharks (although the precise number is unknown). This fatality rate seems quite possible since the Portuguese sailors had to keep huge numbers of sharks away with boat hooks during the rescue operations; also it is unlikely that the shipwrecked men simply drowned because they were young and fit and the sea temperature was warm

enough to have allowed them to wait for help. This is the worst mass shark attack on record, although a substantial number of other shipwrecks are known in which dozens or even hundreds of people have been killed by sharks. Around the world, there are about 50000 victims of shipwrecks every year, at least half of them occurring in sub-tropical and tropical waters – it is impossible to estimate how many of them are taken by sharks.

**Fastest eater** Frogfish (family Antennariidae) are voracious predators that can open their mouths and engulf their prey faster than any other vertebrate. There are more than 40 different species, widespread in tropical and sub-tropical waters around the world. The first spine of the dorsal fin acts as a lure as they lie in wait for any fish or crustacean to pass within striking distance (the strike zone is an area whose radius is roughly two-thirds the length of the frogfish). Then they suck the unsuspecting prey into their large cavernous mouths as effectively as if they were using a vacuum cleaner. It happens so quickly and quietly that other fish nearby are often unaware of what has happened. Research by Theodore W. Pietsch and David B. Grobecker, involving frame-by-frame analysis of high-speed cinematography (filming at 800–1000 frames/s), has shown that the record-breaking time for opening the mouth and engulfing the prey is just under 6 milliseconds – recorded for the hispid frogfish (*Antennarius hispidus*), the striated frogfish (*A. striatus*) and the warty frogfish (*A. maculatus*). The next fastest gape-and-suck feeder recorded is the stonefish

**Australia has recorded more shark attacks than any other country in the world.**

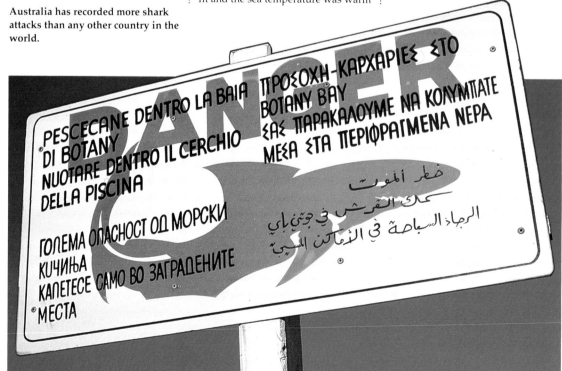

(*Synanceia verrucosa*), which requires a longer 15 milliseconds, although even this is less time than it takes a normal striated muscle to contract.

**Most varied diet** The tiger shark (*Galeocerdo cuvier*) probably has the most varied diet of all fish. It will eat literally anything it encounters in the water: all kinds of bony fish as well as other sharks; sea birds including cormorants, pelicans and frigate birds; marine mammals such as dolphins and seals; marine reptiles including sea turtles, sea snakes and marine iguanas; a wide variety of invertebrates such as lobsters, crabs and octopuses; chickens, rats, dogs, cattle and a variety of other domestic animals (some alive and some dead) that happen to fall in the water; and even apparently inedible objects (unusual items found in the stomachs of tiger sharks include car tyres, sacks of nails, leather coats, canned fish, wristwatches, car number plates and paint cans). Not surprisingly, they have been nicknamed 'garbage-can sharks'.

**Longest fast** The longest known fast by any fish has been recorded in the African lungfish (family Protopteridae), which can remain dormant inside a deep burrow in the muddy bottom of a dried-out swamp for up to four years (*see Survival out of water*).

Sharks are capable of long periods of fasting and even the most active species can survive for 6 weeks or more without food. The record observed in captivity is for a 1 m *39 in* swell shark (*Cephaloscyllium ventriosum*), which survived for 15 months without eating.

**Human parasitism** The 2.5 cm *1 in* long candiru (*Vandellia cirrhosa*) is the only vertebrate known to be an internal parasite of people, although it enters human bodies only accidentally. This tiny South American catfish has the unpleasant habit of entering the human urinary tract (if the victim urinates in the water). Once inside, it cannot be pulled out because of the erectile spines on its head and gill covers; the only way it can be removed is by surgery. It also parasitizes other fish (passing under the gill cover and between the gills) and even uses its spines to pierce the skin of potential hosts to drink their blood.

**Same species parasitism** The deep-sea anglerfish (*Ceratias holboelli*) is one of about 20 species in the family Ceratiidae in which the male is a parasite of the female. This is believed to be unique among vertebrate animals (although parallels can be found among the invertebrates). Once the male has

made contact with a female, he fastens on to her body with his jaws; eventually his blood supply becomes connected to that of his mate and he becomes wholly dependent on her for nourishment and oxygen. There is no fixed place where attachment occurs: the male may be fastened to her side, belly or back, and occasionally two or more males are attached to a single female. In some species, the males and females pair bond for life and remain attached to one another throughout; in others, the males attach themselves to the females only briefly, leaving to resume a free-swimming existence after mating. Female deep-sea anglerfish can grow to 1.2 m *47 in*, but the males are rarely longer than 6 cm *2.4 in*.

**Best shot** The archer fish (*Toxotes jaculator*) and its relatives are able to spit drops of water at insects perched on overhanging leaves and branches and shoot them down. The water is ejected in little droplets, rather like pellets from an airgun, and hits the insects with incredible force and accuracy. An experienced adult can score a direct hit on a victim more than 1.5 m *59 in* above the water's surface – sometimes even when it is in flight. When the insect falls into the water, it is promptly eaten. Living in muddy salt and freshwater habitats in India, Malaysia and northern Australia, the archer fish is almost invisible as it swims towards its prey just below the surface.

**Best fossil site** The world's best site for fish fossils is probably an area of sandstone sediments on the side of the road at Canowindra, central New South Wales, Australia. Fossilized remains of thousands of fish, including at least three previously unknown genera and some close relatives of early amphibians, have been uncovered to date. In places, there are up to 50 fossils per m² *4.7/ft²*. The site was first discovered in 1956 by men working on the road, but was not examined in detail until July 1993 when a research team led by Alex Ritchie, a palaeontologist at the Australian Museum in Sydney, removed 70 tonnes of rock slabs bearing the fossils of more than 3000 fish in a period of only 10 days. It is thought that all the fish died during a drought some 360 million years ago.

**Most variations** Freshwater fish have a greater tendency than almost any other animal to become divided into separate populations, because connecting waterways frequently become impassable. Therefore many species have a range of ecologically and physically distinct variations. The best known

> *Some fish living in south-east Asia get drunk by gorging themselves on the fermented fruit of the chaulmoogra tree when it drops into the water; after 'closing time' they float helplessly in the water until they have had time to sober up.*

example is the brown trout (*Salmo trutta*) of northern Europe, whose breeding habit (returning to the river of birth to spawn) ensures that each population remains genetically isolated as surely as if it were living on an island; consequently, the trout has a great many widely differing populations, both in way of life and appearance. In the past, these have all been divided into as many as 50 different species but, in theory, they are still sufficiently similar genetically to be able to interbreed and therefore modern biologists classify them all as a single species.

**Leading fishing nation** United Nations Food and Agriculture Organisation figures for 1991 (the last year for which comparable data are available) showed the world's leading fishing nation to be China, with a total catch of 13.13 million tonnes (from a world total of 96.92 million tonnes for the same year).

**Largest catch** The record for a single trawler is a 37 897 tonne catch by the Icelandic vessel *Videy* at Hull, Humberside, UK, on 11 Aug 1987, worth £278 798.

The greatest catch ever recorded from a single throw is 2471 tonnes by the purse seine-net boat M/S *Flomann* from Hareide, Norway, in the Barents Sea on 28 Aug 1986. It was estimated that more than 120 million fish were caught in this one shoal.

**Largest rod catch** The largest officially ratified fish ever caught on a rod was a great white shark (*Carcharodon carcharias*) weighing 1208 kg *2664 lb* and measuring 5.13 m *16 ft 10 in* long, which was caught on a 59 kg *130 lb* test line by Alf Dean at Denial Bay, near Ceduna, South Australia, on 21 Apr 1959. A great white shark weighing 1537 kg *3388 lb* was caught by Clive Green off Albany, Western Australia, on 26 Apr 1976 but will remain unratified by the International Game Fishing Association because whale meat was used as bait (expressly forbidden under game fishing rules).

208

# ARACHNIDS

> Hot scorpions sometimes raise their bodies off the ground – a behaviour called 'stilting' – to permit the circulation of air underneath to cool themselves down.

### Arachnida
c. 70 000 species including spiders, scorpions, harvestmen, mites and ticks

**Largest** The largest arachnid in the world is a scorpion called *Heterometrus swannerdami*, from southern India. Males frequently attain a length of more than 18 cm *7 in* from the tips of the pedipalps or 'pincers' to the end of the sting. The record-holder is a specimen that was found in the village of Krishnarajapuram, India, during World War II; it measured 29.2 cm *11½ in* in overall length. Another exceptionally large specimen, collected in Madras Province, India, on 14 Sep 1869 and now housed by the Bombay Natural History Society, measures 24.7 cm *9.7 in* in overall length.

The tropical emperor or imperial scorpion (*Pandinus imperator*) of West Africa is almost as large. Males frequently have a body length of 18 cm *7 in* or more and the largest was an individual caught in Sierra Leone, in 1977, which measured 22.9 cm *9.01 in*. Another male, at 22.8 cm *9 in*, was very nearly the same size; it was caught in

Ghana in 1931 and later presented to London Zoo. Interestingly, the sting of these and other exceptionally large scorpions is virtually harmless (seldom more painful than a bee sting) although allergic reactions are known to occur on occasion and can cause fatalities.

Some of the world's largest spiders have a leg-span of up to 28 cm *11.02 in* (*see Largest spider*). However, their maximum body size is less than one-third of this length and they are much lighter in weight than scorpions.

**Smallest** Most mites (order Acari) are 1 mm *0.04 in* or less in length and, indeed, the smallest arachnids are the gall mites (sub-order Tetrapodili): adults average less than 0.25 mm *0.0098 in* in length. They tunnel through plant tissues and feed on the contents of plant cells.

### SCORPIONS

### Scorpiones
c. 800 species

**Earliest** The earliest known scorpion and, indeed, the earliest known arach-

nid, is a species called *Palaeophonus nuncius*, which lived during the Devonian period more than 400 million years ago. There were scorpions around during the Silurian period, as long as 440 million years ago, but they were quite different to modern-day species (in particular, they had gills and were aquatic). Some prehistoric species, living in the leaf litter of the Carboniferous forests approximately 300 million years ago, reached a record length of 86 cm *34 in*.

**Largest** *see General records for Arachnids.*

**Smallest** The world's smallest scorpion is a species called *Microbothus pusillus*, which measures about 1.3 cm *½ in* in overall length and is found on the Red Sea coast.

**Most venomous** All scorpions have a narrow 'tail' (actually part of the abdomen) with a pair of poison glands and a sting at the end; the sting is used in self-defence and to subdue large or potentially dangerous prey. The venom of most species, while sufficiently toxic to kill small animals, is innocuous to people and causes little more than a sharp burning sensation. However, a number of species are known to possess venom which is sufficiently toxic to cause human deaths. The world's most venomous scorpion is the Palestine yellow or African gold scorpion

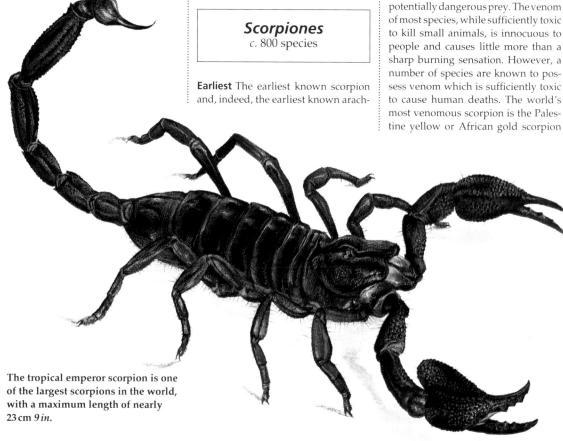

The tropical emperor scorpion is one of the largest scorpions in the world, with a maximum length of nearly 23 cm *9 in*.

(*Leiurus quinquestriatus*), which ranges from the eastern part of North Africa through the Middle East to the Red Sea. Fortunately, the amount of venom it delivers with each sting is very small (typically 0.255 mg *0.000009 oz*) and adult lives are seldom endangered. However, this species has been responsible for a number of fatalities among children under the age of five. Symptoms include intense pain, a tightening of the throat, slurred speech, restlessness, twitching, sweating and vomiting, and blueing of the lips and other tissues.

**Most dangerous** Most scorpions are not aggressive and will only sting if they are touched or frightened. Nevertheless, tens or even hundreds of thousands of people are stung by them every year. The number of fatalities varies according to the species involved and the age of the victim: average mortality rates are under 1 per cent in adults, 5–10 per cent in school-age children and more than 20 per cent in babies. The most dangerous scorpions (measured by the number of human fatalities rather than the toxicity of the venom) tend to be medium-sized species, while the majority of extremely large or small ones are relatively harmless. The most dangerous of them all is generally considered to be the fat-tailed scorpion (*Androctonus australis*), which is found in the drier parts of northern Africa including parts of the Sahara. Its venom is equivalent in toxicity to cobra venom and, if left untreated, its sting can kill a man in under 7 hours and a dog in as little as 7 minutes.

Other notoriously dangerous scorpions include: *Androctonus crassicauda*, from North Africa and the Middle East; three species in the genus *Centruroides*, from Mexico and southern USA; three species in the genus *Tityus*, from northern South America and Trinidad; *Buthus occitanus*, which occurs in many countries around the Mediterranean (although individuals in southern Europe are not considered dangerous to people); and *B. tamalus*, which lives in India and Pakistan.

> *Before mating, scorpions perform a courtship dance during which the male faces the female, holds her by the 'pincers' and then waltzes her back and forth; sometimes, they may continue dancing for hours or even days.*

**Most deaths** More people die from scorpion stings in Mexico than in any other country in the world. The peak number of deaths since 1940 occurred in the year 1946, when 1933 people died. More recently, the number of deaths has decreased thanks to control measures, education and better medical treatment; however, as many as 1000 people still die in Mexico every year from scorpion stings. Most of the victims are youngsters and the main culprits are species belonging to the genus *Centruroides*.

**Water loss** Scorpions are better adapted to high temperatures and dryness than any other animals. Even in the driest conditions, thanks to a sturdy covering of wax, they lose only one part per 10 000 of their body moisture – the lowest recorded for any animal. And when they do dehydrate, they can survive losing as much as 40 per cent of their body fluid.

---

**The goliath bird-eating spider has a record-breaking legspan of up to 28 cm *11.02 in*, which is sufficient to cover a dinner plate.**

## SPIDERS

### *Araneae*
About 35 000 species (as many as 200 000 may still be undiscovered)

**Earliest** Since spiders are soft-bodied creatures they are not easily fossilized and, consequently, there are huge gaps in our knowledge of prehistoric species. The earliest known spider has been identified from fossils dating back to the Devonian period, some 350–400 million years ago. As a group, spiders are believed to have been abundant for the first time during the Carboniferous period, about 300 million years ago.

**Largest** The world's largest known spider is the goliath bird-eating spider (*Theraphosa leblondi*), which lives in the coastal rainforests of Surinam, Guyana and French Guiana (although isolated specimens have also been reported from Venezuela and Brazil). A male collected by members of the Pablo

San Martin Expedition at Rio Cavro, Venezuela, in April 1965, had a body length of 9 cm *3½ in* and a record leg-span of 28 cm *11.02 in* – sufficient to cover a dinner plate.

**Heaviest** Female bird-eating spiders (family Theraphosidae) are more heavily built than the males and in February 1985 Charles J. Seiderman of New York City, USA, captured a female example near Paramaribo, Surinam, which weighed a record peak 122.2 g *4.3 oz* before its death from moulting problems in January 1986. At the time, it had a maximum leg-span of 26.7 cm *10½ in*, a total body length of 10.2 cm *4 in* and fangs measuring 2.5 cm *1 in* long.

**Smallest** The smallest known spiders are the so-called midget spiders (family Symphytognathidae), the tiniest of which is usually quoted as the pale yellow *Patu marplesi* of Western Samoa, south-west Pacific; the type specimen was a male found in moss at an altitude of *c*. 600 m *1968 ft* in Madolelei, Upolu, in January 1965, and measured 0.43 mm *0.017 in* overall – about the size of a full-stop on this page. However, a closely related species, the Columbian forest spider *P. digua*, may be even smaller: the record for a female is 0.59 mm *0.023 in*, but a male has been found with a length of only 0.37 mm *0.015 in*.

The smallest known female spider belongs to a new species, *Anapistula caecula*, recently discovered in leaf-litter in the Taï Forest Reserve, Ivory Coast. This white, blind spider measures just 0.46 mm *0.018 in* long. Since male spiders are generally smaller than their mates, the undiscovered male *A. caecula* may yet beat the current champion as the world's smallest spider.

**Size difference** The greatest size difference between the sexes is found in golden orb-web spiders of the genus *Nephila*. The massive silver, black and yellow females are giants compared to the diminutive brown males: in some tropical species, they can weigh nearly 1000 times as much as their mates. Fortunately, the males are *so* small that they are below the minimum size of the females' normal prey and are therefore in no danger of being eaten.

**Largest web** Only about half of the world's spiders spin webs (the remainder actively hunt their prey or lie in ambush). The largest spider webs are built by tropical golden orb-web spiders in the genus *Nephila*. The largest properly measured was found in the Karrakpur Hills, near Monghyr, central Bihar, India, and was 1.5 m *5 ft* in circumference; it had long supporting guy-lines up to 6.1 m *20 ft* in length.

The largest communal web is built by *Ixeuticus socialis*, from Australia, and can measure up to 3.7 m *12 ft 2 in* in length and 1.2 m *3 ft 11 in* in width.

**Smallest web** The smallest spider webs

**The world's largest and strongest webs are built by golden orb-web spiders; they have been known to measure up to 1.5 m *5 ft* in circumference, with considerably longer supporting guy-lines.**

are built by midget spiders (family Symphytognathidae) and may be less than 10 mm *0.4 in* in diameter.

**Eggs** The number of eggs laid in a single batch varies from just two by *Oonops domesticus*, a small pinkish spider no longer than 2 mm *0.08 in*, to as many as 3000 by certain bird-eating spiders (family Theraphosidae). The eggs range in size from only a fraction of a millimetre in diameter, in the case of *Oonops* and many other species, to the size of a small pea in the case of some of the bird-eating spiders.

**Largest meal** It is unusual for spiders to tackle prey much larger than themselves, although some crab spiders (family Thomisidae) are known to ambush and kill animals several times their own size; for example, an individual no more than 3 mm *1.2 in* will tackle prey as large as bees and butterflies. This is made possible by a very fast-acting venom, which immobilizes the prey quickly and therefore reduces the risk of injury to themselves.

The large tarantulas of South America, particularly those in the genera *Grammostola* and *Lasiodora*, are known to kill and eat 30 cm *11.8 in* pit vipers and 45 cm *17.7 in* rattlesnakes. In the early 1920s, a captive spider in the genus *Grammastola* reportedly killed and ate two frogs, a small rattlesnake and a highly venomous Jararaca snake within the space of just four days.

There is a report from 1919 of a barking spider (*Selenocosima* sp) in Australia dragging a chicken a distance of 16 m *52½ ft* to its hole. Large orb-web spiders in the genus *Nephila* sometimes catch small birds in their webs.

**Longest fast** Spiders have a low metabolic rate, enabling them to survive for many weeks or even months without food. John Blackwell, a British arachnologist, kept a *Steatoda bipunctata* in a closed container from 15 Oct 1829 to 30 Apr 1831, when it eventually died; it had survived a continuous fast, without food or water, of more than 18 months.

**Fastest runner** Spiders are capable of moving swiftly, even after long periods of inactivity, but normally cannot sustain their speed for more than a few seconds at a time. The fastest recorded spider was a female house spider (*Tegenaria atrica*) which reached a maximum speed of 1.90 km/h *1.18 mph* over short distances during a series of experiments held in the UK in 1970. This is exceptionally fast considering that, effectively, the spider covered a distance equivalent to 330 times her own body length in just 10 seconds.

**Most recently discovered** New species of spider are being discovered all the time and it is likely that scientists are still unaware of the existence of many thousands of species. In Britain alone, where spiders have been fairly well studied, more than one new species is added to the national list on average every year.

**Best eyesight** Most spiders have relatively poor eyesight and are able to distinguish little more than day from night; they rely mainly on scents and vibrations to tell them what is happening in the world. The ones with better eyesight tend to be short-sighted, and some day-active species can see surprisingly well at close range. The best eyesight is probably found in the tropical jumping spiders (family Salticidae). They have eight eyes in three rows: the main ones (the two biggest – which are in the middle of the front row) have a very narrow field of vision but can perceive sharp images of objects as far

> **Spider silk is so strong that catching a fly in flight with a web is equivalent to stopping a jet aircraft with a net made of strands a few centimetres thick; some spider webs are even strong enough to catch small birds.**

as 30 cm *12 in* away; and the smaller, secondary ones have a much greater field of vision and enable them to judge distances with a high degree of accuracy. Jumping spiders are also believed to have good colour vision.

**Largest eyes** Ogre-faced or gladiator spiders (in the genus *Dinopis*) have the largest simple eyes of any arthropod, measuring up to 1.5 mm *0.06 in* across. They do not produce very clear images, but do have excellent light-gathering power for night work (equivalent to an f-number of 0.6 and therefore better than most camera lenses – *see p. 218*). When staring at a bright light, their eyes shine like a pair of headlamps.

**Strongest silk** Spider silk is the strongest of all natural and man-made fibres – much stronger than silk from the delicate webs spun by silkworms. It is even stronger than steel: the dragline of a European garden spider (*Araneus diadematus*), for example, can support a weight of 0.5 g *0.02 oz* without snapping, whereas a steel strand of similar thickness will snap under the strain of just 0.25 g *0.01 oz*. Golden orb-web spiders in the genus *Nephila* are believed to produce the strongest of all spider silks.

> *The web of an average garden spider contains 20–30 m 65½–98 ft of silk and yet weighs under 0.5 mg 0.00017 oz.*

**Silk elasticity** Spider silk has a unique combination of strength and elasticity that no existing man-made fibre can match. The most elastic silk of all is produced by the ogre-faced or gladiator spiders (family Dinopidae), which can be stretched six-fold without snapping and then reverts to its normal length without any obvious sign of distortion. For comparison, a steel thread snaps when it is stretched to barely 8 per cent of its original length.

A team of engineers and molecular biologists at the US Army's Natick Research Centre, near Boston, Massachusetts, USA, is working to produce a synthetic spider's silk as good as the real thing – in order to make stronger bullet-proof vests. Army vests are currently made of Kevlar, which can stretch by up to 4 per cent before breaking, while spider silks can stretch by considerably more before breaking; spider silk therefore absorbs much more kinetic energy (from a bullet, for example) without the vest failing. The spider being used in the study is the golden orb weaver (*Nephila clavipes*) from Panama. While it is strapped to a table, the end of the silk protruding from its spinneret is grasped with forceps and then wrapped around a spindle driven by a variable-speed electric motor; on average, a strand about 320 m *1050 ft* long is obtained in one session. According to the researchers, the silking does not hurt the spider, which is ready to be silked again the next day.

**Spitting** There are approximately 50 species of spitting spiders in the genus *Scytodes*, found mainly in the tropics, and many of them literally spit a quick-setting mucilaginous glue over both their prey and potential predators. The glue is produced (in very small amounts) in modified poison glands and then fired in sticky streams from the two fangs. It happens so quickly that it is impossible to see with the human eye – the spider simply seems to shake its head and the prey is left rooted to the spot, struggling to escape. During aggressive encounters, spitting spiders will also spit over one another, typically covering their opponent's head and forelegs with glue; sometimes, the spat-upon spiders are unable to remove the glue, and die. This remarkable hunting and defence technique is unknown in any other group of spiders.

**Most social** Spiders are generally solitary creatures (if they happen to meet they tend to eat one another) and very few are social. Some 20–25 species display primitive social behaviour, varying from little more than mutual tolerance to simple mother–offspring relationships. A further 18 species are known to exhibit truly social behaviour, living in shared nests and even working together to build webs, look after the young and catch prey.

One of the most social species is probably a form of lynx spider

(*Tapinillus* sp) belonging to the family Oxyopidae; it may belong to a new species and is yet to be named formally. It was discovered in 1994 by an American zoologist working in the rainforests of Cuyabeno Nature Reserve, Ecuador, where dozens or even hundreds of the spiders live together. Their three-dimensional communal webs are woven around the ends of tree branches and accommodate equal numbers of adults of both sexes as well as juveniles of different ages. Interestingly, alloenzyme analysis has revealed that all the spiders in a web (apart from a few males) are the offspring of a single pair, suggesting parallels with ants and other social insects.

**Threatened species** Fifteen species of spider are officially listed by the World Conservation Union (IUCN) as known or suspected to be threatened with extinction, although this is likely to be no more than a tiny proportion of the true

---

Spider silk has a unique combination of strength and elasticity that no existing man-made fibre can match.

number. Future research is expected to reveal a host of new, as yet undiscovered, species on the verge of extinction. In the meantime, the two most seriously threatened are the tooth cave spider (*Leptoneta myopica*), from the USA, and the no-eyed big-eyed wolf spider (*Adelocosa anops*), from Hawaii, USA. Although no species of spider is *known* to have become extinct in recent times, it is believed that many are disappearing even before we know of their existence.

**Most dangerous** Spiders are feared and hated far beyond their power to do harm. All of them (except a small number in the family Uloboridae) are venomous – the venom is used both for defence and for killing and digesting their prey – but by far the majority are incapable of biting people. In the spiders that do sometimes inflict injuries (several hundred species altogether), the venom typically causes little more than a small amount of discomfort, normally felt as a slight stinging sensation and persistent irritation, or pain comparable to the sting of a wasp or bee.

Only a very small number of these (around 30 of the 35 000 known spe-

cies) are really dangerous to people – and few bite unless they are provoked. However, their bites can be exceedingly painful: in some cases the intensity of the pain is reported to be almost unbearable and, indeed, people have been known to plead for their bitten limbs to be amputated in a desperate bid for release. The development of antivenoms has dramatically reduced the number of deaths caused by spider bites, although a small number of people (usually young children and the elderly) die every year and thousands of others are laid up for days or even weeks after serious bites.

The world's most venomous spiders are the Brazilian wandering spiders of the genus *Phoneutria*. In particular, the Brazilian huntsman (*P. fera*) is widely believed to have the most active neurotoxic venom of any living spider. Its venom is so potent that only 0.006 mg (*0.00000021 oz*) is sufficient to kill a mouse. Hundreds of accidents involving this species are reported every year, since it frequently enters human dwellings and hides in clothing or shoes; when disturbed, it bites furiously several times. Symptoms include excruciating pain, profuse sweating and salivation, hallucinations, spasms and

The Sydney funnelweb spider is responsible for more serious bites than almost any other species of spider; the individual in this jar is being milked: its venom will be used to produce an antivenom for the treatment of unfortunate human victims.

finally respiratory paralysis. Fortunately, an effective antivenom is available and deaths are now rare.

**Most serious bites** The largest number of *serious* bites are probably caused by the 30 or so species of black widow or red-back spider (*Latrodectus* sp) – which are found in North, Central and South America, southern Europe, Africa, Asia, Australia and New Zealand. Their venom is claimed to be 15 times more potent than the venom of a rattlesnake, they are extremely common and widespread and they frequently come into contact with people. Australia's Sydney funnel-web spider (*Atrax robustus*) and a number of other species are also close contenders. The funnel-web is remarkable in that it is the male which is most dangerous to people – in all other highly poisonous spiders it is the female.

**Largest venom glands** *Photoneutria nigriventer*, the largest and probably the most aggressive spider in South America, also has the largest venom glands of any spider. They each measure up to 10.2 mm *0.4 in* in length and 2.7 mm *0.1 in* in diameter and can hold up to 1.35 mg *0.000044 oz* of venom – enough to kill 225 mice.

**Longest fangs** Fang length is rarely linked with the seriousness of a spider's bite (the nature of the venom is far more important) and, indeed, most spider fangs are relatively short. The longest belong to the bird-eating spider *Theraphosa leblondi* and reach a maximum length of only 1.2 cm *½ in*. By comparison, the fangs of the black widow spider *Latrodectus mactans* are only 0.4 mm *0.016 in* long – yet its bite is far more dangerous than the bite of almost any other spider in the world.

**Most feared** The enormous, furry bird-eating spiders (family Theraphosidae)

> *Spiders are able to taste things with their feet.*

have a fearsome reputation thanks to the popular press and to their starring roles as the great hairy monsters in numerous feature films. Known as baboon spiders in Africa and tarantulas in America, they certainly *look* exceedingly dangerous. But most of the 300 known species, which live mainly in the tropics and sub-tropics, are fairly placid creatures. They are normally reluctant to bite (unless being roughly handled or provoked) and, when they do become aggressive, the bite can be extremely painful but is rarely dangerous.

**Longest lived** Most spiders have an average lifespan of less than a year, although there are some dramatic exceptions. The longest-lived of all spiders are the tropical bird-eaters (family Theraphosidae). As in most spiders, the females tend to live longer than the males; one female collected in Mexico in

1935, at an estimated age of 10–12 years, was kept in captivity for 16 years and therefore died at an assumed age of 26–28 years. It is believed that a 20–25-year lifespan is not unusual for female bird-eating spiders, and for certain trapdoor spiders (family Ctenizidae) putting them among the longest-lived of all terrestrial invertebrates.

**Highest living** Jumping spiders (family Salticidae) hold the world altitude record for spiders. In 1924 the naturalist and explorer R.W.G. Hingston collected several specimens living under stones that were frozen to the ground at a height of 6700 m *21 980 ft* on Mount Everest. Two of these were later named as new species: *Euophrys everestensis* and *E. omnisuperstes* ('highest of all'). They are believed to feed on tiny creatures blown up from lower altitudes.

**INVERTEBRATES**

**Living underwater** The only spider known to live permanently underwater is the 12 mm ½ in long water spider (*Argyroneta aquatica*), which inhabits ponds and slow-moving streams in many parts of temperate Europe and Asia. It collects bubbles of air between its back legs and body and then carries them down to a bell-shaped nest which is firmly anchored, underwater, to aquatic vegetation. Although the spider goes on long hunting expeditions, breathing the air trapped between the hairs on its body, it has no obvious anatomical or physiological adaptations for its unlikely underwater life (inside the nest, it breathes normally as if on land).

Several other spiders are known to be capable of submerging for as long as three weeks, some even absorbing oxygen directly from the water through the skin.

**Most marine** No spider lives in the open sea, but several species live along the seashore. Perhaps the most marine is the 8 mm *0.3 in* long semi-marine spider (*Desis marina*), which lives on exposed coral reefs and on intertidal rocks in Australia and New Zealand. At low tide it hunts sandhoppers and then, when the tide comes in, hides in a disused worm burrow – keeping the water out by blocking the entrance with a woven lid of silk. It is able to survive for several days under water, without a diving bell or a bubble of air.

**Largest family** The largest and most varied of all the 105 known spider families is the Salticidae, or jumping spiders. There are 4400 known species, mostly living in the tropics. Jumping spiders tend to be nomadic daytime hunters and almost never spin webs, because they do not need them for predation.

---

# CENTIPEDES & MILLIPEDES

## *Myriapoda*
*c.* 11 000 species (2800 centipedes and 8000 millipedes)

**Earliest** The earliest land dwellers known from complete fossils were two centipedes and an arachnid found in a layer of rock known as the Ludlow Bone Bed, Shropshire, UK. The fossils, discovered by palaeontologists from the University of Manchester and the University of Wales, are estimated to be 414 million years old. However, it is believed that all three species were fairly advanced predators – and therefore must have been preying on animals that lived on land even before they did.

Indeed, the world's oldest known terrestrial footprints, found in 450-million-year-old rocks in the Lake District, UK, suggest that animals were wandering around on dry land nearly 50 million years earlier. Although no fossils of the creatures themselves have yet been found, the tracks were probably made by animals similar to modern centipedes and millipedes.

**Longest** The longest known species of myriapod is a large variant of the widely distributed *Scolopendra morsitans*, a species of centipede found on the Andaman Islands, in the Bay of Bengal. Specimens up to 33 cm *13 in* in length and 3.8 cm *1½ in* in width have been recorded.

*Graphidostreptus gigas* of Africa and *Scaphistostreptus seychellarum* of the Seychelles, in the Indian Ocean, are the longest known millipedes and have been measured up to 28 cm *11 in* in length and 2 cm *0.78 in* in width.

**Shortest** The shortest myriapod in the world is the British millipede *Polyxenus lagurus*, which measures 2.1–4.0 mm *0.08–0.15 in*. The shortest recorded centipede is an unidentified species measuring only 5 mm *0.19 in*.

**Most legs** Despite their names, centipedes do not have 100 feet (or legs) and millipedes do not have 1000. Nevertheless, millipedes do tend to have more legs than centipedes; they appear to have two pairs per body segment (although, in reality, these are fused segments) compared with just one pair in centipedes. The record is 375 pairs (750 legs) reported for a millipede called *Illacme plenipes*, which is found in California, USA. The centipede with the most legs is a species called *Himantarum gabrielis*, found in southern Europe, which has 171–177 pairs (342–354 legs).

**Least legs** Some centipedes in the subclass Anamorpha have as few as 15 pairs of legs, but the record-holder by a small margin is a millipede which has only 12 pairs.

Pauropods, which are closely related to centipedes and millipedes, usually have nine pairs of legs.

**Fastest** The world's fastest myriapod is probably the house centipede (*Scutigera coleoptrata*), which is a native of southern Europe. With the help of its extremely long legs, it can run at speeds of up to 50 cm/s *20 in/s* (1.8 km/h *1.1 mph*). In warm weather, it can keep this kind of speed up for several metres. Millipedes are significantly slower.

**Most threatened** No species of centipede or millipede is known or suspected to be threatened with extinction, although this situation may change as research progresses. It is believed that no species has become extinct in recent times although, again, it is likely that at least some disappear before the status of their populations has been properly assessed or even before they are known to science – and therefore go unrecorded.

**Most dangerous** All centipedes have poison glands for paralysing or killing their prey, though most are harmless to people. However, certain larger species have a pair of 'fangs' (actually part of a large pair of claws) which can puncture human skin; their 'bites' are highly venomous and can cause excruciating pain. Symptoms include prolonged swelling, soreness of lymph nodes and nausea lasting for up to a week. The appendage at the end of the tail does not inject venom but in some species can be used in defence by pinching.

Millipedes do not possess fangs, but most of them do have poison glands on the sides of the body which can squirt nauseous fluids containing chlorine, iodine and even cyanide. These fluids repel most of the millipede's enemies; on humans, the fluids released by some large tropical species can cause severe irritation when they come into contact with the skin and may even cause temporary blindness if they touch the eyes.

# CRUSTACEANS

## Crustacea

c. 42 000 species, including crabs, lobsters, shrimps, prawns, crayfish, barnacles, water fleas, fish lice, woodlice, sandhoppers, krill

*Most marine crustaceans produce free-swimming larvae that disperse to feed and grow in the plankton.*

**Earliest** The earliest known crustacean is a 12-legged sea spider called *Karagassiema*, which was found in 650 million-year-old rocks in the Sayen Mountains, former USSR.

**Largest** The largest of all crustaceans (although not the heaviest) is the Japanese spider crab (*Macrocheira kaempferi*), named for its superficial resemblance to spiders. Also called the stilt crab or the takaashigani (which means 'tall-leg'), it is found in deep waters off the south-eastern coast of Japan. Its average body size is 25.4 × 30.5 cm *10 × 12 in* (though some individuals attain a length of 45 cm *17.7 in*) and the average leg span is 2.43–2.74 m *8–9 ft*. The record-holder is a specimen with a legspan of 3.69 ft *12 ft 1½ in* and a weight of 18.6 kg *41 lb*. Unconfirmed measurements of up to 5.79 m *19 ft* have been reported. The Japanese spider crab lives on sandy or muddy bottoms in water 30–50 m *98–164 ft* deep, where it feeds on other crustaceans, echinoderms, worms and molluscs. Some crayfish and lobsters have longer bodies (for example, the American lobster *Homarus americanus*) but are much smaller overall.

**Smallest** Many crustaceans are planktonic and less than 1 mm *0.04 in* in length. The smallest of all are the water fleas of the genus *Alonella*, which may measure less than 0.25 mm *0.0098 in* in length. They are normally found in freshwater.

**Largest land crab** The largest (and heaviest) land-living crustacean is the robber or coconut crab (*Birgus latro*), which lives on tropical islands and atolls in the Indo-Pacific. Weights of up to 4.1 kg *9 lb* (the average weight is around 2.5 kg *5 lb 8 oz*) and a leg-span of up to 1 m *39 in* (the average leg-span is

*When a mantis shrimp attacks its prey, using its club-like forelimbs, it can deliver a punch that reaches the impact velocity of a .22 calibre bullet.*

91 cm *36 in*) have been recorded. Unauthenticated weights of up to 15 kg *33 lb* have also been reported. The robber crab is almost entirely terrestrial (although females have to return to the sea to release their eggs) and drowns when submerged in water for any length of time. It feeds mainly on rotting coconuts on the ground, but will eat a variety of other food if coconuts are not available. It has been hunted almost to extinction on many islands in the Indian and Pacific Oceans, because of its sheer size and the fact that it is apparently good to eat.

**Smallest crab** The smallest crabs in the world are the aptly named pea crabs (family Pinnotheridae), which are para-

sitic and live in the mantle cavities of oysters, mussels and other bivalve molluscs; they feed on food collected by the gills of their hosts. Some species have a shell diameter of only 6.3 mm *¼ in*, including the oyster crab (*Pinnotheres pisum*), which is found in British waters.

**Heaviest** The world's heaviest crustacean, and the largest species of lobster, is the American or North Atlantic

**The robber or coconut crab, which is almost entirely terrestrial, is the world's largest and heaviest land-living crustacean.**

**I N V E R T E B R A T E S**

lobster (*Homarus americanus*), which frequently attains a length of about 60 cm *24 in*. On 11 Feb 1977 a specimen weighing 20.14 kg *44 lb 6 oz* and measuring 1.06 m *3½ ft* from the end of the tail-fan to the tip of the largest claw was caught off Nova Scotia, Canada, and later sold to a New York restaurant owner.

**Smallest lobster** The smallest known lobster is the Cape lobster (*Homarus capensis*) of South Africa, which measures 10–12 cm *3.9–4.7 in* in total length.

**Largest freshwater** The largest freshwater crustacean is the crayfish or crawfish *Astacopsis gouldi*, found under logs and vegetation in the deep, slow-

---

The lifespan of crustaceans is poorly known, but some of the larger lobster species may live to the ripe old age of 50–100 years; unfortunately, many succumb to fishing operations long before they grow old.

moving streams and pools of northwest Tasmania, Australia. The average length is less than 40 cm *16 in* and the average weight less than 3 kg *6.6 lb*; however, measurements of up to 61 cm *24 in* and 4.1 kg *9 lb* are not unusual. In 1934 an unconfirmed weight of 6.35 kg *14 lb* was reported for a 73.6 cm *29 in* individual caught at Bridport. The population size has decreased in recent years, probably as a result of habitat alteration.

**Oldest** Little is known about the maximum lifespan of most crustaceans. However, large species tend to live longer than small ones and it is believed that very large specimens of the

American lobster (*Homarus americanus*) may reach an age of as much as 50–100 years.

**Deepest** The greatest depth recorded for any living crustacean is 10 913 m *35 802 ft* for an unidentified red shrimp observed by Lt Don Walsh and Jacques Piccard through the window of the bathyscaphe *Trieste* in the Marianas Trench, near Guam, in the western Pacific, on 23 January 1960.

The greatest depth from which a crustacean has been recovered is 10 500 m *34 450 ft* for *live* shrimp-like amphipods from the Marianas Trench, in the western Pacific, by the US research vessel *Thomas Washington* in

November 1980.

**Highest** Amphipods and isopods have been collected in the Ecuadorean Andes at a height of 4053 m *13 300 ft.*

**Fastest** The world's fastest-*moving* crustaceans are certain lobsters in the genera *Palinurus* and *Homarus*; when escaping from predators, they leap backwards at speeds of up to 8 m/s *26 ft/s* (28.8 km/h *18 mph*). However, this is not considered to be true swimming and therefore the fastest-*swimming* crustaceans are crabs in the family Portunidae, in which the fifth pair of legs is adapted for swimming and flattened into broad paddles to help them chase and catch fish in the open sea. Most crabs cannot swim, but members of this family are exceptional: they can swim sideways, backwards and sometimes forwards with great rapidity. The current record-holder is Henslow's swimming crab (*Polybius henslowi*), which is found in the eastern Atlantic and has been timed at 1.3 m/s *51 in/s* (4.7 km/h *2.9 mph*), although it is likely

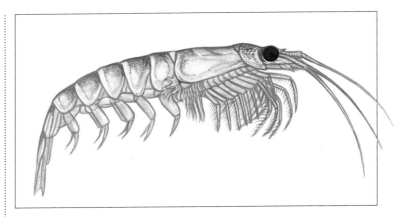

that this and other species attain much greater speeds in the wild.

The fastest-moving crustaceans on land are tropical ghost crabs in the genus *Ocypode*, which live in burrows above the high-tide mark on sandy beaches and among dunes. Some species have been timed at speeds of 2 m/s *79 in/s* (7.2 km/h *4.5 mph*). They always travel sideways and, at top speed, the body is raised well off the ground while two or three pairs of legs do all the running. Strangely, to rest the different muscles in their legs, they frequently stop abruptly and turn around 180° before continuing to run in the same direction.

> *Woodlice are crustaceans – land-living relatives of the crabs and lobsters.*

**Maternal care** The bromeliad crab which lives in the mountain forests of Jamaica, is the only crab known to take care of its young after hatching. For three months after they have hatched, in one of the puddles of rainwater that collect in large leaves of bromeliad plants, the female protects them by chasing away spiders, lizards and other predators – and fetches them cockroaches, beetles and other food to eat.

**Largest concentration** The largest single concentration of crustaceans ever recorded was an enormous swarm of shrimp-like krill (*Euphausia superba*) estimated to weigh 10 million tonnes, which was tracked by US scientists off Antarctica, in March 1981. Vast swarms of this 6.5 cm *2.6 in* crustacean – which is one of the most abundant animals in the world – can often be seen in their Southern Ocean home from satellites in space. Their total weight probably exceeds that of any other animal on Earth. Krill is the staple food of a wide

**Tiny shrimp-like krill are among the most abundant animals on Earth, frequently gathering in swarms so vast that they can even be tracked by satellite.**

variety of Antarctic animals, including baleen whales, seals, penguins and many fish (the word 'krill' actually comes from a Norwegian word meaning 'whale food').

The highest density of crabs in the world is probably on Christmas Island, some 320 km *200 miles* south of Java in the Indian Ocean. An estimated 120 million red crabs (*Gecarcoidea natalis*) live on the 135 km$^2$ *52 miles$^2$* island. They occur nowhere else in the world. The crabs inhabit Christmas Island's tropical rainforests, feeding on flowers and fruit on the forest floor. Every year (appropriately enough from around November until Christmas) millions of the crabs swarm out of their forest burrows and move down to the coast to mate and spawn. Many die on the way, and others are swept away by the waves, but most survive and return to the forest.

**Most threatened** The World Conservation Union (IUCN) lists a total of 158 crustacean species as known or suspected to be threatened with extinction. The species considered to be in most danger are: the Socorro isopod (*Thermosphaeroma subequalum*), Lee County cave isopod (*Liceus usdagalun*), Hay's Spring amphipod (*Stygobromus hayi*), Alabama

> *When spiny lobsters migrate, as many as 60 travel together, walking along the seabed in single file; they are able to cover distances of up to 50 km 31 miles without a rest.*

**INVERTEBRATES**

*Hermit crabs actively encourage sea anemones to live on their shells, because their long stinging tentacles give protection against predators; when the crabs change their shells, they prod and coax the anemones off the old shell and on to the new one.*

cave shrimp (*Palaemonias alabamae*), Kentucky cave shrimp (*Palaemonias ganteri*), California freshwater shrimp (*Syncaris pacifica*), Hell Creek crayfish (*Cambarus zophonastes*), Nashville crayfish (*Orconectes shoupi*) and shasta crayfish (*Pacifastacus fortis*), all of which are found in the USA; and *Engaewa similis*, a crayfish found in Australia. This list largely reflects the greater knowledge of crustaceans in the USA compared to many other parts of the world and it is likely that there are many more threatened crustacean species elsewhere that have yet to be discovered or studied in sufficient detail.

**Extinctions** Four crustacean species are known or suspected to have become extinct since the mid-1800s: the Pasadena freshwater shrimp (*Syncaris pasadenas*), sooty crayfish (*Pacifastacus nigrescens*) and rubious cave amphipod (*Stygobromus lucifugus*), all of which

lived in the USA; and the amphipod *Austrogammarus australis*, which was found in the Melbourne area, Australia. It is likely that at least some species become extinct before the status of their populations has been properly assessed or even before they are known to science – and therefore go unrecorded.

**Most terrestrial crab** The world's most terrestrial crab is the marsupial crab or sidewalker, which lives more than 1600 km *1000 miles* from the sea, in the deserts of the Australian outback. It survives the long dry season in a burrow, living on the little amount of moisture in the air inside and breathing with the help of lungs. When the rains finally come, it immerses itself in the flooded pools and rivers and carries on breathing through gills.

**Largest sperm** Certain mussel shrimps and seed shrimps (class Ostracoda) produce sperm which are considerably longer than themselves. The most remarkable is a species called *Pontocypris monstrosa*, which is less than 1 mm *0.04 in* in length and yet produces sperm as long as 6 mm *¼ in*.

The ghost crab is the fastest-moving crustacean on land, capable of speeds of up to 7.2 km/h *4.5 mph*.

---

**Best night vision** A deep-sea crustacean called *Gigantocypris* sp, which belongs to the class Ostracoda, has better night vision than any other known animal. It surveys its dimly lit world with two parabolic reflectors each of which directs light on to a retina at their centre. The f-number of its eyes is an incredible f-0.25 (the f-number is a measure of light sensitivity used by photographers – the smaller the number the wider the aperture of the lens and therefore the more light will reach the film). For comparison, the f-number of human eyes is about f-2.55 – which makes them many times less sensitive to light than the eyes of *Gigantocypris*. However, *Gigantocypris* has only small eyes and this limits the *quality* of its vision.

**Best colour vision** Certain species of mantis shrimp (order Stomatopoda) are believed to have better colour vision

*The boxer crab gained its name because it 'wears' a sea anemone on each of its pincers, like boxing gloves; the stinging anemones help to ward off potential enemies; unfortunately, though, because the crab's hands are always full, it has to use a pair of its walking legs to feed.*

than any other animal. Their eyes perceive colour through a system based on 10 visual pigments, compared with only three in the human eye and up to five in certain fish and insects. It is believed that their ability to distinguish colours well is important in recognizing other mantis shrimps: each shrimp has distinctive coloured markings inside its 'elbow' and, before a fight, they show their elbows to one another to avoid taking on the wrong opponents.

# HORSESHOE CRABS

## Merostomata
5 species (Atlantic coast of North America and south-east Asia)

> *Coastal American Indians once used the long, serrated tails of horseshoe crabs as fish spear heads.*

**Earliest** Horseshoe crabs or king crabs are among the oldest of the Earth's inhabitants and are often described as 'living fossils'. Their heyday was in the Carboniferous period, some 300–355 million years ago, when there were dozens of different species. It is believed that their appearance has changed very little in about 200 million years (fossils of an almost identical animal are known from late Jurassic rocks).

**Largest** The largest horseshoe crab is the North American species *Limulus polyphemus*, which has an average length (including the tail) of about 50 cm

*Limulus polyphemus*: the largest of the horseshoe crabs alive today.

20 in and can attain a length of 60 cm 24 in. The largest individuals are found in estuaries from Georgia to New Jersey, USA.

The largest of all fossil arthropods were the eurypterids, or giant water scorpions, which also belong to the class Merostomata. They lived from 300–450 million years ago and some reached a length of 3 m 9 ft 10 in.

**Smallest** The smallest horseshoe crab is the south-east Asian species *Carcinoscorpius rotundicauda*, which reaches a maximum length (including the tail) of about 30 cm 12 in.

**Furthest inland** Horseshoe crabs are primarily marine creatures, but *Carcinoscorpius rotundicauda* sometimes occurs in rivers and, on one occasion in India, was reported 145 km 90 miles from the sea.

**Most threatened** The World Conservation Union (IUCN) lists all four species of horseshoe crab as known or suspected to be threatened with extinction. They are still abundant in some areas but have been exploited for many years for animal fodder, bait for eel fishing, fertilizer, for the tourist trade and, most recently, for biomedical research. No species is known or suspected to have become extinct in historical times.

> *The long, mobile tail of a horseshoe crab looks rather dangerous but is never used in defence; it aids forward movement and helps to right the animal if it is accidentally overturned.*

# INSECTS

## Insecta

*c.* 1 million described (*c.* 8–10000 new species discovered annually and an estimated 5–30 million yet to be found), including termites; beetles; ants, bees & wasps; true flies; fleas; butterflies & moths; true bugs; lice; stick insects & leaf insects; grasshoppers, katydids & crickets; cockroaches; earwigs; dragonflies & damselflies; aphids, cicadas & hoppers; mayflies; stoneflies; alderflies; lacewings; caddisflies; mantids etc

*According to some estimates, nearly 90 per cent of all animal species are insects, making them by far the most successful organisms on Earth.*

**Most primitive** The most primitive known insect is a species of springtail (order Collembola) called *Rhyniella praecursor*, which has been found in Devonian rocks at Rhynie, UK, known to be 355–410 million years old. A number of other fossil springtails, rather similar to present-day species, have been found in deposits from Carboniferous and Permian times (250–355 million years ago). Modern springtails, which were named after the forked structure at the end of their abdomen that enables them to jump, are widely distributed throughout the world; they are commonly found in soil, leaf litter, decaying vegetation, grassland, tree bark and even on the surface of freshwater and saltwater pools.

**Most advanced** The most advanced insects are generally considered to be the social ants, bees and wasps of the order Hymenoptera. All ants and some families of bees and wasps have evolved complex cooperative social hierarchies in which there is a division of labour between different castes. The main categories within the hierarchy are the workers (wingless, sterile females which care for the eggs, larvae and pupae, maintain the nest, gather food and deal with intruders); the males (which are winged and have only one function: to mate with the queen); and the queen herself (whose main function in the colony is to lay eggs).

**Longest** Insects can never attain a great size because their breathing system, which is capable of carrying oxygen only over tiny distances, would not work on a grander scale. The longest recorded insect in the world is *Pharnacia kirbyi*, a stick insect from the rainforests of Borneo. The longest known speci-

men is in The Natural History Museum, UK; it has a body length of 32.8 cm *12.9 in* and a total length, including the legs, of over 50 cm *20 in*. In the wild, this species is often found with some legs missing – their great length means that they are easily trapped when the insect sheds its skin.

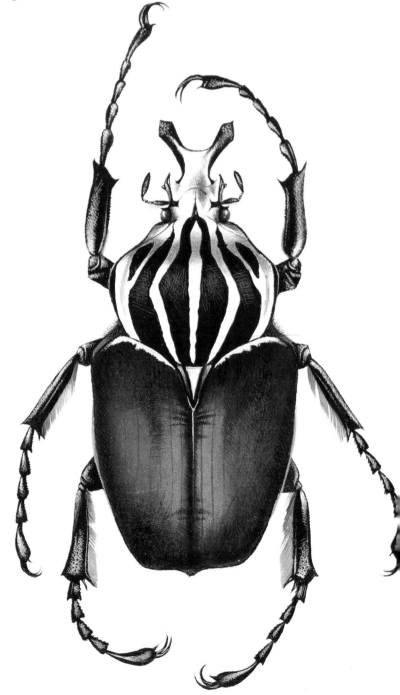

The goliath beetle is the heaviest and bulkiest of all insects; a typical male weighs roughly three times as much as a house mouse.

The rare Queen Alexandra's birdwing butterfly, which lives in Papua New Guinea has the largest wingspan of any butterfly.

**Smallest** The world's smallest recorded insects are the parasitic wasps known as battledore-wing fairy flies (family Mymaridae) and the 'feather-winged' beetles of the family Ptiliidae (=Trichopterygidae). With lengths of as little as 0.21 mm *0.0083 in*, they are even smaller than some species of protozoa (single-celled animals) and much smaller than a pin-head – and yet retain all the external characteristics of insects as well as a full complement of internal organs.

> *One species of earwig lives only in the breast pouch of a bat.*

**Heaviest** The heaviest and bulkiest of all insects are the goliath beetles (family Scarabaeidae) of tropical Africa. The largest members of the family are *Goliathus regius*, *G. druryi*, *G. meleagris* and *G. goliathus* (=*G. giganteus*). Males are generally larger than females and typically weigh from 70 to 100 g *2½–3½ oz* (roughly three times as much as a house mouse); the length (from the tip of the small frontal horns to the end of the abdomen) is up to 11 cm *4.33 in*.

The New Zealand wetapunga (*Deinacrida heteracantha*) comes a very close second. Females are larger than males and, although they are considerably shorter than goliath beetles (up to 8.5 cm *3.4 in* in length), they tip the scales at 70 g *2½ oz*.

**Largest wingspan** The female Queen Alexandra's birdwing butterfly (*Ornithoptera alexandrae*), which is found in Papua New Guinea, has the largest wingspan of any living insect. It can exceed 28 cm *11 in* from tip to tip.

**Largest prehistoric** Fossil remains (impressions of wings) of the dragonfly *Meganeura monyi*, discovered at Commentry, France, indicate a wingspan of up to 75 cm *29½ in*. This giant insect lived about 300 million years ago.

**Fastest flying** Acceptable modern experiments have established that the highest maintainable air speed of any insect, including the deer botfly (*Cephenemyia pratti*), hawk moths (family Sphingidae), horseflies (*Tabanus bovinus*) and some tropical butterflies (family Hesperiidae) is 39 km/h *24 mph*, rising to a maximum of 58 km/h *36 mph* for the Australian dragonfly *Austrophlebia costalis* for short bursts. The widely publicized claim by an American scientist in 1926 that the deer botfly could attain a speed of 1316 km/h *818 mph* was wildly exaggerated; if true, the fly would have had to eat 1½ times its own weight in food every second to acquire the energy that would be needed and, even if this were possible, it would still be crushed by the resulting air pressure.

> *The male death-watch beetle attracts the attention of a female by banging his head against the wall of his tunnel inside a tree.*

**Fastest wingbeat** The fastest wingbeat of any insect under natural conditions is 62 760/min (1046/s) by a tiny midge of the genus *Forcipomyia*. The muscular contraction-expansion cycle in 0.00045 s or 1/2218th of a second, necessary for such rapid wingbeats, also represents the fastest muscle movement ever measured.

**Fastest on land** The world's fastest running insects are certain large tropical cockroaches of the family Dictyoptera. The record is 1.5 m *4 ft 11 in*/s, equivalent to 5.4 km/h *3.36 mph* or 50 body lengths per second, registered by *Periplaneta americana* at the University of California, Berkeley, USA, in 1991. This is equivalent to a human sprinter reaching a speed of about 330 km/h *205 mph*. When travelling at such high speed, the cockroach runs only on its two hind legs.

**Longest lived** The majority of insects live for less than a year, although there are a number of remarkable exceptions.

**I
N
V
E
R
T
E
B
R
A
T
E
S**

The longest-lived of all are the splendour or jewel beetles (family Buprestidae) and there are many authenticated records of them surviving for 30 years or longer. They lay their eggs under the bark of a living tree and, after they have hatched, the young larvae tunnel into the tree and feed on the wood. If the tree is felled, it is not unusual for some of the larvae to survive and then be transported around the world in timber; since some species take many years to reach maturity, the adults may eventually emerge from furniture. The record was broken on 27 May 1983, when a specimen of *Buprestis aurulenta* appeared from the staircase timber in the home of Mr W. Euston, of Prittlewell, Southend-on-Sea, Essex, UK, after at least 47 years as a larva.

In the northern parts of its range, the periodic or seventeen-year cicada (*Magicicada septemdecim*) is known to live underground in the juvenile stage for as long as 17 years (13 years is more typical in the southern parts of its range). The adult cicada lays her eggs in a twig and, when they hatch, the nymphs make their way to the ground where they begin to burrow with their spade-like front legs; they feed underground, on root sap, until they reach the adult stage and then dig their way back up to the surface. They live as adults for no more than a few weeks before dying. Periodic cicadas are found in the woodlands of North America.

A lifespan of 50–100 years has frequently been claimed for queen termites in the genus *Isoptera*, but recent research suggests a more realistic lifespan of up to 25 years.

**Shortest lived** The greater part of an insect's life is generally spent in the larval stage and the adults tend to be extremely short-lived. The most extreme examples are mayflies in the family Ephemeroidea, which may spend 2–3 years as nymphs at the bottom of lakes and streams – and then live for as little as an hour as winged adults.

**Most useful** The most useful insects in the world and, possibly, the most useful of all animals, are the bees (superfamily Apoidea). They are major pollinators of flowering plants which,

*A typical Amazonian tree harbours an amazing 1700 different insect species, mostly ants and beetles.*

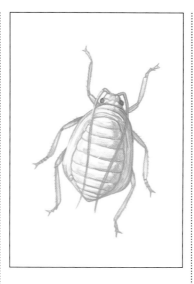

The tiny cabbage aphid is the most fertile animal in the world, capable of reproducing either sexually or by 'virgin birth'.

in turn, feed the world's terrestrial animals and replenish the planet's oxygen. Many plant species are completely dependent upon bees for pollination.

**Most fertile** The most fertile animal in the world (excluding bacteria, which are not really animals) is the cabbage aphid (*Brevicoryne brassicae*). This tiny, pear-shaped, sap-sucking bug is able to reproduce either sexually or by 'virgin birth', a process in which the eggs develop without fertilisation by a male and hatch into exact genetic replicas of the mother. As a result, billions of offspring can originate from just one female aphid. It has been calculated that, in a year with unlimited food and no predators, a single cabbage aphid could theoretically give rise to a mass of descendants weighing 822 million tonnes, or more than three times the weight of the world's human population. The Earth would be covered by a layer of aphids 150 km *93 miles* deep. Fortunately, a variety of natural enemies such as ladybirds, lacewings and insectivorous birds ensure that the aphid's mortality rate is very high.

**Largest egg** The largest egg laid by an insect belongs to the 15 cm *6 in* Malaysian stick insect *Heteropteryx dilitata* and measures an immense 1.3 cm *½ in* in length; this makes it larger in size than a peanut. Some insects, notably mantids (order Mantodea) and cockroaches (order Blattodea) lay egg *cases* which are much larger – but these contain as many as 200 individual eggs.

**Most threatened** The World Conservation Union (IUCN) lists a total of 1184 species of insect that are known or suspected to be threatened with extinction (many more are likely to be added to this list as research progresses). No fewer than 252 of these are considered to be in particularly serious danger, including 190 beetles.

**Extinctions** A total of 73 insect species are known or suspected to have become extinct since the mid-1800s: 2 mayflies, 3 damselflies and dragonflies, 1 katydid, 1 stick insect, 1 stonefly, 2 mealybugs, 18 beetles and weevils, 3 flies, 4 caddisflies and 38 butterflies and moths. However, it is likely that at least some species become extinct before the status of their populations has been properly assessed or even before they are known to science – and therefore go unrecorded.

**Most abundant** The most abundant of all the world's insects are probably the springtails (order Collembola), which are found worldwide from the tropics to the poles and from deserts to the highest mountain tops. They can be extremely common, attaining densities of up to 60 000/m² *5575/ft²* in favoured habitats. A typical area of temperate grassland will be home to some 600 million/ha *243 million/acre*.

Aphids (family Aphididae) are less widespread but, in suitable habitats, there may be as many as 5000 million of them per hectare (*2000 million per acre*).

**Loudest** The loudest of all insects is the male cicada (family Cicadidae). Its 'song' is made by the rapid movement of a membrane or 'tymbal', which oscillates several hundred times a second; behind the membrane is a resonating chamber to amplify the sound. Officially described by the US Department of Agriculture as 'Tsh-ee-EEE-e-ou', the song of many species is detectable from more than 400 m *¼ mile* away. To put this into perspective, a study by scientists at Princeton University, New Jersey, USA, measured the noise produced by thousands of cicadas in a single tree and found it to be 80–100 decibels at a distance of 18 m *59 ft* (compared with 70–90 decibels for a pneumatic drill at a similar distance). The song is designed to attract a female: each of the 1500 species of cicada has its own version. Most female cicadas are mute.

Male mole crickets (family Gryllotalpidae) make an even louder noise, by rubbing their wings together, but they use an artificial chamber as an amplifier. They shape their burrows in such a way that, on a still evening, their

> *Insects do not have backbones or any other internal bones – they wear their skeletons on the outside.*

'singing' can be heard up to 1.5 km *0.9 miles* away; some burrows have twin, flared tunnels leading to the surface from the resonating chamber.

**Most dangerous** The world's most dangerous animals (excluding people) are the single-celled parasites of the genus *Plasmodium*, carried by mosquitos of the genus *Anopheles*, which cause malaria. Excluding wars and accidents, these two creatures combined have probably been responsible directly or indirectly for 50 per cent of all human deaths since the Stone Age. Even today, despite major campaigns to eradicate malaria, at least 200 million people are afflicted by the disease each year. One person dies of malaria, somewhere in the world, every 10 seconds. Eighty per cent of the fatalities are in Africa and, according to estimates published by the World Health Organisation (WHO) in 1993, some 1.4–2.8 million people south of the Sahara die of malaria each year. The most dangerous strain is cerebral malaria – which can strike one day and, unless treated, kill the next. Mosquitos can also transmit diseases such as yellow fever, encephalitis and elephantiasis.

The common housefly (*Musca domestica*) is also highly dangerous, since it is able to transmit more than 30 parasites and diseases to people, including bubonic plague, cholera, leprosy, typhoid, dysentery, smallpox, diphtheria, scarlet fever and meningitis. In the developing world, contamination of food by houseflies and related species (one moment they may be feeding on excreta, the next on food) accounts for more than a million infant deaths every year due to dehydration associated with severe diarrhoea.

The oriental rat flea (*Xenopsylla cheopsis*) – a blood-sucking parasite and carrier of the dreaded bubonic plague (caused by the bacterium *Yersinia pestis*) – has been responsible for the deaths of millions of people in past centuries. Many rodent fleas can carry plague, but this particular species is believed to be responsible for the majority of the world's most catastrophic pandemics. The worst was the Black Death, in the 14th century, which caused the deaths of 25 million people in Europe alone –

approximately one-quarter of the population. Even today, plague still breaks out periodically in human populations.

**Most destructive** Only 1 per cent of known insects are considered to be pests. The single most destructive insect in the world is the desert locust (*Schistocerca gregaria*), which lives in the dry and semi-arid regions of Africa, the Middle East and western Asia. Each locust is only 4.5–6.0 cm *1.8–2.4 in* long (females are slightly larger than males) but is capable of eating its own weight in food every day. More importantly, specific weather conditions induce unimaginable numbers of locusts to crowd together in huge swarms that devour almost every piece of vegetation in their path. A 'small' swarm of some 50 mil-

---

**Mosquitos are the most dangerous animals on Earth, since they transmit malaria and other diseases that have killed hundreds of millions of people over the years; fortunately, the owner of these well-bitten legs suffered nothing worse than severe itching.**

lion locusts can eat, in a single day, food that would sustain 500 people for a year. The largest swarms contain 50 000 million locusts, covering a densely packed area of at least 1000 km² *386 miles²*, and *every day* consume the equivalent *annual* food requirements of nearly half a million people.

**Most profound influence** It is difficult to identify a specific record-holder in this case, since there are so many possibilities. For example, five species of tsetse fly in the genus *Glossina* have had a profound influence on human ecology in Africa. They transmit sleeping sickness (a disease confined to Africa and caused by the protozoan *Trypanosoma gambiense*) which is endemic in the large herds of wild grazing animals and also affects domestic cattle. As a result, it has made cattle ranging impossible in vast tracts of the continent.

**Largest collection** The Natural History Museum, UK, has the largest collection of insects in the world. In early 1995, it included nearly 30 million specimens.

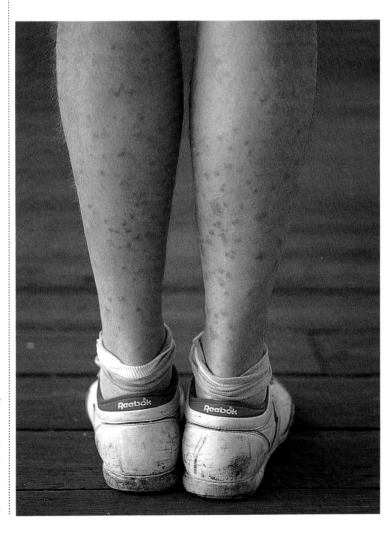

**I N V E R T E B R A T E S**

## ANTS, BEES & WASPS

### Hymenoptera
Nearly 140 000 species, including horntails, sawflies, fairyflies, velvet ants, wasps, ants, bees

**Largest ant** The longest ants in the world are the wingless queen ants of the species *Dorylus helvolus*, which live in South Africa and have a maximum recorded length of 5.1 cm *2 in*. The longest workers are bulldog ants (*Myrmecia brevinoda*), which live in Australia and have been measured up to 3.7 cm *1.46 in*.

Workers of ponerine ants (*Dinoponera gigantea*), which live in Brazil, are bulkier than both *Dorylus* and *Myrmecia*. However, they are shorter and have been known to reach a maximum length of 'only' 3.3 cm *1.3 in* from the top of the relatively short mandibles to the end of the abdomen.

**Smallest ant** The world's smallest ant is the worker of a Sri Lankan species called *Oligomyrmex bruni*, which measures 0.8–0.9 mm *0.031–0.035 in*.

**Largest bee** The world's largest bee is the rare Wallace's giant bee (*Chalicodoma pluto*), which is found only on the islands of Bacan, Soasiu and Halmahera, in the Moluccas, Indonesia. Females are larger than males and attain a maximum length of 3.9 cm *1½ in* (males average about 2.4 cm *1.0 in*). First discovered in 1858, it was not seen again until 1981 and is now believed to be extremely rare.

The leaf-cutter bee (*Megachile pluto*), which is found only on the island of Halmahera, in the Moluccas, Indonesia, is also very large. The record was a 3.8 cm *1½ in* female (females are larger than males).

**Smallest bee** The smallest bee is the Brazilian species *Trigona duckei*, which

> **Worker honey bees perform an elaborate dance inside the hive to tell their nest mates about new sources of food; they are able to pass on information about the distance, direction, type and even quality of food up to 100 m *328 ft* away.**

is stingless and measures only 2–5 mm *0.08–0.20 in* in length.

**Largest wasp** The largest known wasps are members of the genus *Pepsis*, which are found in tropical South America. They are often known as tarantula hawk wasps, because several species are so large that they sting and paralyse tarantula spiders, and then drag them to their burrows for their larvae to feed on. The largest tarantula hawk is probably *Pepsis formosa*, which has a body length of up to 6.7 cm *2.64 in* and a maximum wingspan of 11.4 cm *4½ in*.

**Smallest wasp** *see general records for Insects.*

**Lightest** The parasitic wasp *Caraphractus cinctus* is the lightest insect in the world, though it shares the title with the male blood-sucking banded louse (*Enderleinellus zonatus*). Each wasp may weigh as little as 0.005 mg (*equivalent to 5 670 000 wasps to an oz*) and each of its eggs weighs 0.0002 mg (*141 750 000 to an oz*).

**Largest wasps' nest** The world's largest wasps' nest was discovered on a farm at Waimaukau, New Zealand, in April 1963. Made of a kind of papier-mâché consisting of wood scrapings mashed up with saliva, it measured 3.7 m *12 ft 2 in* in length and 1.75 m *5¼ ft* in diameter and was so heavy that it had fallen to the ground and broken in two pieces. The species responsible is unknown, but is likely to have been the introduced German wasp (*Vespula germanica*) which, in New Zealand, builds much bigger nests than the same species in its native Europe.

**Most advanced** *see general records for Insects.*

**Most useful** *see general records for Insects.*

**Most threatened** The World Conservation Union (IUCN) lists a total of 25 Hymenopteran species that are known or suspected to be threatened with extinction (more are likely to be added to this list as research progresses). These include six species of European red wood ant in the genus *Formica* and 11 sphecid wasps in the family Sphecidae. The only bee currently on the list is Wallace's giant bee (*Chalicodoma pluto*) from the Moluccas, Indonesia; in addition, there is serious concern for a further 64 species of yellow-faced bee in the genus *Hylaeus* (some of which are probably extinct already) but their status has yet to be properly assessed. No extinctions have been recorded, al-

though it is likely that at least some species disappear before the status of their populations has been properly assessed or even before they are known to science – and therefore go unrecorded.

> **A large red ant colony may consume as many as 100 000 aphids and other insects every day.**

**Most dangerous ant** Worker ants of all species have venomous stings or squirting glands, but most of them are too small to be dangerous to people. However, at least two Australian species have been responsible for fatalities: the jumper ant (*Myrmecia pilosula*), which grows to 3 cm *1.2 in* and can jump as far as 20 cm *8 in*; and the bulldog ant (*M. pyriformis*), which gained its name because of its ferocity and determination during an attack. Both species are highly aggressive, show little fear of people and will sting a number of times in quick succession (injecting more venom with each penetration). In an attack, the ant holds on to its victim with long, toothed mandibles, curls its body underneath and then thrusts its long, barbless sting (which is at the end of the tail) into the skin. The sting of both species is extremely painful and, on a few occasions, has been known to kill adults within 15 minutes. A major concern is that, in recent years, increasing numbers of people in Australia are becoming allergic to their stings, which then produce a much more severe reaction.

There have been many claims of huge numbers of ants swarming over people and eating them alive. Columns of army ants (genus *Eciton*) and driver ants (genus *Dorylus*) have certainly killed people in isolated incidents – but there is no evidence of them being a serious threat. (*See Longest column of ants*).

**Most dangerous bee or wasp** Most bees and wasps are able to sting and, although many of their stings can be quite painful, the majority are not particularly dangerous. There are a number of cases of people being stung more than 2000 times by angry swarms of bees, and surviving. The main risk is to people who are allergic to the venom, in which case a single sting by a relatively harmless species can prove fatal. Consequently, many thousands of people die from bee and wasp stings every year.

**The record number of bees settled on a single person is 343 000, on Jed Shaner on 29 Jul 1991; they weighed an estimated 36.3 kg *80 lb*.**

The most dangerous bee is probably a cross between the notoriously ferocious African honey bee (*Apis mellifera*) and various European honey bees (genus *Apis*). A biological experiment in 1957 went tragically wrong when 26 queen African honey bees escaped from a research station at the University of São Paulo, Brazil; by mating with the more docile local bees, their numbers increased rapidly and they began to spread northwards at a steady rate of about 400 km *248 miles* per year. They had reached Panama by 1982, Mexico by 1986 and the USA by 1990 (the first official acknowledgement that the killer bee had arrived in the US was in October 1990, when US Department of Agriculture officials found a swarm on a farm in southern Texas, a stone's throw from the Mexican border). They are expected to reach North Carolina, USA, some time during 1995 and to have inhabited much of the southern half of the US by the end of the decade. In fact, the sting of the Africanized bee is no more potent than the stings of many other bees. But their behaviour is different: they attack people approaching their nests more readily (even if they are more than 1 km *0.6 miles* away) and in far greater numbers. The number of fatalities caused by these bees is unknown, but it is likely that more than 300 people and countless animals have been killed.

**Mantle of bees** During a record-breaking attempt on 29 Jul 1991 Jed Shaner was covered by a mantle of *c.* 343 000 bees weighing 36.3 kg *80 lb* at Staunton, West Virginia, USA. Talking about his experience, he said: 'People say you're crazy, but everyone's crazy in their own way. There are things that other people do that I might think were crazy.'

> *Some bees store up their faeces for weeks or even months before flying away from their hives on 'toilet flights', during which they may lose as much as 40 per cent of their body weights.*

**Slave-taking** In some ant species, the workers do none of the work themselves, but enlist the help of other species by taking slaves. One well-known example is the western slave-making ant (*Polyergus breviceps*), which has been studied in the Chiricahua Mountains, in south-western Arizona, USA. Half a dozen *Polyergus* workers go off in search of potential slave nests (their favourite slave species is *Formica gnava*) and, as soon as they have found one, return to fetch their contemporaries. As many as 1000 workers follow the original search party back to the *Formica* nest and, instead of killing the inhabitants, spray them with a chemical which causes them to flee. They steal as many of the pupae as they can, carry

them back to their own nest and then hand them over to the slave-workers of their own species, who raise the *Formica* ants to serve their *Polyergus* masters.

**Longest column of ants** Army ants in the genus *Eciton*, from Central and South America, and driver ants in the genus *Dorylus*, from Africa, have a reputation for travelling in highly organized columns. These can be up to 100 m *328 ft* long and over 1 m *3 ft 4 in* wide and may contain as many as 600 000 individuals; they frequently take several hours to pass one spot. The reputation these ants have for devouring any animal that is too slow to get out of the way is accurate: they will eat, for example, everything from poisonous snakes to tethered horses. But their reputation for swarming over people and tearing at their flesh is grossly exaggerated. Since they move so slowly (approximately 14 m/h *46 ft/h*) it is easy for everyone to get out of harm's way. There is a report of a column of army ants 1.6 km *1 mile* long and half as wide marching on the town of Goiandira, in central Brazil, in December 1973; supposedly, it devoured several people (including the chief of police) before being driven back into the jungle with the help of a team of people armed with flame-throwers. However, most experts completely disregard this story and it is highly unlikely that ant columns ever reach anything approaching such a size. Army and driver ants do not march all the time, but typically alternate 15 days of marching with 20 days of camping while the queen lays eggs.

**Temperature tolerance** When temperatures in the central Sahara reach 46°C *115°F*, and most creatures are hiding from the midday sun, silver ants (*Cataglyphis bombycina*) leave their nest holes to search for the corpses of other insects that have succumbed to the blazing heat. *Ocymyrmex* ants from the Namib desert do the same. They spend as long as half an hour dashing about in search of their prey – occasionally seeking relief atop dried vegetation where the air is slightly cooler – before having to return to the safety of their burrows. Their own predators, such as lizards, are unable to cope with such extreme heat and are safely hidden underground while the silver ants go about their business. If the temperature rises above 54°C *128°F*, the ants themselves start to suffer, becoming disoriented, losing their coordination and generally stumbling around.

**Memory** In an experiment by French biologists at the University of Paris, in Villetaneuse, worker ants of two different species (*Formica selysi* and *Manica rubida*) were reared together for three months and then separated. It was found that they could recognize one another, probably by the odours on their skin, as much as 18 months later.

---

## BEETLES

---

### Coleoptera
Nearly 400 000 species (almost one third of all described animal species), including beetles, weevils, ladybirds, fireflies

---

**Smallest** *see general records for Insects.*

**Longest** The longest beetles in the world are two species of hercules beetle: *Dynastes hercules* and *D. neptunus*, which are found in Central America and northern South America and on some Caribbean islands. Males have been reliably measured up to 19 cm *7½ in* (*D. hercules*) and 18 cm *7.1 in* (*D. neptunus*) although, in both species, more than half the length is taken up by the long opposing horns, one on the head, the other on the prothorax.

With this in mind, the title for the world's longest beetle should perhaps go to the fittingly named *Titanus giganteus*, from the Amazon region, which does not have long horns and still attains a length of up to 16 cm *6.3 in* (with unconfirmed reports of lengths up to 20.3 cm *8 in*).

**Heaviest** *see general records for Insects.*

**Strongest** In proportion to their size, the strongest animals in the world are the larger beetles of the family Scarabaeidae, which are found mainly in the tropics. In tests carried out on a rhinoceros beetle of the sub-family Dynastinae, it was found that it could support 850 times its own weight on its

---

The world's longest beetles are hercules beetles found in Central and South America and on some Caribbean islands; this individual was photographed on Dominica, in the Lesser Antilles.

back. As a comparison, in a trestle lift a human can support only 17 times his own body weight.

The dor beetle (*Geotrupes stercorosus*) has been observed shifting a load weighing 80 g *2.82 oz* or 400 times its own body weight from one point to another.

**Highest g-force** The highest *g*-force that can be endured by any insect is an average of *400 g* by the click beetle (*Athous haemorrhoidalis*). When the beetle is placed (or falls) on its back it can right itself by jumping into the air. It arches its back (holding this position for a moment with the help of a tiny peg resting on a ridge on the underside of the body) and then, as tension builds up in the body muscles, the peg slips. There is a loud click – and the beetle is suddenly thrown into the air. If the surface is at all uneven, the beetle somersaults several times after take-off and does not necessarily land the right way up – but will keep on trying until it does. The jump is nearly vertical and may reach a height of 30 cm *11¾ in*. One individual measuring 1.2 cm *½ in* in length and weighing 40 mg *0.00014 oz* jumped to a height of 30 cm *11¾ in* and was calculated to have endured a peak brain deceleration of *2300 g* by the end of the movement.

**Longest lived** *see general records for Insects.*

**Longest snout** The long-snouted South African cycad weevil (*Antliarhinus zamiae*) has the longest snout, relative to body size, of any known beetle. On average, the weevil itself is about 3 cm *1.2 in* long and its snout can add a further 2 cm *0.8 in* to its overall length. It is believed that the long snout is needed to drill holes for laying eggs inside cycad seeds.

**Strangest defence** The bombardier beetle (genus *Brachinus*) stores two relatively benign chemicals in a special chamber in its abdomen. When it feels threatened, the chemicals are released into a second chamber, where they mix with an enzyme, resulting in a violent chemical reaction and the release of considerable heat. The concoction may approach 100°C *212°F* and is sprayed from the anus as an explosive puff of irritating gas (which the beetle can aim with remarkable accuracy). The spray can be turned on and off 500 times a second, using a system very similar to the one used in the pulse jet engine that powered the German V-1 flying bomb during World War II; the V-1, however, was capable of pulsing its jet only 42 times per second.

**Most threatened** According to the World Conservation Union (IUCN) there are more threatened insects than any other group of insects: a total of 378 species of which 190 are considered to be in serious trouble. Many more are likely to be added to this list as research progresses. In addition, there is serious concern for several hundred other species whose populations have yet to be properly assessed.

**Extinctions** A total of 18 beetles and weevils are known or suspected to have become extinct since the mid-1800s. The majority of these were found in the USA (reflecting a high level of research as well as a high extinction rate) and include the Mono Lake diving beetle (*Hygrotus artus*), Blackburn's weevil (*Pentarthrum blackburni*) and the Fort Ross weevil (*Trigonoscuta rossi*). However, it is likely that many coleopteran species become extinct before the status of their populations has been properly assessed or even before they are known to science – and therefore go unrecorded.

**Largest family** With over 60 000 species known, the weevils or snout beetles (family Curculionidae) form the largest family in animal kingdom. All of them are plant eaters, and many are pests.

---

## BUGS

### *Hemiptera*
Nearly 90 000 species, including shield bugs, bed bugs, aphids, water boatmen, cicadas, hoppers, pond skaters

---

**Largest** The largest true bugs are giant water bugs in the family Belostomatidae, which can be up to 6.5 cm *2.6 in* long. They feed on both invertebrate and vertebrate prey as large as salamanders and small fish.

Cicadas (family Cicadidae) are also relatively large, attaining lengths of up to 6 cm *2.4 in*.

**Longest lived** *see general records for Insects.*

**Most threatened** According to the World Conservation Union (IUCN), 26 species of bug (order Hemiptera) are known or suspected to be threatened with extinction (many more are likely

to be added to this list as research progresses); the species considered to be in the most danger is the Ash Meadows bug (*Ambrysus amargosus*), which is found in the USA. A further 21 species of hoppers and cicadas (order Hemiptera) are known or suspected to be threatened with extinction; the most threatened of these are three species of periodical cicada in the genus *Magicicada*, all of which are found in North America.

**Extinctions** Only two species in the orders Hemiptera and Homoptera are known or suspected to have become extinct since the mid-1800s. These are both mealybugs in the family Pseudococcidae. However, it is likely that at least some species disappear before the status of their populations has been properly assessed or even before they are known to science – and therefore go unrecorded.

**Most fertile** *see general records for Insects.*

**Loudest** *see general records for Insects.*

---

## BUTTERFLIES & MOTHS

### *Lepidoptera*
*c.* 165 000 known species: including approximately 20 000 butterflies and 145 000 moths

---

**Largest** The largest known butterfly is the rare Queen Alexandra's birdwing (*Ornithoptera alexandrae*) of the Popondetta Plain area, in Northern Province, Papua New Guinea. Females are larger than males and have a front wingspan which may exceed 28 cm *11.02 in* from tip to tip (average 21 cm *8¼ in*) and a weight of more than 25 g *0.88 oz*. This species is seldom seen; it is found only in association with the vine *Aristolochia dielsiana* (its only source of nourishment) and both adults and caterpillars live out of sight 15–40 m *49–131 ft* above the ground in the vine leaves.

*Only male cicadas 'sing': their calls serve to attract females of the same species*

**I N V E R T E B R A T E S**

**The most acute sense of smell in nature is that of the male emperor moth, which can smell females from an almost unbelievable range of 11 km *6.8 miles*.**

There are several moths which match – and may even exceed – the Queen Alexandra's birdwing in size. The Hercules moth (*Cosdinoscera hercules*) of tropical Australia and Papua New Guinea has a wingspan of up to 28 cm *11.02 in* and there is an unconfirmed measurement of 36 cm *14.17 in*, taken in 1948 for a female captured in Innisfail, Queensland, Australia. The rare owlet moth (*Thysania agrippina*), which lives in southern USA and Central and South America, is of a similar size: the record is a female with a wingspan of 30.8 cm *12.16 in*; she was taken in 1934 and is now in the collection of John G. Powers in Ontario, Canada. The enormous Atlas moth (*Attacus atlas*) is often mistaken for a bird, while flying around its rainforest home in south-east Asia, and has a wingspan of up to 25 cm *9.8 in* (although there are unauthenticated records of up to 30 cm *11.8 in*); the male has huge feathery antennae, the largest of any butterfly or moth.

**Smallest** The smallest of the known butterflies and moths is a micro-moth called *Stigmella ridiculosa*, which lives in the Canary Islands. It has a wingspan of 2 mm *0.079 in* and a similar body length. The world's smallest butterfly is the dwarf blue (*Brephidium barberae*) of South Africa. It has a wingspan of 1.4 cm *0.55 in* and weighs less than 10 mg *0.00035 oz*.

**Longest tongue** A characteristic feature of adult lepidopterans is the sucking proboscis or tongue, which is generally rolled up underneath the head when resting and has to be unrolled to feed. It functions like a flexible drinking straw and is used mainly for sucking nectar out of flowers. The longest tongues are found in the hawk moths (family Sphingidae), which use them to feed on the nectar deep inside tubular-flowered orchids.

The longest of all the hawk moth tongues belongs to the Madagascan hawk moth (*Xanthopan morgani praedicta*). Intriguingly, Charles Darwin predicted the existence of this moth more than 40 years before it was actually discovered, in 1903. After examining one of Madagascar's native orchids, a species called *Angraecum sesquipedale*, whose nectar-producing organs are almost 30 cm *11.8 in* deep, he concluded that Madagascar must be home to a butterfly or moth with an exceptionally long proboscis in order to reach the nectar (and thereby brush against the orchid's pollen and effect pollination). As Darwin suspected, the Madagascan hawk moth has a record-breaking 28 cm *11 in* proboscis, which is just enough to reach the nectar which lies in the deepest 4 cm *1.6 in* of the orchid.

It is possible that another species of Madagascan hawk moth, as yet undiscovered, has an even longer proboscis; the Madagascan orchid *A. longicalcar* is even deeper than *A. sesquipedale* and would require a proboscis of 38 cm *15 in* to reach the nectar at the bottom.

**Most acute sense of smell** The most acute sense of smell exhibited in nature is that of the male emperor moth (*Eudia pavonia*) which, according to German experiments in 1961, can detect the sex attractant of the virgin female at an almost unbelievable range of 11 km *6.8 miles*. The female's scent has been identified as one of the higher alcohols ($C_{16}H_{29}OH$) of which she carries less than 0.0001 mg (and only the minutest portion is released into the air at any one time). The chemoreceptors on the male moth's antennae are so sensitive that they can detect a single molecule of the scent; they can also determine the strength of the scent and, as it increases, the moth is able to move along in the direction of the female source.

**Greediest animal** The caterpillar of the polyphemus moth (*Antheraea polyphemus*) of North America consumes an amount of oak, maple and birch leaves equal to 86 000 times its own birth weight in the first 56 days of its life. In human terms, this would be equivalent to a 3.17 kg *7 lb* baby taking in 273 tonnes of nourishment.

> *The monarch or milkweed butterfly is so poisonous and bad-tasting that, if it is eaten, it causes uncontrollable retching in birds and other predators.*

**Noisiest** Butterflies and moths are normally the essence of peace and quiet, but male butterflies in the genus *Hamadryas* make a loud clickety-clickety-clack sound that can be heard up to 30.5 m *100 ft* away. An analysis of high-speed photographs and sound recordings (with the aid of a computer) by biologist Julián Monge-Nájera, working at the University of Costa Rica, has revealed that the males produce the sound when their forewings collide during vigorous flight (normally prior to courtship as they jostle for space along female flight paths).

Some moths make loud ultrasonic clicking sounds (beyond the range of human hearing) when they hear echolocating bats – to make the predators leave them alone. It is unclear exactly how these noises affect the bats, but they may startle them or jam their echolocation systems, or they could even be the acoustic equivalent of warning colours (telling the bats that the moths taste unpleasant).

**Strangest diet** Several hundred tropical and sub-tropical moth species (belonging to six different families) drink the tears of hoofed mammals such as cattle and other bovids, deer, horses, tapirs, pigs and elephants. They have even been known to drink the tears of people, but have yet to be seen visiting carnivores, marsupials, birds or members of any other group of vertebrates. This preference for certain hosts may reflect differences in the chemical composition of tears from different animals – or it may simply be that the most frequent victims are the most placid and tolerant. Tears are believed to be a source of protein and salt, and for most moth species form only part of a much broader diet. However, nearly 10 species feed exclusively on tears and one of the most highly evolved of these is a south-east Asian moth called *Lobocraspis griseifusa*, which actively sweeps the victim's eyeball with its proboscis to stimulate a copious flow of tears.

**Blood drinking** A number of moth species lap up the blood seeping from open wounds on an entirely opportunistic basis. But the vampire moth (*Calyptra eustrigata*) of Malaysia takes this a stage further and is the only lepidopteran known to make its own wound to drink blood. It has an unusually short, sturdy proboscis, which it stabs directly through the skin of large mammals (causing brief pain) and then uses to suck up the blood as if through a drinking straw. This unique feeding behaviour possibly evolved from the fruit-piercing habit of many moths, which have a similar kind of proboscis.

> *Butterflies and moths have some of the strangest names in the animal kingdom; good examples include the silver-topped wallaby grass moth, the green banded Ohe Ohe leaf-roller moth, the pale hockey stick sailer, the death's head hawk moth and the false baton blue.*

**Oldest** The entire lifecycle of a butterfly or moth (egg – caterpillar or larva – chrysalis or pupa – adult or imago) can last for as long as several years. But the lifespan of the adult is usually much shorter than any of the other stages. Most adult butterflies, for example, live for an average of 2–3 weeks (some for as little as one week), giving them little time to complete courtship, mating and egg-laying. A few species that hibernate over winter may live for as long as 12 months – for example the brimstone (*Gonepteryx rhamni*) and peacock (*Inachis io*) – but few remain *active* for so long. The main exceptions are the 38 species of long-winged butterflies in the genus *Heliconius*, which live in the tropical rainforests of the Americas. They can live 25 times longer than most other butterflies and the oldest on record was approximately 9 months when it eventually died.

**Greatest chemists** Recent research suggests that butterflies may be nature's greatest chemists. A team of German and British scientists have found that African milkweed butterflies from the genera *Danaus*, *Tirumala* and *Amauris* can make no fewer than 214 compounds from 14 different chemical classes. Individual milkweed species have a quite distinct mixture of compounds (including some which are unique to the species) with anywhere from 12 to 59 chemicals each. Until this study, some of the chemicals had never been found in nature before. They are produced in the male scent glands and are thought to be used in pheromone production (helping the female to ensure that her potential mate belongs to the right species) and to make the butterflies extremely poisonous to birds and other potential predators.

**Lowest temperature** During the winter, hundreds of insect species are able to survive long periods of freezing without apparent harm, and then thaw in the spring. The record-holder is probably the woolly bear caterpillar (*Gynaephora groenlandica*) of the high Arctic, which is the larval stage of a tiger moth in the family Arctiidae. The caterpillar may spend as much as 10 months of the year frozen solid at temperatures that drop to –50°C –58°F or even lower.

---

Most adult butterflies, such as this swallowtail, live for only a few weeks or months – although their entire lifecycle can last for several years.

**Fastest flying** The fastest-flying lepidopteran is the death's head hawk moth (*Acherontia atropos*), which is found in Europe, Africa and northern Asia. It has a complex wingbeat (involving at least four different wing movements to obtain maximum uplift) and has been credited with bursts of speed of nearly 54 km/h *33½ mph*. Acceptable modern experiments have established that the highest *maintainable* airspeed of any lepidopteran is 39 km/h *24 mph* by several species of hawk moth (family Sphingidae) and some tropical butterflies (family Hesperiidae).

**Longest migration** It is extremely difficult to study the migratory flights of butterflies and moths, because they are too small, too fragile and too short-lived to trace their movements using the standard 'mark and recapture' techniques used so successfully in bird research. However, there have been a few extraordinary successes. The record-holder is a tagged female monarch or milkweed butterfly (*Danaus plexippus*) released by Donald Davis at Presqu'ile Provincial Park near Brighton, Ontario, Canada, on 6 Sep 1986, and recaptured 3432 km *2133 miles* away, on a mountain near Angangueo, Mexico, on 15 Jan 1987. This distance was obtained by measuring a straight line from the release site to the recapture site, but the actual distance travelled could have been considerably longer.

Dr William Hendrix III, of Iowa State University, and Dr William Showers, of the Corn Research Institute in Ankeny, Iowa, USA, have been studying North American migratory moths by investigating the pollen present on their bodies at the end of their journeys. Their findings suggest that two noctuid moths, the black cutworm or dark swordgrass (*Agrotis ipsilon*) and the armyworm (*Pseudaletia unipunctata*), are extreme long-distance fliers. They examined a total of 5755 moths in central Iowa and, with a fair degree of certainty, were able to trace the origins of the pollen of 14 of them. These particular moths had flown at least 1600 km *994 miles* and, in some cases, as far as 2200 km *1366 miles*.

Vast numbers of painted lady butterflies (*Cynthia cardui*) migrate

There is a rule of thumb that butterflies are brightly coloured and fly by day, while moths are drab and fly by night; this is largely true, although there are many exceptions.

northwards from the desert edges of North Africa and Arabia across Europe and, in some years, as far north as Iceland and beyond. In exceptional summers they penetrate far above the Arctic Circle, more than 3000 km *1865 miles* north of their winter breeding grounds. It is unknown whether these long-distance migrations occur in one flight, or over several generations.

**Highest migration** The greatest height reliably reported for migrating butterflies is 5791 m *19 000 ft* for a small flock of small tortoiseshells (*Aglais urticae*) seen flying over the Zemu Glacier in the eastern Himalayas. The Queen of Spain fritillary (*Issoria lathonia*) has reputedly been seen flying at about 6000 m *19 685 ft* in the Himalayas.

**Record fly-past** In 1928/29, an enormous flock of African migrant butterflies (*Catopsilia florella*) took 3 months to fly past the house of an entomologist living in East Africa. The fly-past was apparently continuous: there was always a steady stream and, at times, there were huge swarms.

**Largest colony** Every November, millions of monarch or milkweed butterflies (*Danaus plexippus*) gather in the mature fir, pine and cypress forests along the coasts of California, USA, and Mexico. They spend the winter in the same locations year after year, with only slight shifts in the precise trees chosen depending on weather conditions. Crowded together in dense masses, they often cover every available space on the trunks and branches. The Californian colonies each contain a maximum of approximately 100 000 individuals, but the Mexican ones are considerably larger and may number many millions (concentrations reach

10 million/ha *4 million/acre*). As spring approaches, they begin to leave their roosts and mate before departing in late February or early March to begin their migration north (sometimes flying as far as 3000 km *1860 miles* or more).

**Greatest diversity** The greatest diversity of butterflies known anywhere in the world is in the rainforests of South America. Gerardo Lamas and his colleagues have recorded no fewer than 1209 species within an area of 55 km² *21¼ miles²* in the Tambopata Reserve, in the Rio Madre de Dios drainage, south-eastern Peru. In a similar study at Fazenda Rancho Grande, Rondonia, western Brazil, Thomas Emmel and George Austin have so far identified 800 species in a much smaller forest patch (several km²) and estimate the total number to be 1500–1600. This compares with fewer than 380 species in the whole of Europe.

**Most threatened** The World Conservation Union (IUCN) lists a total of 342 species of butterflies and moths that are known or suspected to be threatened with extinction (many more are likely to be added to this list as research progresses). About 25 of these are believed to be in particularly serious danger, including the Queen Alexandra's birdwing (*Ornithoptera alexandrae*) of Papua New Guinea; the European large blue (*Maculinea arion*); Natterer's longwing (*Heliconius nattereri*) of Brazil; the tawny crescent butterfly (*Phyciodes batesi*) of the USA; and the prairie sphinx moth (*Euproserpinus wiesti*) of the USA. A further 98 sub-species are known or suspected to be threatened.

**Extinctions** Thirty-eight species of butterflies and moths are known or suspected to have become extinct in recent times, including the Xerces blue butterfly (*Glaucopsyche xerces*), which disappeared from the USA in the early 1940s, and the Levuana moth (*Levuana irridescens*) which disappeared from the Hawaiian Islands, USA, in 1929. No fewer than 29 (76 per cent) of all recently extinct lepidopterans used to live in the Hawaiian Islands, USA; however, this figure reflects a high level of research as well as a high extinction rate and it is likely that, in many parts of the world, at least some species become extinct before the status of their populations has been properly assessed or even before they are known to science – and therefore go unrecorded. A further eight sub-species are known or suspected to have become extinct in recent times.

One way to tell a butterfly from a moth is by the way they hold their wings: although there are many exceptions, butterflies tend to hold them vertically over the body while moths fold them horizontally; another distinguishing feature is the antennae, which end in a small club on butterflies but tend to be feathery on moths.

I
N
V
E
R
T
E
B
R
A
T
E
S

## CADDISFLIES

### Trichoptera
Nearly 10 000 species

**Most threatened** The World Conservation Union (IUCN) lists a total of 49 species of caddisfly that are known or suspected to be threatened with extinction (many more are likely to be added to this list as research progresses). Eight of these are found in Australia and the remaining 41 in the USA, indicating areas with a high level of research as well as a relatively large number of threatened species.

**Extinctions** Only four caddisfly species are known or suspected to have become extinct since the mid-1800s: the Castle Lake caddisfly (*Rhyacophila amabilis*), Athens caddisfly (*Triaenodes phalacris*) and the three-tooth caddisfly (*Triaenodes tridonata*), all of which used to live in the USA; and Tobias' caddisfly (*Hydropsyche tobiasi*), which used to live in Germany. However, it is likely that at least some caddisflies disappear before the status of their populations has been properly assessed or even before they are known to science – and therefore go unrecorded.

**Most marine** Caddisflies are normally found near freshwater, but there is an Australian species, *Philanisus plebeius*, which breeds by the sea in rock pools near the low-tide mark.

## COCKROACHES

### Blattodea
Nearly 4000 species

**Largest** The world's largest cockroach is *Megaloblatta longipennis* of Colombia. A preserved female in the collection of Akira Yokokura of Yamagata, Japan, measures 9.7 cm *3.81 in* in length and 4.5 cm *1.77 in* across.

**Most threatened** The only species of cockroach known or suspected to be threatened with extinction is the tuna cave roach (*Aspiduchus cavernicola*), a poorly known species living in Puerto Rico. More cockroaches are likely to be

added to this list as research progresses. No species is known to have become extinct, although it is likely that at least some disappear before the status of their populations has been properly assessed or even before they are known to science – and therefore go unrecorded.

**Fastest** *see general records for Insects.*

> *When threatened, a species of South African cockroach stands on its head and hisses vigorously.*

## CRICKETS, GRASSHOPPERS & LOCUSTS

### Orthoptera
*c.* 20 000 species, including crickets, grasshoppers, wetas, katydids

**Largest** The largest known grasshopper in the world is an unidentified species from the border of Malaysia and Thailand, measuring 25.4 cm *10 in* in length. It is capable of leaping 4.6 m *15 ft.*

**Heaviest** *see general records for Insects.*

**Greatest concentration** A huge swarm of Rocky Mountain locusts (*Melanoplus spretus*), which were once the scourge of western pioneers in North America, covered a *minimum* area equivalent in size to England, Scotland, Wales and Ireland combined. Some estimates put the size of the swarm as high as 514 374 km² *198 600 ml²* as it flew over the state of Nebraska, USA, on 15–25 Aug 1875. It contained an estimated 12.5 trillion (12 500 000 000 000) locusts, weighing in the order of 25–50 million tonnes. (These figures are partly speculative, since the exact characteristics of Rocky Mountain locust swarms are un-

> *Some caddisfly larvae make protective cases from twigs (to prevent fish from swallowing them) and these are known as log cabins*

> *Crickets and grasshoppers do not have ears on their head, but on their abdomen or legs instead; each 'ear' consists of a thin membrane with specialized receptors.*

known: the species mysteriously became extinct in 1902.)

**Most destructive** *see general records for Insects.*

**Most threatened** The World Conservation Union (IUCN) lists a total of 72 species of grasshoppers, crickets, wetas and katydids that are known or suspected to be threatened with extinction (more are likely to be added to this list as research progresses). These include nine species of weta (family Stenopelmatidae) from New Zealand, two monkey grasshoppers (family Eumastacidae) from the USA and the Oahu deceptor bush cricket (*Leptogryllus deceptor*) from the Hawaiian Islands, USA.

**Extinctions** The only orthopteran known or suspected to have become extinct since the mid-1800s is the Antioch Dunes shieldback katydid (*Neduba extincta*), which disappeared from its home in the USA in 1937. However, it is likely that at least some species disappear before the status of their populations has been properly assessed or even before they are known to science – and therefore go unrecorded.

**Highest living** The highest-living orthopteran is a species called *Punacris peruviana*, in the sub-family Tristirinae, which is found in short wiry turf in the dry Peruvian Andes at heights of over 4300 m *14 104 ft.*

**Loudest** *see general records for Insects.*

## DRAGONFLIES & DAMSELFLIES

### Odonata
*c.* 5500 species

**Earliest** The first dragonflies and damselflies appeared during the Carboniferous period, between 280 and 350 million years ago, making them

**I
N
V
E
R
T
E
B
R
A
T
E
S**

(along with mayflies – order Ephemeroptera) the most ancient of flying insects.

**Largest** A damselfly, *Megalopropus caeruleata* of Central and South America, has a wingspan of up to 19.1 cm *7.52 in* and a body length of 12 cm *4.72 in.*

**Largest prehistoric** *see general records for Insects.*

**Smallest dragonfly** The world's smallest dragonfly is *Agriocnemis naia* of Myanmar (Burma). A specimen in The Natural History Museum, UK, has a wingspan of 1.76 cm *0.69 in* and a body length of 1.8 cm *0.71 in.*

**Fastest flying** *see general records for Insects.*

**Most threatened** The World Conservation Union (IUCN) lists a total of 138 species of dragonfly and damselfly that are known or suspected to be threatened with extinction (more are likely to be added to the list as research progresses). The species considered to be in most danger include the San Francisco forktail damselfly (*Ischnura gemina*), from the USA; the Pacific damselfly (*Megalagrion pacificum*), from the Hawaiian Islands, USA; the Ohio emerald dragonfly (*Somatochlora hineana*), from the USA; *Mortonagrion hirosei*, from Japan; *Platycnemis mauriciana*, from Mauritius; and *Mecistogaster pronoti*, from Brazil.

**Extinctions** Only three species of Odonata are known or suspected to have become extinct since the mid-1800s: Jugorum Megalagrion damselfly (*Megalagrion jugorum*) and Edmund's snaketail damselfly (*Ophiogomphus edmundo*), both of which lived in the USA; and *Sympetrum dilatatum*, which used to live on St Helena. However, it is likely that at least some dragonflies and damselflies disappear before the status of their populations has been properly assessed or even before they

are known to science – and therefore go unrecorded.

---

### EARWIGS

### Dermaptera
*c.* 1800 species

**Largest** The largest earwig in the world is the St Helena giant earwig (*Labidura herculeana*), which has a body length of 3.6–5.4 cm *1.4–2.1 in* and additional pincers of 1.5–2.4 cm *0.6–1.0 in*, making a total maximum length of 7.8 cm *3.1 in*. The largest known specimen is a male of 7.8 cm *3.1 in* total length, preserved in the collections of the Musée Royal de l'Afrique Centrale, in Tervuren, Belgium. Females tend to be smaller, with relatively shorter forceps. First described in 1798 and not seen again until 1965, this poorly known insect is extremely rare or even extinct (*see Extinctions*). As its name suggests, it comes from the island of St Helena, in the mid-Atlantic.

---

*Earwigs gained their name because they like to squeeze into any tight crack or crevice and therefore, given the chance, they really do try to get into people's ears; however, they do not tear through the ear drum or hollow out the brain as people used to think.*

**Most threatened** No earwig species is known or suspected to be threatened with extinction, although it is likely that at least some threatened species will be revealed as research progresses.

**Extinctions** The St Helena giant earwig (*Labidura herculeana*) is the only species of earwig believed to be extinct. It was last seen alive by a Belgian Zoological expedition in 1965–67, in a barren area of approximately 1 km² *0.4 mile²* known as Horse Point Plain, in

---

**The largest earwig in the world is the St Helena giant earwig, shown here actual size.**

*The best way to tell dragonflies and damselflies apart is by their wings: dragonflies hold theirs out when resting, while damselflies hold theirs together over their back.*

the extreme north-east of St Helena. The cause of extinction is unknown.

No other earwig species is known to have become extinct since the mid-1800s, although it is possible that some disappear before the status of their populations has been properly assessed or even before they are known to science – and therefore go unrecorded.

## FLEAS

### Siphonaptera
*c.* 2400 species

**Largest** Siphonapterologists recognize 1830 varieties of flea, of which the largest known is *Hystrichopsylla schefferi*, which was described from a single specimen taken from the nest of a mountain beaver at Puyallup, Washington, USA, in 1913. Females are up to 8 mm *0.32 in* long, which is roughly the diameter of a pencil.

**Best jumper** The cat flea (*Ctenocephalides felis*) is believed to be the champion jumper among fleas and has been known to reach a height of 34 cm *13.4 in* in a single jump. This requires an acceleration over 20 times that needed to launch a space rocket. However, other species are capable of equivalent or similar feats. In one American experiment carried out in 1910, a common flea (*Pulex irritans*) allowed to leap at will performed a long jump of 33 cm *13 in* and a high jump of 19.7 cm *7¾ in*. The fleas do not use only muscle power when jumping, but have developed a triggered click mechanism which involves generating and then storing energy. They can release as much as 97 per cent of this stored energy for a massive leap (or a series of leaps) whenever it is required. Many fleas are capable of jumping non-stop for many hours, or even several days, without a rest.

> *All fleas live on a diet exclusively of blood.*

**Most threatened** No fleas are known or suspected to be threatened with extinction, although it is likely that at least some threatened species will be revealed as research progresses. Similarly, none is known or suspected to have become extinct in recent years.

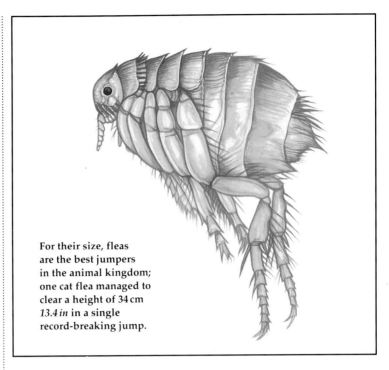

For their size, fleas are the best jumpers in the animal kingdom; one cat flea managed to clear a height of 34 cm *13.4 in* in a single record-breaking jump.

However, it is likely that many species disappear before the status of their populations has been properly assessed or even before they are known to science – and therefore go unrecorded.

**Most dangerous** *see general records for Insects.*

## LACEWINGS

### Neuroptera
*c.* 4500 species of lacewings and antlions

**Most threatened** The World Conservation Union (IUCN) lists a total of seven species of lacewing that are known or suspected to be threatened with extinction (more are likely to be added to the list as research progresses). They are all found in the Hawaiian Islands, USA. No species is known to

> *Some fleas are highly adaptable and can choose from a wide variety of hosts, but many are much more specialized; consequently, there is a beaver flea, a human flea, a penguin flea and even a Tasmanian devil flea.*

have become extinct, although it is likely that at least some disappear before the status of their populations has been properly assessed or even before they are known to science – and therefore go unrecorded.

## LICE

### Phthiraptera & Psocoptera
*c.* 7000 species, including biting lice, sucking lice, book lice, bark lice

**Lightest** The male bloodsucking banded louse (*Enderleinellus zonatus*) is the lightest insect in the world, though it shares the title with the parasitic wasp *Caraphractus cinctus*. Each louse may weigh as little as 0.005 mg (equivalent to *5 670 000 to an oz*).

**Most threatened** According to the World Conservation Union (IUCN), the only species of louse known or suspected to be threatened with extinction is the pygmy hog sucking louse (*Haematopinus oliveri*), which lives in India. Many more species are likely to be added to this list as research progresses. No species is known to have become extinct, although it is likely that at least some disappear before the status of their populations has been properly assessed or even before they are known to science – and therefore go unrecorded.

Pelican lice live inside the throat pouches of pelicans, coming out through the nasal holes of the bill to lay their eggs on the birds' head and neck feathers.

## MANTIDS

### Mantodea
Praying mantises
Nearly 2000 species (most in the tropics)

**Largest** The largest praying mantises are members of the genus *Tenodera* and the species *Archimantis latistyla*, all of which can attain lengths in excess of 15 cm *5.9 in.*

**Smallest** The smallest praying mantis is a species called *Bolbe pygmaea*, which is about 1 cm *0.39 in* in length.

**Most threatened** According to the World Conservation Union (IUCN), the only mantid known or suspected to be threatened with extinction is a species called *Apteromantis aptera*, which lives in Spain. Many more are likely to be added to this list as research progresses. No species is known to have become extinct, although it is likely that at least some disappear before the status of their populations has been properly assessed or even before they are known to science – and therefore go unrecorded.

## MAYFLIES

### Ephemeroptera
*c.* 2100 species

**Most threatened** The World Conservation Union (IUCN) lists a total of 14 mayfly species that are known or suspected to be threatened with extinction (many more are likely to be added to this list as research progresses). The rarest of these is probably the large Blue Lake mayfly (*Tasmanophlebia lacuscoerulei*), which lives in Australia.

**Extinctions** Two species of mayfly are known or suspected to have become extinct since the mid-1800s: the

Pecatonica River mayfly (*Acanthometropus pecatonica*) and the robust burrowing mayfly (*Pantagenia robusta*), both of which lived in the USA. However, it is likely that at least some mayflies disappear before the status of their populations has been properly assessed or even before they are known to science – and therefore go unrecorded.

The shiny, silvery sheen of silverfish is caused by reflectant scales.

## SILVERFISH & BRISTLETAILS

### Thysanura
Silverfish & bristletails
*c.* 400 species

**Most threatened** The World Conservation Union (IUCN) lists only two species in the order Thysanura which are known or suspected to be threatened with extinction: the Hawaiian long-palp bristletail (*Machiloides heteropus*) and Perkin's club-palp bristletail (*Machiloides perkinsi*), both of which live in the Hawaiian Islands, USA. More species are likely to be added to this list as research progresses. No species is known to have become extinct, although it is likely that at least some disappear before the status of their populations has been properly assessed or even before they are known to science – and therefore go unrecorded.

To a female praying mantis, the male is just another potential meal, so he has to be very careful when approaching her to avoid being seized and eaten; if he is careless, she will eat his head first and will start even while they are mating.

## STICK INSECTS & LEAF INSECTS

### Phasmatodea
More than 2500 species

**Longest** *see general records for Insects.*

**Most dangerous** Stick insects are generally harmless creatures and no species can actually sting or bite. Some hiss alarmingly, others attempt to slash predators with their sharp-spurred hind legs, and a few arch their backs to pretend that they are capable of stinging like a scorpion. One of the most 'dangerous' is probably the two-striped walking stick (*Anisomorpha buprestoides*) from Florida, USA, which is able to squirt a milky spray over a distance of up to 20 cm *8 in* that can cause temporary blindness.

**Egg-laying** Females of the species *Acrophylla titan*, a 25 cm *10 in* stick insect from Queensland, Australia, lay more than 2000 relatively large eggs – more than any other species of stick insect.

*In some stick insect species there are no males: the females can produce fertilized eggs without their help through a process called parthenogenesis.*

**Largest egg** *see general records for Insects.*

**Most threatened** No stick insect or leaf insect is known or suspected to be threatened with extinction, although it is likely that at least some threatened species will be revealed as research progresses.

**Extinctions** Only one stick insect is known or suspected to have become extinct since the mid-1800s: the Lord Howe Island stick insect (*Dryococelus australis*), which is believed to have disappeared from its native home on Lord Howe Island, Australia, in the 1970s. However, it is likely that at least some stick insects and leaf insects disappear before the status of their populations has been properly assessed or even before they are known to science – and therefore go unrecorded.

## STONEFLIES

### Plecoptera
Nearly 2000 species

**Most threatened** The World Conservation Union (IUCN) lists a total of 15 species of stonefly that are known or suspected to be threatened with extinction (more are likely to be added to this list as research continues). The species considered to be in most serious danger is the Otway stonefly (*Eusthenia nothofagi*), which lives in Australia.

**Extinctions** The only species of stonefly known or suspected to have become extinct since the mid-1800s is Robert's stonefly (*Alloperla roberti*), which was found in the USA. However, it is likely that at least some species disappear before the status of their populations

Termite mound in Botswana: in proportion to their size, termites build the largest structures of all land-living creatures.

has been properly assessed or even before they are known to science – and therefore go unrecorded.

## TERMITES

### Isoptera
*c.* 2300 species

**Earliest** Fossil termite nests discovered in rocks in Arizona's Petrified Forest National Park, USA, have been dated at 220 million years old. This was a very significant find since the previous earliest indication of their existence was a termite wing fragment just over 100

*When the nests of some termite species are invaded by marauding ants, the soldiers block off the tunnels by swelling up and then exploding – covering their attackers with all their insides.*

**INVERTEBRATES**

*Termites are believed to be more closely related to cockroaches than to ants; strangely, they are often called 'white ants', although they are neither white nor ants.*

million years old and evidence of termite damage in 70-million-year-old wood. The earliest evidence of other social insects – bees and wasps – comes from the late Cretaceous period about 70 million years ago.

**Largest** The largest termite in the world is the African species *Macrotermes bellicosus*. The workers are relatively small, but the queens have hugely swollen bodies (which are basically giant egg-producing machines, capable of making over 30 000 eggs a day) and have been measured up to 14 cm *5½ in* long and 3.5 cm *1.4 in* wide. The queens can barely move and spend their entire lives in a 'royal cell' in the centre of the colony – and do little other than feed and reproduce.

**Largest termite mound** In proportion to their size, termites build the largest structures of all land-living creatures (coral reefs are considerably larger). The *bulkiest* termite mounds are found in northern Australia, where they can be as much as 6.1 m *20 ft* high and 31 m *102 ft* in diameter around the base. However, the *tallest* mounds are built by the African species *Macrotermes bellicosus*; the world record was a mound discovered in Zaire which was 12.8 m *42 ft* high (but a maximum of only 3 m *9 ft 10 in* in diameter). For comparison, the tallest office building in the world is the Sears Tower in Chicago, USA: it rises to 443 m *1454 ft* or about the height of 250 people; in contrast, the highest termite mound is taller than 2000 termite workers laid end to end. When building their intricate nests, the workers painstakingly put each grain of soil in place, one piece at a time, and cement them together with saliva.

**Lifespan** *see general records for Insects.*

**Most threatened** No termite species is known or suspected to be threatened with extinction, although it is likely that at least some threatened species will be revealed as research progresses. Similarly, no species is known to have become extinct since the mid-1800s. However, it is possible that some disappear before the status of their populations has been properly assessed or even before they are known to science – and therefore go unrecorded.

---

## TRUE FLIES

### Diptera
*c.* 120 000 species, including midges, craneflies, mosquitos, gnats, houseflies, bluebottles, horseflies, hoverflies

**Largest** The world's largest fly is *Mydas heros*, from tropical South America, which has been recorded with a body length of 6 cm *2.36 in* and a wingspan of about 10 cm *3.94 in*. This powerful predator tackles prey as formidable and well-armed as bees and wasps by biting them on the neck.

Craneflies (family Tipulidae) have very elongated bodies and long legs (thus the common name 'daddy long legs') but have very little bulk. The body length of some species may reach a maximum 6.5 cm *2.6 in* and the wingspan can exceed 10 cm *3.94 in*. However, with the legs extended, the *overall* length (measured from the tips of the front legs to the tips of the hind legs) of species such as *Holorusia brobdignagius* can probably exceed 23 cm *9.1 in*.

*Each housefly carries between 2 and 3 million bacteria on and inside its body.*

**Fastest wingbeat** *see general records for Insects.*

**Fastest-flying** *see general records for Insects.*

**Most studied** Several species of fruit fly in the genus *Drosophila* are probably the most studied animals in the world. Their small size, ease of culturing on artificial media, high reproduction rate and giant salivary chromosomes make them ideal as laboratory insects in a broad range of studies involving genetics, cytology and physiology. In particular, they have been used for many years in classic genetics experiments in heredity and, indeed, complete gene maps have been made for some species.

---

*A group of flies is sometimes called a 'business'.*

**Most threatened** The World Conservation Union (IUCN) lists 18 species of fly which are known or suspected to be threatened with extinction (many more are likely to be added to this list as research progresses). The most seriously threatened are the giant torrent midge (*Edwardsina gigantea*), found in Australia; the Tasmanian torrent midge (*Edwardsina tasmaniensis*), as its name suggests found in Tasmania, Australia; and Belkin's dune tabanid fly (*Brennania belkini*), found in Mexico and the USA.

*If a pair of houseflies were left to their own devices for a summer, and all the succeeding generations survived, there would be enough flies to cover an area the size of Germany in a mound six storeys high.*

**Extinctions** Only three fly species are known or suspected to have become extinct since the mid-1800s: the volutine stoneyian tabanid fly (*Stonemyia volutina*), *Campsicnemus mirabilis* and the fruit fly *Drosophila lanaiensis*, all of which lived in the USA. However, it is likely that many dipteran species disappear before the status of their populations has been properly assessed or even before they are known to science – and therefore go unrecorded.

**Shortest-lived** *see general records for Insects.*

**Most dangerous** *see general records for Insects.*

**Most profound influence** *see general records for Insects.*

*It is almost impossible to swat a fly because its eyes are extremely sensitive to movement and it has a reaction time of 0.02 s (against the minimum human reaction time of 0.25 s); to a fly, an attempt to swat it must appear to be in slow motion.*

# JELLYFISH & CORALS

## Cnidaria
Jellyfish, hydroids, sea anemones, corals etc.
*c.* 9000 species

Sixty per cent of the world's coral reefs are found in the Indian Ocean (including the Red Sea).

**Earliest** Coral reefs are probably the oldest ecosystems on the planet and, indeed, primitive forms existed at least 450 million years ago. The first 'modern' reef-building corals appeared nearly 230 million years ago and, since evolution on coral reefs is a much more gradual process than in many other less stable environments, they have changed surprisingly little since then. In fact, some fossil reef animals dating back to the age of the dinosaurs, about 100 millions years ago, are represented by creatures in the same genera which are still alive today.

**Largest jellyfish** Most jellyfish have a bell or body diameter ranging from 2–40 cm *0.8–15.8 in*, but some species grow considerably larger. The largest is the Arctic giant jellyfish (*Cyanea capillata arctica*) of the north-west Atlantic. One huge specimen which washed up in Massachusetts Bay, USA, had a bell diameter of 2.28 m *7½ ft* and tentacles stretching to 36.5 m *120 ft*.

**Largest sea anemone** The world's largest sea anemone is a species in the genus *Discoma*, which is found on the Great Barrier Reef, Queensland, Australia. When expanded, its oral disc measures up to 61 cm *24 in* in diameter.

**Most dangerous jellyfish** While all jellyfish are capable of stinging, only a few are considered to be really dangerous to people. The beautiful but deadly sea wasp or box jellyfish (*Chironex fleckeri*) is by far the most dangerous and, indeed, is probably the most venomous animal in the world. Found in the near-shore waters of northern Australia and parts of south-east Asia, its bell can be as a large as a football and it may have as many as 60 stinging tentacles each up to 4.6 m *15 ft* long. Millions of stinging capsules cover the tentacles and discharge venom into the skin of any creature that touches them; other capsules produce a sticky substance to ensure that the tentacles stick to the victim. It takes approximately 3 m *10 ft*

of tentacle to deliver a fatal dose of venom to a human, but the pain of the sting from just a couple of centimetres is normally instant and has often been described as unbearable. In the past century, the box jellyfish's cardiotoxic venom has caused the deaths of at least 70 people in Australia alone – more than the combined toll taken in the same region by sharks and crocodiles – and some of the victims have died within 4 minutes of being stung. A large box jellyfish has enough venom to kill no fewer than 60 adults but, fortunately, an anti-venom was developed in 1970 and this has reduced the

The box jellyfish is by far the most dangerous jellyfish in the world, giving an excruciatingly painful and sometimes fatal sting; many beaches along the north coast of Australia are effectively closed during the stinger season.

238

N
V
E
R
T
E
B
R
A
T
E
S

*The sea anemone looks like an underwater flower, but it is really an animal – with poisonous tentacles instead of petals.*

The Great Barrier Reef in Australia is the largest structure ever built by living creatures; this tiny section of the 2027 km *1260 mile* reef was photographed some miles off the coast of Hayman Island, Queensland.

number of deaths. Strangely, the stings cannot penetrate women's tights and, until proper 'stinger suits' became widely available, lifesavers patrolling problem beaches used to wear them (top and bottom) unashamedly.

**Most dangerous hydroid** The Pacific Portuguese man-of-war (*Physalia utriculus*) and the Atlantic Portuguese man-of-war (*P. physalus*) both carry a virulent poison and are the only hydrozoans known to endanger human life. All stings are extremely painful but massive ones can prove fatal – and dead animals can sting almost as effectively as live ones. The Pacific form usually has a single tentacle, while the Atlantic has several; each tentacle may be 30 m *98 ft* long and is transparent. In one length of tentacle measuring 9 m *29½ ft*, scientists counted about 750 000 nematocysts (stinging organs). Also known as bluebottles, both species are widely distributed, although they are most abundant in warm waters. Although they look like jellyfish, each man-of-war is actually a complex colony of hydrozoans; individual hydrozoans perform different functions within the colony: for example, some are adapted for feeding and others for defence.

**Largest structure** The largest structure ever built by living creatures is the 2027 km *1260 mile* long Great Barrier Reef, off Queensland, north-east Australia. Covering an area of 207 000 km² *80 000 miles²*, it has been built by countless millions of stony corals (the only animals capable of building massive

geological formations). It is not actually a single reef, but consists of thousands of smaller reefs, built over a period of about 18 million years.

**Largest atoll** The world's largest coral atoll (a round or horseshoe-shaped reef with a central sheltered lagoon) is Kwajalein in the Marshall Islands: the 283 km *175 miles* long arc of coral encloses a lagoon of 2850 km² *1100 miles²*.

**Discrete coral** The world's largest known example of discrete coral is a stony colony of *Galaxea fascicularis* found in Sakiyama Bay off Iriomote Island, Japan, on 7 Aug 1982, by Dr Shohei Shirai of the Institute for Development of Pacific Natural Resources. It has a long-axis measurement of 7.8 m *23 ft 9 in*, a height of 4 m *13 ft 1½ in* and a maximum circumference of 19.5 m *59 ft 5 in*.

**Most threatened** According to the World Conservation Union (IUCN), three species of cnidarian are known or suspected to be threatened with extinction: the broad sea fan (*Eunicella verrucosa*), which is found in the Mediterranean Sea and the north-east Atlantic; Ivell's sea anemone (*Edwardsia ivelli*), found in the UK; and the starlet

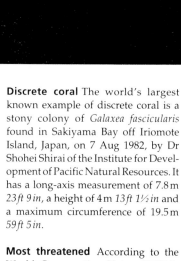

*Sea anemones do not like crowds and will vigorously defend their living space against rivals; their weapons include toxic chemicals, stinging cells on specially elongated tentacles and even special gut extensions that can digest the tissues of an unwanted competitor.*

*A group of jellyfish is called a 'smack'.*

sea anemone (*Nematostella vectensis*), found in the USA, Canada and the UK. It is likely that more species will be added to this list as research progresses.

**Extinctions** No cnidarian is known to have become extinct since the mid-1800s, although it is likely that at least some species disappear before the status of their populations has been properly assessed or even before they are known to science – and therefore go unrecorded.

**Oldest** The longest-lived cnidarians are certain species of sea anemone, including *Actinia mesembryanthemum*, *A. equina* and *Cereus pedunculatus*, which have lived in fish tanks (in captivity) for between 60 and 90 years.

Many coral reefs are extremely old. In the 1970s, it was discovered that a reef can be aged by passing an X-ray through it to reveal annual growth rings like those found in trees. Using this technique, it has been demonstrated that some stony corals (order Madreporaria) on the Great Barrier Reef, in Australia, are 800–1000 years old. However, it is the coral *skeletons* that attain this age – not the living corals themselves. The skeletons are created by succeeding generations of little animals called polyps (average 1–3 mm *0.04–0.12 in* in diameter), which

look rather like miniature sea anemones; each polyp builds a rigid skeleton of almost pure calcium carbonate around itself and, after it dies, the next polyp generation continues the building work.

*Sea anemones anchor themselves to a rock or another hard surface and are dependent upon food coming to them, although most are capable of crawling very slowly and a few of floating or swimming.*

# MOLLUSCS

### Mollusca
More than 60000 species (*c.* 50000 have external shells), including squid, cuttlefish, octopuses, shellfish, snails, slugs, sea slugs, limpets, bivalves

*Octopuses are capable of opening screw-top jars and stoppered bottles to get at food placed inside.*

**Largest invertebrate** The Atlantic giant squid (*Architeuthis dux*) is the world's largest known invertebrate. Most of the exceptional records came from a series of animals which were washed ashore in Newfoundland, Canada, during the period 1870 to 1889. The heaviest ever recorded was a 2 tonne monster which ran aground in Thimble Tickle Bay, Newfoundland, Canada, on 2 Nov 1878. The body length of this giant among giants was 6.1 m *20 ft* (from tail to beak) and the longest tentacles measured 10.7 m *35 ft*, giving it a total length of 16.8 m *55 ft*. Each eye measured about 50 cm *20 in* across and the largest suckers on the ends of the tentacles were 10 cm *4 in* in diameter.

**Longest invertebrate** The longest invertebrate ever recorded (excluding worm-like species) was an 18.9 m *62 ft* giant squid *Architeuthis longimanus* which was washed ashore on Lyall Bay, Cook Strait, New Zealand, in October 1887. It was the first time this particular species had ever been seen. Its two long slender tentacles each measured 16.5 m *54 ft*, but its body was a relatively short 2.4 m *7¾ ft* in length. Unconfirmed reports of giant squid off the coast of Labrador, Canada, measuring in excess of 24 m *79 ft* have never been authenticated.

For centuries, giant squid were considered to be mythical creatures, along with mermaids and unicorns. It is now known that there are a number of species around the world, but many of the horror stories about them attacking ships are still treated with suspicion by experts (they have been known to attack ships – probably mistaking them for whales – but authenticated cases are extremely rare).

**Smallest squid** The world's smallest squid is *Parateuthis tunicata*, which is known only from two specimens collected by the German South Polar Expedition of 1901–03. The larger of the two, which was collected in the Antarctic Ocean at a depth of about 3000 m *9840 ft*, was 1.27 cm *½ in* in length (including tentacles of 4.83 mm *0.2 in*).

**Largest gastropod** The largest known gastropod is the trumpet or baler conch (*Syrinx aruanus*) of Australia. One specimen collected off Western Australia, in 1979, and now owned by Don Pisor of San Diego, California, USA (who bought it from a fisherman in Kaohsiung, Taiwan, in November 1979) had a shell 77.2 cm *30.4 in* long with a maximum girth of 1.10 m *39¾ in*. It weighed nearly 18 kg *40 lb* when alive.

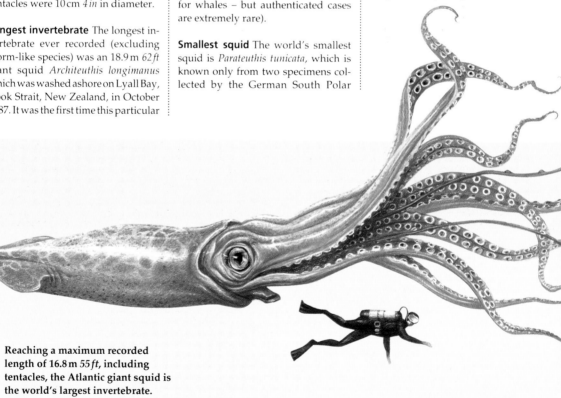

**Reaching a maximum recorded length of 16.8 m *55 ft*, including tentacles, the Atlantic giant squid is the world's largest invertebrate.**

*Squid move through the water by jet propulsion: water is forced from a cavity within the body through a funnel just behind the head by the contraction of muscles in the body wall.*

The African giant snail is the largest known land snail, shown here at only one third of its normal size.

**Largest land snail** The largest known land snail is the African giant snail *Achatina achatina*, which looks like an outsize version of many common garden snails. On average its shell is about 20 cm *8 in* in length. The largest recorded specimen measured 39.3 cm *15½ in* snout-to-tail when fully extended (shell length 27.3 cm *10¾ in*) in December 1978 and weighed exactly 900 g *2 lb*. Named *Gee Geronimo*, this snail was owned by Christopher Hudson (1955–79) of Hove, E Sussex, UK, and had been collected in Sierra Leone in June 1976. African giant snails have been introduced to many parts of the world outside Africa, mainly for their food value, but they have become serious crop pests, particularly in southeast Asia.

**Largest bivalve** The largest of all existing bivalve shells is that of the marine giant clam *Tridacna gigas*, found on the Indo-Pacific coral reefs. One specimen measuring 1.15 m *45.2 in* in length and weighing 333 kg *734 lb* was collected off Ishigaki Island, Okinawa, Japan, in 1956, but was not scientifically examined until August 1984. It probably weighed just over 340 kg *750 lb* when alive (the soft parts weigh up to 9.1 kg *20 lb*) and was therefore the heaviest on record. The longest bivalve mollusc was another giant clam, collected at Tapanoeli (Tapanula) on the north-west coast of Sumatra, Indonesia, before 1817, and now preserved at Arno's Vale, which measures 1.37 m *48 in* in length and weighs 230 kg *507 lb*.

The smallest 'giant clam' is *Tridacna crocea*, which grows to a maximum of only 15 cm *6 in* in length. It also lives in the Indo-Pacific.

**Largest octopus** The Pacific giant octopus (*Octopus dofleini*), which lives in an area from California, USA, northward along the coast to Alaska and off eastern Asia as far south as Japan, is the largest octopus in the world. Its average armspan is believed to be about 2.5 m *8 ft 2 in* and, on average, males weigh about 23 kg *51 lb* and females about 15 kg *33 lb*. The world record-holder is a Pacific giant octopus found off western Canada in 1957, with an exceptional armspan of 9.6 m *31½ ft* and an estimated weight of 272 kg *600 lb*.

Despite earlier reports, there is no evidence for the existence of *Octopus giganteus*, which supposedly spanned 60 m *197 ft* from tentacle to tentacle. Remains washed up on beaches in Saint Augustine, Florida, USA (1896) and Bermuda (1988) are now considered to be a whale and a fish respectively.

**Smallest octopus** The Sri Lankan species *Octopus arborescens* has an armspan of less than 5.1 cm *2 in* on average and is the smallest known octopus in the world.

**Largest sea slug** The largest known sea slug is an individual found by Tamara Double in May 1991, off Les Sept Frères, a group of islands in the Red Sea belonging to the Republic of Djibouti. It belonged to a small population of brilliant pink and peach-coloured nudibranchs, which were previously unknown to science. The largest was 52 cm *20½ in* long and 37 cm *14½ in* wide; it weighed an estimated 2 kg *4 lb 6 oz*. The smallest was 33 cm *13 in* long and 21 cm *8¼ in* wide. It is unclear whether the population represents an extraordinarily large variation of the so-called Spanish dancer (*Hexabranchus sanguineus*) or if it is an entirely new species of *Hexabranchus*.

**I N V E R T E B R A T E S**

Previously, the world's largest recorded sea slug was believed to be a rather compact species called *Tochuina tetraquetra*, which is found off the north-western Pacific coast of the USA and reaches a maximum length of 'only' 30 cm *12 in*.

**Smallest shell** The smallest known shell-bearing mollusc is the marine gastropod *Bittium* sp, which was collected by Mr Zheng Gen Hai from reefs near the Nansha Islands, China. It measures 0.39 mm *0.015 in* in length and 0.31 mm *0.012 in* in width.

**Suspended animation** In 1846 two specimens of the desert snail *Eremina desertorum* were presented to The Natural History Museum, UK, as dead exhibits. They were glued on to a small tablet and placed on display. Four years later, in March 1850, the Museum staff,

suspecting that one of the snails was still alive, removed it from the tablet and placed it in tepid water. The snail moved and later began to feed. This hardy little creature lived for a further 2 years before it fell into a torpor and died.

**Largest eye** The Atlantic giant squid (*Architeuthis dux*) has the largest eye of any known animal – living or extinct. It has been estimated that the record example from Thimble Tickle Bay, Newfoundland, Canada, which had an overall length of 16.8 m *55 ft* also had eyes measuring 50 cm *20 in* in diameter (considerably larger than a long-playing record).

**Most dangerous octopus** The world's most dangerous octopuses are two species of blue-ringed octopus: *Hapalochlaena maculosa*, which is found along the coasts of Australia, and the slightly larger *H. lunulata*, another Australian species which is also found in Indonesia and the Philippines. The relatively painless bite of these deceptively pretty creatures can kill in a matter of minutes although, strangely, some people are only mildly affected. The octopuses carry a venom which includes a component called tetrodotoxin (a paralysing poison identical to the one found in the tissues of pufferfish) and it has been estimated that each individual carries sufficient venom to cause the paralysis of 10 adult men. They are small animals, with a radial spread of just 10–20 cm *4–8 in*, and bite with a parrot-like beak situated at the junction of their eight arms. Victims are often unaware that they have been bitten until the penetration site begins to swell and they feel a tingling numbness around the mouth. Fortunately, blue-ringed octopuses are not considered to be aggressive and normally 'attack' only when they are taken out of the water and provoked.

In the rare event of other octopus species biting people, the result may be some swelling, soreness and numbness, because they all secrete powerful salivary compounds designed to subdue and digest their prey. However, only

**The most venomous gastropods are the cone shells, capable of delivering a fast-acting neurotoxic venom which has been known to kill people.**

the blue-ringed octopuses carry a dangerous venom. The suckers on all octopus tentacles are harmless.

*A group of clams is called a 'bed'*

**Most dangerous snail** Tiny aquatic snails in the genera *Biomphalaria, Bulinus, Physopsis* and *Oncomelania,* form a crucial link in the development of the tropical disease schistosomiasis (bilharzia). Caught by contact with infected water, schistosomiasis is one of the commonest diseases in the world, affecting hundreds of millions of people every year in many parts of Africa, south-east Asia and South America. It can prove fatal. The disease is caused by infestation of the body with the larvae of parasitic flatworms in the genus *Schistosoma.* These flatworms require two hosts in their lifecycle: the larvae undergo part of their development in the body of the snail; then they enter the water and attach themselves to (and then penetrate) the skin of their second host, which is a human or another mammal. The flatworm larvae mature, mate and lay their eggs, which eventually leave the body of the mammalian host in the urine or faeces – and the cycle continues.

The most venomous gastropods are the cone shells in the genus *Conus,* all of which can deliver a fast-acting neurotoxic venom. There are some 400–500 species altogether, ranging from about 1–20 cm *0.4–8 in* in length (the largest on record is 25 cm *9.8 in* long, belonging to a species called *Conus pulcher*). Several species are capable of killing people, but the geographer cone (*Conus geographus*), found in the Indo-Pacific, is considered to be one of the most dangerous. The venom is injected with the help of disposable darts (which are quickly replaced) and symptoms include impaired vision, dizziness and nausea; it can also cause paralysis and death. In the larger species, each dart may be up to 1 cm *0.4 in* long.

No bivalve molluscs are particularly dangerous to people and, despite

**A major threat to molluscs with attractive shells is exploitation for the curio trade; these Queen conch shells were on sale in the Caribbean.**

the harrowing scenes in many adventure films, giant clams (genus *Tridacna*) do not trap people and hold them under water. Some are certainly big enough to trap a person's leg – and they possess tremendous muscular power to lock their shells shut – but they move so slowly that it usually takes several minutes for them to close properly so a diver or swimmer would have to be asleep to get caught.

*Limpets feed on tiny green algae attached to rocks and, like miniature lawn mowers, they move systematically back and forth across the rock surfaces.*

**INVERTEBRATES**

**Oldest** The longest-lived mollusc is believed to be the ocean quahog (*Arctica islandica*), a thick-shelled clam found on both sides of the North Atlantic and in the North Sea. A 10 cm *4 in* specimen with 220 annual growth rings (implying an age of 220 years) was collected in 1982. Not all biologists, however, accept growth rings as a measure of age, so this record is controversial.

> *Before the evolution of fish, cephalopods such as squid, cuttlefish and octopuses were the major predators of the sea and dominated the upper layers of the world's oceans for millions of years.*

**Slowest growth** The deep-sea clam *Tindaria callistiformis*, which is found in the North Atlantic, is believed to have a slower rate of growth than any other animal. A team of scientists working at Yale University, Connecticut, USA, calculated that it takes about 100 years to reach a length of just 8 mm *0.31 in*.

**Fastest learner** Squid, cuttlefish and octopuses (all in the class Cephalopoda) are believed to be more intelligent than any other invertebrate. It is very difficult to measure intelligence but, as an example, one recent experiment illustrates how the octopus *Octopus vulgaris* is able to learn simple tasks by observing other octopuses in action. Italian scientists Graziano Fiorito and Pietro Scotto trained a number of individuals to attack either a red ball or a white ball (since octopuses are colour blind, these differed in brightness rather than colour). When they had learned which ball to attack (they were given food rewards each time they got it right) a second octopus in an adjoining tank was allowed to watch. As a result, the observers learned which ball to attack in less time than it had taken the original octopuses to learn by trial and error. The results of this experiment are highly significant because it is the first time anyone has demonstrated that an invertebrate can learn in a way neurologists consider preliminary to conceptual thought.

**Most popular shell** The most popular shells among conchologists are generally considered to be the cowrie shells (family Cypraeidae), which have a very smooth, glossy, porcelain-like texture, as well as vivid patterning and coloration. There are more than 200 known species and many local variations. The cowries are closely followed in popularity by cone shells (family Conidae), volutes (family Volutidae) and rock shells (family Muricidae).

**Most expensive shell** The value of a sea-shell depends upon many different factors, including its rarity and accessibility, the beauty of its colour and markings, the presence of any interesting abnormalities or deformities, its general condition and its 'collectability' (many conchologists tend to specialize in one group or family). Values are in a constant state of flux because one specimen may be infinitely more desirable than another of the same species and, at the same time, the level of demand changes with sudden crazes and as so-called rare species become more readily available. However, the most sought-after and most valuable shell probably belongs to a cowrie called *Cypraea fultoni*. In 1987 two live specimens were taken by a Soviet trawler off Mozambique, in the Indian Ocean: the larger of the two was later sold in New York to Italian collector Dr Massilia Raybaudi for $24 000 and the other was put up for sale at $17 000. One reason for the exceptionally high value of this particular species is because, until recently, almost all *C. fultoni* shells were collected only from the stomachs of bottom-feeding fish caught off the coast of south-east Africa. However, their value has been halved since 1990 due to the discovery of new habitats off Mozambique.

**Largest pearl** The world's largest natural pearl was taken from a giant clam (*Tridacna derasa*) off the coast of Palawan, in the Philippines, on 7 May 1934. Known as the 'Pearl of Laotze', it weighs 6.4 kg *14 lb 2 oz* and measures 24.1 cm *9½ in* in length and 10.2–14 cm *4.0–5½ in* in diameter. It was auctioned in San Francisco, USA, in 1980, for $200 000 (then £85 000).

**Most threatened** The World Conservation Union (IUCN) lists no fewer than 1215 mollusc species that are known or suspected to be threatened with extinction, of which 309 are considered to be in particularly serious danger. Many other species are likely to be added to this list as research progresses. Threats include pollution, habitat destruction and exploitation for food and for the ornamental shell trade.

**Extinctions** An incredible 286 different mollusc species are known or suspected to have become extinct since the mid-1800s. No fewer than 76 of these used to live in French Polynesia and a further 61 lived in the Hawaiian Islands, USA. Other areas with a high extinction rate include the Ogasawara Islands, in Japan, and St Helena, in the South Atlantic. These figures probably reflect areas with a high level of research as well as areas with genuinely high extinction rates. It is possible that other mollusc species disappear before the status of their populations has been properly assessed or even before they are known to science – and therefore go unrecorded.

> *Cuttlefish have a shell inside their bodies, which acts as a variable flotation device helping them to maintain neutral buoyancy.*

**Fastest** The fastest-moving species of land snail is probably the common garden snail (*Helix aspera*). On 20 Feb 1990 a garden snail named *Verne* completed a 31 cm *12.2 in* course at West Middle School in Plymouth, Michigan, USA, in a record-breaking 2 min 13 s at 0.233 cm/s *0.09 in/s*. To put this into perspective, the snail-racing equivalent of a 4-minute mile would be roughly an 8-day mile.

**Most variable colour** All cephalopods (squid, cuttlefish and octopuses) have the ability to change colour, but cuttlefish (order Sepioidea) are the real experts. They have thousands of small contractible pigment sacs in their skin; each of these is one of three colours and can be enlarged or reduced in size at will to produce rapid or long-term colour changes. Specific patterns have a variety of uses: to deter predators, in courtship displays and to distract prey animals. Ironically, cuttlefish themselves do not have colour vision.

> *Slugs are basically snails that have lost their shells during the course of evolution; however, some still have tiny internal shells and in one family they even have a tiny external shell perched on the end of the tail.*

# SPONGES

## *Porifera*
*c.* 5000 species (only *c.* 150 live in fresh water)

**Earliest** Sponges were the first multicellular organisms to evolve on Earth, appearing some 570 million years ago. The simplest and most primitive multicellular animals alive today, they have neither true tissues nor organs, and their cells display a considerable degree of independence.

*Sponges spend their lives attached to rocks and other hard surfaces and feed by extracting small particles from the surrounding water.*

A barrel-shaped loggerhead sponge, the world's largest sponge.

**Largest sponge** The largest known sponge is the barrel-shaped loggerhead sponge (*Spheciospongia vesparium*), found in the West Indies and in the waters off Florida, USA, which measures up to 1.05 m *42 in* in height and 91 cm *3 ft* in diameter. Neptune's cup or goblet (*Poterion patera*) of Indonesia grows to 1.20 m *48 in* in height, but is far less bulky.

**Heaviest sponge** In 1909 a wool sponge (*Hippospongia canaliculatta*) measuring 1.83 m *6 ft* in circumference was collected off the Bahamas. When first taken from the water, it weighed 36–41 kg *80–90 lb*, but this fell to 5.44 kg *12 lb* after it had been dried and relieved of all excrescences. It is now preserved in the US National Museum, Washington, DC, USA.

For many centuries, sponges were regarded as plants and they were not classified as animals until 1835; they do not look very animal-like but, just like other animals, feed on organic matter and reproduce sexually by means of an egg and a spermatozoon.

**Smallest sponge** The widely distributed *Leucosolenia blanca* is just 3 mm *0.11 in* tall when fully grown.

**Deepest sponge** The deepest living sponges known are members of the family Cladorhizidae, which have been found at depths of up to 8840 m *29 000 ft*.

**Regeneration** Sponges are little more than colonies of individual cells, with very limited coordination or depend-ence between them. Not surprisingly, they have more remarkable powers of regeneration of lost parts than any other animal – and are capable of regrowing from tiny fragments of their former selves. For example, if a sponge is forced through a fine-meshed silk gauze, the separate fragments can reform into a full-size sponge. Alternatively, if a sponge becomes separated into several different pieces, these will reorganize themselves into one or more new sponges.

# STARFISH & SEA URCHINS

The brittle stars' name reflects their readiness to cast off their long, thin arms easily when attacked or roughly handled.

### Echinodermata
*c.* 6000 species, including starfish, brittle stars, sea urchins, sea cucumbers, feather stars, sea lilies

**Earliest** The earliest echinoderms are believed to have resembled the sea lilies or feather stars (class Crinoidea), which are the most primitive living members of the group. Their origins go back at least to the Cambrian period, 510–570 million years ago.

**Largest starfish** The largest of the 1600 known species of starfish is the very fragile brisingid *Midgardia xandaros*. A specimen collected by the Texas A & M University research vessel *Alaminos* in the southern part of the Gulf of Mexico, on 18 Aug 1968, measured a maximum 1.38 m *4½ ft* from the tip of one arm to the tip of another, but its disc was only 2.6 cm *1.02 in* in diameter. Its dry weight was 70 g *2.46 oz*.

**Heaviest starfish** The heaviest species of starfish is the five-armed *Thromidia catalai* of the western Pacific. One specimen collected off Ilot Amédéé, New Caledonia, in the Pacific, on 14 Sep 1969, and later deposited at Nouméa Aquarium, New Caledonia, weighed an estimated 6 kg *13 lb 4 oz*. Its total armspan was 63 cm *24.8 in*.

**Smallest starfish** The smallest known starfish is the asterinid sea star *Patiriella parvivipara*, discovered by Wolfgang Zeidler on the west coast of the Eyre peninsula, South Australia, in 1975. It has a maximum radius of only 4.7 mm *0.18 in* and a disc diameter of less than 9 mm *0.35 in*.

**Oldest starfish** Very little is known about longevity in starfish, although four years is considered to be a good age for most species. The longest-lived species are probably *Asterias rubens* and *Marthasterias glacialis*, which do not reach sexual maturity until they are 5–7 years old.

**Regeneration** All starfish are capable of regrowing lost arms and many species can even recover from losing half their bodies: the two halves 'walk' away from each other and regrow into two new starfish. But members of the family Ophidiasteridae are exceptional in being able to grow an entirely new starfish from nothing more than a tiny piece of arm as little as 1 cm *0.39 in* in length and a portion of the central disc. Regeneration is typically slow and, in some cases, may take as long as a year to be completed.

**Most arms** The majority of starfish and brittle stars have five arms, but a few have more; members of the starfish genus *Heliaster*, living along the west coast of North America, have as many as 50. Feather stars are not directly comparable, since they have an entirely different body structure (most are attached to long stalks and look very plant-like); some primitive species have five arms, but the majority have a total of 10 and a few have as many as 200 (resulting from the repeated forking of each original arm).

**Most destructive** Many marine creatures attack coral, but the crown-of-thorns starfish (*Acanthaster planci*) is the most destructive. Named for the spines which cover its entire body and arms, it is found from the Red Sea across the Indian Ocean and southeast Asia to the Pacific, and is undoubtedly the best-known coral predator in the world. It has 12–19 arms and can measure up to 60 cm *24 in* in diameter (although 30 cm *12 in* is more

The notorious crown-of-thorns starfish is probably the world's most destructive echinoderm – and is the only really venomous starfish.

typical). A single crown-of-thorns starfish eats about half its diameter of reef surface every night and large 'plagues' of them have been known to destroy entire coral colonies. The worst damage seems to have been on the Great Barrier Reef, Australia, but other parts of the world have suffered as well. Scientists are in wide disagreement over the ecological processes leading to crown-of-thorns invasions, but one theory is that overfishing of predatory fish may be the cause in some areas. The crown-of-thorns is the only really venomous starfish – each of its needle-sharp spines is encased in a sheath containing venom cells.

**Largest sea urchin** The world's largest sea urchin is *Sperosoma giganteum*, which is found in deep waters off the coast of Japan. The diameter of the test or shell (measured horizontally) averages 32 cm *12.6 in*.

**Smallest sea urchin** The smallest known sea urchin is *Echinocyamus scaber*, which is found off the coast of

New South Wales, Australia. The diameter of the test or shell (measured horizontally) averages only 5.5 mm *0.22 in*.

**Largest sea cucumber** The bulkiest of the world's 550 species of sea cucumber is *Stichopus variegatus*, which is found in the Philippines; when fully extended, it can be up to 1 m *39 in* in length and 24 cm *9½ in* in diameter. The longest sea cucumbers belong to the genus *Synapta* and can reach almost 2 m *78 in* in length when fully extended, although they are worm-like in appearance and measure only about 1.2 cm *½ in* in diameter.

**Smallest sea cucumber** The world's smallest sea cucumber is *Psammothuria ganapatii*, which is found off the coast of southern India. It rarely exceeds 4 mm *0.16 in* in length.

**Deepest** The greatest depth from which any species of echinoderm has been recovered is an amazing 10 710 m *35 130 ft* for *Myriotrochus bruuni*, which was collected by the Soviet research ship *Vityaz* in the Marianas Trench, western Pacific, in 1958.

The greatest depth from which a starfish has been recovered is 7584 m *24 881 ft* for a specimen of *Porcellanaster ivanovi*, collected by the *Vityaz* in the

Marianas Trench, western Pacific, in 1962.

**Most threatened** The World Conservation Union (IUCN) lists only one echinoderm that is known or suspected to be threatened with extinction: the European edible sea urchin (*Echinus esculentus*), which is found in the north-east Atlantic. It is likely that at least some other echinoderms will be added to this list as research progresses.

**Extinctions** No echinoderm species is known or suspected to have become extinct since the mid-1800s, although it is likely that at least some species disappear before the status of their populations has been properly assessed or even before they are known to science – and therefore go unrecorded.

*When a fish or crab tries to eat a slime star, a kind of starfish found off the Pacific coast of North America, it is instantly 'slimed': the starfish secretes huge amounts of thick, rubbery, poisonous mucous that can completely cover the hapless predator.*

# WORMS & WORM-LIKE INVERTEBRATES

## Nemertea, Annelida, Platyhelminthes & Nematoda

*c.* 65 000 species, including earthworms, leeches, flukes, ribbon worms, tapeworms, roundworms

**Longest** The longest known worm is the boot-lace worm (*Lineus longissimus*), a kind of ribbon worm or nemertine (phylum Nemertea) found in the shallow waters of the North Sea. A specimen which washed ashore after a severe storm at St Andrews, Fife, UK, in 1864, measured more than 55 m *180 ft* in length.

The world's largest leech is the 30 cm *11.8 in* Amazonian species, *Haementeria ghilianii*.

**Longest earthworm** The longest known species of segmented worm (phylum Annelida) is the giant earthworm *Michrochaetus rappi* (=*M. michrochaetus*) of South Africa, which has an average length of 1.36 m *54 in*. A record-breaking giant earthworm of this species, measuring 6.7 m *22 ft* in length (when naturally extended) and 2 cm *0.8 in* in diameter, was collected in the Transvaal in 1937.

Another exceptional individual (presumed to be *Microchaetus*) was reported in South Africa in 1969 to be about 7 m *23 ft* in length, with a diameter of 7.5 cm *2.95 in*. However, such reports are regarded with considerable doubt since an earthworm of that size is probably impossible physiologically: it seems unlikely that the internal hydraulic pressures necessary to move such a large animal could be sustained without damaging internal organs and preventing blood circulation.

**Shortest earthworm** *Chaetogaster annandalei* measures less than 0.5 mm *0.02 in* in length and is the shortest of the world's known annelids. It lives in freshwater, in close association with several species of snail, and is carnivorous (feeding on amoebas, ciliates, rotifers and trematode larvae).

**Most threatened** The World Conservation Union (IUCN) lists 16 worm-like invertebrate species as known or suspected to be threatened with extinction and expresses serious concern about many others (more are likely to be added as research progresses).

The list includes seven species of segmented worm (phylum Annelida), including the medicinal leech (*Hirudo medicinalis*), found in many parts of Europe; the palolo worm (*Eunice viridis*), from the South Pacific; and the giant Gippsland earthworm (*Megascolides australis*), which lives in Australia. The two species considered to be in most serious danger are the Washington giant earthworm (*Driloleirus americanus*) and the Oregon giant earthworm (*Driloleirus macelfreshi*), both of which are found in the USA. In addition, there is serious concern for a number of annelid species for which there has been no proper status assessment: 53 species of South African giant earthworm and 90 species of Southern African acanthodriline earthworm.

A total of six species of ribbon worms (phylum Nemertina) are listed as known or suspected to be threatened with extinction. The two in most serious trouble are: *Antiponemertes allisonae*, from New Zealand; and *Pantinonemertes agricola*, from Bermuda.

Three species of turbellarian worm are also listed (phylum Platyhelminthes): Malheur cave planarian (*Kenkia rhynchida*), Holsinger's groundwater planarian (*Sphalloplana holsingeri*) and Bigger's groundwater planarian (*Sphalloplana subtilis*), all of which are found in the USA.

**Extinctions** One species of worm-like invertebrate is believed to have become extinct in recent years: the Lake Pedder planarian (*Romankenkius pedderensis*), which lived in Tasmania, Australia. However, it is likely that at least some species disappear before the status of their populations has been assessed or even before they are known to science – and therefore go unrecorded.

**Worm charming** The world record for worm charming was set in 1980, at the Willaston County Primary School, Nantwich, Cheshire, UK, when Tom Shufflebotham raised an astonishing 511 earthworms from a 3 m² *32 ft²* plot. His record-breaking attempt took place during the annual World Worm Charming Championship, which has just two basic rules: no refreshment, stimulation or drugs, and no digging. The contestants are allowed 30 minutes to entice as many worms out of the ground as possible. Shufflebotham used a traditional technique called 'twanging', in which a four-pronged pitchfork is placed in the ground and wiggled back and forth to cause special vibrations that apparently persuade the worms to emerge.

**Gender difference** The most striking difference in size between the sexes in any known animal is in the marine worm *Bonellia viridis*, which is found throughout the Mediterranean. The females are 5–12 cm *2–4.7 in* long but have an extendable proboscis which, when fully stretched, may be over 1 m *39 in* long. This compares with 1–3 mm *0.04–0.12 in* for the males, thus making the females thousands of times heavier than their mates. The males live on or even inside the females.

**Most specific parasite** The hippopotamus leech (*Placobdelloides jaegerskioeldi*) is the only leech known to be specific to one mammal. It feeds only on hippo blood. This is more difficult than it sounds, because hippos spend much of their time in deep, fast-flowing water, their skin is thick and they allow birds to search their bodies for tasty ectoparasites such as leeches. One of the leech's many adaptations for this difficult lifestyle is its dark red colour, making it difficult to see against the red viscous fluid that hippos secrete to protect their skin from the burning sun. This is the only known example of camouflaged coloration in leeches.

**Immolation** Some ribbon worms (phylum Nemertina) absorb themselves when food is scarce. One specimen under observation digested 95 per cent of its own body in a few months without apparently suffering any ill effects. As soon as food became available, the lost tissue was restored.

---

*Most earthworms are hermaphroditic, which means that they are both male and female at the same time; they can mate with any adult of the same species.*

# MICROBES

## Viruses, bacteria and protozoans

(Strictly speaking, bacteria, viruses and protozoans are not animals: they are classified in the kingdoms Monera (bacteria) and Protista (protozoans); viruses are not usually ascribed their own kingdom. However, they are included here as living things which provide some interesting comparisons with members of the animal kingdom.)

Most diseases caused by bacteria (including cholera, food poisoning, syphilis, plague and tetanus) can be successfully treated with antibiotic drugs, but most diseases caused by viruses (including AIDS and hepatitis) remain incurable.

**Earliest** The first evidence of life on Earth comes from minute globules preserved in rocks 3800 million years old, believed to be the fossils of primitive bacteria-like organisms. They probably fed on the so-called 'organic soup' – organic molecules in the early oceans.

**Most basic organism** Viruses consist simply of a protein coat protecting a strand of nucleic acid (RNA or DNA – a complex molecule which carries the instructions for replication). They meet the fundamental requirement of all living things: an ability to replicate themselves and pass on instructions to make new individuals from one generation to another. However, they can reproduce only within the cells of other living organisms and therefore, in some ways, are in a grey area between living and non-living things. Even though they are the most basic, the fact that viruses are completely dependent on other living cells is an indication that they are unlikely to have been the first forms of life.

**Largest bacteria** The largest known bacterium is *Epulopiscium fishelsoni*. It was discovered by Israeli researchers in 1985 and first described in 1993 as a symbiont inhabiting the intestinal tract of the brown surgeonfish (*Acanthurus nigrofuscus*), which is found in the Red Sea and around the Great Barrier Reef, Australia. Measuring 0.6 × 0.08 mm *0.023 × 0.003 in* or more (and therefore visible to the naked eye) it is so big that

it was originally thought to be a protozoan. It does not seem to harm the 30 cm *12 in* fish but merely lives quietly (albeit in large numbers) in its digestive tract; indeed, the genus name *Epulopiscium* essentially means 'guest at a fish's banquet'. *Epulopiscium* is a

The most virulent and lethal virus known, the Ebola virus kills as many as 88 per cent of its victims within seven days of exposure.

particularly exciting discovery because it demonstrates that bacteria have the ability to grow much larger than scientists previously thought possible. It is approximately one million times larger than the famous food-poisoner found in the human gut, *Escherichia coli*.

**Largest virus** Viruses are so small (on average about 100 millionths of a millimetre long) that they can only be seen with an electron microscope. The largest known species is the rod-shaped *Citrus tristeza* virus, which measures

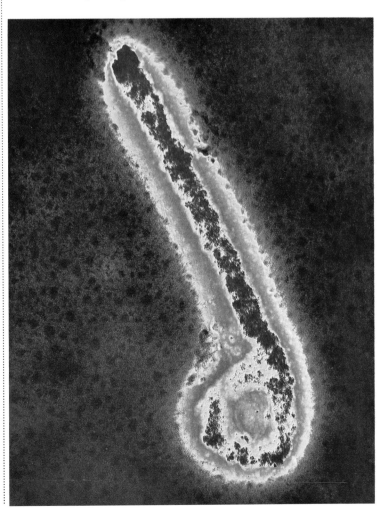

The existence of bacteria was first demonstrated in the 17th century by Anton van Leeuwenhoek; he saw them through a microscope in scrapings of the white film on his teeth.

**M**
**I**
**C**
**R**
**O**
**B**
**E**
**S**

*A single bacterium reproduces by splitting itself into two new cells; some species can divide as often as every 15 minutes, which leads to very rapid population growth.*

0.0006 mm *0.00002 in* length – only twice the size of the smallest known bacteria.

**Largest protozoan** One of the most remarkable events in the history of life on Earth took place about 1500 million years ago, when microscopic organisms – although still single-celled – became many times larger than the bacteria that preceded them. They were the protozoans. The largest-known protozoan is a species of the fan-shaped *Stannophyllum* (Xenophyophorida), which can attain a length of 25 cm *9¾ in*.

The largest prehistoric protozoans were the foraminiferans and the radiolarians, which measured up to 10 cm *3.9 in* in diameter.

**Smallest virus** The smallest known virus measures 0.000018 mm *0.0000007 in* long – about two millionths of a millimetre and 17 times smaller than the smallest bacteria.

**Smallest bacteria** Bacteria each consist of a single *cell* – the smallest biological unit able to function independently. The smallest of all are the only two species in the genus *Chlamydia*, which are no more than 0.0003 mm *0.000012 in* in length.

**Toughest bacteria** Many bacteria are able to tolerate extreme environmental conditions, such as a complete lack of oxygen, high salt concentration or temperatures below freezing. In March 1983 John Barras of the University of Oregon, USA, reported bacteria from sulphurous seabed vents in the East Pacific Rise (latitude 21°N) thriving at temperatures of 306°C *583°F*. Perhaps even more surprising, the bacterium *Micrococcus radiodurans* can withstand atomic radiation of 6.5 million röntgens, or 10 000 times that fatal to the average human.

**Oldest bacteria** In 1991 it was reported that *live* bacteria were found in the carcass of a mastodon (an extinct ancestor of the elephant) which was discovered in an oxygen-free bog by a golf course construction crew in Ohio, USA. According to the results of carbon-dating, the mastodon had been lying in the bog for 11 600 years – yet the bacteria gave the flesh a 'bad smell' even after such a long time. (The evidence of spear marks found on the ribs of the mastodon was also interesting, because it represented the first proof of humans killing a prehistoric animal.)

**Best known** The best understood living creature is probably the bacterium *Escherichia coli*, the famous food poisoner found in the human gut. It has been used in countless studies of genetics, biochemistry and other areas of biology.

**Fastest single-celled organism** By means of a polar flagellum (effectively, the world's smallest motor) rotating at 100 times/s the tiny bacterial predator of other bacteria, *Bdellovibrio bacteriovorus*, can travel 50 times its own length of 0.002 mm *0.00008 in* every second. This is 10 times faster than the maximum travelling speed of its favourite prey, *Escherichia coli*, and would be the equivalent of a human sprinter reaching 320 km/h *200 mph* or a swimmer crossing the English Channel in 6 minutes. *Bdellovibrio bacteriovorus* is known by its admirers as a 'Bdella' (the *'B'* is always silent).

**Most dangerous** The malarial parasites of the genus *Plasmodium*, which are protozoans carried by mosquitos of the genus *Anopheles*, have probably been responsible for half of all human deaths (excluding wars and accidents) since the Stone Age. Eighty per cent of the fatalities are in Africa and, according to estimates published by the World Health Organisation (WHO) in 1993, between 1.4 million and 2.8 million people die from malaria in sub-Saharan Africa each year.

The most virulent and lethal viruses known are the Ebola virus and the Marburg virus, which are classified as Biosafety Level 4 (the AIDS virus is a mere Level 2). They are so contagious that researchers wear protective space suits to handle them. Within seven days of exposure, victims develop a variety of gruesome symptoms from red eyes to raging fever and from haemorrhages to blood spurts, for which there is no vaccine or cure. Marburg, the milder of the two, kills 25 per cent of those infected; Ebola kills as many as 88 per cent.

*Bacteria are best known for causing harmful diseases, but they also play a crucial role in the carbon and nitrogen cycles, they are important in animal digestion and they have been exploited in various industrial processes such as fermentation and cheese-making.*

# INDEX

**I N D E X**